I0137911

Discovering Christ

In

The Gospel Of John

Volume 2

Discovering Christ In The Gospel Of John

Donald S. Fortner

Volume 2

Go *publications*

Go Publications
Gibb Hill Farm, Ponsonby, Seascale, Cumbria, CA20 1BX, United Kingdom

First Published 2017

British Library Cataloguing in Publication Data available

ISBN 978-1-908475-08-4

Printed and bound in Great Britain
By Lightning Source UK Ltd.

Dedication

To Pastor Gary Vance

"our dear fellowservant …
a faithful minister of Christ"

Contents

	Foreword	9
1	Hirelings And The Shepherd – John 10:6-21	11
2	Reprobation Asserted – John 10:19-30	19
3	'they shall never perish' – John 10:27-30	25
4	'thou, being a man, makest thyself God' – John 10:31-42	33
5	Lessons From The Blessed Family At Bethany – John 11:1-57	39
6	Lazarus Raised, Irresistible Grace – John 11:1-12:11	49
7	Where Was Lazarus? – John 11:11-46	55
8	Our Friends Sleep – John 11:11	65
9	Christ Our Resurrection – 11:25, 26	71
10	Astonishing Love – John 11:36	77
11	Sovereignty And Instrumentality – John 11:39	87
12	Seeing The Glory Of God – John 11:40	93
13	Substitution: Christ In My Place – John 11:47-57	103
14	'six days before the passover' – John 12:1-11	113
15	'behold, thy King cometh' – John 12:12-19	121
16	'glorify thy name' – John 12:20-33	133
17	The Crisis Of The World – John 12:31-33	141
18	The Attraction Of The Cross – John 12:32, 33	147
19	'Father, glorify thy name' – John 12:27-30	153
20	'who is this Son of man?' – John 12:31-34	161
21	Responsibility, Reprobation, Ruin – John 12:35-43	167
22	'his commandment is life everlasting' – John 12:44-50	175
23	Loved To Perfection – John 13:1	183
24	Dark Providences Cleared In Due Time – John 13:1-20	193
25	Foot Washing – John 13:1-20	201
26	Christ Our Example – John 13:1	209
27	Judas And The Glory Of God – John 13:18-31	215
28	Preparing For A Fall – John 13:31-14:1	221
29	Relief For Troubled Hearts – John 14:1-3	227
30	Seven Promises – John 14:1-31	233
31	Wondrous Mystery – John 14:1-20	239

32	Warnings Or Promises? – John 15:1-27	253
33	Self-Sufficiency Slain – John 15:1-8	259
34	'so have I loved you' – John 15:9	269
35	No Greater Love – John 15:13	275
36	Electing Love – John 15:16	279
37	'They hated me without a cause' – John 15:22-25	291
38	Equipped For Trouble – John 16:1-33	297
39	The Comforter – John 16:7-16	305
40	The Expedience And The Comfort – John 16:7-14	309
41	The Comfort Of Conviction – John 16:7-11	319
42	The Conviction Of Righteousness – John 16:7-11	323
43	The Lord's Prayer – John 17:1-26	333
44	'this is life eternal' – John 17:3	341
45	The 'I haves' Of Christ – John 17:8	347
46	'Sanctify them' – John 17:17	355
47	'thou … hast loved them as thou hast loved me' – John 17:23	365
48	God's Everlasting Love For His Elect – John 17:24	373
49	God's Love In Us – John 17:26	379
50	Gethsemane's Sovereign – John 18:1-11	387
51	Jesus Taken, And Bound, And Led Away – John 18:12-27	395
52	'To this end was I born' – John 18:28-40	401
53	'Pilate sought to release him' – John 19:1-12	409
54	'Behold the man'! – John 19:5	417
55	The Crucifixion Of Our Lord – John 19:13-37	425
56	Seven Words From The Cross – John 19:25-30	433
57	Christ Crucified And The Scriptures Fulfilled – John 19:28-42	443
58	'It is finished' – John 19:30	451
59	Lessons From The Resurrection – John 20:1-18	459
60	The Tomb Was Not Empty – John 20:1-18	467
61	'Then were the disciples glad' – John 20:18-31	475
62	'on this wise showed he himself' – John 21:1-14	481
63	'lovest thou me?' – John 21:15-17	491
64	'what is that to thee?' – John 21:18-25	497
65	'other things' – John 21:25	505
	Index Of Bible Verses	513

Foreword

The Lord Jesus Christ is wonderfully set forth in the Gospel of John, perhaps here more personally and intimately than in any other single book of holy scripture. The mutual love and familiarity between John and his Master is woven throughout the gospel narrative in modest shades that creates a backcloth upon which are highlighted the clearest and most profound revelations of Christ's human and divine natures.

In many ways, therefore, it is not difficult to find the Lord Jesus in the Gospel of John. He is on every page, the theme of every chapter and verse. Yet, in these two volumes Pastor Don Fortner has done an excellent job in gathering key insights and applications of our Saviour's words and works to remind us of where our focus must lie if we are properly to understand the word of God and the divine purpose.

There is much here for every kind of reader. The material in the following pages is comforting and challenging, simple yet profound, practical yet sublime. It opens up cause for reflection in our own souls yet draws our eyes from ourselves to look upon the One whose ministry and sacrifice brings every good and perfect gift to needy sinners.

These individual chapters were originally delivered as preached sermons to a local congregation of Christian believers, though they have been adapted for print and ease of reading. For that reason you will find a complete and compact message in each chapter, lending the book increased value whether it is used as portions for daily reading, read through in its entirety, or referred to for the meaning of a particular passage. It is not a commentary in the usual sense but a meditation upon and an explanation of John's message, drawing out the story of the narrative, the meaning of the passage but also the personal application and significance for the Lord's people today.

As always, Pastor Fortner's aim has been two-fold. First, to lift up the Lord Jesus Christ and highlight his glory and greatness in the execution and sovereign accomplishment of his plan and purpose to save his people from their sins. Then, secondly, to explain and apply the outworking of free grace in the hearts and lives of God's elect people.

I feel sure that no one who reads these chapters will be left in any doubt but that in these two goals the author has been successful. Consequently, I am very confident the reader will discover something new and thrilling in these pages about the blessed Lord Jesus Christ from the Gospel of John.

Peter L. Meney, Pastor
Sovereign Grace Church
Great Falls, Montana

Chapter 1

Hirelings And The Shepherd

'This parable spake Jesus unto them: but they understood not what things they were which he spake unto them. Then said Jesus unto them again, Verily, verily, I say unto you, I am the door of the sheep. All that ever came before me are thieves and robbers: but the sheep did not hear them. I am the door: by me if any man enter in, he shall be saved, and shall go in and out, and find pasture. The thief cometh not, but for to steal, and to kill, and to destroy: I am come that they might have life, and that they might have it more abundantly. I am the good shepherd: the good shepherd giveth his life for the sheep. But he that is an hireling, and not the shepherd, whose own the sheep are not, seeth the wolf coming, and leaveth the sheep, and fleeth: and the wolf catcheth them, and scattereth the sheep. The hireling fleeth, because he is an hireling, and careth not for the sheep. I am the good shepherd, and know my sheep, and am known of mine. As the Father knoweth me, even so know I the Father: and I lay down my life for the sheep. And other sheep I have, which are not of this fold: them also I must bring, and they shall hear my voice; and there shall be one fold, and one shepherd. Therefore doth my Father love me, because I lay down my life, that I might take it again. No man taketh it from me, but I lay it down of myself. I have power to lay it down, and I have power to take it again. This commandment have I received of my Father. There was a division therefore again among the Jews for these sayings. And many of them said, he hath a devil, and is mad; why hear ye him? Others said, These are not the words of him that hath a devil. Can a devil open the eyes of the blind?' (John 10:6-21).

George Whitefield once declared, 'As God can send a nation or people no greater blessing than to give them faithful, sincere, and upright ministers, so the greatest curse that God can possibly send upon a people in this world, is to give them over to blind, unregenerate, carnal, lukewarm, and unskilled guides. And yet, in all ages, we find that there have been many wolves in sheep's clothing, many that daubed with untempered mortar, that prophesied smoother things than God did allow.'

Wolves in sheep's clothing were prevalent in the days of Isaiah, Jeremiah, and Ezekiel. They were common in the days of our Lord's earthly ministry. They were found in the earliest churches in the days of the apostles. And they are common today. In fact, throughout history, the wolves have always been the majority, the accepted, praised, applauded, and exalted leaders of the religious world; and faithful gospel preachers have always been, and are today, held in contempt, despised, mocked, ridiculed, slandered, and opposed as wolves.

God's servants are shepherds, pastors after God's own heart, given by him to his church for the care of their souls, to feed them with knowledge and understanding (Jeremiah 3:15). Blessed are those people and churches to whom God gives faithful pastors. All false prophets are hirelings. Cursed are they who have for pastors hirelings and false prophets.

In the tenth chapter of John's Gospel, our Lord Jesus spoke pointedly to the religious leaders of his day and identified them as hireling shepherds. Remember, this parable was spoken to those scribes and Pharisees who had just put a man out of the synagogue because he had been healed by the Master. They sat in Moses' seat and assumed the office of shepherds, teaching the sheep the things of God, but without the knowledge of God and without the authority of God. They fed themselves, not the sheep. The Lord Jesus calls them hirelings, thieves, and robbers.

In this parable the sheepfold (v.1) is the Church of God. The Door into the Church and Kingdom of God is Christ, his blood and righteousness (vv. 1, 7, 9). The true shepherd is our Lord Jesus Christ, the Good Shepherd. He gave his life for the sheep. He calls his own sheep by name and leads them out of the wilderness into Canaan, out of darkness into light, out of Babylon into the sheepfold. The Porter who opens the way for Christ and causes the sheep to hear his voice and follow him is God the Holy Spirit. The Sheep are God's elect. Some are in the fold. Some are yet straying from the Good Shepherd and his fold. But all God's elect are Christ's sheep.

'This parable spake Jesus unto them: but they understood not what things they were which he spake unto them. Then said Jesus unto them again, Verily, verily, I say unto you, I am the door of the sheep. All that ever came before me are thieves and robbers: but the sheep did not hear them. I am the door: by me if any man enter in, he shall be saved, and shall go in and out, and find pasture. The thief cometh not, but for to steal, and to kill, and to destroy: I am come that they might have life, and that they might have it more abundantly' (vv. 6-10).

With those words, our Saviour shows a clear distinction between all false shepherds and all true shepherds, using himself as the standard and example of the true shepherd. He continues the same analogy in the following verses, and declares that the one great distinction between hirelings and true shepherds is just this: The hireling cares not for the sheep, because he is just a hireling.

'I am the good shepherd: the good shepherd giveth his life for the sheep. But he that is an hireling, and not the shepherd, whose own the sheep are not, seeth the wolf coming, and leaveth the sheep, and fleeth: and the wolf catcheth them, and scattereth the sheep. The hireling fleeth, because he is an hireling, and careth not for the sheep. I am the good shepherd, and know my sheep, and am known of mine. As the Father knoweth me, even so know I the Father: and I lay down my life for the sheep' (vv. 11-15).

'I am the good shepherd: the good shepherd giveth his life for the sheep.' What blessed words! As you read through the scriptures, it would be both instructive and delightful to mark the many names by which our Saviour describes himself in this blessed book. There are more than a hundred of them; I think 107. There is a good reason why he has so many names. Our all-glorious Christ has so many offices that one name could not represent or explain them all. Indeed, all of them put together do not describe him. Paul said, 'Unto me who am less than the least of all saints is this grace given, that I might preach among the Gentiles the unsearchable riches of Christ.'

Of all the names given, that of a shepherd is, perhaps, the sweetest. Our Saviour was a master Artist. He drew pictures with words that explain things more clearly than volumes of defining words. As this chapter opens, he contrasts himself with a stranger. Here (vv. 11-15), he contrasts himself with an hireling, whose own the sheep are not. Let us look at the passage, marking the contrast between the hireling and true pastors, true shepherds.

A hireling is a person who works only for pay, with little or no concern for the value of the work. A shepherd is a person who tends sheep, a protector, a guardian, a defender, a keeper, one who watches over, provides for, feeds, and carefully guards a flock.

Here Is A Hireling

Our Saviour uses the word 'hireling' to describe all self-serving preachers, pastors, and religious leaders; those men who claim to be God's servants but refuse to enter the sheepfold by the Door, those who climb up some other way.

The hireling, the false shepherd, will not submit himself to the righteousness of God, will not enter by the Door, will not trust Christ alone for righteousness.

The Master tells us plainly that all who climb up some other way are thieves and robbers (v. 1). They come only 'to kill, and to steal, and to destroy' (v. 10). Here are the common features of a hireling preacher.

'But he that is an hireling, and not the shepherd, whose own the sheep are not, seeth the wolf coming, and leaveth the sheep, and fleeth: and the wolf catcheth them, and scattereth the sheep. The hireling fleeth, because he is an hireling, and careth not for the sheep' (vv. 12, 13)

He who is a hireling is one who only seeks his hire. He is only interested in himself. The word of God plainly teaches that every faithful gospel preacher is to be maintained by the generosity of God's people. The fact that a man is supported by the people he serves does not make him a hireling. 'The labourer is worthy of his hire' (Luke 10:7). In fact, a man may be a hireling who receives no financial remuneration from any church. A hireling is a man who is motivated by his own lusts. A true shepherd is motivated by his Master. Sheep control hirelings. True shepherds cannot be controlled by sheep. Yet, the faithful shepherd is to be maintained by the flock he serves. The scriptures are crystal clear about this (1 Corinthians 9:7-14; Galatians 6:6; 1 Timothy 5:17, 18)

The church of God is not a business; and faithful men cannot be hired. Money talks everywhere in the world. And money talks in religious organizations. But money has no voice in God's church. And money has no voice with God's servants. Nevertheless, every faithful pastor is to be supported and maintained in his livelihood by the generosity of God's people.

The hireling is one who seeks the hire and not the flock. This was the most common charge God laid against false prophets in the Old Testament. Isaiah complained of it in his day. 'His watchmen are blind: they are all ignorant, they are all dumb dogs; they cannot bark; sleeping, lying down, loving to slumber. Yea, they are greedy dogs which can never have enough, and they are shepherds that cannot understand: they all look to their own way, every one for his gain, from his quarter' (Isaiah 56:10, 11). Jeremiah said the same thing in his day. 'For, from the least of them even unto the greatest of them, every one is given to covetousness; and from the prophet, even unto the priest, every one dealeth falsely' (Jeremiah 6:13). Ezekiel spoke of the false prophets in exactly the same way, describing the hireling shepherd as one who feeds himself. 'Woe be to the shepherds of Israel that do feed themselves! should not the shepherds feed the flocks?' (Ezekiel 34:2). Paul said exactly the same thing about false prophets in his day. 'For all seek their own, not the things which are Jesus Christ's' (Philippians 2:21).

This is the black mark of the hireling. 'He that is a hireling, and not the shepherd, whose own the sheep are not, seeth the wolf coming, and leaveth the sheep and fleeth.' But it is not merely the seeking of money that marks the hireling. It is seeking things for himself, such as ease, honour, fame, position, power, and influence.

The hireling is one 'whose own the sheep are not'. He has no love for the sheep. The hireling is not part of the family. The hireling is not a son, or a brother, or a father. He has no connection with the sheep. He has no connection with the souls of men. He is one of the 'clergy', a 'reverend', and they are just 'lay people', 'sheep'.

'The hireling fleeth because he is an hireling, and careth not for the sheep.' That is another feature of a hireling. I do not suggest or imply that any man who moves from one congregation to another is a hireling. That is not the case. God may move a man from one place of service to another. But I do mean to say, and our Lord means for us to understand, that the hireling always watches out for number one. He always takes care of himself. If a wolf howls, the hireling flees, because he is a hireling. The hireling is always found on the side of the wolf!

He is not willing to bear any reproach or persecution for Christ and the gospel. He is not a keeper of the flock, as David was who went after the lion and the bear. When they rose up against the sheep, David did not flee, but caught them by the beard and slew them. The hireling is not a keeper of the sheep like the Apostle Paul, who fought with wild beasts at Ephesus, who turned his back on none, who gave place to none, no, not for an hour, that truth might continue.

When a wolf comes, be it Satan, trouble, persecution, opposition, slander, or reproach, the hireling flees, the sheep are scattered, the name of God, his church, and the gospel of the grace of God are dishonoured. But the hireling protects himself and gets 'a call from the Lord', telling him that 'his work in that place is done', and moves on to greener pastures.

The hireling is one who flees when the sheep are most in need of a shepherd, because 'He careth not for the sheep' (vv. 12, 13). His only interest is himself, his name, his reputation, his future. He does not care for the sheep. He does not care what becomes of the sheep. They are just so many pebbles in his road to success.

John Calvin wrote, 'He who looks to the hire, and not to the flock, though he may deceive others, when the Church is in a state of tranquillity, yet when he comes into the contest, will give proof of his treachery.' 'Woe to the idol shepherd that leaveth the flock! the sword shall be upon his arm, and upon his right eye: his arm shall be clean dried up, and his right eye shall be utterly darkened' (Zechariah 11:17).

Here Is The True Shepherd

All that is here said of the hireling, as it identifies the hireling, by contrast identifies the true shepherd, the faithful gospel preacher. The hireling serves himself; but the faithful shepherd serves the sheep (2 Corinthians 2:17; 4:1-7).

The hireling has no personal interest in the sheep. They are not his. The true shepherd has a very personal interest in the sheep. They are his. God's family is his family. God's people are his people. Christ's sheep are his sheep. Faithful pastors stand in a peculiar relation to the Lord's sheep. Faithful shepherds are called fathers (1 Corinthians 4:15; Galatians 4:19; 1 Timothy 1:2; Philemon 10). Like fathers, they are instruments of birth. Like fathers, they provide for the family. Like fathers, they educate the family. Like fathers, they lead the family. Like fathers, they protect the family. Like fathers, they are devoted to the family.

True shepherds, true pastors are set as watchmen who stand on the watch tower. They watch over the souls committed to their trust as they that must give account (Hebrews 13:7, 17). The relationship of faithful gospel preachers and the people they serve is a relationship that outlasts death (1 Thessalonians 2:19; Philippians 4:1; Colossians 1:25-29). God's servants are men to whom the Lord Jesus has entrusted the care of his sheep; and they care for the sheep (Acts 20:31; Romans 1:9; 2 Corinthians 2:4; Philippians 1:3; 4:1; Colossians 2:1; 1 Thessalonians 3:9).

This is the mark of a true shepherd. But a hireling cares not for the sheep; he does not and cannot weep for the sheep; he has no anguish of heart for them. He does not care what happens to them. When the wolf comes, the hireling flees, because 'he is a hireling and careth not for the sheep', but the faithful shepherd will not flee from the wolf, and will not abandon the sheep.

In the word of God the wolf specifically represents both false prophets and heresy (Acts 20:29). The time when the wolf comes is the time to mark who the true shepherd is. He stands to protect the sheep when heresy comes in, or when a persecuting world stretches out its hand towards them. At such times, the true shepherd stands between the fold and trouble (Isaiah 52:7).

Here Is The Good Shepherd

'I am the good shepherd: the good shepherd giveth his life for the sheep … I am the good shepherd, and know my sheep, and am known of mine. As the Father knoweth me, even so know I the Father: and I lay down my life for the sheep' (vv. 11, 14, 15). The Good Shepherd gave his life for his sheep. The sentence was written against us, 'Thou shalt die'. The Lord Jesus Christ stepped in and died for us. 'He was wounded for our transgressions, he was bruised for our iniquities' (Isaiah 53:5). He did it out of free love, just because he loved us. 'He gave himself for us'. 'Hereby perceive we the love of God, because he laid down his life for us: and we ought to lay down our lives for the brethren' (1 John 3:16). When we enter heaven's glory, it will be altogether because of the Good Shepherd who gave his life for the sheep.

The Good Shepherd knows his sheep. He knows his sheep with the eternal knowledge of everlasting love, delight, and approval. He knows his sheep as his sheep, sheep given to him by his Father, redeemed by his blood, and brought to him by his Spirit.

The Good Shepherd is known of his sheep, because he graciously makes himself known to them. We know his voice. We know who he is. We know what he has done. We know where he is. We know what he is doing. We know him!

The Good Shepherd seeks the sheep (vv. 16-18). Christ seeks his sheep, and all true shepherds, all true pastors seek the Lord's sheep. Sheep are the business of Christ's shepherds, his pastors.

A Division

'There was a division therefore again among the Jews for these sayings. And many of them said, he hath a devil, and is mad; why hear ye him? Others said, These are not the words of him that hath a devil. Can a devil open the eyes of the blind?' (vv. 19-21).

Here is a large crowd of religious people divided over doctrine. Religious people always are. What multitudes there are who fight for doctrine, and even divide family and friend while defending 'their position'. Contending about Christ, but never trusting in him! The Lord Jesus was standing in their midst, teaching the gospel publicly, expounding the Old Testament scriptures; but they believed not on him. They were divided over the Saviour's doctrine 'for these sayings' (v. 19). Some said he was a demon-possessed madman. Others objected. They would not go that far. But none believed (v. 25).

Do you trust the Son of God? Has the Lord Jesus Christ made himself known to you? Has he granted you understanding to know him that is true? Are you in him that is true? This is the mark of all his sheep. 'I am known of mine'. The sheep hear his voice. They follow him. They know him and know his voice. They will not follow a stranger.

If you now trust the Son of God, the Good Shepherd has brought you into his fold. The blessed Son of God has claimed you as his sheep, whom he redeemed, whom he has called, whom he will keep. Thus he fulfils his word by the prophet Jeremiah (3:15; 33:12-16).

Chapter 2

Reprobation Asserted

'And it was at Jerusalem the feast of the dedication, and it was winter. And Jesus walked in the temple in Solomon's porch. Then came the Jews round about him, and said unto him, How long dost thou make us to doubt? If thou be the Christ, tell us plainly. Jesus answered them, I told you, and ye believed not: the works that I do in my Father's name, they bear witness of me. But ye believe not, because ye are not of my sheep, as I said unto you. My sheep hear my voice, and I know them, and they follow me: And I give unto them eternal life; and they shall never perish, neither shall any man pluck them out of my hand. My Father, which gave them me, is greater than all; and no man is able to pluck them out of my Father's hand. I and my Father are one' (John 10:19-30).

Reprobation is clearly taught in holy scripture. It is a doctrine which should fill our hearts with praise to God our Saviour, the triune Jehovah. Election is God's choice of some to eternal salvation in Christ. Reprobation is God passing by, not choosing others. Predestination is God's sovereign, eternal purpose of grace toward and for his elect. Reprobation is God leaving all others to themselves. Salvation is God's mighty, wondrous works and operations of grace for, in, and upon his chosen. Reprobation is God abandoning others to themselves. Election is God loving Jacob and all the sons and daughters of Jacob. Reprobation is God hating Esau and all the children of Esau. Eternal life is God refusing to leave you alone. Reprobation is God leaving you alone. Salvation is God not leaving you to your will, your choice, and your way. Reprobation is God leaving you to your will, your choice, and your way.

Believe Not, Because

Read John 10:26. Here the Lord Jesus Christ asserts, with unmistakable clarity, the Bible doctrine of reprobation. 'But ye believe not, because ye are not of my sheep, as I said unto you.' Read those words again. Be sure you read them just as they stand. Read nothing into the text. Leave nothing out of the text. Do not rearrange the words of the text. Read it just as it stands. Here is reprobation asserted by the Son of God, the Lord Jesus Christ, the sinner's Friend. 'But ye believe not, because ye are not of my sheep, as I said unto you.'

What unspeakably solemn words those are! The Lord Jesus is the only man who ever lived who knew who the elect are and who the reprobate are. He alone knows who his sheep are and who the goats are. And here he asserts in the plainest terms possible that these Jews who cavilled at his doctrine in rebellion and unbelief, these men who wilfully stopped their ears and would not hear him, these people who were offended at his doctrine were reprobates. Now that their character was fully manifested, the Lord did not hesitate to tell them that they were abandoned of God, left to themselves, reprobate. What an unspeakably solemn thing this is!

The force of our Lord's words is definite and clear. Yet, preachers and theologians and commentators, in their unbelief, have done their best to cut these words out of the Bible altogether. Almost all the commentators explain away the meaning of our Lord's words in John 10:26 by reversing their order. They rearrange the Master's words to make them mean what they want them to mean. They read the text this way: 'Because ye believe not, ye are not of my sheep'. But the text reads, 'But ye believe not, because ye are not of my sheep, as I said unto you.'

Men always turn the things of God upside down, especially lost religious men. When man comes to something in the word of God he doesn't like, something that does not fit his religious system, something that is contrary to his high opinion of himself, instead of bowing to and receiving that which is written in the book of God, he either ignores it, or rearranges it according to his own whims.

Here the Lord Jesus not only charges these very religious, very devoted Jews with unbelief, but he also tells them why faith had not been granted to them. They were not of his sheep. They were not numbered among the favoured people of God. They were not chosen of God. They were not among God's elect.

Faith in Christ does not make us his sheep. Rather faith in Christ is the evidence that we are his sheep (Hebrews 11:1). If you believe on the Lord Jesus Christ, you believe because you were given to the Good Shepherd as one of his sheep before the world began. If you continue in wilful, obstinate unbelief and perish in your sins, it is because God has left you to yourself, because God has abandoned you to your own will, your own choice, and your own way. You are reprobate.

Confirmation From John 8

'But ye believe not, because ye are not of my sheep, as I said unto you.' What does the Saviour refer to in those words? When had he previously avowed that these people were not numbered among God's elect? When had he formerly declared them reprobates? Look at John 8. There he is talking to the very same people. In verse 48, they rejected his word, rejected his message, and declared him to be a worthless Samaritan, possessed of a devil. In verses 42-45 the Master tells us why they could not believe him.

'Jesus said unto them, If God were your Father, ye would love me: for I proceeded forth and came from God; neither came I of myself, but he sent me. Why do ye not understand my speech? even because ye cannot hear my word. Ye are of your father the devil, and the lusts of your father ye will do. He was a murderer from the beginning, and abode not in the truth, because there is no truth in him. When he speaketh a lie, he speaketh of his own: for he is a liar, and the father of it. And because I tell you the truth, ye believe me not' (John 8:42-45).

Again, in verse 47, the Lord Jesus told them that they believed not because they were not of his sheep. 'He that is of God heareth God's words: ye therefore hear them not, because ye are not of God.' They heard not because they were not of God. They believed not because they were not of his sheep. In each instance he gives this as the reason why they received him not: the solemn fact that they belonged not to God's elect. They were numbered not among God's elect, but among the reprobates. They were not sheep, but goats.

A Division

First, I want us to see the context in which our Saviour's words are found (vv. 19-30). As I pointed out in the previous chapter, here is a large crowd of religious people divided over doctrine! Religious people always are. They were divided over the Saviour's doctrine 'for these sayings' (v. 19). He had plainly taught the sweet, gospel doctrines of sovereign election, covenant mercy, his own suretyship responsibility, limited atonement, irresistible grace, and the holy trinity. Some said he was demon-possessed, others would not go that far. But none believed (vv. 25, 26).

Let us never be surprised if we see the same thing in our own day. Human nature never changes. So long as the heart of man is without grace, so long we must expect it to be enmity against God, ever despising the gospel of Christ (Romans 8:7; 1 Corinthians 2:14).

God's people and God's servants should never think it a strange thing if we go through the same experience as our Master. Our gospel is still the cause of offence and strife in our families and among friends. If you believe and confess the gospel of God, you will endure ridicule, harsh words, and petty persecution from this world. 'If they have called the Master of the house Beelzebub, how much more shall they call them of his household?' (Matthew 10:25).

Sheep

Take special notice of the name our Lord gives to his people. He uses a figurative expression full of deep meaning. He calls us, 'my sheep'.

Without question, the word 'sheep' points to something in the character and ways of God's saints in this world. It speaks of the weakness, helplessness, harmlessness, and usefulness of his elect; all points of resemblance between the sheep and the believer. But the leading, primary thing intended by giving us the name 'sheep' was to remind us of the entire dependence of the sheep upon its shepherd. Just as sheep hear the voice of their own shepherd, and follow him, so do believers follow Christ. By faith we listen to his call. By faith we submit to his guidance. By faith we lean on him, and commit our souls implicitly to his will and his direction. The ways of a shepherd and his sheep beautifully display the relation between Christ and the true Christian. We depend upon our dear Shepherd for everything in grace and in providence.

The expression, 'my sheep', points to the close connection that exists between Christ and his people. We are his by gift from the Father, his by purchase, his by his calling and his choice, and his by the willing consent and submission of our own hearts. In the highest sense imaginable, we are Christ's property. He made us for himself. He chose us to be his own. He bought us with his own precious blood. He sought us, found us, and called us by his grace.

Privileges

Our dear Saviour declares the vast privileges of mercy, love, and grace he has bestowed upon us as his sheep in verses 27 and 28.

Christ knows his sheep with a special knowledge of approbation, approval, and love. Christ gives his sheep 'eternal life'. He has freely bestowed on us a right and title to heaven, pardoning our many sins, clothing us with his perfect righteousness, and making us new creatures by his grace. Money, and health, and worldly prosperity he often wisely withholds from his sheep. But he never fails to give them grace, and peace, and glory.

Christ declares that his sheep 'shall never perish'. Weak as they are, they shall all be saved. Not one of them shall be lost or cast away. Not one of them shall miss heaven. We they err, they shall be corrected. When they stray, they shall be brought back. When they fall, they shall be raised up again. The enemies of our souls may be strong and mighty, but our Saviour is mightier; and none shall pluck us out of our Saviour's hands.

Reprobation

Second, I want to show you the meaning of our Saviour's words in our text (v. 26). 'But ye believe not, because ye are not of my sheep, as I said unto you.' In the next line he says, 'My sheep hear my voice', 'and I know them', 'and they follow me'.

'But ye believe not, because ye are not of my sheep'! What do those words mean? Does the Lord Jesus Christ speak those awful words to you? Obviously, our Lord here asserts the reprobation of those people standing before him who would not believe his gospel. The fact is there are goats as well as sheep in this world. There are reprobates as well as elect sinners among Adam's sons and daughters. There are vessels of wrath and vessels of mercy in this world (Romans 9:10-24; 1 Peter 2:6-8; Jude 4; John 12:39, 40). The same sun that melts the wax hardens the clay; and the same gospel that melts the hearts of God's elect hardens the hearts of the reprobate.

'But ye believe not, because ye are not of my sheep'! What do those words mean? I'll tell you exactly what they mean. Those words mean. I never loved you (Jeremiah 31:3; Romans 9:13). I never knew you (Romans 8:29, 30). I never chose you (Acts 13:48). I never entered into a covenant to save you (Jeremiah 31:31-34). I am not your Surety (Hebrews 7:22). I did not redeem you (Isaiah 53:8; John 10:11, 15). I did not come to save you (Matthew 1:21). I have never prayed for you (John 17:9, 20). I never called you (Romans 8:29, 30; 2 Timothy 1:9). I sent you a strong delusion that you should believe a lie (2 Thessalonians 2:10-12). I have set the world in your heart, so that you cannot find my work and know me (Ecclesiastes 3:11). I have blinded your eyes so that you cannot see (Isaiah 6:9, 10; John 12:39, 40; 2 Corinthians 4:3, 4).

'Ye believe not because ye are not of my sheep'. That means God is determined to destroy you. There is no hope for your soul.

Your Fault

God has mercy on whom he will; and whom he will, he hardens. There is no question about that fact. And your unbelief will not nullify God's purpose or alter his will. Your everlasting damnation will cause no grief in glory. The only person you injure by your rebellion is yourself. You heap upon yourself the fire of hell forever by your unbelief. God will send you to hell because you demanded he leave you alone. God will send you to hell only because you justly deserve to go to hell (Romans 6:23; Proverbs 1:23-33; 29:1). If you go to hell it will be your fault alone. You will have no one to blame but yourself.

Praise

Third, I want us to see that our Lord's assertion of reprobation should inspire praise and thanksgiving in the hearts of his elect (vv. 27-30). The Lord God could have left you to yourself. He could have abandoned you. But he chose you to salvation!

'But ye believe not, because ye are not of my sheep, as I said unto you. My sheep hear my voice, and I know them, and they follow me: And I give unto them eternal life; and they shall never perish, neither shall any man pluck them out of my hand. My Father, which gave them me, is greater than all; and no man is able to pluck them out of my Father's hand. I and my Father are one' (vv. 26-30).

Every time we think about God's just judgment upon poor reprobates, lost forever, forever abandoned by God, let us lift our hearts in praise to our great and glorious Lord God, the God of all grace, the Father of mercies, who has saved us by his grace.

'And for this cause God shall send them strong delusion, that they should believe a lie: That they all might be damned who believed not the truth, but had pleasure in unrighteousness. But we are bound to give thanks alway to God for you, brethren beloved of the Lord, because God hath from the beginning chosen you to salvation through sanctification of the Spirit and belief of the truth: Whereunto he called you by our gospel, to the obtaining of the glory of our Lord Jesus Christ' (2 Thessalonians 2:11-14).

'For who maketh thee to differ from another? and what hast thou that thou didst not receive? now if thou didst receive it, why dost thou glory, as if thou hadst not received it?' (1 Corinthians 4:7).

'But if our gospel be hid, it is hid to them that are lost: In whom the god of this world hath blinded the minds of them which believe not, lest the light of the glorious gospel of Christ, who is the image of God, should shine unto them. For we preach not ourselves, but Christ Jesus the Lord; and ourselves your servants for Jesus' sake. For God, who commanded the light to shine out of darkness, hath shined in our hearts, to give the light of the knowledge of the glory of God in the face of Jesus Christ. But we have this treasure in earthen vessels, that the excellency of the power may be of God, and not of us' (2 Corinthians 4:3-7).

Do you believe on the Lord Jesus Christ? If you do, you believe because you are one of his sheep. You were given to him by the Father in eternity. You were redeemed by him at Calvary, sought and found by him in mercy, called by him in salvation. You are kept by him in grace and shall soon be presented by him before the Father's throne with joy!

Chapter 3

'they shall never perish'

'My sheep hear my voice, and I know them, and they follow me: And I give unto them eternal life; and they shall never perish, neither shall any man pluck them out of my hand. My Father, which gave them me, is greater than all; and no man is able to pluck them out of my Father's hand. I and my Father are one' (John 10:27-30).

We who believe are Christ's sheep; weak, helpless, defenceless creatures. The Lord Jesus Christ, the Son of God, is our Shepherd; wise, good, and strong. Because Christ is our Shepherd, we are secure in him. This is what the Son of God, our dear Shepherd, says concerning all his sheep: 'They shall never perish'! With those words, the Son of God declares the absolute, infallible, unwavering security of God's elect in Christ.

I realise that some pervert the doctrine of holy scripture concerning the eternal security and preservation of God's elect in Christ. Some twist it into a lie to the eternal ruin of their souls. They attempt to justify their ungodliness by claiming to believe in God's sovereignty to the exclusion of all responsibility. They try to soothe their consciences with the delusion that they really are saved, though they live in utter, abhorrent ungodliness. Others cry, 'Such teaching as that promotes lawlessness and antinomianism.' Because they must be ruled by law, they presume that everyone must. Because they are forced servants and mercenary soldiers, they presume that there is no such thing as voluntary obedience to the Son of God.

I regret such perversions; but I will not hold back the truth of God for fear that some godless wretch will pervert it, or be offended by it. Our Lord never hesitated to proclaim the truth, even when he knew the people to whom he was preaching would twist his words, pervert his doctrine, or be offended by the gospel he preached. When our Master preached the fulfilment of the law, his enemies said, 'He is an enemy of the law.' When he preached election, they took up stones to kill him. When the Son of God preached the free forgiveness of sin, they said, 'He is the friend of publicans and sinners, a promoter of licentiousness.' When the Lord Jesus Christ preached moral freedom, freedom of conscience, his enemies said, 'He is a glutton and a wine bibber.'

I want all who read these lines to know and rejoice in the absolute security and preservation of God's elect in Christ. Some of you may be confused by this doctrine. Some may twist and pervert my doctrine to the ruin of their own souls. But, for those who believe God, the doctrine set forth in this chapter will be full of comfort, peace, assurance and joy for their souls.

Perseverance

Without question, the word of God teaches the perseverance of the saints. Those who are born of God must and shall persevere. They will continue in the faith of Christ. God's elect both believe and keep on believing. The true believer begins in faith, lives in faith, and dies in faith. True faith never quits (Matthew 10:22; John 8:31; 1 Corinthians 15:1; Colossians 1:23; Hebrews 3:6, 14). The Bible is very clear in this matter, only those who continue in the faith shall enter into glory. This is the doctrine of final perseverance of the saints.

Preservation

However, the Bible also teaches the preservation of God's elect in Christ. Those who are truly born of God will most certainly persevere in faith, because we are preserved in Christ by almighty grace. Not one of God's elect shall ever perish. The word of God teaches the preservation of the saints just as plainly, just as fully, just as forcibly as it teaches the perseverance of the saints.

Perseverance is the believer continuing in faith. Preservation is God keeping his people in faith. Perseverance is the believer holding Christ by the hand of faith. Preservation is Christ holding the believer by the hand of grace.

Having Christ as our Shepherd, all of God's sheep are absolutely secure in his hands. It is not possible for any true believer to perish, because we are preserved by the grace of God in Christ.

A Divine Distinction

Here is a divine distinction: 'My sheep hear my voice, and I know them, and they follow me.' Let men denounce it as they may, the God of the Bible does distinguish between men. He chooses some and passes by others. He redeems some and leaves others under the curse. He calls some and rejects others. He saves some and does not save others. Grace is God's prerogative. He has mercy on whom he will have mercy (Romans 9:16).

Our Lord clearly teaches his sovereignty in salvation in this chapter. He said to the unbelieving Jews who refused to believe his word, 'Ye are not of my sheep'. And he told them that the reason for their unbelief was the fact that they were not his sheep (v. 26). The gift of faith and all other grace is reserved for God's elect.

Catch these words and let them sink into your heart. God our Saviour says of you and I who believe, 'these people are my sheep'. In everlasting love, by sovereign grace, the Son of God has distinguished us from all other people, and made us to be his own sheep, his own peculiar possession.

All who believe are Christ's sheep by a distinct election. We became his sheep by his own eternal choice. In the covenant of grace God branded his sheep and set a hedge about them, securing their eternal salvation (v. 16). The Lord Jesus says, 'I know them'. And his knowledge is the peculiar knowledge of his own elective, omniscient love. Blessed word of grace this is. Christ knows his sheep! He knows who they are, where they are, what they are, all that they have done and all that they have been, what he will make of them, when he will be gracious to them, and how to bring them home.

We are his sheep by a distinct purchase, too. 'I am the good shepherd: the good shepherd giveth his life for the sheep ... As the Father knoweth me, even so know I the Father: and I lay down my life for the sheep' (vv. 11, 15). The Lord Jesus Christ laid down his life for his sheep, in the place of his sheep, as our Substitute, in our room and stead. He offered himself as a voluntary sacrifice for sin. The Son of God died as a vicarious Substitute, suffering the penalty of the law for his sheep. Our great Saviour accomplished redemption for us as a victorious Saviour.

God's elect are made his own by a distinct call. 'He calleth his own sheep by name, and leadeth them out.' 'My sheep hear my voice, and they follow me.' This is that special irresistible call that Christ issues to his sheep alone. It is always effectual. It always accomplishes salvation. It always brings the sheep to the Shepherd. The good Shepherd calls his own sheep, and no one else (v. 3). He calls his sheep by name. When he calls them, he effectually leads them out. Out of darkness into light! Out of bondage into liberty! Out of death into life! And they follow him. 'These are they that follow the Lamb withersoever he goeth'. Do you hear the Shepherd's voice?

The Lord assures us of something else regarding his sheep. His sheep will not follow a stranger. They know truth from error (v. 5; 1 John 2:20, 27). Those who are his sheep are taught of God; and, being taught of God, they have the mind of Christ and are enabled by his Spirit to discern truth from error in all matters spiritual.

A Divine Gift

Here is a divine gift. 'I give unto them eternal life'. This is one reason why we must believe in the eternal security of God's elect. Eternal life is the gift of God. It is not God's offer to men, but God's operation in men. Eternal life comes to chosen, redeemed sinners as a matter of free grace. Man does not have eternal life by nature. Eternal life does not evolve from man's sinful heart by some mysterious process of 'spiritual evolution'. It is given to men graciously. It is performed in the heart by the power of God's sovereign grace. The very word 'give' forbids the idea that eternal life comes to men as a matter of debt or reward. 'The gift of God is eternal life'. There was nothing in our hearts or conduct, which caused God to bestow eternal life upon us (Jeremiah 31:3; Romans 8:30; Ephesians 2:1-4). And there is nothing in the believer's heart or conduct which can cause God to take away his gift of eternal life (Isaiah 54:10; Psalms 89:30-36).

R. L. Dabney wrote, 'God was not induced to bestow his renewing grace in the first instance by anything which he saw meritorious and attractive in repenting sinners; and therefore the subsequent absence of everything good in them would be no new motive to God for withdrawing his grace.'

It is contrary to the nature and character of God to take away his gifts so freely bestowed (Romans 11:29). This gift of eternal life is a gift freely bestowed. It is in no way dependent upon the contingencies of this present, mortal existence. If we acknowledge that eternal life is entirely the gift of God, in no way earned by or dependent upon the goodness of man, it must be concluded that those to whom eternal life is given are eternally secure in Christ (Ecclesiastes 3:14).

A Divine Promise

Here is a divine promise. 'I give unto them eternal life; and they shall never perish'. Our Lord Jesus here makes a blanket, unconditional promise. It takes into consideration all times, all circumstances, all contingencies, all events, and all possibilities. Our Lord says, concerning all his sheep, I give unto them eternal life', and because they are my sheep and I give eternal life to them, 'they shall never perish'.

What if they are babes in Christ and their faith is weak? 'They shall never perish'. What if they are young men in Christ and their passions are strong? 'They shall never perish'. What if they are old men and their vision grows dim? 'They shall never perish'. What if they are tempted? 'They shall never perish'. What if they are tried? 'They shall never perish'. What if all hell breaks loose against them? 'They shall never perish'. What if they sin? 'They shall never perish'. What if they sin again? 'They shall never perish'. What if they fall? 'They shall never perish'. What if they fall seven times a day? 'They shall never perish'. What if they fall seventy times in a day? 'They shall never perish'!

This promise takes in all the flock. 'They shall never perish'. Not one of Christ's sheep shall ever perish; no, not even one! This is not a distinctive privilege reserved for a favoured few. It is a common mercy to all the chosen flock. If you are a believer, if you trust the Lord Jesus Christ, if you have received eternal life, you shall never perish! Christ himself has promised it. No, you cannot even sin away the grace of God bestowed upon you in Christ. Noah's fall did not alter God's grace. Abraham's weakness did not make God's grace less strong. Lot's wickedness did not make him less righteous before God. David's crime did not cause him to perish. Peter's denial of the Lord did not cause his Lord to deny him. 'Salvation is of the Lord'! Christ's sheep shall never perish.

This doctrine of the believer's security in Christ is in every way consistent with all revealed truth. It is most surely believed among the people of God. Deny this promise and with it you deny every promise of God. If one word from God cannot be believed, no word from God can be believed. Here are seven reasons why the sheep of Christ shall never perish.

The Promise Of God Must Be Fulfilled

'They shall never perish' (2 Timothy 2:19; 1 John 3:19). The purpose of God cannot be frustrated (John 6:37-40). God's covenant cannot be disannulled. God's purpose in election cannot be overturned. The suretyship engagements of Christ cannot be defeated (Hebrews 2:13). The redemptive work of Christ cannot be nullified (Isaiah 53:10, 11).

Substitutionary Redemption

The book of God declares an actual, literal, accomplished, substitutionary redemption. Since Christ died for his sheep, in their room, in their place, they cannot and will not die. He paid all our debts. We have no debt to pay.

He Bore All Our Punishment

There is no punishment left for us to bear. Christ satisfied the offended justice of God for us. There is nothing left for us to bear, and nothing for us to satisfy. Justice pleads as strongly as mercy for the eternal salvation of those people for whom Christ died at Calvary (Romans 5:10; 8:31-34). If even one of those for whom Christ died were to perish, then his purpose in dying for them would be frustrated (Ephesians 5:25-27; Galatians 1:4, 5; Titus 2:14).

Prophetic Fulfilment
If even one of those for whom Christ died were to perish, then he could never see of the travail of his soul and be satisfied (Isaiah 53:10).

Justification Is Accomplished
The believer's justification in Christ is an irreversible act of grace. The trial is over. The court of heaven has pronounced an irreversible verdict upon us 'Justified'! God will not impute sin to a believing soul (Romans 4:8). God has put away our sins forever by the sacrifice of his Son. Our acceptance before God is in Christ. Our justification is free, full, and forever!

Grace Cannot Be defeated
The work of God's grace can never be defeated (Philippians 1:6). That which God has begun he will carry on to perfection. God is willing to complete his work in us. God is wise enough to complete his work in us. God is strong enough to complete his work in us.

Christ's Intercession Will Prevail
The intercessory work of Christ must prevail (John 17:9-11, 15, 20; 1 John 2:1, 2). Our cause can never, never fail, For Jesus pleads and must prevail! The seal of the Holy Spirit cannot be broken (Ephesians 1:13, 14).

A Divine Security
Here is a divine security. 'Neither shall any man pluck them out of my hand'. We are preserved in the heart of his love. And we are preserved in the hands of his power. 'All thy saints are in thy hands'. We are in the hands of Christ our God and Saviour. We are always in his hands. What a blessed place to be! This is the place of our security. These are the hands that were pierced to redeem us. These are the hands of omnipotent power. These are the hands that hold the reins of universal dominion. These are the hands that hold us in life. These are the hands of God himself. 'My Father, which gave them me, is greater than all; and no man is able to pluck them out of my Father's hand. I and my Father are one' (John 10:29, 30).

Man's Response
This blessed doctrine of the believer's security in Christ always draws a strong response from men. The self-righteous religionist says, 'That is a dangerous doctrine. Such a doctrine will lead men into sin.' The presumptuous professor of religion will say, 'Let us sin that grace may abound.' The true believer will say, 'Such marvellous grace compels me to give my heart to Christ in complete

love, praise, and devotion' (cf. Romans 11:33-12:2). Grace produces gratitude; and gratitude produces devotion.

Perhaps you are asking, 'How can I know that this word of grace is for me?' This word of grace is for every self-confessed sinner who trusts Christ alone as Lord and Saviour. If I trust him, it is for me. If you trust him, it is for you. Do you hear the Shepherd's voice? Do you follow Christ? If so, you have eternal life; and you shall 'never perish'.

Without the least presumption, every true believer may gladly sing,

A debtor to mercy alone,
Of covenant mercy I sing,
Nor fear, with Thy righteousness on,
My person and offerings to bring.
The terrors of law and of God
With me can have nothing to do;
My Saviour's obedience and blood
Hide all my transgressions from view.

The work which God's goodness began,
The arm of His strength will complete;
His promise is yea and amen,
And never was forfeited yet:
Things future, nor things that are now,
Not all things below nor above,
Can make Him His purpose forego,
Or sever my soul from His love.

My name from the palms of His hands,
Eternity will not erase:
Impressed on His heart it remains
In marks of indelible grace:
Yes, I to the end shall endure,
As sure as the Earnest is given,
More happy, but not more secure,
The glorified spirits in heaven.

Augustus Montague Toplady

Chapter 4

'thou, being a man, makest thyself God'

'Then the Jews took up stones again to stone him. Jesus answered them, Many good works have I shewed you from my Father; for which of those works do ye stone me? The Jews answered him, saying, For a good work we stone thee not; but for blasphemy; and because that thou, being a man, makest thyself God. Jesus answered them, Is it not written in your law, I said, Ye are gods? If he called them gods, unto whom the word of God came, and the scripture cannot be broken; Say ye of him, whom the Father hath sanctified, and sent into the world, Thou blasphemest; because I said, I am the Son of God? If I do not the works of my Father, believe me not. But if I do, though ye believe not me, believe the works: that ye may know, and believe, that the Father is in me, and I in him. Therefore they sought again to take him: but he escaped out of their hand, And went away again beyond Jordan into the place where John at first baptised; and there he abode. And many resorted unto him, and said, John did no miracle: but all things that John spake of this man were true. And many believed on him there' (John 10:31-42).

In the tenth chapter of John's Gospel our Lord Jesus plainly declared himself to be the Son of God, one with and equal with the Father in all things. The Pharisees who heard his words clearly understood what he said. They took up stones to stone him, not because they did not understand his doctrine, but because they clearly understood it and hated it. They hated his doctrine and hated him for preaching it, because, though they were very religious and very strict in their practice of religion, they hated God.

Before we look at the things revealed in that last section of John 10, let me remind you of the things our Lord Jesus has just declared to this multitude of religious rebels in the temple. These Pharisees and Jews were gathered in Jerusalem at the temple to celebrate one of their many man-made religious festivals and ceremonies, The Feast of the Dedication.[1] In their pomp and pretence, they had gathered to declare and show their dedication to the Lord; but before their festivities were over, they tried to kill the God to whom they claimed to be utterly dedicated!

Why were they so enraged against the Lord Jesus? What made them mad enough to pick up stones and try to murder him in the very temple of God? He declared himself to be the only Door of salvation, saying, 'I am the Door' (v. 9). The Lord Jesus declared himself to be the Good Shepherd God promised to raise up over his elect, by whom he promised to gather his sheep unto himself (vv. 11-15). Then, the Saviour declared to those proud, racially bigoted Jews that the sheep he came to save were not just Jews, but Gentiles, too (vv. 16-18). On top of all that, the Lord Jesus, the man Christ Jesus, plainly asserted that he is God, one with the Father (v. 30).

'Then the Jews took up stones again to stone him'! Can you picture the scene? They were angry when the Lord's discourse began. The more he talked, the more angry they got. Soon, their anger turned to rage, and their rage broke forth in attempted murder. Then, 'Jesus answered them, Many good works have I shewed you from my Father; for which of those works do ye stone me? The Jews answered him, saying, For a good work we stone thee not; but for blasphemy; and because that thou, being a man, makest thyself God' (vv. 32, 33). Let me just call your attention to the things set before us by the Spirit of God in verses 31-42.

Man's Hatred Of God

The first thing here displayed in the most glaring manner is the hatred of God that possesses the heart of every human being by nature. The enraged Jews declare by example that which we read in Romans 8:7. 'The carnal mind is enmity against God'! Oh the extreme wickedness of humanity! Man hates his Maker. The creature hates his Creator. As one of the old writers put it, 'Unconverted men would kill God himself if they could only get at him.'

The unbelieving Jews at Jerusalem were not moved by our Lord's miracles or by his message. They were determined not to have him as their King, as the

---

[1] John Gill tells us, 'This was the feast of dedication, appointed by Judas Maccabaeus and his brethren, on account of purging the temple, and renewing the altar, after the profanation of them by Antiochus; which feast lasted eight days, and began on the twenty fifth of the month Cisleu, which answers to part of our December.'

Christ, the Messiah, the Shepherd of Israel. So 'they took up stones again to stone him', just as they had done back in John 8:59.

Our Lord had done them no injury. He was no robber, murderer, or rebel against the law of the land. He was one whose whole life was spent doing good. He 'went about doing good' (Acts 10:38) for thirty-three years. There was no fault or inconsistency in his character. No crime could be laid to his charge. He was holy, harmless, and undefiled. Such a man, perfect and spotless, had never walked upon the face of this earth. Yet the Jews hated him and thirsted for his blood. How true are the words of scripture, 'They hated me without a cause' (John 15:25; Psalms 35:19).

We should never be surprised when we meet with the same hatred as our blessed Lord met with at the hands of zealous religious people. Many, in their proud self-righteousness, like to convince themselves that men hate them because they are so much more righteous than others, that their righteousness exposes the wickedness in others. That is not the doctrine of this passage, or the doctrine of this book in any other passage.

Do not misunderstand me. I am fully aware that if you are known for behaving uprightly, behaving in a manner that others know is right, and they refuse to do what their own consciences tell them they ought to do, you will invoke their jealousy and rage. But you do not have to be a believer to do what is right in that sense, and enrage people by doing it. And that is not the case here.

These people did not hate our Lord Jesus because of his goodness as a man. They had no quarrel with him for doing good things: feeding the multitudes, healing the sick, raising the dead, calming the storm. They were enraged because he performed his miracles on the Sabbath, but not because he performed them. And no one will ever hate you for doing good things. I never knew anyone to be hated for being honest, telling the truth, being fair in trade, wearing modest clothes, being sober, reading the word of God, praying, giving, charity, attending church, etc..

That which enrages the world against God's elect today is the very same thing that enraged these Jews against our Lord, the very same thing that enraged Cain against Abel; it is the gospel we believe and preach, the testimony of Jesus. Abel's righteous works for which Cain hated him were his works of faith (1 John 3:10-13; Genesis 4:3-8; Hebrews 11:4). Cain was enraged because God accepted Abel by grace, without works, by the merit of a slain lamb, but would not accept him and his works of righteousness. Abel's Righteousness, that is the Lord Jesus Christ, exposed Cain's unrighteousness, the filthy rags of his self-righteous, works religion; and Cain hated Abel because of it (Hebrews 11:4).

The world, especially the religious world, hates God, hates God's saints, and hates the gospel of God. The Jews took up stones to stone the Lord Jesus in the very house of God, because his doctrine, the gospel of God, left them without hope in themselves, exposing their religion as a refuge of lies; and any man will kill you to protect his gods, unless God destroys them in his heart. That which enraged the Jews and enrages lost religious men and women everywhere is the gospel of God's free and sovereign grace in Christ, the gospel of salvation in and by Christ alone. Our Saviour tells us plainly we should always expect the hatred of the world, especially the religious world, if we worship him. 'If the world hate you, ye know that it hated me before it hated you' (John 15:18).

Holy Scripture

The second thing that we should learn from this passage is the high honour the Lord Jesus puts on holy scripture.

'Jesus answered them, Is it not written in your law, I said, Ye are gods? If he called them gods, unto whom the word of God came, and the scripture cannot be broken; Say ye of him, whom the Father hath sanctified, and sent into the world, Thou blasphemest; because I said, I am the Son of God?' (vv. 34-36).

The Lord Jesus quoted Psalms 82:6 in reply to these cavilling imps. Obviously, he was not trying to answer these Pharisees or calm their rage. His words only enraged them more (v. 39). Our Lord's reference here to the book of Psalms was for the benefit of his disciples who were standing by and for the benefit of his people in all ages.

If the Psalmist called men 'gods' and 'sons of the highest', because they were ordained of God to administer justice in his name, as Moses was to Pharaoh, as David was to Israel and her enemies, and as Joseph was in Egypt, surely it cannot be blasphemy for the Lord Jesus Christ to declare himself the Son of God. He is eternally one with and self-existent with the Father, sanctified by his Father to be our Prophet, Priest, and King, he who was in the fulness of time sent into the world to be the author of eternal redemption to the sons of men is himself God (1 John 5:7). Jesus is 'God blessed forever' (Romans 9:5).

Our Lord's purpose here is to show us, as he declares in verse 35, that 'the scripture cannot be broken'. Whatever the scriptures declare on any subject, whether we understand it or not, is true, and is to be received as fact because God declared it. There can be no question about it. The matter is settled and decided. Every jot and tittle of holy scripture is true, and must be received as authoritative and conclusive.

This is a matter of vast importance. Grasp it firmly, and never let it go. Every word of the Bible is inspired of God. Inspiration extends not only to the thoughts and ideas of scripture, but to the very words of holy scripture (2 Timothy 3:16, 17; 2 Peter 1:16-21).

The Master's Miracles

Third, we must not fail to see in this portion of holy scripture what great importance the Lord Jesus Christ attached to the miracles he performed. He appeals to his miracles as irrefutable evidence of his own divine mission as the Son of God and of his manifest deity. He told the Jews to look at them, and deny them if they could.

'Say ye of him, whom the Father hath sanctified, and sent into the world, Thou blasphemest; because I said, I am the Son of God? If I do not the works of my Father, believe me not. But if I do, though ye believe not me, believe the works: that ye may know, and believe, that the Father is in me, and I in him' (vv. 36-38).

We read of our Saviour doing things entirely miraculous more than forty times in the Gospel narratives: healing the sick in a moment, raising the dead with a word, casting out devils, calming winds and waves in an instant, walking on the water as on solid ground, and raising the dead. Some were performed privately among friends; but most were wrought in public, under the eyes of unfriendly witnesses.

We are so familiar with these things that we are apt to forget the lessons they are intended to teach. They teach that he who worked these miracles must be nothing less than very God. They stamp his doctrines and precepts with the mark of divine authority. He alone who created all things in the beginning could suspend the laws of creation at his will. To reject One who confirmed his mission by such mighty works is the height of madness and folly.

The Lord's miracles all say with one voice, 'Jesus of Nazareth is God in human flesh, the Son of God, the Christ; and all who believe on him have everlasting life through his name.' Yet, we see but little into the true worth and importance of the miracles of the Lord Jesus, if we see no more than the proof of his divinity in them. The Lord's miracles do loudly assert the divinity of his Person to the carnal sense of man, and did so even to those who hated and blasphemed him. But the grandeur of these works consisted in this: they were outward testimonies of the far more noble operations of his grace within the soul, which were not to endure for a time only, like their outward signs, but through all eternity.

He gave sight to the blind, that he might testify unto men his sovereign power in giving light and understanding to the mind. He opened the deaf ear, that men might know by whom alone they can hear aright the good news of salvation and live forever. The lame he caused, in a moment, to walk, that his people might learn that we can only move, as well as live, by him, and that without him we can do nothing. He cured the foul leprosy of the body, in order to show that only by him can men be healed of the far more deplorable leprosy of sin, which covers and defiles the soul. All sicknesses vanished at his command, that we might have hope in him as the Restorer of our souls. The poor – the meek – among men are made rich for eternity by him. He cast out unclean spirits and suffered them to possess the swine, who were thereby destroyed, that he might teach his redeemed that he alone delivered and can deliver his elect from the powers of darkness, which, being let loose upon the world, drive them violently and swiftly down the steep course of time into a gulf of endless woe in hell. The hungry multitudes were fed by his miraculous power to explain that he is not only the Giver of spiritual life, but also the constant Sustainer and Nourisher of it from day to day. And he did this by small, insignificant means, that the excellency of the power might be known to be his and not in the creatures, however sanctified, blessed and used. The winds and waves were instantly obedient to his word, that his beloved might rejoice in him as the Stiller of all spiritual waves, the tumultuous madness of this world, the raging of Satan, and the confusion of all things. These can roar and foam no longer than it pleases him; and when they foam and roar at all, it shall turn out in the end for the good of his people. The dead were raised to proclaim his power as our risen Lord, and to declare that the issues also of spiritual life and of endless death are altogether in his hands. 'He quickeneth whom he will.'

Every miracle our Master performed was an act of mercy, by which he revealed, as in parable pictures, countless lessons of mercy, grace, and love. All his works proclaimed him to be both the Creator of all and the Redeemer and Restorer of untold millions that were lost.

Learn from these things, O child of God, what your Lord God has done for your soul. He quickened you when you were dead in trespasses and sins. He gives light and peace to your soul. He feeds you with the Bread of Life. He cures all your spiritual diseases. He quells all your manifold enemies and temptations. He strengthens you with his grace day by day. He does all that is done in you by his grace; and he will never cease working in you both to will and to do of his good pleasure.

'And many resorted unto him, and said, John did no miracle: but all things that John spake of this man were true. And many believed on him there' (vv. 41, 42).

Blessed Spirit of God, graciously cause chosen, redeemed sinners to resort to the Lord Jesus and believe on him unto life everlasting.

Chapter 5

Lessons From The Blessed Family At Bethany

'Now Jesus loved Martha, and her sister, and Lazarus' (John 11:1-57).

On the eastern slope of the Mount of Olives, about two miles east of Jerusalem there was once a small village called Bethany. In this chapter God the Holy Ghost takes us to Bethany, the scene of the great miracle by which our Lord Jesus Christ demonstrated his eternal deity and omnipotent power as God. I want us to glean from the events of that great and notable day some spiritual lessons for the spiritual instruction and edification of our souls. As we do, I trust that our hearts and minds will be focused upon him who is the Resurrection and the Life, our all-glorious Christ, the Son of God, who raised Lazarus from the dead.

He who raised Lazarus from the dead at Bethany continues to raise sinners from death to life today by the power of his grace.

Sickness

Here is the first lesson taught in this chapter. It is a lesson we need to learn, lay to heart and remind ourselves of often; true believers suffer from sickness and disease in this world.

'Now a certain man was sick, named Lazarus, of Bethany, the town of Mary and her sister Martha. (It was that Mary which anointed the Lord with ointment, and wiped his feet with her hair, whose brother Lazarus was sick.) Therefore his sisters sent unto him, saying, Lord, behold, he whom thou lovest is sick. When Jesus heard that, he said, This sickness is not unto death, but for the glory of God, that the Son of God might be glorified thereby' (vv. 1-4).

Sickness is not a sign of God's displeasure or a lack of faith on our part. The fact is, sickness is sent to us by our heavenly Father for our benefit. That which is aggravating to our bodies is often good for our souls. Sickness tends to draw our affections away from the world to Christ. Sickness sends us to our knees, sends us to our Bibles, and sends us to our Saviour. Anything that accomplishes these things is good.

Sickness reminds us that life in this world, at its best, is but a vapour that is soon gone. Sickness forces us to look to the grave, look past the grave to judgment, and look past the judgment to eternity. Whenever sickness comes, be it nothing more than a cold or something as serious as cancer, let us be patient before the Lord, ever mindful of the fact that sickness is the fruit of sin. Sickness is the forerunner of death. Sickness and health, life and death are alike in the hands of our Lord Jesus Christ. For believers sickness is never unto death. And our sicknesses, whatever they are, are for the glory of God.

Faith

Here is the second lesson: True faith submits to the will of God. When Lazarus fell sick, his sisters, Martha and Mary, sent word to the Lord Jesus, their Master and most tender, caring, affectionate Friend, saying, 'Lord, behold, he whom thou lovest is sick' (v. 3). They did not ask him to come to Bethany. They did not ask him to heal their brother, though that is what they obviously hoped he would do. They simply left the matter in his hands, confident that he would do what was best.

Like Eli of old, they said, 'It is the Lord; let him do what seemeth him good.' We would be wise to follow their example. Our best, ablest, wisest, and most considerate Helper is God our Saviour. Christ is our best Friend, especially in time of need. The best thing for us to do in trouble is to fall on our knees and worship, as Job did. Like Hezekiah, let us spread our case before our God.

In the hurry and excitement of trouble and the annoyance and pain of sickness, always remember that none can help like him who 'took our infirmities and bare our sicknesses' (Matthew 8:17). None is so kind, gracious and caring as our Redeemer, who is touched with the feeling of our infirmity.

Faith submits to the will of God. Yet, we must never imagine that perfect faith will be found in any sinner in this world. Though Martha and Mary were true believers, though they were choice companions of our Saviour, there was much weakness and unbelief in them. Both Martha and Mary seem to have misjudged the Master's delay in coming to Bethany and his intentions toward them and Lazarus. Even when he was about to raise Lazarus from the dead, when he commanded them to take away the stone from his tomb, Martha argued with her Lord.

'Jesus said, Take ye away the stone. Martha, the sister of him that was dead, saith unto him, Lord, by this time he stinketh: for he hath been dead four days' (v. 39).

It is very easy to talk about faith when we are healthy and strong and have money in the bank. But it is hard to practice faith when we are sick and weak and broke. When all is darkness, when neither the sun, nor the moon, nor stars appear, it is not easy to be confident. The fact is, the strongest believer's faith is very fragile and apt to break in times of great trial.

Still there is another thing revealed in this chapter about faith. Our Lord tells us plainly (v. 40) that, if we would believe, we would see the glory of God. 'Jesus saith unto her, Said I not unto thee, that, if thou wouldest believe, thou shouldest see the glory of God?' Faith in Christ sees the glory of God in the gospel, in creation, in providence, and in grace. Faith sees the glory of God in the face of the Lord Jesus Christ and in the salvation of sinners by his perfect righteousness and his precious, sin-atoning blood.

The Love Of Christ

Here is the third lesson set before us in this chapter: The Lord Jesus Christ, our God and Saviour, loves all his elect alike. We read in verse 5, 'Now Jesus loved Martha, and her sister, and Lazarus'. Here are three chosen sinners. All were saved by the grace of God. All were alike the objects of electing love, redeeming blood, and saving grace. But they were not all alike. Martha appears to have been a bit too pushy and domineering. Mary appears to have been very spiritual, though perhaps somewhat negligent of earthly responsibilities. Of Lazarus we are told nothing, except that the Lord Jesus raised him from the dead. Yet, we are told plainly that the Lord Jesus loved all three. He loved them all alike he loved them all for the same reason. He loved them all to the same degree.

Our Saviour's love for us is free, sovereign, everlasting, and unchanging. It does not depend upon us, what we are, what we do, or what we fail to do in any way.

We must not undervalue others because they are different from us. Flowers in a garden are all different. But it is their difference that makes their contribution to the garden needful and beautiful. Your children are all different from one another; but loving parents do not care less for one child and more for another because they are different.

Even so, in the Kingdom of God, among God's true children, there are differing degrees of grace, faith, and maturity. But the least, the weakest, and the most feeble of the Lord's disciples are no less the objects of his love than the greatest, strongest, and most steadfast.

'Now Jesus was not yet come into the town, but was in that place where Martha met him. The Jews then which were with her in the house, and comforted her, when they saw Mary, that she rose up hastily and went out, followed her, saying, She goeth unto the grave to weep there. Then when Mary was come where Jesus was, and saw him, she fell down at his feet, saying unto him, Lord, if thou hadst been here, my brother had not died. When Jesus therefore saw her weeping, and the Jews also weeping which came with her, he groaned in the spirit, and was troubled, And said, Where have ye laid him? They said unto him, Lord, come and see. Jesus wept. Then said the Jews, Behold how he loved him' (vv. 30-36).

Those who show kindness to others usually find great blessedness for themselves in doing so. The little house in Bethany was filled with mourners when the Lord Jesus arrived. These mourners probably knew very little about these women and their faith in Christ. But they felt the pain of their neighbours and came in their time of bereavement to do what they could to comfort Martha and Mary. As a result of their kindness, they reaped a rare, rich, unexpected blessing. They were allowed to be eyewitnesses to the greatest miracle performed by our Lord during his earthly ministry. They saw Lazarus raised from the dead. For many of them the raising of Lazarus led to a resurrection in their souls. That was the day of their spiritual birth. 'Then many of the Jews which came to Mary, and had seen the things which Jesus did, believed on him' (v. 45).

These things are written for our learning. There is no healthier employment in the world than to visit the fatherless and the widows in their affliction, to weep with those that weep, to try to bear one another's burdens and lighten one another's loads. One great secret to being happy is to make others happy. The wise man, writing by inspiration, said, 'It is better to go to the house of mourning than to the house of feasting ... The heart of the wise man is in the house of mourning' (Ecclesiastes 7:2, 4). The surest way to make yourself miserable is to live for yourself!

These women shared Martha's and Mary's grief and they shared their joy, too. How much more should we who are already the Lord's disciples care for one another in time of need!

Our Lord Jesus Christ shows us that loving someone is being touched by that which touches them, moved by that which moves them, and grieved by that which grieves them. Our Saviour knew what he was about to do. Yet, he groaned because Martha and Mary were groaning. He wept because they wept. He was touched and moved by that which touched and moved these two women whom he dearly loved. May God give us grace to be like our loving, caring, Master.

Providence

Here is the fourth lesson set before us in this chapter by the Spirit of God: God's time is always the right time. 'When he had heard therefore that he was sick, he abode two days still in the same place where he was' (v. 6).

'These things said he: and after that he saith unto them, Our friend Lazarus sleepeth; but I go, that I may awake him out of sleep. Then said his disciples, Lord, if he sleep, he shall do well. Howbeit Jesus spake of his death: but they thought that he had spoken of taking of rest in sleep. Then said Jesus unto them plainly, Lazarus is dead. And I am glad for your sakes that I was not there, to the intent ye may believe; nevertheless let us go unto him. Then said Thomas, which is called Didymus, unto his fellow disciples, Let us also go, that we may die with him. Then when Jesus came, he found that he had lain in the grave four days already' (vv. 11-17).

Our Lord always knows when it is best for him to intervene, when it is best for him to work, and how. When he heard that Lazarus was sick, he stayed where he was for two days. He knew Lazarus was dying. Yet, he stayed right where he was. For the sake of his church, for the good of his friends, for the salvation of his chosen, and for the glory of God, he stayed where he was until he knew that it was time for him to appear and act. Our Lord always intervenes at the right time.

It was in the fulness of time that Christ came to redeem and save his people. Lazarus was dead for four days before Christ came to raise him from the dead. You know that, according to Peter, one day is with the Lord as a thousand years and a thousand years as one day. By that calculation, there is a picture of our redemption here. Only four days passed (four thousand years) between our sin and death by the fall of Adam in the Garden and Christ's coming to save us from our sins, 'when the fulness of time was come'!

In all the affairs of our lives, we need to realise that God's time is the best time for everything. As J. C. Ryle put it, 'Nothing so helps us to bear patiently the trials of life as an abiding conviction of the perfect wisdom by which everything around us is managed.'

Everything that happens to us is well done, done in the best manner, by the right instrument, and at the right time. We are all naturally impatient when trials come. We want things done now. We cry out like Moses did when Miriam was stricken with leprosy, 'Heal her now, LORD' (Numbers 12:13). We ought to wait. Our God is too wise to err, too good to do wrong, and too strong to fail. Our times are in his hands. It is our greatest wisdom and faith to patiently wait for him to do what he will, when he will. When we are sick, he knows the best time to heal us and the best way. When we are in trouble, he knows the best time to deliver us and the best way. When we need help, he knows the best time to help and the best way.

Death

Here is our fifth lesson and what a wonderful lesson it is. Because Christ is the Resurrection and the Life and we live in him, God's elect shall never die (vv. 11-14, 25, 26).

'These things said he: and after that he saith unto them, Our friend Lazarus sleepeth; but I go, that I may awake him out of sleep. Then said his disciples, Lord, if he sleep, he shall do well. Howbeit Jesus spake of his death: but they thought that he had spoken of taking of rest in sleep. Then said Jesus unto them plainly, Lazarus is dead' (vv. 11-14).

'Jesus said unto her, I am the resurrection, and the life: he that believeth in me, though he were dead, yet shall he live: And whosoever liveth and believeth in me shall never die. Believest thou this?' (vv. 25, 26).

Without question, we must all die in a physical sense. These bodies of clay must return to the dust. And you who are without Christ must die the second death, which is everlasting separation from God in hell. But believers do not die. When our bodies cease to function, when our earthly tabernacle is dissolved, when these houses of clay crumble, we shall be forever with the Lord in life. Those who have experienced the first resurrection, the new birth, shall never taste the second death (Revelation 20:6). For the believer, death is no more than the sleeping of the body for a while. Yet, while the body sleeps, while we shall be absent from the body, we shall be present with the Lord. This is exactly what our Lord Jesus told Martha (vv. 25, 26).

'I am the Resurrection and the Life'. Christ is our Life. We have life from him; and we live in him by virtue of his Resurrection as our Substitute and Saviour. He is our Resurrection. We were raised from the dead with him representatively (Ephesians 2:5, 6). We have been raised from the dead in him spiritually in the new birth (Revelation 20:6). And we shall be raised from the dead literally by his power at the second coming (1 Corinthians 15:42-58; 1 Thessalonians 4:13-18).

'He that believeth in me, though he were dead, yet shall he live'. Though we are all by nature sinners, dead in trespasses and in sins, if we believe on the Lord Jesus Christ, we shall live forever. If we trust in him, we have everlasting life.

'Whosoever liveth and believeth in me shall never die! Believest thou this?' Believers shall never die. God's elect are immune to death. For the believer death is a graduation, an elevation, a freedom, a liberty, an entrance into a life longed for and expected. Then, and not until then our most earnest prayers will be answered, our highest, noblest ambitions will be realised, our trials, temptations, and sorrows will be over.

Salvation

Here is the sixth lesson given to us in this chapter. The salvation of a sinner is accomplished by the life-giving, resurrection power of the Son of God.

'Jesus said, Take ye away the stone. Martha, the sister of him that was dead, saith unto him, Lord, by this time he stinketh: for he hath been dead four days. Jesus saith unto her, Said I not unto thee, that, if thou wouldest believe, thou shouldest see the glory of God? Then they took away the stone from the place where the dead was laid. And Jesus lifted up his eyes, and said, Father, I thank thee that thou hast heard me. And I knew that thou hearest me always: but because of the people which stand by I said it, that they may believe that thou hast sent me. And when he thus had spoken, he cried with a loud voice, Lazarus, come forth. And he that was dead came forth, bound hand and foot with graveclothes: and his face was bound about with a napkin. Jesus saith unto them, Loose him, and let him go' (vv. 39-44).

Here, in broad daylight, before many hostile witnesses, a man who had been dead for four days was raised to life again in a moment by the voice of the Son of God! Here was public proof that our Lord Jesus Christ has absolute power over the material world. A corpse already corrupt and rotting was made alive in an instant. Here was public proof that our Lord Jesus Christ has absolute power over the spirit world. A soul that had left this tabernacle of clay was called back from heaven to earth to live a while longer in mortality.

Yet, great and glorious as these things are, I am certain that these things are recorded here primarily to teach us spiritual lessons about salvation and the way it is accomplished.

Lazarus was dead. That is the spiritual condition of us all by nature. We are all born in a state of spiritual death. That means that we are totally incapable of doing anything to change our condition. If salvation comes, it must come from outside us.

Lazarus was decaying. Just as the dead corpse decays in the earth, so spiritually dead hearts and souls and minds are in a state of unceasing decay, called 'the corruption of this world'. I do not need to prove that statement to anyone. Things that you once never dreamed you would think, now occupy your mind constantly. Things you thought you could never do, you now practice without thought. If the thoughts of your mind were open to public view, you would be ashamed, if not terrified, to show your face in public.

Lazarus was delivered. Lazarus' resurrection from the dead and deliverance from the grave is a vivid picture of our spiritual deliverance from death and sin by the grace of God. First, our Saviour spoke to the people at the tomb. He said, in verse thirty-nine, 'Take ye away the stone'. Why? If he could raise the dead, he could easily roll away the stone. But he is demonstrating the fact that though God always acts sovereignly in the salvation of sinners, he never by-passes the use of means. We cannot raise the dead; but we can take away the stones. Therefore we are responsible to take away the stones. By the preaching of the gospel we fill the ditches in the way, level the hills, make crooked places straight and the rough ways smooth, and 'take up the stumblingblock out of the way' of sinners (Isaiah 40:4; 57:14).

Christ's Prayer

Next, our Saviour spoke to God the Father.

'Then they took away the stone from the place where the dead was laid. And Jesus lifted up his eyes, and said, Father, I thank thee that thou hast heard me. And I knew that thou hearest me always: but because of the people which stand by I said it, that they may believe that thou hast sent me' (vv. 41, 42).

I take that to be a picture of our Saviour's intercession for chosen sinners in heaven. Then, the Lord Jesus spoke directly to Lazarus. 'And when he thus had spoken, he cried with a loud voice, Lazarus, come forth' (v. 43). He called Lazarus out of death exactly as he calls sinners out of death by his grace, with a personal, particular, powerful call. The call of God is always irresistible. When God says, 'Live', the dead are made to live. When God says, 'Come', those who cannot come to Christ come, immediately, to Christ.

After Lazarus was risen, our Saviour spoke to the people again. 'And he that was dead came forth, bound hand and foot with graveclothes: and his face was bound about with a napkin. Jesus saith unto them, Loose him, and let him go' (v. 44). That is the mission of God's church in this world. First, we are to remove the stones which hinder men from coming to Christ. We do that by preaching the gospel of God's free grace. Then, when sinners are saved by the grace of God, it is our job to loose them from the grave clothes of death. We do that by exactly the same means, by preaching the gospel of God's free grace in Christ. Religion loves to bind men with rules and duties. Christ sets sinners free. By the preaching of the gospel, sinners are freed from the grave clothes of religious legalism, self-righteousness, free-willism, and ritualism.

Substitution

All of this would really be meaningless if I failed to show you the last thing revealed in this chapter, because the salvation of our souls is an utter impossibility without the sin-atoning, substitutionary sacrifice and death of the Lord Jesus Christ in the place of his people.

'And one of them, named Caiaphas, being the high priest that same year, said unto them, Ye know nothing at all, Nor consider that it is expedient for us, that one man should die for the people, and that the whole nation perish not. And this spake he not of himself: but being high priest that year, he prophesied that Jesus should die for that nation; And not for that nation only, but that also he should gather together in one the children of God that were scattered abroad' (vv. 49-52).

Here is the seventh lesson given in this chapter by the Spirit of God. The only way sinful men and women can be saved from the wrath of God is by the substitutionary sacrifice, the death in our place, of that Man who is God.

Though he had absolutely no idea what he was saying, Caiaphas the high priest spoke by the Spirit of God as a prophet. He made two statements, said two things that very few preachers, let alone anyone else in this world, ever come to know. But these two things are vital to the gospel. Apart from these two things there is no gospel.

Justice must be satisfied. 'It is expedient for us, that one man should die for the people, and that the whole nation perish not' (v. 50). The Lord Jesus has fully satisfied the justice of God for his elect by his death upon the cursed tree. Since the Lord Jesus Christ has died as our Substitute, fully satisfying the justice of God for us, all for whom he died can never die, all the children of God, all God's elect, every ransomed sinner must be gathered together in everlasting salvation.

Chapter 6

Lazarus Raised, Irresistible Grace

'And when he thus had spoken, he cried with a loud voice, Lazarus, come forth. And he that was dead came forth, bound hand and foot with graveclothes: and his face was bound about with a napkin. Jesus saith unto them, Loose him, and let him go' (John 11:1-12:11).

Do you know anything about the love-calls of our omnipotent Saviour? It is impossible not to know them if you have ever heard them. The soul that hears the voice of the Son of God, though he never heard it before, knows the sweet sound of the Shepherd's voice. When the Saviour speaks to a sinner dead in trespasses and sins, he speaks with a loud voice that cannot be missed (John 11:43), a powerful voice that cannot be resisted 'the voice of the LORD is powerful: the voice of the LORD is full of majesty'! (John 11:44; Psalms 29:3-11), a still small voice that no one hears but the one called (1 Kings 19:9-14), a sweet, loving, winning voice that causes the one called to arise and seek the Lord (Song of Solomon 5:2), and a personal voice that causes the one called to know he is called (Luke 19:5).

Responsibility

It is the responsibility of God's church and of every gospel preacher to preach the gospel to all men as the Lord gives them opportunity (Mark 16:15, 16). I recognise that the greatest privilege that has ever been bestowed upon a man is the privilege of preaching the gospel to men, to speak to men on God's behalf. The highest calling in the world, the greatest privilege that can be given to a mortal man is to be sent of God to proclaim the gospel of redeeming grace to perishing men. But, while this is the greatest privilege in the world, it is also the greatest responsibility in the world. It is an awesome thing to speak to men with immortal souls on the behalf of the eternal God.

In fulfilling this responsibility, basically, three things are required of a man: sincerity, simplicity, and steadfastness. The preacher must be sincere in his motives, free of deceit, serving the souls of men, not himself. He must preach the gospel with simplicity. To preach with simplicity is to preach with bold decisiveness, with clarity, the singular message of redemption accomplished by the sin-atoning sacrifice of Christ. To preach the gospel with simplicity is to preach so as to be understood. And we must be steadfast, never allowing ourselves to be turned aside or diverted in any way from our purpose and our message.

It is the responsibility of all who hear the gospel to repent and believe on the Lord Jesus Christ (2 Corinthians 6:1, 2). 'God commandeth all men everywhere to repent'. I rejoice to declare to all men everywhere, that any sinner in all the world who calls upon Christ in true faith shall be saved. It is written, 'Whosoever shall call upon the name of the Lord shall be saved.' I know that all are responsible before God to believe that which is plainly revealed in his word. And I know that all who believe on Christ shall be saved (Acts 16:31). Indeed, if you believe, God has saved you! 'He that believeth on the Son of God hath everlasting life'!

Yet, I know that no man by nature can or will come to Christ. Fallen man has neither the desire nor the ability to trust Christ (John 5:40; 6:44). It is not within the realm of man's power, and it is not within the scope of his heart's desire to come to Christ. Unless God does for a sinner what that sinner cannot and will not do for himself, he will perish. None can believe, except God create faith in them and cause them to trust his Son.

God's Gift

And we know that true saving faith is the gift of God (Ephesians 2:8; John 6:37-40). This is our Saviour's doctrine. No one can come. Anyone may come. Someone will come. 'Thy people shall be willing in the day of thy power'! And all who do come to him shall be saved forever! 'Blessed is the man whom thou choosest and causest to approach unto thee'.

If any man comes to Christ, believing on him unto life everlasting, he does so because God has drawn him to Christ by the effectual power and irresistible grace of his Spirit. True faith is the result of, not the cause of, divine grace. Saving faith is created in a man's heart by the mighty, sovereign operations of God the Holy Spirit in omnipotent, saving grace. We who believe, believe 'by the greatness of his power' and 'according to the working of his mighty power, which he wrought in Christ Jesus when he raised him from the dead'

(Ephesians 1:19, 20). The faith that we have and exercise in Christ is performed in us by 'the operation of God' (Colossians 2:12).

This creation of faith in the heart, by which a person is drawn to Christ, is what we call 'effectual calling', or 'irresistible grace'. The effectual calling of the Holy Spirit is that sovereign, gracious, irresistible work and operation of God the Holy Spirit, which changes a man's heart and will, causing him to come to Christ and be saved by faith in him. Effectual calling is the tender influence, the overpowering love, the compelling grace and irresistible power of God the Holy Spirit which causes a person to gladly and willingly receive Christ as Lord and Saviour. Those who, left to themselves, would by nature never come to Christ, are made willing to come to him in effectual calling.

There are many, many pictures of this effectual calling and irresistible grace in the scriptures; pictures that beautifully illustrate this blessed act of mercy by which chosen, redeemed sinners are made to experience God's love. They are brought to experience the grace that was given to them in Christ Jesus before the worlds were made. One of the most instructive of these pictures is the resurrection of Lazarus. In the eleventh and twelfth chapters of John's Gospel, the Holy Spirit tells us five things about Lazarus and his call from death to life that picture God's irresistible grace in the salvation of his elect.

His Condition

First, Lazarus' condition is plainly declared in John 11:14. Lazarus was dead. 'Then said Jesus unto them plainly, Lazarus is dead'. That is the state of all human beings by nature; spiritually dead, dead in trespasses and sins, incapable of either knowing or changing their condition (Romans 5:12). The dead cannot move toward God. The dead have neither will nor ability to come to Christ. The dead do not desire God's salvation. The dead cannot see. The dead cannot understand. The dead must be raised from death to life by the power of God; that resurrection is the new birth, the first resurrection (John 5:25; Ephesians 2:1-10; Revelation 20:6). As Lazarus' sickness and death was 'for the glory of God, that the Son of God might be glorified thereby' (v. 3), so our sin and death in our father Adam was 'for the glory of God, that the Son of God might be glorified thereby'.

His Calling

Look at John 11:43 and you will see Lazarus' calling. That is the second thing I want you to see. Lazarus' calling was a picture of our calling, the effectual, irresistible call of God's omnipotent grace by which all who are saved are saved. 'And when he thus had spoken, he cried with a loud voice, Lazarus, come forth'. When the Lord Jesus cried, 'Lazarus, come forth', the dead man arose to life.

There is a general call which goes out to all men whenever the gospel is preached; but this was not a general call. This was a personal, particular, powerful call, irresistible, effectual, and distinguishing. The only way any sinner will ever be saved is if the Son of God, by the power of his Spirit, calls him from death to life. And all who are called by him live by him, with him, and in him (John 5:25). Our election and redemption are made manifest and made sure to our souls by this act of God's omnipotent mercy (1 Thessalonians 1:4, 5).

His Conversion

'And he that was dead came forth, bound hand and foot with graveclothes: and his face was bound about with a napkin. Jesus saith unto them, Loose him, and let him go.' Once he was called, Lazarus was converted. His conversion was both immediate and gradual. He was immediately changed from death to life. But he was gradually freed from his 'grave clothes'. And sinners saved by grace are immediately transformed into a new creation (2 Corinthians 5:17). But throughout our lives we are being saved, gradually, from the 'grave clothes' of sin and unbelief, legalism and self-righteousness, and religious customs, traditions, and rituals (2 Corinthians 7:1). The Saviour's command is, 'Loose him, and let him go' (2 Corinthians 6:14-7:1). And by the preaching of the gospel, saved sinners are loosed, not bound with fetters of law, but loosed in the blessed liberty of grace.

His Communion

Fourth, in chapter 12 we see Lazarus sitting at the table with the Lord Jesus in sweet communion. 'Then Jesus six days before the passover came to Bethany, where Lazarus was which had been dead, whom he raised from the dead. There they made him a supper; and Martha served: but Lazarus was one of them that sat at the table with him' (vv. 1, 2).

Soon after his resurrection, Lazarus is found sitting at the table with his Saviour. Do not miss this: perhaps the house and the table belonged to Lazarus; but the Master of the house was Christ. Lazarus surrendered all to his Lord (Luke 14:25-33). The believing, surrendered heart is the heart with which Christ holds sweet communion. I can almost hear Lazarus' heart, as he sat there at the table with the Lord Jesus …

I am Thine, O Lord! I have heard Thy voice;
And it told Thy love to me;
But I long to rise in the arms of faith,
And be closer drawn to Thee!

Consecrate me now to Thy service, Lord,
By the pow'r of grace divine;
Let my soul look up with a steadfast hope,
And my will be lost in Thine'!

Frances J. Crosby

His Conflict

Fifth, in John 12:9-11, we find Lazarus in the midst of terrible conflict, with men trying to kill him. Because of Lazarus, many others believed; but the Jews sought to kill him. Why? Because he had been raised from the dead. That is all. He had been the blessed recipient of God's great grace, and they had not. Therefore, they sought to kill him. This is the last we hear of Lazarus. His life with Christ was a life of unceasing conflict in this world. And all who believe will find it so with them. That is the way it was in the beginning; and that is the way it shall be until the end (Genesis 4:1-8; John 16:33).

'The Lord said unto Cain, Why art thou wroth? and why is thy countenance fallen? If thou doest well, shalt thou not be accepted? and if thou doest not well, sin lieth at the door. And unto thee shall be his desire, and thou shalt rule over him. And Cain talked with Abel his brother: and it came to pass, when they were in the field, that Cain rose up against Abel his brother, and slew him.'

The Lord God said to Cain, 'If your worship is evil, sin lies at the door of your guilty conscience still, tormenting you. Abel's love for you has not changed. He still desires you as his brother. He still respects you as his elder brother, as the firstborn of your father.' Still, Cain murdered Abel, for just one reason. Abel was accepted of God in and by Christ. Abel believed God; and Cain, trusting his own righteousness, was still guilty before God. And he knew it.

Abel was chosen. Therefore Abel was redeemed. Being chosen and redeemed, Abel was called. Because he was called, Abel believed. Believing on the Son of God, Abel was justified. Justified in Christ, Abel was accepted and his conscience was clear before God.

Do you know anything about the love-calls of our omnipotent Saviour? How I thank God for that sovereign, free, irresistible grace by which I am called! How I praise him that when he called me, he would not take 'No' for an answer! O blessed Holy Spirit, call out chosen sinners! O precious Lord Jesus, blessed Friend of sinners, let the dead now hear your voice that they may live!

Am I called? And can it be?
Has my Saviour chosen me?
Guilty, wretched as I am,
Has He named my worthless name?
Vilest of the vile am I,
Dare I raise my hopes so high?

Am I called? I dare not stay,
Cannot, must not, disobey:
Here I lay me at Thy feet,
Clinging to the Mercy-seat:
Thine I am, and Thine alone;
Lord, with me Thy will be done.

Am I called? What shall I bring
As an offering to my King?
Poor, and blind, and naked I,
Trembling at Thy footstool lie;
Nought but sin I call my own,
Nor for sin can sin atone.

Am I called? An heir of God!
Washed, redeemed, by precious blood!
Father, lead me in Thy hand,
Guide me to that better land,
Where my soul shall be at rest,
Pillowed on my Saviour's breast.

Chapter 7

Where Was Lazarus?

'Our friend Lazarus sleepeth … Loose him, and let him go' (John 11:11-46).

We are now familiar with the story of Lazarus' death and resurrection recorded in John 11. Without question, this mighty display of our Saviour's eternal Godhead was intended by our God to give us pictures of two things. It was, I am sure, intended to show us a picture of the spiritual resurrection of God's elect in the new birth by the effectual call and irresistible grace of God our Saviour (Ephesians 2:1-7; Revelation 20:6). And Lazarus' death and resurrection pictured the death and resurrection of God's elect with Christ. But, have you ever considered this: Between the time that he died and the time that he was raised from the dead by our blessed Saviour, where was he? During those four days that his body slept in the earth, where was he?

When this miracle had been performed, many of the Jews, seeing 'the things which Jesus did, believed on him'. Others believed not, but were only hardened in their enmity and opposition to the Saviour. The same is true throughout the ages. To many, the works of Christ and the power of his grace, when declared by the gospel, are, by the blessing of God, a sweet savour of life unto life. To others, the word of grace is a savour of death unto death. May God the Holy Spirit make his word a sweet savour of life to you who read these lines, for Christ's sake!

Lazarus

Let me say just a few things about Lazarus. First, it should be noted that we are not told in the scriptures that he ever afterwards said anything about the state of his soul while his body was in the grave. In fact, we are told nothing more about him at all, except that he was among those who sat with the Saviour at the table in John 12. Lazarus' silence, and the silence of scripture about his experience should not surprise us. If Paul could not utter words to describe his experience, which was apparently the same as Lazarus', and could not tell us the things he saw in heaven, it is not surprising that Lazarus said nothing about what he saw in heaven. I see divine wisdom in that fact. It is ever the tendency of man to sensationalise everything, especially the supernatural, unexplainable interventions of God. Therefore our God wisely draws a curtain over his most remarkable works. And those who experience them consider them too precious, too sacred, too heavenly to talk about. Those who have experienced anything like a miraculous work of God have very little to say about it.

It is also remarkable that the scriptures tell us absolutely nothing about the feelings of Martha and Mary after Lazarus was raised from the dead. What joy they must have experienced! What gratitude they must have expressed! What humiliation they must have felt because of their unbelief! Yet, we read nothing of these things. The Lord God in infinite wisdom draws a curtain over them, while at the same time giving us a clear picture of their sorrow and grief. The fact is, affliction and sorrow are more profitable for study and meditation than joy.

Yet, the resurrection of Lazarus was one of the most unmistakable and unquestionable revelations of our Saviour's eternal Godhead recorded in holy scripture. If he could raise a man to life who had been dead for four days, truly he is God with whom 'all things are possible'. He who is God our Saviour can raise dead sinners to life, no matter how corrupt they are. And he will raise us up from the grave at his glorious second advent. The voice that called Lazarus from the tomb will, at the last day, call the bodies of his sleeping saints from their graves! Yes, 'the dead shall hear the voice of the Son of man, and they that hear shall live' (John 5:25).

My Thoughts

Now, let me give you some of my thoughts about dying. I say, 'my thoughts', but were they only my thoughts they would not be worth anything. These are my thoughts only because God the Holy Spirit has shown them to me in the book of God and sealed them to my heart. I pray that he will do the same for you.

I write not as a brave man, or as a holy man, but simply as a saved man, as a believing man. Trusting Christ, who alone is all my salvation, I am hopeful that when he comes to receive me unto himself, 'when the Master of the house cometh, at even, or at midnight, or at the cockcrowing, or in the morning', like Mary, I shall rise quickly at the well-known voice of my Beloved and rejoice when it is said, 'The Master is come and calleth for thee'.

I fully realise that the things I have to say in this study cannot be understood by any who do not know our God. Of all spiritual things, these are most spiritual. And the natural man, no matter how brilliant and well-educated he may be, simply cannot know them. They are spiritually discerned (1 Corinthians 2:9-12).

The Body

First, the scriptures tell us much about the bodies of God's saints, when the soul is separated from the body in death. Death for the believer is a temporary separation of our souls from our bodies, but not the least separation of us from our Saviour. That everlasting union that is ours with Christ is an indissoluble, indestructible union. That is the basis and security of every blessing we enjoy in time and in eternity. The scriptures clearly show us that the separation we experience in the death of our souls from our bodies does not separate either the soul or the body of the redeemed from the Redeemer.

Christ's people are as truly his people in death as they are in life. Our union with him is the same. Our interest in him is the same, because he is 'the same, yesterday, and today, and forever'. God's promise does not rot with our bodies in the grave. Indeed, the decay of our bodies as they return to dust is ordered by God's covenant and promise to give occasion for the greater manifestation of Christ's glory, and our everlasting blessedness with him in the resurrection.

Brief Separation

The separation we must sustain in death, the separation of our souls from our bodies, shall be but a brief separation, a brief separation that shall be everlastingly compensated by our Lord in the resurrection (Romans 14:8; 1 Corinthians 3:22). When our Lord Jesus revealed himself to Moses in the burning bush, he revealed himself as the God of Abraham, Isaac, and Jacob, the God not of the dead, but of the living (Exodus 3:6). Then, after hundreds of years, he stated exactly the same thing, asserting plainly that though the patriarchs had long ago died in the flesh, they were not at all separated from him (Luke 20:37, 38). And he declares that this is also an assertion of the fact of the resurrection.

Sleeping

The separation of the soul from the body at death makes no separation of either body or soul from Christ. When our Lord Jesus said, 'our friend Lazarus sleepeth', and the scriptures speak of God's saints sleeping in Christ, there is nothing said about soul sleep. The sleep of God's saints in death refers to their bodies in the grave, sleeping in Christ as they sleep in the earth. And the sleeping bodies of God's saints, 'them which sleep in Jesus', he will awake out of sleep (1 Thessalonians 4:14; Romans 8:11).

Sweet Sleep

Far too little has been said and written about the sleeping of our bodies in the arms of our Redeemer. It is a sweet sleep. There is nothing evil connected with it. It is a good, sweet, unspeakably blessed sleep! Be sure you understand this. Both our bodies and our souls are the objects of Christ's mercy, love, and grace. He has redeemed both my body and my soul. My body is as precious to him as my soul. It is his purchased possession, which is yet to be redeemed, yet to be delivered from the consequences of sin, in the resurrection (Ephesians 1:14; 4:30).

Both my body and my soul are the objects Christ's love, and his purchased possession by blood redemption. Yet the conflicts between them are such as produce an unceasing warfare. From the moment of the new birth, to the moment that the Lord undresses the body for death, 'The flesh lusteth against the spirit; and the spirit against the flesh, and these are contrary the one to the other: so that ye cannot do the things that ye would' (Galatians 5:17).

Groaning

In this body we groan for life. I see nothing but sin in every fibre of my being, and behold what I am in this body of flesh with horror and abhorrence. The leprosy of my body of flesh is loathsome (Job 42:6; Isaiah 6:5; Romans 7:18). Not until I drop this robe of flesh in death, not until my soul is separated from this body, will I be freed from the body of inbred, indwelling corruption and the groaning of my soul, longing for that freedom (2 Corinthians 5:4). Then the very being of sin in this body of flesh will be over forever! No hiding place shall then be found for that loathsome thing now burrowed so deeply in my nature that it corrupts everything about me. The vile cesspool of iniquity, all original and actual corruption, shall be dried up and emptied forever!

I feel the blessedness of this in my soul. The anticipation of it is joyous. The hour rapidly advances when I shall never speak another idle word, never have another vile thought, and never again hurt and injure anyone or anything, when I shall at last cease from sin!

Though I know that the whole troop of iniquity will pursue me, like the Egyptian army pursued Israel to the borders of the sea, yet I know also that the new and living way the Lord there opened for his people has been, and is, and will be opened for my salvation. Death ends the warfare. It is written, 'The

Egyptians whom ye have seen to day, ye shall see them again no more for ever' (Exodus 14:13). Child of God, inconceivable blessedness shall be ours in an instant in the temporary separation of soul and body!

Christ's Glory

But there is something even more wonderful to contemplate. The separation of our souls from our bodies is a means ordained by our God by which our Lord Jesus Christ shall be seen most glorious and triumphant. This shall be the culminating point to crown all. It is in the dust of his saints that the Lord has laid the foundation for manifesting the special conquests of his almighty arm in raising us up to glory.

God's glory is the first and ultimate end of all things. The whole purpose, counsel, will, and pleasure of the triune God, for which he created all things and sustains all things, is the manifestation of 'the glory of his grace' (Ephesians 1:5-7; Proverbs 16:4; Isaiah 43:21; Romans 11:36; Revelation 4:11). It was for this purpose, the purpose that God be visibly glorified before wondering worlds, visibly glorified in his saints, I say, it was for this purpose that the Son of God assumed our nature, redeemed us, and shall come again to gather his saints unto himself (John 1:14; 2 Thessalonians 1:7-10).

What can be more suitable and right than that he, who was 'crucified through weakness', should alone possess the glory of raising the dead? Our bodies must sleep in the dust until that great day for the express purpose of our Lord Jesus Christ being exalted and glorified as our Redemption and our Resurrection! The temporary separation of soul and body of God's elect at death was and is, in the appointment of God, primarily and above every other consideration, for the personal glory of Christ, and secondarily and subordinately, for our everlasting happiness and bliss.

Where was Lazarus for those four days? He was with the Lord, awaiting a greater display of the Lord's glory than had yet been displayed in the earth.

What great and marvellous acts of almighty power shall be executed by our glorious Saviour in that great day of God! Try to imagine the nations sleeping in the dust and the sea, which at his call shall then give up their dead.

All who trust Christ alone as Saviour and Lord have the assurance of God's own word that in that glorious day, when Christ shall come 'to be glorified in his saints, and admired in all that believe', they shall be found among the blessed 'dead which die in the Lord'. Let us therefore await, with holy joy and expectation, the hour of God's appointment, when by death the separation of soul and body shall take place. By this means, he makes us ready for Christ's coming, for his triumph and glory.

Are the personal triumphs of Christ to be manifested before the assembled creation of God in that day? Is the dust of God's saints the preparatory means for the greater display of Christ's power and glory? Does this temporary separation of my soul and body give occasion for my God and Saviour to get glory by me? If so, then it cannot be doubted that death is for us a blessing to be anticipated, not a curse to dread.

Salvation in Christ is worth living for; and the personal glory of Christ in raising me from the dust is worth dying for. May God give me grace, with increasing rapture of soul, to anticipate the time of my appointed departure. It shall be nothing more and nothing less than my body falling asleep in my Saviour's arms at night to be awakened by him in his likeness in the morning.

If a young lady goes to bed tonight, joyfully anticipating that tomorrow she will be married to the man she loves, anticipating the day she has planned for a long time, anticipating that which she ardently desires, she will go to bed with excitement, such excitement that she can hardly sleep. But, oh how sweet her sleep will be, because the morning will bring for her a greatly desired new beginning of life.

Shall not the children of God, heirs of his kingdom, lay down in like manner in the sleep which is to be followed by the resurrection morning, that morning which will open into endless glory? The interval between death and the resurrection shall be but the sweet rest of a brief night. No wonder Paul calls this our 'blessed hope'. The fulfilment of it shall be eternally blessed beyond imagination. Christ will, at his second coming, 'change our vile body, that it may be fashioned like unto his glorious body, according to the working whereby he is able even to subdue all things unto himself' (Philippians 3:21).

The Soul Departed

Now, let us look at the state of the soul while separated from the body. It must be acknowledged that we know very little of the world of the redeemed in heaven. We are in this present, mortal state incapable of knowing much about it. It is impossible for any of us to form any adequate apprehension of heaven's glory. Yet, God the Holy Spirit has graciously given us love tokens in his word of the world to come, by which he draws the hearts of chosen, redeemed, saved sinners to Christ in heaven.

Regarding the immediate effect of our souls being temporarily separated from our bodies at death, we have little information; but the little we have is more precious than mountains of gold. There are some things we know. The body returns to the earth for an appointed time; but the soul lives on in another, higher, more spiritual form of life than we can now imagine. We know that 'to be absent from the body is to be present with the Lord'. This we know by the testimony of holy scripture, and by the testimony of scripture being stamped upon our hearts by grace (Ecclesiastes 12:6, 7; 2 Corinthians 5:1-9).

Immediate Glory

As soon as my soul is separated from my body, I shall be with the Lord in heaven, in a body, a house not made with hands, eternal in the heavens. We are not told and cannot imagine what that form is, but it shall be a body, a house suitable to our souls in that blessed state. In the moment of separation, we shall not be found naked, 'but clothed upon that mortality might be swallowed up of life'. The Lord Jesus said to the dying thief on the cross, 'Today, shalt thou be with me in Paradise'. And Stephen, in his dying moments, when beholding with an eye of faith our all-glorious Christ on the right hand of the throne, cried out, 'Lord Jesus receive my spirit' (Acts 7:55-58). While the body sweetly sleeps in the earth, in the arms of Jesus, until the resurrection morning, the soul is with the Lord. In the conscious assurance of this Paul said, 'For to me to live is Christ, and to die is gain' (Philippians 1: 22).

Freed Of Self

In that moment, we shall at once be rid of and forever freed from self, self-love, and all that selfishness of character which our spirits are encased in in the flesh; freed from that self-love we can never subdue while living in this form. Everything we now enjoy, even of a spiritual nature, is tinged with self. If we meditate upon the glories of our God as he reveals himself to us in Christ, if we enjoy seasons of sweet communion with the Father and with his Son Jesus Christ by some renewed revelation from him, if we give thanks to God for his grace or for some special manifestation of grace, then at once self, self-love, and self-interests corrupt all our thoughts. In heaven, that shall cease to be! There, all selfishness is lost in the love of God, for what he is in himself, independent of all that he is to us and all that he has done for us. This is what Paul speaks of in Romans 5, after declaring the unspeakable blessedness of being reconciled to God by the death of his Son; and much more being reconciled and saved by his life, he adds, 'and not only so, but we also joy in God, through our Lord Jesus Christ' (Romans 5:10, 11).

To 'joy in God', Father, Son, and Holy Ghost, as God, through our Lord Jesus Christ, is a far higher degree of blessedness than all the gifts we can receive from him here. There we shall joy in him, the source of all joy. There self is lost and done away in him. And this is the immediate effect of the soul being temporarily separated from the body.

Face To Face

As soon as my soul is separated from my body, I shall behold my all-glorious Saviour face to face, in open and clear vision, with nothing between my soul and my Saviour. That sums up everything I can conceive of blessedness. This is what our Saviour desires, indescribably more than we do (John 17:24). The thought is rapturous!

Beholding him in all the beauties and glories of his infinite Being is infinitely more than all the benefits we derive from him. We shall be swallowed up and absorbed with beholding him (1 John 3:1, 2). While we are everlastingly and unremittingly engaged in beholding him, all other things will occupy our minds no more. Nothing else will crowd into our hearts. There will be room for nothing but him, and more of him!

The Lord God once hung a star in the sky that arrested the attention of the whole world. It was a bright, glorious star. No one could take his eyes off of it. But that star simply pointed to the place where Christ could be found. Just try to imagine what it will be like, not to see his star, but to see him face to face, who is 'the brightness of his Father's glory, and the express image of his person'! That is the immediate and everlasting experience of every saved sinner, as soon as he falls asleep in his Saviour's arms, and the spirit enters 'into the joy of his Lord'.

Blessed Reunion

This separation of body and soul is but a brief, temporary separation. The body sleeps in Jesus; and the soul lives during the time of separation in the unceasing enjoyment of the presence of Christ. But soon the morning of the resurrection shall come; and the Son of God 'shall descend from heaven with a shout, with the voice of the archangel, and with the trump of God'. Then there shall be a glorious reunion of soul and body, not for me only, not for you only, but for the whole election of grace. All the bodies of all the sleeping saints shall be raised at once, in a moment, in the twinkling of an eye! All shall at once be united to Christ, the glorious Head of the body, united, without the possibility of separation forever, to Christ and to each other!

What will be the joy of the bride in that hour! What will be the triumphs of our Bridegroom, the Lord Jesus Christ himself, when he shall come, 'to be glorified in his saints, and admired in all that believe?' Imagination fails to form the least idea of what must be the feeling in that reunion of soul and body. The two parts of self, separated in a moment of sorrow, bereavement, and death, shall meet and be forever united in the joy and glory of the Lord!

The cold, clammy sweat of death on the body, in which the soul left it, shall be changed into all the warmth of life and immortality! The body, sunk in weakness, shall be raised in power! It was sown a natural body. It shall be raised a spiritual body! The soul shall come down from above with Christ and in the power of Christ, perfumed out of the ivory palaces; and the body shall rise to meet the soul, now by Christ changed from a vile body to a glorified body, as much prepared and as fully qualified for the everlasting enjoyment of

Christ as the soul! That shall be what Paul calls 'the redemption of the purchased possession'. Then Christ shall present us, body and soul, 'faultless before the presence of his glory with exceeding joy'!

He who redeemed my soul, at his own appointed time, regenerated my soul. And my body is no less precious to him than my soul. He who redeemed my body as his purchased possession shall, at the divinely appointed time, regenerate my body, too, with life everlasting!

These have been the thoughts and meditations of my heart for many years, without significant interruption. Needless to say, I've been enjoying life more fully than ever! I pray that I will never have these thoughts far from my mind, that I may continually look for the mercy of our Lord Jesus Christ unto eternal life, crying to the Lord Jesus with his Bride of old, 'Until the day break, and the shadows flee away, turn my Beloved, and be thou like a roe, or a young hart, upon the mountains of Bether' (Song of Solomon 2:17).

'I would not have you to be ignorant, brethren, concerning them which are asleep, that ye sorrow not, even as others which have no hope. For if we believe that Jesus died and rose again, even so them also which sleep in Jesus will God bring with him. For this we say unto you by the word of the Lord, that we which are alive and remain unto the coming of the Lord shall not prevent them which are asleep. For the Lord himself shall descend from heaven with a shout, with the voice of the archangel, and with the trump of God: and the dead in Christ shall rise first: Then we which are alive and remain shall be caught up together with them in the clouds, to meet the Lord in the air: and so shall we ever be with the Lord. Wherefore comfort one another with these words' (1 Thessalonians 4:13-18).

May God the Holy Spirit seal his word to our hearts, giving us faith in Christ and enabling us from this day forward to live in the blessed hope of God's boundless, free, eternal grace in Christ!

Chapter 8

Our Friends Sleep

'These things said he: and after that he saith unto them, Our friend Lazarus sleepeth; but I go, that I may awake him out of sleep' (John 11:11).

That which our blessed Saviour said about Lazarus is true of all those blessed dead who die in the Lord. Their bodies sleep in Christ in the earth.

We have many friends and loved ones whose bodies we have buried in the earth. How many times we have bidden farewell to one we loved, with burning tears running down our cheeks, because we knew they were about to leave this world. But, with regard to those who have died in faith, who have died in Christ, we may say, as our Lord Jesus did of Lazarus, 'Our friends are asleep'.

Background

In the previous verses the Lord Jesus received a touching message from Martha and her sister, Mary, telling him that Lazarus, the one he loved, was sick. Two days later, after Lazarus had died, he headed to Bethany.

The primary thing revealed in John 11 is the fact that our Lord Jesus Christ is 'the resurrection and the life'. Everything in this chapter shows us the blessedness of that revelation. Resurrection can be displayed only where death has come; and that which is emphasized here is the desolation death brings, and man's helplessness in the presence of it.

First, Lazarus died. Then, it became obvious that the Lord Jesus was going to Bethany to be with Martha and Mary. Then, Thomas speaks of the disciples accompanying the Lord to Bethany that they may die with him (John 11:16). Then Martha comes before us. Though in the presence of Christ, she could think only of the death of her brother (John 11:21). The same was true of Mary (John 11:32). Finally, the Jews who had come to comfort the bereaved sisters are seen 'weeping' (John 11:33). And, even as the Lord stands before Lazarus tomb, they have no thought that he was about to raise Lazarus from the dead (John 11:37). What a background this was for our great Saviour to display his wondrous glory as 'the resurrection and the life'!

Spiritual Death

We have before us a picture of physical death, the death of the body. But that is only the figure and the result of something far more solemn, tragic, and dreadful. The natural man is dead in trespasses and sins. And 'the wages of sin is death'. When the first man, our father Adam, sinned, he received those fearful wages. In the day that Adam ate of the forbidden fruit he died, died spiritually. Death was passed upon him and upon all men, as the penal sentence of divine justice. Adam died not only as a private individual, but as the public head and federal representative of all his race.

If you cut down a tree, severing the trunk of the tree from its roots, it dies. Its branches, twigs, and leaves wither. In like manner, the fall of Adam dragged every member of the human race with him into death. That means that every child born into this world enters it 'alienated from the life of God' (Ephesians 4:18), lost, and spiritually dead.

All men by nature, the world over, are spiritually dead. There is in no one even a spark of life which might be fanned into a flame. Fallen man is dead. Being dead, if he is to live, something must be done for him that he cannot do for himself. 'Ye must be born again'! Life must be given to you from without, by the mighty work of God. Life must be imparted to you. Christ, who is life, must be formed in you. How is it that dead sinners are given life? How can the dead be made to live? The Lord Jesus must come to raise the dead by the merit of his blood, the power of his Spirit, and the word of his grace.

That is what we see so strikingly and beautifully illustrated here in John 11. Lazarus was dead; and the Master said, 'I go that I may awake him'. How utterly helpless we are in the presence of death! You who are dead are helpless. Your friends are helpless. The preacher is helpless. But, blessed be God, there is One who is able to save to the uttermost! Christ is not helpless. He can cause the dead to live.

If the sin problem was merely a matter of ignorance in the sinner, we might overcome that by clearly reasoned statements of the truth. If it was merely a stubborn will that stood in the way of the sinner's salvation, we could depend upon our powers of persuasion. If the sinner was only sick, we could induce him to accept some remedy. But in the presence of death we are impotent.

'With men this is impossible; but with God all things are possible' (Matthew 19:26), our Saviour said in answer to the disciples' question, 'Who then can be saved?' Here the light breaks in and shines forth 'for the glory of God, that the Son of God might be glorified thereby' (v. 4). Man is helpless before death; but Christ is not helpless. Lazarus could not raise himself to life. His loving sisters could do nothing for him. His sorrowing friends could weep; but their weeping was neither heard nor meaningful to Lazarus. He was dead. Then, he who is himself, 'the resurrection and the life' steps into the picture and everything changes.

What did he do? He did that which must have seemed terribly strange to all who were present. He cried to the dead man with a loud voice, 'Lazarus, Come forth'! What nonsense! If Lazarus had the power to come forth from the tomb, he would have walked out four days earlier. Had Mary or Martha, or any of the apostles cried, 'Lazarus, Come forth', he would have remained dead. No man's voice is able to pierce the depths of the tomb; but here is a Man who is God. When he cries, 'Lazarus, Come forth', the same omnipotent lips that called a world into existence caused the grave to give up its victim, 'and he that was dead came forth'! That is exactly how the Lord Jesus Christ saves chosen, redeemed sinners by his omnipotent mercy and irresistible grace. He calls them from death to life in the day of his power by a personal, particular, distinguishing call. 'Lazarus, Come forth'! His call of grace is an omnipotent, irresistible, effectual life-giving call. 'And he that was dead came forth'!

Death Compared To Sleep

But, between the time that he died and the time he came forth in resurrection life, our Saviour tells us that Lazarus was sleeping. His body was sleeping in the earth in the arms of his Saviour who loved him. The Lord Jesus announced that Lazarus was no longer in the land of the living, referring to his death as 'sleep'. The scriptures often speak of the death of believers, during that brief period between death and the resurrection, while the soul is separated from the body, as 'sleep'. In the New Testament, this figure is only used with reference to believers (1 Corinthians 15:20, 51; 1 Thessalonians 4:14; 5:10). This sleep refers not to some imaginary sleep of the soul, but to the sleep of the body in the earth. Let me show you seven things about this 'sleep'.

Harmless

First, sleep is completely harmless. There is nothing fearful about sleep, but much for which to be thankful. Sleep is a friend, not a foe. So it is with death for every believer. David sang, 'Yea, though I walk through the valley of the shadow of death I will fear no evil'. Such ought to be the triumphant language of every child of God. The 'sting' has been taken from death (1 Corinthians

15:56, 57). It has no more power to hurt the redeemed than a hornet has after its stinger has been extracted.

Relief

Second, sleep comes as a welcome relief after the sorrows and toils of the day. As the wise man declared, 'The sleep of a labouring man is sweet' (Ecclesiastes 5:12). Death for believers is simply the door through which we pass from this scene of sin and turmoil into the world of everlasting glory and bliss. 1 Corinthians 3:22 tells us, 'death' is ours. Sleep is a merciful provision, greatly appreciated when it cannot be found. Equally merciful is death for one who is washed in the precious blood of Christ. How thankful I am that I shall soon 'sleep with Jesus', and that I will not live as long as Methuselah! 'He giveth his beloved sleep' (Psalms 127:2). What a promise! 'I will both lay me down in peace, and sleep: for thou, LORD, only makest me dwell in safety' (Psalms 4:8).

Death is separation from the body. It must come. But it will be a welcome separation. It will be a separation from a troublesome and hateful companion. Richard Baxter said, 'It is like taking off a shoe that hurts my foot. It will be a welcome relief.' To put this body aside will be like laying aside a worn out tool when all its work is done. It will be dismissing a servant when his service is ended.

This body has been my greatest enemy. As much as I have loved and over-loved it, I must leave this body of flesh to the grave. There it must lie and rot in darkness as a neglected and hateful thing. These eyes must see no more. These hands must move no more. These feet must walk no more. This tongue must speak no more. From the dust it came, and to the dust it must return; earth to earth, water to water, air to air, ashes to ashes. This is the fruit of sin. But, thank God, this body is only my shell, my tabernacle, my tent, my clothing, and not myself.

It has caused me pain, and toil, and sorrow. It has required my constant care and attention. I will be glad to put it aside. I know by long experience that this body of flesh has been a painful lodging for my soul.

When I am free of this body, I will be free from the bondage of corruption and the prison of sin (Romans 7:24). By reason of sin, this body has become mortal, beastly, and vile. We must learn to treat this body as a perishing thing. I do not mean that we should be reckless about our health. That would be a great evil. But I do mean that we spend too much time, care, and money pampering, soothing, and satisfying this body. Soon, very soon, it will rot in the grave. It is your soul that is important. 'What shall it profit a man if he gain the whole world, (for the comfort of his body) and lose his own soul?' (See 1 Timothy 6:6-8).

Brief

Third, sleep is just for a short time. We lie down and soon rise again. Sleep is brief and gets more brief with the passing of years. We sleep for just a few hours snatched from the day. In the morning we awaken and rise to a new day. Death is a brief sleep. Soon comes a morning of awakening and resurrection to a new day. 'Them that sleep in the dust of the earth shall awake, some to everlasting life, and some to shame and everlasting contempt' (Daniel 12:2).

On the glorious resurrection morning, the dead in Christ shall be awakened, to sleep no more, but live forever throughout the perfect day of God (1 Thessalonians 4:13-18). 'So shall we ever be with the Lord'!

Rest

Fourth, sleep is a time of rest. The work of the day is exchanged for sweet repose of the night. This is what death means for God's saints. 'Blessed are the dead which die in the Lord from henceforth: Yea, saith the Spirit, that they may rest from their labours' (Revelation 14:13).

This applies only to the intermediate state, between death and resurrection, while our bodies sleep in the earth. When we receive our glorified bodies in the resurrection, there will be new ministries for us to engage in, for it is written, 'his servants shall serve him (Revelation 22:3).

Shuts Out Troubles

Fifth, sleep shuts out the sorrows of life. In sleep we are mercifully unconscious of the things which trouble us and cause us pain, sorrow, and grief throughout the day. The sleep of night gives us welcome relief from that which troubles us by day. So it shall be in death. Those who are with Christ in Paradise know nothing of the tears which are shed on earth. Holy scripture does seem to indicate that God's saints in heaven are keenly aware of what is transpiring here. They are certainly made to rejoice when the salvation of sinners is heralded on high (Luke 15:7, 10). And they appear to be watching us in our race, aware of what we must face and overcome, but altogether without sorrow, fear, or tears (Hebrews 12:1, 2).

Easily Awakened

Sixth, a sleeping man is easily awakened. Death is compared to a sleep to emphasize the ease with which the Lord will awaken our bodies. To raise the dead, impossible as it seems to the sceptic, will be simpler to our Saviour than rousing a man from sleep. Nothing so quickly awakens one who is asleep as the voice of another, especially the voice of one who is dearly loved. So we are told 'the hour is coming, in the which all that are in the graves shall hear his voice, and shall come forth' (John 5:28, 29).

Preparation

Seventh, sleep is a time of preparation, a time when the body is fitted for the duties of tomorrow. When a man is awakened from sleep he arises refreshed and invigorated, and ready for what lies before him. In like manner, the resurrected believer will be endued with a new power. The limitations of this mortal body will no longer exist. That which was sown in weakness shall be raised in power (1 Corinthians 15:40-49). What is 'a spiritual body'? I do not have a clue; and I doubt anyone else has a clue. But it seems obvious to me that it must be a body without the limitations with which we are now encumbered. Luther suggested that the resurrection body be as agile as thought. Augustine said in the resurrection body we will move to any place as soon as we will. Jerome Zanchius wrote, 'As birds being hatched, do fly lightly up into the skies, which being eggs, were a heavy and slimy matter; so man, being hatched by the resurrection, is made pure and nimble, and able to mount up into the heavens.'

No wonder the Apostle calls this our 'blessed hope'. The fulfilment of it shall be eternally blessed beyond imagination. Christ will, at his second coming, 'change our vile body, that it may be fashioned like unto his glorious body, according to the working whereby he is able even to subdue all things unto himself' (Philippians 3:21).

No Hope

But O how vastly different that day shall be for you who are without Christ. If you die in your sins, if you die without Christ, after the death of your body, nothing awaits you but 'the second death', your everlasting separation from God in hell, among the torments of the damned! No sweetness, just ever-increasing bitterness! No rest, just ever-increasing toil! No blessedness, just ever-increasing cursedness! No hope, just ever-increasing hopelessness!

Yes, you, too, shall be raised from the dead, but it will be unto 'the resurrection of damnation', not 'the resurrection of life'. Your body will be raised only to suffer more acutely the eternal torments of the damned in the lake of fire. What an inconceivable, everlasting nightmare hell must be! The thick darkness! The undying worms! The unquenchable fires! May God the Holy Spirit graciously give you life in Christ; may he graciously give you faith in the Son of God, and cause you to flee from the wrath to come! Seek the Lord while he may be found. There is no hope beyond the grave.

O Spirit of God, O Almighty God of all grace, O blessed Saviour, come, snatch chosen, redeemed sinners as brands from the burning, for the glory of your own grace!

Chapter 9

Christ Our Resurrection

'Jesus said unto her, I am the resurrection, and the life: he that believeth in me, though he were dead, yet shall he live: And whosoever liveth and believeth in me shall never die. Believest thou this?' (John 11:25, 26).

How important is the resurrection? Many seem to think it is irrelevant. But the fact is there is no aspect of gospel doctrine that is more important than the resurrection. I live in hope of the resurrection. With Paul, I say, 'If in this life only we have hope in Christ, we are of all men most miserable' (1 Corinthians 15:19). In making that statement Paul does not mean the believer's life in this world is a sad, morbid life. The apostle certainly does not mean that it is really more delightful and pleasurable to live in this world without faith. And he does not mean that were it not for the hope of eternal glory, the people of God would prefer not live as they do in obedience and submission to our heavenly Father. God's saints are not mercenary. We do not serve our God for gain!

When Paul says, 'If in this life only we have hope in Christ, we are of all men most miserable', he simply means this: If there were no eternal life in Christ, no eternal bliss of life with Christ in glory, and no resurrection, then the believer would be the most miserably frustrated person in the world. We would never have that which we most earnestly desire. We would never see the end of our hope. We would never embrace Christ, or be embraced by him. We would never see our Redeemer.

Such thoughts are unbearable. I cannot imagine anything more distressing than to be without Christ! Nothing could be more cruel and miserable than to live in hope of seeing Christ, of being like Christ, and spending eternity with Christ, only to die like a dog! 'If in this life only we have hope in Christ, we are of all men most miserable'. What a horrible thought! What a tormenting supposition! But, bless God, it is not so.

Hope Of Resurrection

We live in hope of the resurrection; and our hope is both sure and steadfast. 'For I know that my Redeemer liveth, and that he shall stand at the latter day upon the earth: and though after my skin worms destroy this body, yet in my flesh shall I see God: whom I shall see for myself, and mine eyes shall behold, and not another; though my reins be consumed within me' (Job 19:25-27). In sickness we are calm, because we live in hope of the resurrection. In sorrow we are peaceful, because we live in hope of the resurrection. In trial and affliction we are at ease, because we live in hope of the resurrection. In bereavement we are confident, because we live in hope of the resurrection. And we hope to die in confidence and joy, because we live in hope of the resurrection.

Our assurance of the resurrection is much more than belief in a point of theological orthodoxy. It is a very personal thing, the most personal thing in the world. In fact, when we talk about the resurrection, we are not really talking about a doctrine, but about a person. When we think about the resurrection, we ought to be thinking about a person. The Lord Jesus Christ himself, the Son of God, our glorious Mediator is the Resurrection.

The blessed hope of the resurrection is not some fool's philosophy. It is not a mere religious tranquilizer by which we are able to cope with the trials of life. This is the calm, confident assurance of believing hearts. It is the necessary, inevitable result of faith in Christ. That is what our Lord Jesus teaches us in these words: 'Jesus said unto her, I am the resurrection, and the life: he that believeth in me, though he were dead, yet shall he live: And whosoever liveth and believeth in me shall never die. Believest thou this?' (John 11:25, 26)

Representative Resurrection

We live in hope of the resurrection, first, because we have been resurrected in union with Christ representatively (Ephesians 2:5, 6). While he lived on this earth, in obedience to God as our Representative, we lived in him. When Christ died, all God's elect died in him. And when he arose from the dead, taking his seat in heaven, we arose with him, and have been seated with him in glory (Ephesians 2:4-6).

Christ Our Resurrection

Hail! sacred union, firm and strong,
How great the grace, how sweet the song!
That worms of earth should ever be
One with incarnate Deity!

(One in the tomb, one when He rose,
One when He triumphed o'er His foes,
One when in heaven He took His seat,
While seraphs sang all hell's defeat.)

John Kent

Nothing in all the world is more wondrous, more profound and more comforting than the teaching of holy scripture about our union with Christ. Union with Christ is the very heart of salvation. Union with Christ is central to everything revealed in scripture. Without this union of our souls with Christ and the union of Christ with our souls, there is no salvation. Our union with Christ is an eternal union, secret and unknown to us until it is brought to light by the gospel (Romans 8:28-30; Ephesians 1:3-6; 2 Timothy 1:9-11). Our union with Christ is a legal, representative union (Romans 5:12, 18-21). Our union with Christ is a living, vital union, a union made manifest when Christ is formed in us in the new birth (Colossians 1:27). And our union with Christ is an everlasting union of life and grace (John 17:22, 23).

When the Lord Jesus Christ arose from the grave, he arose as our Representative. All that he has done and all that he has experienced, all of God's elect have done and experienced in him, by virtue of our representative union with him. His obedience to the law was our obedience (Romans 5:12, 18-21). His death as a penal sacrifice for sin was our death (Romans 6:6, 7, 9-11; 7:4). His death is our atonement!

Our Lord's resurrection was our resurrection. This is our life! The resurrection of Christ is an indisputable fact of revelation and history upon which we rest our souls (1 Corinthians 15:1-8). Disprove the resurrection and you disprove the gospel. 'If Christ be not raised, your faith is vain; ye are yet in your sins' (1 Corinthians 15:17). In 1 Corinthians 15, God the Holy Spirit inspired Paul to mention six distinct appearances of the Lord Jesus. In all, the scriptures record twelve separate times that the risen Lord appeared to his own. There may have been more appearances (Acts 1:3); but these twelve are recorded.

To Mary Magdalene (John 20:11-18).
To the women (Matthew 28:9, 10).
To Cleopas and his companion (Luke 24:13-35).
To Simon (Luke 24:34; 1 Corinthians 15:5).
To the disciples, Thomas being absent (John 20:19-23).
To the disciples, Thomas being present (John 20:24-29).
To the Seven at the Sea of Galilee (John 21:1-14).
To the Disciples on the mountain in Galilee (Matthew 28:16-20).
To the five hundred (1 Corinthians 15:6).
To James, the Lord's brother (1 Corinthians 15:7).
To the disciples on Olivet, near Jerusalem (Acts 1:4-11; Luke 24:50, 51).
To Paul on the road to Damascus (Acts 9:3-7).

The bodily, physical resurrection of the Lord Jesus Christ necessitates the resurrection of all who are in Christ. That which has been done for us mystically and representatively must be experienced by us personally. We are members of Christ's mystical body, the Church. If one member of the body were lost, the body would be maimed (1 Corinthians 12:12, 27). If one member of the body were lost, the Head would not be complete (Ephesians 1:22, 23). These bodies of ours must be fashioned like unto his glorious body (Philippians 3:21; John 17:24).

The Lord Jesus was raised as the firstfruits of them that sleep (1 Corinthians 15:20). The full harvest must follow! Christ is the Last Adam. As we have borne the image of our first covenant head, we must bear the image of the second (1 Corinthians 15:21, 23, 47-49). Our Redeemer, the Captain of our Salvation, has obtained the victory over all that could hinder the glorious resurrection of his people; sin, death, hell, the grave, and the devil (Colossians 2:13-15; Hebrews 2:14, 15). The covenant engagements of Christ as the Surety of God's elect are not complete until the hour of our resurrection (John 6:37-40).

Spiritual Resurrection

Second, we live in hope of the resurrection, because we have experienced the resurrection of Christ in regeneration. We know, assuredly, that Christ is the Resurrection and the Life, because we have been raised from the dead and Christ lives in us.

The new birth is nothing less than a resurrection from the dead. To be born again by the Spirit of God is the first resurrection (Revelation 20:6; John 5:25; 11:25, 26; Ephesians 2:1-10; Colossians 2:9-15; 3:1-3).

Resurrection Hope

Third, we live in hope of the resurrection, because we believe the revelation of God concerning the resurrection (John 5:28, 29). God's elect never die! There is a day coming when all that are in the grave shall be raised by the voice of the Son of God; and for all who trust the Lord Jesus Christ, it shall be a resurrection of life. There shall be a resurrection of life at the second coming of Christ (1 Corinthians 15:35-44, 51-59; 1 Thessalonians 4:13-18; 2 Thessalonians 1:7-10; Philippians 3:21). This will not be some secret rapture, but a glorious resurrection, a resurrection with and by our Lord Jesus Christ.

Soon must this body die,
This mortal frame decay;
And, yes, my body must return
To ashes, air, and clay.

Corruption, earth, and worms
Shall but refine this flesh,
Till my triumphant spirit comes
To put it on afresh.

God my Redeemer lives!
My Saviour from the skies
Looks down, and watches all my dust,
Till he shall bid it rise.

Arrayed in glorious grace
My body then shall shine,
(United body, spirit, soul!),
In life by pow'r divine.

This blessed hope I owe
To Jesus' dying love.
My Life and Resurrection, too,
I'll live with Christ above.

Dear Lord, accept the praise
Of this poor mortal's song,
Till tunes of nobler sound I raise
With an immortal tongue!

Isaac Watts (adapted)

Let us comfort one another with these words. And let us be steadfast, unmovable, always abounding in the work of the Lord. Our labour is not in vain in the Lord!

The Resurrection Of The Damned

There shall also be a resurrection of damnation (John 5:29). The wicked and unbelieving shall be raised by the power of Christ in order to be judged and condemned. The believer shall be raised by virtue of his union with Christ, in order to be judged worthy of and rewarded with everlasting glory. The wicked shall be raised in wrath. The believing shall be raised in love. The wicked shall be raised for execution. The righteous shall be raised for a wedding. 'Prepare to meet thy God'! Soon you and I will stand before the living God in judgment (2 Corinthians 5:10, 11).

Chapter 10

Astonishing Love

'Then said the Jews, Behold how he loved him'! (John 11:36).

The tears of the Lord Jesus at the tomb of Lazarus produced such astonishment in the minds of the Jews who stood before the tomb, that they exclaimed, 'Behold, how he loved him'! But had they known what every heaven-born sinner knows of the love of the Son of God, their astonishment would have been indescribably greater. Oh, that we might know, with ever increasing astonishment, the length, and breadth, and height, and depth of the love of God that passes knowledge, the unquenchable love of God in Christ Jesus!

What a huge volume shall be read over in eternity of the Saviour's love to our souls! His distinct and distinguishing, express, personal, particular love! Truly, my Saviour, 'Thy love is better than wine'! We are astonished that the Son of God should ever even cast a glance in our direction, that the Holy One of Israel should choose to look upon us, but that he should love us; that is utterly astonishing!

In eternity, seeing as we cannot now see, knowing as we cannot now know, as we look back over the days, and weeks, and months, and years of our lives, as we scan the ages of time and the wonders of providence, as the whole purpose and work of God is revealed to his creation, all creation shall look upon each chosen, redeemed sinner with astonishment, and we shall look upon ourselves with astonishment, and all the universe shall say of each saved sinner, 'Behold, how he loved him'!

We see sweet tokens and evidences of that love throughout our sojourn here, not only in his tears of sympathy, but in the precious blood that he so freely shed for us, and in all his manifold works of mercy and grace toward us, upon us, and in us. As often as we think of his love to us, we ought to cry with astonishment, 'Behold how he has loved us'!

If we were in a right state of heart and mind, we would often remind one another how wondrously the Saviour loves us. If we were in a better frame, our conversations with one another would often be taken up with this blessed subject. We waste far too much of our time upon trifles. How much better it would be if the Saviour's love so engrossed our thoughts that it became the constant theme of conversation with one another. What a blessing we would be to one another if whenever we met, we spoke of some sweet, blessed, fresh experience of the love of Christ that passes knowledge! Let us talk less about sports and more about the Saviour, less about politics and more about providence, less about business and more about blood, less about money and more about mercy, less about revelling and more about redemption, less about the recession and more about the Redeemer, less about the President and more about the King!

Soon, in that land beyond the river, when we are seated with the saints in light, we will want no other theme for conversation. There everything will serve to remind us how the Saviour loves us. I want to remind you of the Saviour's astonishing love to our souls. Love is known best by its deeds. So, let me remind you of our great Saviour's great deeds of love, love deeds wrought for us and in us by our blessed Redeemer.

Suretyship

First, give a little thought to the great deeds of love our blessed Saviour has performed for us from everlasting. When did Christ's love begin to work for us? It was long before we were born, long before the world was created. 'Behold, how he loved us'! Way, way back in eternity our Saviour gave the first proof of his love to us by espousing and undertaking our cause as our blessed Surety. He beheld humanity as a palace that had been plundered and broken down. In the ruins of the palace, he saw every unclean thing. Who could restore the palace? Who could restore that which was lost? Who could build again that which was fallen? Who was there to undertake the great work of restoring that ruined palace? No one but the Word, who was with God, and who was God. 'And he saw that there was no man, and wondered that there was no intercessor: therefore his own arm brought salvation unto him; and his righteousness, it sustained him' (Isaiah 59:16).

Before the angels began to sing, or the sun, and moon, and stars cast out their first beams of light across primeval darkness, Christ the Lord stood forth to espouse the cause of his people, and pledged himself not only to restore to us all the blessings that we would lose in the sin and fall of our father Adam, but also to add to them richer favours that could never have been ours except through him and in him. Yes, from everlasting his delights were with the sons of men; and to everlasting his delights with his chosen shall continue.

When I think of the Son of God, in that far-distant past of which we cannot even form an idea, becoming 'the head over all things to the church' (Ephesians 1:22), which then existed only in the mind of God and in union with him, my soul cries out in a rapture of delight, 'Behold how he loved us'!

'Behold, how he loved us'! In the secret, eternal councils of the triune God, the Lord Jesus Christ became the Representative and Surety of his chosen. The Son of God, knowing well all that his suretyship would involve, undertook to be the Surety for our souls, to fulfil all the covenant on our behalf, to meet all its demands for us. He swore to his own hurt, and (blessed be his name forever!) he stuck to it (see Psalms 15:4).

'Behold, how he loved us'! In the covenant of grace, before the world began, the triune God gave his elect into the hands of Christ, as his righteous Servant. He trusted all his chosen sheep into the hands of the Good Shepherd. He gave Christ the charge of and charge over all things as our Surety (Ephesians 1:3-14). Yes, God the eternal Son covenanted to redeem all his elect, to keep them all by his grace, and to present them 'faultless' before the presence of his Father's glory with exceeding joy. Thus, as Jacob became accountable to Laban for the whole flock committed to his charge, the Lord Jesus Christ, 'that great shepherd of the sheep, through the blood of the everlasting covenant' (Hebrews13:20), undertook to redeem and guard the whole flock entrusted to his care, so that when, at the last great muster, they should pass under the rod of him that counts the sheep, not one of them would be missing. He and he alone became responsible for the sheep trusted to Him; and he and he alone shall have the praise of our everlasting salvation. In that great day the blessed Shepherd-Son-Surety, our dear Saviour, will say to his Father, 'Those that Thou gavest me I have kept, and not one of them is lost.'

It was in the everlasting covenant that our Lord Jesus Christ became our Representative and Surety, and engaged on our behalf to fulfil all his Father's will. As we think of this great mystery of mercy, surely all who are truly his must exclaim with grateful adoration, 'Behold how he loved us'!

Incarnation

'Behold, how he loved us'! In the fulness of time, our Lord Jesus Christ left the glories of heaven and took upon himself our nature. We know so little of what the word 'heaven' means that we cannot adequately appreciate the tremendous sacrifice that the Son of God made in order to become the Son of man. The holy angels could understand far better than we can what their Lord and ours gave up when he, the Son of the Highest, stooped to be the Seed of women, to be born of a woman.

Yet, there were mysteries about the incarnation the angels of God could not fathom. As they followed the footprints of the Son of man on his wondrous way from the manger to the cross and to the tomb, they must often have been in utter astonishment (2 Corinthians 8:9). The matters of our redemption by Christ, Peter tells us, are 'things the angels desire to look into'. And well they might! 'Without controversy great is the mystery of godliness: God was manifest in the flesh'. The omnipotent Creator took the nature of the creature into indissoluble union with his divine nature. Marvel of marvels! 'He took not on him the nature of angels; but he took on him the seed of Abraham.'

'Behold, how he loved us'! O glorious Bridegroom of our hearts, there never was any other love like thine. That the eternal Son of God should leave his Father's side and stoop so low as to become one with us, so that as Paul declares, 'We are members of his body, of his flesh, and of his bones', is such a wonder of condescending grace and mercy that we can only exclaim again and again, 'Behold how he loved us'!

Redemption

Then, 'being found in fashion as a man' he became obedient unto death, even the death of the cross, bearing all our sicknesses, and all our sufferings, and all our sins under the white hot fury of God's holy wrath and justice! If you want to see the love of Christ, if you want to behold how he loved us, go to Gethsemane, Gabbatha, and Golgotha! Go to Mount Calvary. By faith gaze upon him when he took upon himself all the sins of all his elect, as Peter writes, 'who his own self bare our sins in his own body on the tree'.

The Lord God 'hath made him to be sin for us, who knew no sin; that we might be made the righteousness of God in him' (2 Corinthians 5:21). 'Christ hath redeemed us from the curse of the law, being made a curse for us: for it is written, Cursed is every one that hangeth on a tree: That the blessing of Abraham might come on the Gentiles through Jesus Christ; that we might receive the promise of the Spirit through faith' (Galatians 3:13, 14). How could one who was so pure, so absolutely perfect ever bear so foul a load? How could he who knew no sin, did no sin, and could never sin, be made sin? No mortal can conceive such a thing. Yet, bless his name, he who knew no sin was made sin for us, that he might die the Just for the unjust, and bring us to God by the sacrifice of himself!

'Behold, how he loved us'! 'The Lord hath laid on him the iniquity of us all.' 'He hath made him to be sin for us, who knew no sin; that we might be made the righteousness of God in him.' In fulfilment of the great everlasting covenant of grace, and in prospect of all the glory and blessing that would follow from Christ's atoning sacrifice, 'it pleased the LORD to bruise Him; he hath put him to grief'. We cannot have the slightest conception of what that bruising and that grief must have been, when the Son was forsaken by the Father! We cannot imagine what our Lord's physical and mental agonies must have been. Yet they were only the shell of his sufferings. His soul-agony was that which made him cry, 'My God, my God, why hast thou forsaken me?' Then it was that the precious 'corn of wheat' fell into the ground and died, and dying, brought forth 'much fruit', of which heaven and eternity alone can tell the full tale. 'Behold how he loved us'!

Joint-heirs

Still, there is more. The Lord Jesus Christ has so completely given himself to us that all that he has is ours. The Spirit of God declares that we are 'heirs of God and joint-heirs with Jesus Christ'. He is the glorious Husband, and his Church is his bride, the Lamb's wife; and there is nothing that he has which is not also hers even now, and shall be to eternity. He possesses nothing that is not ours forever! By a marriage bond which cannot be broken, 'for he hateth putting away', the Son of God, our Saviour, has espoused his chosen bride unto himself in righteousness and in truth; and she shall be one with him throughout eternity.

He has gone up to his Father's house to take possession of the many mansions there, not for himself, but for his people. His intercessory prayer is, 'Father, I will that they also, whom thou hast given me, be with me where I am; that they may behold my glory, which thou hast given me: for thou lovedst me before the foundation of the world.' 'Behold how he loved us'!

Preservation

Think often upon the Lord's dealings with us in the days of our unregeneracy. Oh, how he loved us! How persevering is the love of Christ! He called us again and again, but we would not come to him. The more lovingly he called us, the more resolutely we hardened our hearts and refused him. With some of us, this refusal lasted for years; and we wonder now that the Lord waited for us so long.

Yet, he waits to be gracious to the objects of his everlasting love. 'Therefore will the LORD wait, that he may be gracious unto you, and therefore will he be exalted, that he may have mercy upon you' (Isaiah 30:18). Not only did our Saviour persevere in his love, enduring our insults, he also, all the days of our rebellion while we passionately pursued our adulterous lovers, provided for us, protected us, hedged us about, and equally passionately pursued us. That is what is pictured for us by his prophet in Hosea 1-3.

Regeneration

At last, the blessed Saviour conquered us by his grace, made us partakers of his own divine nature in regeneration, and came to us not as he comes to the world, but to live in us and dwell in us, one in living union with us! Many days have passed since then, and I ask you now to recall what Christ has done for us since we first trusted in him. Has his love for you cooled in the slightest degree? We have all tried that love by our wanderings and our waywardness; but we have not quenched it; and its fire still burns just as vehemently as at the first.

We sometimes fall so low that our hearts are like adamant, incapable of emotion. Yet, the Lord Jesus loves us still, and forsakes us not. We are like the insensible grass which calls not for the dew, yet the dew of his love gently falls upon us and refreshes our souls. He endures our indifference. He bears with our provocations. He forgives all our transgressions. Though our hearts are as ice toward him, his heart burns with love for us. Though we shut the door against him, he puts his hand in by the hole of the door and draws our hearts to himself. Oh, 'Behold how he has loved us'!

Unquenchable

We who are God's are all monuments to the unquenchable love of God our Saviour.

'Who is this that cometh up from the wilderness, leaning upon her beloved? I raised thee up under the apple tree: there thy mother brought thee forth: there she brought thee forth that bare thee. Set me as a seal upon thine heart, as a seal upon thine arm: for love is strong as death; jealousy is cruel as the grave: the coals thereof are coals of fire, which hath a most vehement flame. Many waters cannot quench love, neither can the floods drown it: if a man would give all the substance of his house for love, it would utterly be contemned' (Song of Solomon 8:5-7).

What a description this is of the love of Christ, the 'love that passeth knowledge'! It is Christ who speaks in verse 5, 'I raised thee up under the apple tree'. And it is Christ who says, 'I have loved thee with an everlasting love, and with loving-kindness have I drawn thee.' It is God our Saviour who declares, 'I drew them with cords of love, and with the bands of a man.' He found us in a desert land, and in a waste, howling wilderness. 'Christ loved the Church, and gave himself for it'.

The Lord Jesus here declares his love to his church, and she replies, 'Set me as a seal', not only on your heart, but also on your arm the place of your love and the place of your strength the place of the most tender emotion and deepest passion, and the place of power, safety, and work.

Who shall separate us from the love of Christ? His love is invincible and irresistible as death. It is a jealous love, as unyielding and unalterable as the grave. It is comparable to fire, coals of fire, the very flame of Jehovah.

Here, then, is the love of Christ! Its breadth, length, height, and depth are absolutely immeasurable. Our Saviour's love is unquenchable love. No other love is really unquenchable, but our Saviour's love is. His love is eternal and everlasting, immutable and unalterable. The love of Christ is infinitely beyond that of a father or a mother, or a brother or a sister, or a husband or a wife. The love of Christ is the one and only love that passes knowledge; the one love that nothing in heaven, or earth, or hell is able to extinguish or cool; the one love whose dimensions are beyond all measure (Ephesians 3:14-19).

Our Redeemer's love is here compared to fire that cannot be quenched. As such, it is affirmed that 'waters', 'many waters' cannot quench it. Christ's love for us is a thing of life which the floods cannot drown (Psalms 69:15, 93:3).

The waters of shame and suffering sought to quench and drown it. They would have hindered its outflowing, and come, like Peter, between the Saviour and the cross; but his love refused to be quenched on its way to Calvary. Herein was love! It leaped over all the barriers in its way. It refused to be drowned. Its fire would not be quenched. Its life could not be extinguished.

The waters of death sought to quench it. The waves and billows of death went over the great Lover of our souls. The grave sought to cool and chill his love; but it proved itself stronger than death. Neither death nor the grave could alter or weaken his love for us, it came out of both death and the grave as strong as before. Love defied death, and overcame it.

The waters of our unworthiness could not quench nor drown the love of Christ for our souls. Love is usually attracted to that which is loveable. When something ugly, unlovely, unattractive comes, love, so called, withdraws from its object. Not so here. All our unfitness and unloveableness could not quench or drown the love of Christ. It clings to the unlovely, and refuses to be torn away.

The waters of our long rejection sought to quench it. I repeat myself; but the repetition is needed. Is it not? How soon we forget! Though the gospel showed us that personal unworthiness could not arrest the love of Christ, we continued to reject him and his love. We continued to hate him and despise his love. Yet, his love for us rose above our enmity to him, rose above our unbelief and survived our hardness. In spite of everything we are and have done his love was unquenched.

Though he has saved us by his matchless grace, the waters of our daily inconsistency seek to quench his love; but, blessed be his name, without success. Even after experiencing his adorable grace, we are constantly spurning his love! What inconsistencies, coldness, lukewarmness, unbelief, worldliness, hardness, and utter ungodliness daily rushes out of us against the Saviour's love, like a mighty flood to quench its fire and drown its life! Yet it survives all; it remains unquenched, unquenchable, and unchanged!

All these infinite evils in us are like 'waters', 'many waters', like 'floods', torrents of sin, waves and billows of evil, all constantly labouring to quench and drown the love of Christ! They would annihilate any other love, any love less than his. But our Saviour's love is unchangeable and everlasting. 'Behold, how he loved us'!

When the Jews saw our Lord weeping at Lazarus' tomb, they were astonished. To them, his tears were an evidence of special love. But to us, the great token of our Lord's special love is his shed blood (Romans 5:6-8; 1 John 4:9-11). It might well be said of each blood-bought believer, 'Behold how he loved him'! Child of God, Jesus Christ, your Lord, loves you eternally. There never was a time when he did not love you. His love for his own is without beginning and without end. It is eternal. The Son of God loves his own peculiarly. The love God has for his own elect is a special, particular, family love, a love he has for none but his own. He loved Jacob, but hated Esau. So it is. So it ever has been. So it ever shall be.

The Lord loves his people perseveringly. Though we sinned in Adam, were born in sin, and lived in sin by deliberate choice, his love for us was never broken. Though we sin still after experiencing his grace, his love does not cease or grow cold. His love is patient, longsuffering, lasting, and enduring. God will never cease to love those whom he has always loved. His love is immutable. Our Saviour loves us sacrificially. 'Hereby perceive we the love of God, because he laid down his life for us.' He so loved us that he voluntarily laid down his life in our place. So mighty is his love that when he knew the price of our souls was his own precious blood, he willingly poured out his life's blood to redeem us!

The Lord Jesus Christ loves all of his people savingly. The love of Christ for us is much more than a wishful emotion. He so loves his own that he desires their salvation. And what he desires he has the power and wisdom to accomplish. His love is not helpless, but powerful. He will not stand idly by and allow one soul whom he loves to perish when he has the power to save that soul!

The Lord Jesus Christ loves his people satisfyingly. His love will be satisfied. He will never lose the object of his love. Hosea's love did at last conquer Gomer's heart. And the love of Christ will in the end conquer the hearts of all his elect. 'Thy people shall be willing in the day of thy power'. This special, free, and sovereign love of Christ's will satisfy all his people. He will give us all that we can need or desire for all of eternity. He will withhold no good thing from his own. In that great day which is yet to come, God's creation will stand back in awe and wonder and say, concerning his redeemed people, BEHOLD HOW HE LOVED THEM!

Bow down, my soul, while pondering the wondrous love of Christ and the rich, boundless mercy and grace that love fetches to me in free salvation, and give all the praise and all the glory to him alone. His love and his free grace, not my merit, is the sole cause of all. After experiencing such distinguishing, free mercy, grace, and love, how increasingly astonishing it is that all my repeated and aggravating transgressions have not extinguished this love toward me. Rather, he loves me still, just as he did from the beginning! Oh, love unequalled, love past finding out! When shall this base, this shameful heart of mine so love you as to live to your glory, O Lord Jesus? What love is thine! What vileness is mine!

Truly, it must be said of God our Saviour, he is love; and without him we are nothing (1 Corinthians 13). The more we meditate upon his great love to us, its character, its fulness, its blessedness, the more our hearts are compelled to acknowledge, 'We love him because he first loved us'.

Chapter 11

Sovereignty And Instrumentality

'Jesus said, Take ye away the stone' (John 11:39).

'Salvation is of the Lord'! Salvation is the work of God's free and sovereign grace in Christ. From start to finish, salvation is by grace alone. This is the message we preach to all men. You cannot save yourself. You cannot contribute anything to the work of salvation. And you cannot keep yourself saved. No preacher can save you. No church can save you. No religious system can save you. No priest can save you. No ceremony can save you. God alone can save you. Salvation is by God's grace alone.

Salvation originates with the sovereign will of God the Father. 'It is not of him that willeth, nor of him that runneth, but of God that showeth mercy' (Romans 9:16). Salvation, as it is revealed in the Bible, begins with election, predestination, and the covenant of grace ordered in all things and sure. Salvation was earned and purchased for God's elect by the obedience and death of God the Son as the sinner's Substitute, our covenant Surety. 'Christ hath redeemed us from the curse of the law, being made a curse for us: for it is written, Cursed is every one that hangeth on a tree' (Galatians 3:13). Christ Jesus came into the world to save sinners. He came to save his people from their sin; and he did what he came to do. The Son of God has saved his people. He brought in an everlasting righteousness for us. He obtained eternal redemption for us. And he entered into heaven as our Forerunner to claim the prize of eternal glory for us. Salvation is effectually applied to chosen, redeemed sinners by the irresistible grace, omnipotent mercy, and sovereign power of God the Holy Spirit. 'It is the Spirit that quickeneth; the flesh profiteth nothing' (John 6:63). The Holy Spirit of God calls sinners from death to life, creating in those whom he calls repentance toward God and faith in Christ. He seals to our hearts all the blessings of God's grace, and seals us in grace forever, so that those who are born of God can never perish.

If today you trust Christ, if you are a child of God, it is not because of your will and work, but because of God's will and work. If you believe on the Lord Jesus Christ, it is because God the Father chose you, God the Son redeemed you, and God the Spirit gave you faith in Christ. 'Salvation is of the Lord'!

Our Responsibility

There lies Lazarus in the tomb. He is dead, helplessly dead. It is obvious to any sane man that Lazarus could do nothing to change his condition. He is dead! His sisters, though they loved him dearly, could do nothing to help him. All the disciples standing by could not breathe life into his body, or call back the departed spirit of their friend, Lazarus. Dust had already begun to return again to dust. His body had already begun to decay. But the Lord Jesus was there. He was about to perform a great miracle. Soon the voice of God who created Lazarus would be heard speaking with life-giving power, 'Lazarus, come forth'! And this dead man would begin to live again. But, before our Lord would perform this great miracle, which only he could perform, he required his disciples to do something. 'Jesus said, Take ye away the stone'. Is that strange? No, not really.

Without question, he who by the mere power of his word can cause the dead to live could have removed the stone from the mouth of the tomb with great ease. But he chose to use his disciples. He gave them a work to do, which was essential to the resurrection of Lazarus, essential because he required it. The removal of that stone could not give life to Lazarus. Only God can give life to the dead. But the Lord would not raise Lazarus from the dead until his disciples took the stone away.

When 'Jesus said, Take ye away the stone', at first the disciples hesitated. Human reason got in the way. Martha said, 'Lord, by this time he stinketh: for he hath been dead four days' (v. 39). Human reason will have either human instrumentality or divine sovereignty, but not both. God's word teaches both. Our Lord gently corrected Martha's unbelief (v. 40). 'Then they took away the stone' (v. 41). When they rolled away the stone, those disciples demonstrated three things. First, submissive obedience to the will and word of their Lord. Second, faith in Christ's power to raise the dead (v. 40). Third, an anticipation of Lazarus' resurrection for the glory of God.

There are some things that you and I must do for the salvation of God's elect. We look to Christ alone as the Giver of Life and the Saviour of men. But we do not fold our arms in indifference and say, 'God will save his elect no matter what.' That which we can do we must do. We must look for opportunities to be instruments in the hands of God for the salvation of sinners. Wouldn't you like to have been the one who rolled away that stone from Lazarus' tomb that day? Well, we cannot go back to Lazarus' tomb. But there are many like Lazarus around us who are dead in sin. And you and I can do some things to help them. There are some stones for us to take away!

A Word For The Dead

Here is a word for the dead. Fallen sinners are in the same condition spiritually as Lazarus was in physically. They are spiritually dead; but spiritual death is no excuse for neglect, indifference, or even unbelief. Poor, lost sinners are dead spiritually and legally. Yet, all are both physically and morally alive and responsible. There are some things dead sinners can and must do. Dead in sin, fallen, depraved men and women cannot save themselves, redeem themselves, put away their sins, or give themselves life. But there are some things sinners can do. And what you can do you must do.

Was the Ethiopian Eunuch dead in sin? He certainly was. Yet, he did not neglect his soul. He did what he could (Acts 8:26-39). That Ethiopian Eunuch bought a Bible and began to read it. You can do that, too. That African earnestly sought the Lord. You can do that, too. He went up to the place where the Lord promised to reveal himself (Matthew 18:20). It was a long, costly, dangerous journey. But he was in trouble. He was a sinner in need of a Saviour. So he made the trip from Ethiopia to Jerusalem. Though he did not find the Saviour at first, he was not discouraged. When he left Jerusalem, he was still seeking the Lord. He was reading Isaiah 53. He did not seek to know the mysteries of scripture, or the deep doctrines of the Bible. He was seeking a Person! No doubt, he prayed much. And while he was seeking the Lord, God sent him a gospel preacher. What mercy! He heard! He believed! He was baptised! 'He went on his way rejoicing'!

He walked in the light God gave him, did what he knew he could do and had to do; and God gave him more light. If you care for your soul, seek the Lord while he may be found and call upon him while he is near. 'The Lord is good to the soul that seeketh him'! (Lamentations 3:25). Ask, and it shall be given you; seek, and ye shall find; knock, and it shall be opened unto you (Matthew 7:7). There are no exceptions. If you seek the Lord, he will save you. If you do not seek him, you will not find him.

It is true, the Lord God declares, 'I am found of them that sought me not' (Isaiah 65:1). Yes, it is true that the Holy Spirit searches for the lost coin; and the good Shepherd seeks his lost sheep. But that prodigal son must return to his Father's house. You must seek the Lord. 'Wherefore he saith, Awake thou that sleepest, and arise from the dead, and Christ shall give thee light'

(Ephesians 5:14). Without question, if you seek the Lord, it is because he is seeking you; but seek him you must (Jeremiah 29:12, 13).

A Word For The Preacher

Second, here is a word for the preacher. As a gospel preacher, as the servant of God in this world, there are some things every gospel preacher can and must do for the souls of men. I know that whenever God is pleased to save a sinner, he sends a gospel preacher to the sinner he is determined to save to proclaim the gospel of his grace. We do not exalt the ministry of the gospel into a popish priesthood. But we dare not despise it as a needless thing. The preaching of the gospel is essential to the salvation of God's elect, because, 'it pleased God by the foolishness of preaching to save them that believe' (1 Corinthians 1:21; Romans 10:13-17). C. H. Spurgeon once said, 'We cannot turn dry bones into living men, but we can prophesy upon them, and, blessed be God, we can also prophesy to the four winds, and so by our means the dead may live.'

Not everyone can or should preach. God has not called and gifted all of his people to be preachers. But he has called and gifted some for the work. It is the responsibility of all who are called and gifted of God for this blessed work to give themselves whole-heartedly and conscientiously to the work of preaching the gospel (1 Corinthians 9:16). They must be diligent in study and preparation, diligently seek God's message in prayer, and avail themselves of every means and opportunity to preach the gospel to this generation.

There is a work to be done for the souls of men before they are converted. Before Lazarus was raised from the dead, our Lord required those who were standing by to take the stone away from his tomb. God's servants have no power to make dead sinners live. But we are responsible to remove the stones which have been laid over their tombs. Like those men who were sent out to clear all debris from the road leading to the City of Refuge, gospel preachers must 'Prepare the way of the LORD, make straight in the desert a highway for our God' (Isaiah 40:3). The Lord God commands us, 'Cast ye up, cast ye up, prepare the way, take up the stumblingblock out of the way of my people' (Isaiah 57:14).

Some do not come to Christ because the huge stone of ignorance prevents them. There are some things you must know in order to trust Christ. You cannot trust an unknown Saviour. Therefore, we are sent to preach the gospel that men may know who Christ is, what he accomplished as our Substitute, and how he saves sinners by his almighty grace. Many others do not come to Christ because they have been entombed beneath the heavy stone of religious error. They are blinded by false religion and the doctrines of men. Therefore, a faithful gospel preacher must continually combat and expose religious error. And some do not come to Christ because Satan holds them under the heavy, black stone of despair. There is no cause for any sinner to despair of grace. Grace is free and unconditional, 'him that cometh unto me I will in no wise cast out' (John 6:37).

There is much to be done for sinners before they believe; and there is much that must be done by God's servant for people after they believe. Before they are converted, the Lord's word to his servants is, 'Take ye away the stone'. Once the dead are given life, his word is, 'Loose him, and let him go' (v. 44). Christ's says to his servant, 'Feed my lambs' (Jeremiah 3:15; 1 Peter 5:1-3).

Young plants in the vineyard must be tenderly watered and nurtured. Newborn babes must be fed the sincere milk of the word. The children of God must be brought into the glorious liberty of the sons of God. And the men of grace must be fed with strong meat. New converts must be set free from religious tradition, the grave clothes of legalism, and the oppressive care of the world, as well as the chains of sin. God's children must be fed and nurtured and cared for, so that they may enjoy the freedom of fellowship with Christ and his people. This loosing of God's people is a life-long process. It requires the constant, faithful, loving, and knowledgeable ministry of the gospel. Gospel preachers are ascension gifts of Christ to his church, given to lead sinners to Christ, instruct saints in faith, establish churches in doctrine, guide pilgrims in their sojourn, comfort believers in their troubles, and protect God's sheep in their pasture.

A Word For The Believer

Third, here is a word for the believer. There are some things you who are saved by the grace of God can and must do for the souls of men (see Mark 2:1-5). Perhaps God has not called you to preach. You are not gifted, perhaps, for that work. But God has given you a sphere of influence with some, and gifted you with the ability to do some things that no one else can do. That which God has given you the ability to do and the opportunity to do you must do.

You can do for the unbelieving what Mary and Martha did for their dead brother. You can call upon the Master on their behalf.

Brethren, see poor sinners round you,
Slumbering on the brink of woe.
Death is coming, hell is moving,
Can you bear to let them go?

George Atkins

As God gives you opportunity, you can tell what you know (John 9:11). You can tell your friends, relatives, neighbours, and acquaintances what you have seen, heard, felt, and experienced of the grace of God in Christ. 'What great things God hath done unto thee'! You can use what God has given you for the support of the gospel ministry (3 John 5-8). You can make a decided effort to distribute tracts, tapes, CDs, DVDs, bulletins, books, and articles to the people you come into contact with. You can work to prepare a place for others to hear the gospel. You can find a way to bring men and women with you to hear the gospel of Christ. And you can exemplify the grace of God in your life before the people of this world.

A Word For Us All

Fourth, here is a word for us all. That which we can do, before God, we are responsible to do (Ezekiel 33:7-9).

'So thou, O son of man, I have set thee a watchman unto the house of Israel; therefore thou shalt hear the word at my mouth, and warn them from me. When I say unto the wicked, O wicked man, thou shalt surely die; if thou dost not speak to warn the wicked from his way, that wicked man shall die in his iniquity; but his blood will I require at thine hand. Nevertheless, if thou warn the wicked of his way to turn from it; if he do not turn from his way, he shall die in his iniquity; but thou hast delivered thy soul.'

Necessity is laid upon me. I must preach the gospel (1 Corinthians 9:16). We are under the constraint of Christ's grace and love; we must be his witness (John 20:21). What are you doing for the glory of Christ and the souls of men? Be your own judge in this matter. Men and women are perishing for lack of knowledge. I see zeal and enthusiasm for everything in this world, except for the gospel of Christ. How very sad! The time is short. Dedicate yourself to the Master's work. Throw yourself into it today!

Chapter 12

Seeing The Glory Of God

'Jesus saith unto her, Said I not unto thee, that, if thou wouldest believe, thou shouldest see the glory of God?' (John 11:40).

That which is the only thing worth seeing, that which will fill and gladden the soul when it is seen and known, that in comparison with which all other sights are nothing is 'the glory of God'. That which righteous men of old desired to see, but saw only in brief, shadowy glimpses; that for which Moses prayed in the tabernacle, when he saw the Lord face to face; that for which we who believe most earnestly and constantly pray; that without which our longing hearts can never be satisfied is 'the glory of God'. That which everything in heaven and earth is intended to reveal, which our eyes were made to behold and our minds were formed to appreciate, for which sin was allowed to come into the world that it might be expelled by righteousness, and for which death came to be succeeded by everlasting life; that for which the Son of God came into the world; lived, died, and rose again to reveal, is 'the glory of God'.

At The Tomb

Our Lord Jesus is standing before the tomb of with Lazarus's sisters, Martha and Mary. It appears that Martha questioned both the Saviour's wisdom and his power. She seems to have questioned the Lord's wisdom in providence, because he had not come sooner to prevent her brother's death (v. 21). And she seems to have questioned his power and ability to raise Lazarus from the dead (v. 39). Without question, Martha was a believer. She was loved of God and born of God. But, like us, she was weak, faltering, and failing. She struggled with unbelief. She looked at her present situation and what she saw told her that Lazarus, who had been dead for four days, was beyond hope. She had grace to believe for the future. She said, 'I know that he shall rise again in the resurrection at the last day' (v. 24). But she did not trust Christ for the present. She walked by sight, not by faith. She acted according to reason, not revelation.

Then, 'Jesus saith unto her, Said I not unto thee, that, if thou wouldest believe, thou shouldest see the glory of God?' The only thing preventing Martha from seeing the glory of God on this occasion was her unbelief. Our Lord said, 'if thou wouldest believe, thou shouldest see the glory of God'. These words were not spoken for Martha's sake alone. They were not intended to reprove and instruct Martha alone. They are recorded for our learning and admonition as well. This is what the Lord Jesus says to you and me, 'if thou wouldest believe, thou shouldest see the glory of God'.

In another place our Lord says, 'Blessed are the pure in heart, for they shall see God.' But here the Saviour is not speaking of seeing God himself, but rather of seeing the glory of God. He is talking about the revelation of that which is in God. Horatius Bonar said, our Lord is talking about seeing 'some display of the invisible excellences that are in him.' The glory of God is that which shows him to be the glorious Being that he is. It is through the knowledge of his glory, through seeing his glory, that we reach the knowledge of God himself. 'For God, who commanded the light to shine out of darkness, hath shined in our hearts, to give the light of the knowledge of the glory of God in the face of Jesus Christ' (2 Corinthians 4:6).

The glory of God is spread out before us in all his wonderful works. It is revealed in creation's handiwork. 'The heavens declare the glory of God; the firmament showeth his handiwork' (Psalms 19:1). It is written out plainly in the book of holy scripture. It is embodied in Christ, the incarnate Son, who is the image of the invisible God and the brightness of his glory. And it is the glory of God, above all else, that is proclaimed in the gospel of his grace.

The glory of God is the thing we desire. That is the thing we long to see, and must see. We who believe have dedicated our hearts, our lives, and all that we possess to the glory of God. Every time we bow our heads in prayer, both in private and in public, our hearts cry out for a manifestation of God's glory. Why then do we see so very little of the glory of our God? The only thing that keeps us from seeing the glory of God is our own unbelief. Here is the high, high honour that God our Saviour puts upon faith in himself. He says, 'If thou wouldest believe thou shouldest see the glory of God'!

God's Purpose

First, let us understand that it is God's purpose to reveal his glory. The supreme, ultimate purpose of God in creation, providence, redemption, and grace is to reveal himself and to show forth his glory. The prophet Isaiah says, 'So didst thou lead thy people, to make thyself a glorious name' (Isaiah 63:14). For his own sake and for our sake, God is pleased to manifest his glory. God reveals himself and shows forth his glory for his own name's sake, so that he might receive the honour and praise that rightfully belongs to him from all his wonderful works. And God reveals himself and shows forth his glory for our sakes as well, so that we might know and enjoy him as God.

Particularly, in John 11:40, our Lord Jesus speaks of God's glory being seen in bringing life out of death. It was for this cause that Christ came into the world, that he might reveal the glory of God in abolishing death by his own death on the cross. Christ came to remove the penalty of sin which is death, to undo the work which death had done, to destroy him which had the power of death, to swallow up death in victory. This work of redemption is altogether the work of God's free grace. Its accomplishment is a marvellous manifestation of his glory.

Even God's strange work, his acts of judgment, is designed of God to show forth his greatness and his glory. 'For the scripture saith unto Pharaoh, even for this same purpose have I raised thee up, that I might show my power in thee, and that my name might be declared throughout all the earth' (Romans 9:17). Vessels of wrath, made unto dishonour, shall show forth the glory of the great Potter and serve his purpose, just as fully as the vessels of mercy 'which he had afore prepared unto glory' (Romans 9:21-24).

Everything in God's creation is designed, ordained, brought to pass, and ruled by God in his total sovereignty to glorify himself, and to reveal his glory to his creatures. Nothing happens by chance. Everything, the bad as well as the good, is ruled by God for the glory of his own name. This is plainly the doctrine of holy scripture. 'Surely the wrath of man shall praise thee: the remainder of wrath shalt thou restrain' (Psalms 76:10). 'The LORD hath made all things for himself: yea, even the wicked for the day of evil' (Proverbs 16:4). 'For of him, and through him, and to him are all things: to whom be glory forever. Amen' (Romans 11:36). 'Thou art worthy, O Lord, to receive glory and honour and power: for thou hast created all things, and for thy pleasure they are and were created' (Revelation 4:11). It is the purpose of God to reveal his glory in all things. To that end he ordained all things, made all things, and rules all things.

Mediator's Desire

Second, the scriptures reveal that it is the desire of the one Mediator between God and men, the Lord Jesus Christ, our Substitute, the God-man our Saviour, that we see the glory of God (John 1:18). Sin has hidden God's glory from fallen man. Christ Jesus came to unveil the Father's face, to make known the Father's character, to manifest the Father's glory. 'No man hath seen God at any time; the only begotten Son, which is in the bosom of the Father, he hath declared him' (John 1:18). This was the errand upon which Christ came. It is true he came to save his people from their sins. But his purpose in saving us was that he might reveal the glory of God, that God might be glorified in us and by us (John 12:27, 28; 17:1, 4; Ephesians 1:6, 12, 14, 2:7).

The Lord Jesus seeks our eternal blessedness; and he knows that our blessedness is to be found in beholding the glory of God. What are we without this glory? We are nothing. Our existence is meaningless, vain, and empty. We are like a world without a sun, a bee without a hive, or a well without water. Will you not look to Christ and behold the glory of God? The Son of God delights to show sinners the glory of God. It was for this purpose that he came into the world, lived in righteousness, died in agony, and rose again in triumph. Will you not turn and behold the glory of God in the face of Jesus Christ, that in beholding him, your soul may be filled with heavenly light and gladness?

To say that Christ desires the salvation of sinners, the holiness of his elect, and the comfort of his saints is to say much. But to say that he desires to make known to men the glory of God is to say much more. To say this is to declare that the Son of God desires and delights in men beholding that which, as soon as it is beheld, will bring life, gladness, holiness, and comfort to your heart and soul. When the Lord Jesus says, 'Come unto me and I will give you rest', his meaning is, 'Come unto me and I will show you that which will immediately cause you to rest.' When he says, 'If any man thirst, let him come unto me and drink', his meaning is, 'Come unto me, and I will show you that which is more refreshing to your soul than a fountain of water to a thirsty man.'

Our Unbelief

We have seen that it is the purpose of God in all things to reveal his glory. The word of God makes that fact crystal clear. And the book of God shows us plainly that Christ Jesus, the Mediator, desires for men and women to see and know and enjoy the glory of God. Why is it, then, that so few see the glory of God, and that those few see so little of God's glory? To answer that question, let me show you a third fact, plainly revealed in the word of God. It is our unbelief, only our unbelief that keeps us from seeing the glory of God.

This is the reproof given in our text. Our Lord Jesus said, 'If thou wouldest believe, thou shouldest see the glory of God'. The one, singular evil about which our Lord complained most often while he was upon the earth was unbelief. He found wretched unbelief not only in the Pharisees and the common people of the world, but also among his own disciples. They were slow of heart to believe God! How often they shut both their eyes and stopped both their ears against the wonders performed in their midst and spoken in their presence by the Son of God! They would not believe the message of free-grace, redeeming love, and eternal life! They would not believe, therefore, they could not see the glory of God revealed in Jesus Christ!

But we must not be too quick or severe in our judgment regarding those early disciples. That which was their shame and crime is ours as well. How slow we are to believe our God! And, like Israel in the wilderness, like Martha, like those before whom the incarnate God walked upon the earth, it is our unbelief that keeps us from seeing the glory of God today. It is unbelief alone that keeps sinners from Christ. It is unbelief alone that keeps God's saints from enjoying the privileges that are ours in Christ. It is unbelief alone that keeps redeemed, regenerate sinners from the joy of full assurance. It is unbelief alone that keeps God's children from that peace that passes understanding. It is unbelief alone that keeps you and me from enjoying the fulfilment of God's promises.

Matthew Henry said, 'Unbelief is at the bottom of all our staggerings at God's promises', and Robert Traill wrote, 'A great many believers walk upon the promises at God's call in the way to heaven even as a child upon weak ice, which they are afraid will crack under them and leave them in the depth.' John Calvin tells us, 'Our own unbelief is the only impediment which prevents God from satisfying us largely and bountifully with all good things.' It is unbelief that prevents our minds from soaring into the celestial city and walking by faith with God across the golden streets. Oh, wretched, sinful, shameful unbelief! God grant us grace to overcome this weakness and infirmity of the flesh.

It is unbelief that hinders Christ from performing those works in our midst which would show us the glory of God. That is an incredible statement, contrary to all human reason. I would not dare think of making such a statement, were it not for one thing. It is plainly given in the word of God. Can a child's hand smother the sun? Can a withered leaf, fallen into a mighty river, stop its flow, or dry up its waters? Can the breath of a man extinguish the stars of heaven? Of course not! Yet, the word of God plainly informs us that unbelief prevents Christ from performing his mighty works in our midst, by which the glory of God might be seen. Matthew tells us that when the Lord Jesus 'was come into his country … he did not many mighty works there because of their unbelief' (Matthew 13:58). Mark uses stronger language, telling us, 'he could there do no mighty work, save that he laid his hands upon a few sick folk, and healed them, and he marvelled because of their unbelief' (Mark 6:5, 6).

The hand of God is not prevented from working in our midst by our unworthiness, or by the multitude of our sins, or by our inability, but only by our unbelief. What wonders God might perform for us, among us, in us, and with us if we would simply take him at his word! It was unbelief that prevented the Son of God from performing his mighty works in Galilee. Unbelief lays hold of Christ's hand, and says, 'Work not here.' Unbelief despises the grace and power of God and says, 'Depart out of our coasts.'

It is unbelief that prevents us from seeing the glory of God in his works, even though they are wrought before our very eyes. Christ's hand is not always stayed by man's unbelief. Thank God for that! Where he wills to work, he will work. Man's will cannot overthrow his will. And man's unbelief cannot frustrate, nullify or even alter God's eternal purpose. Very frequently the Lord Jesus did work the works of God, works in which the glory of God was evidently revealed before the eyes of unbelieving men. Multitudes saw the works performed by the Lord Jesus; but, because of their unbelief, they could not see the glory of God in those works. They saw the healing of the leper, but did not see the glory of God in the leper's healing. They saw the opening of the blind man's eyes, the unstopping of deaf ears, the giving of feet to the lame, the casting out of devils and even the resurrections of Jarius's daughter and of the widow's son; but they did not see the glory of God in these things. They no more saw the glory of God in the works of Christ than they did in Christ himself. Even after Lazarus was raised from the dead, some who saw that mighty miracle did not see the glory of God in the miracle (John 11:43-46).

In John 6 there were five thousand men, not counting the women and children, who were fed with five barley loaves and two small fish. A mighty miracle was performed. Those people ate the bread and the fish. They both saw the miracle and partook of its benefits. But they did not see the glory of God in it all. They ate from the hand of him who is the Bread of Life and knew it not. They followed the Master for a while, because of the abundance of loaves and fish he gave them. But they saw nothing glorious in him, or in his works. The glorious God was standing before them; but they could not see him. And the Lord told them plainly, 'Ye seeks me, not because ye saw the miracles', that is to say, not because you saw the glory of God in the miracles I have performed, 'but because ye did eat the loaves, and were filled' (John 6:26).

The glory that is wrapped up in God's works can be perceived only by faith. Faith draws aside the veil. Faith sees the glory of God in his works, for faith sees the glory of God in the face of Jesus Christ. Faith eats the Bread of Life and drinks from the Fountain of Living Water, and is refreshed by the abundance of grace, which all of Christ's miracles portrayed. The charismatic looks for and sees nothing but carnal miracles; and Satan gives him his desire. The believer sees in every miracle performed by Christ a picture of God's grace; and in that grace he sees the glory of God. We do not look for carnal signs of grace, which is what the miracles were. We have the word of grace;

and believing the word of grace, we see the glory of God in all his works of grace.

Unbelief keeps us from enjoying the glory of God even after we have in some measure seen it. The Lord's disciples saw the glory of God in his wondrous works. Yet, after all they had seen, heard, and experienced, they realised very little. The glory of God seems to have been seen by them at intervals, in glimpses, but not continually. Like men with a telescope at their side, sometimes using it to look far beyond the scope of natural vision, and sometimes not using it at all, these disciples seem to have exercised great faith at times, and virtually no faith at other times. There was more unbelief in their history than faith. They had faith enough to show them something. But their unbelief kept much more hidden from them. They entered but little into the glory they acknowledged and at times enjoyed.

How much like those disciples we are! Like Martha, we have seen the glory of God in Christ yesterday. And we have hope of seeing more tomorrow. But for today, where is the faith to see the glory of God? We have seen the glory of God in the death, resurrection, and exaltation of our Lord Jesus Christ. Our eyes rest upon him who is the glory of God. But, oh, how faintly do we behold him! And the reason is our shame. We see but little of the glory of God, because we believe but little. Unbelief is the thing that grieved our Lord. Unbelief is what he reproves in us more than anything else. Unbelief dishonours God, quenches the work of the Spirit, and keeps us from usefulness for the glory of God and the souls of men.

But our dear Saviour's words in John 11:40 are much more than a reproof. The Lord Jesus is calling us to faith. 'Jesus saith unto her, Said I not unto thee, that, if thou wouldest believe, thou shouldest see the glory of God?' He is saying, 'Have faith in God. Only believe. Be not faithless, but believing. Trust God in everything and for everything, in the most trying circumstances, say, "Is anything too hard for the Lord?"'

Faith honours God, and God honours faith! He always has and he always will; ask Job (Job 1:20-23; 2:9, 10; 42:10), ask Noah (Genesis 7:23), ask Abraham (Genesis 22:8, 13, 14; Romans 4:20-22), ask Hannah (1 Samuel 2:1), ask Naomi (Ruth 4:14, 15), ask David (1 Samuel 17:45-51), ask the Widow of Zarephath (1 Kings 17:14-16). Faith honours God, and God honours faith!

Believe And See

Fourth, if we would believe, we would see the glory of God. Martha and Mary were placed in hard, trying circumstances. Their beloved brother was dead. What could they hope might be done? Had the Lord arrived earlier, they might have hoped that he would have healed Lazarus. But it appeared that he had arrived too late. Lazarus was dead. They comforted themselves with the hope of the great resurrection. But for the present, Martha was full of despair. Then the Lord spoke to Martha, saying, 'Said I not unto thee, that, if thou wouldest believe, thou shouldest see the glory of God?' It is as much as if he had said, 'Martha, Martha, if you would just trust me, I would do for you far greater things than you could ever think or ask. If you would but trust me, there is nothing I would not do for you, no length to which I would not go, no limit to the power I would exercise on your behalf to show you the glory of God.'

And he says the same thing to you and me. Child of God, you may be enduring some great trial right now. But your trial is no greater than Abraham's, when he was called to offer up his son, Isaac. If he believed and staggered not, if he hoped against hope and was strong in faith, giving God the glory, why should we not do the same? Are we the children of Abraham, to whom the 'God of glory' appeared? Is it not reasonable for our Lord, who is always faithful to us, to expect faith from us? After all he has done, can we be hesitating, fearful, and distrustful? God forbid! This is his promise: 'If thou wouldest believe, thou shouldest see the glory of God.'

If we would believe, we would see the glory of God in salvation by Christ our Substitute (Exodus 33:18-23). The glory of God can be seen only by those who are standing upon the mount of sacrifice, looking through the blood of Christ slain upon the cursed tree (Romans 3:24-26). In the cross of Christ, in his death as the sinner's Substitute, I see the glory of God. There 'mercy and truth have met together; righteousness and peace have kissed each other' (Psalms 85:10). We see the glory of God most fully in the substitutionary sacrifice and sin-atoning death of the Lord Jesus Christ, because in his death all the glorious attributes of God are plainly revealed: his sovereignty and his grace, his righteousness and his goodness, his inflexible justice and his pardoning mercy, his unmitigated wrath and his everlasting love (Exodus 33:19, 34:5-7).

If you will believe on the Lord Jesus, you will see the glory of God in the sacrifice of his Son. But if you believe not, you never can. Reason may see the doctrine of the cross; but only faith can see the glory of the cross. Only faith can see the glory of God in the face of Jesus Christ.

If we would believe, we would see the glory of God in his wise and good providence (Romans 8:28; 11:36). If Martha had believed, she would have seen the glory of God in Lazarus' sickness and death and in her own grief as well. All things are of God; but only faith can see the glory of God in all things. How adorable his providence is! Faith sees the glory of God in providence.

If we would believe, we would see the glory of God in the works he performs in our midst. God's glory is seen in his works. And faith perceives both his work and his glory in his work. God's glory is to be seen in what he has done, in what he is doing, and in what he shall do.

If we would believe, we would see the glory of God in the fulfilling of his promise. 'Put me in remembrance: let us plead together: declare thou, that thou mayest be justified' (Isaiah 43:26). I wonder how much spiritual blessedness we miss simply because we do not believe God. Because we insist upon having much goods laid up for many years, we miss the blessedness of seeing God raining manna from heaven, giving us each day our daily bread.

If we would believe, we would see the glory of God in his resurrection power (John 5:25-29). I know that God works in total sovereignty. He depends upon us for nothing. His work depends upon us for nothing. But I know this also, God works in his sovereignty by the faith of his people (Ezekiel 36:33-38). I take Ezekiel's prophecy to mean that if we would but believe God, we would see his glory in spiritual resurrections, we would see God save his elect. Yes, God will save all his elect, when and where it pleases him. But I am certain that in the Church of God we lack for conversions only because we lack faith. It is written, 'When Zion travailed, she brought forth her children' (Isaiah 66:8). And if we believe, we shall see the glory of God in the resurrection of our bodies at the last day (Job 19:25, 26).

God's Gift

Fifth, be sure you understand that faith to behold the glory of God is itself the gift of God's grace and a work in which his glory is to be seen (Ephesians 1:19; 2:8; Colossians 2:10-12). We believe only by the working of God's mighty power in us, only by the gift of his grace. If you now believe God, it is by that very same power that raised our Lord Jesus from the dead. Yet, our Lord Jesus Christ declares, 'If thou wouldest believe thou shouldest see the glory of God'! Believe God! Believe and you shall see the glory of God (Mark 9:23, 24).

Faith is the gift of grace alone,
My God, how can it be
That you should choose, in saving love,
To give that gift to me?

Faith owes its birth to sovereign grace,
And lives beneath the throne,
Where grace maintains her dwelling place,
And reigns supreme alone!

A sinner saved by sovereign grace,
My praise I cannot hold:
Hail, sovereign, free, unchanging grace!
'Salvation's of the LORD'!

Chapter 13

Substitution: Christ In My Place

'Then gathered the chief priests and the Pharisees a council, and said, What do we? for this man doeth many miracles. If we let him thus alone, all men will believe on him: and the Romans shall come and take away both our place and nation. And one of them, named Caiaphas, being the high priest that same year, said unto them, Ye know nothing at all, Nor consider that it is expedient for us, that one man should die for the people, and that the whole nation perish not. And this spake he not of himself: but being high priest that year, he prophesied that Jesus should die for that nation; And not for that nation only, but that also he should gather together in one the children of God that were scattered abroad. Then from that day forth they took counsel together for to put him to death. Jesus therefore walked no more openly among the Jews; but went thence unto a country near to the wilderness, into a city called Ephraim, and there continued with his disciples. And the Jews' passover was nigh at hand: and many went out of the country up to Jerusalem before the passover, to purify themselves. Then sought they for Jesus, and spake among themselves, as they stood in the temple, What think ye, that he will not come to the feast? Now both the chief priests and the Pharisees had given a commandment, that, if any man knew where he were, he should shew it, that they might take him' (John 11:47-57).

How hard, how desperately wicked, how utterly depraved the heart of man is! A mighty miracle had been wrought just a short distance from Jerusalem. A man who had been dead for four days was raised to life in the sight of many witnesses. The fact was unmistakable, and could not be denied. Yet, the chief priests and Pharisees and the multitudes under their influence would not believe. They shut their eyes and stopped their ears. Fearful of losing their ecclesiastical power, they would not bow to God's revelation. Rather than bowing to Christ, they 'took counsel to put him to death'.

Read this passage again, and behold the insanity with which men reason when they set themselves against God. These elevated fools reasoned that the only way they could preserve their nation was to destroy Christ, his church and his gospel. They rushed madly down the path they chose; and the very thing they feared came to pass. In just a few short years, the Roman armies did come, destroyed Jerusalem, burned the temple, and carried away the whole nation into captivity.

The religious hypocrites held before us in this passage clearly exemplify the fact that lost people, with hearts full of sin, with hearts completely filled with hatred for God, often love religion, religious traditions, and religious ceremonies. Here is a great multitude (v. 55), in the throes of plotting to murder the Lord Jesus while meticulously purifying themselves for the observance of the Passover!

'The Jews' passover was nigh at hand … Then sought they for Jesus, and spake among themselves, as they stood in the temple, What think ye, that he will not come to the feast?' He will, indeed, come. He created the world for this hour. Before this feast was ended, Christ our Passover would be sacrificed for us. The subject presented to us here is Substitution. I want to show you from the word of God what substitution is, and show you the efficacy of Christ's substitutionary work.

One Subject

The Bible is a book with one subject, and that subject is substitution. The singular theme of the holy scripture is the substitutionary work of the Lord Jesus Christ, by which he obtained eternal redemption for his elect and secured the everlasting salvation of his people. The one purpose and object of the word of God is to reveal the glory of Christ in the performance and accomplishment of his great substitutionary work. If you miss, or fail to understand the gospel message of substitution, you cannot understand anything written upon the pages of inspiration.

I know that the Bible teaches us many blessed truths. I love to study and preach Bible doctrine. I am not embarrassed or uneasy when someone refers to me as a 'doctrinal preacher'. If I were not a preacher of gospel doctrine, I would not pretend to be a preacher. But all the blessed doctrines of the sacred volume may be summed up and set forth in the doctrine of substitution. No truth of holy scripture, no part of the Bible can be understood apart from the doctrine of substitution.

The very first doctrine of the Bible, the doctrine of creation, can be understood properly only when we realise that all things were created by the Lord Jesus Christ, our Substitute. The doctrine of divine providence is a precious truth of holy scripture. We rejoice to 'know that all things work together for good to them that love God, to them who are the called, according to his purpose.' But providence can only be understood when we realise that all things are upheld and governed by the word and power of Christ our Substitute. We believe the glorious doctrines of eternal election and sovereign predestination. And we are not at all bashful about proclaiming them. But election is in Christ. We were chosen in the Substitute. Predestination is to the end that we should be conformed to the image of the Son of God, our Substitute. How we rejoice and glory in the doctrine of the atonement! But if there were no Substitute, no Mediator between God and man, if there was no one who could satisfy the needs of fallen man and the justice of a holy God, if there were no suitable Substitute, there would be no atonement. The doctrines of the resurrection and the glorification of the saints cause our hearts great joy before God. This is the glorious expectation of the sons of God. But we would have no hope of future glory, if there were no Substitute into whose likeness we must be made.

The theme of the Bible is substitution. The whole purpose of divine revelation is to teach us that God will not speak to, nor will he be spoken to by any man, apart from a Substitute. God only deals with men through a Substitute. Your eternal salvation, or your eternal damnation will be determined by your relationship to God's appointed Substitute, the Lord Jesus Christ. Everything in the Bible sets forth Jesus Christ, the Son of God, the incarnate God-man as the one, the only, the all-sufficient Substitute for sinners (Luke 24:44-47).

Sinner's Hope

Substitution is the sinner's only hope. The substitutionary sacrifice of the Lord Jesus Christ is the only hope we have, the only hope God's elect have ever had, and the only hope sinners ever shall have. In the Old Testament church God's elect believed on and trusted the Substitute who was to come, the One promised, prophesied, and pictured in the Old Testament scriptures, and they were redeemed and justified, forgiven and accepted in their Substitute, 'the Lamb slain from the foundation of the world' (Genesis 3:15; 4:1-4; 22:8-14; Exodus 12:13; Psalms 22; Isaiah 53; Daniel 9:24; 12:10; Malachi 4:1, 2; ; Luke 2:25; John 1:29; Acts 10:43, Revelation 13:8).

As the Church of the Old Testament had but one foundation upon which to rest its hope before God, so today we have no hope of acceptance with God but this, 'In due time Christ died for the ungodly'. In both the Old Testament era and in this gospel era, the Christ we trust, the Substitute by whom we are redeemed is Christ, 'the Lamb slain from the foundation of the world', whose 'works were finished from the foundation of the world' (Hebrews 4:3).

The book of God makes it perfectly clear that the only hope any sinner has of eternal salvation is substitution. Our only hope of acceptance with God is through the substitutionary work of the Lord Jesus Christ. Every ritual, every garment of the priesthood, every sacrifice, every article of furniture within the tabernacle, the tabernacle itself, all the laws of the Old Testament, the temple, the temple service, and all the prophets of God, all have but one message, and they all speak it very plainly. Their message is substitution and that is the message of every man called and sent of God to preach the gospel. Substitution means Christ in my place.

A Substitute Is ...

You know what a substitute is. A substitute is one who stands in the place of another. A substitute assumes the obligations and responsibilities of another person. This is what the Lord Jesus Christ has done for us, as our Substitute. The Son of God assumed our nature and took upon himself the sins of God's elect. He stood in the place of sinners at Calvary so that all who trust him might stand in his place eternally accepted before God. Since I fully trust my soul upon the merits of Christ and him alone, resting my soul upon him for everything before God, I have good reason to believe that Jesus Christ is my Substitute. I want to tell you about Christ my Substitute. I want to show you how he has stood, is standing, and shall forever stand in my place before God. I want you to know, trust, love and worship my glorious Saviour, the Lord Jesus Christ, the sinners' Substitute.

A Perfect Substitute

Who is our Substitute? (John 1:1; 1 Timothy 3:16; 6:14-16). His name is Immanuel, 'God with us'. The sinners' Substitute must be a real man; and he must be the infinite God. Were he only God, he could not suffer. Were he only man, he could not satisfy. But the God-man can both suffer and satisfy.

And the Substitute must be perfect (Leviticus 22:21). In Leviticus 21 and 22, the Lord instructed Moses and Aaron with the most vital and fundamental information on how to approach and worship him. The high priest must have no defect, deformity or blemish of any kind (Leviticus 21:16-21). And the sacrifice must have no blemish at all (Leviticus 22:17-24). If the priest had no defect, but brought a sacrifice with blemishes it would not be accepted, for it 'must be perfect to be accepted' (Leviticus 22:21). Likewise, if the sacrifice had no blemish, but the priest who offered it had any blemish, the sacrifice would not be accepted at all, for it 'must be perfect to be accepted'.

The purpose of those ancient Levitical laws was to declare the gospel of the Lord Jesus Christ in the ceremonial pictures of the law. Christ is our perfect, great High Priest without spot, blemish, defect, deformity or sin (Hebrews 4:14, 15; 7:26; 8:1). And he is the perfect Sacrifice. He is the Lamb without blemish and without spot (John 1:29; 1 Peter 1:18-20). It is only in the Lord Jesus Christ and his glorious sacrifice that we can be and are justified from all sin (Acts 13:38, 39; Hebrews 9:12).

In the Lord Jesus Christ every believer is a priest with no blemish, no sin (Revelation 1:5, 6; 5:9, 10). In Christ's precious blood atonement we approach the throne of grace with boldness (Hebrews 4:16; 10:19-22), because we have a perfect sacrifice that fully, eternally satisfies the holy justice of God (Romans 3:24-26; Colossians 1:19-22; Jude 24, 25).

It is in, by, through, and with Christ our Substitute, the perfect Priest and perfect Sacrifice, that we meet God's standard of perfection. 'It must be perfect to be accepted'. And this is all 'To the praise of the glory of his grace, wherein he hath made us accepted in the beloved' (Ephesians 1:6).

Saviour's Mission

Why did our Substitute, the Lord Jesus Christ, come into this world? What was his purpose in coming? What was his mission? He said that he came to do his Father's will. He said that he came to seek and to save that which was lost. Our Lord Jesus Christ came into this world, taking upon himself our nature, so that he might do that which was committed to him by his Father in the covenant of grace before the world began. Christ came to redeem unto himself a people and to glorify his Father in doing so. 'This is a faithful saying, and worthy of all acceptation, that Christ Jesus came into the world to save sinners; of whom I am chief' (1 Timothy 1:15). In order for God, in his infinite holiness, to save fallen, guilty sinners, God's own Son must become the sinners' Substitute. Righteousness must be established. Sin must be punished. Justice must be maintained and satisfied. Christ assumed our nature and came into this world so that God might be both just and the Justifier of his people.

Mission Accomplished

What did the Lord Jesus Christ accomplish while he was in this world? He brought in an everlasting righteousness. He satisfied the law and justice of God. He put away all the sins of his people. He redeemed a people unto himself (Galatians 3:13; Hebrews 9:12; 10:10-14).

'For the law having a shadow of good things to come, and not the very image of the things, can never with those sacrifices which they offered year by year continually make the comers thereunto perfect. For then would they not have ceased to be offered? because that the worshippers once purged should have had no more conscience of sins. But in those sacrifices there is a remembrance again made of sins every year. For it is not possible that the blood of bulls and of goats should take away sins. Wherefore when he cometh into the world, he saith, Sacrifice and offering Thou wouldest not, but a body hast Thou prepared me: In burnt offerings and sacrifices for sin Thou hast had no pleasure. Then said I, Lo, I come (in the volume of the book it is written of me,) to do thy will, O God. Above when he said, Sacrifice and offering and burnt offerings and offering for sin thou wouldest not, neither hadst pleasure therein; which are offered by the law; Then said he, Lo, I come to do thy will, O God. He taketh away the first, that he may establish the second. By the which will we are sanctified through the offering of the body of Jesus Christ once for all. And every priest standeth daily ministering and offering oftentimes the same sacrifices, which can never take away sins: But this man, after he had offered one sacrifice for sins for ever, sat down on the right hand of God; From henceforth expecting till his enemies be made his footstool. For by one offering he hath perfected for ever them that are sanctified' (Hebrews 10:1-14).

Substitute Accepted

Where is Christ now? (Hebrews 1:1-3). Yonder, beyond the skies, I see him, seated at the right hand of the Majesty on high, as our Substitute. Our great Substitute has finished the work of redemption; and now he reigns as the exalted Monarch of the universe, performing the final salvation of those people for whom he died, the sinners he has redeemed with his own precious blood. The sovereign Ruler of this universe is that one who suffered and bled and died as the sinners' Substitute! (Isaiah 53:10-12; John 17:2).

Eternal Substitute

The Lord Jesus Christ stood as our Substitute in eternity past as our Surety in the everlasting covenant of grace. Christ is an eternal Substitute. It is always smart to begin in the beginning. And if you want to know what the book of God teaches about salvation, you must understand it is a work finished from eternity in our Substitute. By God's own oath in the counsels of eternity, 'Jesus was made a Surety of a better testament' (Hebrews 7:22). Before I was a sinner, Christ stood as my Saviour. Before I broke God's law, Christ stood as my Redeemer. Before I was a transgressor, Christ stood as my Righteousness. Before I fell in Adam, I was accepted in Christ my Substitute. Before I became a slave, Christ stood as my Ransom. Before I became a debtor, Christ stood as my Surety.

From everlasting, the God of glory said, concerning his elect, 'I will be their God, and they shall be my people'. In the covenant of grace the salvation of God's elect was planned, purposed, provided for, made sure, and completely accomplished (2 Samuel 23:5; Ephesians 1:3-14; 2 Timothy 1:9). All the blessings of the covenant and all of God's elect were entrusted to the hands of the Lord Jesus Christ as the Surety of the covenant (John 6:39; Ephesians 1:13). He voluntarily took upon himself all responsibility for us, just as Judah became surety for Benjamin and assumed all responsibility for Benjamin (Genesis 43:8, 9). With Christ standing as our Substitute and Surety, in the mind and purpose of God, our salvation was from eternity a thing already complete. In very plain, unmistakable words, God the Holy Spirit declares that the whole work was done in Christ before the world began (Romans 8:29, 30; Ephesians 1:3-7; 2 Timothy 1:9; Hebrews 4:3). Christ, the Lamb of God, was slain as our Substitute before the foundation of the world (Revelation 13:8). We were 'accepted in the Beloved', our Substitute, from eternity (Ephesians 1:6). God has always looked upon his elect in Christ, the Substitute, and always will!

Obedient Substitute

Christ is an eternal Substitute. He stood in our place and we were in him from eternity. The Lord Jesus Christ is our obedient Substitute. He stood as our Substitute while he lived in this world. For thirty-three years the Lord Jesus Christ lived as the federal Head and Representative of his people in this world. It is written, 'By the obedience of one shall many be made righteous' (Romans 5:19). As we were made sinners by the disobedience of Adam, we were made righteous by the obedience of Christ. In the course of his earthly life the Lord Jesus Christ restored that which he took not away, righteousness.

Understand this, the sinless life of Christ was as necessary for our redemption and salvation as his death at Calvary. In his life Christ fulfilled the holy law of God as our Substitute, establishing perfect righteousness (Romans 3:22), without which we could never be accepted before God. By his life of obedience, he brought in an everlasting righteousness for us. His name is, Jehovah-tsidkenu, 'The Lord our Righteousness' (Jeremiah 23:6). Our Lord voluntarily submitted himself to every law and ordinance of God to fulfil all righteousness as our Representative. All that the Lord Jesus Christ did in his life, he did as our Substitute. His righteousness is imputed to us because it is ours. All who are represented by him, all for whom he obeyed the law as their Substitute, obeyed the law in him. We often say, 'It is just as though we did it', and that is true; but there's more to this than a 'just as though'. The book of God reveals a real Substitute and real substitution (compare Jeremiah 23:6 and 33:16). God demands that we fulfil the law in perfect righteousness; and we who believe have fulfilled the law of God in our Substitute (Romans 3:28-31; 8:3, 4).

Crucified Substitute

We have seen, first, Christ is an eternal Substitute. He stood in our place, and we were in him from eternity. Second, the Lord Jesus Christ is our obedient Substitute. He stood as our Substitute while he lived in this world. Third, The Lord Jesus Christ, the Son of God, stood in our place as our Substitute at Calvary. He is our crucified, sin-atoning Substitute.

Our dear Saviour died under the penalty of God's law, bearing our sin, our shame, our guilt, and the wrath of God due unto us. He died in our place, satisfying the wrath of God for us, so that we, God's elect, the objects of his everlasting love, would never be required to die. That is Substitution; and that is the doctrine of holy scripture (2 Corinthians 5:21; Galatians 3:13, 14; 1 Peter 2:24; Isaiah 53:4-8; Psalms 40:12; 69:3-6, 9, 19, 20).

Child of God, when you think of the redemptive work of Christ, remember these four facts, rejoice in them, and let nothing move you from them.

1. The death of Christ was a vicarious sacrifice (2 Corinthians 5:21).

2. The death of Christ was for a particular people. 'For the transgression of my people was he stricken' (Isaiah 53:8). 'The good shepherd giveth his life for the sheep' (John 10:11).

3. The death of Christ was an effectual satisfaction of justice, an effectual atonement, an effectual redemption. 'By his own blood he entered in once into the holy place, having obtained eternal redemption for us' (Hebrews 9:12). Christ has put away all the sins of all his people. The Lord Jesus has redeemed God's elect. Our Substitute has silenced the claims of God's law against us, by fully satisfying it. Our great Substitute, the Lord Jesus Christ, has justified, perfectly and completely, all of those people for whom he died as a Substitute.

4. And the death of Christ was final. 'Now once in the end of the world hath he appeared to put away sin by the sacrifice of himself' (Hebrews 9:26).

Present Substitute

But there is more. Our Lord Jesus is an eternal Substitute. He is an obedient Substitute. He is a crucified, sin-atoning Substitute. And, blessed be his name, our dear Saviour is a present Substitute! See him yonder in glory. Jesus Christ the righteous stands in our place today as our Substitute and Advocate with the Father in heaven (1 John 2:1, 2). His five precious wounds, the merit of his righteousness and the merit of his blood effectually secure the present and eternal welfare of his people. God will not charge his own elect with sin; and the law cannot require any punishment of God's elect because of sin, because Christ, the risen Lord, our Substitute, stands as our Advocate with the Father. Child of God, do not sin! But when you do sin, do not despair! Our Advocate on high holds up his hands, as often as his child sins, and he says, 'Father, do not charge my redeemed one with sin. I paid the price for his iniquity, transgression, and sin. See, here are the wounds.'

God will never charge his people with sin for four reasons. In Christ we cease to be accountable for sin, because, 1. God himself has accepted our Substitute (Hebrews 6:20; 10:12). 2. Our Substitute is perfectly righteous, 'Jesus Christ, the Righteous'. 3. Our Advocate has made satisfaction for our sin. 'He is the propitiation for our sins'. 4. In Christ we have no sin. Christ has taken our sins away! 'Ye know that he was manifested to take away our sins; and in him is no sin' (1 John 3:5).

Judgment Substitute

First, Christ is an eternal Substitute. He stood in our place and we were in him from eternity. Second, the Lord Jesus Christ is our obedient Substitute. He stood as our Substitute while he lived in this world. Third, the Lord Jesus Christ, the Son of God, stood in our place as our Substitute at Calvary. He is our crucified, sin-atoning Substitute. Fourth, Jesus Christ the righteous stands in our place today as our Substitute and Advocate in heaven. He is our present Substitute. And, fifth, the Lord Jesus Christ himself will stand in our place, as our Substitute before the bar of the thrice holy Lord God on the day of judgment.

In that great day, when God judges all men, Christ will present all of his people, even you, even me; holy, unblameable, unreproveable, and perfect before the glorious majesty of the triune God, saying, 'Behold I and the children which God hath given me' (Hebrews 2:13; Ephesians 5:27; Jude 24, 25). When God examines us with the omniscient eye of his strict justice, truth, and holiness, he will find no spot or blemish in us, because his own Son performed in our place, as our Substitute, perfect righteousness and obedience and thoroughly washed away our sins in his blood (Jeremiah 50:20).

Trusting Christ as my Substitute, I fully expect to hear God say, 'This is my Beloved Son in whom I am well pleased'. And looking upon me in his Son, my Substitute, I fully expect to hear him say to me, 'Well done, Thou good and faithful servant; Come, inherit the kingdom prepared for you from the foundation of the world.'

Come, poor, guilty, helpless sinner! Come, you who are dirty, corrupt, bankrupt sinners, come to Christ. Trust your soul upon the merits of the Substitute, the Lord Jesus Christ; and, like the publican of old, find free, full, perfect justification in the Christ of God.

Child of God, how this gospel message of substitution ought to inspire our hearts with love for, praise to, adoration of, and devotion to the Lord Jesus Christ, our divine Substitute, the one who is, was, and shall forever be in our place!

Chapter 14

'six days before the passover'

'Then Jesus six days before the passover came to Bethany, where Lazarus was which had been dead, whom he raised from the dead. There they made him a supper; and Martha served: but Lazarus was one of them that sat at the table with him. Then took Mary a pound of ointment of spikenard, very costly, and anointed the feet of Jesus, and wiped his feet with her hair: and the house was filled with the odour of the ointment. Then saith one of his disciples, Judas Iscariot, Simon's son, which should betray him, Why was not this ointment sold for three hundred pence, and given to the poor? This he said, not that he cared for the poor; but because he was a thief, and had the bag, and bare what was put therein. Then said Jesus, Let her alone: against the day of my burying hath she kept this. For the poor always ye have with you; but me ye have not always. Much people of the Jews therefore knew that he was there: and they came not for Jesus' sake only, but that they might see Lazarus also, whom he had raised from the dead. But the chief priests consulted that they might put Lazarus also to death; Because that by reason of him many of the Jews went away, and believed on Jesus' (John 12:1-11).

May God the Holy Spirit, whose word we have before us, graciously take the things of Christ and apply them to our hearts as only he can. As we open our Bibles to the twelfth chapter of John's Gospel, we come to the end of our Lord's public earthly ministry. Everything else recorded in John's Gospel, until his arrest in the Garden of Gethsemane, tells us about our Saviour's private instructions given to his beloved disciples during the last six days of his life on this earth.

John 12 is really a climactic chapter. For three years, without wavering, the Lord Jesus had declared and proved his manifold perfections. He had manifested his blessed person in public and private; and he had verified every claim he ever made as the Son of man by his words, by his deeds, and by his behaviour. And the result among his own disciples was a deepening knowledge of him. They began to see and appreciate more fully who he really is. After the resurrection of Lazarus from the dead, his chosen ones, the sheep of his fold, had a more confident awareness that this is indeed the Son of God. Yet, the unbelieving were more completely hardened in their unbelief. The very same things that had in those three years melted the hearts of God's elect only hardened the Lord's enemies; and their hatred intensified with every passing day (2 Corinthians 2:14-16).

Blessed Company

The event described in the passage before us is recorded no less than three times in the Gospel narratives of our Lord's earthly life. Obviously, the Holy Spirit intends for us to learn much from it and meditate often upon it. First, we have a sweet picture of the blessed company of the redeemed (vv. 1-3).

'Then Jesus six days before the passover came to Bethany, where Lazarus was which had been dead, whom he raised from the dead. There they made him a supper; and Martha served: but Lazarus was one of them that sat at the table with him. Then took Mary a pound of ointment of spikenard, very costly, and anointed the feet of Jesus, and wiped his feet with her hair: and the house was filled with the odour of the ointment'.

With the observance of this passover, the legal, Old Testament ordinance ceased forever. The passover here mentioned was the fourth during our Lord's earthly ministry. The Lord Jesus was looking forward to it with peculiar delight. He was anxious to eat it with his disciples before his death (Luke 22:15), because he was anxious to fulfil his Father's will and complete his covenant engagements as our Surety, anxious to finish the mission for which he had come into the world, anxious to save his people from their sins! With the celebration of this passover, the ordinance of it was to cease forever, because Christ our Passover was about to be sacrificed for us. Once the substance came, the shadow died away (1 Corinthians 5:7, 8; Colossians 2:16, 17).

Six days before the final passover our Lord Jesus came again to Bethany, the town of Martha, Mary, and Lazarus. They made a special supper for him. Martha, who was always a busy, active woman, served the Lord and the guests. Lazarus, who had been raised from the dead, sat at the table with Christ and the others. Then, we read (v. 3) that Mary, whom we saw sitting at the

Saviour's feet and hearing his word in Luke 10, took a pound of very costly and fragrant ointment, anointed his feet and wiped them with her hair. When she did, the house was literally filled with the fragrance of the ointment.

We read (v. 2) that 'they made him a supper'. That is what we should seek to do every time we come together in his house, every time we gather our families to pray, and every time we enter into our closets. O Holy Spirit, make it so. Public and private worship, gathering together in his name, more than anything else, is to gather for his honour, to make him a feast (Song of Solomon 1:7, 13). If we make him a feast, he will come in and sup with our souls (Revelation 3:20; Song of Solomon 5:2)

Here we see three things, three great features, which ought to characterise every believer and every gospel church. First, communion with Christ, as portrayed in Lazarus sitting at the table with the Saviour. Second, worship, as portrayed by Mary anointing his feet. And third, service to Christ and his people, portrayed in Martha serving the table.

The work was harmonious: no envy and no self-exaltation. Each were in their place. The workers were one, 'they made him a supper'. How blessed God's Church is when the Holy Ghost gives us grace so to serve our Saviour! Let us ever seek grace to do so (Philippians 2:1-5, 14-18).

Lazarus At The Table

John just casually mentions the fact that Lazarus, whose body just a few days earlier was rotting in the tomb, was sitting at the table with the Lord Jesus, his family, and friends, and a good many neighbours, including the chief priests and Pharisees. So the second thing we see here is the fact that our Saviour's wondrous works are as undeniable as they are unexplainable. There sat Lazarus!

No one could pretend that his resurrection was a mere optical delusion, and that the eyes of the bystanders must have been deceived by a spirit or vision. There sat Lazarus, in the flesh, eating and drinking and talking with other men.

The very same things are true with regard to our Saviour's resurrection from the dead. Lazarus was seen by the people of Bethany, going in and coming out among them, so was the Lord Jesus. Lazarus ate food before the eyes of his friends, so did the Lord Jesus eat and drink before his ascension.

We should mark this and remember it in this age of abounding unbelief and scepticism. Our Lord's resurrection will bear any weight we can lay upon it. Just as he placed beyond reasonable doubt the resurrection of Lazarus, so he placed beyond doubt his own victory over the grave. If we believe that Lazarus rose again, we need not doubt that the Lord Jesus rose again also. If we believe that Christ rose from the dead, we need not doubt that he raised Lazarus from the dead, and will raise us from the dead. All of our Saviour's wondrous works, his incarnation, his sinless, perfect obedience, his supernatural, substitutionary death, his resurrection and ascension are both undeniable and unexplainable.

Mary's Anointing

Next, John gives a brief description of Mary's very instructive act of anointing the Saviour's feet. 'Then took Mary a pound of ointment of spikenard, very costly, and anointed the feet of Jesus, and wiped his feet with her hair: and the house was filled with the odour of the ointment' (v. 3).

There are several things that are both striking and instructive here. When we consider who Christ is, we ought to be overwhelmed at his wonderful condescension in allowing this woman to anoint and bathe his feet! You and I who are his should be astounded that he condescends to allow us to serve him (1 Corinthians 1:26-29). When we realise who Mary was (Luke 7:37) what a great privilege this was for her! This was an act of great love and devotion, displayed in extraordinary, sacrificial generosity. Mary poured out 'a pound of ointment of spikenard, very costly'. It was worth 300 pence, about a year's wages (Matthew 20:2). Love never counts the cost. Love never weighs the consequence. Love never considers lost what is given to one who is loved.

This was an act of great humility. Mary wiped the blessed Saviour's feet with her hair. The whole thing was motivated and inspired by gratitude. The Lord Jesus had just raised her brother from the dead. Though it was a spontaneous act of love, this sacrifice and anointing required thoughtful, deliberate preparation. Our Master tells us here that Mary had specifically kept this precious ointment for this occasion. And Mary did this thing without calling any attention to herself. C. H. Spurgeon wrote, 'Silent acts of love have musical voices in the ears of Jesus. Sound no trumpet before thee, or Jesus will take warning and be gone.' Mary's love and gratitude produced her humility and generosity. To whom much is given and forgiven, the same will give, forgive, and love much (Luke 7:47).

This anointing of our Lord Jesus by Mary is also a beautiful picture of gospel preaching. The word of God is a casket, a treasure chest, containing the costly spikenard of Christ crucified. The gospel preacher breaks open the casket and pours out the spikenard. And the sweet odour of Christ crucified fills the house.

Mary's Opposition

In verses 4-6 we are told that Judas Iscariot, who had no love for Christ, but rather was a hypocrite and a covetous person, said, 'Why was not this ointment sold for three hundred pence and given to the poor?' Judas did not care for the poor. He was interested in money and material things. What he really had in mind was that Mary should sell the ointment and give the money to him as the treasurer of the twelve. Of course, he could not suggest his real thoughts; so he tried to impress the Lord and the others with his piety and concern for the poor.

The fourth thing we see in this passage is the fact that anyone who seeks the honour of Christ and seeks to serve the interest of his honour will meet with opposition, often in the most unsuspected places. Mary anointed the feet of our Lord with precious ointment and wiped them with the hair of her head. The ointment was not poured out with a niggardly hand. She did it so liberally and profusely that 'the house was filled with the odour of the ointment'. She did it under the influence of a heart full of love and gratitude. She thought nothing too great and good to bestow on such a great Saviour. Sitting at his feet in days gone by, hearing his words, she had found peace for her conscience and pardon for her sins. At this very moment she saw Lazarus, alive and well, sitting by her Master's side, her own brother, Lazarus, whom he brought back to her from the grave. Greatly loved, she thought she could not show too much love in return. Having freely received, she freely gave.

But there were some present who found fault with her conduct and charged her with wasteful extravagance. Judas led the charge; but all the other apostles joined his opposition of Mary and her devotion. Many, like Judas, who have no interest in the cause of Christ, except in pretence and show, openly oppose true devotion at every opportunity. Sadly, many truly faithful disciples are influenced by them and follow their lead. We must never allow ourselves to be moved from 'patient continuance in well-doing' by such people.

Mary's Defender

Fifth, the Lord Jesus comes to Mary's defence. Our God promises, them 'that honour me I will honour'. He is as good as his word. 'Then said Jesus, Let her alone: against the day of my burying hath she kept this. For the poor always ye have with you; but me ye have not always' (vv. 7, 8).

Mary often sat at his feet and heard his words. She listened much and said little. She knew that his death was near; and she took this opportunity to anoint him for that day, fearing that once the Pharisees laid hold on him, she would not be able to anoint him (Matthew 26:12; Mark 14:6-9).

Mary believed the word of God which she saw fulfilled in the Lord Jesus. In a day when few understood his doctrine, Mary believed, and believing, she understood. Faith is simply trusting Christ, taking God at his word, believing him. That faith which stands in the word of man is not faith at all. True faith stands in the word of God alone. Our Lord Jesus told his disciples that he must die and rise again. Mary simply believed him, and came as a poor, broken-hearted, forgiven sinner to anoint him for his burial. Where does your faith stand? What is the basis of your faith? Is it your feeling? Your experience? Or, is it the word of God?

Faith believes the word of God (1 John 5:7-12). The basis of our faith is the word of God, and the word of God alone. I agree with Martin Luther,

> Feelings come and feelings go,
> And feelings are deceiving.
> My warrant is the word of God;
> Naught else is worth believing!

With David, I say, 'My soul fainteth for thy salvation: but I hope in thy word'. 'Thou art my hiding place and my shield: I hope in thy word'. 'Remember the word unto thy servant, upon which thou hast caused me to hope'. 'I wait for the LORD, my soul doth wait, and in his word do I hope' (Psalms 119:49, 81, 114; 130:5). Our feelings are no basis for hope. Our hope is in that which God has caused to be written in holy scripture. If I have 'a good hope through grace', I ought to be able to turn to some text, or fact, or doctrine of God's word as the source and basis of it. Our confidence must arise from something that God has said in his word, that we have received and believed with our hearts. 'The heart is deceitful above all things' (Jeremiah 17:9). 'He that trusteth in his own heart is a fool' (Proverbs 28:26). Good feelings are deceiving, unless we can point to, 'Thus saith the LORD' as the basis of our hope. Our hope is found in, arises from, and is based upon the book of God. 'For whatsoever things were written aforetime were written for our learning, that we through patience and comfort of the scriptures might have hope' (Romans 15:4). The book of God was written specifically to give believing sinners an assured hope of grace, salvation, and eternal life in Christ Jesus, our Lord (1 John 5:1-3).

The basis of hope is the word of God. And that which is revealed in the word of God which gives us hope is the person and work of the Lord Jesus Christ, our Substitute (Romans 8:34, 35; 2 Corinthians 5:17-21). Christ is the Foundation upon which we are built. 'Christ is our Hope' (1 Timothy 1:1). We 'hope in our Lord Jesus Christ' (1 Thessalonians 1:3). 'The LORD is my portion, saith my soul; therefore will I hope in him' (Lamentations 3:24). Our hope is in Christ, our Covenant Surety, our blessed, sin-atoning Redeemer, our Righteousness, and our Advocate and High Priest in heaven. 'I know whom I have believed, and am persuaded that he is able to keep that which I have committed unto him against that day' (2 Timothy 1:12).

The basis of our hope is the word of God. That which is revealed in this book that gives us hope is the person and work of the Lord Jesus Christ. And I want you to see that the good hope of grace and salvation that God gives to his elect is something that is felt in us, felt inwardly in our hearts. The Apostle

Paul speaks of God's saints as people 'rejoicing in hope' (Romans 12:12). We read in Romans 5:5, 'Hope maketh not ashamed, because the love of God is shed abroad in our hearts by the Holy Ghost which is given unto us.'

The Lord Jesus undertook Mary's cause, came to her defence, and held her up as an example of faith and devotion. I say with David, 'Be thou my strong rock, for an house of defence to save me' (Psalms 31:2), 'Plead my cause, O LORD, with them that strive with me' (Psalms 35:1), and with the prophet, 'O LORD, I am oppressed; undertake for me' (Isaiah 38:14). 'I would seek unto God, and unto God would I commit my cause' (Job 5:8). 'Plead my cause, and deliver me: quicken me according to thy word' (Psalms 119:154).

In verse 8 the Saviour says, 'There will always be poor people in the church and in the world for you to take care of and provide for; but I will not be with you very long in the flesh, and you will not have these opportunities to show your love and devotion to me so directly.' However, in these days he tells us that what we do for others in his name is done unto him (Matthew 25:34-40). We should never forget that, and ever look for opportunities to serve the spiritual and eternal, and physical and emotional needs of others.

Desperate Hardness

Sixth, we see what desperate hardness and unbelief there is in the heart of man. 'Much people of the Jews therefore knew that he was there: and they came not for Jesus' sake only, but that they might see Lazarus also, whom he had raised from the dead' (vv. 9-11).

Multitudes who came to Jerusalem for the passover journeyed to Bethany, which was only two miles from Jerusalem. It was reported that the Lord Jesus was there; but they came to Bethany not so much to see Christ as to see Lazarus, whom he had raised from the dead. How dull and dark is the understanding of the natural man, who is more interested in the curious than in the Creator, more interested in Lazarus than in the One who gave him life!

Here, again, we are reminded that while miracles are a witness of the deity and power of Christ, they do not beget saving faith. Faith is the gift and operation of God the Holy Spirit, bestowed upon and wrought in the hearts of sinners by the preaching of the gospel (Luke 16:29-31). While it is said that many of these people believed, they were like those in John 2:23-25, who were impressed by the miracles he performed (John 12:37-40).

The chief priests were not impressed, but rather angered because of the notoriety that Jesus had received, and because the people were flocking to him. They took counsel that they might not only put Christ to death, but Lazarus, too. 'But the chief priests consulted that they might put Lazarus also to death; Because that by reason of him many of the Jews went away, and believed on Jesus' (vv. 10, 11). Their hearts were totally hardened. They wanted to murder the Son of God and erase every trace of his ministry from the face of the earth. They wanted to murder Lazarus because Lazarus' very existence was a witness to Christ as Saviour, Lord, and Messiah, and exposed them as pretentious, religious hypocrites.

What hardness of heart possessed Judas Iscariot! An apostle and a preacher of the kingdom of heaven, Judas proved himself to be both a thief and a traitor. So long as the world stands, that reprobate man will stand as a lasting proof of the depth of human corruption. That anyone could follow Christ as a disciple for three years, see all his miracles, hear all his doctrine, receive at his hand repeated kindnesses, be counted an apostle, and yet prove rotten at heart in the end, at first sight appears incredible and impossible. Yet the case of Judas shows plainly that the heart of man is 'deceitful above all things and desperately wicked'. No mortal knows the extent of the desperate hardness and unbelief there is in the heart of man. Let us thank God if we know anything of faith, and can say, with all our sense of weakness and infirmity, 'I believe on the Son of God'. Then 'let him that thinketh he standeth take heed lest he fall' (1 Corinthians 10:12).

This act performed upon the Lord Jesus was an act of singular respect and honour. It showed great humility on the part of this woman. More importantly, it was a literal fulfilment of the love gift (Song of Solomon 1:12) 'While the king sitteth at his table, my spikenard sendeth forth the smell thereof'. What this woman did for the honour of Christ, every gospel preacher must do every time he stands to preach the gospel. The word of God is like a sacred chest containing precious spikenard, the rich, fragrant spikenard of Christ crucified. As this dear women broke open her box of spikenard, it is the privilege and responsibility of the gospel preacher to break open the word of God, that the sweet, sweet aroma of Christ may fill his house. The gospel of Christ is as ointment poured forth. The sweet savour of the knowledge of Christ is diffused in the house of God when Christ is preached.

Let every ransomed sinner anoint the Son of God spiritually, by faith in him, giving him the honour he so richly deserves. Anoint him as your sovereign King with the kiss of allegiance. Anoint him as your glorious Saviour with the kiss of repentance. Anoint him as your Beloved with the kiss of affection.

Mary lost nothing. Her oil was not wasted. Her labour was not spent in vain. She got by it that good name which Solomon says is 'better than precious ointment'. You can count on this: those who honour Christ, Christ will honour (1 Samuel 2:30). 'Whether therefore ye eat, or drink, or whatsoever ye do, do all to the glory of God' (1 Corinthians 10:31).

Chapter 15

'behold, thy King cometh'

'On the next day much people that were come to the feast, when they heard that Jesus was coming to Jerusalem, Took branches of palm trees, and went forth to meet him, and cried, Hosanna: Blessed is the King of Israel that cometh in the name of the Lord. And Jesus, when he had found a young ass, sat thereon; as it is written, Fear not, daughter of Sion: behold, thy King cometh, sitting on an ass's colt. These things understood not his disciples at the first: but when Jesus was glorified, then remembered they that these things were written of him, and that they had done these things unto him. The people therefore that was with him when he called Lazarus out of his grave, and raised him from the dead, bare record. For this cause the people also met him, for that they heard that he had done this miracle. The Pharisees therefore said among themselves, Perceive ye how ye prevail nothing? behold, the world is gone after him' (John 12:12-19).

This passage of scripture, at first glance, appears to be out of step with the rest of our Lord's earthly life and ministry. It is unlike anything else recorded of him in the New Testament. It tells us of the only recorded event in the life of our Lord Jesus which he intentionally made public to the highest possible degree. It is recorded four times in the New Testament. Obviously, the scene before us is one which ought to be studied carefully and frequently. May God the Holy Spirit give us grace and wisdom to learn the things taught here, so that we may properly love, trust, serve, and honour our great King, the Lord Jesus Christ.

The narrative reads like the account of some royal conqueror returning to his own city. 'Much people', 'a great multitude' swelling to 'multitudes' (some estimate the crowd to have been more than 300,000), accompanying the Lord Jesus Christ in what is described as his 'triumphal entry' into Jerusalem. Loud cries of praise and expressions of adulation rang through the air. 'All the city was moved'. Everyone wanted to know, 'Who is this?'

Everything in this passage seems to contradict the whole tenor of our Lord's earthly life and ministry. It seems to be altogether unlike him who would not cry, nor strive, nor lift up his voice in the streets. He always withdrew from the crowd, hid from applause, and urged those who were healed by his power to tell no one what he had done for them.

Yet, our Lord's public, triumphal entry into Jerusalem at this time is just what we should expect to see. He knew well that the hour of his death, the hour of his glory, the hour of his manifestation was near. The time of his humiliation and earthly ministry were drawing to a close. The hour was rapidly approaching when he must finish the work he had come into this world to perform. His last great, supreme work was before him. There was nothing left for him to do except make atonement for and redeem his people by the sacrifice of himself upon the cursed tree. Having assumed our nature, and having fulfilled all other things written in the book of God concerning him, the Lord Jesus must now finish his work; he must fulfil all righteousness by his sin-atoning death. Now, he must satisfy justice and put away our sins by the sacrifice of himself.

His Hour

The Saviour's long anticipated hour had arrived. The time had come at last when Christ was to die for his people. The time had come when the true Passover Lamb must be slain, when the true blood of atonement must be shed, when Messiah was to be 'cut off' according to the prophecy of Daniel (Daniel 9:26), when the way into the holiest must be opened for needy sinners by the true High Priest.

Knowing all this, our Lord Jesus purposefully drew attention to himself. Knowing this, he placed himself prominently under the notice of the whole Jewish nation. It was only right that this thing not be 'done in a corner' (Acts 26:26). If ever there was a transaction in our Lord's earthly ministry which was public, it was the sacrifice he offered upon the cross of Calvary. He died at the time of year when all the tribes were assembled at Jerusalem for the passover feast. By divine, providential arrangement, according to the purpose of God in eternal predestination, our blessed Saviour died within a week of his remarkable, public, triumphal entry into Jerusalem, by which he had caused the eyes of all Israel to be fixed upon him. Within a week of this public pronouncement of the multitudes who 'Took branches of palm trees, and went forth to meet him, and cried, Hosanna: Blessed is the King of Israel that cometh in the name of the Lord', this same multitude cried, 'Crucify him! Crucify him! His blood be on us, and on our children.'

Our Lord deemed it proper that every eye should be fixed upon him as he came to be offered up as the Lamb of God. He would have his great work of redemption known and advertised by everyone in Jerusalem. The sin-atoning blood of the Son of God was about to be shed. Therefore, he who had deliberately spent most of his life in secrecy, secluded from public view, he who would not allow his admirers to make him a king, now comes to announce himself King in the most public manner imaginable. His death would be his entrance into his kingdom. He made a royal procession through the streets of Jerusalem. This was our Lord's public declaration that he is indeed the Christ of God, and that he was about to enter into his kingdom.

The King

The Lord Jesus Christ, our Redeemer and Saviour, God the Son, the second person of the blessed trinity, is the King of Glory and the King of the Universe.[2] The Lord Jesus Christ is King over all things by virtue of his obedience to God as our Substitute (Psalms 2:8; John 17:2; Romans 14:9; Ephesians 1:21, 22; Philippians 2:9-11). Let us ever worship and obey him as our great King. Let us ever throw off our filthy garments of self-righteousness before him and worship him, saying, 'Hosanna to the son of David: Blessed is he that cometh in the name of the Lord; Hosanna in the highest'!

The word 'Hosanna' is an exclamation of adoration and praise; but it is more than that. The word means 'save me'. We worship and adore Christ as our Saviour only when we bow to him as our King; and we bow to him as our king only when we worship and trust him as our Saviour, laying everything at his feet, just as these multitudes 'spread their garments in the way; others cut down branches from the trees, and strawed them in the way' before the King.

Voluntary Sacrifice

The first thing that strikes me in this passage is the obvious fact that our Lord's sacrifice of himself as our Substitute was a voluntary sacrifice. His sufferings were voluntary. His death was voluntary. That which is written here displays as clear as the noonday sun, and as the scriptures universally declare, that the

[2] Our Lord Jesus Christ is, always was, and always shall be King over everybody and everything by virtue of the fact that he is God. The one true and living God is King everywhere. He always has his way and does his will. But in this text, we have a presentation of Christ as our Mediatorial King, which is a kingship and dominion given to him as the God-man by the triune Jehovah as the reward of his obedience unto death as our Mediator

Lord our God, our great Saviour, holds a sovereign, mysterious influence over the minds and wills of all men. Nothing else can account for the effect his entrance into Jerusalem had upon the multitudes who surrounded him. They were moved and carried forward by the secret constraining power of the sovereign Lord God to do his will, though they knew him not. At what other time did the common people in Israel act in defiance of the bulk of their religious leaders? But here, they are defiant, declaring Jesus of Nazareth to be the Messiah, the Christ, though the Chief Priests and the Pharisees had made it known that he was to be put to death (John 11:57).

Just as he made winds, and waves, and diseases, and devils obey his will, so he turned the minds of men according to his will; and he still does.

The man Christ Jesus, our Saviour, exercised this power that belongs to God alone while he walked upon this earth. The men of Nazareth could not hold him when he 'passing through the midst of them, went his way' (Luke 4:30). The angry Jews of Jerusalem could not detain him when they would have laid violent hands on him in the temple; but, 'Jesus … going through the midst of them, … passed by' (John 8:59). Above all, the very soldiers who apprehended him in the garden, at first 'went backward and fell to the ground', when he revealed himself as Jehovah, the 'I AM' (John 18:6).

In each of these things there can be but one explanation. The only possible explanation is the thing God taught Nebuchadnezzar in Daniel 4. 'The heavens do rule'! And he who walked on earth in human flesh was and is God on his throne in the highest heaven! Throughout our Saviour's earthly ministry, we see these mighty acts which displayed a mysterious 'hiding of his power' (Habakkuk 3:4).

If he is God almighty, the omnipotent Jehovah, why did he not resist his enemies? Why did he not scatter the band of soldiers who came to arrest him, like chaff before the wind? There is but one answer. He was a willing Substitute! His sacrifice was a willing, voluntary sacrifice. His death was the death of one who wanted to die in the stead of chosen sinners, loved by him with an everlasting love. He freely laid down his life in our place that he might make atonement for our sins and redeem us from all iniquity. He had undertaken to give his own life as a ransom that we might live forever, and he laid it down upon the cursed tree with all the desire of his heart. J. C. Ryle says,

> He did not bleed and suffer and die because he was vanquished by superior force, and could not help himself, but because he loved us and rejoiced to give himself for us as our Substitute. He did not die because he could not avoid death, but because he was willing with all his heart to make his soul an offering for sin.

O my soul, forever rest upon this blessed Saviour and Redeemer! Forever let us rest our hearts on this sweet revelation of grace. Our Lord Jesus is a willing Saviour, a voluntary Redeemer. It was his delight to do his Father's will. It was his delight to make a way for poor, lost, guilty sinners to draw near to God in peace. He loved the work he undertook as our Surety in old eternity. He delights in mercy and rejoices in forgiving sin. He is willing to save, willing to receive all who come to God by him. He who was willing to suffer all the horrid, ignominious agony of the cursed death he endured in our stead, he who was willing to be made sin for us, he who was willing to be made a curse for us is willing to save all who come to God by him!

Prophecy Fulfilled

First, we see in our text that our Lord Jesus Christ was a voluntary Substitute. Second, our text stands before us as an undeniable assurance that this book, the Holy Bible, is in truth the inspired, inerrant word of God. In fact, in Matthew's account (Matthew 21:4, 5), the Holy Spirit specifically tells us that all this was done that the scriptures might be fulfilled. 'All this was done', not because our Lord Jesus was incapable of walking the distance to Jerusalem, but 'that it might be fulfilled which was spoken by the prophet', the King of glory rode into Jerusalem on 'an ass's colt' Then the Holy Spirit puts two Old Testament passages together (Isaiah 62:11; Zechariah 9:9; Matthew 21:4, 5).

'And Jesus, when he had found a young ass, sat thereon; as it is written, Fear not, daughter of Sion: behold, thy King cometh, sitting on an ass's colt' (John 12:14, 15).

Yes, this book, the Bible, is, without question, the word of God, fully and perfectly inspired and without error (2 Timothy 3:16, 17; 2 Peter 1:20, 21). Zechariah's prophecy was made more than 550 years before this event; and it is here fulfilled in every detail. Once more, we see a clear example of the complete harmony of the Old and New Testament scriptures.

Faith's Object

Third, and this is very, very important; our text shows us that faith's object is Christ himself. Do not misunderstand me. It is important what you believe. I make no apology for declaring that it is impossible for anyone to be saved believing a false gospel. The scriptures are crystal clear in this regard (Galatians 1:6-8; 5:2-4; 1 John 2:23, 24; 4:2; 5:1). If you do not believe that Jesus Christ is come in the flesh, if you do not believe that the Lord Jesus Christ actually accomplished all that the prophets said he would accomplish, if you do not believe that the Lord Jesus brought in everlasting righteousness, put away sin, and saved his people from their sins, obtaining eternal redemption for all God's elect by the sacrifice of himself, you are not born of God.

There is no such thing as a saved, will-worshipping Arminian. If you believe that Christ is a failure, that he tries to save people who are ultimately lost forever in hell, because they would not let him have his way, or because they did something he could not overcome, or because they did not do something he left undone, you are yet without hope. The christ you trust is anti-christ. But the object of faith is not what you know about Christ. The object of saving faith is Christ himself (John 17:3).

'These things understood not his disciples at the first: but when Jesus was glorified, then remembered they that these things were written of him, and that they had done these things unto him' (v. 16). These disciples, including the Apostles, did not at this time understand the things our Lord taught them from the scriptures about his death and resurrection. Henry Mahan said,

> They saw Christ riding into Jerusalem on the ass, the people scattering the palm branches and their clothes before him, crying, 'Hosanna to the King of Israel' but to what purpose this was done and what prophecies were fulfilled they understood not; for, like the others, they thought of the Messiah as a Jewish ruler. But after Christ died and rose again, they began to remember his words concerning these things and why they were done, as Peter clearly preached at Pentecost (Acts 2:32-36).

John tells us that the disciples did not understand Zechariah's prophecy and our Lord's doctrine, until later. Sadly, there are many who know the Lord's doctrine, and know it very precisely, but do not know the Lord. Balaam stands as a clear beacon of this fact. And there are some true believers, men and women who trust Christ, whose understanding of his doctrine is not very clear. Apollos was a man mighty in the scriptures; but he knew only the teachings of John the Baptist, until Pricilla and Aquila took him into their hearts and instructed him in the way of the Lord more perfectly (Acts 18:24-28). Cornelius was a devout man, one who feared God. The Lord himself sent an angel to him, assuring him that his prayers and alms came up as a memorial to God. Yet, Cornelius did not even know that Christ had come. He knew only the Old Testament scriptures until Peter came and preached the gospel to him (Acts 10); but clearly he was a believer. It is not what you believe that is saving, but who. Christ alone is the object of saving faith, not doctrine, feelings, experiences, or knowledge.

Only after our Lord's resurrection, ascension, and exaltation, once he was enthroned as the King of Zion, did things begin to fall into place. Then the disciples began to understand what he had really meant by the things he did and said.

For those early disciples, the things they remembered must have been sort of like reading a good novel. As you read a novel, in the early chapters you wonder why this character was introduced, what that comment means, why the person did this or that, and why this thing or that happened. Then, when you get to the last chapter, everything unfolds and falls into place. I suspect that is the way it was for the apostles after the resurrection. Lights went on everywhere. There must have been a hundred things about which they said, 'That is what the Master meant. This is what he was telling us. So that is what he was talking about when he said 'Destroy this temple, and in three days I will raise it up' (John 2:19). 'Verily, verily, I say unto you, Except a corn of wheat fall into the ground and die, it abideth alone: but if it die, it bringeth forth much fruit' (John 12:24). 'The stone which the builders rejected, the same is become the head of the corner' (Matthew 21:42). 'A little while, and ye shall not see me: and again, a little while, and ye shall see me, because I go to the Father' (John 16:16). 'If David then call him Lord, how is he is son?' (Matthew 22:45)

All of our Saviour's words and deeds shined with new and clear meaning in the light of his resurrection and exaltation. Not only that, once the Lord Jesus was enthroned as King and poured out upon them his Spirit, the Old Testament popped open. When our Lord Jesus rode into Jerusalem on an ass's colt, John tells us the whole thing went over their heads. They did not have a clue what was happening at the time. But later, Zechariah's prophecy flamed with light, as they realised that they had witnessed its actual fulfilment on that day when they saw the Saviour riding into Jerusalem.

How thankful we ought to be for the blessed gift of God the Holy Spirit, who alone can open to our dull hearts and minds the things of Christ (John 7:39; 14:26).

Thy King Cometh

Let us go back to Zechariah's prophecy (Zechariah 9:9), and see fourthly, the blessedness of this gospel declaration. 'Behold, thy King cometh'! Zechariah 9:9 begins with a command to rejoice. 'Rejoice greatly, O daughter of Zion; shout, O daughter of Jerusalem'! Zion is simply another name for Jerusalem. Zechariah repeats himself for emphasis. The phrases 'daughter of Zion' and 'daughter of Jerusalem' refer to the citizens of Zion and Jerusalem. This command to rejoice is given to the church of God. It is God's command to us.

He is telling us to draw our waters out of the Well of Salvation with joy. And he tells us why we should do so.

'Behold, thy King cometh'. Zechariah is talking about the Lord Jesus Christ, Messiah the Prince, as Daniel called him (Daniel 9:25). This is the sum of all the good news in the world. 'Behold, thy King cometh'! Let this blessed fact swallow up every sorrow, and cause songs of joy to burst from our hearts (Jeremiah 31:12). 'Hosanna in the highest; Blessed is he that cometh in the name of the Lord'! Let every believer be sure to read the prophecy as the promise of God to you personally. 'Behold, thy King cometh unto thee'. There is no king like our King. Christ Jesus, your Lord and your King comes to you, for your everlasting benefit.

The church, the city of God, is here called to gladness and shoutings of joy. Babylon may mourn; but Zion must rejoice. Egypt may howl; but Jerusalem must shout. O child of God, 'rejoice and be exceeding glad'. Be not of a heavy heart. 'Whosoever believeth that Jesus is the Christ is born of God' and all who are born of God are citizens of the joyous city, the city of the great King.

Jerusalem has a King. He is 'the great King', 'King of kings and Lord of lords', 'King of Israel', 'King of nations', 'the Prince of the kings of the earth'. His name is Jesus of Nazareth. He is 'the Word made flesh', the God-man, 'Emmanuel, God with us', 'thy King'. It is written, in Psalms 149:2, 'Let the children of Zion be joyful in their King'!

Nothing is said here of Zion being joyful in what their King had done for them. Those things in their proper place are truly sweet subjects of praise. But the subject of Zion's praise is, first and foremost, the King, Christ Jesus himself. Let us never forget this apparently small, but most important distinction. The Lord is gracious in his gifts, gracious in his love, gracious in his salvation. Everything he gives is from his mercy and to be acknowledged with praise and thanksgiving. But it is Christ himself, not his gifts, that is the Object of our faith, hope, love and joy. It is the Lord Jesus Christ himself I want and must have. In him I have all things and abound. Without him I am lost forever!

'Rejoice in the Lord alway: and again I say, Rejoice. Let your moderation be known unto all men. The Lord is at hand. Be careful for nothing; but in every thing by prayer and supplication with thanksgiving let your requests be made known unto God. And the peace of God, which passeth all understanding, shall keep your hearts and minds through Christ Jesus. Finally, brethren, whatsoever things are true, whatsoever things are honest, whatsoever things are just, whatsoever things are pure, whatsoever things are lovely, whatsoever things are of good report; if there be any virtue, and if there be any praise, think on these things' (Philippians 4:4-8).

Present Tense

Read the prophecy as it is written in the present tense. 'Behold, thy King cometh unto thee'! For four thousand years he was 'the coming one'. For four thousand years the promise spoke of his coming. Now he has come. But, I like to read the word of God with personal application. 'Behold, thy King cometh unto thee'! (Song of Solomon 2:8; 3:6). In his word, by his Spirit, in his house, in his ordinances, in saving grace, in reviving mercy, in restoring goodness, in great faithfulness, tender-mercy, and lovingkindness, 'Behold, thy King cometh unto thee'! O child of God, 'thy King cometh unto thee' and he bids you come to him (Matthew 11:28-30).

'He is just, and having salvation'. He is just that he might justify us by his righteousness and save us by his merit and his grace. He is the just God and our Saviour, just and the Justifier of all who trust him. He is our Saviour, because he is our Justifier, because he is the Just One. He has a righteous salvation for unrighteous men. It is salvation to the uttermost, because he is mighty to save and just to save. Jesus Christ the righteous came into the world to save sinners.

He comes to us 'having salvation'! Oh, how I love those words 'having salvation'. Don't you? He comes to our poor souls with salvation in his hand to bestow. He had the salvation of our souls in his heart from eternity. It was entrusted to his hands as our Surety before the worlds were made. The covenant of grace, in which salvation is the principal article, was made with him; and he, as Surety of that covenant, undertook the work. In the fulness of time, being sent of the Father, he came into the world to save his people from their sins. Entering once into heaven with his own blood, he obtained eternal redemption for us. And now, 'thy King cometh unto thee having salvation'!

Zechariah continues to describe our King, telling us how he came to redeem us and how he comes to save us. 'Lowly, and riding upon an ass, and upon a colt the foal of an ass'. Our great King was meek and lowly; even when he came to Jerusalem in triumph. He showed his meekness by the way he came. No troops of soldiers, no guards, no procession, no banners waving! No chariot, no war horse! He rides upon an ass, and alongside there is the colt, the foal of an ass, just as they were found, unprepared and unadorned. He is at once the most lofty and the most lowly of the sons of men. None ever came from such a height, or went down to such a depth as he (2 Corinthians 8:9).

O sinner, come and learn of this lowly one. He will give you rest. Give him your fullest confidence, in spite of all the evil, and the darkness, and the folly that is in you. Keep ever near his side. Look at him, love him, speak to him, trust him. Does he frown? Does he turn away? No, he bids us welcome; and the more we need him, the more welcome we are.

An Allegory

Fifth, I want us to view this entire picture allegorically. There is more to be learned from this prophecy than just its historic fulfilment by our Lord's triumphal entry into Jerusalem. There are spiritual things revealed here that tell us how it is that God our Saviour saves his elect. As the Holy Spirit tells us in Galatians 4 that the story of Sarah and Hagar is an allegory, this too is an allegory. It is a prophecy of a true, historical event; but it is more. It portrays God's free, sovereign, saving grace in and by our Lord Jesus Christ.

We must never spiritualise holy scripture. I mean by that statement that we must never twist the scriptures into whatever it is we want them to teach. To do so is to treat the word of God with horrible irreverence. Yet, when we read the word of God, we are always to look for the spiritual meaning, the gospel message each particular passage is intended to convey. This is, in my opinion, especially true when we read the Gospel narratives of our Lord's life and ministry, knowing that every event in the earthly life of our Saviour and every miracle performed by him is written in the book of God to give us a picture, an object lesson about his great salvation.

When we read the book of God in this way, it comes to life. When my grandson, Will, was just a couple of years old, he walked over to the office one Sunday morning and crawled up on my lap, while I was preparing to preach. Pointing to my opened Bible, he asked, 'Poppy, is this where Jesus lives?' I gave him a longer answer, but the fact is, the answer to his question is, 'Yes, the Lord Jesus lives right here in this blessed book.'

Every word he spoke, every movement he made, every step he took was predetermined before the world began for the salvation of his elect and was designed by God's eternal decree to show us something of God's sovereign, electing, redeeming, saving, mercy, love and grace through Christ our Redeemer. Even the small details, those things that appear to be no more than records with information, show forth his great salvation.

Blessed be his holy name, the Lord Jesus still comes 'riding upon an ass' when he comes to save his own. When we think of our Lord Jesus riding the wild ass's colt through the streets of Jerusalem, we ought to see it as a picture of his sovereign, electing, fetching, irresistible, saving grace.

The Apostle John, quoting the prophet Zechariah, shows us here that when Christ rode into Jerusalem, his triumphal entry was made in the way it was to display the character of his kingdom and his work as our King. He came riding 'an ass, and upon a colt, the foal of an ass' to show himself in the infinite humility of his grace as one who is 'just and having salvation'. He comes to break the bow of war and 'speak peace unto the heathen', and to do so in universal dominion 'from sea to sea, even to the ends of the earth'.

The Wild Ass's Colt

In Job 11:12 we see who the wild ass's colt is, upon whom the King of glory rides through the streets of Jerusalem in triumphant grace. The wild ass's colt, an ass upon which no man ever before sat, the ass upon which our Saviour rode through Jerusalem is in scripture a picture of fallen man. You and I are all born by nature 'like a wild ass's colt', foolish, senseless, stubborn, and wild, given to lust and debauchery. As the wild ass will not bear the yoke, so none will ever bow to the yoke of Christ, except the Son of God break him. Man by nature is like 'a wild ass used to the wilderness, that snuffeth up wind at her pleasure' (Jeremiah 2:24; Job 39:5).

In the movies we see old men and women riding donkeys, and get the idea that they are nice, gentle, sweet animals, the kind you would like to have for pets, if you just had the room. But that is never the case by nature. It is their nature to be mean. If you try to get one to ride, to carry a load, to pull a cart, he will buck and kick and bite until he is broken and tamed. If all else fails, he will just sit down.

That is a pretty good picture of fallen man. Made by God and made for his glory, all men ought to gladly give thanks to him, submit to his rule, worship him, and give him his due. But when you try to get one to worship God, watch him kick. Tell sweet, religious wild asses the truth about man, about God, about Christ, about redemption and grace, and they will buck and bite. But when the King of grace mounts the wild ass, he is broken and gladly ridden.

I once read that one of the rarest mammals in the world is the African wild ass. There are not more than a few hundred in the world. I am not really very interested in that. But I am interested in the people represented in our text by the wild ass's colt. I can tell you that they are very, very rare.

> To understand these things aright,
> This grand distinction should be known:
> Though all are sinners in God's sight,
> There are but few so in their own.
> To such as these our Lord was sent;
> They're only sinners who repent.
>
> What comfort can a Saviour bring
> To those who never felt their woe?
> A sinner is a sacred thing;
> The Holy Ghost hath made him so.
> New life from Him we must receive,
> Before for sin we rightly grieve.

This faithful saying let us own,
Well worthy 'tis to be believed,
That Christ into the world came down,
That sinners might by Him be saved.
Sinners are high in His esteem,
And sinners highly value Him.

Joseph Hart

Chapter 16

'glorify thy name'

'And there were certain Greeks among them that came up to worship at the feast: The same came therefore to Philip, which was of Bethsaida of Galilee, and desired him, saying, Sir, we would see Jesus. Philip cometh and telleth Andrew: and again Andrew and Philip tell Jesus. And Jesus answered them, saying, The hour is come, that the Son of man should be glorified. Verily, verily, I say unto you, Except a corn of wheat fall into the ground and die, it abideth alone: but if it die, it bringeth forth much fruit. He that loveth his life shall lose it; and he that hateth his life in this world shall keep it unto life eternal. If any man serve me, let him follow me; and where I am, there shall also my servant be: if any man serve me, him will my Father honour. Now is my soul troubled; and what shall I say? Father, save me from this hour: but for this cause came I unto this hour. Father, glorify thy name. Then came there a voice from heaven, saying, I have both glorified it, and will glorify it again. The people therefore, that stood by, and heard it, said that it thundered: others said, An angel spake to him. Jesus answered and said, This voice came not because of me, but for your sakes. Now is the judgment of this world: now shall the prince of this world be cast out. And I, if I be lifted up from the earth, will draw all men unto me. This he said, signifying what death he should die' (John 12:20-33).

'And there were certain Greeks among them that came up to worship at the feast' (v. 20). The Passover Feast was one of the great, important holy days God commanded the Jews to keep every year. It was a week-long festival, which culminated in the slaying of the paschal lamb. Jews from everywhere were gathered at Jerusalem for this holy festival. Among the Jews there was also a large multitude of Gentile proselytes, Gentiles who had been converted to the Jews' religion. The men mentioned in this verse were Greeks who had turned from their heathen idols and were seeking the knowledge of the one true and living God.

They were allowed to come to the temple, but only to the Gentile court. In the Old Testament Gentiles were never allowed the privileges of full acceptance with the Jews. Thank God, in Christ's spiritual kingdom, the Church, the Israel of God, there are no racial, social, economic, or ceremonial separations. We are all one in him! 'There is neither Jew nor Greek, there is neither bond nor free, there is neither male nor female: for ye are all one in Christ Jesus' (Galatians 3:28). 'For in Christ Jesus neither circumcision availeth anything, nor uncircumcision, but a new creature' (Galatians 6:15). In the new creation of grace, 'there is neither Greek nor Jew, circumcision nor uncircumcision, Barbarian, Scythian, bond nor free: but Christ is all, and in all' (Colossians 3:11).

Gentiles Seeking Jesus

These Greeks came to Jerusalem to worship God. While they were there they heard about a man, a mighty miracle-worker, a prophet, whom a few fishermen worshipped as the Christ, the Messiah. 'The same came therefore to Philip, which was of Bethsaida of Galilee, and desired him, saying, Sir, we would see Jesus' (v. 21). These Greeks came to Philip and requested an audience with the Lord Jesus. They had heard about the Saviour's many miracles. Most notably, they had heard about the resurrection of Lazarus (John 12:9), who was a great type of every regenerate soul being raised from death to life by Christ (John 5:25; Ephesians 2:1-5). Being Gentiles, these men were reluctant to approach the Master personally. So they took their request to Philip, who was from Bethsaida, and was perhaps a neighbour. It seems likely that they knew Philip and knew that he was one of the Lord's disciples. Look at verse 22:

'Philip cometh and telleth Andrew: and again Andrew and Philip tell Jesus'. Philip talked this matter over with Andrew. Then he and Andrew together brought the matter before the Lord Jesus. Why do you suppose such a simple request presented such a problem? Let me suggest three reasons why this thing seemed to greatly disturb Philip and Andrew.

First, things were in great turmoil at Jerusalem. The chief priests talked about killing Lazarus (v. 10). The people talked about making Jesus of Nazareth king (vv. 12, 13). The Pharisees were worried and angry about losing their position, power, and influence (v. 19).

Second, the Lord's disciples simply did not yet understand the necessity of his death and resurrection as their Substitute and the true, spiritual nature of

God's kingdom. They trusted the Lord Jesus. They knew him; but they knew little of his doctrine. They knew very little of what he had taught them day and night for more than three years. They knew that he was their Saviour; but they do not appear to have known that his death upon the cursed tree was necessary for their redemption and salvation. 'These things understood not his disciples' (v. 16). They wanted Christ to live, not to die. They wanted an earthly, Jewish kingdom (Luke 24:21; Acts 1:6). But the Son of God must be crucified, or God's elect could not be saved (Romans 3:24-26).

Third, Philip may have thought that if the Master received these Gentiles, that would be the last straw. That, he may have thought, would give the Pharisees the excuse they were looking for to kill him. I can almost hear his counsel, 'Lord, these Greeks are asking for an audience with you. Andrew and I have discussed it. And, well, we just do not think it would be wise to receive them right now. The priests are talking about killing Lazarus. The Pharisees are worried sick, afraid of losing their hold over the people. But the people are for you. They want to make you king! To receive these Greeks now would spoil everything.' Then, in verses 23-33 the Master himself speaks. He seized the opportunity to instruct and challenge his disciples.

The Purpose Of His Incarnation

'And Jesus answered them, saying, The hour is come, that the Son of man should be glorified' (v. 23). Here our Saviour shows us again the purpose of his incarnation. He said, 'The hour is come'! The crisis he had been telling them about had arrived (John 2:4; 7:30). This was not the hour when the King of Israel must be glorified as the Son of God, over all, blessed forever. This was not the hour when the Judge of all men must be made manifest. This was not the hour when the Son of man must be glorified as the God of glory. This was not the hour when men must own our dear Saviour as the King of kings and Lord of lords. All these things will come in due time; but this was not the time. This was the hour of the Son of man, the last Adam (1 Timothy 2:5; John 17:1-5). This was the hour of redemption (Daniel 9:24). This was the hour for which the Son of God came into this world (Hebrews 10:5-10).

The Meaning Of His Death

'Verily, verily, I say unto you, Except a corn of wheat fall into the ground and die, it abideth alone: but if it die, it bringeth forth much fruit' (v. 24). Here our Saviour shows us the meaning of his death. He portrays himself as a grain of corn, or wheat. It has much potential. There is in this one grain much corn, but only if it dies. If it dies, it will bring forth much fruit, but only if it dies. If it does not die, it must abide alone. So our Lord has many people in him (Ephesians 1:3-6). He must die, or he must abide alone. But if he dies all who are in him will come to life; and all shall be like him. The corn sown and the corn reaped are identical. That is the blessed hope that fills our souls with joy (Jude 24, 25). Thus the Son of man will be glorified (v. 23; Isaiah 53:10-12).

The Way Of Salvation

'Except a corn of wheat fall into the ground and die, it abideth alone: but if it die, it bringeth forth much fruit.' What a blessed illustration of his redemptive, life giving death! But he does not stop there. He had a death to die. And all who would be his disciples also have a death to die. The same principle is involved. Next, the Lord Jesus shows us the way of life and salvation in him. Do you ask, 'How can I be saved?' Here is the answer. If you would save your life, you must lose it.

'He that loveth his life shall lose it; and he that hateth his life in this world shall keep it unto life eternal. If any man serve me, let him follow me; and where I am, there shall also my servant be: if any man serve me, him will my Father honour' (vv. 25, 26).

Let me show you what these things mean. A farmer has a bushel of wheat, good wheat. It is his. He can keep it for a little while. He can eat it. Or he can feed it to his hogs. But if he keeps it, uses it to satisfy his carnal appetite, uses it only for passing, momentary purposes, or wastes it, he will lose it, and lose it very soon. However, if with an eye to the future, he takes that corn and casts it away from himself into the ground, keeping only what is necessary for the present, he will soon have an abundant harvest of corn.

I have a life. You do, too. What shall I do with it? Keep it? Love it? Protect it? Shield it from danger and difficulty? Pamper it? Cater to it? I can. It is my life. You can, too. But if I keep my life, I will lose it; and the same is true of you. However, if I give my life to Christ, if you give your life to Christ, we will have an indescribable abundance of life, even eternal life, here and in the world to come.

The fact is, no man can have two masters. No man can both love Christ and the world. No man can walk in two directions. If you love this world and this life, you will lose it. If you lose your life to Christ, love, trust, and follow him, you gain eternal life. You cannot do both (Acts 20:28; 2 Timothy 1:12).

'If any man serve me, let him follow me'. To believe on the Lord Jesus Christ is to serve him and follow him. Faith in Christ is giving ourselves entirely to the Lord Jesus Christ, as bond slaves of old, to follow and serve him, it is to be consecrated to him. What a challenge! I am talking about putting your hand to the plough and never going back, never looking back! I am talking about Jephthah's commitment (Judges 11). I am talking about Ruth's resolve (Ruth 1:16, 17).

'Where I am, there shall also my servant be'. Here our Lord Jesus explains what it is to follow him. It is not mine to determine where he is, or what he does, but by his word and Spirit to find out where he is and what he does, and follow him. There is no guess work involved. He is about his Father's business. He is seeking his sheep (Luke 19:10). He is ministering to the needs of men. He is among his people. He is washing his disciples' feet. He is in prayer (John 7:53-8:1). 'Every man went to his own house'. But the Saviour went out to the mount to pray. He is despised and hated by this world. They took him outside the city and nailed him to the tree. 'Let us go unto him, without the camp'! He is nailed to a cross. 'God forbid that I should glory save in the cross of our Lord Jesus Christ'. Let me with my Saviour be crucified to the world and the world to me. He is risen and seated in the heavens.

Take the world, but give me Jesus.
All its joys are but a name!
But His love abideth ever,
Through eternal years the same!

Take the world, but give me Jesus,
Sweetest comfort of my soul;
Then throughout my pilgrim journey,
I can sing while billows roll.

O the height and depth of mercy!
O the length and breadth of love!
O the fulness of redemption,
Pledge of endless life above!

Frances J. Crosby

Then, our Master says, 'If any man serve me, him will my Father honour', and he will, both here and hereafter (1 Samuel 2:30).

The Object Of His Life

Then, our Saviour shows us by example what he meant. Here, he shows us the object of his life. He lived for and served the will and glory of God.

'Now is my soul troubled; and what shall I say? Father, save me from this hour: but for this cause came I unto this hour. Father, glorify thy name. Then came there a voice from heaven, saying, I have both glorified it, and will glorify it again' (vv. 27, 28).

O Spirit of God, give me the grace of my Lord Jesus Christ, graciously, effectually, teaching me to live in this world only to serve the will of God and the glory of God!

The Accomplishments Of His Death

The Lord tells us of the accomplishments of his death. 'The people therefore, that stood by, and heard it, said that it thundered: others said, An angel spake to him. Jesus answered and said, This voice came not because of me, but for your sakes. Now is the judgment of this world: now shall the prince of this world be cast out. And I, if I be lifted up from the earth, will draw all men unto me. This he said, signifying what death he should die' (John 12:29-33).

Our Saviour's death upon the cursed tree was the judgment of this world and his long-anticipated triumph over Satan, crushing the serpent's head (Genesis 3:15) (v. 31). Thus, by the accomplishment of redemption for us, the Son of God effectually draws chosen, redeemed sinners to himself in this, the day of his power (v. 32) (Psalms 110:3). The Lord Jesus Christ is the Pearl of Great Price. Will you buy this Pearl, or will you pass it by?

An Apocryphal Story

A wealthy man and his son loved to collect rare works of art. They had everything in their collection, from Picasso to Raphael. They would often sit together and admire the great works of art. When the Vietnam conflict broke out, the son went to war. He was very courageous and died in battle while rescuing another soldier. The father was notified and grieved deeply for his only son. About a month later, just before Christmas, there was a knock at the door. A young man stood at the door with a large package in his hands. He said, 'Sir, you don't know me, but I am the soldier for whom your son gave his life. He saved many lives that day, and he was carrying me to safety when a bullet struck him in the heart and he died instantly. He often talked about you, and your love for art.' The young man held out this package. 'I know this isn't much. I'm not really a great artist, but I think your son would have wanted you to have this.' The father opened the package. It was a portrait of his son, painted by the young man. He stared in awe at the way the soldier had captured the personality of his son in the painting. The father was so drawn to the eyes that his own eyes welled up with tears. He thanked the young man and offered to pay him for the picture. 'Oh, no sir, I could never repay what your son did for me. It's a gift.'

The father hung the portrait over his mantle. Every time visitors came to his home he took them to see the portrait of his son before he showed them any of the other great works he had collected. The man died a few months later. There was to be a great auction of his paintings Many influential people gathered, excited over seeing the great paintings and having an opportunity to purchase one for their collection. On the platform sat the painting of the son. The auctioneer pounded his gavel. 'We will start the bidding with this picture of the son. Who will bid for this picture?' There was silence. Then a voice in the back of the room shouted, 'We want to see the famous paintings. Skip this one.' But the auctioneer persisted. 'Will somebody bid for this painting. Who will start the bidding? $100, $200?' Another voice said angrily. 'We didn't come to see this painting. We came to see the Van Gogh's, the Rembrandt's. Get on with the real bids.' But still the auctioneer continued. 'The son! The son! Who'll take the son?' Finally, a voice came from the very back of the room. It was the long-time gardener of the man and his son. 'I'll give $10 for the painting.' Being a poor man, it was all he could afford. 'We have $10, who will bid $20?' 'Give it to him for $10. Let's see the masters'. '$10 is the bid, won't someone bid $20?' The crowd was becoming angry. They didn't want the picture of the son. They wanted the more worthy investments for their collections. The auctioneer pounded the gavel. 'Going once, twice, SOLD for $10'! A man sitting on the second row shouted, 'Now let's get on with the collection.' The auctioneer laid down his gavel. 'I'm sorry, the auction is over.' 'What about the paintings?' 'I am sorry. When I was called to conduct this auction, I was told of a secret stipulation in the will. I was not allowed to reveal that stipulation until this time. Only the painting of the son would be auctioned. Whoever bought that painting would inherit the entire estate, including the paintings. The man who took the son gets everything.'

So it is with the Christ of God. He who gets the Son gets everything.

Chapter 17

The Crisis Of The World

'Now is the judgment of this world: now shall the prince of this world be cast out. And I, if I be lifted up from the earth, will draw all men unto me. This he said, signifying what death he should die' (John 12:31-33).

'My thoughts are not your thoughts, neither are your ways my ways, saith the Lord. For as the heavens are higher than the earth, so are my ways higher than your ways, and my thoughts than your thoughts' (Isaiah 55:8, 9). This is never more clearly and extraordinarily demonstrated to be the truth than by these statements which fell from the lips of our Saviour. It is a great marvel to me that God should, in his infinite wisdom, choose to judge the world, destroy the devil, and save his elect by sending his Son to become a man that he might suffer and die upon the cursed tree! Oh, mystery of mysteries, 'God hath made him to be sin for us, who knew no sin, that we might be made the righteousness of God in him.' Oh, the height of God's love! Oh, the depth of his mercy! Oh, the breadth of his wisdom! Indeed, his ways and his thoughts are beyond us, as high as the heavens are above the earth.

In this chapter 12 of John our Lord Jesus rehearsed his sin-atoning death with his disciples before it actually took place. He saw those Greeks who came to Philip, and whom Philip and Andrew brought to him; and his heart was filled with joy. This, he knew was to be the result of his death, that the Gentiles would be gathered to him. That thought reminded him of his approaching crucifixion. It was now very near. Only a few days were to pass; and then he would die upon the cursed tree.

Our Troubled Saviour

In anticipation of Calvary, Christ's soul was full of trouble. It was not that he feared death; but his death was to be a very peculiar one. Death is the penalty of sin; but he had done no sin. Death was due to the sons of Adam; but he is the Son of God. He was to die the Just for the unjust. He was to bear our sins in his own body upon the cross. Is it any wonder that his pure and holy soul should shrink from contact with sin, let alone from being made sin? To stand in the sinner's place, to hang before his holy Father as a horrid mass of iniquity, to endure the Father's wrath, justly, as a guilty man deserving his wrath, were thoughts astonishing to him. He was, as a man, very faint of heart, and cried, 'What shall I say? Father save me from this hour: but for this cause came I unto this hour. Father, glorify thy name.' Here we see the Saviour of the world, the eternal Son of God troubled and disturbed in mind. We see him, who could heal diseases with his touch, cast out demons with a word, command the waves to obey him, and call the dead to life, in great agony and conflict. Nothing can ever explain our Lord's agony here, and later in Gethsemane, except that he felt the great burden of all the sins of his people pressing him down. Without any repining at his Father's will, he saw how terrible that will was; and he shuddered at what it included. Here the God-man was sipping that bitter cup which he was to drink until he could cry, 'It is finished', and give up the ghost.

When our blessed Saviour was in this great distress of mind in anticipation of the terrible sufferings he was about to endure, his Father spoke to him out of heaven saying, 'I have both glorified it, and will glorify it again.' How beautifully this shows that the intimate relation and union of God the Father and God the Son was unbroken during the whole course of the Saviour's pilgrimage. This was also a testimony to those who stood by that God the Father completely approved of his eternal Son as the Messiah, the Redeemer, and the Saviour of men.

Child of God, here is a word of encouragement for you when you are in distress. In your hour of trial God will speak to you, as he did to his Son. If you are his child, when the weakness of your flesh seems to prevail over your spirit, you, too, shall have the reassuring voice from heaven.

The Saviour seems to have recovered himself at once; and bracing himself, he once again indulged his heart with the vision of the glorious results of his death. Here he assured his disciples, and assures us that by his death upon the cross he would seal every purpose of God for the world, the devil, and his elect.

Success In Death

You will recall that on the Mount of Transfiguration Moses and Elijah spoke to our Redeemer about 'the death he should accomplish at Jerusalem'. Here, in verses 31, 32, our Saviour tells us about all he would accomplished and did accomplish in his death as our sin-atoning Substitute. The Lord Jesus declared the sure and certain success of his death. 'Now is the judgment of this world: now shall the prince of this world be cast out. And I, if I be lifted up from the earth, will draw all men unto me' (vv. 31, 32).

As the Son of God anticipated his sufferings and death, he spoke as though they were already accomplished, and sums up the consequences in these three points: 'Now is the judgment of this world', 'now shall the prince of this world be cast out', and 'if I be lifted up, I will draw all men unto me.'

Judgment Of The World

First, the death of Christ was the judgment of this world. What does that mean? The word translated 'judgment' is the Greek word from which our English word 'crisis' is derived. So our Lord's words might be accurately translated, 'Now is the crisis of this world.'

Indeed, the death of Christ was the crisis of the world. The cross of Jesus Christ was the turning point, the hinge of the world's history. The death of Christ was the death of sin, the crushing of the serpent's head, and victory over death. And by his death upon the cursed tree, our blessed Saviour secured the regeneration of the earth (Revelation 21:5).

The death of Christ was also the judgment of the world. The world was convicted of guilt (Acts 2:23; John 1:4, 5, 10, 11). The world hated perfect love and perfect righteousness, and murdered the Son of God! Men of the world would pull God off his throne and slay him, if they had it in their power. The world is not good, but guilty. How dare we embrace the world!

The world was sentenced to death when it put to death the Lord of glory. The death of Christ is the clearest possible display of the heinousness of sin; and the death of Christ is the clearest possible display of divine justice. If the Lord Jesus, God's darling Son, escaped not the Father's wrath in bringing many sons to glory, when sin was found upon him, if sin is found on you, surely you must die! God must be just. That means that if you die without Christ, there is no hope. If you have no propitiation by the blood of Jesus, God must slay you.

By the cross you are judged; and by the cross you shall be judged! By the cross God judged the world. By the cross, let us judge the world, its religion, its favour, its frowns, its fame, and its friendship (1 John 2:15-17; Galatians 6:14).

It is the cross of our Lord Jesus Christ 'by which the world is crucified unto me' (Galatians 6:14). Faith in Christ, the assurance of redemption by Christ, caused the Apostle Paul to look upon the world as a thing crucified. He knew that he had no more reason to fear his most implacable enemies in this world than a man would have reason to fear someone crucified and dead. Happy are those who learn this. Because our Lord Jesus Christ, by his death upon the cross as our Substitute and Redeemer, has overcome the world, conquered Satan, the prince of this world, and cast him out, and vanquished death, hell, and the grave. Since he has put away our sins by the sacrifice of himself, we are more than conquerors in him (Romans 8:32-39). We have nothing to fear in this world or from this world. As the children of Israel looked upon Pharaoh and the Egyptian army slain by God in the Red Sea, and sang praise to him, so we ought to look upon all that opposes us in this world as dead, and sing praise to God our Saviour who has 'triumphed gloriously'. Let us neither love the world, nor the things that are in the world, but look upon them as dead things. The gospel of the grace of God experienced in the soul teaches us to despise the riches, honours, and applause of the world. The profits, pleasures, and praises of dead men are as worthless as dung. That is exactly how they are to be looked upon and counted by all who seek Christ (Philippians 3:7-15).

But, as Paul uses the term 'world' here in the book of Galatians, he is specifically referring to 'the weak and beggarly elements of the world' (Galatians 4:3-9), the carnal ordinances and ceremonies of the law. He is declaring that since 'Christ is the end of the law' (Romans 10:4), the law's sabbath days, sacrifices, and services are to be looked upon by us as dead things (Romans 6:15; 7:4; Galatians 2:19, 20). Our all-glorious Redeemer took 'the handwriting of the ordinances that was against us, which was contrary to us, out of the way, nailing it to his cross' (Colossians 2:14).

'The world is crucified unto me, and I unto the world'. As the world had no more attraction for Paul than a dead corpse, so he had no attraction for the world, but was despised by it for Christ's sake. It shall ever be so with those who follow Christ. As the law was dead to him and had no power over him, so he was dead to the law by the sacrifice of Christ. He had nothing to do with those weak and beggarly elements of bondage.

Satan Cast Out

The second result of Christ's death is this: The prince of this world is cast out. It is certain that by crucifying the Lord of glory, men by their wicked hands cast out Christ, the only true Prince of this world. They cast out the Creator! But, here our Saviour is describing his accomplishments, not the imagined accomplishments of his foes. He is telling us that he, the woman's Seed, has crushed the serpent's head.

Christ has answered Satan's accusations against the believer (Revelation 12:7-10). The Lord Jesus Christ, by his cross, spoils Satan of his universal monarchy. He casts Satan out of the hearts of believers. Yes, Satan still roars as a lion; but his power is crippled. We are no longer under his dominion. Christ Jesus will bruise Satan under your heels shortly (Romans 16:20). Our

Saviour will, one day soon, thoroughly destroy our enemy. Thank God for the bruising of the Saviour's heel, for it was the crushing of the serpent's head!

The Great Attraction

The third result of the Lord's death is this, the cross has become the centre of attraction. 'And I, if I be lifted up from the earth, will draw all men unto me'! What attracts sinners to the Saviour is the preaching of the cross (1 Corinthians 1:17-2:2). The preaching of the cross is the centrepiece of all true Christianity, the revelation of the gospel, and the centre of attraction in God's Church. By the death of Christ upon the cursed tree, the scope of God's mercy was manifestly widened to include Gentiles. This is the grand display of God's amazing, infinite love (John 3:16; Romans 5:8; 1 John 3:16, 4:9). Through the cross, by the death of Christ as our sin-atoning Substitute, we have all blessings of grace; forgiveness, justification, sanctification, reconciliation, acceptance and preservation, eternal life and heavenly glory.

God's Magnet

Consider briefly the significance of our Saviour's declaration 'And I, if I be lifted up from the earth, will draw all men unto me. This he said, signifying what death he should die' (vv. 32, 33). Our Lord Jesus Christ went to his death with a clear view of what it was. He fully knew what it meant. He went to his cross knowing that his cross was the means of his exaltation (Philippians 2:8-11; John 17:2). Our Saviour knew that his cross would supply our every need.

From the cross, the Lord Jesus draws sinners like a magnet draws iron. He draws sinners who cannot come to him. He draws sinners who will not come to him. He draws sinners to himself. The preaching of the cross attracts sinners to the Saviour. We need no other attraction. The preaching of the cross is God's means of saving sinners (Romans 1:15, 16; 10:17; 1 Peter 1:23-25).

The Lord Jesus knew that he would live again to exercise his dominion as Lord (Psalms 16:9, 10; Isaiah 53:10-12). He knew he would be surrounded by a mighty company, who would overcome by his cross. Lift your eyes yonder to glory, and behold the power of the preached cross (Revelation 7:9-17).

'God forbid that I should glory, save in the cross of our Lord Jesus Christ (Galatians 6:14). By the cross of our Lord Jesus Christ, the world is judged, Satan is vanquished, sinners are drawn to the Saviour, and Christ our Lord is exalted. Let us live by the cross.

> The way of the cross leads home!
> There's no other way but this.
> I shall ne'er get sight of the gates of light,
> If the way of the cross I miss.

Chapter 18

The Attraction Of The Cross

'And I, if I be lifted up from the earth, will draw all men unto me. This he said, signifying what death he should die' (John 12:32, 33).

That is Christ's own testimony to the power of his death upon the cross. There is in the cross of our Lord Jesus Christ that saving, effectual power that draws sinners to him in faith. Christianity is a religion about a cross. The cross of Christ is the key of knowledge which gives us understanding in holy scripture. Martin Luther said, 'There is not a word in the Bible which can be understood without reference to the cross.' Everything we believe has the cross for its base, structure, and covering. The cross of Christ is the essence of all biblical doctrine and the motivation for all biblical precepts. We look to the cross for the forgiveness of all sin, for justification and acceptance with God. We look to the cross for sanctification, to be made holy before God. We look to the cross for motivation, as our rule of life in this world. We look to the cross for our entrance into heaven's glory, as the door of hope regarding the life to come.

For the believer, the cross of our Lord Jesus Christ is all. We say with Paul, 'God forbid that I should glory save in the cross of our Lord Jesus Christ'.

The Cross

It is not necessary for me to remind you of what I mean when I talk about the cross. I am not talking about the Roman gibbet upon which our Lord was crucified, or about the idolatrous crucifix which has become a piece of jewellery to so many, or about some imaginary magical sign of the cross which papists use. I am talking about the glorious doctrine of the cross as it is set forth in the word of God. I am talking about the atonement of sin by the death of Christ upon the cursed tree. I am talking about the putting away of sin by the suffering, bleeding, and dying of the Lord Jesus as the sinner's Substitute.

This is the cross our Lord was talking about when he said, 'I, if I be lifted up from the earth, will draw all men unto me.' The doctrine of Christ crucified has a marvellous, saving power. The power of the cross is not destructive power, but saving power. It is not punitive power, but forgiving power. It is not repulsive power, but drawing power. The cross of Christ is not harsh or compulsive, but attractive. Horatius Bonar wrote, 'The sun draws up the vapours from the sea, and then hangs a brilliant rainbow upon them; so Christ draws up the sons of men from the depths of our low world, and glorifies them.'

If the attraction of the cross is like that of the sun, it is also like the attraction of a magnet. As the far distant North Pole, by some unseen influence, lays hold of the motionless needle in a compass and turns it to itself, so the cross of Christ lays hold upon the hearts of the sons of men and turns them to himself, by the unseen power of his omnipotent mercy and irresistible grace. Have you felt the magnetic power of the cross? Does it now turn your heart to Christ?

It is not simply Christ himself who is the magnet; it is Christ crucified. It is our Lord's crucifixion and death upon the cross that has imparted to him this power to draw sinners to himself. It is not Christ without the cross, nor is it the cross without Christ, but both together which draws us to him.

The Power Of The Cross

Now notice the greatness of the power of the cross. It draws all men to him. Obviously, that does not mean that every person in the world will be drawn to Christ as the result of his death upon the cross. There are millions in hell who were not drawn to Christ. And there are millions upon the earth who shall never be drawn. How can they be drawn who have never heard? Yet, there is marvellous, saving power and efficacy in the cross which extends to the entire world, so by virtue of his death on the cross, our Lord Jesus Christ draws some from all mankind to himself. He draws Jews and Gentiles, men and women, black and white, bond and free, rich and poor, learned and unlearned. Behold the wondrous power of the cross. In the last day there shall be some of all men, some out of every nation, kindred, tribe, and tongue gathered around the throne of the Lamb, all drawn to our Lord Jesus Christ by the power of the cross.

The cross of our Lord Jesus Christ is the centre from which divine omnipotence goes forth in the saving operations of grace. It is the place from which the saving power of God goes out to arrest sinners and bring them to Christ. What gives the cross of our Lord Jesus Christ such magnetic, drawing power? What is the attraction of the cross? Obviously, that is a bigger question than I can answer; but I want to show you seven things about the cross of our Lord Jesus Christ, by which the crucified Christ draws sinners to himself through the preaching of the gospel.

The One Who Died

This is the first attraction of the cross. The One who died upon the cross was no ordinary man. Many men died by Roman crucifixion before our Lord Jesus was crucified. Two men died when he died. Many were crucified after him. But this man was and is the Son of God (Matthew 27:54).

Someone said, 'The wonder of the cross is not the blood, but whose blood, and to what purpose.' If that man who died upon the cross is himself God over all and blessed forever, as he most assuredly is, two things are certain. One, the Lord Jesus Christ died as a willing Substitute, by his own voluntary consent (Luke 9:51; John 10:17, 18), and two, whatever he intended to accomplish in his death upon the cross, he has fully accomplished (Isaiah 42:4; 53:10, 11).

He shall see his seed. He shall see all his chosen seed, all his redeemed justified, sanctified, and glorified seed. He shall see them with himself in heaven's everlasting bliss. He shall prolong his days. That is to say, he shall live again in resurrection glory. The pleasure of the Lord shall prosper in his hand. He will rule the universe to accomplish the triune Jehovah's eternal purpose of grace. He shall see of the travail of his soul and be satisfied. By his knowledge he shall justify all of those whose iniquities he bore.

The Love Of God

The second attraction of the cross is this, the cross of our Lord Jesus Christ is the revelation of the love of God (John 3:16; Romans 5:6-8; 1 John 3:16; 1 John 4:9, 10).

> Could we with ink the ocean fill,
> And were the skies of parchment made,
> Were every stalk on earth a quill,
> And every man a scribe by trade,
> To write the love of God above,
> Would drain the ocean dry.
> Nor could the scroll contain the whole,
> Though stretched from sky to sky.
>
> Frederick M. Lehman

The cross of Christ proclaims what the law could never reveal, 'God is love'. In the cross of Christ we see 'what is the length, and breadth, and depth, and height' of the love of God. The breadth of God's love encompasses a world of perishing sinners. The length of God's love spans eternity. The depth of God's love reaches down to dregs of fallen humanity. The height of God's love lifts us up to eternal glory. The cross of Christ shows how far men will go in sin. We crucified the Son of God. But it also shows how far God will go for man's salvation. He gave his only begotten Son! We could never have known the love of God as we now do, had we not fallen in Adam that we might be redeemed by Christ.

Righteousness Vindicated
The third attraction of the cross is this, the cross of Christ is a vindication of God's righteous character and his strict justice (Isaiah 45:20-22; Romans 3:24-26). Here, in the cross of our Lord Jesus, mercy and truth meet together, righteousness and peace kiss each other, and while the indescribable fury of God's wrath is completely satisfied by the death of his Son, his infinite saving mercy is poured out upon all for whom his Son was slain.

God's Being
The fourth attraction of the cross is the fact that the cross of our Lord Jesus Christ is the ultimate revelation of God's being (John 1:18; Psalms 85:9-13). 'By mercy and truth iniquity is purged' (Proverbs 16:6). Creation tells us that God is great. Conscience tells us that God is righteous. The law tells us that God is just and holy. But only the cross of Christ reveals the entirety of God's character. In the cross we see that God is holy and merciful, just and gracious, righteous and good, immutable and wise, omnipotent and kind, omnipresent and compassionate, omniscient and forgiving.

Covenant Ratified
Here is a fifth attraction. The cross of our Lord Jesus Christ is the centre of God's purposes and the ratification of God's covenant. The death of our Lord Jesus Christ was not an afterthought with God. It was not something God did as the result of man's disobedience to and rejection of his Son's claims as the Messiah. Far from it! The cross of Christ is the reason for which God made the world and the object which he had in mind when he created man upon it.

The cross of Christ is the centre and focal point of God's eternal purposes and decrees (Acts 2:23; 1 Peter 1:18-25). The cross of Christ was the central object of all the types and prophecies of the Old Testament scriptures. 'To him give all the prophets witness' (Acts 10:43). And the cross of Christ ratified, confirmed, and fulfilled the everlasting covenant of God's grace (Hebrews 9:14-17; 8:10-12).

Redemption Accomplished
Here is the sixth attraction of the cross, the cross of Christ is a proclamation of redemption fully accomplished (John 19:30; Hebrews 9:12; Isaiah 40:1, 2).

The cross of Christ declares to sinners everywhere, atonement is made, justice is satisfied, sin is put away. Believe and live!

Transforming Power

There is yet a seventh attraction in the cross. The cross of our Lord Jesus Christ has a marvellous healing and transforming power. There is healing in the cross. He who looks to Christ is healed, healed in every part of his being, completely healed. The healing begins now in the soul; it is completed hereafter in the resurrection body. Jesus Christ, the crucified and risen One is our Healer. His name is Jehovah-rophe, 'The Lord that healeth thee' (2 Corinthians 5:17-21). 'The saving power of the cross', J. I. Packer wrote, 'does not depend on faith being added to it. Its saving power is such that faith flows from it.'

In the cross of Christ is life eternal, propitiation with God, reconciliation to God. Here I find rest from all my labour, inspiration for my life on earth, and hope for the world to come. The cross of Christ, the gospel, is the power of God unto salvation to all who believe. The cross irresistibly draws our hearts to Christ. The cross of our Lord Jesus Christ is the theme of our preaching and praise here. And the cross shall be the theme of our song in glory! 'God forbid that I should glory, save in the cross of our Lord Jesus Christ, by whom the world is crucified unto me, and I unto the world' (Galatians 6:14).

Chapter 19

'Father, glorify thy name'

'Now is my soul troubled; and what shall I say? Father, save me from this hour: but for this cause came I unto this hour. Father, glorify thy name. Then came there a voice from heaven, saying, I have both glorified it, and will glorify it again. The people therefore, that stood by, and heard it, said that it thundered: others said, An angel spake to him. Jesus answered and said, This voice came not because of me, but for your sakes' (John 12:27-30).

This chapter opens with John's description of a good work done for the Lord Jesus Christ (John 12:1-7). In fact, this is the only work our Saviour ever commended as a good work (Matthew 26:10; Mark 14:6). It was a work motivated by love, inspired by faith, a work requiring great sacrifice, and a work done just for the Lord Jesus.

The next day our Saviour made his triumphal entry into Jerusalem, 'sitting on an ass's colt'. Mary had anointed him for his burial in anticipation of his death, resurrection, ascension, and exaltation as King of kings and Lord of lords. Now, the very next day, the Lord God compelled the very people who would soon cry, 'Crucify him', to spread palm branches before him and cry, 'Hosanna! Blessed is the King of Israel that cometh in the name of the Lord' (v. 13). Then ...

'And there were certain Greeks among them that came up to worship at the feast: The same came therefore to Philip, which was of Bethsaida of Galilee, and desired him, saying, Sir, we would see Jesus. Philip cometh and telleth Andrew: and again Andrew and Philip tell Jesus. And Jesus answered them, saying, The hour is come, that the Son of man should be glorified. Verily,

verily, I say unto you, Except a corn of wheat fall into the ground and die, it abideth alone: but if it die, it bringeth forth much fruit. He that loveth his life shall lose it; and he that hateth his life in this world shall keep it unto life eternal. If any man serve me, let him follow me; and where I am, there shall also my servant be: if any man serve me, him will my Father honour' (John 12:20-26).

Soul Trouble

Now, hear the Son of God, as he speaks of his heavy, heavy soul trouble, as he anticipates being made sin for us, bearing the furious wrath of an angry God in our place and dying in our stead upon the cursed tree.

'Now is my soul troubled; and what shall I say? Father, save me from this hour: but for this cause came I unto this hour. Father, glorify thy name. Then came there a voice from heaven, saying, I have both glorified it, and will glorify it again. The people therefore, that stood by, and heard it, said that it thundered: others said, An angel spake to him. Jesus answered and said, This voice came not because of me, but for your sakes' (John 12:27-30).

'Father, glorify thy name.' I cannot think of a prayer more suitable for the children of God in all seasons than that which our Saviour here prayed. May God the Holy Ghost make it the cry of my heart and of yours for Christ's sake. 'Father, glorify thy name.'

Context

Before I try to explain the meaning of this prayer, which was first spoken and offered to the Father by our Saviour, we should look at the things which preceded and led up to it. Our Lord Jesus had performed a very remarkable miracle in raising Lazarus from the dead. The fame of that miracle spread like wildfire. Multitudes flocked to see this man Jesus, this prophet who, claiming to be the Son of God, both healed the sick and raised the dead to life by the mere word of his power. Enthusiastic crowds gathered in such huge numbers that the Pharisees exclaimed to one another, 'The world hath gone after him.'

Following this and the other miracles performed by our Lord, the people wanted to make him king in Israel. As he rode into Jerusalem, a great multitude met him waving palm branches, and crying, 'Hosanna! Blessed is the King of Israel that cometh in the name of the Lord.' But our Saviour passed through the streets of the ancient city in humility, riding an ass's colt, just as the prophet Zechariah had prophesied he would. This public manifestation, the well-known miracles, the resurrection of Lazarus from the dead, and the general talk of the people stirred the interests of many. Many strangers began to ask questions about this man who was called 'the Christ'.

'Father, glorify thy name'

Certain Greeks asked Philip to introduce them to the Master, saying, 'Sir, we would see Jesus' (v. 21). Obviously, these men did not simply desire to see the Saviour physically. They could do that without Philip's assistance. These Greeks wanted to know the Christ of whom they had heard so much.

The sight of these Greeks must have brought joy to the Saviour's heart. Here were men coming out of great darkness to him who is the Light of the world. These were Gentiles seeking their Saviour. No doubt, he saw in these men a reminder of that which he had come to accomplish: the salvation of his elect out of the nations of the world. He must have looked upon these strangers with delight, regarding them as representatives of the countless multitudes who would come to him from the ends of the earth and the islands of the seas to behold the glory of God in his face. How his heart must have laughed with joy! This was the joy set before him, for which he was about to endure the cross, despising the shame (Hebrews 12:2).

Then, as he began to address the crowds before him, a solemn thought seems to have seized his holy mind. He seems to have thought to himself 'Multitudes are to be gathered unto me. Both Jew and Gentile shall be saved by me. But they cannot be born into my kingdom without my soul's travail. They cannot be saved except I satisfy the justice of God for them. These people cannot live except I die and redeem them with my life's blood.'

It appears that this fact came vividly before the Saviour's heart and mind. It seems to have rushed upon his holy soul like a raging storm. He saw that he could not become the seed of a great harvest until he first fell into the ground and died. That is what he says in verse twenty-four. He was and is that one grain of wheat upon whom all depended. He must be slain and buried in the earth, or else he must abide alone and have no fruit. Apart from his death as our Substitute there is no way for the holy Lord God to save fallen, guilty sinners. Justice must be satisfied, or sinners could never be saved.

Our Saviour saw the vicarious sufferings he must endure as the sinner's Substitute, how that he must be made sin for us that we might be made the righteousness of God in him; and his soul was exceedingly troubled. He said in verse twenty-seven, 'Now is my soul troubled; and what shall I say? Father, save me from this hour: but for this cause came I unto this hour.'

Yet, we must never imagine that our Saviour feared and dreaded death. Obviously, the Son of God did not fear death. His courage and strength of mind were infinitely superior to that possessed by any of his servants, many of whom have welcomed death. We have read of many of the martyrs who endured death in the most terrifying forms imaginable without fear, even expressing delight and glorifying God in their mortal agony. I have seen many of God's saints leave this world, welcoming death as a blessed thing. Our Lord was not less courageous or weaker than they.

He did not fear death; but his was to be a very peculiar death. Death is the penalty for sin; but he knew no sin. Death is the curse of God's broken law; but he never broke the law. Death is the out-pouring of divine wrath upon fallen man; but he is the delight of his Father's heart. Death had no claim upon him. He is holy, harmless, undefiled, and separate from sinners.

The Son of God died as the Sin-bearer. His death was the vindication of God's holiness and the satisfaction of his justice. Our Lord Jesus Christ died voluntarily as our Sacrifice and sin-atoning Substitute. He died in the place of sinners, being made sin, being made the object of his Father's holy wrath and furious justice.

This is altogether different from the death that we must die as pardoned, justified believers. We shall have the privilege of passing out of this world resting upon the atonement of Christ, sustained with the confidence that we are reconciled to God by the blood of the cross. Our Lord Jesus died bearing the enormous load of our guilt! The dark hue of human corruption, sin, and guilt must soon blacken his holy soul! He must be made sin for us! His sinless, sensitive, holy soul must be made guilty before his Father!

When we die, our death is precious in the eyes of the Lord. When Christ died, his death was peculiarly and distinctly cursed by God (Galatians 3:13). He died the cursed death of the cross that all the blessings of God's free grace might flow down to his redeemed people through the merits of his blood.

Not one of us can perceive the agony our Redeemer endured for us when he died in our place at Calvary. Yet, he saw it all clearly, even before it took place. He knew exactly what lay before him, what he must do, and what he must suffer, in order to 'see of the travail of his soul and be satisfied'.

Inward Struggle

When he began to anticipate the horror of bearing our sins in his own body on the tree, there was a struggle in his soul. That struggle was witnessed by the crowds gathered before him, and is here recorded by John for our learning.

The Greeks wanted to see the Lord Jesus; and see him they did. They saw him as no one had ever seen him. They saw him and heard him 'in the days of his flesh' offering 'up prayers and supplications with strong crying and tears unto him that was able to save him from death'. Yes, as the Spirit of God tells us in Hebrews 5:7, they saw the Lord Jesus Christ in fear. They must have been astonished by what they saw. They expected to see a King; and they did behold his royal soul; but they saw him in a depth of grief that no words can describe. They wanted to see the greatness of his spirit and the power of his mind. They did see it; but it was a greatness of spirit and a power of mind that filled the incarnate God with agony!

Gethsemane

On this public occasion, our Saviour seems to have rehearsed that which later took place in Gethsemane. His soul was troubled. His heart was heavy. His spirit was in agony. In his inmost being, the Son of man was going through a time of deep, deep distress and great trouble. Our text is the culminating point of his trouble, the climax of his anguish, and the conquest of his soul over his distress. 'Now is my soul troubled; and what shall I say? Father, save me from this hour: but for this cause came I unto this hour.'

When he had spoken those words, reminding himself of his purpose in life to accomplish the will of God, he seems to have shaken himself free of fear. He emerged victorious, with his face set like a flint, he was determined to go forward to the bitter, but glorious end. This was his prayer, his motive, his rule of life, and the desire of his heart and soul in all things and at all times. 'Father, glorify thy name.'

Using our Saviour's own words and example, let us understand that as the glory of God is the ultimate end of all things, it ought to be the constant motive and ambition and desire of our hearts in all things. Our Lord Jesus Christ sought the glory of God above all else. May he give us grace to walk in his steps. This was his prayer when his soul was troubled. This is my prayer. It is the daily cry of my heart to my God. I trust it is yours as well. 'Father, glorify thy name.'

A Prayer Of Faith

Here is a prayer of faith. 'Father, glorify thy name.' Our Lord Jesus Christ, above all others, lived in this world by faith, believing God. His faith in God was exemplified in his perfect faithfulness to God in all things as a man. Both his faith and his faithfulness are displayed in this prayer.

This is a prayer that arose from our Saviour's great trouble of soul as a man. I am always fearful when I try to speak about the inner conflicts of our Redeemer's holy soul. Jealousy for his honour makes me reluctant to speak of such things. Yet, this event and this prayer are recorded here by divine inspiration for our learning.

Our Saviour's great soul was full of trouble. His heart was heavy. Here is God the Son, the Saviour of the world, bowed down with woe. His mind, his soul, his heart in conflict vexed him. He who could heal diseases with the touch of his hand, cast out demons with a word, calm the raging sea and tempestuous winds, and call the dead back again to life is in agony! How can such a thing as this be explained?

'Is it nothing to you, all ye that pass by? behold, and see if there be any sorrow like unto my sorrow, which is done unto me, wherewith the LORD hath afflicted me in the day of his fierce anger … The yoke of my transgressions is bound by his hand: they are wreathed, and come up upon my neck: he hath made my strength to fall, the Lord hath delivered me into their hands, from whom I am not able to rise up' (Lamentations 1:12, 14).

He knew what lay before him in Gethsemane. He knew what Judas was about to do. He knew how Peter would deny him. He knew how his disciples would all forsake him. He knew that he must soon be made sin for us. The weight of our sins began to press upon his soul. Our Redeemer knew full well what he must suffer for his elect. He knew that all the sins of all his people must be transferred to him and made his. He knew that all the fury of God's justice and wrath must be completely poured out and fully exhausted upon him. He knew that he must be abandoned by his Father at the very height of his obedience, when he would be made sin for us.

I find here both a deep mystery and a comforting truth. Though our Saviour suffered trouble and fear, he knew no sin. There was trouble in his soul, but no doubt in his heart, fear, but no fretting or cowardice, distress, but no despair, sorrow, but no unbelief.

Our Saviour entered into our manhood fully. He experienced everything we experience, every trial, every temptation, and every heartache. Though he knew no sin and did no sin, though he was altogether without sin, he was now about to be made sin for us. If he would be our merciful and faithful High Priest, if he would be touched with the feeling of our infirmities, if he would be able to succour them that are tempted, he must be made sin for us (Hebrew 2:9, 10, 17, 18). Blessed be his name, our all-glorious Christ is a merciful and faithful, sympathizing High Priest, in all things touched with the feeling of our infirmities!

Our Redeemer overcame his great trouble of soul with the determination of his committed, consecrated heart. 'Now is my soul troubled; and what shall I say? Father, save me from this hour: but for this cause came I unto this hour. Father, glorify thy name.' The time of his suffering and sorrow had been appointed for him; and he knew it. 'The hour is come.' He had come to Jerusalem specifically because his hour had come. The hour appointed to him by the Father's decree, the hour agreed to in the covenant of grace (John 10:16-18), the hour for which he came into the world (Hebrews 10:5-10) had arrived. Our Lord Jesus Christ was determined to suffer all the wrath of God for us at the appointed hour (Isaiah 50:5-7).

Be sure you understand how Christ died. He did not die as a helpless victim of circumstances beyond his control, but as a voluntary, vicarious, victorious Redeemer and Substitute (John 10:16-18). The cause of our Lord's holy determination is evident. Why was he resolved to die? Was it to save men? Indeed, it was. Yet, that was not the chief reason. His prayer here is not, 'Father, save thy people', but 'Father, glorify thy name.' This is what I want us to see, the primary object of our Saviour's life, that which inspired, motivated, and invigorated his holy soul, was and is the glory of the Father. He came into the world for the glory of his Father. He lived here for the glory of his Father. He died at Calvary for the glory of his Father. He reigns upon his throne for the glory of his Father. He saves sinners for the glory of his Father.

A Promise From God

Here is a promise from God. 'Then came there a voice from heaven, saying, I have both glorified it, and will glorify it again'. The grand result of our Saviour's life, death, resurrection, and exaltation is the glory of God. Here the Father speaks from heaven both of the past and the future.

Three times, during the days of our Lord's earthly life and ministry, we hear the Father speak from heaven. All three times, the issue at hand was the death of Christ his Son as our Substitute: at his baptism (Matthew 3), at his transfiguration (Matthew 17), and here in John 12. In all that is past, our heavenly Father declares that he has glorified himself. Without a doubt, the primary thing declared here is that the Father was glorified in all things done by the Son. The glory of the Father is always in the Son; and the glory of the Son is always in the Father (John 13:31, 32). Therefore, we are assured by Christ himself that all who honour the Son honour the Father also (John 5:20-24). God's primary purpose in all things is his own glory (Psalms 106:8; Proverbs 16:4; Romans 11:36; Revelation 4:11).

God glorified himself in the covenant of grace. God glorified himself in the creation of the world. He glorified himself in all the laws and ceremonies and events of Old Testament history. He glorified himself in the incarnation and birth of his Son. God glorified himself in the life of his Son upon the earth. Christ is the Revelation of the triune God. Christ is the Embodiment of the triune God. Christ is the Fulness of the triune God. Christ is the Glory of God. Jesus Christ, the Man, is himself God!

Yet, here, the Father also speaks to the Son a word of promise, saying, 'I will glorify my name again.' This promise filled our Saviour with joy and courage. Let it do the same for you. Is your soul downcast? Are you concerned about the future? Hear the promise of God and take comfort. 'I will glorify it again.'

God's name was glorified in and by the death of his Son as our Substitute. When we read the context carefully, we cannot fail to see that the glory of God is vitally connected with the cross of Christ. Sin was judged at Calvary. Satan was bound at Calvary. God's elect were redeemed at Calvary. The crucified Christ draws sinners to himself. All the attributes of God meet together and are honoured in the cross (Psalms 85:9-13).

'The people therefore, that stood by, and heard it, said that it thundered: others said, An angel spake to him. Jesus answered and said, This voice came not because of me, but for your sakes. Now is the judgment of this world: now shall the prince of this world be cast out. And I, if I be lifted up from the earth, will draw all men unto me. This he said, signifying what death he should die' (John 12:29-33).

God's name was glorified by our Saviour's resurrection and ascension (Psalms 68:18-20). God's name is glorified in Christ by the preaching of the gospel (2 Corinthians 2:15, 16). God's name is glorified in the salvation of sinners by Christ (Ephesians 2:7-9). And, blessed be his name, there is a day coming when God Almighty will glorify his name in and by all things. Christ will come again with the glory of the Father. All men will bow to and confess Christ as Lord to the glory of God (Philippians 2:8-11). The earth shall be filled with the glory of God, when Christ makes all things new. The wicked will be judged and forever damned for the glory of God. The righteous will be saved, forever saved, for the glory of God. And all things will be reconciled to God by our great Saviour 'to the praise of the glory of his grace'! If I am in Christ, if you are in him, we may take this word in the most personal way possible, applying it to ourselves in every detail of our lives. In all that is past, God has glorified himself. In all that shall come, our God will glorify himself.

A Principle Of Grace

Here is a principle of grace. This is the principle by which our Saviour lived in this world. It is the principle by which we should always strive to live. 'Father, glorify thy name.' Let this ever be the prayer, desire, ambition, and governing principle of our lives in this world. 'Father, glorify thy name' (Proverbs 3:5, 6). Seek his will. Surrender to his will. Trust his will. Delight in his will.

'Trust in the LORD with all thine heart; and lean not unto thine own understanding. In all thy ways acknowledge him, and he shall direct thy paths' (Proverbs 3:5, 6). 'Whether therefore ye eat, or drink, or whatsoever ye do, do all to the glory of God' (1 Corinthians 10:31).

Then, let us live in the expectation of his promise being fulfilled. 'I will glorify it again'. This is our confidence, our hope, and our ultimate satisfaction. 'I will glorify it again'.

Would you glorify God? Are you interested in the glory of God? Let me give you four simple words of direction. Do these four things, and you will glorify the name of God: trust Christ, follow Christ, live for the honour of Christ, serve Christ.

With the dawn of every day, as we anticipate that which lies before us in the providence of God, may God the Holy Spirit make this our souls' ambition, desire, and prayer. 'Father, glorify thy name.'

Chapter 20

'who is this Son of man?'

'Now is the judgment of this world: now shall the prince of this world be cast out. And I, if I be lifted up from the earth, will draw all men unto me. This he said, signifying what death he should die. The people answered him, We have heard out of the law that Christ abideth for ever: and how sayest thou, The Son of man must be lifted up? who is this Son of man?' (John 12:31-34).

In holy scripture, our Lord Jesus is called 'the Son of Mary' only once (Mark 6:3). Truly, he is the Son of Mary, the woman's Seed, conceived in the womb of the virgin by God the Holy Spirit, without an earthly father. We rejoice to know that. But the only time our Lord was ever called 'the Son of Mary', he was called that by godless, reprobate men, who were offended by his doctrine. That fact should speak volumes to us about that idolatrous religion that promotes the worship of Mary, ever referring to God our Saviour as 'the Son of Mary'.

Our Redeemer is called 'the Son of David' sixteen times. He is called the Son of David, because he was directly descended from David as a man. Being David's Son, it was his lawful right to sit upon David's throne as the king of Israel. Indeed, he is that Son of David whom God promised to raise up to set upon his throne forever. The Son of David has come. He is now reigning upon his throne, the King of God's Israel, the King of glory forever.

Then, our blessed Saviour is called 'the Son of God' forty-seven times. Yes, Jesus of Nazareth, the baby of Bethlehem, the Son of David, is himself the Son of God, the second Person of the holy trinity. Our Saviour is God.

Were he anything less than God over all, blessed forever, he could not be our Saviour. Because he is God the Son, he is God our Saviour.

But in the book of God the Lord Jesus Christ is called 'the Son of man' eighty-eight times. This is the name he used in reference to himself more than any other. In fact, this name, 'the Son of man', is used almost exclusively by Christ himself. Yet, none of his disciples ever called him 'the Son of man' until after his exaltation, and then only two of them did so. Stephen, when he saw heaven opened, said 'Behold, I see the heavens opened, and the Son of man standing on the right hand of God' (Acts 7:56). John, in the Book of Revelation, wrote, 'And in the midst of the seven candlesticks one like unto the Son of man, clothed with a garment down to the foot, and girt about the paps with a golden girdle' (Revelation 1:13). Then, in Revelation 14:14, we read, 'And I looked, and behold a white cloud, and upon the cloud one sat like unto the Son of man, having on his head a golden crown, and in his hand a sharp sickle'.

Why did the Lord Jesus Christ constantly refer to himself as 'the Son of man'? How can he be both the Son of God and the Son of man? When our Saviour spoke in John 12:34 of the Son of man being lifted up to suffer and die, and yet declared that by means of his death he would save men and women throughout the world, the people who heard it were confused. 'The people answered him, we have heard out of the law that Christ abideth forever'. You say that you are the Christ, the Messiah. 'And how sayest thou, the Son of man must be lifted up' to die upon the cursed tree?

'Who is this Son of man?' To find the answer to this question, we must search the scriptures, taking the word of God alone as our source of information, asking God the Holy Spirit, whose word the Bible is, to be our Teacher. As it is used in the New Testament, the term 'Son of man' never refers to anyone except the God-man, our Mediator, the Lord Jesus Christ. This term, 'the Son of man', always refers to the person and work of the Lord Jesus Christ as the Mediator between God and men.

Hear The Saviour

'Who is this Son of man?' First, let the Son of man himself tell us who he is. Of the eighty-eight times this term, 'the Son of man', is used in the New Testament, eighty-four times it was uttered by the Lord Jesus Christ in reference to himself. Who better than he can tell us who he is?

'Then answered Jesus and said unto them, Verily, verily, I say unto you, The Son can do nothing of himself, but what he seeth the Father do: for what things soever he doeth, these also doeth the Son likewise. For the Father loveth the Son, and sheweth him all things that himself doeth: and he will shew him greater works than these, that ye may marvel. For as the Father raiseth up the dead, and quickeneth them; even so the Son quickeneth whom he will. For the Father judgeth no man, but hath committed all judgment unto the Son: That all men should honour the Son, even as they honour the Father. He that honoureth not the Son honoureth not the Father which hath sent him. Verily, verily, I say unto you, he that heareth my word, and believeth on him that sent me, hath everlasting life, and shall not come into condemnation; but is passed from death unto life. Verily, verily, I say unto you, The hour is coming, and now is, when the dead shall hear the voice of the Son of God: and they that hear shall live. For as the Father hath life in himself; so hath he given to the Son to have life in himself; And hath given him authority to execute judgment also, because he is the Son of man' (John 5:19-27).

In these verses our Lord calls himself 'the Son', 'the Son of God', and 'the Son of man'. This alone is enough to assure us that there is no contradiction between the titles 'Son of God' and 'Son of man'. Both names refer to the same person, the Lord Jesus Christ. The one refers to his divinity and the other to his humanity. Our Saviour is both God and man, as truly God as though he were not man, and as truly man as though he were not God, the Godman.

John 6:62 says, 'What and if ye shall see the Son of man ascend up where he was before?' (See John 17:1-5). The Lord Jesus here declares that he existed in heaven as the Son of man before he came into the world in our nature. Though his human body and soul were created in time, he was the Son of man, our Mediator, the Surety of the everlasting covenant from eternity. He was, in the mind and purpose of God, the Son of man before any man was made. He says to the Father, 'My substance was not hid from thee, when I was made in secret, and curiously wrought in the lowest parts of the earth. Thine eyes did see my substance, yet being unperfect (unmade, uncreated); and in thy book all my members were written, which in continuance were fashioned, when as yet there were none of them' (Psalms 139:15, 16).

In John 3:13 our Saviour said to Nicodemus, 'No man hath ascended up to heaven, but he that came down from heaven, even the Son of man, which is in heaven.' Even while he was upon the earth, in human flesh, the Son of man was the omnipresent Son of God. His humanity, his physical form, can only be in one place at a time. Yet, he is God, everywhere present at all times. Our Mediator, the Son of man, is the Lord, Jehovah, our God, omniscient, omnipotent, and omnipresent. This One who is the Son of man is God, the Lord of the Sabbath (Mark 2:28). He is the Son of man and the Son of God, who has power on earth to forgive sin (Luke 5:17-26).

Matthew 25:31 reads, 'The Son of man shall come in his glory, and all his holy angels with him, then shall he sit upon the throne of his glory'. The Son of man came to seek and to save that which was lost. The Son of man came to minister and to give his life a ransom for many. The Son of man lived for us.

The Son of man died for us. The Son of man arose, ascended back into heaven, and sat down in glorious exaltation on our behalf. The Son of man is making intercession for us. The Son of man rules the world for us. The Son of man has opened a way of access to God for sinful men, by the blood of his cross. The Son of man is coming again in glory. The Son of man is our Saviour. And the Son of man is the Son of God!

Hear His Disciples

'Who is this Son of man?' We have heard the Saviour answer the question. Now, secondly, let us hear what his disciples have said about him. Whenever our Lord's disciples thought of him as the Son of man, or heard him call himself by that name, they never looked upon it as a pretty title, implying only that he was a good man, a prophet, a miracle worker or a social reformer. To the disciples, this title, 'the Son of man', implied authority, exaltation, glory, power, dominion, and tenderness.

The Apostle Peter certainly understood the title, 'the Son of man', to be a title just as noble, honourable, and distinct as the title 'the Son of God'. When the Lord Jesus called himself 'the Son of man', Peter called him 'the Son of God', and the Saviour took Peter's confession as an honour done to him by Peter (Matthew 16:13-17). The writer of Hebrews used this title, 'the Son of man', to ascribe glory to Christ, the Son of God (Hebrews 1:1-3, 6-9; 2:6-9). Stephen, the first martyr, saw the Lord Jesus standing as 'the Son of man' at the right hand of God (Acts 7:54-59).

'Who is this Son of man?' His disciples tell us that he is the Christ, the Messiah, the Son of the living God. His disciples tell us that he is the exalted, sovereign Saviour of the sons of Abraham, God's elect, touched with the feeling of our infirmities, able to help us, always delighted to call us his brethren, determined to save us. His disciple, Stephen, that blessed martyr, tells us that he is a faithful friend and our faithful God!

Hear His Enemies

'Who is this Son of man?' Let us now consult with his enemies, and hear what they have to say. Our great God, in his wise and adorable providence, makes even the enemies of his Son to be witnesses for his Son. In this passage (John 12:31-34) the Jews understood that the Messiah would be called 'the Son of man' (See Psalms 80:17; Daniel 7:13, 14). Those who raised this question, 'Who is this Son of man?' looked upon the terms 'Son of God' and 'Son of man' as synonymous terms. When they heard the Lord of glory call himself the 'Son of man', they understood his meaning to be, 'I am God'. Therefore, they crucified him (Matthew 26:63-67). When they said, 'Thou, being a man, makest thyself God' (John 10:33), the Lord Jesus replied, 'Say ye of him, whom the Father hath sanctified, and sent into the world, thou blasphemest; because I said, I am the Son of God?' (John 10:36). 'Who is this Son of man?' He is God over all and blessed forever. And he is man, bone of our bone and flesh of our flesh. There is no lack of efficacy in his blood and no lack of power in his grace. He can save to the uttermost all who come to God by him. Trust him and you will find his grace sufficient for you.

Ten Reasons

Still the question needs to be answered, 'Why is the Lord Jesus Christ called 'the Son of man'? To the best of my very limited ability I have shown you who the Son of man is. Now, let me show you ten reasons the Lord of glory is called 'the Son of man'.

1. Christ is called the Son of man because he is the original Man. Our Lord Jesus Christ is the man who is the image of the invisible God, in whose image and after whose likeness man was made in the beginning. God created Adam in the image of Christ, that man who was to come, who is the image of God (Genesis 1:26, 27; Colossians 1:15; Hebrews 1:3). Adam was created and made in the physical image of our Redeemer, his moral and intellectual image, and in his authoritative image, having dominion over all creation. And the first Adam was made in the mediatorial image of the last Adam, our divine Mediator.

2. The Lord Jesus is called the Son of man because he is the representative Man. He is the last Adam, the second Man, the Lord from heaven; as such he is distinguished from the first man, the first Adam, who was of the earth, earthy (1 Corinthians 15:45, 47). In all things Christ is the Surety, the Representative, the Mediator, the Substitute of an elect race, just as Adam was the representative of all our physical race in the garden (Romans 5:12-19).

3. Our Saviour is called the Son of man because he is the prophesied Man. He is the man of whom all the prophets spoke, the man who is God's equal (Psalms 89:19; Isaiah 9:6; 32:2; 53:1-12; Zechariah 13:7).

4. The Lord Jesus Christ is called the Son of man because he is the ideal Man. He is the only man who ever fulfilled perfectly God's will, and fulfilled the purpose of God in creating man. That purpose was and is threefold; to live in righteousness, to glorify God, to have dominion over God's creation. In Christ we fulfil God's purpose for manhood (Genesis 1:26-28).

5. Our Redeemer is called the Son of man because he is the justice satisfying Man. No mortal could ever satisfy the justice of God. Not all the race of manhood could satisfy God's offended justice for sin. But the Son of man, with one tremendous draught of love, drank damnation dry, when he suffered the wrath of God in our place (Isaiah 53:9; Ephesians 5:2).

6. Christ Jesus is called the Son of man because he is the exalted Man (Philippians 2:9-11).

> The head that once was crowned with thorns
> Is crowned with glory now.
> A royal diadem adorns
> The mighty Victor's brow.
>
> Thomas Kelly

7. Our great Saviour is called the Son of man because he is the Godman.

> God could not suffer. God could not die.
> And man could never satisfy.
> But Christ, the God-man suffered and died.
> And He God's justice satisfied.

8. The Lord Jesus is called the Son of man because he is the saving Man. The Son of man is the Saviour of men. 'The Son of man is come to seek and to save that which was lost' (Luke 19:10).

9. Christ Jesus is called the Son of man because he is the coming Man. 'The Son of man cometh' (Matthew 24:44; 25:13; Luke 12:40; 18:8) to save his own, to judge the world, and to finish his mediatorial work (1 Corinthians 15:24-28).

10. And our dear Saviour, the Lord Jesus Christ, the Son of God, is called the Son of man because he is the sympathizing Man (Hebrews 2:17, 18; 4:15; 5:2; 7:25).

Why is Christ called the Son of man? He is called the Son of man so that lost men might look to him, the God-man, for grace and life, and believing men might look to him, the God-man, for comfort and peace.

Chapter 21

Responsibility, Reprobation, Ruin

'Then Jesus said unto them, Yet a little while is the light with you. Walk while ye have the light, lest darkness come upon you: for he that walketh in darkness knoweth not whither he goeth. While ye have light, believe in the light, that ye may be the children of light. These things spake Jesus, and departed, and did hide himself from them. But though he had done so many miracles before them, yet they believed not on him: That the saying of Esaias the prophet might be fulfilled, which he spake, Lord, who hath believed our report? and to whom hath the arm of the Lord been revealed? Therefore they could not believe, because that Esaias said again, he hath blinded their eyes, and hardened their heart; that they should not see with their eyes, nor understand with their heart, and be converted, and I should heal them. These things said Esaias, when he saw his glory, and spake of him. Nevertheless among the chief rulers also many believed on him; but because of the Pharisees they did not confess him, lest they should be put out of the synagogue: For they loved the praise of men more than the praise of God' (John 12:35-43).

Soon, we must meet God in judgment! You know it; and I know it. Soon, very soon, we will stand before the holy Lord God in judgment. We are going to spend eternity somewhere, either in the everlasting torments of the wicked in hell, or in the everlasting bliss of the saints in heaven, either with the damned under the infinite wrath of God, or with the saved in the indescribable blessedness of God's goodness; but we will spend eternity somewhere. You know it; and I know it (2 Corinthians 5:10, 11).

When Christ ascends His judgment throne,
And bids all worlds draw near;
Men's hearts shall melt, with sighs and groans;
And trembling souls shall fear.
Then as the solemn, opened books,
Disclose the dreadful day;
Jehovah's frowns and angry looks,
Will wicked souls dismay.

Omniscience will, with truth, expose,
Their secret thoughts to view;
Their crimes God's justice will expose,
And conscience own them true.
God's wrath shall seize the guilty souls
Of unconverted men,
While all God's books, the judgment scrolls,
Accuse, convince, condemn!

But, there in Jesus' gracious hand,
The Book of Life is placed.
The names of His elect there stand,
Nor can they be erased!
As He unfolds the sacred seals,
With God's decrees all done,
With one decisive word, He will
Welcome His ransomed home!

Joseph Irons

If you and I are saved, if we go to heaven, if the Lord God receives us into his Kingdom, if we enter into the everlasting bliss of heaven's glory with Christ, it will be by the work and grace of the triune God alone. 'Salvation is of the LORD'! Salvation comes to sinners by the will, decree, and purpose of God the Father, the righteousness, redemption, and intercession of God the Son, and the regeneration, calling, and preservation of God the Holy Spirit (Ephesians 2:8-10).

If we perish in our sins, if we die without Christ, without God's salvation, without hope, if we go to hell and suffer the horrid wrath of God in the pit of the damned forever, it will be our own fault. We will have no one to blame, but ourselves; and we will blame ourselves forever! It is written, 'The wages of sin is death; but the gift of God is eternal life through Jesus Christ our Lord' (Romans 6:23). Everlasting death in hell is something we earn. Eternal life is the free gift of God to poor sinners in our Lord Jesus Christ.

I want to show from the scriptures, and particularly from this passage of scripture, that it is our responsibility to believe on the Lord Jesus Christ, and that if you refuse to trust the Son of God, your wilful, obstinate unbelief will be the just cause of your everlasting damnation.

Responsibility

First, our Saviour shows us that it is our responsibility to believe on his name, to trust him as our only God, our only Lord, and our only Saviour.

'Then Jesus said unto them, Yet a little while is the light with you. Walk while ye have the light, lest darkness come upon you: for he that walketh in darkness knoweth not whither he goeth. While ye have light, believe in the light, that ye may be the children of light. These things spake Jesus, and departed, and did hide himself from them' (vv. 35, 36).

I take a back seat to no one in declaring the gospel of God's free and sovereign grace in Christ. Divine sovereignty, absolute predestination, total depravity, unconditional election, limited atonement, irresistible grace, and perseverance of the saints are in our house of worship like salt and pepper on the table. We never have a meal without them. These are not things discussed only in the secrecy of the pastor's study. They are openly declared from the pulpit without apology or abatement. Arminianism is a heretical form of evil that cannot be denounced in terms too severe. Will worship, under any name or in any form, is damning to the souls of men, and must be denounced with absolute dogmatism. However, we must not distort the truth of God and the plain teachings of holy scripture, even in denouncing the heresies of Arminian, free-will, works religion.

Many, attempting to guard the doctrine of God's sovereignty, completely deny the responsibility of men. They reason, as one wrote a while back, 'If we preach that a sinner is responsible to repent, we must declare that he is able to repent. If we teach that sinners are responsible to believe on Christ, we must also teach that they are able to believe.' They deduce, in what appears to be a very reasonable and logical manner, that responsibility implies ability. The problem with this reasoning is that it attempts to mould the word of God to a theological system; and that we dare not do!

We must never try to make the word of God fit into any humanly devised system of doctrine or theology. We must build our doctrine upon the plain statements of holy scripture alone. If the plain statements of scripture contradict, or even destroy our theological system, so be it. If we have to throw away every doctrinal creed, every confession of faith, and every catechism that has ever been written by men in order to be faithful and true to the word of God, then let us throw them away.

This is one reason why, in our congregation, we do not require members to sign or agree to a confession of faith. Our creed, our confession of faith is the holy, inspired word of God. If that seems to others to be too simple, too non-intellectual, or too pietistic, we can live with their disapproval. We bow to and build our doctrine upon the word of God alone, even when it seems to contradict human reason and philosophy. 'To the law and to the testimony: if they speak not according to this word, it is because there is no light in them' (Isaiah 8:20).

Here are two facts which simply cannot be denied or refuted: God Almighty is absolutely sovereign in salvation. He has mercy on whom he will have mercy. He is gracious to whom he will be gracious. He saves whom he will. 'So then it is not of him that willeth, nor of him that runneth, but of God that sheweth mercy' (Romans 9:16). Second, all men are responsible under God to walk in the light he gives them. The Lord God has fixed it so that those who perish in their sins, those who die in rebellion and unbelief are altogether without excuse. No one goes to hell by accident. Unbelief is not a passive thing. If you go to hell, you will have to scratch and claw your way there, fighting to your last breath against the light God has given you. Men and women do not go to hell because they are ignorant. People go to hell because they are rebels (Romans 1:18-20). 'The wages of sin is death'. You earn that. 'But the gift of God is eternal life'. That is his work.

'Yet a little while is the light with you'. Christ is the Light. The gospel he preached is the light. The revelation of his divine person and work is the light. But that light, he declared, would be taken away. Certainly, this primarily refers to his own death, resurrection, and ascension. He was about to go back to the Father. When that happened, judicial blindness was sent upon the nation of Israel by the judgment of God upon them.

But that is not all that our Lord's words mean. They have meaning for us as well. Our Lord Jesus is telling us that the light he gives us in this world is light that is given only for a specific space of time. He has given us the light of his grace and glory revealed in the gospel; but the light will not always shine before us. The Lord Jesus says, 'Yet a little while is the light with you'.

'Walk while ye have the light'. When our Lord says, 'Walk while ye have the light', his meaning is 'Believe in the light, while ye have the light', as he states in verse 36. 'While ye have light, believe in the light'. Soon we must die; and there is no light of grace in the grave.

This is to you who read these lines in this day of grace and salvation. There may not be another. God may never speak to you again by his gospel, by his Spirit, or by the voice of his servant. The darkness of old age, senility, gospel-hardness, false religion, and false refuges leave people only to stumble about in confusion and darkness, with no light. 'Behold, now is the accepted time; behold, now is the day of salvation'![3] When the light is taken away, darkness comes; and when the darkness of God's judgment comes upon you, you cannot walk in the light. When God sends darkness, he sends darkness; and you cannot see. Oh, how great is that darkness!

John Gill said, 'So it is with a man in a state of unregeneracy, and more especially under judicial blindness. He is not aware of the pits and snares that lie in his way, or of the dark mountains on which he stumbles; and though destruction and misery are in his ways, he knows not that he is going thereunto.'

'While ye have light, believe in the light, that ye may be the children of light. These things spake Jesus, and departed, and did hide himself from them.' Our Lord then departed from them and hid himself, leaving them to their thoughts and ways. 'He that hath ears to hear, let him hear.' When the Light leaves, nothing remains but darkness. This will be the torment of the damned forever, they loved darkness rather than the Light. Therefore they inherit the darkness of hell. God give me grace to believe the Light, to walk in the Light of Christ, the light of his purpose, his presence, his providence, and his gospel.

The galling, tormenting remembrance of lost and misspent opportunities will be the very essence of hell!

Reprobation

The scriptures clearly teach both election and reprobation. Reprobation is the act of abandoning, or state of being abandoned, to eternal destruction. It is a term applied both to the eternal decree of God to punish all who die in unbelief, and to the judicial act of God in abandoning, or casting off those who refuse to walk in the light God gives them, who refuse to believe the gospel, who refuse to believe on the Lord Jesus Christ.

The scriptures speak of God giving men over to a reprobate mind (Romans 1:28). That is God's act of judgment, casting men off, shutting them up in unbelief, because they harden their hearts against him (Proverbs 1:23-33; 29:1; Romans 10:21). When God shuts the door, it is shut forever.

The scriptures also speak of reprobation as an eternal act of God in predestination (Romans 9:11-24; 1 Peter 2:7, 8; Jude 4). Just as there are vessels of mercy 'afore prepared unto glory', there are vessels of wrath 'fitted to destruction'.

Our Lord Jesus speaks of both eternal reprobation by the decree of God and judicial reprobation by the justice of God in our text, in verses 37-41.

[3] What a privilege it is to have the light of the gospel, to have a place to hear the gospel, to have a messenger from God to preach the gospel! God can take the light away in a moment!

Reprobation is both the decree of God in eternity and the judicial act of God in time. God hardened Pharaoh's heart and Pharaoh hardened his own heart; but Pharaoh's hardening of his own heart was the cause of God's judgment upon him (Exodus 8:32-9:3). So it is with all who are lost.

'But though he had done so many miracles before them, yet they believed not on him: That the saying of Esaias the prophet might be fulfilled, which he spake, Lord, who hath believed our report? and to whom hath the arm of the Lord been revealed? Therefore they could not believe, because that Esaias said again, he hath blinded their eyes, and hardened their heart; that they should not see with their eyes, nor understand with their heart, and be converted, and I should heal them. These things said Esaias, when he saw his glory, and spake of him.'

Be sure you do not miss the order in which God the Holy Spirit dictated these statements of inspiration. The order here given is very significant. First, we are told that those before whom our Lord had performed so many miracles would not believe (v. 37). Then the Spirit of God refers us to Isaiah 53:1, and tells us that the unbelief of these people was a fulfilment of divine prophecy (v. 38). Their unbelief did not take God by surprise, or nullify his purpose. Rather, their unbelief was the fulfilment of God's purpose (Romans 3:3, 4). Third, because they would not believe, we are told that the Lord God fixed it so that they could not believe. 'Therefore they could not believe, because that Esaias said again, he hath blinded their eyes, and hardened their heart; that they should not see with their eyes, nor understand with their heart, and be converted, and I should heal them' (vv. 39, 40). God blinded their eyes and hardened their hearts in retribution, a just retribution and judgment, for their unbelief. And this was all according to God's eternal purpose. Fourth, in verse 41, John tells us that Isaiah had this revealed to him when he saw the Lord's glory, when the he saw sovereign mercy, and justice executed, redemption accomplished, Christ exalted, free forgiveness by the accepted sacrifice of Christ (Isaiah 6:1-13).

How hardened in rebellion the heart of man is by nature, how deceitful, how desperately wicked! Though numerous, undeniable wonderful miracles were performed before their eyes, they would not believe. They would not believe because they could not believe; and they could not believe because they would not believe. Miracles performed before the eyes of men, undeniable miracles, will never produce faith. Faith comes by hearing the gospel, not by signs and wonders. Yet, the most orthodox, perfect, pure preaching of the gospel will not produce faith without the accompanying power and grace of God the Holy Spirit. 'It is the Spirit that quickeneth: the flesh profiteth nothing'! The dead must be given life before they can believe. Even then, the faith we exercise as living men is, as Paul puts it, 'the faith of the Son of God who loved me and gave himself for me' (Galatians 2:20). Our faith is the work of God in us, not our work for God. Faith in Christ is the gift of and operation of God's free and sovereign grace (Ephesians 1:19, 20; 2:8; Philippians 1:29; Colossians 2:14).

All things that come to pass in time, even the rebellion, unbelief, and everlasting ruin of reprobate sinners is according to the unalterable, everlasting purpose of God in predestination (Romans 9:11-24; 1 Peter 2:7, 8; Jude 4; Romans 3:3, 4). Yet, divine judgment is always just. It is always the just retribution of God upon ungodly rebels. It comes upon men because of deliberate, wilful rebellion and unbelief. 'The wages of sin is death'! If you go to hell, it will be your own fault; and you will forever be tormented by your own conscience screaming 'Amen' to your everlasting damnation.

No one goes to hell because of Adam's transgression. 'The soul that sinneth, it shall die' (Ezekiel 18:20). No one goes to hell who does not personally deserve eternal damnation. God will not condemn the just (Proverbs 17:15). If you go to hell, you will go to hell kicking, fighting, opposing, and warring with your own conscience all the way, transgressing everything you know by nature, providence, and the word of God. You will go to hell kicking God, as it were, out of your way, with your fingers in your ears, deliberately hardening your heart against everything holy, pure, and spiritual. Still, you will not escape, alter, or in any way hinder God's eternal purpose and decree in predestination. You will only fulfil it! When Isaiah saw the Lord's glory (Isaiah 6), he saw his glory both in the salvation of chosen, ransomed sinners by his free grace, and in the everlasting ruin of reprobate sons and daughters of Adam who harden their hearts and will not believe on the Son of God.

Ruin

Third, we see that religion without Christ is the ruin of multitudes.

'Nevertheless among the chief rulers also many believed on him; but because of the Pharisees they did not confess him, lest they should be put out of the synagogue: For they loved the praise of men more than the praise of God' (vv. 42, 43).

These men were convinced fully that Jesus is the Christ, the Son of God. They believed; but they did not believe. They had a faith about Christ, but no faith in Christ. Their heads were forced to acknowledge truth; but their hearts could not receive the love of the truth.

Reason, and intellect, and mind, and conscience forced them secretly to admit that no man could do the miracles Jesus of Nazareth did, unless God was with him, and that the preacher of Nazareth really was the Christ of God. But they would not confess him. They would not identify themselves with Christ, his gospel, and his people. They dared not face the ridicule and persecution, which confessing Christ might entail. Like the cowards they were, they held their peace and kept their convictions to themselves.

What was the reason for this cowardice? 'They loved the praise of men more than the praise of God'! What multitudes there are like these! What will it take to overcome this love of the praise of men? What will it take to melt a sinner's hard heart? What will it take to bring proud rebels to their knees before God? What will it take to make sinners 'believe in the light, that they may be children of the light'?

This I know, if God leaves us to ourselves, we will never walk in the Light, we will never trust the Lord Jesus, we will never obey the command of the gospel, which we are responsible to obey. The only way any sinner will ever believe on the Son of God, the only way any child of darkness will ever walk in the Light is if, like Isaiah of old, God Almighty gives that sinner the saving revelation of his grace and glory in Christ. O Lord God, force yourself upon poor, needy sinners. Show us your glory, and sweetly force us to walk in the Light of the knowledge of the glory of God shining in the face of Jesus Christ.

Chapter 22

'his commandment is life everlasting'

'Jesus cried and said, he that believeth on me, believeth not on me, but on him that sent me. And he that seeth me seeth him that sent me. I am come a light into the world, that whosoever believeth on me should not abide in darkness. And if any man hear my words, and believe not, I judge him not: for I came not to judge the world, but to save the world. He that rejecteth me, and receiveth not my words, hath one that judgeth him: the word that I have spoken, the same shall judge him in the last day. For I have not spoken of myself; but the Father which sent me, he gave me a commandment, what I should say, and what I should speak. And I know that his commandment is life everlasting: whatsoever I speak therefore, even as the Father said unto me, so I speak'(John 12:44-50).

He who is God is the King, your King, the King of the universe. His message is not a suggestion, or an offer, or even an opportunity. His message, God's word to you, is a command. 'And', the Lord Jesus declares, 'I know that his commandment is life everlasting'! I call your attention to seven things in our Saviour's declaration in this portion of holy scripture.

Faith in Christ is faith in God (v. 44). 'Jesus cried and said, he that believeth on me, believeth not on me, but on him that sent me'.

Faith in Christ is faith in God; and there is no faith in God except faith in his Son, the Lord Jesus Christ. Any other pretended faith in God is a damning delusion. He has no faith in God, who does not trust the Lord Jesus Christ as his only Lord and Saviour. Righteousness, atonement, salvation, and life are found only in Christ.

In this passage our Lord Jesus is describing, for the very last time, to the Jewish nation who he is and what he came into this world to do as the God-man Mediator. He is not talking about himself as God the Son, the second person of the holy trinity. Neither is he talking about himself merely as a man. Rather, he here speaks of himself as the God-man, Immanuel, our Mediator, Jehovah's righteous Servant.

'Jesus cried with a loud voice', speaking distinctly and clearly, that he might be heard, leaving the Jewish nation and people, the Pharisees, Sadducees, priests, and religious lawyers, without excuse. He cried with a loud voice, expressing both the bold earnestness and openness with which our Saviour preached to men. He spoke to be heard and understood. His words were so plain that they could not be mistaken.

'He that believeth on me, believeth not on me'. Obviously, these words are not to be understood in an absolute sense, for that would be a contradiction in terms. We who believe in Christ do believe in him personally; and it is right for us to believe in him. Christ is the object of all true faith. It is Christ who is set before us in the gospel. It is the Father's will and counsel that we believe in his Son. We believe on the Lord Jesus Christ as the sent one of the triune God. Thus, believing him, we believe God; and our faith in him is our assurance that we are born of God and taught of God (John 6:45; 1 John 2:22, 23; 1 John 4:2, 15; 5:1).

'He that believeth on me, believeth not on me, but on him that sent me.' If an ambassador is sent by an earthly ruler to a foreign court, anything done to him is done to the one he represents. An affront to the ambassador of a king is an affront to the king. So it is with the Lord Jesus, the God-man, as Jehovah's Servant. If we despise Christ, we despise God. If we receive Christ, we receive God. If we refuse to believe Christ, we make the triune God a liar. If you believe Christ, you believe the triune Jehovah.

The Lord Jesus Christ is the invisible God made visible (v. 45). 'And he that seeth me seeth him that sent me.'

What a wonderful statement! We may never fully realise it. Christ is the seeable God. God is not visible; but when we see the Christ, we see all of God. The invisible God made himself visible in Christ. 'For God was in Christ reconciling the world to himself'. 'In him dwelleth all the fulness of the Godhead bodily' (Colossians 2:9, 10).

But our Saviour is not talking about seeing him with the natural eye. Multitudes saw him physically, who never saw and never knew God. They saw nothing divine in him. When our Saviour talks about people seeing him, he is talking about seeing him with the God given eyes of the soul, the eyes of faith. To see him is to believe him. All who truly see Christ with an eye of faith, see his glory, as 'the glory of the only begotten of the Father, full of grace and truth', 'as the brightness of his Father's glory', having the fulness of the Godhead dwelling in him. Therefore, he declares, 'He that hath seen me hath seen the Father' (John 14:1, 6-10).

Faith in Christ is faith in the triune God. To see Christ is to see God; for Christ is God incarnate, God made visible and knowable to man, God in our nature.

Faith in Christ, true, saving faith in the Lord Jesus Christ sheds light upon everything. 'I am come a light into the world, that whosoever believeth on me should not abide in darkness' (v. 46).

Faith in Christ sheds light on everything concerning which light is desirable. We are made to understand things when we believe in Christ. Until we believe, we understand nothing. It is no surprise to me that those who believe not doubt everything and question everything. They have no light. They walk in darkness. I do not expect them to see. But believers walk in the Light. And the Light in which we walk is Christ, the Sun of Righteousness, the Light of faith. If you have no light, you cannot see. Faith in Christ sheds light on everything. 'He that followeth me shall not walk in darkness, but shall have the light of life' (John 8:12). Believers understand all things (Proverbs 28:5).

Other people are vexed and confused by the word of God, the ways of God, and the works of God; but God's saints understand all things. This is not a matter of supposition, but the plainest possible declaration of inspiration. 'They that seek the Lord understand all things.' The wise man tells us that, 'Evil men understand not judgment'. Then he asserts, 'but they that seek the Lord understand all things.' I do not suggest that religious people understand all things; but the Lord God himself asserts that his people, all who know him by the saving operations of his grace, all who are born of God and taught of God, understand all things (1 Corinthians 2:12-16; 2 Corinthians 4:6).

Darkness To Light

Like all others, God's elect, while in a state of unregeneracy and unbelief, are in darkness. When Christ shines in upon them and infuses the light of faith into them, they are no longer in darkness. The darkness is past and the true Light shines. In that true Light we see the light of the glory and grace of the triune God in Christ. In and by Christ we see the invisible realities of the world to come. Walking in the light of his grace, we no longer walk in the darkness of sin, ignorance, and unbelief; but walk in the light of truth, faith, and holiness, until the perfect day comes, when all the shadows of remaining darkness will flee away.

Believers understand that the origin of all things is God. We understand that the end of all things is the salvation of God's elect and the glory of his great name. God's people understand that the nature of all things here is temporal. Everything here in this sin-cursed earth is temporal and vanishing. Every relationship in this world is just temporal.

Most importantly, those who are taught of God understand all things spiritual. This is what the Apostle John tells us. 'But ye have an unction from the Holy One, and ye know all things' (1 John 2:20). All who are born of God and taught of God have the mind of Christ and understand all things vital and necessary to the saving of their souls.

All Things In Salvation

All upon whom the Lord God shines the Light of his grace understand how God saves sinners in, by, and through the Lord Jesus Christ. We rejoice to know that salvation is and only can be by the purpose of God in unconditional election, the effectual accomplished redemption of God's elect by Christ's precious blood, and the irresistible power and grace of God the Holy Ghost in regeneration and effectual calling.

Thanks For All Things

We understand that it is both the responsibility and the joy of believers to give thanks to God for all things. We are taught to give 'thanks always for all things unto God and the Father in the name of our Lord Jesus Christ' (Ephesians 5:20). In the context Paul is talking about walking in the Spirit and being filled with the Spirit. The Spirit-filled life is the life of a believer giving thanks to God. 'In everything give thanks: for this is the will of God in Christ Jesus concerning you' (1 Thessalonians 5:18). It is both our duty and our great privilege to give thanks to God always, and for all things. It glorifies God for us to praise him and give thanks to him. It breeds joy and peace in our own hearts and among our brethren for us to ever give thanks to God for all things.

Restitution Of All Things

We also understand that there is a day coming called 'the restitution of all things' (Acts 3:21). It is written, 'Repent ye therefore, and be converted, that your sins may be blotted out, when the times of refreshing shall come from the presence of the Lord; And he shall send Jesus Christ, which before was preached unto you: Whom the heaven must receive until the times of restitution of all things, which God hath spoken by the mouth of all his holy prophets since the world began.' In that great and glorious day, when all things are brought to their final end, when time shall be no more, all things will glorify our God! Everything that has been, is now, or shall hereafter be, all things, all events, all creatures, and all the actions of all creatures, whether good or evil, will praise him, and will prove to have been good. Everything, even you and I, will glorify the triune God, one way or another. We will either glorify his grace in Christ in our everlasting salvation; or, like Pharaoh, we will glorify his power and wrath in our everlasting destruction; but we will all glorify God.

Inherit All Things

In Revelation 21:7 we read, 'He that overcometh shall inherit all things; and I will be his God, and he shall be my son.' All true believers may rightfully sing, 'We shall overcome some day'! We shall at last, by the grace of God, completely overcome sin and all its consequences. We shall in the end overcome this world, all its lusts, and all its charms, by the power and grace of our God. By God's free grace in Christ, we shall overcome Satan, too.

Many years ago, when my doctors thought I was about to die, and I was fairly certain that they were right, I got a card from a friend that lifted my spirit to heaven itself. It was totally blank, except for a scripture reference. On the inside, my friend simply wrote the reference Romans 16:20. When I turned to it and read the text, my soul melted within me and leaped with joy in the realisation of the promise contained in that text. If you are a believer, this is God's word to you. 'And the God of peace shall bruise Satan under your feet shortly'! Then, we shall inherit all things, by the grace of God. We shall inherit all things with Christ, in Christ, and for Christ's sake.

End Of All Things

We who are taught of God also understand that 'the end of all things is at hand' (1 Peter 4:7). 'Behold, he cometh'! When our great and glorious Christ appears the second time, without sin, unto salvation, then the end of all things will come: the end of all our troubles, the end of all our struggles, the end of all our toils, the end of all our trials, the end of all our temptations, the end of all our sorrows, the end of all our sins!

Done All Things Well

God's saints all understand this, too. The Lord our God has done all things well! When the end of my days on this earth comes, when I look over my life's finished story, I am confident this will be my final word then. And when the end of all things has come, and time shall be no more, this will be the final word of all history, and of all rational creatures, 'He hath done all things well' (Mark 7:37). This I declare now; and this I will declare in that great day, when time shall be no more. 'He hath done all things well' with me and mine. 'He hath done all things well' with his church. 'He hath done all things well' with his world. 'He hath done all things well' with you and yours.

This is not the day of judgment, but the day of grace (v. 47). 'And if any man hear my words, and believe not, I judge him not: for I came not to judge the world, but to save the world.'

'If any man hear my words and believe not'. Men may hear the gospel of Christ, and not understand it. They may understand it literally and grammatically, but understand nothing spiritually and experimentally. If that is the case, they do not believe, but rather reject and deny the gospel. Though faith comes by hearing, not all who hear are given faith (Hebrews 2:1-3).

'If any man hear my words and believe not, I judge him not: for I came not to judge the world, but to save the world.' At his first coming, the Lord Jesus did not appear as a judge, but as a Saviour. He did not accuse, condemn, or judge men, but would leave them to another day, when righteous judgment shall take place.

This present dispensation is not the time of judgment. The Lord leaves the reprobate to themselves. He has not yet come to judge them. There is a second coming, a day of judgment, when he will be both Judge and Witness, and Condemner, of those who have rejected him; but this present gospel age is the day of grace (Ezekiel 33:11; Micah 7:18). 'behold, now is the accepted time, behold, now is the day of salvation.'

There is a day of judgment appointed by God. 'He that rejecteth me, and receiveth not my words, hath one that judgeth him: the word that I have spoken, the same shall judge him in the last day' (v. 48).

The gospel itself will judge the wicked at the last day. We know that the Lord Jesus Christ shall judge the world, as Paul said, 'according to my gospel'. Those who are against the gospel involve themselves in the most solemn condemnation. The greatest guilt is theirs; and the greatest punishment shall be theirs! The heathen, who perish without the gospel, shall be damned by the witnesses of creation and nature, by the witness of the law written upon their own hearts and consciences. Those who had only the revelation of the Mosaic law shall be judged and damned by the witness of creation, conscience, and the law written upon tables of stone. But those who perish under the sound of the gospel shall have the greater condemnation, being damned by the witness of creation, conscience, law, and the gospel they choose to despise!

They have been favoured with the revelation of the gospel, but have rejected and denied it. The gospel they despise will judge them at the last day. The Judge will act by its declaration, and proceed, as it stands in Mark 16:16. 'He that believeth and is baptised shall be saved; but he that believeth not shall be damned.' The gospel they have heard and despised will rise up in judgment against them. It will be their souls' relentless tormenter in hell forever!

For those who hear the gospel, neutrality is impossible. Either we believe on Christ, trusting him for all righteousness, grace, atonement, salvation, sanctification, acceptance with God, and everlasting life, or we reject him. There is no middle ground. We either receive his words and trust him, or we trust in ourselves and despise him. We either enter in by Christ the Door, or we are still trying to come to God another way. Only the blood of Christ can satisfy divine justice. Only the obedience of Christ can meet the demands of God for righteousness. Only the holy Christ can make sinners holy before God.

But if any do not believe, Christ is not the reason they are under condemnation. He said, 'I came not to judge the world, but to save the world' (John 3:17, 18). Every sinner was already condemned when Christ came. Those who believe not were condemned before they ever began to hear the word of truth. Man's wilful rejection of the gospel and of Christ is but the outward display of his inward heart enmity toward God (John 3: 19, 20).

All men do what their nature determines they will do. The natural man is conceived with an evil nature and does evil. He hates Christ the Light and will not come to Christ the Light, for he does not want his deeds, his very being, reproved as being evil. Confusion and shame will not allow him to admit that he is a sinner. The same ignorance convinces him he is himself righteous, or has something God will accept and receive. Yet, deep down inside he knows, even in his abominable self-righteousness, it is a refuge of lies. His bed is too short; he cannot rest. His covering is too narrow; he cannot cover himself. He has no ease in his soul, no comfort in his heart, no peace with God. Still, he works to make himself better. But that is his condemnation: he loves darkness and hates light. He loves evil and hates Christ the Light. What an awful condition to be in!

'But he that doeth truth cometh to the light, that his deeds may be made manifest, that they are wrought in God' (John 3:21). Be sure you understand our Lord's words. The heaven-born soul is regenerated, given a new nature, born from Christ the incorruptible Seed, by God the Holy Spirit. That new-born soul is one with Christ the Truth. Indeed, that new man created in you is 'Christ in you, ... the new Man, created in righteousness and true holiness'. Those born of God do truth by coming to Christ the Light. The chosen, redeemed sinner is given faith in Christ and repentance toward God. The conscience is purged. The prisoner is set free. The adopted child is made to rejoice in Christ. The forgiven soul is made to be ashamed of fig-leaf righteousness. The believing soul is confidently assured that all that God requires of him Christ is for him and he is in Christ (2 Corinthians 5:19-21; Galatians 2:20; Romans 8:1-4).

In that great and terrible day of judgment the Lord Jesus Christ, the God-man Mediator, will be either your everlasting Executioner or your everlasting Saviour (v. 49). 'For I have not spoken of myself; but the Father which sent me, he gave me a commandment, what I should say, and what I should speak'.

Here is the divine authority of the gospel. Our Lord Jesus, as the God-man Mediator, did only that which he was commanded to do and spoke only that which he was commanded to speak as our Covenant Surety, as Jehovah's own

Fellow, and the Servant of the Lord. Christ, as a man, as our Mediator, had his mission and commission, his instructions and commandments from his Father to preach the gospel unto men and gather his sheep into the fold of grace (John 10:16-18). He was appointed to the work from eternity. He agreed to accomplish all the work as our Surety. He was anointed for it by the Holy Ghost. He was prepared for the work in the incarnation. He finished the work at Calvary. And he was accepted into heaven as our Forerunner, and rewarded for his obedience, when he ascended on high.

In the light of these things, I urge you to obey God's commandment, I urge you to believe on the Lord Jesus Christ, because God's commandment is life everlasting (v. 50). 'And I know that his commandment is life everlasting: whatsoever I speak therefore, even as the Father said unto me, so I speak.'

God's commandment is that we believe on the Lord Jesus Christ (1 John 3:23, 24; John 6:28, 29; Romans 3:31; Ezekiel 33:14-16, 19). The only way any sinner can do what is 'lawful and right' is by offering God what he requires, what he only can give Christ. The only way we can restore the pledge, give back what we took away, the only way a sinner can make restitution to God is by faith in Christ, by bringing Christ to God in the hands of faith.

God's commandment is the gospel; and the gospel of Christ is life. It is the ministration of life, the means by which God gives life to dead sinners (1 Peter 1:23-25), the power of God unto salvation (Romans 1:16; 1 Corinthians 1:18). When the gospel comes home to the chosen, redeemed sinner in the mighty power of God the Holy Spirit, it gives life.

How will my heart endure
The terrors of that day
When earth and Heav'n before His face
Astonished shrink away?

But 'ere that trumpet shakes
The mansions of the dead,
Hark from the Gospel's cheering sound
What joyful tidings spread:

Ye sinners, seek His grace
Whose wrath ye cannot bear;
Fly to the shelter of His cross
And find salvation there.

Philip Doddridge

Chapter 23

Loved To Perfection

'Now before the feast of the passover, when Jesus knew that his hour was come that he should depart out of this world unto the Father, having loved his own which were in the world, he loved them unto the end' (John 13:1).

The Lord Jesus was on his way to Calvary, where he must be made sin for us. There, upon the cursed tree, 'bearing our sins in his own body on the tree', he must suffer and die as the cursed thing, the thing specifically cursed of God. In just a few hours, the holy Lamb of God must go through Gethsemane's darkness. There he would anticipate being made sin, being forsaken by his Father in those three hours of darkness. In Gethsemane, he will begin to drink the bitter cup. His very heart crushed within him, he will sweat great drops of blood, falling to the ground. In less than twenty-four hours, those very hands that washed the disciples' feet would be nailed to the cross, and he who spoke so tenderly to his little band of followers would be in his death agonies, suffering all the horror of hell, all the horror of God's infuriated wrath in the room and stead of his people.

What was on his mind? What were his thoughts? It is important to know what is on a man's heart when he comes to the end of his life, when he knows he is about to leave this world. Someone long ago wrote, 'The ruling passion is strong in death.' The ruling passion of a person's life is strong in death, be that passion hypocrisy or sincerity, whether it be selfish or magnanimous, 'the ruling passion is strong in death.' As men are leaving this world, they usually reveal what is the chief, ruling passion by which they have lived.

That was certainly the case with our blessed Saviour. He had almost reached the end of his earthly life. He now came to a time of great trouble and agony of heart and soul. He was about to endure the great and terrible death of the cross, by which he would purchase and obtain eternal redemption for all God's elect. What was uppermost in his mind? What filled his heart? What did he think of his disciples in that hour, when he had so many things to occupy his mind? What thoughts occupied his heart? What moved his soul? These questions are answered in the most amazing way imaginable in John 13:1.

'Now before the feast of the passover, when Jesus knew that his hour was come that he should depart out of this world unto the Father, having loved his own which were in the world, he loved them unto the end.'

The Saviour's love burned as brightly at the Passover Supper as it had ever burned before. Behold how he loved his disciples! Even at the end of his life he still loved them. 'Having loved his own which were in the world, he loved them unto the end.' I want to do the best I can to expound this marvellous revelation of God line by line and word by word. I do not want to miss, or lightly pass over anything in this text that is bursting with life.

Before The Passover

First, John connects the Saviour's love for his own with the Passover. 'Now before the feast of passover ...' The feast of passover was the annual celebration of redemption, the celebration of God redeeming Israel out of Egyptian bondage. The feast was instituted by God himself. The great day of the feast, the highest holy day in Israel, was the Day of Atonement, when the paschal lamb was slain and its blood sprinkled upon the mercy-seat by God's high priest.

But God's purpose in giving that commemorative celebration was much, much more than a mere reminder of what he had done. The whole feast was, when kept by believing men and women, a blessed celebration of faith, anticipating what he would do. It was a picture of Christ our Passover being sacrificed for us.

> Paschal Lamb, by God appointed,
> All our sins were on Thee laid;
> By almighty love anointed,
> Thou hast full atonement made.
> All Thy people are forgiven
> Through the virtue of Thy blood;
> Opened is the gate of heaven,
> Peace is made for us with God.

Saviour, hail! Enthroned in glory,
There forever to abide;
All the heavenly hosts adore Thee,
Seated at Thy Father's side;
Worship, honour, power, and blessing,
Thou art worthy to receive;
Loudest praises, without ceasing,
Meet it is for us to give.

John Bakewell

The Lord Jesus had his mind fixed upon the purpose for which he had come into the world. He came here to give his life a ransom for many, that we might receive the forgiveness of sin in him.

Jesus Knew

Second, we are told that the Lord Jesus knew he was about to depart out of this world. 'Now before the feast of the passover, when Jesus knew that his hour was come that he should depart out of this world unto the Father …' Oh, what a change was now coming over our dear Redeemer! Though it is stated in the most tender terms possible, the Spirit of God here tells us that our Lord Jesus knew he was about to die. He had come to die. He knew he must to die. He knew all he must suffer in dying. Yet, such is the fulness of his love that even as he anticipated the wormwood and the gall, his heart was upon his people. 'Having loved his own which were in the world, he loved them unto the end'! He set his face like a flint to go to Jerusalem; but there was no flint in his heart.

The Lord Jesus undertook the work of our redemption, as our covenant Surety before he made the worlds. He must go through with it. Death itself could not change his love. Truly, his 'love is strong as death' (Song of Solomon 8:6) and stronger than death. His love for us was stronger than that death of deaths, which he deigned to die that he might make us live. This was his great 'hour' of trial; but he was true to 'his own' even in this dreadful hour. He was about to die; but he still loved 'his own'.

The blessed Saviour was about to depart out of this world, to go away from his disciples. Soon, they would see him no more. Soon, they would hear his voice no more. It may be true that 'absence makes the heart grow fonder' but men often forget those they profess to love when they are separated from them. Many hearts are shamefully, but completely, dependent on sight. But it is not so with Christ. All the distance between earth and heaven was soon to intervene between our Lord and his disciples; yet he loved them; and he loves them still.

No distance makes any difference between him and 'his own'. 'Having loved his own which were in the world, he loved them unto the end.'

He was going to the Father. None of us have the slightest idea what that involved. I will not attempt to describe the heavenly splendours of his throne, the glories which his redeemed delight to lay at his feet, the songs which angels continually sing in his presence. His glory, now that he has returned to his Father, is glory no mortal heart can imagine, and no mortal mind can conceive.

Now though He reigns exalted high,
His love is still as great;
Well He remembers Calvary,
Nor lets His saints forget.

Isaac Watts

I cannot describe the wondrous experiences of our Lord Jesus, from life to death, from death to resurrection, from resurrection to ascension, from ascension to the glories of his Father's throne. But all those changes made no change in him, none of them. 'Having loved his own which were in the world, he loved them unto the end.'

'having loved'

Third, we are given a full description of how the Lord Jesus had loved his own up to this point in time: 'having loved his own'. How much can be done with one stroke of a pen! With those four words John gives us the whole history of Christ's dealings with his disciples, 'having loved his own'.

Remember, that is how he began with them; and that is how he began with us. They were poor and insignificant; but he loved them. He showed his love for them by calling them to be his own. That love wrought effectually upon their hearts, and made them obedient to his call. He began his relationship with them by loving them. The Lord Jesus loved my soul out of the pit. I do not know a better way to describe conversion and salvation than that. Do you? Christ has loved us out of the pit! The love of God loves us up out of the pit, and loves us to Christ. Thus Christ loved his people from the beginning, with an everlasting love, and proves his love by drawing them to himself; and the cords he uses to draw them to himself are the bands of his own love for them.

Having begun by loving them, he taught them. And all his teaching was love, for they were, like you and me, very slow learners, quick to forget and slow to remember. Yet, he went on teaching them because he loved them. Had he not loved them, he would not have tolerated them. Did he not love us, he would soon cast us aside, and looked for a people more worthy.

'Have I been so long time with you, and yet hast thou not known me, Philip?' What massive love there is in that question! So it was when he was dealing with Thomas. In his tenderness he submitted without question to the doubting disciple's test. He said to him, 'Reach hither thy finger, and behold my hands; and reach hither thy hand, and thrust it into my side: and be not faithless, but believing.' All his teaching, all his doctrine dripped with mercy, love, and grace. All his lessons were lessons of love.

The Lord kept on loving his disciples, though they were sinners still and far from being perfect disciples. What weaknesses and infirmities they had, all of them! When in the tempest, they were fearful and suspected the Lord Jesus of caring nothing for them. Yet, he loved them. When he told them of his certain death and resurrection, they understood not the words that he spoke. Yet, he loved them still. When he looked into the future and saw they all would soon be cowardly and faithless, he loved them still. He said, 'All ye shall be offended because of me this night' and so it came to pass, for 'they all forsook him'. He told Peter he would deny him thrice; and so it came to pass. Yet, 'Having loved his own which were in the world, he loved them unto the end'!

In spite of all their weaknesses, sins, failures, rebellions, inconsistencies, and ignorance, the Lord Jesus kept on loving them! He had made up his mind to love them, and he never ceased to love them as long as he was with them; and he has gone on loving them ever since. When he was about to depart out of the world unto the Father, they still needed to have their feet washed; and he still loved them. He loved them enough to stoop before each one and wash their feet! All the infirmities, the imperfections, the carnality, the dullness, the unbelief, and the hardness of their hearts, which he saw in them did not cause his love for them to cool or diminish in the least. 'Having loved his own which were in the world, he loved them unto the end.'

That sums it all up. There was never the slightest touch of hate, the slightest hint of anger, the least sign of weariness, or the slightest lukewarmness in the Saviour's love. It was always just the same. 'Having loved his own which were in the world, he loved them unto the end.'

That is the love of Christ to his chosen; and that is the love of Christ to me! I never knew, I never heard of such a lover as he is. I never dreamed he could be such a lover as he has been and is to me. Oh, how I have vexed and grieved his gracious heart! But never, never, never once have I found anything from him but love! 'Having loved his own'. That expression sums up the whole of Christ's conduct towards his chosen people. It reveals every feature of his character. There it is, all of it. You may use a microscope, and look as long as you like, but you will find that it is all there. 'Having loved his own'.

'his own'

Fourth, John identifies the objects of the Saviour's love as 'his own'. That is a very brief description; but it is magnificent and full. 'Having loved his own which were in the world, he loved them unto the end.' Do you know how they came to be 'his own'?

He chose them as his own before the worlds were made. As long as the scripture stands, the doctrine of election can never be eradicated from it. Before the day-star knew its place, or planets ran their rounds, Christ had made his choice, and, having made it, he stood to it. He chose them for his love; and he loved them for his choice.

Having loved them and having chosen them, he espoused them unto himself. 'They shall be mine', said he; 'I will be married to them, I will be bone of their bone, and flesh of their flesh'. Therefore, in the fulness of time, he came here, made one with our humanity, that he might be seen to be a true Husband to 'his own', by his own choice, espoused to him from everlasting!

They were 'his own' by divine gift, too. His Father gave them to him. The Father committed them into his hands. 'Thine they were', said the Saviour, 'and thou gavest them me'. The Father loved the Son and committed all things into his hands; but he made a special committal of his own chosen people. He gave them to him, and entered with him into suretyship engagements on their behalf, that as they were his sheep, committed to his charge, he would deliver them up into the heavenly fold; and not one of them would be torn by the wolf, or die of the frost or the heat, but that all would pass again under the rod of him who counts the sheep. He has sworn, 'I will cause you to pass under the rod, and I will bring you into the bond of the covenant' (Ezekiel 20:37).

The great Shepherd of the sheep will take care of the whole flock that was entrusted to his care. He will not lose one of his sheep. In the last day he will say, 'Father, here I am, and the children that you gave me; of all that you gave me I have lost none.' Thus, they are 'his own' by his own choice, 'his own' by espousal, and 'his own' by his Father's gift.

And all the Lord Jesus calls 'his own' are his by a wondrous purchase, by the purchase of his own life's blood. He looked upon their redemption as being already accomplished, for in his prayer he said to his Father, 'I have finished the work which thou gavest me to do'. Truly, the work was finished from the foundation of the world; and in just another twenty-four hours, our blessed Lord Jesus would cry, 'It is finished'! Think often my brother, my sister, how dearly bought you are. Think that you belong to Christ, you are numbered among 'his own' by the price of his own blood. 'Ye are not your own; ye are bought with a price'. Oh, what a price he paid!

He loved us better than he loved himself. He paid the purchase price for us that was demanded by the law and justice of the triune Jehovah, the price required that we might be made the righteousness of God in him. Well may he call us 'his own' when it cost him so much to redeem us.

And we have become 'his own' by his conquest of his love. He called his disciples by his grace. He drew each one of them by cords of love. And they ran after him. That is just the way it is with you and me, with all who are his. You remember when he drew you; do you not? Can you ever forget when, at last, you yielded to the power of those bands of love, those cords of a man? How gladly we now sing,

O happy day, that fixed my choice
On Thee, my Saviour and my God!
Well may this glowing heart rejoice,
And tell its raptures all abroad.

O happy bond, that seals my vows
To Him who merits all my love!
Let cheerful anthems fill His house,
While to that sacred shrine I move.

'Tis done: the great transaction's done!
I am the Lord's and He is mine;
He drew me, and I followed on;
Charmed to confess the voice divine.

Now rest, my long divided heart,
Fixed on this blissful centre, rest.
Here have I found a nobler part;
Here heavenly pleasures fill my breast.

High heaven, that heard the solemn vow,
That vow renewed shall daily hear,
Till in life's latest hour I bow
And bless in death a bond so dear.

Phillip Doddridge

We are 'his own' because of the force of his irresistible love. His love has conquered our hearts. 'We love him because he first loved us'! There is no greater joy to our souls than the knowledge that we belong to Christ, that we are 'his own'. The fact that we truly are Christ's is the fountain of innumerable pleasures and blessings. The Son of God calls us 'his own', his own sheep, his own disciples, his own friends, his own brethren, the members of his own body. What a title for such things as we are to wear, 'his own'! We are HIS OWN! He owns us. He calls us 'his own'. With those two magnificent words, he distinguishes us from the rest of mankind, and sets us apart unto himself. 'My name shall be named on them', he says, 'his own'. Surely, that is the highest honour that can be put upon us even in the last great day. 'They shall be mine, saith the LORD of hosts, in that day when I make up my jewels.'

Oh, the wondrous sovereignty of divine love! Oh, the wondrous mystery of it! Oh, the wondrous majesty of it! Loved and chosen! Loved and redeemed! Loved and called! Loved and kept! 'Having loved his own which were in the world, he loved them unto the end.'

'which were in the world'

Fifth, the Spirit of God reminds us where 'his own' are who are loved by the Lord Jesus. 'Having loved his own which were in the world'. There is something wondrous about this declaration, 'which were in the world'. As a pastor, maintained in my livelihood by the generosity of God's saints, I live a very secluded life. I am very seldom confronted with the people among whom you live every day. You live in the midst of heathendom. The sooner we believe that terrible truth the better, because it is really so; and the Church of God in the world is nothing but a travelling tent in the midst of a world that lives in wickedness. We are 'in the world'. Like Lot was in Sodom, you are in the world, vexed day by day in your righteous soul with all that is paraded before you every hour, in every place. To be 'in the world' is to be in the midst of unrestrained idolatry, abounding wickedness, and relentless blasphemy.

Being in the world, these disciples soon began to be persecuted. They were stoned, imprisoned, and dragged into the amphitheatre to be torn of lions. Yet, 'having loved his own which were in the world, he loved them unto the end.' 'Who shall separate us from the love of Christ? shall tribulation, or distress, or persecution, or famine, or nakedness, or peril, or sword? As it is written, For thy sake we are killed all the day long; we are accounted as sheep for the slaughter. Nay, in all these things we are more than conquerors through him that loved us. For I am persuaded, that neither death, nor life, nor angels, nor principalities, nor powers, nor things present, nor things to come, nor height, nor depth, nor any other creature, shall be able to separate us from the love of God, which is in Christ Jesus our Lord.'

In the world we are tempted. In the world we are afflicted. In the world we suffer. In the world we are in pain. In the world we sin. In the world we get sick. In the world we are bereaved. In the world we die. We have losses and crosses because we are 'in the world'. God's curse still rests upon the earth, 'Thorns also and thistles shall it bring forth to thee'. Nothing else! You may do what you like with it; but you cannot make it stop bringing forth thorns and thistles. They will continue to spring up as surely as the dust will return to the dust from whence it came. Yet, we read that the Lord Jesus, 'having loved his own which were in the world, he loved them unto the end.' All the things we experience in the world come upon us and are brought to pass by him who loved us from everlasting, loved us at Calvary, and loves us now.

'to the end'

Here is the sixth thing revealed in our text. Our Saviour loves his own who are in the world unto the end. 'Having loved his own which were in the world, he loved them unto the end.' He who loved us from everlasting will love us always. 'He loved them unto the end.' What does that sentence mean? Without question, it must be asserted that the Lord Jesus loved his own unto the end of his obedience, unto the end of the law's demands, unto the end of the curse, unto the end of their transgressions, and unto the end of God's wrath.

But the text specifically means that his love is constant, immutable, and unending. The Hebrew phrase, 'his mercy endureth forever', might be rendered, 'his mercy endureth to the end'. His mercy endures to the end which has no end, for there never will be an end to his mercy; and his love is continual, everlasting love; it will never come to an end. Having loved them while he was in the world with them, he loves them right straight on, and always will love them when time shall be no more.

The words of our text might be translated, 'having loved his own which were in the world, he loved them unto the uttermost.' He loves his people to the utmost stretch of love. He loves us to the utmost length of our need. He loves us without measure.

The sentence might also be rendered, 'He loved them to perfection.' 'Having loved his own which were in the world, he loved them unto perfection.' The Lord Jesus loves us perfectly. The knowledge of his perfect love casts out all fear. And the sure and certain result of his love is the everlasting, glorious perfection of all 'his own'. Yes, he loves us unto perfection (Ephesians 5:25-27; Jude 24, 25). 'Keep yourselves in the love of God, looking for the mercy of our Lord Jesus Christ unto eternal life' (Jude 21).

Chapter 24

Dark Providences Cleared In Due Time

'Now before the feast of the passover, when Jesus knew that his hour was come that he should depart out of this world unto the Father, having loved his own which were in the world, he loved them unto the end. And supper being ended, the devil having now put into the heart of Judas Iscariot, Simon's son, to betray him; Jesus knowing that the Father had given all things into his hands, and that he was come from God, and went to God; he riseth from supper, and laid aside his garments; and took a towel, and girded himself. After that he poureth water into a bason, and began to wash the disciples' feet, and to wipe them with the towel wherewith he was girded. Then cometh he to Simon Peter: and Peter saith unto him, Lord, dost thou wash my feet? Jesus answered and said unto him, What I do thou knowest not now; but thou shalt know hereafter. Peter saith unto him, Thou shalt never wash my feet. Jesus answered him, If I wash thee not, thou hast no part with me. Simon Peter saith unto him, Lord, not my feet only, but also my hands and my head. Jesus saith to him, he that is washed needeth not save to wash his feet, but is clean every whit: and ye are clean, but not all. For he knew who should betray him; therefore said he, Ye are not all clean. So after he had washed their feet, and had taken his garments, and was set down again, he said unto them, Know ye what I have done to you? Ye call me Master and Lord: and ye say well; for so I am. If I then, your Lord and Master, have washed your feet; ye also ought to wash one another's feet. For I have given you an example, that ye should do as I have done to you. Verily, verily, I say unto you, The servant is not greater than his lord; neither he that is sent greater than he that sent him. If ye know these things, happy are ye if ye do them. I speak not of you all: I know whom I have chosen: but that the scripture may be fulfilled, he that eateth bread with me hath lifted up his heel against me. Now I tell you before it come, that, when it is come to pass, ye may believe that I am he. Verily, verily, I say unto you, he that receiveth whomsoever I send receiveth me; and he that receiveth me receiveth him that sent me' (John 13:1-20).

How many times have you seen or known some terribly painful, traumatic, almost devastating thing, and thought to yourself, 'What good can come of this? How is this going to work for good? How will this benefit anyone? Can this be honouring to God?'

We know that our heavenly Father is too wise to err, too strong to fail, and too good to do wrong. Yet, when tragedies come close to home, we cannot help asking, 'Why did this thing happen?' We may not openly say it, but we ask in frustration, perhaps in anger or resentment, 'God, what are you doing?'

Here in John 13 God the Holy Spirit has preserved by divine inspiration a word from our dear Saviour that should help to prepare for such times. As the Lord Jesus began to wash his disciples' feet, Peter was confused by the Master's conduct, and said to him in verse 6, 'Lord, Dost thou wash my feet?' Then, in verse 7, 'Jesus answered and said unto him, What I do thou knowest not now; but thou shalt know hereafter.'

When Jacob awoke from his dream, he said, 'Surely the Lord is in this place; and I knew it not' (Genesis 28:16). When Samson's strength was gone, we are told, 'He wist not that the Lord was departed from him' (Judges 16:20). What is said of our Saviour's presence and absence, his goings and comings, may also be said of his doings. 'What I do', he says, 'thou knowest not now; but thou shalt know hereafter.'

Specifically this word from our Saviour in John 13:7, 'What I do thou knowest not now; but thou shalt know hereafter', refers to our Lord's act of washing his disciples' feet. But it is a statement that is clearly applicable to God's providence. The design or intention of God's works of providence are often, if not usually, hidden from his people; but they shall be revealed in due time.

Immutable Love

First, we see that the love of Christ for us is immutable and incessant. 'Now before the feast of the passover, when Jesus knew that his hour was come that he should depart out of this world unto the Father, having loved his own which were in the world, he loved them unto the end' (v. 1). The love of Christ for his elect is a love surpassing thought. There is nothing like it in this world below. The narrow, self-centred thoughts, and words, and deeds of humanity cannot comprehend it. Our Saviour knew that his disciples would all soon forsake him. Yet, he loved them to the end. His love for us is from everlasting (Jeremiah 31:3). His love for us is for everlasting (Romans 8:39). In matchless, free love the Lord Jesus Christ delights to receive sinners (Luke 15:2). So great, so free, so immutable is the love of Christ for our souls that having embraced us in his arms from everlasting, he will never reject us or cast us away for any reason (John 6:37).

God's Absolute Dominion

Second, learn this, God's dominion over all things is absolute. Even the most base, vile, and despicable acts of reprobate men and women are under the absolute rule of our God and heavenly Father (vv. 2, 3). Even the work of Satan himself is under the rule and control of our God and Saviour (Psalms 76:10; Proverbs 16:4). Yes, our heavenly Father wisely and sovereignly uses his enemies and ours, contrary to their will, to do that which will advance his cause, as when the Philistines were constrained to send the ark of God back to Israel (1 Samuel 5:1-7:17). Ralph Erskine rightly observed, 'He employs the wicked themselves to carry on his work, and make their wicked designs to contribute to advancement of his holy and glorious design; as he did make the treason of Judas, the sentence of Pilate, the malice of the Jews, to contribute for the work of redemption'.

Judas's Brazen Hypocrisy

Third, nothing in all the world is more corrupt or more callous than the heart of a hypocrite. There sat Judas at the table with the Son of God and his disciples. But he had already struck his deal with the Jew's priests to betray the Saviour (v. 2). What brazen hypocrisy!

Judas stands as a beacon to warn us of what deep corruption may be found in the hearts of very religious people. He shows us how far a man may go in religion and yet be rotten at heart. He shows us how much a person may know about the things of God and yet not know God. He shows us how high one may rise in the eyes of men and in religious office and yet be unconverted. Judas shows us how confident a person may be that he is saved, even when he is on the brink of hell!

We must not be surprised, overwhelmed, or overly disturbed when we find such hypocrites among God's saints. Not all who are washed in the waters of baptism have been washed in the blood of Christ (v. 10). 'They are not all Israel which are of Israel' (Romans 9:6).

'Jesus saith to him, he that is washed needeth not save to wash his feet, but is clean every whit: and ye are clean, but not all' (John 13:10).

'Examine yourselves, whether ye be in the faith; prove your own selves. Know ye not your own selves, how that Jesus Christ is in you, except ye be reprobates?' (2 Corinthians 13:5).

'Wherefore the rather, brethren, give diligence to make your calling and election sure: for if ye do these things, ye shall never fall' (2 Peter 1:10).

Blood Washed

Fourth, we are reminded again that we must be washed in the blood of Christ. The only way we can be saved is by being washed in the blood of Christ. The only saved sinner is the blood-washed sinner (vv. 8-10).

'Peter saith unto him, Thou shalt never wash my feet. Jesus answered him, If I wash thee not, thou hast no part with me. Simon Peter saith unto him, Lord, not my feet only, but also my hands and my head. Jesus saith to him, he that is washed needeth not save to wash his feet, but is clean every whit: and ye are clean, but not all.'

What can wash away my sins?
Nothing but the blood of Jesus!
What can make me whole again?
Nothing but the blood of Jesus!
Oh, precious is the flow
That makes me white as snow!
No other fount I know
Nothing but the blood of Jesus!

Robert Lowry

'In that day there shall be a fountain opened to the house of David and to the inhabitants of Jerusalem for sin and for uncleanness' (Zechariah 13:1).

'Forasmuch as ye know that ye were not redeemed with corruptible things, as silver and gold, from your vain conversation received by tradition from your fathers; But with the precious blood of Christ, as of a lamb without blemish and without spot: Who verily was foreordained before the foundation of the world, but was manifest in these last times for you, Who by him do believe in God, that raised him up from the dead, and gave him glory; that your faith and hope might be in God' (1 Peter 1:18-21).

'But if we walk in the light, as he is in the light, we have fellowship one with another, and the blood of Jesus Christ his Son cleanseth us from all sin ... If we confess our sins, he is faithful and just to forgive us our sins, and to cleanse us from all unrighteousness' (1 John 1:7-9).

We cannot be saved unless Christ has washed us in his blood (1 Corinthians 6:9-11). We must be washed in the blood judicially. That took place for all God's elect when the Lord Jesus Christ accomplished our redemption and obtained eternal redemption for us at Calvary (Hebrews 1:3). And we must be washed in the Saviour's blood experimentally. That takes place in regeneration and effectual calling, when God the Holy Spirit applies the cleansing blood to our hearts, giving us faith in Christ, purging our consciences of guilt before God, bringing life and immortality to light by the gospel (Titus 3:5; Hebrews 9:14). Even those who are cleansed and forgiven need a daily application to the blood of Christ for daily pardon. 'The blood of Jesus Christ his Son cleanseth us from all sin' (1 John 1:7, 9).

Humility Exemplified

Fifth, in this passage of scripture the Lord Jesus gives us a blessed example of genuine humility and love (vv. 5-17).

'After that he poureth water into a bason, and began to wash the disciples' feet, and to wipe them with the towel wherewith he was girded. Then cometh he to Simon Peter: and Peter saith unto him, Lord, dost thou wash my feet? Jesus answered and said unto him, What I do thou knowest not now; but thou shalt know hereafter. Peter saith unto him, Thou shalt never wash my feet. Jesus answered him, If I wash thee not, thou hast no part with me. Simon Peter saith unto him, Lord, not my feet only, but also my hands and my head. Jesus saith to him, he that is washed needeth not save to wash his feet, but is clean every whit: and ye are clean, but not all. For he knew who should betray him; therefore said he, Ye are not all clean. So after he had washed their feet, and had taken his garments, and was set down again, he said unto them, Know ye what I have done to you? Ye call me Master and Lord: and ye say well; for so I am. If I then, your Lord and Master, have washed your feet; ye also ought to wash one another's feet. For I have given you an example, that ye should do as I have done to you. Verily, verily, I say unto you, The servant is not greater than his lord; neither he that is sent greater than he that sent him. If ye know these things, happy are ye if ye do them.'

True humility and love willingly condescends to do whatever is needed to meet the needs of those who are the objects of our love. Though it is apparent that our Saviour washed Judas's feet, too, the message is in what he did for his disciples. The Son of God stooped to wash his disciples' feet, and he still does! When he shows us the foulness of our feet (our sin), and then graciously causes us to dip our feet in the fountain of his blood (Zechariah 13:1), and when he enables us with tears of repentance to wash and kiss his feet (Luke 7:38; Ezekiel 16:63), our dear Saviour still washes his disciples' feet (1 John 1:9; 2:1, 2). William Cowper wrote,

The dying thief rejoiced to see
That fountain in his day;
And there may I, though vile as he,
Wash all my sins away!

This self-denying, loving service is our responsibility to one another in this world (vv. 14, 15). In all things, Christ's example is our rule of life (1 John 3:16, 17). And all who follow our Lord's example find happiness and satisfaction in doing so. 'If ye know these things, happy are ye if ye do them' (v. 17). Nothing brings greater joy to devoted saints than the privilege and grace of obedience to Christ and usefulness to his people.

Providence Cleared

Sixth, all the dark mysteries and painful experiences of God's providence will be cleared up for God's saints in God's time. 'Jesus answered and said unto him, What I do thou knowest not now; but thou shalt know hereafter' (v. 7).

Jacob lamented, 'All these things are against me'! But before the Lord took him out of this world, the old saint learned better and said, 'God fed me all my life long. The Angel of the LORD redeemed me from all evil.' Joseph must have been horribly confused by all his woes. But before he left this world he understood that he was in the place of God. When Moses first came to deliver Israel out of Egypt, the Egyptians only increased their torment. But in the end Israel sang God's praise for all his goodness, triumphing over Pharaoh at the Red Sea, and thoroughly spoiling the Egyptians. Haman erected gallows for Mordecai; but it was Haman who was hanged upon them, and Mordecai was exalted. How confusing it must have been for Paul to be imprisoned at Philippi; but how he must have rejoiced when he baptised his jailor! The shipwreck that landed them upon the island of Melita, the bitter cold, and the bite of the asp all must have appeared to be acts of divine disfavour; but they were all acts of great mercy, opening the way for the salvation of a barbarian chieftain and many others. Truly, 'thy way, O God, is in the sanctuary; thy way is in the seas, thy paths in the great waters, and thy footsteps are not known' (Psalms 77:13, 19). 'Thy righteousness is like the great mountains; thy judgments are a great deep' (Psalms 36:6). 'The works of the Lord are great; sought out of all them that have pleasure therein' (Psalms 111:2).

Sometimes God's providence appears to contradict his promises (Exodus 5:21-23). Sometimes God's acts of mercy and grace in providence look and feel like acts of wrath and judgment. Sometimes God appears to be favourable to the wicked and indifferent, at best, to the righteous (Psalms 73). Many, many things in this world are confusing to God's people. When God gave Abraham a son, he required Abraham to sacrifice his son. When Moses brought Israel up to Canaan, God refused to let him take Israel in to possess the land. When time came to build the temple, David died. God often lifts up with one hand and casts down with the other; heals with one and wounds with the other. Blessed Holy Spirit, let us at all times understand and rest our souls upon this promise of God our Saviour to our souls. 'What I do thou knowest not now; but thou shalt know hereafter.'

When we think the Lord is doing nothing, he is working for us. When we think he has forsaken us, he is with us still. When we think everything is against us, everything is loaded down with mercy for us. Our Lord will not let us walk by sight here. He demands and deserves that we walk by faith. 'What I do now thou knowest not; but thou shalt know hereafter.' In due time, he will inform us.

'O the depth of the riches both of the wisdom and knowledge of God! How unsearchable are his judgments, and his ways past finding out! For who hath known the mind of the Lord? or who hath been his counsellor? Or who hath first given to him, and it shall be recompensed unto him again? For of him, and through him, and to him, are all things: to whom be glory forever. Amen' (Romans 11:33-36).

Often I wonder why I must journey,
Over a road so rugged and steep.
Why all the darkness? Why all the heartache?
Why must Your chosen so often weep?
Farther along we'll know more about it.
Farther along we'll understand why;
Cheer up, believer, trust your great Saviour.
We'll understand it all by and by.

Chapter 25

Foot Washing

'Now before the feast of the passover, when Jesus knew that his hour was come that he should depart out of this world unto the Father, having loved his own which were in the world, he loved them unto the end. And supper being ended, the devil having now put into the heart of Judas Iscariot, Simon's son, to betray him; Jesus knowing that the Father had given all things into his hands, and that he was come from God, and went to God; he riseth from supper, and laid aside his garments; and took a towel, and girded himself. After that he poureth water into a bason, and began to wash the disciples' feet, and to wipe them with the towel wherewith he was girded. Then cometh he to Simon Peter: and Peter saith unto him, Lord, dost thou wash my feet? Jesus answered and said unto him, What I do thou knowest not now; but thou shalt know hereafter. Peter saith unto him, Thou shalt never wash my feet. Jesus answered him, If I wash thee not, thou hast no part with me. Simon Peter saith unto him, Lord, not my feet only, but also my hands and my head. Jesus saith to him, he that is washed needeth not save to wash his feet, but is clean every whit: and ye are clean, but not all. For he knew who should betray him; therefore said he, Ye are not all clean. So after he had washed their feet, and had taken his garments, and was set down again, he said unto them, Know ye what I have done to you? Ye call me Master and Lord: and ye say well; for so I am. If I then, your Lord and Master, have washed your feet; ye also ought to wash one another's feet. For I have given you an example, that ye should do as I have done to you. Verily, verily, I say unto you, The servant is not greater than his lord; neither he that is sent greater than he that sent him. If ye know these things, happy are ye if ye do them. 'I speak not of you all: I know whom I have chosen: but that the scripture may be fulfilled, he that eateth bread with me hath lifted up his heel against me. Now I tell you before it come, that, when it is come to pass, ye may believe that I am he. Verily, verily, I say unto you, he that receiveth whomsoever I send receiveth me; and he that receiveth me receiveth him that sent me' (John 13:1-20).

The things recorded in John 13, 14, 15, 16, and 17 are things that God the Holy Spirit inspired John alone to record. Neither Matthew, Mark, nor Luke mention the things recorded in these five chapters. We can never be sufficiently thankful that God the Holy Spirit caused them to be written here for our learning and admonition and for our edification and consolation. The things here revealed have been meat and drink for thirsty souls for more than two thousand years. They provide strength and comfort for Zion's pilgrims in every age and land as they are blessed to the hearts of God's elect by the gracious influence of the Holy Spirit.

What was the intent of our Lord Jesus in performing this very menial task of washing his disciples' feet? What does he teach us in this passage?

Blessed Departure

First, we learn that as our Saviour looked upon his rapidly-approaching death as a blessed departure out of this world unto the Father, so we who believe should anticipate the death of the body. 'Now before the feast of the Passover, when Jesus knew that his hour was come that he should depart out of this world unto the Father' (v. 1). Our blessed Saviour expressed a great ambition to eat this last Passover feast with his disciples, that he might fulfil its typical significance by dying in our place, as our Passover Sacrifice, to make atonement for the sins of his elect. Our Lord Jesus was anxious to die as our Substitute and accomplish our redemption by the sacrifice of himself.

Though he must die the shameful, painful, ignominious death of the cross, though he must be made sin for us, though he must die as a man cursed of God, when he was made sin for us, our Saviour knew that his departure out of this world would be the end of sin and the end of suffering, the end of shame and the end of the curse, the end of wrath and the end of sorrow, both for him and for us, 'for he that hath suffered in the flesh hath ceased from sin'! Therefore, his death as our Substitute would be his accomplished exodus (Luke 9:31) out of this world unto the Father.

Because he died for us, 'the just for the unjust, that he might bring us to God', he has delivered us from the fear of death. That is to say, death for God's saints is but removing from one place to another. It is the quiet, sweet, longed-for departure out of this world unto the Father. As John Trapp put it, 'It is to the saints no more than a passage to the Father, an inlet to eternal life.' One aged believer long ago said, as he was dying, 'The Father loves me, the Son redeemed me, the Holy Ghost comforts me; how then can I be cast down at the approach of death?'

As a specific time and hour was fixed for our Saviour's entrance into this world from eternity, so the time and hour of our entrance into this world was fixed from eternity. As the specific time and hour of our Redeemer's departure out of this world was fixed from eternity, so the time and hour of our departure out of this world was fixed from eternity. Bless God, we shall soon depart out of this world! And when we depart out of this world, we will be departing unto our Father, to dwell forever in his house.

Incomparable Love

Second, the Holy Spirit here speaks of our Saviour's great love for his people as an incomparable love of indestructible and patient perseverance. 'Having loved his own which were in the world, he loved them unto the end' (v. 1).

The objects of his love are described as 'his own'. Those words do not refer to all men, though all are his property by creation. The words 'his own' do not refer to the Jews, who were his own nation and countrymen according to the flesh. And they do not merely refer to the twelve apostles, whom he had chosen. These two, sweet, sweet words 'his own', refer to all the hosts of God's elect, those who are his own by his own choice of them, the Father's gift of them to him, the purchase he made of them with his blood, and his effectual call of them by his grace.

Our Saviour's love is specifically said to be a love for 'his own which were in the world'. That means that our Saviour loves us in our present state and condition, whatever that state and condition may be. He loves his own in this present, evil world. Though we live in this body of sin and death, though we are liable to many snares and temptations, though we are weak and frail, faltering and failing, sinful and shameful, still, we are and always will be the objects of the love and care of Christ Jesus our Lord.

The acts of his love toward us are expressed both in time past and in time to come. 'Having loved' us, he loved us from everlasting, with a love of complacency and delight, which he showed by espousing us to himself from eternity, undertaking our cause as our Surety in the covenant of grace, taking upon himself all responsibility for us as our Substitute, Representative, and Mediator, from everlasting, and by assuming our nature in the incarnation; and, having done all this, 'he loved them to the end.'

Yes, the Lord of glory died for us, because he loved us; and he continues to show that incomparable love for us by interceding for us in heaven, by supplying us with all grace, and by preserving us unto glory. And he will at last bring us into his kingdom and glory. There we shall be forever with him.

Imagine that! And try to get hold of this, that same love for our souls continues not only to the end of our lives in this world, but to the end of the world, and forever! The Lord Jesus loves us; no, he loved us continually from everlasting and to everlasting!

Eternal Dominion

Third, we are here taught that our Saviour's dominion as our Mediator is an eternal dominion. As he is 'the Lamb slain from the foundation of the world', in whom all God's elect were blessed and accepted from everlasting, so the triune Jehovah trusted him from everlasting as the Mediator-Saviour of his elect; and all things were given into his hands as Lord from everlasting. Notice that the language here speaks of that which was already done. We cannot even think like this really; but all the works of God were finished before the world began (Hebrews 4:3).

Christ was our accepted Sacrifice from eternity (Revelation 13:8). We were accepted in him from eternity (Ephesians 1:6). We were blessed with all the blessings of grace in Christ from eternity (Ephesians 1:3-6). The book of God says we were saved in Christ from eternity (2 Timothy 1:9). And Christ was made Lord over all things as our Mediator from eternity, made Lord over all flesh to give eternal life to all the objects of his love from eternity. And all the works of God, 'finished from the foundation of the world', are brought to light, made manifest, and openly performed in due time, to the praise of his glory.

But the primary purpose of verse three is to show us that our Saviour understood and was fully aware of his own great, indescribable dignity and superiority as a man. 'Jesus knowing that the Father had given all things into his hands, and that he was come from God, and went to God'. By telling us this, and then telling us about our Lord washing his disciples' feet, the Holy Spirit is emphasizing the Lord's act as a matter of great, indescribable condescension.

In the very moment when he, as God-Man Mediator, knew himself to be the Lord, Proprietor, and Governor of heaven and earth, the Lord Jesus did that which few among the sons of men will ever perform. It is obviously the Holy Spirit's intention that we have before us a sense of Christ's unbounded condescension as we consider the things that follow.

Then, the Holy Spirit inspired John to tell us that our Saviour also knew that he 'was come from God, and went to God' (v. 3). He came from the triune God upon a mission as Jehovah's Servant, to save his people from their sins. And the Saviour knew that his work would soon be done. When he had finished all that he was sent to accomplish, he would return to the triune God as our God-man Mediator. With these thoughts before him, our dear Saviour stooped to wash his disciples' feet. Only now, only under these conditions could he give such a vivid picture of his undying love for those very people for whom he was about to die. He was now about to return to his Father. For a while, they would see him no more (John16:10).

Indescribable Humiliation

Fourth, our Saviour's act of washing his disciples' feet was intended to set before them and us a picture of his indescribable humiliation as our sin-atoning Substitute. I have no doubt that we have before us in this chapter a very clear and vivid picture of the self-abasing, condescending service we ought to gladly render to one another. What the Lord Jesus did for us, we should gladly do for one another. Does he serve us? Let us serve one another. Does he refresh us? Let us refresh one another. Does he stoop to meet our needs? Let us stoop to meet one another's needs. Did he empty himself to fill us? Let us empty ourselves to fill one another. Did he abase himself to meet our needs and lift us up? Let us abase ourselves to meet the needs of others and lift up others. Does he love us? Let us love one another. Did he lay down his life for us? Let us lay down our lives for one another.

The foot washing described in this chapter portrays the loving services we ought to render to the church and kingdom of our God and the humility of mind with which we should gladly serve one another in this world (Philippians 2:1-11). And the Master's washing of the disciples' feet may well be intended to be a declaration of the high esteem with which God's servants should be esteemed by his people. Our Lord's statement in verse 20 certainly implies that he intended that we understand it this way. 'Verily, verily, I say unto you, he that receiveth whomsoever I send receiveth me; and he that receiveth me receiveth him that sent me.' The washing of his disciples' feet and not their hands was, perhaps, a ceremonial presentation of them as his Apostles, as preachers of the gospel (Isaiah 52:7, 8; 1 Thessalonians 5:12, 13).

But the primary thing intended by this marvellous act of humiliation was to give us a picture of the great, indescribable condescension and humiliation of our Saviour, the Lord Jesus Christ, when he stooped to redeem us.

'He riseth from supper, and laid aside his garments; and took a towel, and girded himself. After that he poureth water into a bason, and began to wash the disciples' feet, and to wipe them with the towel wherewith he was girded' (John 13:4, 5).

This is a great and beautiful picture of the Son of God laying aside his glory, which he had with the Father before all worlds, and taking upon him the form of a servant, when he came to wash his people from their sins in his blood (Philippians 2:5-8; 2 Corinthians 8:9; 5:21).

This is truly the one thing needful, the one thing that is absolutely necessary for our souls. We must be washed in the Saviour's precious blood. The Lord Jesus said, emphatically, to Peter, 'If I wash thee not, thou hast no part with me.' Though our Saviour baptised no one, and made a point of stressing that fact (John 4:2), as if to tell us that baptism has no saving merit or efficacy of any kind, he says to you and me, as he did to Peter, 'If I wash thee not, thou hast no part with me.' 'Without shedding of blood is no remission' (Hebrews 9:22). We must be washed judicially (Romans 3:24-26). We must be washed experimentally (Titus 3:4-7; Zechariah 3:1-9). And we must be washed continually (1 John 1:7, 9).

Inward, Not Outward

Fifth, the fact that the Lord Jesus washed Judas's feet is very instructive. Are you not astonished by the fact that Judas's feet were washed by the Son of God, in common with the other Apostles? It is almost shocking. Isn't it? It shouldn't be. Our Lord Jesus did this deliberately; and his deliberate act of washing Judas's feet was obviously intended to teach us much.

True, saving grace is inward, not outward. Judas was washed ceremonially, outwardly, but not spiritually, not inwardly, not experimentally. There is no saving benefit, merit, or efficacy in any outward ordinance, even if the ordinance were administered by Christ himself. God's people, true believers, are never injured or kept from spiritual benefit by the presence of devils in our assemblies of worship. Judas's defilement did not corrupt Peter, James, or John. Robert Hawker rightly observed,

> As the presence of Judas had no effect to injure the Apostles in those hallowed seasons with their Lord, so neither can devils, or bad men, hinder the blessed manifestations which the Lord makes to his own, when handing to them their portions in secret, and causing them to eat of the 'hidden manna' (Revelation 2:17).

When devils like Judas raise their ugly heads and manifest themselves in our midst, we should be reminded of God's distinguishing grace. The only difference between Judas and the others was God's free, sovereign, electing, distinguishing grace; and the same is true today (vv. 18, 19; 1 Corinthians 4:7).

Application

What a picture of grace we have before us! What an endearing portrait God the Holy Ghost has given us by the pen of his servant John of our Lord Jesus Christ! Can the imagination conceive anything equally lovely as in thus beholding the Son of God in our nature, washing the feet of poor fishermen?

The picture was drawn at that moment, above all others, when the Lord Jesus 'knew that the Father had given all things into his hands'! Ponder it well. What a lesson is here taught to mortify the pride of our hearts!

While the great ones of the earth carry themselves so proudly, and will hardly condescend to look upon the poor, the destitute, the homeless, and the wicked, the King of heaven stoops to the lowest humiliation and washes his disciples' feet. Let us never lose sight of this unequalled condescension of our Lord. Shall you, or I, or shall any poor sinner, in the view of such clemency, ever imagine that it is beneath the dignity of the Son of God to regard his people in our low estate. Did the Lord Jesus wash their feet, and will he not wash my soul? Did the Son of God, unasked, yea, even when Peter refused him, persist to perform such an act of grace; and will he turn a blind eye to our needs or a deaf ear to our earnest petitions? Can any child of God, in the contemplation of such love in our Saviour and Lord, say, I am too low, too abject, too unworthy for his care?

By this act of washing his disciples' feet before his departure, our blessed Saviour intended to convince us that his love is the same now as it was when he walked here in our flesh, as when he lived for us, and as when he died in our stead at Calvary. His very last act on earth, before suffering for them, was to wash his disciples' feet. And with that act he declared his complete devotion to them. Neither time, nor place, nor circumstances can alter his love for our souls.

May God the Holy Spirit cause us to keep these things always in remembrance. It will not be long until he who washed his disciples' feet will bring us home to glory, washed from all our sins in his blood, and present us to himself, sanctified and cleansed, 'a glorious church, not having spot, or wrinkle, or any such thing; but ... Holy and without blemish' (Ephesians 5:25-27). Soon, the Son of God, our Saviour, will 'present you faultless before the presence of his glory with exceeding joy' (Jude 24).

Chapter 26

Christ Our Example

'For I have given you an example, that ye should do as I have done to you' (John 13:1).

What is the believer's rule of life? By what standard must our lives be governed, as the children of God in this world? How should we behave? What principles are we to live by, as we walk before God and men in this world? By what law are we to live?

These are questions which concern all of God's children. None of God's people are lawless, rebellious antinomians. All who trust Christ want to honour God. All who are born of God want to do the will of God. We want to do what is right before God and men. The grace of God experienced in the soul teaches us to live 'soberly, righteously, and godly in this present world' (Titus 2:12). As we are admonished in holy scripture, saved sinners want to 'be blameless and harmless, the sons of God, without rebuke, in the midst of a crooked and perverse nation, among whom ye shine as lights in the world' (Philippians 2:15).

A man or woman who is chosen, redeemed, and regenerated by the grace of God has a principle of godliness and righteousness created in his or her heart. Such a person wants to live in a manner that will be pleasing and honouring to God, for the glory of Christ. If you do not love God's law, you neither know God nor love God. Your religion is a refuge of lies. Your pretence of faith is a delusion.

Antinomian Slander

Because we preach the gospel of God's free and sovereign grace in Christ, declaring incessantly and everywhere that salvation is free, that grace is unconditional, and that God's elect are free from the law, that God will never charge his own with sin, as the scriptures everywhere assert, we are slandered by religious legalists as antinomians, as promoters of licentiousness. These work-mongers, who had already crept into the church in Jude's day, have multiplied through the ages. Pretending to preach the grace of God, they attempt to mix law and grace together and blasphemously assert that the preaching of free grace leads to licentiousness (Jude 4).

Of course, nothing could be further from the truth. The gospel of God is the gospel of godliness. It teaches all who know it to 'lead a quiet and peaceable life in all godliness and honesty' (1 Timothy 2:2). It is 'wholesome doctrine which is according to godliness' (1 Timothy 6:3).

Three Statements

Here are three things we need to learn, as we seek to live in this world for the glory of God our Saviour.

1. Believers are not under the law, period. There is absolutely no sense in which believers are under the yoke of bondage. We are not under the ceremonial laws of Israel. We are not under the civil laws given to Israel. We are not under the dietary laws given to Israel. We are not under the economic laws given to Israel. And we are not under the moral law, the Ten Commandments, that was given to Israel.

The law was given to Israel alone. No one else was commanded, or even allowed to observe the Jewish sabbath days, ceremonies, and ordinances. The law was given to point to Christ. The law was a schoolmaster unto Christ. The law is not our rule of life! We have no commitment to the law, no curse from the law, and we are not constraint by the law (Romans 6:14, 15).

The law promises reward for obedience and threatens punishment for disobedience; but God's saints are not mercenaries. We do not serve our God for gain, or because of fear. God's elect are not motivated by such things. Our service to God is motivated by love, grace, and faith. God requires and accepts heart obedience. He will not accept the mere outward, pretentious show of the hypocrite. The Almighty sees through the Pharisee's show!

Did you hear the scriptures? 'We are not under the law, but under grace'! The law makes men slaves. It produces bondage and bondage creates strife. Law work promotes pride, self-righteousness, and judgmental attitudes. We are expressly and repeatedly warned not to be brought in bondage to the law (Romans 7:1-4; Galatians 3:24-26; Romans 10:1-4; Galatians 5:1-4; Colossians 2:14-16). The reason the law was given at Sinai was to point sinners to Calvary. The law was given to point us to Christ, who alone obeyed its requirements and satisfied its justice as the sinner's Substitute.

2. God's people in this world must not allow themselves to be ruled by the self-righteous standards, traditions, laws, and customs imposed by religious men (1 Timothy 4:1-5; Romans 14:5, 11-17).

It is customary in our day for men to set themselves up as judges of other men's spirituality, dedication, and devotion. They call it 'fruit inspecting'. But the standard by which they judge is a very faulty one. It changes from one place to another, from one time to another, and from one circumstance to another. But you can be sure of this: anything that is right is always right; and anything that is wrong is always wrong. True godliness is not outward, but inward. It is a matter of the heart. The fruit of the Spirit is heart fruit (Galatians 5:22, 23.

3. Yet, we are not left without law. We have a law by which to live (1 John 3:23; 2 Corinthians 5:14-16). The whole of God's holy law teaches two things: faith and love, faith in Christ and brotherly love. By these two rules we live. The just live by faith, faith which worketh by love.

We have an example of that law of love in John 13:15. I realise that such frail creatures of the dust as we are need some example by which to live, some pattern to copy. Our sinful flesh requires that we be ruled by some law. We do not suggest that every man do that which is right in his own eyes. But what example are we to follow? What law must we submit to and obey? What is the rule by which we must live? The answer is found right here.

'So after he had washed their feet, and had taken his garments, and was set down again, he said unto them, Know ye what I have done to you? Ye call me Master and Lord: and ye say well; for so I am. If I then, your Lord and Master, have washed your feet; ye also ought to wash one another's feet. For I have given you an example, that ye should do as I have done to you' (John 13:12-15).

The Lord Jesus Christ, our blessed Saviour, 'suffered for us, leaving us an example, that we should follow in his steps' (1 Peter 2:21). If I want to know how to live in this world, I need only to read the four gospels, look to Christ my Example, and follow him.

What kind of father should I be? Look to Christ.
What kind of mother should I be? Look to Christ.
What kind of child should I be? Look to Christ.
What kind of friend should I be? Look to Christ.
What kind of husband should I be? Look to Christ.
What kind of wife should I be? Look to Christ.
What kind of neighbour should I be? Look to Christ.

How should I treat my enemies? Look to Christ.
How should I pray? Look to Christ.
How should I forgive men? Look to Christ.
How should I deal with men in business? Look to Christ.
Should I pay my taxes? Look to Christ.
How can I know the will of God? Look to Christ.
How can I overcome temptation? Look to Christ.
How should I treat the poor? Look to Christ.
What is humility? Look to Christ.
What is sin? Look to Christ.
How should a believer suffer? Look to Christ.
What is faithfulness? Look to Christ.
How much should I give? Look to Christ.
What is patience? Look to Christ.
How much of this world's goods should I seek? Look to Christ.
What is it to live by faith? Look to Christ.
What is love? Look to Christ.

If you have any other questions pertaining to life in this world, look to Christ. And if you would learn how to die, when your life is over, look to Christ. In all things, Christ is our Law, our Teacher, our Guide, our Example. All who want to live in this world for the glory of God need only to follow the example of our Lord Jesus Christ.

Constant Love Portrayed

John 13 records one of the most instructive incidents in the earthly life and ministry of our Lord. Here we see the Son of God washing his disciples' feet. This picture of our Lord Jesus Christ washing his disciples' feet is a picture of our Saviour's constant love toward us. Really, verse one is a text for the sermon which our Lord acted out in verses 2-17. Here we see our Lord acting as a gracious Host to his disciples. He gives them bread to eat and wine to drink. He even takes a towel and a bowl of water and stoops down to wash their feet!

This was a custom in the old Eastern countries. If a man had honoured guests in his home, he provided them with food, wine, and cool water to wash their feet. Abraham had some water brought for the angels who visited him to wash their feet. Joseph had his servant to wash the feet of his brothers when they came to Egypt. But Christ himself so highly honoured his disciples that he washed their feet.

It is still true today that our Lord tenderly cares for our every need as our constant, gracious, loving host (Romans 8:28; Psalms 57:2).

This act of love performed by our Saviour shows me three things. First, the Lord Jesus Christ looks after our smallest cares and concerns with great interest. So tender is his love that he even washes his disciples' feet. He takes notice even of a little soil on their heels.

> He who sovereignly rules all things
> Takes care of our smallest affairs:
> The Almighty Lord, King of kings,
> Would have us cast on Him our cares.

Second, our Lord Jesus tenderly provides refreshment for the children of his love. In hot climates, nothing is more refreshing, after a long walk or a long day of work, than to have your feet bathed in cool water. Truly, there are many pools of cool water from which the Son of God refreshes our weary souls such as, his salvation, his promises, his presence, his faithfulness, his word, his ordinances, his gospel, his throne of grace. And there are special, specific seasons when he refreshes us. Before we enter the hard labour of trial, he graciously prepares his own for the trials they must endure, with sweet refreshments of grace. In the midst of our journey, our Saviour comes to us, as he did to the disciples on the Emmaus Road, opens to us the scriptures, and causes our hearts to burn within us, as he talks to us by the way. When we arrive home in heaven, he will refresh our souls as never before (Luke 12:37; Revelation 8:1).

Third, our blessed Lord Jesus carefully tends to the spiritual welfare of each of his disciples. He washes our feet. He washes us from the defilements of the world and the soil of worldly care.

It seems to me that the public ordinances of the gospel are especially designed for this purpose. In baptism and in the Lord's Supper we are reminded again of our Saviour's great sacrifice of himself for us, and have our feet washed again. The blood is freshly applied by the Holy Spirit; and we are freshly washed in the preaching of the gospel, in the songs of Zion, in the reading of the word, and in the prayers and praises of God's elect.

We need to be washed daily, constantly. 'Purge me with hyssop, and I shall be clean: wash me, and I shall be whiter than snow' (Psalms 51:7). And our dear Saviour is always ready to wash us.

An Example To Follow

This picture of Christ washing his disciples' feet is an example of love for us to follow (vv. 12-15).

'So after he had washed their feet, and had taken his garments, and was set down again, he said unto them, Know ye what I have done to you? Ye call me Master and Lord: and ye say well; for so I am. If I then, your Lord and Master, have washed your feet; ye also ought to wash one another's feet. For I have given you an example, that ye should do as I have done to you'.

We do not physically observe foot washing as an ordinance, because our Lord did not instruct us to do so. The New Testament gives no hint that our Saviour's disciples ever practiced such an ordinance, the early church did not do so, and we have no instruction about such an ordinance in the New Testament.

Our Lord Jesus did not institute foot washing as an ordinance for the church. He gave us an example to live by as a rule of life. He gave us a pattern to follow. He said, 'Do as I have done to you.' Our Lord Jesus here shows us how we ought to serve one another, and how we ought to allow ourselves to be served by our brethren. Some of us are too proud to wash someone else's feet; and some of us are too proud to have our feet washed by someone else.

Three lessons are clearly taught by our Saviour's example in this portion of holy scripture: First, we should carefully maintain love for one another (John 13:35; 1 John 4:8; 1 Corinthians 13:1-13). Second, love is serviceable. Love does not say. Love does! No service is too great for love. No service is too small for love. No service is too demanding for love. No service is too costly for love. Third, love is the never ending, abiding law of Christ's church (John 13:34, 35).

Our dear Saviour himself shows us how to love (1 John 3:16, 17; 4:9-11). Deeds of love and kindness are understood by all men. And love is all the law fulfilled and all the law needed. 'For all the law is fulfilled in one word, even in this; Thou shalt love thy neighbour as thyself' (Galatians 5:14).

'If there be therefore any consolation in Christ, if any comfort of love, if any fellowship of the Spirit, if any bowels and mercies, Fulfil ye my joy, that ye be likeminded, having the same love, being of one accord, of one mind. Let nothing be done through strife or vainglory; but in lowliness of mind let each esteem other better than themselves. Look not every man on his own things, but every man also on the things of others. Let this mind be in you, which was also in Christ Jesus: Who, being in the form of God, thought it not robbery to be equal with God: But made himself of no reputation, and took upon him the form of a servant, and was made in the likeness of men: And being found in fashion as a man, he humbled himself, and became obedient unto death, even the death of the cross' (Philippians 2:1-8).

'If ye know these things, happy are ye if ye do them' (John 13:17).

Chapter 27

Judas And The Glory Of God

'I speak not of you all: I know whom I have chosen: but that the scripture may be fulfilled, he that eateth bread with me hath lifted up his heel against me. Now I tell you before it come, that, when it is come to pass, ye may believe that I am he. Verily, verily, I say unto you, he that receiveth whomsoever I send receiveth me; and he that receiveth me receiveth him that sent me. When Jesus had thus said, he was troubled in spirit, and testified, and said, Verily, verily, I say unto you, that one of you shall betray me. Then the disciples looked one on another, doubting of whom he spake. Now there was leaning on Jesus' bosom one of his disciples, whom Jesus loved. Simon Peter therefore beckoned to him, that he should ask who it should be of whom he spake. He then lying on Jesus' breast saith unto him, Lord, who is it? Jesus answered, he it is, to whom I shall give a sop, when I have dipped it. And when he had dipped the sop, he gave it to Judas Iscariot, the son of Simon. And after the sop Satan entered into him. Then said Jesus unto him, That thou doest, do quickly. Now no man at the table knew for what intent he spake this unto him. For some of them thought, because Judas had the bag, that Jesus had said unto him, Buy those things that we have need of against the feast; or, that he should give something to the poor. He then having received the sop went immediately out: and it was night. Therefore, when he was gone out, Jesus said, Now is the Son of man glorified, and God is glorified in him' (John 13:18-31).

John 13 begins with a declaration of God the Holy Spirit, by which he describes the everlasting love of the Lord Jesus Christ for his elect. 'Having loved his own which were in the world, he loved them unto the end.' Our Saviour's love for his people is here described as a sovereign, eternal love 'Having loved', a special, distinguishing love, 'Having loved his own', and a steadfast, unchanging, immutable love 'Having loved his own which were in the world, he loved them unto the end.'

Do you remember what our Saviour said, in Psalm 109, about this great love of his, which charms our hearts and ravishes our souls? 'They compassed me about also with words of hatred; and fought against me without a cause. For my love they are my adversaries: but I give myself unto prayer' (Psalms 109:3, 4). The Lord Jesus here declares that the reason for man's opposition to him and his people is his love for his people. Yes, he declares that men and women everywhere hate God because God loves his people. That is the reason Cain hated his brother Abel and murdered him. Ishmael persecuted Isaac because God loved Isaac. That is why Esau despised Jacob. God loved Jacob and hated Esau. Men and women everywhere hate God because God loves his people. Nothing enrages the heart of man like the fact of God's free, sovereign, saving love bestowed upon chosen sinners in Christ (Romans 9:4-23).

There are among the fallen sons of Adam only two groups of people: the elect and the reprobate, the seed of Christ and the seed of the serpent, vessels of mercy afore prepared to glory by whom and in whom God makes known the riches of his glory, and vessels of wrath fitted to destruction by whom and in whom God makes his power known. The greatest, most glaring example of those vessels of wrath fitted to destruction is the betrayer of our Lord Jesus, Judas Iscariot.

Election And Predestination

The portion of holy scripture before us begins with our Lord Jesus assuring his disciples of their election and the certainty of God's purpose of grace in sovereign predestination. How I thank God for electing love! How I praise him for absolute predestination! The Saviour is about to tell his disciples that one of their number is a devil, a betrayer, a reprobate vessel of wrath; but first he assures them and us that God's purpose of grace is sure (vv. 18, 19). He says, 'I know whom I have chosen'. He declares, 'The scripture must be fulfilled, he that eateth bread with me hath lifted up his heel against me' (See Psalms 41.9). Divine prophecy must be fulfilled. The purpose of God must and shall be accomplished. Our Lord made his reason perfectly clear for telling his disciples exactly what God's purpose was for Judas. He said, 'Now I tell you before it come, that, when it is come to pass, ye may believe that I am he.'

The Betrayer

The Lord God our Saviour knows whom he has chosen. The purpose of God is sure. Everything God does he does to make all men know that he is God, to glorify himself in Christ, and make all men know and confess that the man Christ Jesus is Jehovah God, the 'I Am'!

Now, with those assurances given, let us see clearly what God the Holy Spirit here reveals to us about Judas Iscariot, the betrayer. The lessons set before us in the character and conduct of that vile, base, reprobate man are many and alarming. Yet, we are specifically told that the things written here were given by the inspiration of God the Holy Spirit for our consolation (Romans 15:4).

First, lost people often enjoy great advantages by which their guilt is aggravated and their condemnation is increased. Certainly that was the case with Judas. Judas Iscariot was given many great advantages over other men. He had the privilege of being in the company of the Lord Jesus Christ almost constantly for nearly three and a half years. He saw all the miracles performed by our Lord Jesus. He heard our Saviour's sermons in public, and the private instructions given just to his disciples. Judas was in the daily habit of conversing with the Son of God, of conversing with that Man 'who spake as never man spake'.

Those were great advantages indeed; but Judas enjoyed even greater privileges and advantages. If we consider nothing except what is before us in this chapter, what countless tokens of our Saviour's kindness, goodness, mercy, and grace Judas observed. The Lord Jesus washed his feet!

When the betrayer again took his seat at the table, the Lamb of God spoke so gently in declaring that one of those sitting at the table with him would betray him, that the Saviour's words would have broken any man's heart and would have stung any conscience to the quick, except the hard, obstinate heart and seared conscience of Judas Iscariot. Could any arrow of conviction have reached his heart, surely the words spoken by our Redeemer in this chapter and the deeds he performed would have pierced the steel of his soul. But there he sat, hard and unmoved by the most tender words and actions imaginable, hardened with determined guilt.

While all the other Apostles trembled with horrid fear at the bare thought that one of them could do such a thing, that one of them could betray the Master, Judas sat, like a volcano, with all the fire of hellish malice burning within, until the Lord Jesus finally gave him the fatal sop by which the traitor was marked. Then, only then, he withdrew.

Still, the hardness of his heart, the determination with which he pursued his hatred of the Lord Jesus is made manifest in what he did as soon as he left the table. Though it was now night, and what night, what darkness possessed his soul, Judas went immediately to Jerusalem, a two mile walk from Bethany. There he made his pact with the chief priests (Matthew 26:14-16).

As he walked by night to perform his dastardly deed, all through that long, solitary walk, it appears that Judas did not have so much as a slight pricking of conscience, not the slightest compunction. In fact, judging by the only records we have (Matthew, Mark, Luke, and John), there is no indication that Judas felt or knew even the slightest measure of hesitation for the next two days and nights. There is no indication that his heart was even momentarily softened.

On the contrary, the very next thing we see him doing is taking his place with the Lord Jesus and the other Apostles at the Passover, and actually receiving the Lord's Supper from the hands of the Lord Jesus Christ, whom he had already agreed to betray, as if a he were a faithful disciple! The Saviour washed his feet. The Lord Jesus gave him the bread and wine. Judas joined in the closing hymn!

As all tenderness was lost upon that hardened wretch, so the alarms of judgment had no effect upon him. When Judas daringly led that band of men and officers who came to arrest the Lord Jesus in Gethsemane, and they all fell to the ground when the Lord Jesus asked, 'whom seek ye?' and then declared himself to be Jehovah, the 'I AM', as they all fell away backward to the ground, Judas was among them (John 18:2-9).

But neither miracles, nor acts of kindness, nor privileges, nor acts of judgment could penetrate or even affect Judas's hard heart. Satan completely possessed the man, because the Lord himself had given Satan the possession of him. And the last state of that man was worse than the first (Luke 11:26).

Distinguishing Grace

The greatest of opportunities will never convert a sinner. The highest privileges will never give life to a dead sinner. The best of good company cannot save a soul from hell, or even from itself. The best preaching in the world cannot create life and faith in the soul, except it be made effectual by omnipotent grace. Life is God's gift. Conviction is the Spirit's work. Faith is by God's operation. Repentance is God turning the soul to himself. 'Salvation is of the Lord'!

Second, the only difference between Judas and you, the only difference between Judas and me, the only difference between Judas Iscariot and all the host of God's elect is the difference God himself has made and makes by his distinguishing grace. Read the history of that reprobate man of whom the Lord Jesus said, 'good were it for that man if he had never been born' (Mark 14:21). There is a line of everlasting distinction drawn between the precious and the vile, between the righteous and the wicked, between 'him that serveth God, and him that serveth him not' (Malachi 3:18). And that line of distinction, drawn by the finger of God from everlasting, is continually drawn by the finger of God in providence and in grace (1 Corinthians 4:7; 1 Thessalonians 5:9).

Though all God's elect were ruined in the sin and fall of our father Adam, though all are born with the same depraved nature, both the elect and the reprobate, the word of God clearly distinguishes the seed of the serpent and the seed of Christ (Jude 4-11).

God's elect, because we are blessed of God to be in an everlasting union of grace with Christ, are sanctified by God the Father, preserved in Jesus Christ, and called. But Jude tells us that the reprobate were of old ordained to this condemnation. And, as the descendants of Cain, they have run and do run greedily after the error of Balaam and shall perish in the gainsaying of Core.

The Lord Jesus himself declares of all the Judas-seed of Adam's apostate race, 'Ye are of your father the devil, and the lusts of your father ye will do' (John 8:44). The Apostle John makes this same distinction (1 John 3:5-12).

Judas was not merely tempted of the devil, he was a devil; and Satan entered into him and took complete possession of him (John 6:70). Yet, you and I are exactly like Judas. We are in every way as vile, hard, and unrelenting in wickedness and determined evil as he was. Why, then, is Judas an heir of everlasting darkness and torment, while you and I to whom God has given faith in Christ are heirs of light and everlasting blessedness? Only one answer can be found. The Saviour says, 'I know whom I have chosen'! Oh, thank God for electing love!

'For God hath not appointed us to wrath, but to obtain salvation by our Lord Jesus Christ' (1 Thessalonians 5:9).

'But we are bound to give thanks alway to God for you, brethren beloved of the Lord, because God hath from the beginning chosen you to salvation through sanctification of the Spirit and belief of the truth: Whereunto he called you by our gospel, to the obtaining of the glory of our Lord Jesus Christ. Therefore, brethren, stand fast, and hold the traditions which ye have been taught, whether by word, or our epistle. Now our Lord Jesus Christ himself, and God, even our Father, which hath loved us, and hath given us everlasting consolation and good hope through grace, comfort your hearts, and stablish you in every good word and work' (2 Thessalonians 2:13-17).

God's Glory

Our Saviour assured us that God's purpose of grace in election and predestination is firm and unalterable. Then we are given a picture of both man's depravity and God's distinguishing grace in Judas the betrayer. Now, look at verses 30, 31, and rejoice in the fact that even Judas and his horrid betrayal of the Lord Jesus Christ was ordained of God, overruled by God, and used by God our heavenly Father to accomplish our redemption and the glory of God in our redemption by Christ.

'He then having received the sop went immediately out: and it was night. Therefore, when he was gone out, Jesus said, Now is the Son of man glorified, and God is glorified in him.'

The Lord Jesus Christ, the Son of man, was glorified by the accomplishment of redemption in his death, by Judas betrayal. And the redemption of our souls by the sin-atoning death of our Lord Jesus Christ was and is the glorifying of the triune God.

Chapter 28

Preparing For A Fall
(And Christ Glorified In His People)

'Therefore, when he was gone out, Jesus said, Now is the Son of man glorified, and God is glorified in him. If God be glorified in him, God shall also glorify him in himself, and shall straightway glorify him. Little children, yet a little while I am with you. Ye shall seek me: and as I said unto the Jews, Whither I go, ye cannot come; so now I say to you. A new commandment I give unto you, That ye love one another; as I have loved you, that ye also love one another. By this shall all men know that ye are my disciples, if ye have love one to another'.

'Simon Peter said unto him, Lord, whither goest thou? Jesus answered him, Whither I go, thou canst not follow me now; but thou shalt follow me afterwards. Peter said unto him, Lord, why cannot I follow thee now? I will lay down my life for thy sake. Jesus answered him, Wilt thou lay down thy life for my sake? Verily, verily, I say unto thee, The cock shall not crow, till thou hast denied me thrice. Let not your heart be troubled: ye believe in God, believe also in me' (John 13:31-14:1).

In this passage we find the Lord Jesus alone at last with his eleven faithful disciples. The traitor, Judas Iscariot, has left the room. He has gone out to do his wicked deed of darkness. Freed from the betrayer's painful company, our Lord opens his heart to his little flock more fully than he had ever opened himself to them before. Speaking to his disciples for the last time before his arrest, his mock trial, his sufferings, and his death as our blessed Substitute, our dear Saviour begins a discourse which is unsurpassed by any portion of holy scripture. The message begins in John 13:31 and runs through John 16:33, and is concluded with the Lord's great High Priestly prayer in John 17.

In the portion of scripture now before us, our Lord Jesus declares that he is glorified as the Son of man, that the triune God is glorified in him, and that the triune God glorifies him in himself. Then he shows us how he glorifies himself in his people. May God the Holy Spirit, whose word we have before us, be our Teacher.

Just The Family

First, we see the Lord Jesus being alone with his family. 'Therefore, when he was gone out ...' (v. 31). No sooner was Judas gone out, than the Lord Jesus said, 'Now is the Son of man glorified, and God is glorified in him.' When the traitor finally departed, the Saviour was left alone with his beloved family, his children, his mystical body, his Church. In these eleven disciples, his chosen Church, the Lord Jesus was glorified; and they were made everlastingly happy and blessed in him. The three Persons of the triune God were glorified in the Man, Christ Jesus, as our Mediator and Covenant Surety; and the triune Jehovah is glorified in his people.

These eleven disciples were at that time the representatives of Christ's whole body the Church. As such, when Judas, representing his father the devil and all the seed of the serpent, was gone out, the Lord Jesus was left alone with his family. Thus, Christ was glorified. So it will be in that great day, when sin, and Satan, and all the seed of the serpent, all the Judases of every generation, shall be gone out forever. What a glorious day of God and our souls that eternal day will be, when God our Saviour makes all things new, when he has removed the very slime of the serpent from all his creation (Isaiah 60:14; Psalms 125:3).

Christ's Glory

Second, we see Christ's glory as our Redeemer, as the Son of man, and him glorifying the triune Jehovah, our God (vv. 31, 32).

'Therefore, when he was gone out, Jesus said, Now is the Son of man glorified, and God is glorified in him. If God be glorified in him, God shall also glorify him in himself, and shall straightway glorify him.'

The Saviour's words here may and should be applied to many things; but it seems obvious to me that he is specifically talking about his own crucifixion and death upon the cross as the thing by which he has been and is glorified and by which the triune God is glorified. It is as though he had said, 'The time of my crucifixion is at hand. My work on earth is finished. An event is about to take place tomorrow, which, however painful to you who love me, is in reality that which is most glorifying both to me and my Father.'

How dark and mysterious those words must have been to the Lord's disciples! Obviously, none of them understood what the Lord was talking about.

Even if they had understood that he was talking about dying on the cross, hanging naked for six hours between two thieves, in all the agony of that cursed death, in all the shame, ignominy, and humiliation it entailed, there was no appearance of glory in it. Nor was there even a hint of anything glorious in all that they saw and heard the next day. On the contrary, all they saw in the Saviour's death at the time it took place was shame, disappointment, and dismay. Yet, our Lord declares that this is his glory and his Father's glory.

The death of Christ upon the cursed tree brought glory to God the Father. It glorified his wisdom, faithfulness, holiness, and love. It showed him wise, in providing a way whereby he could be just, and yet the Justifier of the ungodly. It showed him faithful, in keeping his promise, that the Seed of the woman should bruise the serpent's head. It showed him holy, in requiring his law's demands to be satisfied by our great Substitute. It showed him loving, in providing such a Mediator, such a Redeemer, and such a Friend for sinners as Christ is (Romans 5:6-8; 1 John 3:16; 4:9, 10).

The death of our Lord Jesus Christ, the Son of man, as our Mediator and Covenant Surety, brought glory to God the Son. It glorified his compassion, his patient obedience, and his power. It showed him compassionate, loving, and gracious in laying down his life for us, suffering in our stead, being made sin and a curse for us, and obtaining our redemption by the price of his own precious blood. It showed his patient obedience, in not dying the common death of most men, but in willingly submitting to such horrors and unknown agonies as no mind can conceive, when with a word he could have summoned his Father's angels, and been set free. He was 'obedient unto death, even the death of the cross'! Christ our Saviour glorified God the Father in his death by his obedience unto death, by our obedience unto death in him, and by his success in the accomplishment of redemption by his death. Our Saviour's accomplished death at Calvary showed him powerful, in vanquishing Satan and despoiling him of his prey, even as he bare in his body all the weight of all our transgressions and all our guilt!

The death of our Lord Jesus Christ glorified God the Holy Spirit in that Christ was justified in the Spirit. It is the glory of God the Holy Spirit to take the things of Christ and show them to chosen, redeemed sinners, to apply the Saviour's blood to his redeemed, to make the ransomed of the Lord new creatures in Christ in the new birth, to make us partakers of the divine nature, to seal and comfort God's elect, and to keep and preserve us in Christ unto everlasting glory.

Forever let us cherish such thoughts about the sacrifice and death of our blessed Saviour. The idolatrous paintings and sculptures of men can never portray what took place at Calvary. The length and breadth and depth and height of the work transacted on the cross, the honouring of God's law, our sins borne and punished in a Substitute; transferred sin and transferred guilt, are things that can be known only by divine revelation, only by the experience of grace. They cannot be explained, only believed, adored, and praised. 'God forbid that I should glory, save in the cross of our Lord Jesus Christ' (Galatians 6:14).

A Time Of Separation

Third, in verse 33, our Lord Jesus tells us that there must be a time of separation between us and him. 'Little children, yet a little while I am with you. Ye shall seek me: and as I said unto the Jews, Whither I go, ye cannot come; so now I say to you.' How greatly we feel the separation!

'For to me to live is Christ, and to die is gain. But if I live in the flesh, this is the fruit of my labour: yet what I shall choose I wot not. For I am in a strait betwixt two, having a desire to depart, and to be with Christ; which is far better: Nevertheless to abide in the flesh is more needful for you' (Philippians 1:21-24).

Our Saviour said, 'Whither I go ye cannot come' in verse 33; but, oh, how we ought to thank God that his words do not end there. He expands his meaning in verse 36. 'Simon Peter said unto him, Lord, whither goest thou? Jesus answered him, Whither I go, thou canst not follow me now; but thou shalt follow me afterwards.'

We cannot follow him now; but we shall follow him soon. The Lord Jesus leaves us here for a set time. And he has left us here for specific purposes. During this time of separation, while we are in this world, our blessed Lord Jesus glorifies himself in us by proving in us the sufficiency of his grace (1 Corinthians 10:13), the blessedness of his gift of faith, and his own faithfulness. It is during this time of separation that our Saviour allows us to serve him and the interests of his kingdom, glorifying himself in the use of such things as we are (1 Corinthians 1:26-31). But when our work on earth is done, then, we shall depart to be with Christ forever!

In the last worship service he was able to attend, just a few days before the Lord called him home to glory, Pastor Scott Richardson said to the saints at Fairmont, West Virginia,

'I've come across some things that helped me and I want to pass them on to you. We understand more about what heaven is and will be to us, by what it is not, and will not be. There will be no more sin, no more darkness, no more pain, no more sorrow, no more jail, no more crying, no more war, no more sickness, no more heartache, no more dying in a ditch, no more fear, no more confusion, no more lacking anything, no more vanity, no more waiting, no more going astray, no more reproach, no more affliction, no more darkness, no more trouble, no more curse, no more dishonouring God. Our name will no more be called Jacob. We'll be the children of the Living God.

'And there shall be no more curse: but the throne of God and of the Lamb shall be in it; and his servants shall serve him: And they shall see his face; and his name shall be in their foreheads. And there shall be no night there; and they need no candle, neither light of the sun; for the Lord God giveth them light: and they shall reign for ever and ever.

'And when we take our last breath and go out into that world, we'll feel good about it since we know a little more about it, what it will be. And I myself, experience it every day. I know that I'm going to die, not very long; and I'll be glad if I make one turn over in bed tonight and go to sleep. I'll be happy about it, because heaven is my happiness. The Lord bless us.'

Oh, what a day that will be when the company of Judas is no more; and when the Judas of my own wretched heart is gone forever!

A New Law

Fourth, in verses 34, 35, our Lord Jesus gives his chosen a new law by which our lives are to be governed in all things. The Lord Jesus glorifies himself in us by putting his law in our hearts, causing us to walk in his steps, motivated and governed by that love wherewith he loved us.

'A new commandment I give unto you, That ye love one another; as I have loved you, that ye also love one another. By this shall all men know that ye are my disciples, if ye have love one to another.'

If you are at all familiar with your Bible, you know that is not a new commandment. Even the rich young ruler understood that the essence of the law is that we love God with all our hearts and love our neighbours as ourselves. So why did the Saviour say, 'A new commandment I give unto you, That ye love one another; as I have loved you, that ye also love one another'?

The old law said, 'Thou shalt love thy neighbour, as thyself.' Here the Saviour says, 'Love one another, as I have loved you.' 'As I have loved you.' That is the example we are to follow. 'As I have loved you.' That is the motivation. 'As I have loved you.' That is the inspiration of love.

This new law is the law of God now written upon the hearts of God's elect in the new birth, not the old law written upon tables of stone. This new law of love arises from and always accompanies faith in Christ (1 John 3:23, 24; 2 Corinthians 5:14, 15).

Preparation For A Fall

Fifth, the Lord Jesus very graciously prepares his beloved disciple, Peter, for a terrible fall.

'Simon Peter said unto him, Lord, whither goest thou? Jesus answered him, Whither I go, thou canst not follow me now; but thou shalt follow me afterwards. Peter said unto him, Lord, why cannot I follow thee now? I will lay down my life for thy sake. Jesus answered him, Wilt thou lay down thy life for my sake? Verily, verily, I say unto thee, The cock shall not crow, till thou hast denied me thrice' (John 13:36-38).

Peter was far too confident in himself. He said, 'I will lay down my life for thy sake.' The Lord Jesus warned him of that terrible fall by which Peter's pride would and must be broken. 'Jesus answered him, Wilt thou lay down thy life for my sake? Verily, verily, I say unto thee, The cock shall not crow, till thou hast denied me thrice.' But never was our Saviour more glorious in the exercise of his free grace and matchless goodness than in his next word to Peter. 'Let not your heart be troubled: ye believe in God, believe also in me' (John 14:1).

O how greatly our great Saviour glorifies himself by his restoring mercy, love, and grace! Read Mark 16:7 and John 21:15-17. Bless his holy name forever, his covenant is sure. He will not let the objects of his love destroy themselves!

'And they shall be my people, and I will be their God: And I will give them one heart, and one way, that they may fear me for ever, for the good of them, and of their children after them: And I will make an everlasting covenant with them, that I will not turn away from them, to do them good; but I will put my fear in their hearts, that they shall not depart from me. Yea, I will rejoice over them to do them good, and I will plant them in this land assuredly with my whole heart and with my whole soul' (Jeremiah 32:38-41).

Chapter 29

Relief For Troubled Hearts

'Let not your heart be troubled: ye believe in God, believe also in me. In my Father's house are many mansions: if it were not so, I would have told you. I go to prepare a place for you. And if I go and prepare a place for you, I will come again, and receive you unto myself; that where I am, there ye may be also' (John 14:1-3).

The three verses before us are rich in precious gospel truth. For more than 2000 years, they have been peculiarly precious to God's elect throughout the world. Many are the hospital rooms which they have lightened. Many are the dying hearts which they have cheered. May God the Holy Spirit give us the comfort these precious words spoken by our dear Lord Jesus are intended to convey.

Heart Trouble

First, we have in this passage very precious relief for a very old problem. The problem is heart trouble. The relief is faith in Christ. 'Let not your heart be troubled: ye believe in God, believe also in me' (John 14:1).

Heart trouble is the most common thing in the world. No rank, or class, or condition is exempt from it. No bars, or bolts, or locks can keep it out. Heart trouble comes partly from inward things and partly from outward things, partly from the body and partly from the mind, partly from that which we love and partly from that which we fear, partly from things we cherish and partly from things we despise.

The journey of life is full of trouble. Even the most faithful believer has many bitter cups to drink between grace and glory. Even those who walk in the closest communion with the Saviour find this world a vale of tears. All of Zion's pilgrims must pass through waters of trouble, rivers of pain, and fires of adversity. 'We must through much tribulation enter into the kingdom of God' (Acts 14:22). There are Philistines without and Canaanites within who constantly wage war against our souls. Sooner or later, we all must face the Giant Despair. Sooner or later, we all must walk through Doubting Castle. Sooner or later, we all must be bound in the Dungeon of Darkness. Sooner or later, we all must be sifted as wheat.

No Break

When we read John 14, we should always consciously remember that there is no break between chapters 13 and 14. Our Lord Jesus is continuing the discourse he began after washing the disciples' feet and the scene of Judas leaving him and the eleven faithful disciples to make his plans to betray the Master.

There may have been a slight pause after Judas left, as he turned again to the whole body of the Apostles; but there may have been no pause at all, as if to indicate that what Judas was about to do was in no way contrary to his purpose. Be that as it may, the place, the time, and the audience are all the same.

Our Lord's great object throughout this and the two following chapters seems clear. His intent is to comfort, stablish, and build up his downcast, heart-troubled disciples. Our blessed Saviour saw that their hearts were troubled by many things. They had seen him, their Master, whom they loved so dearly, 'troubled in Spirit' (13:21). Their carnal, Jewish expectations of a temporal kingdom under a temporal Messiah were now shattered. The Lord Jesus had just told them that one of them would betray him. They had all watched Judas get up and walk out of the room. The Lord Jesus had just announced that he would only be with them a little while longer. Then, at last, he told them that they could not go with him. And the Lord Jesus had just told Peter that he would deny him three times before the rising of the morning sun. 'The cock shall not crow, till thou hast denied me thrice. Let not your heart be troubled: ye believe in God, believe also in me.'

For all these reasons, this little band of weak believers was disquieted, troubled at heart, cast down, anxious, and fearful. The Master saw it and proceeded to give them this sweet, blessed word of encouragement: 'Let not your heart be troubled'. Note this, too, our blessed Redeemer used the singular, 'your heart', not the plural, 'your hearts'. He was saying particularly to Peter, 'Let not your heart be troubled: ye believe in God, believe also in me.' He was saying to them all, collectively, 'Let not your heart be troubled: ye believe in

God, believe also in me.' And he was saying to you and me, to all his own, 'Let not your heart be troubled: ye believe in God, believe also in me.'

Only One Relief

Faith in the Lord Jesus is the only real relief for troubled hearts. To believe more thoroughly, trust more entirely, rest more unreservedly, lay hold more firmly, lean back more completely upon him is the prescription our Master gives all his beloved disciples. No doubt, the members of that little band which sat round the table at the last supper were believers already. They had proved the reality of their faith by giving up everything for Christ's sake. Yet, once more, he presses on them and on us the old, much needed lesson, the lesson with which they first began: 'Believe! Believe more! Believe on me!' 'As ye have therefore received Christ Jesus the Lord, so walk ye in him' (Colossians 2:6).

Our Saviour's words, 'Ye believe in God, believe also in me', have caused much confusion to some; but the confusion is needless. The Lord Jesus was not implying that faith in God, and faith in him as the God-man Mediator were different. There is no faith in God apart from faith in Christ. Abel, Enoch, Abraham, Moses, and David, like all believers in the Old Testament, believed in the Saviour, just as we do.

So why did our Master say to his disciples, 'Ye believe in God, believe also in me'? The words should be read as a double imperative. The Master was saying, 'Believe! Believe! Believe God! Believe me'! They might even be read as a double indicative: 'You believe God and you believe me. So stop letting your heart be troubled.'

Still, we should never forget that between faith in Christ and strong faith in Christ there is a great gulf. There are degrees of faith. Some believers are weak in faith, and some are strong in faith. Those who are strong in faith are very often very weak in faith. And those who are weak in faith are often strong in faith. Some of the martyrs who were burned at the stake recanted at first; but later proved themselves strong, and sealed their testimonies with their blood.

We have all had to say, with the man who brought his demon possessed son to the Saviour, 'Lord, I believe; help thou mine unbelief' (Mark 9:24). But the weakest faith in Christ is saving faith. It should never be despised. Yet, weak faith is often the cause of great heart trouble. Vagueness and dimness of perception, fearfulness and fretfulness are the defects of weak faith. The disciples on the storm-tossed sea were, at the time, weak in faith, though they were truly strong believers. The Master said to them, 'How is it that ye have no faith?' (Mark 4:40).

When we are doubtful and weak in faith, we do not see clearly whom we believe, what we believe, and why we believe. At such times, more faith is the one thing needed. Like Peter on the water, we need to look more steadily and firmly, more confidently and fully to the Lord Jesus, and less at the waves and wind. It is written, 'Thou wilt keep him in perfect peace whose mind is stayed on thee, because he trusteth in thee' (Isaiah 26:3).

Faith in Christ is the only real relief there is for heart trouble (1 Peter 5:6, 7; Psalms 121:1-8).

Our Heavenly Home

We have, secondly, in this passage a very sweet and comfortable description of heaven and the blessed abode that awaits us on the other side of the grave. What a home our eternal home in heaven must be! We understand very little about heaven while we are here in the body. And the little that is revealed to us in the scriptures is revealed more by negative than by positive statements. We know much more about what will not be there than we do about what will be there. But here the Lord Jesus assures us of four distinct things about our heavenly home. 'In my Father's house are many mansions: if it were not so, I would have told you. I go to prepare a place for you'.

Heaven is the 'Father's house'. 'In my Father's house'! Heaven is the house of that God of whom the blessed Saviour said, 'I go to my Father and your Father'. Heaven is our Father's house. In other words, heaven is home: the home of Christ and his people. This is a sweet and touching expression. Home is the place where we are loved for our own sakes, and not for our gifts or possessions. Home is the place where we are always loved, and loved to the end. Home is the place where we are never forgotten, and always welcome. We are in a strange land here. In heaven we will be home. In the life to come we will be at home forever.

Heaven is a place of 'mansions'. It is a place of rich, lavish, lasting, permanent, and eternal dwellings. Here in the body we are in temporary lodgings; tents, and tabernacles. In these tabernacles of clay we experience many changes, both bad and good, both painful and pleasing. In heaven we shall be settled at last, and go out no more. 'Here we have no continuing city' (Hebrews 13:14). Our house not made with hands shall never be taken down. It shall never undergo change (2 Corinthians 4:17-5:9).

Heaven is a place of 'many mansions', not just mansions, but 'many mansions'. There will be room for all believers and room for all sorts, for little saints as well as great ones, for the weakest believer as well as for the strongest. The feeblest child of God need not fear there will be no place for him. None will be shut out but impenitent sinners and obstinate unbelievers. In heaven there are many mansions, because a great multitude shall dwell there with the Lord forever (Revelation 5:11-14; 7:1-17; 14:1-4; 19:1-9).

Heaven is a place where Christ himself dwells forever. And he is not content to dwell there without us! 'Where I am, there ye shall be also' is his promise. We should never imagine that we are alone, or that we shall ever be alone or neglected. Christ is our ever present God and Saviour; and he shall be with us and us with him forever (John 17:24). 'To be absent from the body is to be present with the Lord'. Our Saviour, our elder Brother, our Redeemer, who loved us and gave himself for us, shall be in the midst of us forever. What we shall see and whom we shall see in heaven, we cannot yet fully conceive, while we are in the body. But one thing is certain: we shall see Christ. And 'when we see him, we shall be like him; for we shall see him as he is'!

O blessed hope! O sweet consolation! To the worldly and careless and unbelieving these things may seem to be the empty dreams of deluded and ignorant men and women full of religious superstition; but to all who feel in themselves the workings of the Spirit of God, to all in whom the Son of God dwells, they are full of unspeakable comfort, and fill our souls with joyful anticipation, as we look 'for the mercy of our Lord Jesus Christ unto eternal life' (Jude 21).

Good Things To Come

Thirdly, we have in verse 3 solid ground for expecting good things to come. 'I go to prepare a place for you'. Sweet, sweet promise! Heaven is a prepared place for a prepared people: a place which the Lord Jesus Christ himself has made ready for us. He has prepared it by procuring a right for every sinner who believes to enter in by the merit of his obedience and the merit of his blood. None can stop us and say we have no business there. Our Lord Jesus has prepared it by going before us as our Head and Representative, and taking possession of it as our Forerunner; the Head, Representative, and Forerunner of all the members of his mystical body, the Church. As our Forerunner, he has marched in, leading captivity captive, and has planted his banner in the land of glory. He has prepared it by carrying our names with him as our High Priest into the holy of holies and making angels ready to receive us. When we enter the gates of heaven, we will find that we are neither unknown nor unexpected.

'I will come again and receive you unto myself'. Our Lord Jesus Christ will not wait for us to come up to him. He will come down to us, to raise us from our graves and escort us to our heavenly home. As Joseph came to meet Jacob, so the Lord Jesus will come to call his people together and guide us to our eternal inheritance in heaven.

The second advent ought never to be forgotten. We do not think of it as we should, with constant expectation, standing as it were upon the tiptoe of faith and expectation. Great is the blessedness of looking back to Christ coming the first time to suffer and die for us as our sin-atoning Substitute. But let us never forget the glory that must and shall follow his sufferings (1 Corinthians 15:51-58; 1 Thessalonians 4:13-18; 2 Thessalonians 1:7-10).

'Let not your heart be troubled: ye believe in God, believe also in me. In my Father's house are many mansions: if it were not so, I would have told you. I go to prepare a place for you. And if I go and prepare a place for you, I will come again, and receive you unto myself; that where I am, there ye may be also.'

Chapter 30

Seven Promises

'Let not your heart be troubled: ye believe in God, believe also in me ... But that the world may know that I love the Father; and as the Father gave me commandment, even so I do. Arise, let us go hence' (John 14:1-31).

All the promises of God are in Christ Jesus; and all the promises of God in Christ Jesus are sure promises. They are all 'yea and amen'. Here in John 14 we have seven of God's great yea and amen promises that fell from the lips of our blessed Saviour just before he died as our sin-atoning Substitute at Calvary. Grace was poured into his lips when he stood forth as our covenant Surety before the world was made (Psalms 45:2); and grace poured out of his lips as he prepared his disciples for the troubles they would face in this world.

Everything in this blessed chapter is intended by our dear Saviour to comfort our hearts, strengthen our souls, and steady our spirits in a world of woe. May God the Holy Spirit graciously write them upon our hearts.

First, let us note, our blessed Saviour, the Lord Jesus Christ, is coming again (vv. 1-3). I find it delightful that the very first thing our Redeemer promised his disciples, after telling them that he was going away, was 'I will come again'! He was going away to die for us, to obtain eternal redemption for us, to prepare a place for us, to be our Advocate and High Priest in heaven, to make intercession for us, going away to save all his chosen, blood-bought people by the power of his grace. But the very first thing our Redeemer promised his disciples, after telling them that he was going away, was 'I will come again'!

'Let not your heart be troubled: ye believe in God, believe also in me. In my Father's house are many mansions: if it were not so, I would have told you. I go to prepare a place for you. And if I go and prepare a place for you, I will come again, and receive you unto myself; that where I am, there ye may be also.'

'I will come again and receive you unto myself'. Christ will not wait for us to come up to him. He will come down to us, to raise us from our graves and escort us to our heavenly home. As Joseph came to meet Jacob, so the Lord Jesus will come to call his people together and guide us to our eternal inheritance in heaven. Spirit of God, give us grace ever to live in the immediate expectation of our Saviour's glorious second advent, anticipating the fulfilment of the 'blessed hope', the glorious appearing of the great God and our Saviour (1 Corinthians 15:51-58; 1 Thessalonians 4:13-18; 2 Thessalonians 1:7-10).

There is a way to God, a way to heaven, a way to eternal life and salvation (vv. 4-11).

There is a sure way of salvation for poor, needy sinners; and that Way is Christ himself. Jesus Christ himself is Salvation (vv. 4-11).

'And whither I go ye know, and the way ye know. Thomas saith unto him, Lord, we know not whither thou goest; and how can we know the way? Jesus saith unto him, I am the way, the truth, and the life: no man cometh unto the Father, but by me. If ye had known me, ye should have known my Father also: and from henceforth ye know him, and have seen him. Philip saith unto him, Lord, shew us the Father, and it sufficeth us. Jesus saith unto him, Have I been so long time with you, and yet hast thou not known me, Philip? He that hath seen me hath seen the Father; and how sayest thou then, Shew us the Father? Believest thou not that I am in the Father, and the Father in me? the words that I speak unto you I speak not of myself: but the Father that dwelleth in me, he doeth the works. Believe me that I am in the Father, and the Father in me: or else believe me for the very works' sake.'

Christ is the Way. Without him there's no going. He is the Way, not a way, the Way of salvation. Salvation is by his obedience alone. Salvation is by his death alone. Salvation is by his grace alone. 'Salvation is of the Lord'!

Christ is the Truth. Without him there's no knowing. He alone is the Truth, the very embodiment of all Truth. He alone reveals the Truth. He alone makes God known to men. And he alone is faithful and true.

Christ is the Life. Without him there's no living. Christ is the Author and Giver of life: natural, spiritual, and eternal. He is the only Way of life, 'the living way'. He always has been, and ever will be the Way, the Truth, and the Life. All who are in the Way, know the Truth, and have the Life. None shall ever be put out of the Way. None shall ever depart from the Truth. And none shall ever die who have the Life!

'No man cometh unto the Father but by me.' Christ is the only way of access to the Father. There is no coming to God by your works. There is no coming to God by religious duties and ceremonies. There is no coming to God without a Mediator; and the only Mediator between God and man is the man Christ Jesus.

The Lord Jesus promises us that his cause in this world is never in jeopardy. The purpose of God never alters. The cause of God is never injured. The Church of God is always safe. And the glory of God is always sure (vv. 12-14).

'Verily, verily, I say unto you, he that believeth on me, the works that I do shall he do also; and greater works than these shall he do; because I go unto my Father. And whatsoever ye shall ask in my name, that will I do, that the Father may be glorified in the Son. If ye shall ask any thing in my name, I will do it.'

As if to endear himself yet the more to our hearts and to convince us that his whole heart and soul is ours (Jeremiah 32:41), our Lord Jesus urges us to continually send our hearts' desires and prayers to him in heaven, that he might present them to his and our Father (Hebrews 4:16). And he assures us, that whatsoever we should ask the Father in his name he will do it for us, that the Father might be glorified in the Son. What a promise!

He who is possessed by the desire that God may be glorified has in this assurance a wondrous promise before him of successful, effectual prayer. To pray in Christ's name is to identify ourselves with him who ever seeks the fulfilment of the will and purpose of God. Such prayer is always effectual prayer.

God the Holy Spirit will abide with us, dwell in us, keep us, and comfort us forever.

'If ye love me, keep my commandments. And I will pray the Father, and he shall give you another Comforter, that he may abide with you for ever; Even the Spirit of truth; whom the world cannot receive, because it seeth him not, neither knoweth him: but ye know him; for he dwelleth with you, and shall be in you' (vv. 15-17).

Throughout the days of our sojourn through this vale of tears, our blessed Saviour has promised that he will come to us with his all-sufficient grace. This is the promise set before us in verses 18-24.

'I will not leave you comfortless: I will come to you. Yet a little while, and the world seeth me no more; but ye see me: because I live, ye shall live also. At that day ye shall know that I am in my Father, and ye in me, and I in you. He that hath my commandments, and keepeth them, he it is that loveth me: and he that loveth me shall be loved of my Father, and I will love him, and will manifest myself to him. Judas saith unto him, not Iscariot, Lord, how is it that thou wilt manifest thyself unto us, and not unto the world? Jesus answered and said unto him, If a man love me, he will keep my words: and my Father will love him, and we will come unto him, and make our abode with him. He that loveth me not keepeth not my sayings: and the word which ye hear is not mine, but the Father's which sent me.'

'I will not leave you comfortless: I will come to you.' The Son of God promises to come to each of his elect in the power of his saving grace and to come to every believing sinner, every sinner saved by his grace, in restoring mercy when he falls, reviving grace when his soul languishes, and sufficient grace as needed. Then he says, 'Yet a little while, and the world seeth me no more; but ye see me.' We see him by faith, through the eyes of faith he created in us, and by the light he gives us. And then our dear Saviour declares, 'Because I live, ye shall live also. At that day ye shall know that I am in my Father, and ye in me, and I in you.' O blessed, wondrous, indescribable union!

Our Saviour promises us that God the Holy Spirit, the Divine Comforter, will be our Teacher.

'These things have I spoken unto you, being yet present with you. But the Comforter, which is the Holy Ghost, whom the Father will send in my name, he shall teach you all things, and bring all things to your remembrance, whatsoever I have said unto you' (vv. 25, 26).

He comforts us by teaching us all things, by giving us the mind of Christ, by giving us spiritual understanding, by bringing to our remembrance the sweet revelations of grace in the gospel (Isaiah 40:1, 2).

The Son of God has promised to keep us in peace. 'Peace I leave with you, my peace I give unto you: not as the world giveth, give I unto you. Let not your heart be troubled, neither let it be afraid. Ye have heard how I said unto you, I go away, and come again unto you. If ye loved me, ye would rejoice, because I said, I go unto the Father' (vv. 27, 28).

If they had known, how they would have rejoiced! He was going to the Father as our Surety and Saviour, as our God-man Mediator, as Jehovah's Righteous Servant, having accomplished all his covenant engagements, to obtain eternal redemption by his blood! Read on …

'For my Father is greater than I. And now I have told you before it come to pass, that, when it is come to pass, ye might believe. Hereafter I will not talk much with you: for the prince of this world cometh, and hath nothing in me. But that the world may know that I love the Father; and as the Father gave me commandment, even so I do. Arise, let us go hence' (vv. 28-31).

Blessed Lord Jesus, Almighty Preacher, give us grace to sit at your feet and hear by faith your sweet, omnipotent voice in this great message, in each of these great promises. Graciously cause them to sink deep into our hearts. You are indeed the Way, and the Truth, and the Life. By you alone we have access to God. We own none but you. We claim none but you. We plead none but you.

Thank you, blessed Saviour, for the gift of your Spirit, God our Comforter! Thank you, O Holy Ghost, for constantly showing us the things of Christ, for constantly reminding us of him who loved us and gave himself for us, for constantly turning us to him, even as we turn ourselves from him! Thank you for sealing us with your grace and never leaving us.

O Father of mercies, God of all grace, we bless and praise your holy name forever for your free, everlasting love by which you have given us your dear Son and all the grace of your Holy Spirit. 'Thanks be unto God for his unspeakable gift'!

Chapter 31

Wondrous Mystery

'Let not your heart be troubled: ye believe in God, believe also in me. In my Father's house are many mansions: if it were not so, I would have told you. I go to prepare a place for you. And if I go and prepare a place for you, I will come again, and receive you unto myself; that where I am, there ye may be also.'

'And whither I go ye know, and the way ye know. Thomas saith unto him, Lord, we know not whither thou goest; and how can we know the way? Jesus saith unto him, I am the way, the truth, and the life: no man cometh unto the Father, but by me. If ye had known me, ye should have known my Father also: and from henceforth ye know him, and have seen him. Philip saith unto him, Lord, shew us the Father, and it sufficeth us. Jesus saith unto him, Have I been so long time with you, and yet hast thou not known me, Philip? He that hath seen me hath seen the Father; and how sayest thou then, Shew us the Father? Believest thou not that I am in the Father, and the Father in me? the words that I speak unto you I speak not of myself: but the Father that dwelleth in me, he doeth the works. Believe me that I am in the Father, and the Father in me: or else believe me for the very works' sake.'

'Verily, verily, I say unto you, he that believeth on me, the works that I do shall he do also; and greater works than these shall he do; because I go unto my Father. And whatsoever ye shall ask in my name, that will I do, that the Father may be glorified in the Son. If ye shall ask any thing in my name, I will do it.'

'If ye love me, keep my commandments. And I will pray the Father, and he shall give you another Comforter, that he may abide with you for ever; Even the Spirit of truth; whom the world cannot receive, because it seeth him not, neither knoweth him: but ye know him; for he dwelleth with you, and shall be in you.'

'I will not leave you comfortless: I will come to you. Yet a little while, and the world seeth me no more; but ye see me: because I live, ye shall live also. At that day ye shall know that I am in my Father, and ye in me, and I in you' (John 14:1-20).

God the Holy Spirit tells us that there are two things revealed in the gospel that are great mysteries, just two. There are many mysteries revealed in the gospel; but only two are singled out with special emphasis by the Spirit of God as 'great' mysteries. The first is the mystery of the incarnation.

'And without controversy great is the mystery of godliness: God was manifest in the flesh, justified in the Spirit, seen of angels, preached unto the Gentiles, believed on in the world, received up into glory' (1 Timothy 3:16).

The union of deity and humanity is a mystery no mortal can comprehend. We believe it. We rejoice in it. We hang our souls upon it. 'The Word was made flesh and dwelt among us'! But no man can fully understand, let alone explain the great mystery of godliness.

Ephesians 5 sets the second great mystery of the gospel before us. 'Husbands, love your wives, even as Christ also loved the church, and gave himself for it; That he might sanctify and cleanse it with the washing of water by the word, That he might present it to himself a glorious church, not having spot, or wrinkle, or any such thing; but that it should be holy and without blemish. So ought men to love their wives as their own bodies. He that loveth his wife loveth himself. For no man ever yet hated his own flesh; but nourisheth and cherisheth it, even as the Lord the church: For we are members of his body, of his flesh, and of his bones. For this cause shall a man leave his father and mother, and shall be joined unto his wife, and they two shall be one flesh. This is a great mystery: but I speak concerning Christ and the church' (Ephesians 5:25-32).

This is truly a great mystery. Like the mystery of the incarnation, it is one no mortal can comprehend. We believe it. We rejoice in it. We hang our souls upon it. 'We are members of his body, of his flesh, and of his bones', spiritually bone of his bone and flesh of his flesh! But no man can fully understand, let alone explain the great mystery of the union of God's elect with Christ.

The depths of this subject are utterly unfathomable. The most brilliant, the most well-taught, the most spiritual mind can never find the bottom of this great ocean. May God the Holy Spirit take us by the hand and lead us as we wade around in these sweet, refreshing waters of grace. Paul tells us in Colossians 1:27 that this is a mystery that is both rich and glorious. There is a world of glorious riches in this matchless mystery!

Three Great Unions

In the passage before us (John 14:1-20) our Lord Jesus declares that this great mystery is the thing that God the Holy Spirit reveals in us and to us, by which he gives us the comfort and assurance of grace and salvation. Look at verse 20, particularly. 'At that day', at that day when God the Holy Spirit is given to you, on the day he creates faith in you, at the time he comes into you as the Spirit of life, to abide in you forever and comfort you, 'at that day', the Son of God says, 'ye shall know' these three things.

1. 'I am in my Father'. By divine revelation all who are taught of God the Holy Spirit understand there is a union between the man Christ Jesus and God the Father, between our humanity and the Son of God. We understand the man who is our Saviour and the eternal God are one. Sweet comfort it is to our souls! It is the foundation of all comfort to our souls.

2. 'Ye (are) in me'. Every sinner taught of God, who are given life and faith in Christ, are made to understand that Christ is their Representative and Substitute. We rejoice to know, by divine illumination, that God the Father made his Son a public person; the Representative, Surety, and Substitute of our souls from everlasting (Proverbs 8). That means that he stood in our room and place; he stood in our stead from eternity.

3. 'And I (am) in you'. The Saviour is saying, 'You shall know, in the very day that I give my Spirit to you, that I am in you.'

Eternal Union

The Puritan, Thomas Goodwin, wrote that this 'union of Jesus Christ and his saints is a great and eminent mystery of the gospel, and the greatest hope of glory.' 'At that day ye shall know that I am in my Father, and ye in me, and I in you.' As God is in Christ and Christ is in him, so we who are born of God are in Christ and Christ is in us. That is the one thing I want to communicate to you in this study. If you trust the Lord Jesus Christ, if you are born of God, you and Christ are one. Imagine that. You and Christ are one, not two, one!

By God's sov'reign grace united
To His Son eternally,
I can never be divided
From my cov'nant Surety.
God's free love, from everlasting,
Made me one with His dear Son.
Blessed union, strong, unchanging,
I am with my Saviour one!

Once in Christ, in Christ forever.
Thus His promise ever stands.
Life and death and hell together
Cannot tear me from His hands!
Oft I fall, but God unchanging,
Faithful to His cov'nant stands.
He will never charge with sinning
Those for whom His Son was slain.

One with Jesus, one with Jesus,
By eternal union one!
One with Jesus, one with Jesus,
O what wonders grace has done!
One with Christ from everlasting!
One with Him upon the tree!
One with Him on high ascending!
One with Him eternally!

In the New Testament the nature of the union of Christ and his church is set before us everywhere. It is so constantly and so clearly set forth that it cannot be missed, except by those who choose not to see it. Every act of Christ on earth is set forth in the scriptures of truth as being, in some way, connected with his union with us and our union with him. Was he circumcised? We are circumcised in him (Colossians 2:11). Was he crucified? We are crucified with him (Galatians 2:20). Did he die? We died with him (Romans 6:8). Was he buried in the tomb? We are buried with him (Romans 6:4). Was he raised up from the dead? We are risen together with him (Colossians 2:12). Did he ascend on high and sit down in glory? God has made us sit together in heavenly places in him (Ephesians 2:6). Does he live? He lives in me (Galatians 2:20).

In the book of God this union of Christ and his members is traced out in everything our Lord did, in every act of obedience, and in everything he suffered during his transitory abode upon earth, and in everything he has received in his glory because of his obedience to the Father as our Surety and Substitute. The scriptures show us, in the clearest and most prominent light, that there is an eternal union between Christ and his beloved people.

'Twixt Jesus and the chosen race
Subsists a bond of sovereign grace,
That hell, with its infernal train,
Shall ne'er dissolve nor rend in vain

Wondrous Mystery

This sacred bond shall never break,
Though earth should to her centre shake;
Rest, doubting saint, assured of this,
For God has pledged His holiness.

He swore but once the deed was done;
'Twas settled by the great Three One;
Christ was appointed to redeem
All that the Father loved in Him.

Hail! sacred union, firm and strong,
How great the grace, how sweet the song,
That worms of earth should ever be
One with incarnate Deity!

One in the tomb, one when He rose,
One when He triumphed o'er His foes,
One when in heaven He took His seat,
While seraphs sang all hell's defeat.

This sacred tie forbids their fears,
For all He is or has is theirs;
With Him, their Head, they stand or fall,
Their life, their surety, and their all.

The sinner's Peace, the Daysman He,
Whose blood should set His people free;
On them His fond affections ran,
Before creation's work began.

Blest be the wisdom and the grace,
Th' eternal love and faithfulness,
That's in the gospel scheme revealed,
And is by God the Spirit sealed.

John Kent

This union that exists between us and our Saviour is an eternal union. It is a union of pure, free grace, established in the beginning, before ever God made the heavens and the earth, when the Lord Jesus stood forth and was accepted as your Surety in the covenant of grace (Ephesians 1:3-6).

Vital Union

The old writers used to refer to this union as 'a vital union', and they were right in doing so. It is a union that is vital both to Christ and to us. It is vital to us because we cannot exist apart from him, any more than branches severed from the vine can exist apart from the vine (John 15:1-6). Yet, this union is vital to Christ as the God-man Mediator, too. God the Holy Ghost describes us, as being 'the fulness of him that filleth all in all' (Ephesians 1:22, 23). Commenting on that remarkable declaration of God, John Calvin wrote,

> This is the highest honour of the Church, that, until he is united to us, the Son of God reckons himself in some measure imperfect. What consolation is it for us to learn, that, not until we are with him, does he possess all his parts, or wish to be regarded as complete.

John Trapp said essentially the same thing.

> Christ, who having voluntarily subjected himself to be our Head, accounts not himself complete without his members. In which respect we have the honour of making Christ perfect as the members do the body.

God's elect are the fulness of him in whom is all fulness. As the triune God could not be complete without him, he cannot be complete without his people.

Life Union

This union of Christ and our souls is a union of life, life in Christ, life with Christ, and life by Christ, by the mysterious, wondrous extraction of life from Christ.

'And the LORD God said, It is not good that the man should be alone; I will make him an help meet for him. And out of the ground the LORD God formed every beast of the field, and every fowl of the air; and brought them unto Adam to see what he would call them: and whatsoever Adam called every living creature, that was the name thereof. And Adam gave names to all cattle, and to the fowl of the air, and to every beast of the field; but for Adam there was not found an help meet for him.'

'And the LORD God caused a deep sleep to fall upon Adam, and he slept: and he took one of his ribs, and closed up the flesh instead thereof; And the rib, which the LORD God had taken from man, made he a woman, and brought her unto the man. And Adam said, This is now bone of my bones, and flesh of my flesh: she shall be called Woman, because she was taken out of Man. Therefore shall a man leave his father and his mother, and shall cleave unto his wife: and they shall be one flesh' (Genesis 2:18-24).

Whether Adam fully understood the implications of his words or not I cannot say. But our Lord Jesus Christ knows perfectly well the origin of his spouse. He knows where his church came from. He still wears the mark in his side and the memorial in the palms of his hands and on his feet. Whence came this new Eve, this new mother of all living? Whence came this spouse of the second Adam? She came of the second Adam. She was taken from his side, from his very heart! Have we not read, 'Except a corn of wheat fall into the ground and die, it abideth alone; but if it die, it bringeth forth much fruit'? Had the Lord Jesus never died, he would have abode forever alone, with no help-meet for him, no spouse upon whom to pour out his love. But, since he died, he has brought forth much fruit; and his church, taken from his side, has her life from him, in him, and with him. She is truly bone of his bones, and flesh of his flesh! We sprang out of Christ, even as Levi sprang from the loins of Abraham. We live because we receive life from him.

As bone of his bones and flesh of his flesh, we are the possession of our Husband, the purchase of his blood, the property of his love, and the object of his relentless devotion and care. Wondrous thought! We belong to the Son of God. We are his peculiar possession! The property of his heart! I belong to Christ alone. He bought me with his blood. I am a member 'of his body, of his flesh, and of his bones'!

Manifest Union

This vital union is an eternal union of life, life extracted from him who is Life. Yet, it is a secret union until God the Holy Spirit is given to the chosen, redeemed sinner in the saving operations of his omnipotent grace. And this union of life with Christ is a union that is made manifest in the new birth. The birth of a child is not the beginning of life, but the manifestation of life. So, too, the birth of a new man 'created in righteousness and true holiness' in regeneration is not the beginning of life, but life and immortality brought to light by the gospel (2 Timothy 1:9, 10).

'At that day ye shall know that I am in my Father, and ye in me, and I in you.' Pastor Chris Cunningham once wrote, 'I believe men will argue about the new nature up until the time that they have one, and then they will just be grateful to the God of all grace, who makes all things new.' That is exactly what our Saviour says in John 14:20. When a sinner has a new nature, in the very day he is born of God, he knows it. You may not have known what to call it, or how to describe it; but you knew from the beginning of your new life in Christ that it was a new life, that Christ had come into you.

The Warfare

It is this impartation of Christ, the new creation in us, that begins the warfare inside, with which all God's people struggle in this world. How beastly we are by nature! How often God's saints in this world are compelled, like John Newton of old, to sigh,

> If I love, why am I thus?
> Why this dull and lifeless frame?
> Hardly sure can they be worse,
> Who have never heard His name.

Many of the doubts and fears God's people experience regarding their saving interest in Christ arise from a failure to realise that every heaven-born soul lives in this world with two natures. In scripture these two natures are referred to as 'the old man, which is corrupt according to the deceitful lusts', and 'the new man, which after God is created in righteousness and true holiness' (Ephesians 4:22-24), 'flesh' and 'spirit' (Galatians 5:16, 17). These two natures are constantly at war, the flesh lusting against the spirit and the spirit against the flesh.

Regeneration Not Reformation

It is commonly assumed that in the new birth man, that is, the natural, carnal man, is changed; that the old man is sanctified, that he who once loved sin is made to love holiness, that the enmity of the heart is slain, and that the old man renewed by grace grows more and more holy in progressive sanctification, until he is ripe for glory and the Lord takes him home.

That fanciful dream deludes multitudes, until, after being born again, they suddenly discover that the old lusts are still there. The discovery is sometimes shocking, simply because we have been taught that they would not be there any longer. How many there are who live in constant turmoil, knowing the abiding evil of their nature, but never daring to acknowledge it, lest they be scorned by others who pretend to be holy.

The new birth is not a re-formation, but a re-generation. The new birth is not reforming the old nature of fallen man, but a re-creation of life in man by the Spirit of God. It is not transforming what is sinful into what is righteous, but imparting a new, righteous nature. In the new birth Christ is formed in us, and we are made new in him (Colossians 1:27; 2 Corinthians 5:17).

Two Natures

In every believer there are two natures (sin and righteousness), two men (the old man Adam and the new man Christ), two principles (sin and holiness); and these two constantly oppose one another. This fact is plainly declared in scripture (Romans 7:14-24; Galatians 5:16-22; Colossians 3:9, 10; Ephesians 4:22-24). The old man, Adam, can never be sanctified; and the new man created in righteousness and true holiness, 'Christ in you the hope of glory', cannot sin (1 John 3:9).

Adam lives in us by birth. By natural generation we are made partakers of Adam's nature. Christ lives in us by the new birth. By regeneration we are made 'partakers of the divine nature' (2 Peter 1:4).

Creation And New Creation

God created man in his own image and after his own likeness (Genesis 1:26, 27). When the Lord God had formed a body for Adam from the dust of the ground, he then 'breathed into his nostrils the breath of life and man became a living soul' (Genesis 2:7). Genesis 5:1, 2 tells us that all men were created at one time in the creation of Adam. That is to say, every living soul descends by natural generation from Adam, partaking of his nature. All his sons and daughters are begotten in the image of their father, generation after generation (Genesis 5:3; Psalms 51:5; 58:3; Romans 5:12).

Every living soul was created in and simultaneously with 'the first man Adam'. Being born of Adam, we are all partakers of his nature; and we are called by his name, 'Adam' (Genesis 5:1, 2). As it was in the original creation, so it is in the new creation.

As 'the first man Adam was made a living soul; the last Adam was made a quickening Spirit' (1 Corinthians 15:45). All quickened spirits were created in and simultaneously with Christ, the 'last Adam'. Of course, Christ is not a creature of God. He is God the eternal Son. Yet, he was made our Mediator and covenant Surety. All, being born of him, being 'born of God', are made partakers of his nature, as the Holy Spirit declares (2 Peter 1:4). The children of the 'first Adam' are born of the flesh and are earthy in all their feelings and affections. The children of the 'last Adam' are born of the Spirit and are heavenly, or spiritual in their feelings and affections. The children of the first Adam are born for the earth. The children of the last Adam are born for heaven. Those of the first are born of corruptible seed. Those of the last are born of incorruptible seed.

In the original creation we were made partakers of Adam's human nature. In the new creation of grace we are made partakers of the last Adam's nature, 'the divine nature'. That is the cause of the warfare within. These two natures are contrary the one to the other. We wear our Saviour's name. He has given it to us in free justification. We have his nature. He gives that to us in free sanctification, regeneration. Christ is the Lord our Righteousness in justification (Jeremiah 23:6; 33:16), and the Lord our Holiness in sanctification (Hebrews 12:14).

Just As Necessary

In Hebrews 12:14 the Spirit of God tells us that there is a 'holiness without which no man shall see the Lord'. In Ephesians 4:24 he declares that all who are born of God are born new creatures in Christ Jesus, 'created in righteousness and true holiness'. The holiness without which none can enter into heaven is the righteousness of God and this is imparted to the heaven-born soul in regeneration. It is the divine nature of Christ of which we are made partakers by grace (2 Peter 1:4). This is the experience of the new birth; and it is just as necessary to the salvation of our souls as the righteousness of Christ imparted to us in justification.

Without question, the new birth is the certain result of our Saviour's accomplishments in his death as our Substitute; but if we have no living union with Christ, his mediatorial accomplishments at Calvary cannot effect our deliverance from the wrath to come. Be sure you understand my meaning. You cannot go to heaven without a righteous nature (imparted righteousness in sanctification) any more than you can without a righteous record (imputed righteousness in justification). Some have said, 'If you believe that, you're a lunatic.' If that is so, call me, the Apostle Paul (Ephesians 4:24; Hebrews 12:14), the Apostle Peter (2 Peter 1:4), the Apostle John (1 John 3:9; Revelation 21:27), and the Son of God (John 14:20) lunatics!

Born Of The Spirit

Though the obedience of Christ unto death met all the claims of the law and satisfied divine justice for all the chosen seed, that obedience does not impart to the redeemed a qualification for the enjoyment of heaven. For that we must be born again. 'Except a man be born of water and of the Spirit, he cannot enter into the kingdom of God. That which is born of the flesh is flesh; and that which is born of the Spirit is spirit' (John 3:5, 6).

Here we are presented with two distinct births from two distinct elements, necessarily producing two distinct beings. The flesh produces beings incapable of entering into the kingdom of God. The flesh cannot enter into, understand, or enjoy that which is spiritual, let alone that which is heavenly. As one old writer put it, 'If the unregenerate man could enter heaven, he would be so unhappy in heaven that he would ask God to let him run down to hell for shelter.'

But God the Spirit produces beings capable of entering into the kingdom of God, capable of entering, understanding and enjoying that which is spiritual, making all who are born of the Spirit 'meet to be partakers of the inheritance of the saints in light' (Colossians 1:12). By the new birth God's elect are brought into an open and manifest union with Christ by faith; but our experience of it is not the beginning of this union.

The believer's vital union with Christ the Mediator is an everlasting union of grace. This union between Christ and our souls is, as Spurgeon put it, 'the nearest, dearest, closest, most intense, and most enduring relationship that can be imagined.' We live because Christ lives; and our lives are hid with Christ in God. This is a relationship that is closer than that of a husband and wife, or children and their parents.

Mystical Union

This union of Christ and his people is one of the greatest mysteries revealed in the book of God. 'We are members of his body, of his flesh, and of his bones' (Ephesians 5:30). It is a mystical union of grace. We are members of Christ. We form his mystical body. This is the closest relationship imaginable. It is such a close relationship, such a close union, that the Lord Jesus Christ would be as incomplete without us as we would be without him (Ephesians 1:23; Colossians 2:9, 10). We are identified with him; and he is identified with us. He has made us essential to himself, just as he has made himself essential to us! He is the head of the body; and we are the members of that body. That is a truly vital union. 'We are members of his body.'

Partakers Of Christ

As Eve derived her life from Adam (Genesis 2:18-25), so we derive our life from Christ. As Eve was made partaker of Adam's nature, so we are made partakers of Christ's nature. As Eve's life was but an extension of Adam's life, so our life is but an extension of Christ's life. He is eternal life; and we have eternal life by the gift of God. That eternal life is 'Christ in you' (Colossians 1:27). We are partakers of his life. Our spiritual life proceeds from and is sustained by Christ. It is the source of our present spiritual life, and of our eternal life in glory with Christ.

Let us never diminish one aspect of our Saviour's work to make another appear more glorious. All that Christ is made to us and all that he does for us is vital. We cannot be saved without his work for us; and we cannot be saved without his work in us. Both are vital.

Astonishing But Real

This union of Christ and our souls is real. Yes, it is a mystical, spiritual union, a union that is indescribably beyond the scope of our puny brains; but it is a real union. There are three great mystical unions revealed in holy scripture.

The union of the three persons of the Godhead, being one God, is the doctrine of the trinity (1 John 5:7).

The scriptures also reveal the union of divinity and humanity in the person of our Lord Jesus Christ. 'The Word was made flesh' (John 1:14).

And the book of God reveals this vital union of God's elect with Christ. Nothing can be more astonishing; but nothing is more real than our union with Christ.

Child of God, try to grasp the reality of this union you possess with your Saviour. You are one with the Christ of God! You were 'buried with him in baptism unto death', wherein also you have risen with him. You were crucified with him upon the cursed tree. You have gone up into heaven with him. God has raised us up together, and made us to sit together in the heavenly places in Christ Jesus. You are one with Christ! I am one with Christ!

Be astonished, O my soul! Being one with him, the Lord Jesus himself assures us that the Lord God our Father loves us as he loves him! He loves me to the same degree, with the same love, and for the same reason he loves his Son as my Mediator. He loves me and his Son with an everlasting love (John 17:23).

Since we are members of his body, he will one day present us to himself without spot, or wrinkle, or blemish. We will be perfect even as he is perfect. We will enter into the eternal joy in the Lord. We are joint heirs with Christ; therefore whatever he has we shall have.

Faith Union

This is a union that is ours, in the sweet experience of God's saving grace by faith in Christ.

'If ye love me, keep my commandments. And I will pray the Father, and he shall give you another Comforter, that he may abide with you for ever; Even the Spirit of truth; whom the world cannot receive, because it seeth him not, neither knoweth him: but ye know him; for he dwelleth with you, and shall be in you.'

'I will not leave you comfortless: I will come to you. Yet a little while, and the world seeth me no more; but ye see me: because I live, ye shall live also. At that day ye shall know that I am in my Father, and ye in me, and I in you' (John 14:15-20).

Do you ask, 'How can I keep his commandments?' The answer is found in 1 John 3:23. 'And this is his commandment, That we should believe on the name of his Son Jesus Christ, and love one another, as he gave us commandment.' We keep his commandments by faith in Christ. Believe on the Lord Jesus Christ and rejoice in this sweet assurance 'I am my beloved's and my beloved is mine'! As Christ is in the Father, I am in him and he is in me; and nothing can separate me from him'!

'Because I live', my Saviour says,
'You, too, shall live.' So, I'm secure.
His Word this blest foundation gives
Immutable, forever sure!

Here, O my soul, unshaken dwell,
Though vexed by sin, God's promise stands
Not all the powers of earth and hell
Can tear me from my Saviour's hands!

I'm one with Christ! Whate'er oppose,
Still, I am His and He is mine!
Not sin, nor hell, nor all my foes,
Can make His love for me decline!

O let me never doubt You, Lord!
Faith must upon Your Word rely
Immutable, eternal Word!
The Word that built both earth and sky!

Dead to the law and sin I am,
With Christ who bought me with His blood,
And risen with the risen Lamb,
My life is hid with Him in God!

Chapter 32

Warnings Or Promises?

'I am the true vine, and my Father is the husbandman ... And ye also shall bear witness, because ye have been with me from the beginning' (John 15:1-27).

On that solemn night before the Lord of life and glory was delivered into the hands of wicked men, he gave his disciples everything that might be needed to comfort their hearts, as he anticipated the trouble that was before them. His final discourse and his final actions, recorded by divine inspiration in John 13-18, are filled with things that are intended by him to encourage our faith in him, to give us confidence and assurance in him. Throughout these chapters, his word to us is, 'Let not your heart be troubled, neither let it be afraid'. If ever there was a time during the whole of our Saviour's earthly ministry in which he wanted to minister comfort and peace to the hearts of his beloved disciples, it was on that solemn night before his sin-atoning death as our Substitute. As with Psalm 23, these chapters are recorded in the book of God to minister to our souls in times of greatest trouble.

On that solemn night, he said to those disciples whose faith he knew must soon be greatly tried, 'I have chosen you' (13:18; 15:16, 19). How sweet a pillow that is for our aching hearts! He told them that one of them was a betrayer who would deliver him up to be crucified. He did so that, when it came to pass, their faith might not be shaken by it (13:18). He told them again of his impending death, assuring them of what he would accomplish in his death, and how God would be glorified in him and he would be glorified by the Father (13:31-33). Then, he told them that Satan desired to have them, that he might sift them as wheat, and assured them that their faith would not fail, because he had prayed for them (Luke 22:31, 32). After that, he turned to Peter and told him plainly that before the night was over he would deny him three times. That assertion was immediately followed by the assurance that his faith would not fail, that he would be recovered (converted) from his horrible fall, and encouraged still to believe him. 'The cock shall not crow, till thou hast denied me thrice. Let not your heart be troubled: ye believe in God, believe also in me' (13:38-14:1).

Throughout the night, he said to these disciples, all of whom would forsake him, as he anticipated their great fall, 'Believe me! Believe me! Believe me!' He did not say, Believe in me. He did not say, believe my doctrine. He said, 'Believe me!' And he assured them that he was going to prepare a place for them in heaven, and that he would bring them to that place, in spite of all that they would be, and do, and experience in the next few hours (14:1-3).

I remind you, again, that the difference between Judas's sin, which was for him sin unto death, and the sin that would be committed by Peter and the rest of the disciples (as well as yours and mine) was not their deeds, or the extent of their guilt, or the aggravating circumstances of their crimes, or even that one sinned against greater light or more persistently than the other. The only difference between Judas's fall and Peter's, between these disciples forsaking the Lord and Judas betraying him was this: the Lord prayed for Peter, those disciples, and us, that their faith and ours fail not; but he did not pray for Judas.

He assures us, though we must ever be kept aware of our sinfulness, that we might ever trust him that he would hear and answer our prayers and give us our hearts' desire (14:13, 14). As he anticipated all the weakness, failure, and sin that those beloved disciples would display in just a few hours, as he anticipated all the weaknesses, failures, and sins we would experience and display in this world, the Lord Jesus assured them and assures us that he will never leave us comfortless, that he will come to us, and that he, and his Father, and his Spirit will abide with us forever (14:16-20). What? Does the Son of God intend for sinners saved by his grace to be assured of his grace even when we fall? Indeed, he does (1 John 2:1, 2).

Then, he assures us of his abiding love and tells us that he will manifest himself to us (14:21). Repeatedly, he promised that he would give us his blessed Holy Spirit to be our Comforter, assuring us that he will teach us all things. Again, he says, I tell you all these things 'that ye might believe', that your faith be not shaken, that your confidence and assurance of my mercy and grace may never be shaken.

Vine And Branches

Then, in chapter 15, the Lord Jesus gives us this wonderful description and assurance of our everlasting union with him. 'I am the vine, ye are the branches'.

'I am the true vine, and my Father is the husbandman. Every branch in me that beareth not fruit he taketh away: and every branch that beareth fruit, he purgeth it, that it may bring forth more fruit. Now ye are clean through the word which I have spoken unto you. Abide in me, and I in you. As the branch cannot bear fruit of itself, except it abide in the vine; no more can ye, except ye abide in me. I am the vine, ye are the branches: he that abideth in me, and I in him, the same bringeth forth much fruit: for without me ye can do nothing. If a man abide not in me, he is cast forth as a branch, and is withered; and men gather them, and cast them into the fire, and they are burned' (vv. 1-6).

The first thing to be learned from this passage is the fact that there is a blessed union between Christ and his people that can never be broken. The word of God is filled with illustrations of the eternal union of Christ and his Church. This union of Christ and his elect is both eternal and vital. It is vital to us because without him we cannot live. It is vital to him as our Mediator because without us he would not be complete (Ephesians 1:23).

In the Song of Solomon, when the Bride sang her nuptial love song, she refers to her beloved as the vine. 'My beloved is unto me as a cluster of camphire in the vineyards of Engedi' (Song of Solomon 1:14). Our blessed Saviour is not just a blessing, but a cluster of blessedness (Ephesians 1:3-6; 1 Corinthians 1:30, 31). The word here translated 'cluster' means 'the man that is all things', or 'the man that has atoned and is all things of blessing'. That is what Christ is to us. 'All things are yours, for ye are Christ's.'

Our Lord Jesus, when he would sing his nuptial love song to us, his Bride, his Beloved, uses the very same imagery. 'I am the vine, ye are the branches'. So real and absolute is this union of our souls and our Saviour that we are spoken of in the book of God as the vine (Psalms 80:8-19; Song of Solomon 7:11, 12; 8:11-13). As the vine and the branches are one, so Christ and his people are one.

The union between Christ and believers is just as close and just as real as the union of the vine and the branches in the vine. In ourselves we have no life, or strength, or spiritual power. All we are and have comes from Christ. We are what we are, and feel what we feel, and do what we do, because we draw a continual supply of grace and help from him. Being grafted into Christ by grace, joined to him by faith, and united in mysterious union with him by the Spirit, we live, drawing the sap of life from him.

And, because we are one with him, vitally joined to him, we bring forth fruit from him and by him. Grace is not a self-operating principle, but the continual operation of God (Hosea 14:8). Of Christ's fulness we continually receive grace for grace. He declares, 'From me is thy fruit found' (Hosea 14:8).

The picture before us is as delightful as it is comforting. Believing sinners never have reason to be in doubt of eternal salvation. Our Saviour will never leave us to ourselves, to our own strength, or our own ability. It is God who works in us, both to will and to do of his good pleasure. Our root is Christ; and all there is in the Root is for the benefit of the branches. Because he lives, we shall live also. Weak as we are in ourselves, our Root is in heaven, and never dies. 'When I am weak', Paul said, 'then am I strong' (2 Corinthians 12:10). And his strength is demonstrated to be perfect through our weakness.

In the second verse we see that there are many, like Judas, who are in Christ the vine by profession only. They are fruitless branches that appear to be in the vine, but they are not. They do not abide in the Vine. They have not been grafted into the Vine, but are only attached to the Vine in outward appearance. Consequently, they bear no fruit and are useless. They shall be cast forth and burned as useless debris that is found in the vineyard. Are you like that? Are you attached to the Vine, but not in the Vine? Attached to the Vine by ritual, but not in the Vine by regeneration? Attached to the Vine by profession, but not in the Vine by power? Attached to the Vine by a creed in your head, but not in the Vine by circumcision of the heart? Let each answer for himself. Am I merely attached to the Vine? Believers are in Christ the true Vine. We are branches growing out of the Vine. Are you in Christ? If you trust him, you are in him.

The Assurances

Look at the sweet assurances given to us in this tremendous, instructive passage of holy scripture. 'Now ye are clean through the word which I have spoken unto you' (v. 3). 'As the Father hath loved me, so have I loved you: continue ye in my love' (v. 9). 'These things have I spoken unto you, that my joy might remain in you, and that your joy might be full' (v. 11). 'Greater love hath no man than this, that a man lay down his life for his friends' (v. 13). 'Henceforth I call you not servants; for the servant knoweth not what his lord doeth: but I have called you friends; for all things that I have heard of my Father I have made known unto you' (v. 15). 'Ye have not chosen me, but I have chosen you, and ordained you, that ye should go and bring forth fruit, and that your fruit should remain: that whatsoever ye shall ask of the Father in my name, he may give it you' (v. 16). 'But when the Comforter is come, whom I will send unto you from the Father, even the Spirit of truth, which proceedeth from the Father, he shall testify of me' (v. 26). 'And ye also shall bear witness, because ye have been with me from the beginning' (v. 27).

Warnings Or Promises?

Those sweet assurances are commonly overlooked, because there are several things in this chapter that are commonly interpreted as great, fearful warnings. 'Every branch in me that beareth not fruit he taketh away: and every branch that beareth fruit, he purgeth it, that it may bring forth more fruit' (v. 2). 'Abide in me, and I in you. As the branch cannot bear fruit of itself, except it abide in the vine; no more can ye, except ye abide in me' (v. 4). 'I am the vine, ye are the branches: he that abideth in me, and I in him, the same bringeth forth much fruit: for without me ye can do nothing' (v. 5). 'If a man abide not in me, he is cast forth as a branch, and is withered; and men gather them, and cast them into the fire, and they are burned' (v. 6). 'If ye abide in me, and my words abide in you, ye shall ask what ye will, and it shall be done unto you' (v. 7). 'Herein is my Father glorified, that ye bear much fruit; so shall ye be my disciples' (v. 8). 'If ye keep my commandments, ye shall abide in my love; even as I have kept my Father's commandments, and abide in his love' (v. 10). 'Ye are my friends, if ye do whatsoever I command you' (v. 14).

Are we to understand these statements by our Saviour as conditions that must be met by us? Are we to understand that if we fail to meet these conditions we will perish at last? Not hardly! Pastor Rupert Rivenbark made this tremendously helpful observation about such passages as these. He said, 'If all the 'ifs' in the Bible hang on Christ, the believer can claim them all as promises'. That helps, does it not?

When our Saviour says, 'Abide in me, and I in you', and these other statements commonly interpreted as conditions to be met if we are to have union with him, he is not setting out obligations, but on the contrary, supplying blessed promises of grace. We abide in him because he abides in us. Our Saviour is assuring us that we shall, by the sealing of his blessed Spirit, as our Comforter, abide in him. When our Lord Jesus 'breathed on them, and said unto them, Receive ye the Holy Ghost' (John 20:22), he was not giving a command to obey, but communicating grace. And here, he is telling us that he will continually communicate grace to us by his Spirit, our Comforter, who will continually testify to the believing soul the things of Christ; constantly affirming them to us and in us.

When he says, 'Abide in me and I in you', the Lord Jesus assures us that he undertakes for us, that we shall abide in him, and he in us. How else could we ever hope to abide in him? It is as much as if he had said, 'Ye shall abide in me; and I shall abide in you.' All this is in perfect conformity to that everlasting covenant of grace of which he is the Surety (Jeremiah 32:38-41). This is blessed, absolute, indestructible security. Our Saviour says, 'I will not and they shall not.'

Perhaps, you ask, 'But are we not to look to our evidences for assurance?' Be sure you get the answer. NO! Never! The anchor of our souls is altogether outside ourselves (Hebrews 6:16-20; 11:1). Our hope is in the Vine! Only in the Vine. Be sure you are joined to the Vine.

Chapter 33

Self-Sufficiency Slain

'I am the true vine, and my Father is the husbandman. Every branch in me that beareth not fruit he taketh away: and every branch that beareth fruit, he purgeth it, that it may bring forth more fruit. Now ye are clean through the word which I have spoken unto you. Abide in me, and I in you. As the branch cannot bear fruit of itself, except it abide in the vine; no more can ye, except ye abide in me. I am the vine, ye are the branches: he that abideth in me, and I in him, the same bringeth forth much fruit: for without me ye can do nothing. If a man abide not in me, he is cast forth as a branch, and is withered; and men gather them, and cast them into the fire, and they are burned. If ye abide in me, and my words abide in you, ye shall ask what ye will, and it shall be done unto you. Herein is my Father glorified, that ye bear much fruit; so shall ye be my disciples' (John 15:1-8).

Does it glorify God? That is the litmus test by which all doctrine, all preaching, and all teaching must be proved. All the heresies which have arisen in the history of the church have had a decided tendency to dishonour God and to flatter man. Their aim is always the exaltation of man and the abasing of God, the exaltation of man's imaginary 'free will' and the denial of God's sovereign will, the uplifting of man and the mockery of God. Robbing God of the glory which is due unto his name, false prophets attempt to put a counterfeit lustre upon the head of the rebellious and depraved creature.

Human religion magnifies man; but the gospel of the grace of God sinks the creature very low and presents the Lord God, the triune Jehovah, before us as One sitting upon a throne, high and lifted up. This fact is so evident that the most uneducated believer, even if he is incapable of refuting the heresies men everywhere proclaim, is able to spot the devil's lie with ease. If it glorifies man, it is not of God. By this test you may judge, and judge infallibly, truth from error. By this rule you may determine whether any doctrine is true or false; orthodox or heretical. Does it glorify God? If it does, it is true. Does it exalt man? If it does, it is false.

All gospel doctrine lays man low in the dust and speaks of him in terms which are intended to make him feel his degradation as a sinful, ruined, depraved, helpless, hopeless, undone, God-hating rebel. All gospel doctrine puts the crown upon the head of God, not upon the head of man's free-will, or free agency, or good works. Test everything I preach, and everything preached or written by any other man, by this rule: Does it glorify God?

John 15:1-8 should utterly destroy every thought of self-sufficiency. Because Christ is the true Vine in whom is all life, and grace, and strength, and we are but branches in the Vine, without him we can do nothing. 'Not that we are sufficient of ourselves to think anything as of ourselves; but our sufficiency is of God' (2 Corinthians 3:5).

The True Vine

'I am the true Vine' (v. 1). The Lord Jesus compares himself to many things, by which he condescends to teach us who he is, what he has done, is doing, and shall hereafter do for his chosen people. By the use of these images, very familiar and simple, the Saviour graciously uses common, everyday things to remind us constantly of himself. He said, 'I am the door; by me if any man enter in he shall be saved.' There is no other Door. He said, 'I am the true bread from heaven.' He alone is the Bread of Life we must have, upon whom our souls live. Our Saviour says, 'I am the water of life.' He who drinks of this Water shall never thirst. The Master declares, 'I am the way, the truth, and the life.' Everything that God has for sinners is in Christ. All things spiritual and eternal are in Christ, by Christ, and through Christ (John 3:35; Colossians 2:9; 1 Corinthians 1:30).

Acceptance, forgiveness, salvation, justification, eternal life, redemption, sanctification, propitiation, pardon, peace with God, holiness here and heaven hereafter, all are ours by a living union with Christ. He is the true Vine. All life is in the Vine and from the Vine.

Try to imagine the condescension of our Lord Jesus in using this imagery. The Lord of glory compares himself to a vine to show us the lowliness and meekness of his person. Isaiah described him 'as a root out of a dry ground'. Nothing in the field appears less promising than a dry vine in the winter. Truly, in the vine there is 'no form nor comeliness that we should desire him'. Yet, our blessed Saviour calls himself 'the true vine'. He could not have chosen an image more appropriate.

Zechariah said that when the Saviour would come with salvation, he would be meek and lowly. Nothing is lower than the vine that spreads its branches along the ground. Nothing is weaker and nothing more feeble than the vine. It has to have something to prop it up, a stake to support it.

Yet, by this comparison, when our Saviour says, 'I am the true vine', he also assures us of his own super-abounding grace and infinite fruitfulness and love to us as the people of his choice. What can be more useful to the branches growing out of it than the fruitful vine? Our great 'Joseph is a fruitful bough, even a fruitful bough by a well; whose branches run over the wall' (Genesis 49:22). The fruit of this Vine is like the wine of Lebanon (Hosea 14:7), reviving, exhilarating, and rich. Truly, the Lord Jesus Christ, our great Saviour, is that Plant of Renown God promised by his prophet Ezekiel (Ezekiel 34:29).

The Husbandman

'My Father is the Husbandman'. With those words, our Saviour gives us another word of sweet assurance, that his joy might remain in us and that our joy might be full (v. 11). Christ is the Vine. We are the branches. The vineyard is the Lord's. It belongs to and is unceasingly tended by the Almighty God, our heavenly Father. He is the Husbandman, the Vinedresser. He who purposed the Vine planted and supported it for the purposes of his will and for his own glory.

He planted the Vine in the incarnation (Hebrews 10:5; Galatians 4:4, 5). He filled the Vine with his Spirit. He upheld and supported the Vine, and made it strong for himself (Psalms 80:15, 17). The Father made Christ our Vine and made us branches in the Vine, putting everything in him for his own glory (Ephesians 1:11, 12). He takes infinite delight in the Vine, this Plant of Renown, 'his pleasant plant' (Isaiah 5:7).

'Every branch in me that beareth not fruit he taketh away: and every branch that beareth fruit, he purgeth it, that it may bring forth more fruit' (v. 2). This is the Father's work, as the Husbandman. Robert Hawker suggests that the opening words of this verse would be more accurately translated, 'Every branch that beareth not fruit in me.' Without question, that is our Lord's meaning. It is not possible that any can be truly in him and not bear fruit (Galatians 5:22, 23).

But there are many who appear to be in him who are not; Judas, Simon Magus, Demas, Diotrephes, etc.. They appear to be in Christ by association, outward profession, and the performance of religious duties; but they bear no spiritual fruit (Galatians 5:22, 23). Religious duties and what men call good works, works of religious austerity, may be produced without any true spiritual union with Christ (Luke 16:15). Carnal professors are lost religionists; and, as such, are dead branches which will eventually be exposed and taken away.

There are myriads of professing Christians in the world whose union with Christ is only outward and formal. There are some in every local church. Some are joined to Christ by baptism and church-membership. Some go further and are regular in attendance. Many talk loudly about religion and doctrine. But they all lack 'the one thing needful'. They have no grace in their hearts, no faith in Christ, no inward work of the Holy Spirit. They are not one with Christ. They are not in Christ; and Christ is not in them. Their union with him is only outward. It is not real. They have 'a name to live', but they are dead. Their end will be destruction. They will be separated from the company of true believers, and cast out, as withered, useless branches, into everlasting fire. They will find at last, whatever they thought in this world, that there is a worm that never dies and a fire that is not quenched.

The true branches, those who are savingly rooted in, joined to, and one with Christ by the Father's will and work, always bring forth fruit by the power and grace of his Spirit. The fruit of the Spirit is grace in the soul (Galatians 5:22, 23). It is not something men can produce. The fruit of the Spirit is not something men can see. And the fruit of the Spirit is not something men are competent to discern. You and I are incapable of determining which branches are in the Vine and which are just hanging on the Vine. God alone knows and can distinguish the false from the true.

Dead, withered, fruitless branches that are hanging on the Vine by mere profession, the Vine dresser takes away and burns. Those living branches savingly in the Vine he constantly prunes, cleanses, and purges by trials, afflictions, and instruction that they may grow and bring forth more fruit (James 1:2-4; 1 Peter 1:7; Psalms 119:71).

The Lord God declares, 'From me is thy fruit found' (Hosea 14:8). Let us never forget it. Christ is the Vine. Every portion of life and fruitfulness comes from him. Grace is not a self-acting principle. Grace is not an evolutionary process. Grace is God's gift and God's work. All our springs are in him. Of his fulness we receive grace for grace. That is to say, we get grace from Christ's fulness day by day, hour by hour, and moment by moment. 'All my springs are in thee' (Psalms 87:7).

Clean Through The Word

'Now ye are clean through the word which I have spoken unto you' (v. 3). The Lord Jesus had told his disciples in John 13:10 that they were 'clean, but not all', because Judas was then still among them. Judas was now purged from the Vine, the Saviour says to the eleven, 'ye are clean'. They were made clean, not by works, not by law, not by baptism, not by ceremonies, but by grace.

They were, as all who are born of God are, clean, regenerated, sanctified, and justified by the precious blood of Christ, by the Spirit of God, through the word preached and believed (Zechariah 13:1; 1 Corinthians 6:9-11; Titus 3:4-7). Believing on the Lord Jesus Christ we purify our hearts by faith (Acts 15:9). God's elect are blood-bought and blood-bathed (Zechariah 13:1; 1 Corinthians 6:9-11; Titus 3:4-7).

These men were all true branches in the true Vine, Christ Jesus. By the grace of God, they believed in Christ, loved Christ, and were in Christ, never to be separated from him. So it is with all who are born of God (John 10:27-30; Ecclesiastes 3:14; 1 Peter 1:3-5).

Abiding In Christ

In verse 4 our Saviour says, 'Abide in me, and I in you. As the branch cannot bear fruit of itself, except it abide in the vine; no more can ye, except ye abide in me.' I remind you, this is a promise of grace, not a precept of law. How can you abide in him and he in you, except by his own work? Our Lord is not warning us that if we decide no longer to abide in him, we will cease to bear fruit, wither, die, and be burned forever in hell. I have no idea how that misunderstanding of this verse could cause his joy to remain in anyone, or make anyone's joy full. Remember, that is our Lord's intention in this passage (v. 11). This verse must be understood in the light of that stated intention as a promise of grace.

Our Lord's intent is that his joy remain in us and that our joy be full. That being the case, our Lord's words here must mean: you shall abide in me; and I will abide in you. That is exactly what he promised in his everlasting covenant (Jeremiah 32:38-41). Our abiding in Christ is not a condition which we fulfil before Christ gives us life, but the result of Christ's gift of life. 'By the grace of God I am what I am' (1 Corinthians 15:10; 2 Corinthians 5:17).

Self-Sufficiency Slain

Remember, we are looking at a parable, the parable of a vine and branches. And remember that a parable is an earthly picture of a spiritual lesson. The parable may suggest many thoughts; but it is intended to show us just one thing. Read verse 5, and you will see what our Lord's intent is in giving us this parable. 'I am the Vine, ye are the branches: he that abideth in me, and I in him, the same bringeth forth much fruit: for without me ye can do nothing.' This parable is intended to slay every thought of self-sufficiency. The Lord Jesus says, 'Without me ye can do nothing'! The sooner we learn that, the better. The more fully we realise it, the better. The more broadly we apply it, the better. 'Without me ye can do nothing'!

I know this in theory, as well as I know that I am a sinner; but I am forever failing in this knowledge, when I come to put it into practice. Teach me, O Holy Spirit of God, teach me how to live in the constant realisation of this fact.

'Without me ye can do nothing'! It is a fact that cannot be denied that neither the judgments of God nor his mercies have the slightest effect upon the heart of man, without his grace. Robert Hawker wrote,

> Behold the prosperous sinner bathing in a full river of blessings, himself in health, his circumstances flourishing, his children like olive-branches round his table, wealth pouring in upon him from every quarter; and yet he lives without God, and without Christ in the world; and as he lives, so he dies, in the vanity of his mind. See him amidst distinguishing preservations, in battles by sea or land, still preserved, while floating carcasses, or opened graves, are all around him: do these things bring his heart to God? Not in the least. The sum total of his character may be comprised in a few words; 'God is not in all his thoughts.'
>
> Look at him in the opposite side of the representation; let such an one be visited with chastisements, in his own person sickness, in his family misery, in his substance want; in short, in all that concerns him, a life of sorrow, care, anxiety, disappointment, ruin. Perhaps to all these, a body long the dwelling-place of some loathsome disease, under which he groans, and at length dies, and dies the same unawakened sinner as he had lived. And suppose these accumulated evils had been distinguished also with some more peculiar maladies, in perils in the sea, in perils in the war, in perils among men; nay, let him be maimed in his limbs, let him be rotting in a prison, let him be worn out with misery from evil upon evil, like waves of the sea following each other; yet still he continues the hardened, unsubdued sinner under all, and as unconscious of God's rods as the prosperous sinner before described is of God's blessings.
>
> Are these things so, my soul, and hast thou seen them? Yes, in numberless instances. Oh then, learn, that without Jesus thou canst do nothing. Outward circumstances, unaccompanied with inward grace, leave men just where they found them; and plain it is, that grace alone can change the heart. Lord Jesus, let these loud and crying truths, day by day lead my soul to thee! Be thou 'all in all', my hope, my guide, my strength, my portion; for 'without thee I can do nothing'.

'Without me ye can do nothing'! Outward circumstances, unaccompanied with inward grace leave men just as they find them. Only Christ can change the heart. Only Christ can convert the sinner. Only Christ can save. I say we should apply these words of our Saviour as broadly as possible to all things spiritual. 'Without me ye can do nothing'! 'Without me ye' cannot believe. 'Without me ye' cannot pray. 'Without me ye' cannot watch. 'Without me ye' cannot learn, know, or understand anything spiritual. 'Without me ye' cannot know the meaning of my word. 'Without me ye' cannot preach. 'Without me ye' cannot worship. 'Without me ye' cannot hear me speak by the gospel. 'Without me ye' cannot persevere. 'Without me ye' cannot withstand the devil. 'Without me ye' cannot resist temptation. 'Without me ye' cannot resist sin. 'Without me ye' cannot stand. 'Without me ye' cannot recover when fallen. 'Without me ye can do nothing'! 'So then it is not of him that willeth, nor of him that runneth, but of God that sheweth mercy' (Romans 9:16).

As these words apply to all men, believers and unbelievers, they are especially applicable to preachers. Let every gospel preacher understand that the Lord Jesus is speaking to him, when he says, 'Without me ye can do nothing'. Pastor Henry Mahan wrote,

> I suppose the most difficult thing any believer has to learn is that 'Without him we can do nothing'. This is our creed but not our experience! We will never be effectually used for God's true glory until it becomes our experience. God will never use men that are proud enough to think themselves necessary or capable. He will throw away the vessel which begins to boast in itself or allows others to boast in it. Whatever is our strength in the flesh is sure to become our weakness in the spirit whether it be our intelligence, our morality, our length of service, our doctrine, our courage or whatever. Gideon feared the Midianites because of the small number of his soldiers, but the Lord said, 'Your soldiers are yet too many for me'. I wonder if we will ever become weak enough, empty enough, and ignorant enough for God to use us for his glory! The logic of the Lord is strange to the natural mind. 'For when I am weak, then am I strong' (2 Corinthians 12:10). 'Most gladly therefore will I rather glory in my infirmities, that the power of Christ may rest upon me' (2 Corinthians 12:9). The Lord must go back to the seashore and raise up some fishermen. We've all become masters and doctors, wise men in theology and great counsellors. I disqualify myself for God's use when I become qualified. My fine talents and lofty credentials become hindrances rather than helps. I thought to prepare myself for great things, only to learn that it was the rough voice in the wilderness he planned to use, not the polished preacher; it was the weak, impulsive shepherd with the sling he

planned to use, not the mighty warrior with his armour of wit and arsenal of facts, doctrines, and learning. It may not be too late for some, but most are too proud to become expendable. If we don't pour contempt on ourselves God will!

Fruitless Professors

In verse 6 our Lord tells us again that all fruitless professors of religion shall perish in hell. 'If a man abide not in me, he is cast forth as a branch, and is withered; and men gather them, and cast them into the fire, and they are burned.' Soon, your refuge of lies will be swept away and you will perish without hope.

'Wherefore hear the word of the LORD, ye scornful men, that rule this people which is in Jerusalem. Because ye have said, We have made a covenant with death, and with hell are we at agreement; when the overflowing scourge shall pass through, it shall not come unto us: for we have made lies our refuge, and under falsehood have we hid ourselves: Therefore thus saith the Lord GOD, Behold, I lay in Zion for a foundation a stone, a tried stone, a precious corner stone, a sure foundation: he that believeth shall not make haste. Judgment also will I lay to the line, and righteousness to the plummet: and the hail shall sweep away the refuge of lies, and the waters shall overflow the hiding place. And your covenant with death shall be disannulled, and your agreement with hell shall not stand; when the overflowing scourge shall pass through, then ye shall be trodden down by it. From the time that it goeth forth it shall take you: for morning by morning shall it pass over, by day and by night: and it shall be a vexation only to understand the report. For the bed is shorter than that a man can stretch himself on it: and the covering narrower than that he can wrap himself in it' (Isaiah 28:14-20).

Effectual Prayer

Then, in verse 7 our Lord assures us that because we are one with him, ever abiding in him, inseparable from him, our prayers are accepted before God and effectual with God. 'If ye abide in me, and my words abide in you, ye shall ask what ye will, and it shall be done unto you.'

Abiding or living in Christ is expressed here simply as 'my words abide in you'. His word is called 'the word of life' (Philippians 2:16; Hebrews 4:12; John 6:63). It is the seed of life (1 Peter 1:23-25; Luke 8:11-15). You cannot separate the incarnate Word and the written word. It is impossible for a man to abide in Christ who knows not, loves not, and obeys not his word.

Then, the Lord Jesus says, 'Ye shall ask what you will and it shall be done unto you'. This must not be understood of temporal things, such as riches, honours, material wealth, and earthly luxuries. Prayer is not putting covetousness in pretty words. The person who abides in Christ, in whom his word abides, desires and seeks the will of God, and the glory of God, and prays accordingly (Matthew 6:9-13; 7:7-11; Romans 8:26; Philippians 4:19; 1 Corinthians 3:21-23).

God Glorified

'Herein is my Father glorified, that ye bear much fruit; so shall ye be my disciples.' What do you want more than anything else? Is it or is it not the glory of God? Unless I am totally deceived by Satan, I want the glory of my God more than anything in this world. Nothing in the world could give me such fulness of joy as the certain knowledge that by some means or another, I have done something by which I have glorified God. Wonder of wonders! O matchless, wondrous, unfathomable grace! Here our Saviour assures every sinner who trusts him, he assures every branch in the Vine that our God is and shall be forever glorified in us!

He chose us that we might bring forth much fruit, and that our fruit might remain (v. 16). He redeemed us, regenerated us, and called us that we might be the firstfruits unto God (Romans 8:23; James 1:18; Revelation 14:4). He has given us his Spirit of Life, by whom we bear fruit unto our God (Galatians 5:22, 23). The Lord God sees to it that we bring forth fruit, as our great Husbandman. And he is glorified in us by that which he works in us by his grace (Ecclesiastes 9:7-10).

Just in case you do not know what to call that, let me tell you. That is called 'Grace! Free, sovereign, omnipotent, effectual, saving grace'! May the God of all grace make his grace yours!

Chapter 34

'so have I loved you'

'As the Father hath loved me, so have I loved you: continue ye in my love' (John 15:9).

I can think of nothing more miserable on this earth than living with the thought, the firm persuasion, that no one loves you, or even cares about you. But I can think of nothing more joyful than the knowledge of Christ's love for me. It is my soul's delight to contemplate it. Think of it. 'The Son of God loved me, and gave himself for me'! Truly, with Charles Hutchinson Gabriel, we sing,

> I stand amazed in the presence
> Of Jesus, the Nazarene,
> And wonder how He could love me,
> A sinner, condemned, unclean!

Again,

> O love surpassing knowledge,
> O grace so full and free!
> I know that Jesus loves me
> And that's enough for me!
>
> O wonderful salvation
> From sin Christ set me free
> I feel the sweet assurance
> And that's enough for me!

O blood of Christ so precious
Poured out at Calvary
I feel its cleansing power
And that's enough for me!

Elisha A. Hoffman

Meditate for a while on the great, immeasurable, incomprehensible love of Christ for our souls, as he declares it in John 15:9. 'As the Father hath loved me, so have I loved you: continue ye in my love.' Here are green pastures, in which the Great Shepherd makes his sheep lie down, in which we find rest for our souls. Here are still waters beside which he graciously leads us to refresh our spirits. Here are paths of righteousness, in which our Lord graciously causes us to walk. Here is the table he prepares for us in the presence of our enemies. 'As the Father hath loved me, so have I loved you: continue ye in my love.' What sweet rest I have found in this blessed assurance of his love. 'As the Father hath loved me', the Son of God says to this poor sinner, 'so have I loved you.'

The love of Christ is the great cause of our redemption and salvation. It is, as C. H. Spurgeon put it, 'as the sun in the midst of the heavens of grace'. May God the Holy Spirit enable us to plunge into these deep waters, and drink, and drink, and drink, until our souls are satiated and overflowing. 'As the Father hath loved me so have I loved you.' I want to know, and I want you to know 'the love of Christ that passeth knowledge, that we may be filled with all the fulness of God' (Ephesians 3:14-19).

There is such depth and mystery in the love of Christ that it simply cannot be comprehended, much less explained. All we can do is taste it, experience it, believe it, and rejoice in it. Oh, that we may experience it more fully! Blessed Saviour, bring us into your banqueting house; let us see the banner of your love and rejoice, as we drink from this blessed fountain. 'Thy love is better than wine'! Come, O Holy Spirit, come! Take the things of Christ and show them to us by your grace. Show us, now, our Saviour's love!

I want you to see and be assured of this one thing: every sinner who trusts Christ is loved by him, even as Christ himself is loved by God the Father! 'As the Father hath loved me, so have I loved you: continue ye in my love.'

Believe It

The first thing I would say to you about the love of Christ is this: 'Believe it'! May God enable us to believe it. May he give us grace and faith to believe it unquestioningly. If we trust the Son of God as our Saviour, we have every reason to believe that which he here declares to us. 'As the Father hath loved me, so have I loved you: continue ye in my love.'

He loves us personally, and loves us infinitely! Others like to talk about his love as a general, meaningless love of benevolence toward all men. But our Saviour here speaks to his own, and says, 'As the Father hath loved me, so have I loved you'. He assures us of his peculiar, distinct, and distinguishing love for his own elect, to whom he says in verse 16, 'Ye have not chosen me, but I have chosen you'.

If we are in him, as the branches are in the vine, we are the objects of the Saviour's peculiar love. He speaks to us personally as his church and his choice bride, and says, 'As the Father hath loved me, so have I loved you.'

Does the Son of God speak thus to you? Are those words addressed to me? Have we taken hold of Christ by faith? Has he saved us by his grace? Do we draw life from him? Is he our hope, our joy, our all? If he is, these words are spoken to us. With his own lips, and here in his word, our Saviour takes us into his arms and whispers in our ears, as a man does the wife he adores, 'As the Father hath loved me, so have I loved you.'

That he truly loves us, we may confidently believe. Though we might and do rightfully conclude that he loves us, when we begin to see what he has done for us, our Saviour does not leave it as a matter to be inferred. No. He speaks the words. 'As the Father hath loved me, so have I loved you.' Let me never doubt his words. They were spoken in the solemn night of his agony, and are expressly and purposefully recorded here in the book of God.

The Parallel

As if to confirm his love to us and seal it to our hearts, that we may be absolutely assured of it and know something of its indescribable greatness, our Saviour draws a parallel to his love. He does not say, 'I love you as a man loves a woman.' He does not say, 'I love you as a mother loves her child.' He says, 'As the Father hath loved me, so have I loved you.' Would you dare doubt the love of the Father to his Son? I know you would not do so. The Father's love for his Son is one of those unquestionable things we can never dream of questioning.

Our blessed Saviour would have us place his love for us in the same category with the Father's love for him. He would have us be just as confident of the one as of the other. How does the Father love the Son?

God the Father loves his darling Son as one with himself. The Father and the Son are, with the Holy Spirit, one God; one in an eternal, essential, indestructible union. As such, the Father loves the Son with a boundless, immeasurable love. The Lord Jesus loves us just that way, as one with himself, bone of his bone and flesh of his flesh, boundlessly and immeasurably! That is exactly how the Holy Spirit describes his love for us in Ephesians 5:23-32. Think about that, and be assured of your Saviour's love! Loving you, the Son of God loves his own body!

Because of his love for Christ, the Father chose him as his Servant. 'Behold, my servant, whom I uphold; mine elect, in whom my soul delighteth' (Isaiah 42:1). So it is that our Saviour loves us, with an everlasting, eternal love. Because he loved us, he chose us to be his own. Do you remember how he puts it in the seventh chapter of Deuteronomy?

'For thou art an holy people unto the LORD thy God: the LORD thy God hath chosen thee to be a special people unto himself, above all people that are upon the face of the earth. The LORD did not set his love upon you, nor choose you, because ye were more in number than any people; for ye were the fewest of all people: But because the LORD loved you, and because he would keep the oath which he had sworn unto your fathers, hath the LORD brought you out with a mighty hand, and redeemed you out of the house of bondmen, from the hand of Pharaoh king of Egypt.'

He loved you because he loved you! Divine election flows from the fountain of God's everlasting love. It was in love that he predestinated us unto eternal life and accepted us in the Beloved (Ephesians 1:3-6).

'Blessed be the God and Father of our Lord Jesus Christ, who hath blessed us with all spiritual blessings in heavenly places in Christ: According as he hath chosen us in him before the foundation of the world, that we should be holy and without blame before him in love: Having predestinated us unto the adoption of children by Jesus Christ to himself, according to the good pleasure of his will, To the praise of the glory of his grace, wherein he hath made us accepted in the beloved.'

O my brother, my sister, hear this and rejoice. The Son of God loved you before the world began, just because he would love you! He loved you in order that he might manifest his love to you. He loved you in order that you might be conformed unto his image, that he might be the firstborn among many brethren, and that you might forever be one with him in his glory, heir of God and joint-heir with himself!

The Father loves the Son because he is his Son. So Christ loves us (1 John 3:1). The Father loves the Son because of his perfect obedience unto death, because of the righteousness he brought in and the satisfaction he has made (John 10:16-18; Philippians 2:5-11). So Christ loves us. The Father loves the Son as the rightful heir of all things (John 3:35). So the Son loves us (Romans 8:17, 18). The Father loves the Son and shows him all things (John 5:20). So the Son loves us (John 15:15). The Father loves the Son because he is glorified in him (John 17:4, 5). So the Son of God loves us (Ephesians 2:7).

The Father loves his Son as one who is worthy of his love, as one in whom his soul delights; and our Lord Jesus loves us as a people worthy of his love, made worthy by his love, as a people in whom his soul delights (Colossians 1:12; Romans 8:29, 30; 1 Corinthians 6:11).

Because Of His Love

Because of his great love, having chosen us in love, so great was the love of our Lord that he became a Man, became one with us, that we might be one with him. He, who 'counted it not robbery to be equal with God', became a Man that he might execute his eternal purposes of love toward us. It is written, 'For this cause shall a man leave his father and shall cleave to his wife, and the two shall be one flesh.'

That is what Christ did for us. He left his Father that he might become one flesh with his chosen bride. He took our nature so that he might be able to do for us and suffer for us what, otherwise, he could not have done and suffered. By taking upon himself our nature, the Lord of glory established a nearer and sweeter union with his beloved bride than could otherwise have existed. If he had never become the Babe of Bethlehem and the Man of Nazareth, how could he have been made in all points like unto his brethren? What love brought the Lord of glory from highest Heaven to become the Man of Sorrows for me!

Having become a Man for us, the Lord Jesus died as our Substitute, in our room and stead, under the fury of God's holy wrath and infinite justice, because of love. 'Greater love hath no man than this, that a man lay down his life for his friends' (John 15:13). The laying down of his life is the proof of his love. He died for us voluntarily, in all the pain, shame, and ignominy of sin, being made sin for us, forsaken of God and cursed, because he loved us. Behold how he loved us! Blessed Saviour, let me never doubt your great love for me! He died, 'the just for the unjust, to bring us to God'.

It was because of his great love for us that the Son of God gave us life by the power of his grace. Read Ezekiel 16 again. There you will see the condition we were in when he came to us in 'the time of love'. We were deserted, cast out, filthy, dead, without one to pity us. There we were, lost, helpless, ruined, dead, and no one cared. Oh, but he cared! Our Saviour came to us and drew us by effectual, irresistible love to himself (Jeremiah 31:3; Ezekiel 16:1-14).

Because of his great love for us, the Lord Jesus Christ, God's darling Son, has forgiven us, blotting out all our iniquities. He has justified us and sanctified us; and he has kept and keeps us in his love! As I look back upon my own life, I am filled with adoring gratitude and thanksgiving. Surely, goodness and mercy have followed me all the days of my life! When all the days of my life are threaded on time's string, what a bracelet of mercies they make! What shall I say of my Lord's love? If I liken it for height to the mountains, I see summits piled on summits. 'Your mercy, O God, is in the heavens.' If I compare it to the sea, I can only cry, 'O the depth'! Let us not doubt his love. He has proved it beyond sufficiency. Has he not? Let us, then, be ravished with his love!

Because of his love for us, our Saviour has made us one with himself. Who can describe this union of love and grace? It is inexpressible. We are married to him, joined to him, cemented to him, grafted in him, built upon him, members of his body, one with him in a living, loving, lasting union! He has made us to be identical with himself. I can hear some screaming when they read, 'He has made us to be identical with himself.' 'You just can't say that. People will carry it too far! You've got to explain that. You've got to qualify it. People will carry it too far!' I reply, go ahead and try. Try to carry that too far! He has made us to be identical with himself.

The righteousness of our Surety is our righteousness! His obedience is our obedience! His death is our death! His life is our life! His future is our future! His glory is our glory! This is love, indeed! Our Saviour says, 'As the Father hath loved me, so have I loved you'! 'Who shall separate us from the love of God, which is in Christ Jesus our Lord?' This eternal oneness is the security both of grace and glory to our souls. The saints of God around the throne are not more fully loved than we are; and they have no stronger reason to be assured of our Saviour's love than we do.

What more can I say? What more can he say? 'As the Father hath loved me, so have I loved you.' Personally. Freely. Eternally. Intimately. Immutably. Without beginning. Without end. Without change. Completely. With complete complacency, satisfaction, and delight. Faithfully. Immeasurably. Amazingly.

Continue In

Our Saviour says to you and me, 'As the Father hath loved me, so have I loved you: continue ye in my love'. I take that to mean, 'Ever abide in the confident awareness of my love, never doubt it, never call it into question.' I know that is what this means, because he says as much in verses 10-16.

Continue in the Saviour's love, and you will find his love to be a balm for all your woes, a consolation in all your sorrows, strength for your journey, a fire to melt you, make you tender, and inspire you, and a delight to rejoice your heart. This, truly, is perfect love! And the assurance of our Saviour's perfect love for us takes away all fear (1 John 4:15-19). Therefore, our Saviour says, 'Continue ye in my love', ever abide in the confident awareness of my love, never doubt it, never call it into question. 'Keep yourselves in the love of God, looking for the mercy of our Lord Jesus Christ unto eternal life' (Jude 21). Child of God, sinner washed in the Saviour's blood and saved by his grace, walk in this light all the days of your life. 'As the Father hath loved me, so have I loved you: continue ye in my love.'

Chapter 35

No Greater Love

'Greater love hath no man than this, that a man lay down his life for his friends' (John 15:13).

The whole purpose of our Saviour in this chapter is to assure believing sinners of his great love. Every word, every phrase, every illustration is intended to assure us of his love, that we may continually live in the confidence of his love. He begins the chapter by telling us that he is the true Vine and we are the branches, assuring us of our union with him. Then, he tells us that the One who takes care of the vineyard of grace is God, his Father and our Father, saying, 'My Father is the husbandman'. In verse 9 our Saviour assures us of his great love for us, with these sweet words: 'As the Father hath loved me, so have I loved you.' His next word is 'Continue ye in my love.' That is to say, 'Now, go on living in the confident assurance of my love, ever trusting me.' Then, our dear Saviour says, 'Greater love hath no man than this, that a man lay down his life for his friends.'

There is truly no greater love than the love of our blessed Saviour for us! Because of his great love for us, without any compulsion, except the compulsion of his love, the Son of God freely laid down his life for us.

He not only came down from heaven and laid aside his glory and royal majesty, but he laid down his life for us. Nothing is dearer to a man than his life. That is his all. He who gives his life gives everything. But our Lord's life was not the common life of a common man. His was the life of a man who is himself God. It was the Lord of glory, the Prince of life, who was crucified and slain in our place upon the cursed tree.

Voluntary Sacrifice

His life was not taken from him. He laid down his life, and freely gave his life for us, in our room and stead, as a ransom for us, because he loved us. The Lord of glory laid down his life for us who were his enemies, because he had from eternity called us his friends, and was determined to make us his friends. He laid down his life; the Son of God voluntarily died for us, because of his great love for us, a people who deserved to die, a people who hated him and wished that he should be made to die, a people from whom he would get no love in return, except he create it.

Being our Surety and Substitute, standing in our place, he took our sins to be his own, and was made sin for us. Bearing our sins in his own body on the tree, our Lord Jesus bore the curse of the law, sustained his Father's wrath, and all the punishment due to our sin. He willingly suffered the painful, shameful death of the cross, the just for the unjust, that he might bring us to God. This he did for us when we were sinners, without strength, his implacable enemies, and enmity itself to him. And by the blood of his cross, he has reconciled us unto himself, because he chose us for his friends. He pitched his heart upon us from eternity and resolved to make us his friends. Now, by the regenerating grace and saving power of his Spirit, he has made us his friends forever.

Greater Love

Here, our blessed Saviour tells us that his love, which caused him to lay down his life for us, is greater than any love known to man. The Son of God, our all-glorious, ever-gracious Christ, laid down his life for his enemies, freely and voluntarily, without any selfish motive. Men may and do die for men, but only because they cannot avoid it, or because they look upon the one for whom they die as being worthy of their sacrifice, or even because they desire the praise and applause of others as self-sacrificing heroes. But our Lord's sacrificial obedience unto death, even the death of the cross, was the free, voluntary sacrifice of our loving and lovely Surety and Substitute (Romans 5:6-8).

Willing Bondslave

We have a clear, instructive picture of our Lord's obedience unto death as our Substitute in Exodus 21:1-6.

'Now these are the judgments which thou shalt set before them. If thou buy an Hebrew servant, six years he shall serve: and in the seventh he shall go out free for nothing. If he came in by himself, he shall go out by himself: if he were married, then his wife shall go out with him. If his master have given him a wife, and she have born him sons or daughters; the wife and her children shall be her master's, and he shall go out by himself. And if the servant shall plainly say, I love my master, my wife, and my children; I will not go out free: Then his master shall bring him unto the judges; he shall also bring him to the door, or unto the door post; and his master shall bore his ear through with an awl; and he shall serve him for ever.'

That is exactly what the Lord Jesus Christ, the Son of God, did for us in the covenant of grace. Christ became Jehovah's voluntary Servant that he might redeem and save his people by his free obedience to God as our Substitute. This is what our blessed Saviour says of himself, as he describes himself in Isaiah 50:5-7, and as he describes his work in John 10:16-18.

'The Lord GOD hath opened mine ear, and I was not rebellious, neither turned away back. I gave my back to the smiters, and my cheeks to them that plucked off the hair: I hid not my face from shame and spitting. For the Lord GOD will help me; therefore shall I not be confounded: therefore have I set my face like a flint, and I know that I shall not be ashamed' (Isaiah 50:5-7).

'And other sheep I have, which are not of this fold: them also I must bring, and they shall hear my voice; and there shall be one fold, and one shepherd. Therefore doth my Father love me, because I lay down my life, that I might take it again. No man taketh it from me, but I lay it down of myself. I have power to lay it down, and I have power to take it again. This commandment have I received of my Father' (John 10:16-18).

Much we talk of Jesus' blood;
But how little's understood!
Of His sufferings, so intense,
Angels have no perfect sense!

Who can rightly comprehend
Their beginning, or their end?
'Tis to God, and God alone,
That their weight is fully known.

See the suffering Son of God
Panting, groaning, sweating blood!
Boundless depths of love divine!
Jesus, what a love was Thine!

Though the wonders Thou hast done
Are as yet so little known
Here we fix, and comfort take:
Jesus died for sinners' sake!

Joseph Hart

Chapter 36

Electing Love

'Ye have not chosen me, but I have chosen you, and ordained you, that ye should go and bring forth fruit, and that your fruit should remain: that whatsoever ye shall ask of the Father in my name, he may give it you' (John 15:16).

Did you know that the Bible talks about a special, distinct group of people called 'the chosen'? These chosen ones are God's elect, the people he has chosen unto salvation. They were redeemed by the precious blood of Christ, because they are the chosen. They must and shall be regenerated, called, and saved, because they are the chosen. They shall be preserved unto everlasting glory; they cannot perish, because they are the chosen. They cannot be lost, because they are the chosen. They cannot be condemned, because they are the chosen. The chosen are uniquely special to God, because they are the chosen.

Do you rejoice in that? Do you rejoice in electing love? Paul did. He said, 'Blessed be the God and Father of our Lord Jesus Christ who hath blessed us with all spiritual blessings in heavenly places in Christ, according as he hath chosen us in him before the foundation of the world' (Ephesians 1:3, 4). 'We are bound to give thanks alway to God for you, brethren beloved of the Lord, because God hath from the beginning chosen you to salvation through sanctification of the Spirit and belief of the truth' (2 Thessalonians 2:13).

Do you rejoice in electing love? Peter did. He said, 'Ye are a chosen generation, a royal priesthood, an holy nation, a peculiar people; that ye should show forth the praises of him who hath called you out of darkness into his marvellous light ... Elect according to the foreknowledge of God the Father' (1 Peter 2:9; 1:2).

Do you rejoice in electing love? David did. He leaped and danced before the ark of God, because God had chosen him above Saul. He said, 'Although my house be not so with God, yet he hath made with me an everlasting covenant, ordered in all things and sure: for this is all my salvation and all desire' (2 Samuel 23:5).

Do you rejoice in electing love? Our Lord Jesus did. He said, 'I thank thee, O Father, Lord of heaven and earth, because thou hast hid these things from the wise and prudent, and hast revealed them unto babes: Even so, Father, for it seemed good in thy sight' (Matthew 11:25, 26). Yes, our Lord Jesus Christ taught the doctrine of divine election plainly and clearly. He rejoiced in it and gave thanks for it.

On the night before his crucifixion, in order to comfort and strengthen his disciples, he told them about his marvellous electing love in these words: 'Ye have not chosen me, but I have chosen you and ordained you, that ye should go and bring forth fruit, and that your fruit should remain: that whatsoever ye shall ask of my Father in my name, he may give it you' (John 15:16).

Do you rejoice in electing love? Surely, every true believer should be filled with joy and praise toward God when he hears the good news of God's electing love in Christ. Indeed, every believer, as he reads the word of God and is taught of God the Holy Spirit, understanding the gospel of God's free and sovereign grace in Christ, does rejoice in electing love: God's eternal choice and election of his people in Christ unto salvation and eternal life.

Election is the source and fountain of all the blessings of grace. All the blessings of divine mercy flow down to needy sinners from the throne of God, through the mediation of our Lord Jesus Christ, 'according as he hath chosen us in him before the foundation of the world'.

Do you rejoice in electing love? I hope that you have learned to do so. I hope that your heart is as full of joy at the thought of divine election as David's was. When he thought about God's eternal, electing love, he sang, 'Blessed is the man whom thou choosest, and causest to approach unto thee, that he may dwell in thy courts: we shall be satisfied with the goodness of thy house, even of thy holy temple' (Psalms 65:4). Josiah Conder wrote,

'Tis not that I did choose Thee,
For Lord that could not be,
This heart would still refuse Thee,
Hadst Thou not chosen me.
Thou, from the sin that stained me,
Hast cleansed and set me free,
Of old Thou hast ordained me,
That I should live to Thee.

'Twas sov'reign mercy called me
And taught my op'ning mind;
The world had else enthralled me,
To heav'nly glories blind.
My heart owns none before Thee,
For Thy rich grace I thirst;
This knowing, if I love Thee,
Thou must have loved me first.

Context

In John 15:9 our Saviour assures us of his infinite, eternal love for us. He says, 'As the Father hath loved me, so have I loved you'. Then he says, 'continue ye in my love'. That is to say, 'Now, go on living in the confident assurance of my love, ever trusting me'. Our ever blessed Saviour tells us in verse 11 that he spoke these sweet words of grace to us, that his joy might remain in us and that our joy might be full. Then, in verses 13-15, he tells us some things that ought to, sure enough, make our joy full.

'Greater love hath no man than this, that a man lay down his life for his friends. Ye are my friends, if ye do whatsoever I command you. Henceforth I call you not servants; for the servant knoweth not what his lord doeth: but I have called you friends; for all things that I have heard of my Father I have made known unto you'.

Then, in verse 16, our Lord Jesus tells us the source, the fountain, the cause of all these blessed works of his marvellous, free grace. He laid down his life for us; he has made us his friends; he makes all things known to us and bestows all grace upon us, because of his free, electing love.

'Ye have not chosen me, but I have chosen you, and ordained you, that ye should go and bring forth fruit, and that your fruit should remain: that whatsoever ye shall ask of the Father in my name, he may give it you'.

This is what I want you to see clearly from our text and from the scriptures as a whole. This is the doctrine taught throughout the book of God. Our Saviour's choice and election of his people is not the result of something we do, have done, or might do, but the cause of everything he does, has done, and will yet do for us.

Psalms 65:4

That is what we are told in Psalms 65:4. 'Blessed is the man whom thou choosest, and causest to approach unto thee, that he may dwell in thy courts: we shall be satisfied with the goodness of thy house, even of thy holy temple'.

Here election is spoken of as being in the present tense, though it was done before the world began, because this great work of grace is known and experienced in time. No one knows his election until he has been effectually called by the Holy Spirit to life and faith in Christ.

Notice the progression of grace running through this verse of scripture. 'Blessed is the man whom thou choosest'. That is election. God chose to save some in eternity; and those whom he chose to save in eternity he graciously cuts out from the rest of mankind in time, like a rancher cutting his cattle out of the many roaming the open range. They were his cattle before. He simply rounds them up at the appointed time.

'And causest to approach unto thee'. That refers to irresistible, saving grace, the effectual call of God the Holy Spirit. Election both precedes and is the source and cause of this call.

'That he may dwell in thy courts'. Sinners chosen and called by grace are caused to dwell, not to visit, but to dwell in the courts of divine worship. Those who are chosen and called by the grace of God to life and faith in Christ are kept and preserved by that same grace unto eternal glory. We shall forever abide in our Saviour's love, because he declares, 'I have chosen you'.

But there is more. Election is the source and cause of the everlasting happiness and satisfaction of God's saints in heaven. 'We shall be satisfied with the goodness of thy house, even of thy holy temple.' The house and temple of God in the Old Testament were typical of and representations of Christ and heaven, of God's salvation, and our everlasting nearness to and worship of him. This is true blessedness; and this blessedness rises from and is effectually caused by God's election of his people unto salvation in Christ before the world began.

No wonder David sang, 'O the blessedness of the man whom thou choosest and causest to approach unto thee'! No wonder God's election was so much on David's heart. It was the thought of God's election that made him leap and dance before the ark of God (2 Samuel 6:21). And it was the fact of his election by God unto salvation and eternal life in Christ that sustained his heart and rejoiced his soul as he lay upon his deathbed. Indeed, this is a doctrine full of joy and comfort to every child of God.

I want you to look into the word of God and see what God teaches us about this glorious gospel doctrine of election. I want you to see seven things revealed in this book about God's election.

Eternal Election

First, God chose some to salvation and eternal life in Christ before the world began. There are some who will tell you, 'The Bible does not teach the doctrine of election.' Those who make such foolish statements either have never read the scriptures, or have totally forgotten what they read, or they are out and out liars. Election is taught everywhere in the book of God.

The scriptures speak of 'elect angels', an 'elect nation', an 'elect lady', and 'elect churches'. God chose some angels, and passed by others. Of the first two men born in the world, Cain and Abel, the Lord God chose one and passed by the other. He chose Noah and his family, and left the rest of the world to perish. He chose Abram, but no one else in his father's house. He chose Jacob, but not is brother, Esau. God chose Israel, the smallest of all nations, to be the nation to whom he would reveal himself. All other nations were left in utter darkness. He chose Joseph, but not Pharaoh.

No one can, with any measure of integrity, teach that the word of God does not teach the doctrine of election. That is too obvious to even discuss. However, the question of importance is this: does the Bible teach the election of some to salvation to the exclusion of others? Does the word of God declare that God chose some, but not all of the sons and daughters of Adam to be the heirs of grace and glory in Christ? Indeed it does (Matthew 20:16; 22:14; Romans 9:11-18; 11:5-7).

There is absolutely no question about the fact that the Bible clearly and distinctly teaches the doctrine of election. God chose to save some and passed by others. So, really, the only question to be answered is this. What does the Bible teach about election?

God's Purpose

Second, the purpose of God in all things is the salvation of his elect (Romans 8:28-30). We recognise, of course, that the word of God teaches the doctrine of God's glorious, sovereign predestination. Like election, it is a truth so plainly revealed in holy scripture that it simply cannot be denied by honest men. For that matter, I cannot imagine why anyone would want to deny it.

Predestination is the all-inclusive purpose of our great and glorious God in which he sovereignly determined all things that come to pass in time for the salvation of his elect. In other words, everything that has been, is now, and hereafter will be, was purposed by God in eternity and is brought to pass by God in time for the salvation of that great multitude whose names were inscribed in the Lamb's book of life in sovereign election before the world began. No one ever, since the apostles, stated the doctrine more beautifully than Isaac Watts did in his hymn,

> Keep silence all created things,
> And wait your Maker's nod;
> My soul stands trembling while she sings
> The honours of her God.

Life, death, and hell, and worlds unknown;
Hang on His firm decree;
He sits on no precarious throne,
Nor borrows leave to be.

Chained to His throne a volume lies
With all the fates of men,
With every angel's form and size
Drawn by th' eternal pen.

His providence unfolds the book,
And makes His counsels shine;
Each opening leaf, and every stroke
Fulfils some bright design.

Here He exalts neglected worms
To sceptres and a crown;
And then the following page He turns,
And treads the monarch down.

Not Gabriel asks the reason why,
Nor God the reason gives;
Nor dares the favourite angel pry
Between the folded leaves.

My God, I would not long to see
My fate with curious eyes,
What gloomy lines are writ for me,
Or what bright scenes may rise.

In Thy fair book of life and grace
May I but find my name,
Recorded in some humble place
Beneath my Lord the Lamb!

This is the Bible doctrine of predestination. I give it to you in the very language of holy scripture. 'In love', God our Father 'predestinated us unto the adoption of children by Jesus Christ to himself, according to the good pleasure of his will, To the praise of the glory of his grace, wherein he hath made us accepted in the beloved ... In whom also we have obtained an inheritance, being predestinated according to the purpose of him who worketh all things after the counsel of his own will: That we should be to the praise of his glory, who first trusted in Christ' (Ephesians 1:4-6, 11, 12).

God chose some to salvation; and the purpose of God in all things is the salvation of all the chosen, whom he loved with an everlasting love.

Purpose Performed

Third, I want you to see that the purpose of God shall be accomplished. All that God has purposed, God will perform. The Bible never talks about God purposing what he does not perform, trying to do what he does not do, willing that which he never actually brings to pass, or of him in any way trying to prevent anything that does come to pass. God Almighty does not try. He does! He does not wish. He accomplishes! He does not plan. He purposed!

Men talk about God's plan, because men can do nothing but plan. God does not talk like that. God talks about his purpose. His purpose of grace is much more than some imaginary plan of salvation. A plan may be interrupted, hindered, altered, or utterly rejected. That is not God's purpose of grace. God's purpose is the eternal determination of his heart, the holy, eternal determination of his very Being, to save the people of his love, whom he chose to salvation before the world began.

That purpose cannot be frustrated, altered, or even hindered to any degree. Not even the rebellion of Lucifer or the fall of Adam hindered God's purpose of grace. Oh, no! Those events were just part of that which was and is necessary to accomplish God's sovereign purpose of grace according to election (Isaiah 14:24, 26, 27; 46:9-11, 13; Romans 9:11).

In Christ

Fourth, election is in Christ (Ephesians 1:1-14). Everything God does for, gives to, and requires from sinners is in Christ. God does nothing for us, requires nothing from us, and gives nothing to us apart from Christ. I want you to see three things in this passage of scripture concerning our election in Christ.

1. Election took place in eternity, before the worlds were made. God's love for us did not begin yesterday. It is from everlasting to everlasting. He chose us in Christ before time began. He inscribed our names in the book of life from the foundation of the world.

2. Our eternal election in Christ is the source and cause of all the other benefits and blessings of grace. Apart from election there are no blessings of grace here or of glory hereafter; but for the elect, all the blessings and blessedness of grace and glory are sure. Read verses three and four again. God's blessings of grace and glory flow to sinners 'according as he hath chosen

us in him before the foundation of the world'. Adoption, acceptance with God, redemption and forgiveness, regeneration, preservation, resurrection, and the heavenly glory of the inheritance awaiting us, all are ours, all are sure to all the elect, according to the election of grace! All the chosen shall obtain all these things according to the purpose of God in election.

Do you see this? Everywhere people talk about the fact that Christ came into the world, but few have any idea who he is or why he came. Very few indeed realise that the cause of his coming here to live and die for sinners is to be found in God's electing love and his sovereign purpose of grace. The Son of God came here to save his people (the people chosen by and given to him by God the Father in eternal mercy) from their sins (Matthew 1:21).

3. Election is for the glory of God. Here is the reason why God chose to save sinners, why he chose some unto eternal life, and why he saves us in a manner that clearly demonstrates both his supreme sovereignty and his glorious grace. It is, as Paul here declares three times, 'That we should be to the praise of his glory'! 'That in the ages to come he might show the exceeding riches of his grace in his kindness toward us through Christ Jesus' (Ephesians 2:7). God chose to save some. God's purpose of grace in all things is the salvation of his elect. God's sovereign purpose according to election shall stand. Election is an eternal work and benefit of God's grace in Christ.

Unto Salvation

Fifth, the word of God teaches us plainly that God's election of sinners in Christ is unto salvation (2 Thessalonians 2:13, 14; 1 Peter 1:2). Without question the Bible teaches the eternal salvation of all God's elect. There is a sense in which all who are saved in time were saved from eternity. Romans 8:28-30, Ephesians 1:4-6, and 2 Timothy 1:9-11 plainly and emphatically declare that all God's elect were in Christ, redeemed, accepted, justified, sanctified, and glorified from eternity by the purpose, and decree of God. But do not ever think of election as salvation. Election, by itself, is not salvation. Election, by itself, saves no one. Election is unto salvation. Be sure you get the language of the scriptures. Put 2 Thessalonians 2:13, 14 together with 1 Peter 1:2, and you will see the following things about God's election.

1. Election is a cause for great thanksgiving and praise to God.

2. Election is according to the foreknowledge of God, according to his everlasting love and sovereign foreordination. The word foreknowledge in 1 Peter 1:2 is the exact same word translated foreordain in verse 20.

3. Election is a personal, distinguishing work of grace. 'God hath from the beginning chosen you'!

4. Election is unto salvation. I realise that there is a sense in which some are elected from eternity to specific service in the kingdom of God. Not all are

prophets, apostles, evangelists, pastors, teachers, and deacons. Those who are, if they hold their offices in faithfulness, were chosen to their work by God. However, the biblical doctrine of election is not election to service, but election unto salvation.

5. We were chosen to be saved in a manner consistent with and honouring to the holiness, justice, and truth of God. Peter tells us that we were chosen by God 'unto obedience and sprinkling of the blood of Jesus Christ'. That is to say, no one, not even the elect, could ever be saved apart from the obedience and death of Christ by which redemption was accomplished. The sprinkling of his blood in 1 Peter 1:2 has a double significance. Both are necessary to the salvation of God's elect. It refers to the sprinkling of his blood in heaven, and to the sprinkling of his blood upon our hearts

6. We were chosen to salvation through the sanctification of the Spirit. In other words, no one can ever be saved who is not born again, regenerated, sanctified by God the Holy Spirit, election and predestination notwithstanding.

7. We were chosen to salvation through the belief of the truth. Not only has God ordained who will be saved; he has also ordained the means by which they shall be saved; and the means he has ordained is the hearing of faith. Those who were chosen of God in eternity and redeemed by Christ at Calvary must and shall be regenerated and called by the Holy Spirit through the preaching of the gospel (2 Thessalonians 2:13, 14).

Unconditional Election

Sixth, in 2 Timothy 1:9 we are taught that God's eternal choice of his people to salvation in Christ was an unconditional election of grace. God did not choose us and he does not save us because of our works. His choice of us was not based upon foreseen merit, or our foreseen choice of Christ, or our foreseen faith in him. Oh, no! Our only merit before God is Christ. Our choice of him is the result of his choosing us. Our faith in him is the fruit and result of his election.

'Twas with an everlasting love
That God His own elect embraced,
Before He made the worlds above,
Or earth on her huge columns placed.

O love, how high thy glories swell,
How great, immutable, and free!
Ten thousand sins, as black as hell,
Are swallowed up, O love, in thee!

Loved when a wretch defiled with sin,
At war with heaven, in league with hell,
A slave to every lust obscene,
Who, living, lived but to rebel.

Believer, here thy comfort stands,
From first to last salvation's free;
And everlasting love demands
An everlasting song from thee.

John Kent

I hope each of you see and clearly understand these things regarding God's election. God chose some to be saved. God's purpose in all things is the salvation of his elect. The purpose of God according to election shall stand. Election is an eternal work of grace in Christ. Election is unto salvation. Election is unconditional.

Effectual Election

Seventh, God's electing grace is always effectual. That simply means it gets the job done. All who were chosen in eternity shall be called and saved in time, by the irresistible power and grace of God the Holy Spirit through the gospel because …

God 'hath saved us, and called us with an holy calling, not according to our works, but according to his own purpose and grace, which was given us in Christ Jesus before the world began, But is now made manifest by the appearing of our Saviour Jesus Christ, who hath abolished death, and hath brought life and immortality to light through the gospel:' (2 Timothy 1:9, 10).

We have no way of knowing until God makes it manifest, but perhaps the reason you are reading these words now is God's election. It may be that he has graciously and sovereignly caused you to do so that he might bring life and immortality to light in your soul through the gospel you have read.

Do you now find yourself trusting the Lord Jesus Christ as your only, all-sufficient Lord and Saviour? If you do, if you truly trust the Son of God, it is because 'God hath from the beginning chosen you to salvation'!

Let every child of God give praise, honour, and glory to him forever for his free, electing love and favour, sovereignly and graciously bestowed upon us from eternity in Christ. He who chose us, redeemed us, called us, and gave us life and faith in Christ will keep us unto eternal glory by his grace.

Who shall condemn to endless flames
The chosen people of our God,
Since in the book of life our names
Are written in the Saviour's blood?

Christ for the sins of His elect
Has full, complete atonement made;
And justice never can expect
That the same debt should twice be paid.

Neither the craft and power of hell,
According to God's faithful Word,
Nor all the sins that in us dwell,
Can separate us from our Lord.

Nothing in life, nothing in death,
No powers on earth, no powers above,
(Our God has sworn, the God of truth!)
Can change His purposes of love.

His sovereign mercy knows no end,
His faithfulness shall yet endure;
And those who on His Word depend
Shall find His Word forever sure!

Benjamin Beddome

How I thank God for his free, electing love! How sweet, how immeasurably sweet it is to hear my Saviour say to me, as I look to him in faith, 'Ye have not chosen me, but I have chosen you'! Loved by Christ! Redeemed by Christ! Befriended by Christ! Taught by Christ! All because I was chosen by Christ before the worlds were made! Now, his joy remains in me and my joy in him is full!

'Not unto us, O LORD, not unto us, but unto thy name give glory, for thy mercy, and for thy truth's sake' (Psalms 115:1).

Chapter 37

'They hated me without a cause'

'If I had not come and spoken unto them, they had not had sin: but now they have no cloke for their sin. He that hateth me hateth my Father also. If I had not done among them the works which none other man did, they had not had sin: but now have they both seen and hated both me and my Father. But this cometh to pass, that the word might be fulfilled that is written in their law, They hated me without a cause' (John 15:22-25).

The hottest place of hell's everlasting torment is reserved for sinners who hear but refuse to believe the gospel! Oh, what a dangerous thing it is for you to be raised under the faithful preaching of the gospel of God's free and sovereign grace in Christ! If you stop your ears, shut your eyes, harden your heart, and run madly to hell shoving God out of your way, the hottest place in hell shall be yours forever! If the gospel you hear does not lift you to the highest heaven, it will sink you into the lowest hell! It will be to you either that by which the Lord God gives you life everlasting in Christ, or that by which the God of glory damns you forever. If you go to hell with the gospel of Christ ringing in your ears, it would be better for you never to have been born! Oh, may God the Holy Spirit give you ears to hear, eyes to see, and a heart to believe the gospel, for Christ sake! It is my heart's desire and prayer to God for you that you might be saved by his wonderful grace!

The Son of God declares, 'If I had not come and spoken unto them, they had not had sin: but now they have no cloak for their sin.' The sin our Lord speaks of here is the sin of Israel and the religious Jews in rejecting him, God's

Messiah, the One sent to them (Acts 3:25, 26; John 1:11). If he had not come in his incarnation, in fulfilment of all their law and prophets, and with undeniable proof of his person, they would not be under such strong judgment for their particular sin; but he has come, and they have no excuse. Therefore, God has cast them off (Romans 11:7-10). In a word, it is every person's responsibility to walk in the light God gives him. Our Saviour is here telling us that those who have greater light, and refuse to walk in the light God gives them shall have greater condemnation. If God cast off the whole nation of Israel because they refused to bow to his Son, you can be certain he will cast you off (Proverbs 1:22-33; 29:1).

Next, the Lord Jesus tells us, 'He that hateth me hateth my Father also.' Many pretend to know, love, and worship God, while rejecting and despising the Lord Jesus Christ. But our Saviour tells us that all who hate him, the Christ of God, hate God who sent him. God the Father and God the Son are One (John 5:23; 10:30). The hatred of the world is toward the Father, the Son, the Holy Ghost, and all who love the triune Jehovah.

In verse 24 we read, 'If I had not done among them the works which none other man did, they had not had sin: but now have they both seen and hated both me and my Father.' By his works, as well as by his words, his gospel, the Lord Jesus was evidently set forth before that generation as the Christ of God. Yet, they despised him. They are, therefore, without excuse. Has the Lord Jesus Christ been evidently set before you? Has he made it clear to you that he is the Christ of God, the Lamb of God, the Saviour of the world? Are those facts indisputably, irrefutably clear to you? If they are, your unbelief is inexcusable!

We see man's sin everywhere. It is in our newspapers and on television every day. Murder, rape, incest, sodomy, adultery, paedophilia, terrorism: all these evils we look at with utter disgust, crying out for law and justice. But, if you want to see the evil of depraved humanity most fully exposed and revealed, you will find it plainly set before you in John 15:25. 'But this cometh to pass, that the word might be fulfilled that is written in their law, They hated me without a cause.'

When we think about the sin of our fallen race, we ought always to think of it in terms of deicide. Here is the essence of sin. It is the murder of God! Man, because of his hatred for his Creator, nailed the Son of God to a cross and threw a hellish party as they watched him die! That is the master crime of hell-bent humanity, the pinnacle of man's guilt. Sin outdid itself when it slew the Lord of glory, who came on earth to die in the place of fallen men. Never does sin appear so exceedingly sinful as when we see it nailing the Lamb of God to the cursed tree, whom it hated without a cause!

Most Hated

First, let me remind you that there has never been a man so hated as the God-man, our Saviour, the Lord Jesus Christ. Our Lord Jesus here refers us to two verses in the Psalms (Psalms 35:19; 69:4), affirming plainly that the Psalms, though written by men from their own experiences, were written by divine inspiration as prophecies of our Saviour.

From the time that he entered into this world, until the hour that he was hanged upon the cursed tree, the Son of God was the constant, unceasing object of man's cruel hatred. The word 'they' refers to all who refused to believe our Saviour. Though they had no reason to do so, they hated him.

No human being was ever so lovely as our Saviour. It would seem almost impossible not to love him. Yet, lovely, loving, and loveable as he was, 'Yea, he is altogether lovely'! no creature ever endured such a relentless hatred. As soon as he was born, Herod sought to kill him; and that was just the beginning. All the days of his life he was 'despised and rejected of men, a man of sorrows and acquainted with grief.'

Man's hatred for the Saviour displayed itself in different ways. Sometimes it was in overt deeds, as when they took him to the brow of the hill, and would have cast him down headlong, or when they took up stones again to stone him, because he declared that he is God. At other times, the hatred showed itself in words of slander. 'He is a drunken man and a wine-bibber, a friend of publicans and sinners'. Sometimes it was manifest in looks of contempt, as when they looked suspiciously at him, because he ate with publicans and sinners, and sat down to eat with unwashed hands. At other times, the hatred was silent, entirely in their thoughts, as when they thought within themselves, 'This man blasphemeth', because he said to the woman taken in adultery, 'thy sins be forgiven thee.'

But the hatred was always there. Even when they tried to make him their king, it was not because they loved him, or even admired him. It was because they thought they could use him for their own advantage, nothing more. Remember, it was the same men who tried to make him their king who, just a little while later cried, 'Crucify him, crucify him'!

'They' who hated him were all men, men of every rank and in all quarters of society. The rich and the poor, the men and the women, the old and the young, the Pharisees and the Sadducees, the governor and the slave, the learned and the ignorant, the powerful and the powerless, the prince and the pauper, all hated him!

Here was a man who walked among men, who loved men, who spoke to rich and poor as though they were, as indeed they are, on one level in his sight. Yet, all conspired against him in unified hatred. They admired his eloquence, and frequently would have fallen prostrate in worship before him, on account of the wondrous deeds he did. Yet, they all conspired together to put him to death, nailing him to the tree, wagging their heads, taunting him, jeering at him, mocking him, spitting in his face, jerking out his beard, beating him, and laughing at him, as if they were being entertained by a comedian!

No Reason

Anyone who bothers to read history, let alone the word of God, knows that the Lord Jesus was the object of man's cruel hatred. But why did they hate him? They had no reason. Yet, three times we read, 'They hated me without a cause.'

There is nothing that can be, or ever has been pointed to in the life of our Redeemer that was even objectionable, let alone a cause for hatred. Our Lord Jesus was perfect in his character. In his conduct he was without flaw. His doctrine was pure and good. The law of God which he upheld, obeyed, and exemplified is, in the opinion of all sane men, good. The doctrine he taught was pure doctrine. All his works were works of mercy. His kindness, sympathy, and tenderness were obvious to all. Yet, though there was no cause for it, the Lord of glory was hated of all men in this world, and still is.

Enmity Against God

Third, the cause of man's hatred for Christ was and is altogether in himself. Here is the cause of man's hatred for Christ, 'the carnal mind is enmity against God: for it is not subject to the law of God, neither indeed can be. So then they that are in the flesh cannot please God' (Romans 8:7, 8). Men hated him without a cause, because they hate God who sent him, and everything about the Lord Jesus stirred man's hatred for God against him. They hated him, because of the gospel he preached. Their hatred of him was and is drawn forth and made manifest by the fact that …

1. He declared himself to be God, one with the Father and equal to the Father (John 10:25-33).
2. He exposed the evil of their hearts and the hypocrisy of their religion (Mark 7:20-23; Luke 16:15; John 8:40).
3. He openly proclaimed God's sovereignty in the exercise of his mercy and grace (Luke 4:25-32).
4. He preached redemption, righteousness, and salvation by grace alone, through faith alone, in him alone (John 6:37-40, 44, 45, 47-51, 53, 61-65).
5. They hated him, because he forgave sinners of their sins freely and fully, while refusing to accept and honour their works of righteousness.

For all these things they hated him. Yet, had they believed him, the gospel he preached would have saved them (Matthew 11:25-30).

By Divine Purpose

Fourth, all this was done that the scriptures might be fulfilled, according to our God's sovereign, eternal purpose of grace toward us. 'But this cometh to pass, that the word might be fulfilled that is written in their law, They hated me without a cause.' The hatred of men for Christ resulted in him being crucified upon the cursed tree as our Substitute (Acts 2:23, 36; Acts 4:27, 28). By this means, by his sin-atoning death as our Substitute, the Lord Jesus declares, 'Then I restored that which I took not away' (Psalms 69:4). Yet, the guilt rests on men, for they did what they wanted to do. Nothing in him gave them cause for this hatred. The evil was altogether in them. Be sure you understand this. Wicked men are responsible for all the havoc they attempt to wreak upon the kingdom of God, and shall be judged accordingly; but let us never imagine that they have the power to accomplish their evil designs. It is written, 'Whoso hearkeneth unto me shall dwell safely, and shall be quiet from fear of evil … Jerusalem shall dwell safely' (Proverbs 1:33; Jeremiah 23:6).

Freely Saved

Fifth, the Lord Jesus Christ, our God and Saviour is hated by men without a cause, and that is exactly how he saves sinful men and women who hate him 'without a cause', that is, 'freely' (Hosea 14:4; Romans 3:19-24; 8:32).

A Question

Now, I have a question for you. Do you hate him, or do you love him? I speak frankly to you, and tell you what the word of God plainly declares. If you refuse to trust him, if you refuse to bow to him and believe him, your unbelief reveals your hatred for the Son of God (1 John 5:10). If you trust him, your faith in him causes you to love him. 'Unto you, therefore, which believe, he is precious'. 'Lord, thou knowest all things; thou knowest that I love thee'.

'We love him, because he first loved us' (1 John 4:19). Believing him, trusting him, loving him, I am confident that he loves me, even as he is loved by his Father, with an everlasting love. And his love for me casts out all fear.

Be Reconciled

May God the Holy Ghost now cause you, by his omnipotent mercy, to be reconciled to God, giving you life and faith in the Lord Jesus Christ!

'Come now, and let us reason together, saith the LORD: though your sins be as scarlet, they shall be as white as snow; though they be red like crimson, they shall be as wool' (Isaiah 1:18).

'Ho, every one that thirsteth, come ye to the waters, and he that hath no money; come ye, buy, and eat; yea, come, buy wine and milk without money and without price' (Isaiah 55:1).

'Incline your ear, and come unto me: hear, and your soul shall live; and I will make an everlasting covenant with you, even the sure mercies of David' (Isaiah 55:3).

'Seek ye the LORD while he may be found, call ye upon him while he is near: Let the wicked forsake his way, and the unrighteous man his thoughts: and let him return unto the LORD, and he will have mercy upon him; and to our God, for he will abundantly pardon' (Isaiah 55:6, 7).

'Come unto me, all ye that labour and are heavy laden, and I will give you rest. Take my yoke upon you, and learn of me; for I am meek and lowly in heart: and ye shall find rest unto your souls. For my yoke is easy, and my burden is light' (Matthew 11:28-30).

'For we must all appear before the judgment seat of Christ; that every one may receive the things done in his body, according to that he hath done, whether it be good or bad. Knowing therefore the terror of the Lord, we persuade men; but we are made manifest unto God; and I trust also are made manifest in your consciences' (2 Corinthians 5:10, 11).

'Therefore if any man be in Christ, he is a new creature: old things are passed away; behold, all things are become new. And all things are of God, who hath reconciled us to himself by Jesus Christ, and hath given to us the ministry of reconciliation; To wit, that God was in Christ, reconciling the world unto himself, not imputing their trespasses unto them; and hath committed unto us the word of reconciliation' (2 Corinthians 5:17-19).

'Now then we are ambassadors for Christ, as though God did beseech you by us: we pray you in Christ's stead, be ye reconciled to God. For he hath made him to be sin for us, who knew no sin; that we might be made the righteousness of God in him' (2 Corinthians 5:20, 21).

'We then, as workers together with him, beseech you also that ye receive not the grace of God in vain. (For he saith, I have heard thee in a time accepted, and in the day of salvation have I succoured thee: behold, now is the accepted time; behold, now is the day of salvation.)' (2 Corinthians 6:1, 2).

Quit fighting God. Be reconciled to God by faith in his darling Son, the Lord Jesus Christ!

Chapter 38

Equipped For Trouble

'These things have I spoken unto you, that ye should not be offended ... These things I have spoken unto you, that in me ye might have peace. In the world ye shall have tribulation: but be of good cheer; I have overcome the world' (John 16:1-33).

Anyone who knows anything about public speaking knows that the most important parts of any public speech are the first thing and the last thing spoken. There are good reasons for this. If the speaker does not get your attention when he begins, he is not likely to get it at all. And people tend to remember the first thing a speaker says and the last thing he says.

The same thing applies to preaching. I had very few really good professors while I was in college. In Bible colleges and seminaries as in most colleges and universities, those who cannot do the work are hired to teach the courses. But I did have a few very good professors. One of them was my Homiletics/Pastoral Theology professor, Dr Billy Martin. He constantly stressed the need for careful study and preparation. He taught us that in sermon preparation preachers should always give as much attention to the sermon's introduction and conclusion as to the main points of a message.

If you read sermons, especially those men wrote out for their own use, and never intended to have them published, the good ones, those from which people really benefit, almost always they have three parts: the introduction, the main body containing doctrinal points and exposition, and the conclusion, or application.

In the sixteenth chapter of John's Gospel we have the conclusion of our blessed Saviour's last sermon just before he suffered and died as our Substitute at Calvary.

The sermon's introduction in chapter 13 was a picture of redemption by the institution of the Lord's Supper. In chapters 14 and 15 the Saviour's doctrine is all grace. He promises abiding, immutable grace to all who trust him (14:1-3). He teaches and encourages us to trust him, assuring us of his goodness (14:4-14). He promises to send the Holy Spirit to be our abiding, indwelling Comforter and Teacher (14:15-31). The Lord Jesus then shows us the wonder of our union with him in chapter 15. Then, when we come to chapter 16, we come to the conclusion of this great sermon. Here our Saviour graciously applies all that he has said to our lives.

Expedient Departure

As we look at this sixteenth chapter of John's Gospel the Saviour himself applies the message to us. Our dear Redeemer here tells us that his departure out of this world by the sacrifice of himself upon the cursed tree was a matter of expediency for us. He said, 'It is expedient for you that I go away'. As we read this chapter, it is obvious that the Lord's attention was altogether on us. He said nothing about the joy that was before him in returning to his Father. There is not a word about the felicity to which he was going, as he returned to the Father's house: nothing about the Father's reception of his Son, his Servant, our Saviour, nothing about the saints' reception of their Redeemer, and nothing about the angels' reception of their Lord! We hear of none of those things in the Lord's farewell sermon.

Everything is about the Saviour's dear children whom he was about to leave behind in this world of trouble. As he was about to endure all the agonies of his sufferings and death as our Substitute, as he was about to enter into his glory as our Mediator-King, our Saviour's whole heart was on us and our needs in this world of woe. I find that fact wondrously amazing. In the hour of his greatest sorrow and in the anticipation of his greatest glory, our Saviour's heart was on us (Psalms 69:1-7).

In this chapter, as our Saviour concludes his last sermon before his crucifixion, he tells us the reason for all that he has taught from chapter 13 to this point. We see this in the very first verse of the chapter. 'These things have I spoken unto you, that ye should not be offended' (John 16:1). All that he has been telling us, all that he has been teaching has been to prepare us for the trouble he knew we must face in this world of woe. He does so that we should not be offended (v. 1), that we might remember his doctrine (v. 4), and that we might have peace in him (v. 33).

Our Lord's intention here is that all who follow him, all who trust him, all who seek to live for him in this present evil world might be equipped for the trials, temptations, and troubles we must face in this world of woe. In these 33 verses of Inspiration our blessed Saviour gives us seven comforting promises, promises by which he would prepare and equip us for the troublesome times we must face in this world.

'These things have I spoken unto you, that ye should not be offended' (v. 1). How considerate our Saviour is! We might presume that he would be angry with us if he suspected that we could be offended by anything that he did or suffered. We might presume that he would be angry if he suspected that the things we suffer for him might cause us to stumble; but our presumption would be wrong. 'He knoweth our frame. He remembereth that we are dust'! Our blessed Lord knows the weakness of our flesh; and he sympathizes with us in our deplorable weakness. How gracious he is! He prepares us ahead of time for the trouble we shall encounter so that we might not be offended, might not stumble, and might not fall.

'They shall put you out of the synagogues: yea, the time cometh, that whosoever killeth you will think that he doeth God service. And these things will they do unto you, because they have not known the Father, nor me. But these things have I told you, that when the time shall come, ye may remember that I told you of them. And these things I said not unto you at the beginning, because I was with you' (vv. 2-4). As long as the disciples enjoyed the Saviour's physical presence, he was like a wall of fire round about them. They did not sense any other need of protection from danger, as long as he showed himself in their midst, as long as he was manifestly aware of their danger.

Our Lord has not told us yet some of the things which he will reveal and do at the time appointed, because the trial has not come; but when the trial comes, he will give us grace sufficient for the hour.

In every condition, in sickness in health,
In poverty's vale, or abounding in wealth,
At home, or abroad, on the land, on the sea,
As your days may demand so your succour shall be!

If you are the Lord's, the Lord will supply you with the grace needed when it is needed. Do not torture yourself fretting about tomorrow and tomorrow's trouble. 'Sufficient to the day is the evil thereof;' and sufficient is his grace for every day. He promises, 'My grace is sufficient for thee.'

'But now I go my way to him that sent me; and none of you asketh me, Whither goest thou? But because I have said these things unto you, sorrow hath filled your heart' (vv. 5, 6). The disciples were filled with sorrow because the Lord Jesus told them he was about to leave them; but none of them thought to ask 'Why?' Had they known, had they understood ahead of time, that which he would make them look back upon with joy unspeakable, they would have rejoiced in the prospect as much as they did in the remembrance. What a lesson for us! Blessed Holy Spirit, give me faith to trust my God for tomorrow as well as for yesterday. If we would but trust him implicitly, we would rejoice in the Lord always.

'Nevertheless' (v. 7). I have learned to love that word 'nevertheless'. Read how it is used in the book of God and you will find reason to rejoice and give thanks to God for his great goodness, mercy, love, and grace in Christ Jesus (Psalms 31:21-23; 73:22, 23; 89:28-34; 106:43-45).

In the rest of this chapter our Lord Jesus gives us these seven great promises. Seven things promised to every believer, things by which the Son of God equips his elect for life in this world of woe.

Blessed Comforter

First, the Lord Jesus promised to give his redeemed a blessed, Divine Comforter. Of course, you know that Comforter is God the Holy Ghost. Most everyone who even casually reads the Bible knows that; but very few understand or appreciate that by which he the Holy Spirit comforts God's elect. Yet, our Saviour plainly tells us that the comfort by which he comforts the redeemed is the revelation of God's grace in Christ.

'Nevertheless I tell you the truth; It is expedient for you that I go away: for if I go not away, the Comforter will not come unto you; but if I depart, I will send him unto you. And when he is come, he will reprove the world of sin, and of righteousness, and of judgment: Of sin, because they believe not on me; Of righteousness, because I go to my Father, and ye see me no more; Of judgment, because the prince of this world is judged' (vv. 7-11).

The comfort of the Spirit is that sweet work of his grace in us, creating faith in Christ, by which he seals to us all the blessings of the covenant (Galatians 3:13, 14; 4:4-6; Ephesians 1:12-14).

Spiritual Discernment

Second, the Lord Jesus promised that he would grant every saved sinner spiritual knowledge, discernment, and understanding.

'I have yet many things to say unto you, but ye cannot bear them now. Howbeit when he, the Spirit of truth, is come, he will guide you into all truth: for he shall not speak of himself; but whatsoever he shall hear, that shall he speak: and he will shew you things to come. He shall glorify me: for he shall receive of mine, and shall shew it unto you. All things that the Father hath are mine: therefore said I, that he shall take of mine, and shall shew it unto you' (vv. 12-15).

This is the Spirit that 'searcheth all things' (1 Corinthians 2:9, 10). John tells us that if we have Christ, we have the unction of the Spirit and know all things, for the anointing teaches you all things (1 John 2:20-27). Paul tells us that we have the mind of Christ and know all things (1 Corinthians 2:12-16). We should expect God the Holy Spirit to do his work in us just as effectively as Christ has done his work for us.

Hear the Saviour's promise and rejoice. In this world of religious confusion and chaos, the Spirit of Truth guides believing sinners into all truth. He shows us, by his word, that which the Lord Jesus actually accomplished at Calvary. 'He will show you things to come' (v. 13). He glorifies Christ and shows us the things of Christ (vv. 14, 15).

Sweet Reunion

In verses 16-22 the Saviour promised his sorrowing disciples that shortly after his departure they should look forward to a sweet reunion with him.

'A little while, and ye shall not see me: and again, a little while, and ye shall see me, because I go to the Father … Verily, verily, I say unto you, That ye shall weep and lament, but the world shall rejoice: and ye shall be sorrowful, but your sorrow shall be turned into joy … And ye now therefore have sorrow: but I will see you again, and your heart shall rejoice, and your joy no man taketh from you'.

The sight of our Saviour and of our blessed union with him makes our hearts rejoice. We see him as our successful Substitute, our unrivalled Sovereign, and our coming King. This was literally fulfilled when he rose from the dead. 'Then were the disciples glad when they saw the Lord' (John 20:20). But there is a wider, complete fulfilment of this promise awaiting his suffering, sorrowing disciples in these latter days. He has promised, 'I will come again and receive you unto myself, that where I am, there ye may be also' (John 14:3).

Effectual Prayer

The fourth promise is found in verses 23, 24. Our Saviour equips us for the trials and heartaches, the temptations and troubles we must endure in this world by promising that our hearts' prayers shall never fall on deaf ears in heaven, by promising us that our prayers to our God are effectual prayers.

'And in that day ye shall ask me nothing. Verily, verily, I say unto you, Whatsoever ye shall ask the Father in my name, he will give it you. Hitherto have ye asked nothing in my name: ask, and ye shall receive, that your joy may be full.'

Our Lord made this promise three times in this one message (John 14:13; 15:16, 16:23). I presume he intends for us to understand that our God will never ignore the cries of our hearts, that our God will give us our hearts' desire, that our joy may be full. 'Whatsoever ye shall ask of the Father in my name, he will give you; ask and ye shall receive that your joy may be full'. 'Open thy mouth wide and I will fill it' (Psalms 81:10).

What is it, my brother, my sister, that you want from God? Uninterrupted communion with Christ? Complete consecration to Christ? Perfect conformity to Christ? It shall be yours!

Blessed Advocacy

Fifth, our Saviour assures us of his blessed advocacy on our behalf as our Intercessor in heaven.

'At that day ye shall ask in my name: and I say not unto you, that I will pray the Father for you: For the Father himself loveth you, because ye have loved me, and have believed that I came out from God' (vv. 26, 27).

Our Lord said, 'I say not unto you, that I will pray the Father for you', because there was no need. He had already promised this (John 14:16). Never forget this, child of God, 'We have an Advocate with the Father, Jesus Christ the righteous; and he is the propitiation for our sins' (1 John 2:1, 2). What thanksgiving and confidence this should bring to our hearts! Christ is pleading for us with the Father who loves us. Nothing in heaven, earth, or hell can harm us or prevent his will being done in us, for us, and with us.

Peace

Sixth, the Saviour promises peace; blessed, sweet, abiding peace. 'These things have I spoken unto you, that in me ye might have peace' (v. 33). He has made peace by the blood of his cross. He has spoken peace by the grace and power of his Spirit. This peace is not of ourselves. It is not the result of something we do. It is not conditioned by our circumstances. It is not affected by our disappointments or tribulations. The world cannot give it nor take it away. Christ himself is our Peace. He is our Peace; and in him we have peace: peace with God, peace from God, and the peace of God, the peace of propitiation, the peace of pardon, the peace of providence, and the peace of his presence! This peace is as real, as abiding, and as eternal as Christ himself. 'In me ye shall have peace'.

Certain Triumph

The seventh promise given by our Lord before he left his beloved disciples in the world of woe, the seventh promise by which he equips us for all that lies before us between here and eternity is sure and certain triumph in him. 'In the world ye shall have tribulation; but be of good cheer, I have overcome the world' (v. 33).

It is true, 'All that will live godly in Christ Jesus shall suffer persecution' (2 Timothy 3:12). But persecution, mockery, or even death does not mean defeat. The fact is, all of God's elect must through much tribulation enter the kingdom of God (Acts 14:22); but out of their tribulation they shall come forth into everlasting glory with robes washed and made white in the blood of the Lamb (Revelation 7:14). Nothing can separate us from the love of God in Christ Jesus, in whom, by whom, and with whom we are more than conquerors (Romans 8:35-37). The powers of the world are impotent before God's saints. It is written, 'Greater is he that is in you than he that is in the world' (1 John 4: 4). Christ has already overcome the world; and your life is hid with Christ in God. 'Thanks be unto God which always causeth us to triumph in Christ' (2 Corinthians 2:14; Revelation 19:1-9).

Chapter 39

The Comforter

'Nevertheless I tell you the truth; It is expedient for you that I go away: for if I go not away, the Comforter will not come unto you; but if I depart, I will send him unto you. And when he is come, he will reprove the world of sin, and of righteousness, and of judgment: Of sin, because they believe not on me; Of righteousness, because I go to my Father, and ye see me no more; Of judgment, because the prince of this world is judged. I have yet many things to say unto you, but ye cannot bear them now. Howbeit when he, the Spirit of truth, is come, he will guide you into all truth: for he shall not speak of himself; but whatsoever he shall hear, that shall he speak: and he will shew you things to come. He shall glorify me: for he shall receive of mine, and shall shew it unto you. All things that the Father hath are mine: therefore said I, that he shall take of mine, and shall shew it unto you. A little while, and ye shall not see me: and again, a little while, and ye shall see me, because I go to the Father' (John 16:7-16).

Four times in his final discourse before leaving this world our blessed Saviour promised his disciples that he would send the Holy Ghost to be our Comforter (John 14:16, 26; 15:26; 16:7). God the Holy Spirit is the Divine Comforter who dwells in every heaven-born soul, teaching us, guiding us, and comforting us by showing us our Lord Jesus Christ and the things of Christ, ever glorifying our blessed Saviour. I want to show you seven things our Saviour promised in these wonderful statements about the person and work of God the Holy Ghost.

The Comforter

The Holy Spirit is the gift of God to his church and people through the mediation of the Lord Jesus Christ, our exalted Lord and King. Our Lord Jesus distinctly refers to the Spirit of God as 'The Comforter'. That is the first thing we should see in this passage. Just as the Son of God, in his office capacity as our Mediator and Covenant Surety, is called our Saviour, the Spirit of God is our Comforter.

'And I will pray the Father, and he shall give you another Comforter, that he may abide with you for ever; Even the Spirit of truth; whom the world cannot receive, because it seeth him not, neither knoweth him: but ye know him; for he dwelleth with you, and shall be in you' (John 14:16, 17).

This title given to God the Spirit, 'The Comforter', is a very broad, meaningful title. It means one who comforts, who pleads, who exhorts, one who calls us to his side, as a father would call his child to his side when he has something personal to say to him. Our Lord Jesus has given us his Spirit to dwell in us as our ever abiding Comforter. What a gift of grace!

Another Comforter

Second, our Saviour calls the Holy Spirit 'another Comforter'. 'I will pray the Father, and he shall give you another Comforter'. The word 'another' is also very significant. It means another of the same kind, another just like me, one distinct from me, but exactly like me. Here are the three persons of the holy trinity working together for our souls (1 John 5:7), the three persons of the triune Jehovah, linked together and united in covenant solidarity for the salvation of our souls, constantly engaged in the work of saving chosen sinners (Ephesians 1:3-14).

The Holy Ghost is 'another Comforter' in addition to Christ, who is called 'the consolation of Israel' (Luke 2:25). The Lord Jesus tells us that he is another instead of me. I am going, but he is coming. He will fill up my place; my place of fellowship, counsel, comfort, and love. He will be to you for consolation what I have been to you for consolation. He is another like me. He will be another, and yet not another; one in mind and sympathy with me toward you. In having him, you have me; and he will be another in addition to me. I am still with you, though I go away; and in addition to my presence, you shall have the presence of another like me, another who is God, just as I am God.

Father's Gift

Third, this gift of the Holy Ghost as our Comforter is the Father's gift to every chosen, redeemed sinner. 'I will pray the Father, and he shall give you another Comforter'. It is he of whom the Lord Jesus spoke when he said to the woman at the well, 'If thou knewest the gift of God' (John 4:10). He said, 'If ye, who are evil, know how to give good gifts to your children, how much more shall your heavenly Father give the Holy Spirit to them that ask him'. God the Holy Spirit, our Comforter, is the gift promised to Abraham and his seed (Galatians 3:13, 14), by which the Lord God seals all covenant blessings to his chosen (Ephesians 1:13, 14). It is the Father's good pleasure that we have the Holy Ghost. Having him we live in the Spirit, and walk in the Spirit, and pray in the Spirit (Romans 8:1-17).

Christ's Intercession

Fourth, God the Holy Spirit is bestowed upon all the redeemed by the merit and efficacy of Christ's intercession on our behalf. He said, 'I will pray the Father, and he will give you another Comforter'. At the appointed time of love, God the Father sends his Spirit to every chosen, redeemed sinner in almighty, irresistible grace in regeneration, giving us life and faith in Christ (Ezekiel 16:6-8; 36:27; 37:14; Zechariah 12:10).

Abiding Comforter

Fifth, the Lord Jesus promised that he would give us this Comforter forever, 'that he may abide with you forever'! The Comforter is ours forever, unconditionally ours forever! For as long as time shall last, for as long as we are in this world of woe, God the Holy Ghost shall be our abiding Comforter. As the shekinah glory filled the temple, abiding on the mercy-seat, so God the Holy Spirit abides in us as the Spirit of Life. We live in the sweet 'communion of the Holy Ghost' all the time (2 Corinthians 13:14). Though often we may grieve him, we shall never be deprived of him. Though we may quench him, we cannot lose him!

Spirit Of Truth

Sixth, in John 14:17 our Saviour describes the Comforter as 'the Spirit of truth'. He is the Spirit who communicates the truth to the soul. Christ is the truth he gives and communicates to us, the truth revealed in us by the Holy Spirit. The gospel of Christ is the truth into which he guides us. The word of Christ, holy scripture, is the truth by which he directs our paths.

The world cannot receive him. To the world God sends a strong delusion that they should believe a lie (2 Thessalonians 2:11, 12); but we know him; and by him dwelling in us, we know our election of God. The seed of the serpent cannot receive the Spirit of truth. Jude describes the ruin of the world like this. He says they are 'sensual, having not the Spirit' (Jude 19). What a sad picture of lost men and women! They are without God, without Christ, without life, and without hope, having not the Spirit!

Divine Teacher

Seventh, I want us to look briefly at what our Saviour tells us about the Holy Spirit as our Comforter in John 14:26. 'But the Comforter, which is the Holy Ghost, Whom the Father will send in my name, he shall teach you all things, and bring all things to your remembrance, whatsoever I have said unto you'.

This Divine Comforter, God the Holy Ghost, is our teacher. It is God the Holy Spirit and God the Holy Spirit alone who teaches spiritual truth. He takes the things of Christ, the things that Christ taught and did, brings them to our remembrance, and causes us to see and understand them. 'He shall testify of me', our Saviour told us (John 15:26; 1 John 5:1-13). Sealing the word of God to our hearts, causing us to hear the gospel of our own salvation by Christ (Ephesians 1:13, 14), giving us faith in Christ, the Spirit of God bears witness in our spirits that we are born of God.

What is it that the Holy Spirit teaches poor, needy sinners, by which he causes the chosen to know they are chosen, by which he causes the redeemed to know they are redeemed, by which he causes the called to know they are called? What is it that God the Holy Spirit teaches us and brings to our remembrance that gives us the sweet comfort of assured mercy, love, and grace in Christ?

1. Redemption accomplished: he convinces the sinner that redemption is accomplished by Christ (John 16:7-11).

2. Things to come: he convinces us of 'things to come', that is to say of things that must come as the result of Christ's obedience unto death as our Substitute and Surety (John 16:12, 13; 1 John 3:1-9; 4:17). What comfort the Spirit gives when he convinces a poor sinner of all that Christ has obtained and secured for him by his obedience and death as his Substitute: eternal redemption, absolute forgiveness and justification, perfect righteousness, full sanctification, eternal life, the resurrection of our bodies and certain glory!

3. Christ glorified: God the Holy Ghost comforts the hearts of chosen, redeemed sinners by convincing us that Christ is glorified (John 16:14-16). He glorifies Christ by showing us the things of Christ. God the Holy Spirit always points men to Christ. By the preaching of the gospel he shows the things of Christ, effectually revealing Christ in the called, and thereby glorifies him. The gospel we preach is the good news of the glory of Christ (2 Corinthians 4:6).

Not only does he glorify Christ by showing us his glory as our Redeemer, he shows us that Christ is glorified by the triune Jehovah as our Redeemer (John 16:15, Philippians 2:9-11). This is our comfort: Redemption is accomplished! Salvation is sure! Christ is glorified! All things are in the hands of him who loved us and gave himself for us! Christ is on his Throne: all is well. Christ is glorified: all is well!

Chapter 40

The Expedience And The Comfort

'Nevertheless I tell you the truth; It is expedient for you that I go away: for if I go not away, the Comforter will not come unto you; but if I depart, I will send him unto you. And when he is come, he will reprove the world of sin, and of righteousness, and of judgment: Of sin, because they believe not on me; Of righteousness, because I go to my Father, and ye see me no more; Of judgment, because the prince of this world is judged. I have yet many things to say unto you, but ye cannot bear them now. Howbeit when he, the Spirit of truth, is come, he will guide you into all truth: for he shall not speak of himself; but whatsoever he shall hear, that shall he speak: and he will shew you things to come. He shall glorify me: for he shall receive of mine, and shall shew it unto you' (John 16:7-14).

Here our blessed Saviour tells us that his death upon the cursed tree as our Substitute was for us a matter of expedience, something needful and profitable for our souls. Then he tells us why that is so. The sin-atoning death of the Lord Jesus Christ is the only way sinners could ever obtain God's salvation, the only way we could ever know God, the only way fallen man could ever live in communion with the triune Jehovah. In Galatians 3:13, 14 the Spirit of God tells us exactly the same thing.

'Christ hath redeemed us from the curse of the law, being made a curse for us: for it is written, Cursed is every one that hangeth on a tree: That the blessing of Abraham might come on the Gentiles through Jesus Christ; that we might receive the promise of the Spirit through faith'.

The Expedience

First, let me show you the expedience of our Saviour's death. Then, I will tell you a little about the comfort of his Holy Spirit.

'Nevertheless I tell you the truth; It is expedient for you that I go away: for if I go not away, the Comforter will not come unto you; but if I depart, I will send him unto you' (John 16:7).

It was necessary for the Lord Jesus Christ to go away. He must be lifted up upon the cursed tree. He must suffer and die. He must rise from the dead, ascend back into heaven and appear in the presence of God for us. Otherwise, we could never have been saved. The purpose of God, the word of God, the promises of God, and the covenant of grace would all have been defeated and proven a lie. This is what our Saviour meant when he said, 'It is expedient for you that I go away'.

Behold the Lord Jesus, hanging upon the cursed tree, and learn the meaning of those words. Standing at the foot of the cross, as I behold the Holy One nailed to the cursed tree, covered with his own blood and the spit of an enraged mob, made to be sin, forsaken and cursed of God his Father, yet, realising that this is the work of God's own hand, I am lost in astonishment! I am filled with reverence and awe (2 Corinthians 5:21; Galatians 3:13). Samuel Stennett says,

Yonder (amazing sight!) I see
The incarnate Son of God
Expiring on the cursed tree,
And weltering in His blood.

Behold, a purple torrent run
Down from His hands and head,
The crimson tide puts out the sun;
His groans awake the dead.

The trembling earth, the darkened sky,
Proclaim the truth aloud;
And with the amazed centurion, cry,
'this is the Son of God'!

Awed as I am with reverence for my crucified Lord, still there is a question that I cannot suppress, a question that reason and sound judgment cannot fail to ask. The question is, Why? Why did the Son of God suffer such a death? Why did God so torment his beloved Son and kill him in such a horribly ignominious way? Was it to save my soul? I know that he died that I might live. He suffered, the Just for the unjust, that he might bring me to God. But was there no other way for the omnipotent God to save me? Was all this done to demonstrate the greatness of God's love to me? Indeed it was (Romans 5:8; 1 John 3:16; 4:9, 10). Anne Steele wrote,

> Jesus, who left His throne on high,
> Left the bright realms of bliss,
> And came to earth to bleed and die,
> Was ever love like this?

But, surely, God could have revealed his love to me in some other way. Why did he slay his Son? What necessity was there for the Son of God to suffer and die upon the cursed tree? What was the expedience of his death?

Only one answer can be found to that question. The justice of God had to be satisfied. There was no necessity for God to save anyone. Salvation is altogether the free gift of his grace. But, having determined to save his elect from the ruins of fallen humanity, the only way God could save his people and forgive their sins was by the death of Christ. 'Without shedding of blood is no remission' (Hebrews 9:22). The justice of God had to be satisfied in order for God to save his people; and the only thing that could ever satisfy the justice of God is the blood of Christ.

'If I go not away, the Comforter will not come unto you; but if I depart, I will send him unto you'. Had Christ not gone away the Holy Spirit would never have come in his office capacity as the Comforter of his people, Reprover of the world, Teacher of truth, and Glorifier of Christ. There would have been nothing for him to do! Had Christ not gone away, there would have been no blood to sprinkle, no righteousness to reveal, no salvation to bestow, and no Mediator to glorify.

Without question, the Holy Spirit was in the world from the beginning (Genesis 1:2; Psalms 51:11). Without him, the prophets could not have prophesied and the Old Testament saints could not have been saved. But he was not poured out upon all flesh (the Gentile world), for the gathering of God's elect from the four corners of the earth, until Christ died and ascended back to heaven. This coming of the Holy Spirit was the direct result of Christ's accomplished redemption and his exaltation and glory as our Saviour (Galatians 3:13, 14; John 7:39; Psalms 68:18; Joel 2:32; Acts 2:33).

One Condition

In the infinitely wise and orderly arrangements of the covenant of grace all the blessings of the covenant were conditioned upon one thing. And that one thing was the obedience of Christ as the Surety of God's elect, his righteousness and blood atonement. As God the Holy Spirit is the Conveyor of all grace, he could not come to convey to us the blessings of grace promised in the covenant until our Surety had earned and purchased them for us. The sending of the Spirit was the fruit of Christ's purchase. Therefore, he could not come until the purchase was made. But, inasmuch as Christ has by his blood purchased God's elect from under the curse of the law and purchased for us all the blessings of the covenant, the Spirit of God must and shall come to every redeemed sinner in irresistible, saving power. He comes to seal to us all that the Father promised and the Son purchased by giving us life and faith in Christ, and preserving us in grace until the resurrection day.

Our Lord had just told his disciples that he must suffer, die, rise from the dead, and ascend back to his Father in heaven, that there he would prepare a place for them, and that at the time appointed he would come again to receive them unto himself. Then he assured them that, upon his ascension back into heaven, he would send the Comforter, the Holy Spirit, to minister to them.

These things are all recorded in John 13, 14, and 15. They should have flooded the disciples' hearts with joy. The disciples should have been full of questions about these great, mysterious, and wonderful things. Instead, sorrow filled their hearts. Then the Saviour spoke to quieten their fears and show them the necessity of his going away, his death upon the cursed tree, his resurrection, his ascension, and his heavenly exaltation. He said, 'Nevertheless I tell you the truth; it is expedient for you that I go away: for if I go not away, the Comforter will not come unto you; but if I depart, I will send him unto you'.

Pause a moment and learn a lesson: Those things that appear to be most grievous in their experience are often most expedient in their end. Thank God that he does not deal with us according to the folly of our own wills, but graciously gives us what he knows is good for us! An expedience is that which is, being constrained by necessity, the best course to follow. Our Lord in this place is essentially saying, 'It is both necessary and good for you that I should suffer, die, rise from the dead, and go back to my Father in heaven'.

The expedience of our Saviour's death should be obvious to anyone: had he not gone away, had he not suffered and died as our Substitute upon the cross and ascended back to heaven, we could not have been saved. He could not have finished the work he had come to do (Hebrews 10:5-10). God could not be just and yet justify them that believe (Romans 3:24-26; Isaiah 45:21). There would have been no atonement for sin (Hebrews 9:22). We could never have obtained the forgiveness of sin, reconciliation to God, peace, pardon, and righteousness (Colossians 1:20-22). We would have no Forerunner, High Priest, and Advocate in heaven (1 John 2:1, 2). There would have been no way of access to God for guilty sinners (Hebrews 10:19). Christ could never have saved his people from their sins (Matthew 1:21).

The Comfort

Now, let me show you just a little about the comforting work of the Holy Spirit. How does God the Holy Spirit comfort chosen, redeemed sinners? Hear what the Lord Jesus tells us in the next verse (John 16:8). 'When he is come, he will reprove the world of sin, and of righteousness, and of judgment'. This is the errand upon which the Spirit of God has been sent into the world. This is the work of the Holy Spirit as the Comforter of God's elect. He is the Spirit of Truth. He reveals to and teaches chosen men and women the truth of God. Apart from the illumination of the Spirit, no one can know the truth. He is the Spirit of Reproof. By the preaching of the gospel, the Spirit of God speaks to the hearts of his people to rebuke, reprimand, and reprove them for their sin and unbelief. And he is the Spirit of Conviction. By the preaching of the gospel, he effectually convinces God's elect of their sin, Christ's righteousness, and of God's judgment of sin by Christ.

Legal Term

The word that is translated here 'reprove', and in the margin 'convince' is a legal term. It speaks of the work of a jury in a court of law. When a man is charged with a crime, upon hearing the testimony of others and weighing the evidence, if the jury sees that the man is beyond any reasonable doubt guilty, being convinced by the evidence given, they find the man guilty; and he is convicted. Feelings may enter into their emotions. But feelings must not enter into their judgment. You see, feelings have nothing to do with conviction. Conviction is the result of unanswerable arguments and irrefutable evidence.

When God the Holy Spirit comes upon a sinner in saving grace and power, he convicts him, by the unanswerable, irrefutable word of God, of sin, righteousness, and judgment. This conviction is the sovereign prerogative of God the Holy Spirit. He accomplishes it by almighty, irresistible grace. Man may open the word and preach it. But only the Spirit of God can effectually open the heart, apply the word, and convict the sinner.

When our Saviour says, 'He will reprove the world', he is not suggesting that every person in the world will be the object of the Spirit's work. That would make his work a failure, for all are not convinced. Our Lord's meaning is that the Holy Spirit will effectually and savingly convict his elect throughout all the world, Gentiles as well as Jews, some of every age, some in every nation. He will savingly convict every elect, redeemed sinner by the irresistible power of his grace.

Holy Spirit Conviction

The comfort of the Spirit is Holy Spirit conviction; and Holy Spirit conviction is essential to saving faith in Christ. I do not say that Holy Spirit conviction is a prerequisite, or condition that must be met before a person can trust Christ. That is a dreadful mistake in the thinking of many. Our Lord never calls upon sinners to be convicted and then believe on him. You must simply trust Christ. Trust him and you are saved, forgiven of all sin, and have eternal life. There are no conditions to faith in Christ. There are no prerequisites for you to meet, doctrinally, experimentally, or emotionally, before you can believe.

However, our Lord tells us plainly that one distinguishing characteristic of saving faith is that it is always accompanied by Holy Spirit conviction. Where there is no conviction, there is no conversion, there is no faith, there is no knowledge of Christ. Where there is no conviction there is no saving union with Christ. Wherever there is true, saving faith in the Lord Jesus Christ, there is Holy Spirit conviction. And wherever there is true Holy Spirit conviction, there is true, saving faith in Christ. The two always go together.

The question that must be answered is this: what is Holy Spirit conviction? I have heard and read many answers given by men to that question which have no foundation in the word of God. Most people think that Holy Spirit conviction is a feeling of deep remorse for sin, a dreadful sense of one's lost condition, a terrifying fear of God's wrath, an ardent desire to be saved. These things may, and very often do accompany Holy Spirit conviction; but nowhere in the word of God is conviction described in such terms.

If we would know what Holy Spirit conviction is, we must look to the word of God alone, putting out of our minds the opinions of men. What you and I may think and feel about the matter is of no importance. We only want to know what God says. And this is the way God our Saviour describes Holy Spirit conviction, 'When he is come, he will reprove the world of sin, and of righteousness, and of judgment; of sin, because they believe not on me; of righteousness, because I go to my Father; of judgment, because the prince of this world is judged' (John 16:8-11).

Sin

Holy Spirit conviction deals with these three things: sin, righteousness, and judgment. 'He will reprove the world of sin'. When God the Holy Spirit comes to a sinner's heart in saving power and grace, this is the first thing he does: he reproves, convinces, and convicts the sinner that he is a sinner, deserving eternal damnation. Where there is no Holy Spirit conviction of sin, there is no saving faith in Christ. When a man experiences real conviction of sin, he takes sides with God against himself, justifying God in his own condemnation (Psalms 51:4, 5). The Spirit of God so thoroughly convinces a man of his sinfulness that he gladly takes his place with the publican and cries, 'God be merciful to me, I am the sinner.'

He convinces us of the fact of sin. We have sinned against God. In our father Adam we rebelled against God, we were born with hearts of rebellion and sin, and we have chosen the path of rebellion against God. We are all sinners by nature, sinners at heart, sinners by choice, and sinners by deed.

The Holy Spirit convinces us of the fault of sin. Our sin is much more than an act of evil against man. Sin is an affront to God. It is an attack upon the throne of God. It is a denial of God's right to be God. Sin is a monstrous attempt to rape God, to rob him of his dignity and glory as God. 'Against thee, thee only have I sinned, and done this evil in thy sight.'

In conviction, the Holy Spirit convinces us of the folly of sin. It is the most foolish thing in the world that a man should sin against God. Sin is utter madness. What fool will dare to stand against the Almighty?

God the Holy Spirit convinces us of the filth of sin. He shows us that sin has made us loathsome and obnoxious in the sight of God. It has rendered both me and all that I do unacceptable to a holy God.

The Spirit of God convinces us of the fountain of sin. Sin arises from our own evil hearts. Sin is not so much what we do as it is what we are. Because man's heart is a fountain of evil, it brings forth nothing but corruption, vileness, and sin.

And the Holy Spirit convinces us of the fruit of sin. 'The wages of sin is death'. The just reward of my sin is eternal damnation.

Specifically, our Saviour declares that God the Holy Spirit will convince sinners of sin, 'because they believe not on me'. That is to say, he convinces us of the folly of attempting to save ourselves by our own works. Salvation does not come by anything the natural man can do. A person cannot be saved by repeating a prayer, by walking a church aisle, by making a decision, by being baptised and joining the church, or by obedience to the law of God. Salvation comes to helpless, dead sinners only by faith in Christ, faith wrought in the heart by the mighty, effectual operations of God the Holy Spirit. Salvation is the result of Holy Spirit conviction. Our Lord Jesus declares that when the Spirit of God comes in saving grace to a sinner he will convince that person 'of sin, because they believe not on me'.

When the Spirit of God convicts a person of his sin, the convicted sinner is graciously forced to see and acknowledge his guilt before the holy God (Psalms 51:3-5). And he sees that he is utterly without ability to change his nature. I know that the whole world has sinned and is guilty before God. But the Lord God has graciously shown me that I am guilty, deserving of his wrath, and without excuse before him. The evidence is all in. It is irrefutable. I am convinced. I am guilty. From the depths of my filthy soul I cry, 'God be merciful to me, the sinner'! This conviction is contrary to nature. It is the work of God the Holy Spirit.

The specific issue of conviction is unbelief. All men know by nature that such things as robbery, adultery, and murder are sin. But it is a supernatural work of God the Holy Spirit that convinces us that unbelief is sin. Indeed, unbelief is the greatest of all sins, and the most damning. Unbelief is the heart of man declaring that God is a liar (1 John 5:10). Every sin is damning. But no sin is as damning as unbelief. The heathen are lost for want of knowledge. But those who upon hearing the gospel refuse to believe on the Lord Jesus Christ are lost for want of faith, by their wilful, obstinate unbelief. So their unbelief shall be their condemnation. It is unbelief that keeps them from entering into rest. Unbelief deserves and shall have the unmitigated, everlasting wrath of Almighty God in hell. Blessed is the man or woman who by the Spirit of God is convicted of sin and turned from unbelief to faith in Christ!

Righteousness

When the Spirit of God comes in saving power to a sinner, he convicts the sinner of righteousness. 'Of righteousness, because I go to my Father, and ye see me no more' (John 16:10). The basis of this conviction is the fact that Christ has ascended back to his Father in heaven. What is this conviction of righteousness? It is the conviction that God demands righteousness, that I cannot produce righteousness, and that the Lord Jesus Christ has brought in an everlasting righteousness by his obedience to God as the sinners' Substitute. Blessed be God, our Saviour's name is JEHOVAH-TSIDKINU, THE LORD OUR RIGHTEOUSNESS!

Behold the crucified Christ, slain under the penalty of sin, buried, risen again, ascended back into heaven, exalted to the throne of everlasting glory, and be convinced that he has brought in an everlasting, all-sufficient righteousness for all who trust him. 'There is therefore now no condemnation to them which are in Christ Jesus ... For what the law could not do, in that it was weak through the flesh, God sending his own Son in the likeness of sinful flesh, and for sin, condemned sin in the flesh: That the righteousness of the law might be fulfilled in us ... Who is he that condemneth? It is Christ that died, yea rather, that is risen again, who is even at the right hand of God, who also maketh intercession for us' (Romans 8:1, 3, 4, 34).

The Lord Jesus Christ fulfilled all the requirements of righteousness by his obedience to God as our Representative (Romans 5:19). As a man, he did all that God in his law requires of men. And he did it for his people, to work out a righteousness that God might impute to and bestow upon his elect.

In his death as our Substitute Christ satisfied the righteous and just penalty of God's law due to our sins (Galatians 3:13). He redeemed us from the curse of the law by being made a curse for us. He was made to be sin for us. Our sins were imputed to him. And God punished him, to the full satisfaction of justice, for our sins, so that he might in justice forgive our sins (Romans 3:24-26).

Because Christ was made sin for us and died for our sins, all for whom he died are made the righteousness of God in him. Every sinner who trusts Christ is righteous before God, made righteous by righteousness imputed in justification and by righteousness imparted in sanctification. Just as the Lord Jesus Christ was made sin for us by God's work alone, we are made the righteousness of God in him by God's work alone.

Judgment

'And when he is come, he will reprove the world of sin, and of righteousness, and of judgment: of sin, because they believe not on me; of righteousness, because I go to my Father, and ye see me no more; of judgment, because the prince of this world is judged' (John 16:8-11).

Looking upon my own heart, in the light of God's word, I am thoroughly convinced of my own depravity, guilt, and sin before God. I know I deserve his infinite wrath. Looking upon that Man in heaven who is God, who was once made to be sin for sinful man and is now freed from sin, I am thoroughly convinced that his righteousness is infinitely meritorious and sufficient to give all who trust him eternal, immutable acceptance with the holy God. And looking upon Christ's conquest over Satan by his death upon the cursed tree, I am thoroughly convinced of judgment, convinced that judgment is finished for all for whom this great and glorious Saviour died at Calvary. This is the work of the Holy Spirit. When he saves a sinner, he convinces him of sin, of righteousness, and of judgment. This conviction of judgment is threefold.

God will judge all sin (Acts 17:31). As the Lord God judged Satan for sin, casting him out of heaven, binding him by the cross of Christ, and sentencing him to everlasting destruction in hell, so he will judge the sins of all men and women in the last day. None shall escape the justice and wrath of Almighty God. 'The soul that sinneth, it shall die'!

God's judgment of men for sin is just. Sin is more than an act. It is a principle of enmity against God in the heart of every man. It is treason against the King of heaven and malice against our Creator. The goodness and justice of God demand that wickedness be put out of the earth and that sinners be punished with everlasting destruction (Psalms 11:4-7). Should God punish me forever in hell, he is perfectly just to do so. Should he punish you forever in hell, he is just. We deserve eternal damnation.

For God's elect, judgment is over! The Lord God judged our sins in his Son, the Lord Jesus Christ. He made his dear Son to be sin for us, and punished us for sin, to the full satisfaction of his holy justice, in his darling Son. The proof that judgment is over for the believer is the fact that Christ has taken Satan into captivity, delivering us from the fear of death (Hebrews 2:15).

If you believe on the Lord Jesus Christ, you have nothing to fear from God, his law, or his justice. Your sins are forever forgiven. You have been made perfectly righteous in Christ. You are complete in him. And for you, judgment is over.

Divine Guidance

'I have yet many things to say unto you, but ye cannot bear them now. Howbeit when he, the Spirit of truth, is come, he will guide you into all truth: for he shall not speak of himself; but whatsoever he shall hear, that shall he speak: and he will shew you things to come. He shall glorify me: for he shall receive of mine, and shall shew it unto you' (John 16:12-14).

God the Holy Spirit comforts us by revealing the gospel to us; and he comforts us by guiding us, sweetly, effectually into all truth. Matthew Poole rightly observed that the word here translated 'guide' implies that the Holy Spirit both reveals the truth to God's saints and bows our wills to the truth he reveals. He not only shows us what the truth is, he bows us to the truth.

Though this text is primarily a declaration of apostolic inspiration, it clearly has application to all believers. The Spirit's work in a person is not over when he has been convicted. The Holy Spirit graciously guides all believers into all truth that is needful, useful, and profitable for them. He does so through the ministry of the word, causing saints to grow in the grace and knowledge of Christ (Ephesians 4:11-16). It is written, 'Ye have an unction from the Holy One, and ye know all things' (1 John 2:20). This is not a promise of universal, spiritual knowledge. But it is a promise of true spiritual knowledge. As the Spirit of God, through the word of God, shows us the things of Christ, he guides us into truth, for Christ is 'all truth' (John 14:6). And all who are saved by his grace bow to, receive, and love his truth.

'He will show you things to come'. These 'things to come' are things that will assuredly follow as the result of Christ's accomplished redemption: the sure salvation of all the redeemed, the complete forgiveness of all my sin, the resurrection glory of the redeemed, the everlasting praise of the Redeemer.

'He shall glorify me'. Here our Saviour tells us that 'all truth' revealed and taught by the Spirit of God glorifies Christ. Anything that is of God glorifies Christ; not the preacher, not the church, not a man, but Christ. By this you may determine whether any doctrine or ordinance, religious work or religious experience is of God: does it, or does it not glorify Christ alone? God the Holy Spirit gives comfort to our souls by glorifying our blessed Redeemer in his accomplishments as our Saviour (1 Corinthians 1:30, 31). Blessed expedience! Blessed Comfort! Blessed Saviour! Blessed Comforter!

Chapter 41

The Comfort Of Conviction

'Nevertheless I tell you the truth; It is expedient for you that I go away: for if I go not away, the Comforter will not come unto you; but if I depart, I will send him unto you. And when he is come, he will reprove the world of sin, and of righteousness, and of judgment: Of sin, because they believe not on me; Of righteousness, because I go to my Father, and ye see me no more; Of judgment, because the prince of this world is judged' (John 16:7-11).

Do you know anything about Holy Spirit conviction? Holy Spirit conviction is the very first work of God's grace in sinners. Holy Spirit conviction is as essential to the salvation of our souls as blood atonement. But there are few who know anything about it. When was the last time you heard a preacher preach about Holy Spirit conviction? What do you know about it? Have you experienced it?

On August 13, 1833, Robert Murray M'Cheyne, a young, 20 year old preacher in Scotland, wrote these words in his diary, 'Clear conviction of sin is the only true origin of dependence on another's righteousness, and therefore (strange to say!) of the Christian's peace of mind and cheerfulness.' That is precisely the doctrine of our Lord Jesus Christ in John 16. The Holy Spirit comforts sinners by convincing us of sin.

To understand God's word aright
This grand distinction must be known:
Though all are sinners in God's sight,
There are but few so in their own.
To such as these our Lord was sent;
They're only sinners who repent.

What comfort can a Saviour bring
To those who never felt their woe?
A sinner is a sacred thing;
The Holy Ghost hath made him so.
New life from Him we must receive,
Before for sin we rightly grieve.

This faithful saying let us own,
Well worthy 'tis to be believed,
That Christ into the world came down,
That sinners might by Him be saved.
Sinners are high in His esteem,
And sinners highly value Him.

Joseph Hart

Sins Of Ignorance
In Leviticus chapters 4 and 5 the Lord God gave detailed instructions concerning 'sins of ignorance'. Six times the Lord told Moses that once any sin of ignorance was made known, atonement must be made by the divinely appointed sacrifice, and once atonement was made the offence would be forgiven. That is exactly the order of things in our experience of God's saving grace in Christ.

Sin must be made known. The sinner must be convinced of his sin. Atonement must be made. The convinced sinner must bring the sacrifice God requires, Jesus Christ crucified. The sinner convinced of his sin, the sinner for whom atonement has been made, is forgiven of his sin. That is the comfort of conviction promised by our Saviour in John 16:7-11.

The fact is none of us know our sin, except as God the Holy Spirit causes us to know it. None can or will confess his sin, except God the Holy Spirit convince him of his sin. Here are five things involved in the saving operations of God the Holy Spirit.

The Commission Of The Spirit
The Lord Jesus says, 'I will send him unto you' (v. 7). 'I will pray the Father, and he shall give you another Comforter, that he may abide with you forever' (John 14:16). As the Lord Jesus came into the world as our Mediator, with a commission from the Father to redeem and save his elect, so too God the Holy Spirit comes to chosen sinners as our divine Comforter with a commission. He

is sent of the Father and sent of the Son to effectually apply the blood of Christ to the redeemed, to effectually apply the salvation Christ obtained with his blood, to sprinkle the blood upon the redeemed. The Spirit of God comes as the Seal of the covenant (Ephesians 1:13, 14). He comes with covenant commission to regenerate, call, sanctify, and preserve every chosen, redeemed sinner. His commission is to make sinners new creatures in Christ (2 Corinthians 5:17). His commission is to unite the Redeemer and the redeemed. His commission is to bring us to Christ. The Lord Jesus sends his Spirit to his chosen as David sent Ziba to get Mephibosheth, with a work to do: 'Fetch him'! And when he comes, he fetches the redeemed to the Redeemer.

The Coming Of The Spirit

At the appointed time of love, the Lord Jesus sends his Spirit to give life to his redeemed and bring his ransomed 'into the bond of the covenant' (Jeremiah 29:11-13; Ezekiel 16:6-8; 20:37; 37:1-14; John 3:3-8). 'Ye must be born again'! When God the Holy Spirit comes in omnipotent mercy, the chosen, redeemed sinner is born again, Christ is revealed, and faith is created in the sinner, causing him, by irresistible grace, to come to the Saviour. This is what we call the effectual call of the Spirit (Ephesians 1:3-14). The work of God the Holy Spirit by which he causes chosen, redeemed sinners to trust the Lord Jesus is performed in us by causing us to hear 'the word of truth, the gospel of your salvation' (v. 13). That is what our Lord Jesus says in John 16:7-11.

The Conviction Of The Spirit

When God the Holy Spirit comes in saving power, he causes the sinner to know his sin, to know the atonement made for his sin, and to know the forgiveness of his sin by Christ Jesus (John 16:7-11). When we are made to know our sin, seeing Christ crucified for us, we confess our sin, the Fountain of cleansing is opened before us, and we are washed and made clean in our consciences before God (Zechariah 12:10; 13:1; 1 John 1:7-10).

The Conquest Of The Spirit

'Howbeit when he, the Spirit of truth, is come, he will guide you into all truth: for he shall not speak of himself; but whatsoever he shall hear, that shall he speak: and he will shew you things to come' (John 16:13).

The word translated 'guide' is, as Matthew Poole wrote, 'a word of great emphasis; it strictly signifieth to be a guide of the way, not only to discover truth as the object of the understanding, but the bowing of the will to the obedience of it.' When God the Holy Spirit saves a sinner, he does so by conquering the rebel, by sweetly forcing us to bow to Christ, who is all Truth, and bow to all the truth revealed in him: the truth about ourselves, the truth about our Saviour, and the truth about his salvation.

The Comfort Of The Spirit

But how does this conviction work of the Spirit give us comfort? First, this convicting work of the Spirit is the revelation of God's love in Christ (1 John 4:9, 10). Second, this convicting work of the Holy Spirit gives comfort to our souls by shedding abroad the love of God in us, which gives us 'good hope through grace' (Romans 5:5-11). Third, Holy Ghost conviction causes us to rest in God's perfect love, which casts out all fear (1 John 4:16-19).

All hail! Atoning Lamb,
Whose off'ring once for all,
Appointed by the great I AM,
Redeemed us from the fall.

Your efficacious blood,
By pow'r Divine applied,
Makes perfect all the Church of God,
By free grace sanctified.

No condemnation now,
Against the chosen race,
Perfect, forever, Lord we bow,
And triumph in Thy grace.

Here then my soul shall rest,
With Jesus' blood applied,
Redeemed and perfect, ever blest,
In Him I'm satisfied.

So I will make my boast
In Jesus crucified:
Perfected with the heav'nly host,
I shall be glorified!

Chapter 42

The Conviction Of Righteousness

'Nevertheless I tell you the truth; It is expedient for you that I go away: for if I go not away, the Comforter will not come unto you; but if I depart, I will send him unto you. And when he is come, he will reprove the world of sin, and of righteousness, and of judgment: Of sin, because they believe not on me; Of righteousness, because I go to my Father, and ye see me no more; Of judgment, because the prince of this world is judged' (John 16:7-11).

When the Spirit of God comes in saving power to a sinner, he convicts the sinner of righteousness. 'Of righteousness, because I go to my Father, and ye see me no more' (John 16:10). Do you know anything about that? Do you know anything about righteousness?

In his mighty, saving operations of grace, God the Holy Spirit convicts sinners of righteousness. The basis of this conviction is the fact that Christ has ascended back to his Father in heaven. What is this conviction of righteousness? It is the conviction that God demands righteousness, that I cannot produce righteousness, and that the Lord Jesus Christ has brought in an everlasting righteousness by his obedience to God as the sinners' Substitute. Blessed be God, our Saviour's name is JEHOVAH-TSIDKENU, 'THE LORD OUR RIGHTEOUSNESS' (Jeremiah 23:6; 33:16).

Behold the crucified Christ, slain under the penalty of sin, buried, risen again, ascended back into heaven, exalted to the throne of everlasting glory, and be convinced that he has brought in an everlasting, all-sufficient righteousness for all who trust him (Romans 8:1, 3, 4, 34).

In his Sermon on the Mount the Lord Jesus tells us what God requires of us. If you will look at the last verse of Matthew 5, you will see that God's requirement is more than sincerely endeavouring to do that which is good, and more than sincerely desiring to be righteous. 'Be ye therefore perfect, even as your Father which is in heaven is perfect' (Matthew 5:48).

How good does a person have to be to go to heaven? The answer could not be more plainly given. The Son of God says, 'Be ye therefore perfect, even as your Father which is in heaven is perfect.' This requirement of perfection, perfect holiness, is given by our God repeatedly throughout the scriptures (Leviticus 19:1, 2; 20:7; 1 Peter 1:15, 16; Hebrews 12:14; Revelation 21:27). This is still God's word to us today. 'Ye shall be holy: for I the Lord your God am holy.' Because the Lord our God is holy, he requires that we also be holy.

The Pharisees

In Matthew 5:20 our Saviour declares, 'Except your righteousness shall exceed the righteousness of the scribes and Pharisees, ye shall in no case enter into the kingdom of heaven.' The scribes and the Pharisees were regarded by the ancient Jews as the most devoted, most spiritual, and most holy of all men. They were men of such high esteem and reputation that the Jews had a saying about them: 'If but two of all the world were to go to heaven the one would be a scribe and the other a Pharisee.'

Insofar as outward, religious righteousness was concerned no one excelled those two groups of men. In works of piety they made long public prayers on the corners of streets, so that all could see and hear their devotion. In works of charity they gave alms, blowing the trumpet, so that all would be impressed by their generosity. In works of equity they paid their tithes, counting out ten percent on their gross income. In works of courtesy and hospitality they often held banquets, even for the Lord Jesus and his disciples (Luke 7).

Three Lessons

Yet, the Saviour declares that our righteousness must exceed, not match but exceed, the righteousness of the scribes and Pharisees. If it does not, we cannot be saved. Our Saviour clearly teaches us three things in Matthew 5:20:

(1) There will be no admission into heaven without righteousness.

(2) A legal, Pharisaical righteousness will never be accepted of God.

(3) The only hope a sinner has of being saved is through the righteousness of a divinely appointed and accepted Substitute and Representative.

And that Substitute and Representative is the Lord Jesus Christ, the Lord our Righteousness (Jeremiah 23:6; 1 Corinthians 1:30, 31; 2 Corinthians 5:21; Romans 9:31-10:4). Christ is that holiness we must have, without which no man shall see the Lord (Hebrews 12:14).

The only way a guilty sinner can be saved and obtain righteousness before God is through faith in Jesus Christ, JEHOVAH-TSIDKENU – THE LORD OUR RIGHTEOUSNESS. Because there is so much ignorance and confusion about righteousness, because most people, like the Jews of old, being ignorant of God's righteousness, are going about to establish their own righteousness and refuse to submit themselves to Christ alone for righteousness, it is a subject of immense importance and one that should be of great interest to every eternity bound sinner. Here are six things revealed in the word of God about this matter of righteousness.

God's Requirement

First, as we have seen already, the book of God universally declares that the holy, Lord God requires righteousness. Righteousness is demanded by him. God is holy. Being perfectly holy, he demands perfect holiness. He requires perfect righteousness. Anything and anyone that is not perfectly holy will be consumed by the fire of his glorious holiness. He declares, 'I am Almighty God; walk before me and be thou perfect' (Genesis 17:1). 'It shall be perfect to be accepted; there shall be no blemish therein' (Leviticus 22:21). 'Be ye holy; for I am holy' (1 Peter 1:16). We read in Hebrews 12:14 that there is a holiness to be pursued, without which no man shall see the Lord. God demands character holiness. We are required to be holy on the inside, in heart, at the very core of our being, 'The Lord looketh on the heart' (1 Samuel 16:7). He demands conduct holiness. We must be holy on the outside, in behaviour, 'Be ye holy in all manner of conversation' (1 Peter 1:15). In a word, God demands complete holiness. We must be entirely without sin. 'The soul that sinneth, it shall die' (Ezekiel 18:20).

God demands holiness; but we cannot produce holiness. Not one of us can do one good thing before God. It is written, 'There is none that doeth good, no not one' (Romans 3:12). Purity cannot come from our corrupt nature. We cannot even seek the Lord on our own, much less correct our past record, change our present wretchedness (Psalms 51:1-5), or control our future thoughts and deeds (Galatians 3:10).

The whole purpose of God's law is to show us our utter inability to keep it and to convince us of our need of a Substitute (Galatians 3:24). And the first work of God the Holy Spirit in a sinner's heart is to convince him of sin, of his need of a Substitute.

A person's definition of righteousness depends entirely upon his understanding of who God is. The problem with this religious generation is that they have never seen the holy, righteous, just character of God Almighty. They have never seen the absolute holiness of God. No one will ever see the holy character of God until he sees what happened at the cross (Isaiah 6:1-7).

How good does a person have to be to get to heaven? He must be as good as God. 'It must be perfect to be accepted.' God cannot and will not accept anything short of perfection. 'Who shall ascend into the hill of the Lord? or who shall stand in his holy place? He that hath clean hands, and a pure heart; who hath not lifted upon his soul unto vanity, nor sworn deceitfully' (Psalms 24:3, 4), and no one else. Yet, it is written, 'They that are in the flesh cannot please God'. 'Cursed is everyone that continueth not in all things written in the book of the law to do them' (Galatians 3:10).

No Righteousness

Second, let me remind you that you and I have no righteousness of our own. We lost all righteousness in the sin and fall of our father Adam. 'There is none righteous'! We have no ability to produce righteousness, or even to make any contribution toward it. 'There is none that doeth good; no, not one'! The sons and daughters of Adam are all sinners. We lost all righteousness before God in the garden. We are all totally depraved. We have all gone astray from the womb speaking lies. We all drink iniquity like water. So thorough and complete is the depravity of man that even our works of righteousness are filthy rags before the holy Lord God. We are all at our best altogether vanity (Psalms 14:2, 3; Psalms 51:5; Jeremiah 17:9; Matthew 15:19; Romans 5:12).

The fact is, the natural man has absolutely no idea what righteousness is, where it is to be found, or how it can be obtained; but he thinks he does. 'Ye are they which justify yourselves before men; but God knoweth your hearts: for that which is highly esteemed among men is abomination in the sight of God' (Luke 16:15).

This is the first thing to be established. We have no righteousness, and no ability to produce righteousness. Yet, our Lord said, 'Except your righteousness shall exceed the righteousness of the scribes and Pharisees, ye shall in no case enter into the kingdom of heaven'. In making that statement our Lord declared that there has never been one son or daughter of Adam on this earth good enough, righteous enough, or holy enough to inherit and inhabit the kingdom of heaven. There is not now and never will be one person in heaven who is there because he was good, righteous, and holy in this world. 'Man at his best estate is altogether vanity'. 'Our righteousnesses are as filthy rags in God's sight'.

We must get the idea of 'righteousness' out of our minds, and get the word 'righteousness' out of our vocabulary, insofar as any human works are concerned in God's sight. Our righteousnesses are filthy rags before the holy Lord God (Isaiah 64:6; Isaiah 1:16-20). Every imagination of the thoughts of man's heart is only evil continually (Genesis 6:5). Read the book of God and you will discover that every man in the book who knew God, who knew the righteous character of God, and had been made righteous in Christ, lamented his own utter wickedness.

Still, God requires perfect righteousness. The fact that we cannot produce righteousness does not mean that righteousness cannot be produced. God can do it. Man cannot please God; but God can please God. Man cannot produce righteousness; but God can produce righteousness.

Christ's Righteousness

Third, the Lord Jesus Christ has established and brought in everlasting righteousness by his obedience and death as our Substitute and Surety. The Lord Jesus Christ came into this world to fulfil all righteousness, not for himself, but for us (Matthew 3:15; 5:17). 'The LORD is well pleased for his righteousness' sake', because he magnified the law and made it honourable (Isaiah 42:21). He did for us exactly what Daniel 9:24 said he would do. He finished the transgression. He made an end of sin for us, putting away our sins by the sacrifice of himself. He made reconciliation for iniquity by satisfying the justice of God as our Substitute. And he brought in everlasting righteousness by his obedience to the will of God in all things as our Representative and Federal Head.

In his life Christ Jesus rendered perfect obedience to the law as our Representative. And in his death he satisfied the claims of the law as our Substitute. Therefore, the prophet of God declares of Christ, 'This is the name whereby he shall be called, the Lord our Righteousness', and of us, 'This is the name whereby she shall be called, the Lord our Righteousness' (Jeremiah 23:6; 33:16). That is the message that is set before us and sweetly declared in 2 Corinthians 5:21 and Romans 5:18-21).

The Lord Jesus Christ is our only righteousness, and it is our joy to confess that he is. 'Of him are ye in Christ Jesus, who of God is made unto us wisdom, and righteousness, and sanctification, and redemption: That, according as it is written, he that glorieth, let him glory in the Lord' (1 Corinthians 1:30, 31).

Imputed Righteousness

The fourth aspect of righteousness revealed in the book of God is the fact that the righteousness of Christ is imputed to all who trust him alone for righteousness in free justification. The only way a sinner can be made righteous is by the holy Lord God making him righteous. In justification God imputes the righteousness of Christ to his people in exactly the same way as he made his darling Son sin for us (Romans 5:18, 19; 2 Corinthians 5:21). How are sinners made to become the righteousness of God in Christ? Freely! I appeal to the word of God alone for the answer to that question. The opinions of men are totally irrelevant. What does the book say? Nothing else matters.

'Therefore by the deeds of the law there shall no flesh be justified in his sight: for by the law is the knowledge of sin. But now the righteousness of God without the law is manifested, being witnessed by the law and the prophets; Even the righteousness of God which is by faith of Jesus Christ unto all and upon all them that believe: for there is no difference: For all have sinned, and come short of the glory of God; Being justified freely by his grace through the redemption that is in Christ Jesus: Whom God hath set forth to be a propitiation through faith in his blood, to declare his righteousness for the remission of sins that are past, through the forbearance of God; To declare, I say, at this time his righteousness: that he might be just, and the justifier of him which believeth in Jesus' (Romans 3:20-26).

When Christ was made sin for us, that was a one time, once for all act accomplished in the past, a work in which he was personally involved. But when the Holy Spirit speaks of us being 'made the righteousness of God in him', the word he uses for 'made' is another word altogether. It is a present tense, passive verb, implying total passivity on our part, and means 'continually cause to become'. He is telling us that, God continually causes those for whom Christ was made sin to become the righteousness of God in him, without them doing a thing. Let me show you how he does it.

1. Eternally: our great, all-wise, eternally gracious God made us righteous before the world was made, in his sovereign, eternal purpose of grace in Christ, the Lamb slain from the foundation of the world (Romans 8:28-30; Ephesians 1:3-6; 2 Timothy 1:9, 10; Jude 1). If we were blessed of God with all spiritual blessings before the world began and accepted in the Beloved from everlasting, it was not as unrighteous but as the righteousness of God in Christ.

2. Judicially: we were made to become the righteousness of God judicially, in a legal sense, when the Lord Jesus died as our Substitute under the wrath of God, satisfying divine justice for us. When he had put away sin by the sacrifice of himself, he obtained eternal redemption for us; and we were made to become the righteousness of God in him by divine imputation in justification, 'being justified freely by his grace through the redemption that is in Christ' (Romans 4:25; 5:12, 17-21).

3. Experimentally: but this matter of being made the righteousness of God in Christ, while it is something with which we have no involvement, is not just a matter of law, any more than Christ's being made sin was just a matter of law. It is not something that takes place altogether outside our experience, any more than Christ being made sin was outside his experience. Sinners are made the righteousness of God in Christ experimentally in the new birth, when we are made 'partakers of the divine nature' (2 Peter 1:4). That holy thing in us that is born of God, that John tells us cannot sin (1 John 3:9), is 'Christ in you, the hope of glory' (Colossians 1:27). We experience this blessed thing of being

made the righteousness of God, in the inmost depths of our souls, in the constant assurance of our access to, acceptance with, and forgiveness of our sins by our God (1 John 1:7-2:2). We are in Christ, in whom alone God is well pleased. That means he is well pleased with us (Matthew 17:5). Our sacrifices are accepted of God as a sweet-smelling savour in Christ (1 Peter 2:5). Our sins are never imputed to us, but perpetually forgiven, because we are one with him who was once made sin for us, in whom we are perpetually made to become the righteousness of God.

Absolutely: believing on the Lord Jesus Christ, every sinner who trusts him is made to become the righteousness of God in him absolutely (2 Corinthians 5:17; Colossians 1:12). Discerning the Lord's body, that is to say, knowing our need of a Substitute and knowing the Substitute himself, trusting his finished work and trusting him, sinners like you and me are worthy to enter his church, worthy to call upon his name, worthy to receive the Lord's Table, and worthy to enter into and possess forever his glory!

Everlastingly: we shall be made to become the righteousness of God everlastingly in the last day in resurrection glory. We shall be raised in righteousness. We shall be declared righteous according to the record book of heaven at the day of judgment (Revelation 20:11-15; Jeremiah 50:20). In that great day we shall be declared righteous to wondering worlds to the glory of our God forever (Ephesians 2:7). Then, we shall forever begin to enjoy, in such experimental reality as words cannot describe, the blessedness of being made to become the righteousness of God in Christ (Revelation 21:2-5; 22:1-6).

I am lost in wonder! All this, all that Christ has as the God-man my Mediator, we have in him. All that he is, we are in him. All that he enjoys, soon, I shall enjoy forever in him, because,

'If any man be in Christ, he is a new creature: old things are passed away; behold, all things are become new. And all things are of God, who hath reconciled us to himself by Jesus Christ, and hath given to us the ministry of reconciliation; To wit, that God was in Christ, reconciling the world unto himself, not imputing their trespasses unto them; and hath committed unto us the word of reconciliation. Now then we are ambassadors for Christ, as though God did beseech you by us: we pray you in Christ's stead, be ye reconciled to God. For he hath made him to be sin for us, who knew no sin; that we might be made the righteousness of God in him' (2 Corinthians 5:17-21).

'He that spared not his own Son, but delivered him up for us all, how shall he not with him also freely give us all things?' (Romans 8:32).

Imparted Righteousness

Fifth, not only is the righteousness of God imputed to us in justification, the righteousness of God in Christ is imparted to every chosen, redeemed sinner in sanctification, by the regenerating work of God the Holy Spirit. In regeneration we are sanctified, made holy, by righteousness being imparted to us by the Spirit of God (Galatians 5:23, 24; 2 Peter 1:4; Colossians 1:27; 1 John 3:5-9). Believers are people with two natures (Romans 7:14-24), that holy seed which is born of God and cannot sin (1 John 3:9), and the flesh which is nothing but sin (Romans 7:18). These two natures, the flesh and the spirit, are constantly at war with one another so long as we live in this world.

When God saves a sinner, he does not renovate, repair, and renew the old nature. He creates a new nature in his elect. Our old, Adamic, fallen, sinful nature is not changed. The flesh is subdued by the spirit; but it will never surrender to the spirit. The spirit wars against the flesh; but it will never improve the flesh. The flesh is sinful. The flesh is cursed. Thank God, the flesh must die! But it will never be improved.

This dual nature of the believer is plainly taught in the word of God. It is utterly impossible to honestly interpret the fifth chapter of Galatians, the seventh chapter of Romans, and 1 John 3 without concluding that both Paul and John teach there is within every believer, so long as he lives in this world, an old Adamic nature that can do nothing but sin, and a new righteous nature, born of God, that cannot sin, that can only do righteousness.

The Holy Spirit's work in sanctification is not the improvement of our old nature, but the maturing of the new, steadily causing the believer to grow in the grace and knowledge of Christ and bring forth fruit unto God.

Every believer knows the duality of his nature by painful, bitterly painful experience. Ask any child of God what he desires above all things, and he will quickly reply, 'That I may live without sin in perfect conformity to Christ, perfectly obeying the will of God in all things.' But that which we most greatly desire is an utter impossibility in this life.

Is it not so with you? Though you delight in the law of God after the inward man, there is another law of evil in your members, warring against you. You would do good; but evil is always present with you, so that you cannot do the things you would. Even your best, noblest, most sincere acts of good, when honestly evaluated, are so marred by sin in motive and in execution that you must confess, 'All my righteousnesses are filthy rags'!

It is this warfare between the flesh and the spirit more than anything else that keeps the believer from being satisfied with life in this world. Blessed be God, we shall soon be free! When we have dropped this robe of flesh, we shall be perfectly conformed to the image of him who loved us and gave himself for us! Yet, the Lord God reckons us righteous, absolutely and perfectly righteous before him; and, what is more, he tells us to reckon ourselves to be what he reckons us to be in Christ (Romans 5:9-11; 6:11; 1 Peter 4:1).

Rewarded Righteousness

Here is the sixth aspect of righteousness revealed in this blessed book. May God the Holy Spirit enable us to get hold of it and live in the joyous prospect of it until it, at last, comes to pass. Every sinner who trusts Christ as his Saviour, being made the righteousness of God in him, shall be rewarded for his perfect righteousness with everlasting glory in heaven.

In the last day, every believer shall enter into heaven and obtain the inheritance of everlasting glory; and that will be righteousness rewarded. Immediately after the resurrection we must all be judged by God, according to the record of our works (Revelation 20:12, 13). 'It is appointed unto men once to die, but after this the judgment' (Hebrews 9:27). The Judge before whom we must stand is the God-man, whom we have crucified (John 5:22; Acts 17:31; 2 Corinthians 5:10). We will be judged out of the books, according to the record of God's strict justice. And this is God's declaration.

'In those days, and in that time, saith the LORD, the iniquity of Israel shall be sought for, and there shall be none; and the sins of Judah, and they shall not be found: for I will pardon them whom I reserve' (Jeremiah 50:20).

Will God judge his elect for their sins and failures committed after they were saved and expose them in the day of judgment? No, never. There is absolutely no sense in which those who trust Christ shall ever be made to pay for their sins! Our sins were imputed to Christ and shall never be imputed to us again (Romans 4:8). Christ paid our debt to God's law and justice; and God will never require us to pay. God, who has blotted out our transgressions, will never write them again. He who covered our sins will never uncover them!

Those who are found perfectly righteous, righteous according to the record of God himself, shall enter into eternal life and inherit everlasting glory with Christ. Because we have in Christ done good, nothing but good, perfect good, without any spot of sin, wrinkle of iniquity, or trace of transgression, we shall enter into life everlasting, because we are worthy to enter in (Revelation 22:11).

Who are these perfectly righteous ones? They are all who are saved by God's free and sovereign grace in Christ (1 Corinthians 6:9-11; Romans 8:1, 32-34). Heaven was earned and purchased for all God's elect by Christ. We were predestined to obtain our inheritance from eternity (Ephesians 1:11). Christ has taken possession of heaven's glory as our Forerunner (Hebrews 6:20). We are heirs of God and joint-heirs with Jesus Christ (Romans 8:17). Our Saviour gave all the glory he earned as our Mediator to all his elect (John 17:5, 20). And in Christ every believer is worthy of heaven's glory (Colossians 1:12).

Glorification shall be but the consummation of salvation; and salvation is by grace alone. That means no part of heaven's bliss and glory is the reward of our works, but all the reward of God's free grace in Christ. All spiritual blessings are ours from eternity in Christ (Ephesians 1:3), and all shall be ours in and with him forever.

Christ is our Righteousness. He is that righteousness that exceeds the righteousness of the scribes and Pharisees. And, if we trust him, he is ours. Because his righteousness is ours, we shall enter into the kingdom of heaven. He is that Holiness without which no man shall see the Lord. If we believe on the Son of God, that Holiness is ours, and we shall see the Lord our God face to face in Christ. Then, oh, blessed day, he shall wipe all tears from our eyes forever!

'And I saw a new heaven and a new earth: for the first heaven and the first earth were passed away; and there was no more sea. And I John saw the holy city, new Jerusalem, coming down from God out of heaven, prepared as a bride adorned for her husband. And I heard a great voice out of heaven saying, Behold, the tabernacle of God is with men, and he will dwell with them, and they shall be his people, and God himself shall be with them, and be their God. And God shall wipe away all tears from their eyes; and there shall be no more death, neither sorrow, nor crying, neither shall there be any more pain: for the former things are passed away. And he that sat upon the throne said, Behold, I make all things new. And he said unto me, Write: for these words are true and faithful' (Revelation 21:1-5).

'And there shall be no more curse: but the throne of God and of the Lamb shall be in it; and his servants shall serve him: And they shall see his face; and his name shall be in their foreheads. And there shall be no night there; and they need no candle, neither light of the sun; for the Lord God giveth them light: and they shall reign for ever and ever. And he said unto me, These sayings are faithful and true: and the Lord God of the holy prophets sent his angel to show unto his servants the things which must shortly be done' (Revelation 22:3-6).

Chapter 43

The Lord's Prayer

'These words spake Jesus, and lifted up his eyes to heaven, and said, Father, the hour is come; glorify thy Son, that thy Son also may glorify thee' (John 17:1-26).

In these 26 verses of holy scripture we have the high priestly prayer of the Lord Jesus Christ, our great High Priest, spoken as he was about to enter into the holy of holies in heaven, with his own blood, to obtain eternal redemption for his people. Our blessed Saviour left us the full text of this prayer. He prayed frequently while he was here on the earth in our flesh; but this is the only prayer of our Lord Jesus that is recorded in its entirety. This is Christ our God-man Mediator, our great High Priest, praying to the heavenly Father on our behalf, interceding for us. He left us the full text of this prayer as an example of his intercession, which even now he carries on for his people at the Father's right hand.

The scripture says that when the Lord Jesus Christ died on the cross, and was buried and raised again, that he ascended to heaven and is seated at the right hand of the Father to intercede for us. There he prays or makes intercession for his people. This prayer is the prayer of our High Priest, our Mediator, which he is praying for us at this moment, as he makes intercession for us in heaven (Romans 8:34).

In Hebrews 7:25, we read that, 'He is able to save them to the uttermost that come to God by him; seeing he ever liveth to make intercession for them'. So, this is the prayer of the great High Priest, the one Mediator between God and men. The scripture says, 'There is one God and one mediator', one who prays for us and only one. That is our Lord Jesus Christ. This is his effectual prayer of intercession.

It is the Lord Jesus himself who is praying here. The fact that he prayed, prayed often, and prayed earnestly ought to encourage us to pray (Hebrews 4:14-16). Prayer doesn't change God or change the will of God. It finds the will of God. Prayer not only finds the will of God, it bows us to the will of God. Prayer rejoices in the will of God and changes us, causing us to know and to follow the will of God. If our Master prayed, his servants certainly ought to pray.

Three Statements

In John 16:28 the Lord Jesus summed up his life and ministry, his person and work, in three plain and simple statements. Look at them.

First, 'I came forth from the Father'. Who is this man who declares that he came forth from God the Father? That declaration certainly indicates at least these two things about who he is: first, if he came forth from the Father, he must have been with the Father and in the Father (John 1:1, 18). Second, if he came forth from the Father, he must have been sent by the Father for a specific purpose, to accomplish a specific work (Matthew 1:21; Hebrews 10:5-10).

Second, 'I am come into the world'. He is not of this world, but came into this world. How did he come into this world? He came through the womb of a virgin, by supernatural, divine intervention. The Son of God came into this world by incarnation, conceived in the womb of the virgin, and brought forth into the world by the power of God the Holy Spirit. The eternal God assumed into union with himself our nature. God came into the world as a man (Philippians 2:5-7).

Why did he come into this world? He came here to redeem and save his people, to put away our sins, to justify and sanctify us by his own life's blood, which he poured out to God as a sin-atoning sacrifice for us (Galatians 4:4-6).

What did he do while he was in this world? He did what he came to do. He brought in everlasting righteousness for us by his obedience to the Father (Romans 5:19) and satisfied the law and justice of God for our sins by his death as our Substitute (Romans 3:24-26). The Lord Jesus Christ effectually redeemed his people from their sins and delivered us from the curse of God's holy law (Galatians 3:13).

Third, 'Again, I leave the world and go to the Father'. He must have completed what he came here to do. Otherwise, he would not have left. If upon his leaving the world he went to the Father, from whom he was sent, it is evident that the work he was sent here to do was finished and that the Father approved of and accepted him, his work, and his people (Hebrews 10:11-14).

The Book of Hebrews begins with these same three facts, facts that define the person and work of our Lord Jesus Christ. 'God, who at sundry times and in divers manners spake in time past unto the fathers by the prophets, hath in these last days spoken unto us by his Son, whom he hath appointed heir of all things, by whom also he made the worlds; who being the brightness of his glory, and the express image of his person, and upholding all things by the word of his power, when he had by himself purged our sins, sat down on the right hand of the Majesty on high' (Hebrews 1:1-3)

The Lord Jesus Christ, the Son of God, is our sin-atoning Sacrifice and Substitute, by whom our redemption has been accomplished. He is our great High Priest who makes intercession to the Father for those people he has redeemed. And he is our Almighty Saviour, by whom grace is conveyed to us, and by whom we shall be carried into the very glory of heaven itself. Perhaps the best commentary on who Christ is, what he did, why he did it, and where he is now is to be found here in John 17 in his high priestly prayer, that great prayer which he made to God the Father for us just before he went forth to the cross to accomplish our redemption.

Four Requests

In this seventeenth chapter of John our great High Priest makes four mighty requests, requests which the Father cannot deny. Not one of these requests can be denied, because they are made upon the basis of Christ's finished work. Really, these four requests are more than requests. They are the claims of Christ, our sovereign Redeemer, claims made by him when he had finished the work the Father gave him to do. They teach us much about the person and work of our Lord Jesus Christ.

Glorify Me

His first request is this: 'And now, O Father, glorify Thou me with Thine own self with the glory which I had with thee before the world was' (v.5). That is the request that he makes as our mighty Mediator and Substitute. This is not just an ambition for personal exaltation. It is a prayer for power and dominion as a man for the salvation of chosen men. And the basis of the request is his fulfilment of all the stipulations of the covenant of grace by him as specified in verses 1-4.

'These words spake Jesus (the words spoken to his disciples in the preceding chapters), and lifted up his eyes to heaven, and said, Father, the hour is come (the hour he so often spoke of, the hour for which the world was made, the hour for which he came into the world); glorify thy Son, that thy Son also may glorify thee'. As the Son of God, he needed no glory to be given to him; but he is here praying as our Mediator, as a man. He is here praying that God the Father would uphold and sustain him in the work he was about to accomplish upon the cursed tree, that he might thereby glorify his every attribute.

'As thou hast given him power over all flesh, that he should give eternal life to as many as thou hast given him'. The Father has given the Son, as our Mediator and Saviour, all authority, dominion, and power over all flesh (John 3:35; Matthew 28:18). This total, sovereign dominion, power, and authority belongs to him by divine, eternal decree, both as our Creator and our Redeemer. He is the appointed and rightful Administrator of the Father's will, purpose, and kingdom.

Our Lord Jesus Christ holds and exercises this absolute power so that he may 'give eternal life to as many as thou hast given him' (John 6:37-39). This is a very important phrase. Our Lord refers to his people, those given to him by the Father, six times in this prayer (vv. 2, 6, 9, 12, 24).

'And this is life eternal, that they might know thee the only true God, and Jesus Christ, whom thou hast sent'. Eternal life is knowing God in Christ. Eternal life is not a religious experience. Eternal life is not a moral or religious reformation of conduct. Eternal life is spiritual life. It is life given to dead sinners by God the Holy Spirit in sovereign regeneration. Eternal life is not knowing that there is a God, but knowing God. It is having God revealed in you and to you by his Spirit. It is understanding who God is by personal acquaintance (John 14:6-9; 1 John 5:20).

'I have glorified thee on the earth: I have finished the work which thou gavest me to do'. No one but the Lord Jesus Christ could ever make this claim. Here is a man who literally loved, obeyed, and honoured the eternal God all the days of his life. In his life and in his death, our Saviour glorified God's law, God's will, God's justice, and God's grace. He did it for us, that God might be both just and the Justifier of his people (Romans 3:24-26).

When our Lord says, 'I have finished the work which thou gavest me to do', I have no doubt that he is referring to three things. The righteousness he brought in, established, and finished for his people by his perfect life (Jeremiah 23:6). The redemption he was about to accomplish and finish at Calvary (John 19:30). The kingdom he will at last finish when he has given eternal life to all the Father gave to him from eternity (1 Corinthians 15:24-28; Hebrews 2:13).

It is upon the basis of this finished work that our Saviour prays, 'And now, O Father, glorify thou me with thine own self with the glory which I had with thee before the world was' (v. 5).

Keep My People

Second, in verses 6-19 our Saviour makes this great request for his people: 'And now I am no more in the world, but these are in the world, and I come to thee. Holy Father, keep through thine own name those whom thou hast given me, that they may be one, as we are' (v. 11). His prayer is this: Father, preserve and keep my believing people; but notice how the Son of God describes his believing people. Here are twelve things which are true of all God's people in this world.

1. Believers are people to whom God Almighty has been made known. 'I have manifested thy name unto the men which thou gavest me out of the world: Thine they were, and thou gavest them me; and they have kept thy word'. God's name is his character, his attributes. His name is who he is. It is written, 'Whosoever shall call upon the name of the Lord shall be saved'. That means, whosoever shall believe God, worship God, trust God, as he has manifested and revealed himself in Christ shall be saved. His name is ...

Jehovah-jireh (Genesis 22:13, 14 'The Lord will provide').
Jehovah-rophe (Exodus 15:26 'The Lord that healeth thee').
Jehovah-nissi (Exodus 17:8-15 'The Lord our banner').
Jehovah-mkadesh (Exodus 31:13 'The Lord that sanctifieth thee').
Jehovah-shalom (Judges 6:24 'The Lord our peace').
Jehovah-ra-ah (Psalms 23:1 'The Lord is my shepherd').
Jehovah-tsidkenu (Jeremiah 23:6 'The Lord our righteousness').
Jehovah-shammah (Ezekiel 48:35 'The Lord is there').

2. Believers know that the man Jesus of Nazareth is the Christ, the Son of the living God. 'Now they have known that all things whatsoever thou hast given me are of thee'. We recognise that the Father and the Son are one. We know that everything Christ did and said, and everything he shall yet do is of God the Father. This is the confidence we must have. It is the confidence we do have (2 Corinthians 5:19-21; Acts 17:30, 31).

3. Believers are people who receive the word of God and, receiving the word of God, know who Jesus Christ is, the Sent One of God in whom is all our hope and all our salvation. 'For I have given unto them the words which thou gavest me; and they have received them, and have known surely that I came out from thee, and they have believed that thou didst send me'.

4. Believers are sinners chosen by God the Father in eternity and given to Christ in effectual grace as the special objects of his mercy, love, and grace. 'I pray for them: I pray not for the world, but for them which thou hast given me; for they are thine'. Everything Christ has done, is doing, and shall hereafter do is for his people. To speak of God's love as universal love for all men is to make God's love utterly meaningless. God loves his elect. Christ redeemed his elect. The Holy Spirit calls, regenerates, and keeps his elect. Everything God does in providence and in grace is for his elect (Romans 8:28).

5. Believers are those people in whom the Lord Jesus Christ is glorified. 'And all mine are Thine, and Thine are mine; and I am glorified in them'. Christ is glorified by his own operations of grace for us and in us, our faith in and obedience to him, and by our final, consummate salvation and everlasting glory by him (Ephesians 1:6, 12, 14; 2:7; Revelation 5:9-13).

6. Believers are kept in life, grace, and faith in Christ. 'And now I am no more in the world, but these are in the world, and I come to thee. Holy Father, keep through thine own name those whom thou hast given me, that they may be one, as we are. While I was with them in the world, I kept them in thy name: those that thou gavest me I have kept, and none of them is lost, but the son of perdition; that the scripture might be fulfilled'. God's saints are here described as a people in the world, in hostile enemy territory, kept by God's grace and power, and united as one body in Christ (Ephesians 4:4-6).

7. Believers are those who shall have Christ's joy fulfilled in themselves. 'And now come I to thee; and these things I speak in the world, that they might have my joy fulfilled in themselves'. This joy is the joy of his grace (1 John 1:3, 4) and the joy of his salvation (John 16:20; Hebrews 12:1, 2). 'Your sorrow shall be turned into joy'!

8. Believers are, because of their faith, the objects of the world's hatred. 'I have given them thy word; and the world hath hated them, because they are not of the world, even as I am not of the world'. The gospel we believe, the Saviour we serve, the God we worship is despised by this world.

9. Believers are left in this world to preach the gospel amid much evil and under the relentless assault of the evil one. 'I pray not that thou shouldest take them out of the world, but that thou shouldest keep them from the evil'. Let nothing hinder faithful obedience to Christ. Our God will keep us from evil and from the evil one!

10. Believers are sinners who have been sanctified (set apart and distinguished from the world) by the word and truth of God. 'They are not of the world, even as I am not of the world. Sanctify them through thy truth: thy word is truth'.

11. Every believer, every child of God is sent into this world as the servant of God Almighty to do his will, glorify his name, and serve the interests of his Kingdom. 'As thou hast sent me into the world, even so have I also sent them into the world'.

12. You and I, God's elect, sinners who trust the Lord Jesus Christ, are the special objects of all that the Lord Jesus Christ came to do. 'And for their sakes I sanctify myself, that they also might be sanctified through the truth'. The Son of God set himself apart to be a sin offering that we might be sanctified by hearing and believing the gospel. Our sanctification is threefold. We are sanctified by God the Father in election (Jude 1), God the Son in redemption

(1 Corinthians 1:2; Hebrews 10:10), and God the Holy Ghost in regeneration (1 Peter 1:2; 2 Thessalonians 2:13), through the instrumentality of the word of God.

Save My Redeemed

Third, in verses 20-23, our Saviour turned his attention specifically to us, his people yet to be saved. His prayer is this: Father, save my redeemed ones.

'Neither pray I for these alone, but for them also which shall believe on me through their word; That they all may be one; as thou, Father, art in me, and I in thee, that they also may be one in us: that the world may believe that thou hast sent me. And the glory which thou gavest me I have given them; that they may be one, even as we are one: I in them, and thou in me, that they may be made perfect in one; and that the world may know that thou hast sent me, and hast loved them, as thou hast loved me'.

Give Me My Reward

Then, in verses 24-26, the Lord prays, Father, give me the reward of my labour.

'Father, I will that they also, whom thou hast given me, be with me where I am; that they may behold my glory, which thou hast given me: for thou lovedst me before the foundation of the world. O righteous Father, the world hath not known thee: but I have known thee, and these have known that thou hast sent me. And I have declared unto them thy name, and will declare it: that the love wherewith thou hast loved me may be in them, and I in them'.

Soon, our Saviour's prayer shall be fully answered. He will have all his people with him in glory; and we shall have his joy fulfilled in us. In that great, glorious day, our sorrow shall be turned into joy; and our joy shall be full!

'And I heard a great voice out of heaven saying, Behold, the tabernacle of God is with men, and he will dwell with them, and they shall be his people, and God himself shall be with them, and be their God. And God shall wipe away all tears from their eyes; and there shall be no more death, neither sorrow, nor crying, neither shall there be any more pain: for the former things are passed away. And he that sat upon the throne said, Behold, I make all things new. And he said unto me, Write: for these words are true and faithful. And he said unto me, It is done. I am Alpha and Omega, the beginning and the end. I will give unto him that is athirst of the fountain of the water of life freely. He that overcometh shall inherit all things; and I will be his God, and he shall be my son' (Revelation 21:3-7).

Chapter 44

'this is life eternal'

'And this is life eternal, that they might know thee the only true God, and Jesus Christ, whom thou hast sent' (John 17:3).

When Moses approached the burning bush, the Lord God said to him, 'Put off thy shoes from off they feet, for the place whereon thou standest is holy ground' (Exodus 3:5). That is exactly how I feel every time I read, or attempt to preach from chapter 17 of John. This is the 'Lord's Prayer', the intercessory prayer of our great High Priest, the Lord Jesus Christ. As he anticipated his death upon the cross, the glorious consummation of his obedience to God as our Substitute, these are the words he spoke to God the Father on our behalf.

'Father, the hour is come'. The hour he is talking about is the hour of his death, the hour of our redemption, the hour for which the world was made.

'Glorify thy Son'. He elaborates on this in verse 5. 'Glorify thou me with thine own self, with the glory which I had with thee before the world was'. Exalt me to your throne; give me the dominion over all things; magnify me as Lord over all and King forever; give me pre-eminence.

'That thy Son also may glorify thee'. Give me the rule of the world as the Mediator of my people, as their Head and Representative, that I may save all the people of thy love, all elect sinners, for the everlasting praise, honour, and glory of thy name. We know this is the meaning of verse 1 because he says so in verse 2.

'As thou hast given him power over all flesh'. This power was given to Christ our Surety in the covenant of grace, as the result of his pledged obedience unto death. When he finished the work of redemption and ascended back into heaven, the triune Jehovah turned over to him, the God-man our Redeemer, the reins of the universe, 'power over all flesh'.

'That he should give eternal life to as many as thou hast given him'. The purpose of Christ's exaltation, power, and dominion is that he might, by the power of his omnipotent grace, give eternal life to chosen sinners, redeemed by his blood.

Life Begins Here

Eternal life, in the experience and knowledge of it, begins here on earth. Though it is eternal (without beginning or end), it begins in us as soon as we are born again. When you trust Christ, you receive from him the same life that you shall have throughout eternity, his life! It is 'Christ in you, the hope of glory'!

The life of a new born child of God, who has just a moment ago begun to call upon the name of the Lord, is the very same life that is possessed by Enoch, Noah, Abraham, Moses, and Elijah, who have been in heaven for thousands of years. Eternal life is like a mighty river. It deepens and widens as it flows. But it is the same river which began when Christ, the Water of Life, first sprang up in your soul. We 'grow in grace', but you have to have life to grow. 'We see through a glass darkly:' but we do see. And you have to have life to see. It is true, we only 'know in part;' but we do know. And you have to have life to know.

When the believer dies, he does not suddenly enter into a new life. Death simply rids us of this cumbersome body of flesh, the body of sin, the old nature, which hampers our enjoyment of life. When we drop this body of flesh, then we shall fully enjoy eternal life, the life of Christ imparted to us in the new birth (Romans 7:24, 25).

Eternal life begins here, in the new birth. It is not something awaiting us in heaven. It is 'Christ in you'! To have eternal life is to be made, by the grace of God, a 'partaker of the divine nature'. It is to have Christ formed in you.

God's Gift

This eternal life is the gift of God the Father! 'The wages of sin is death, but the gift of God is eternal life through Jesus Christ our Lord' (Romans 6:23). 'This is the record that God hath given to us eternal life, and this life is in his Son' (1 John 5:11). We were born in spiritual death. We deserve eternal death. But God has decreed and promised to give chosen sinners eternal life.

This eternal life is the purchase of God the Son! 'For God so loved the world that he gave his only begotten Son, that whosoever believeth in him should not perish, but have everlasting life' (John 3:16). 'He that believeth on the Son hath everlasting life: and he that believeth not the Son shall not see life; but the wrath of God abideth on him' (John 3:36). With his own blood, the Lord Jesus entered in once into the holy place, having obtained eternal life for us. Our Saviour said, 'I am come that they might have life'! (John 10:10). 'Christ also hath once suffered for sins, the just for the unjust, that he might bring us to God, being put to death in the flesh, but quickened by the Spirit' (1 Peter 3:18).

This eternal life is the work of God the Holy Spirit. 'It is the Spirit that quickeneth; the flesh profiteth nothing' (John 6:63). Eternal life is bestowed upon helpless, dead sinners by the sovereign, irresistible work of God the Holy Spirit (John 1:11-13; 3:3-8).

Given To God's Elect

This eternal life, the gift of the Father, the purchase of the Son, the work of the Spirit, is given by Christ to all those the Father gave to him in the everlasting covenant of grace. Eternal life is the gift of the triune God to his elect.

Our Saviour is not a beggar, waiting for you to let him come into your heart. He is the Almighty; sovereign King of kings and Lord of lords! He is not in your hands. You are in his hands! He says, 'All power is given unto me in heaven and in earth' (Matthew 28:18). 'Thou hast given him power over all flesh, that he should give eternal life to as many as thou hast given him'. There are many who have been given to Christ from eternity, whom he must and will save (John 6:37-40). All whom Christ had given to him in eternity he will give eternal life in time (John 10:24-28). The evidence and proof of a person's election in eternity is the gift of eternal life in time (1 Thessalonians 1:4, 5; Acts 13:48).

What Is It?

'And this is life eternal'. What is it? What is eternal life? Can it be defined? Can it be described? Hear what the Son of God says, 'This is life eternal, that they might know thee, the only true God, and Jesus Christ, whom thou hast sent'. Eternal life is the knowledge of God in Christ.

Knowing God

Eternal life is knowing the Lord God, the only true God. Before Adam sinned, he knew God. He walked in God's presence and talked with God, as a man talks with his own familiar friend. But when he fell, Adam lost everything. He lost life. He lost righteousness. He lost all light regarding all things relating to and about God. He lost the knowledge of God. He lost peace.

No man by nature knows or can know God. Our Lord said, 'Neither knoweth any man the Father, save the Son, and he to whomsoever the Son will reveal him' (Matthew 11:27). 'Ye neither know me, nor my Father' (John

8:19). All men think they know God, and know all about God; but no man by nature knows God!

Yet, man must have a god. As a dog must have a master, so man must have a god; and he will find a god of some kind. Man's ignorance of God has led him into every imaginable form of idolatry and superstition. There is hardly a creature, a power, or an element of nature that man has not worshiped as god! All men by nature 'worship and serve the creature more than the Creator' (Romans 1:25). And, the more educated and brilliant the man, the more ridiculous and base is his idolatry (Acts 17:22, 23).

Man's ignorance of God is such that he always rejects light and chooses darkness, and turns from the truth of God to vain philosophy, heathen superstition, and religious tradition. Did not our Saviour tell the Pharisees this? 'I am come in my Father's name, and ye receive me not: if another come in his own name, him ye will receive' (John 5:43). 'My thoughts are not your thoughts, neither are your ways my ways, saith the Lord' (Isaiah 55:8). The wisdom of God is foolishness to man. 'There is a way which seemeth right unto a man', and he pursues it with all his heart, 'but the end thereof are the ways of death' (Proverbs 14:12).

What is it to know the only true God? Knowing God is not just having a god. Everybody has a god. Our Lord says eternal life is knowing the only true God. Knowing God is not just believing that there is a God. Whether they acknowledge it or not, everybody believes that there is a God. To know God, the only true God, is to know him as God.

Who is God? He is the great, infinite, invisible, omnipotent, omniscient, omnipresent, eternal Jehovah, who made heaven and earth (Isaiah 45:12). He is God, the incomprehensible trinity (1 John 5:7).

C. H. Spurgeon wrote, 'I would not worship a god that I could fully understand … If I could put my religion in my pocket, like a box of lozenges, I should soon suck it all away'! There is in God an infinite depth of mystery, an infinite height of wonder, an infinite wideness of fulness that no man can comprehend. He is God who 'upholds all things by the word of his power'! He is God 'who worketh all things after the counsel of his own will'! He is God 'in whom we live, and move, and have our being'! He is God who reigns everywhere, over all things, 'who doeth according to his will in the army of heaven and among the inhabitants of the earth', whose will and power no man can resist!

To know the only true God is to know him as my God! The God I have just described is God to me! God is great, sovereign, good. God is holy. God is just. And, blessed be his name, God is personal and he is mine! I bow before his throne. I am aware of his presence. I worship him with reverence and awe. I believe him. I trust his word and love his law. I trust his Son.

To know the only true God is to know him as my Father! 'Ye have received the Spirit of adoption, whereby we cry, Abba (Father!) Father'! (Romans 8:15). We pray to 'our Father which art in heaven' (Matthew 6:9). My Father is one whom I both trust and obey, one whom I both love and fear! I am conscious of his power and his peace, his righteousness and his redemption, his justice and his mercy. If God Almighty is my Father, all is well, always! You may strip me, but I shall still be clothed in his righteousness. You may put me in prison, but I shall still be free in Christ. You may pluck out my eyes, but I shall still see his glory. You may cut out my tongue, but I'll still sing his praise. You may forsake me, but I am never alone. I may be sick in body, but it is well with my soul. I may be pressed under the load of a thousand cares, but all will work together for my good. I may be at death's door, but it will lead me into his everlasting presence!

To know the only true God is to have a life worth living. Before I knew him, I cursed the day of my birth, but now I thank him for a life to live. Before I knew him, I felt like a galley slave pulling his oars for no reason, with no future; but knowing him I have a reason for life and see a reason for every event in life. If I did not know God, I would be in utter confusion regarding life and death, heaven and hell, justice and mercy; but in Christ I see his wisdom in all things. If I did not know God, I would tremble at the prospect of old age, sickness, and death; but knowing him, I face these realities with peace. If I did not know God, there would be no joy for today, no satisfaction with yesterday, and no hope for tomorrow. To those who do not know God, the future is a blank. They call themselves 'agnostics' and they name themselves well. An agnostic is a person who knows nothing! But the man who knows God knows him 'of whom, through whom, and to whom are all things'! 'And this is life eternal, that they might know thee, the only true God, and Jesus Christ, whom thou hast sent'!

Knowing God In Christ

Eternal life is knowing the only true God, as he is revealed in Jesus Christ, his Son. Eternal life is knowing God in Christ. Many foolishly talk about knowing God in many mysterious ways, in what they call, 'mystical, spiritual experiences'. But that is all nonsense.

To know God apart from Christ would not be life eternal, for God apart from Christ is an infinitely holy being, whose law I have broken. He could not bless me, whose law I have violated. He could not walk with me, for I am unclean. He could not smile upon me in my sin. But Christ is my Wisdom, Righteousness, Sanctification and Redemption. And I am accepted in him, 'accepted in the Beloved'!

It would be death, not eternal life, to know God apart from Christ, because the holy, just Lord God must punish sin. He will 'in no wise clear the guilty'! 'The soul that sinneth, it shall die'! But Isaiah 53:5, 6 tells me that Christ paid for all my sins. Hebrews 9:26 tells me that he put them all away. Romans 8:32-34 tells me that I am justified and shall never come into condemnation!

It would not be life to know God apart from Christ, for without Christ my body would rot in the grave and never rise again. I must forever die! 'If Christ be not raised, our preaching is vain … your faith is vain; ye are yet in your sins' (1 Corinthians 15:14, 17). But because he lives we shall live also (John 14:1-3). 'This is life eternal, that they might know thee the only true God, and Jesus Christ, whom thou hast sent'!

Three Essentials

Here are three things that are essential to eternal life. 1. Eternal life must be implanted by grace. As God breathed life into Adam's nostrils and made him a living soul, so God the Holy Spirit must breathe into you the breath of eternal life (John 3:8; Ezekiel 16:8). 2. Eternal life must be revealed by the Holy Spirit. God the Holy Spirit must show you the things of Christ. No one else can. He must reveal your sin to you, the cause of death. He must reveal Christ's precious blood, the price of life! 3. And eternal life must be received by faith in Jesus Christ. I do not say that faith is, in any way, the cause of life. Faith is the result of life. I do not say, if you believe you will live. But I do say, if you live you believe. If you believe on the Son of God you have eternal life. If you do not trust Christ you do not have eternal life; you are yet in the gall of bitterness, dead in trespasses and in sin; and the wrath of God is upon you! 'He that believeth on the Son hath everlasting life; and he that believeth not the Son shall not see life; but the wrath of God abideth on him' (John 3:36).

To believe on the Lord Jesus Christ is to realise the glory of his person. 'God was in Christ, reconciling the world unto himself'. God was and is that Man who died at Calvary! In him God and man are reconciled. To believe on the Lord Jesus Christ is to trust the efficacy of his blood. 'The blood of Jesus Christ, God's Son, cleanseth us from all sin'! (See 1 Peter 1:18-20). To believe on the Lord Jesus Christ is to rest in the merit of his righteousness (Jeremiah 23:6). To believe on the Lord Jesus Christ is to rely upon the power of his intercession! 'He is able to save them to the uttermost that come unto God by him' (Hebrews 7:25). To believe on the Lord Jesus Christ is to bow to his sovereign rule as your Lord.

'This is life eternal, that they might know thee, the only true God and Jesus Christ, whom thou has sent'! 'Believe on the Lord Jesus Christ, and thou shalt be saved'! May God the Holy Spirit cause you to believe on the Lord Jesus Christ!

Chapter 45

The 'I haves' Of Christ

'For I have given unto them the words which thou gavest me; and they have received them, and have known surely that I came out from thee, and they have believed that thou didst send me' (John 17:8).

There is nothing written in the book of God more sacred, more instructive, more comforting, more spiritual than the chapter before us. We have before us John's inspired record of our Lord's high priestly prayer for his elect. What a blessed passage of scripture this is! Here God the Father beheld the perfect, pure devotion of his Son, the Son of his love. Here the disciples heard the most intimate expressions of the Saviour's love for them and for God the Father, as he carried their needs upon his heart to his Father's heart. Here you and I are allowed to hear the Lord of glory, who loved us and gave himself for us, making intercession for us according to the will of God at the throne of God, intercession based upon the plea of his perfect obedience and righteousness.

Unique Prayer

This seventeenth chapter of John is unique. The things spoken here by the Son of God were spoken in the ears of the Father. Yet, they were spoken for the hearts of his people and in their hearing, for their learning and consolation. Indeed, they were spoken and are written here in the word of God for our hearts' and souls' edification in the knowledge of our dear Saviour.

That which is written here is written in the language of prayer; but this is a prayer like no other prayer. We pray because we have sinned and because we are sinners, sinners in need of mercy, grace, and forgiveness. Our prayers are carried before the throne of God with blushing hearts, filled with shame, contrition, confession, and want. The prayers of our all-glorious Saviour were founded upon perfect compliance with his Father's will in all things.

His Father

This prayer is replete with righteousness, every line bursting with the goodness, grace, and glory of God in Christ. It shows forth the perfect obedience of God the Son to his Father as our Mediator in whom the triune God is revealed and known. There is in the Gospel of John a special manifestation of the tender, precious relation between God the Son and God the Father. Notice how often our Saviour uses the endearing name 'Father' to enrich these sacred lines. As the Father constantly filled his heart, his name seems constantly to flow from his lips: twenty-three times in chapter 14, ten times in chapter 15, twelve times in chapter 16, six times in chapter 17.

In verse eleven the Son prays for the Father to keep and preserve his people through his own name, by the power of his name, and for the sake of his name. When he does, he calls him, 'Holy Father'.

In verse twenty-five, when he speaks of knowing the Father, our Redeemer calls him by that name by which he has ever known and forever knows his Father, the name by which all Spirit-taught people know him, saying, 'O righteous Father'. The world does not and never can know him in his righteous character because he has hidden himself from them (Luke 10:21). But all believers know and love God their Father, first and foremost as their righteous Father because he has in his infinite, sovereign love revealed himself to us in Christ as our righteous Father.

His People

Notice how our Lord distinctly identifies his people to the Father in this prayer. It simply blessed my soul to listen to these terms of grace falling from his lips, as he spoke to his Father and my Father about me. He called us, his elect …

A Divinely Given People (v. 2).
A Divinely Kept People (vv. 11, 12).
A Divinely Taught People (v. 14).
A Divinely Sanctified People (vv17-19).
A Divinely United People (vv. 20, 21).
A Divinely Blessed People (v. 22).
A Divinely Perfected People (v. 23).
A Divinely Loved People (v. 23).

Look carefully at John 17:8. 'For I have given unto them the words which thou gavest me; and they have received them, and have known surely that I came out from thee, and they have believed that thou didst send me'. We will look at these words in the order in which they are given. May God the Holy Spirit take the things of Christ revealed in this single verse and show them, effectually show them, to all who read these lines.

Know The Son

The opening word of verse 8, 'For', takes us back to verse seven. In verse seven we are told that the sure and certain result of God's words being communicated to his people by the power and grace of his Spirit and the mediation of his Son is this: God-taught sinners know the Son of God. There is no such thing as a saved sinner who does not know Christ in his true character as the all-glorious Son of God. Is that not what verse seven says? 'Now they have known that all things whatsoever thou hast given me are of thee'. This is a simple fact of divine revelation. Faith without knowledge is nothing but a leap in the dark. It is not salvation. It is not God given faith. True, saving faith involves knowing Christ. 'This is life eternal, that they might know thee the only true God, and Jesus Christ whom thou hast sent' (v. 3). You cannot trust an unknown Saviour (Romans 10:13-17).

When God the Holy Spirit takes the things of Christ and shows them to us, we know from whom they proceed. They come to us from the Father's eternal purpose of grace, unfailing and everlasting love, and that covenant of love and grace made for us between the Father and the Son and the Holy Ghost before time began (Psalms 25:14).

'The grace of God that bringeth salvation' is effectual, teaching grace. Grace gives us an education which fits us for communion with God, our holy and righteous Father, for it teaches us to worship and adore him as the God of all grace. God-taught sinners know the Son of God. Now, look at the next two words of John 17:8 …

Nine I Haves

How I love the finality with which our Saviour speaks when he talks about what he has done as the God-Man, our Mediator and Surety. He does not say, 'I wanted', 'I tried', or 'I desired', but 'I have'! It will do our souls good to pause a little while and drink from this deep well. Here are nine 'I haves' our Saviour speaks of in this chapter. What faith, confidence, and encouragement they ought to inspire in believing hearts.

Come my soul, fall down at the feet of this all-glorious Saviour and trust him, as a true worshipper, for all things and in all things. Grace was poured into his lips as our covenant Surety before the world began. Here grace pours forth from his lips like a gushing fountain as our covenant Surety who has done all that he said he would do.

1. 'I have glorified thee on the earth' (v. 4). Everything he did as a man he did according to the will of God and for the glory of God. When he was but a boy, he went about doing his Father's business. When he taught us to pray, he taught us to pray for the glory of God. 'Hallowed be thy name.' When he was tempted in Gethsemane, he sought the will of God for the glory of God. When he was about to die, he sought only the glory of God (John 12:28).

2. 'I have finished the work which thou gavest me to do' (v. 4). I never finished anything in my life. He finished everything! When I bow before my Father's throne, I am compelled to confess, 'I have done what I ought never to have done and left undone what I ought always to have done.' Not my Saviour! He says, 'I have finished' to absolute perfection and completion 'the work which thou gavest me to do'. He finished his work of establishing righteousness as a man by his perfect obedience. He finished his work of atonement and redemption by his substitutionary sacrifice upon the cursed tree in our place.

3. 'I have manifested thy name unto the men which thou gavest me out of the world' (v. 6). Christ is the Revelation of the Father, the One in whom and by whom alone God is known. When the Son manifests the Father's name to chosen sinners, he assures us of our adoption. He makes us to know that God is our Father, that he is our Elder Brother, that God the Holy Spirit is our Comforter, and that Heaven is our home, assuring us that we are 'heirs of God and joint-heirs with Christ'!

4. 'Those that thou gavest me I have kept, and none of them is lost, but the son of perdition; that the scripture might be fulfilled' (v. 12). The son of perdition was lost that the scriptures might be fulfilled (Psalms 109:6-8). He was the son of perdition. The sons of God can never be lost. Otherwise the scriptures could never be fulfilled (John 10:27, 28). The purpose of God cannot be nullified. The promise of the Father cannot be broken. The blood of the Son cannot be made of none effect. The seal of the Spirit cannot be broken.

5. 'I have given them thy word' (v. 14). When our Saviour here speaks of the 'word' of God, he is talking about the whole revelation of God, the whole truth of God. When he talks about the 'words' of God, he is discussing the many parts which compile the whole. He is describing the many doctrines of holy scripture by which the whole truth of God is revealed. 'Word' means the whole. 'Words' speak of the many parts that make up the whole. God's truth is one. Yet, according to his wisdom and prudence, it is revealed in many parts. When our Redeemer says, 'I have given unto them thy word', he is declaring that the whole of the revelation and knowledge of God and his will is in him and comes from him. More than that, he is telling us that all who are saved by him are made to know the whole truth of God.

He is not telling us that believers know God in the entirety of his Being. No finite creature can know the infinite Creator in the entirety of his Being! But he is telling us that all who are born of God know God entirely, in all his revealed character as God: the righteous God; the holy God; the just God; the sovereign God; the saving God.

6. 'As thou hast sent me into the world, even so have I also sent them into the world' (v. 18). Every child of God, every believer is sent by Christ, not out of the world, not away from the world, but into the world, armed with his word, his Spirit, and faith in him, to do his will, honour his name, build his kingdom, and spread his word. As he is God's anointed Messenger, so we are his anointed messengers. As he was the Father's Representative, we are his representatives in this world.[4]

7. 'And the glory which thou gavest me I have given them' (v. 22). Every time I read that text, I think to myself, 'That is just too much for my puny brain to grasp'. But, oh, how I enjoy trying! This much is certain: Everything which Christ now possesses as our Mediator, all the glory given to him by his Father as the result of his obedience unto death as our Substitute, he has given to all his people in all its fulness forever!

What a Saviour our dear Saviour is! He has honoured his Father in all things for us. He has proved himself faithful and true in all things as Jehovah's Righteous Servant, the Steward of his Father's house, the Trustee of his Father's will, and the Shepherd of his Father's sheep. He has saved his people and will continue to save his people until he has no more people to save! He has supplied all our need and will continue to supply all our need until we come to glory land where we shall have no need. He has glorified his people and will continue to glorify his people until all his people have all his glory in all its fulness! 'Heirs of God and joint-heirs with Christ'!

8. 'I have known thee' (v. 25). It is written, 'No man knoweth the Father but the Son and he to whomsoever the Son will reveal him'. Yet, here is a Man who says, 'I have known thee'. The Son knows his Father's nature, perfections, and glory, his secret thoughts, purposes, and designs, his covenant, promises, and blessings, his love, grace, and goodwill to his people, and his whole mind and will. This gives special power and meaning to verse 26.

9. 'And I have declared unto them thy name, and will declare it: that the love wherewith thou hast loved me may be in them, and I in them.' He who alone knows God has declared to us the mind, purpose, and will of God, so that the same love the Father has to him may be in us, and that he who is God may himself, in the fulness of his infinite love, manifestly dwell in us forever!

Now, go back to verse eight.

[4] Godliness is not isolation from the world's people, but from the world's ways. We are to live for Christ in this present evil world.

Salvation God's Gift

'I have given'! How my needy soul delights in those three indescribably enriching words of grace falling from the grace filled lips of our all-glorious Christ! 'I have given'! Salvation is the gift of God's free grace to sinners in and by Christ Jesus. The Son of God stamps these three words of grace upon the whole of God's salvation and upon every part of it. 'I have given redemption, regeneration, faith, justification, sanctification, preservation, and heavenly glory.

He who gave himself gives all! The gospel of the grace of God does not present an offer of salvation or a proposal of grace, but the gift of God, which is eternal life in Jesus Christ our Lord!

God's Words

'I have given unto them the words which thou gavest me'. Carnal, fleshly, human religion feeds upon, and rests in, signs, symbols, feelings, emotions, and notions. True religion, spiritual religion lives upon the verities, facts, and realities of divine revelation. Most people look for God and grace in their experiences, ceremonies, rituals, visions, and dreams. Believers look for God in his word. As Thomas Bradbury put it, 'God as the Father of his elect, redeemed, and regenerate people is only known in the Son of his love by the Spirit of life and light, and all this only by the words of Jesus Christ.'

It is Christ our Prophet who effectually teaches us by his Spirit and gives us the words of God, causing us to live by them (Deuteronomy 18:18, 19). The Lord Jesus gives chosen, redeemed sinners the words of God as words of life (John 6:63). When he sends his word in effectual, saving power, in the power of his Spirit to his redeemed ones in the time of love, it is to them a word of life, creating life and faith in them by the power of his Spirit. 'Thou hast the words of eternal life'! His words are to his own people life-giving words, life-restoring words, and life-preserving words (1 John 1:1; Ephesians 1:13, 14; 1 Thessalonians 1:5; James 1:18; 1 Peter 1:23-25).

To those who believe not, the words of Christ are words of judgment and condemnation (John 8:26-28). It is worth observing that our Lord (by effectual, irresistible, saving grace) gives, sovereignly gives, his words to his people. To the unbelieving and reprobate he merely speaks his words! If the word of God only comes to your ears, it will be a word of condemnation and death (2 Corinthians 2:14-16; 3:5). Oh, may he be pleased to give you his word!

That which our Master spoke in John 8 was unacceptable to the Jews, but speak it he must, because these words of God formed a part of his commission which he had received from his Father. He who was and is the Truth knew full well what the consequences of his message would be. Yet, he faithfully declared that which would only add to the guilt and condemnation of those who refused to hear his words.

Our Lord told the Jews that the time would come when they would know him, but only to their eternal sorrow. The words at which they quibbled would be the very words by which they would be forever damned and tormented. Do you understand that?

Faithful men are faithful to the word of God, no matter what the consequences may be ((2 Corinthians 2:17). You may ridicule, scorn, and reject Christ's words, but you will never get rid of them or even silence them. They will follow you to the judgment seat, and follow you forever through hell (John 12:47-50).

The Saved

Now, read the rest of verse eight. All saved sinners receive God's words, know God's Son, and believe God's revelation of himself in Christ. I have deliberately used the bulk of my space in this study describing the One who saves, because he is infinitely more important than those who are saved by him. But here our Saviour speaks about those who are saved by his grace. Here he declares what is always the result of his saving operations of grace. Whenever God comes in saving power and grace to chosen, redeemed sinners, this is what happens. These words describe saved sinners under these three characteristics. All saved sinners 'receive' the words of God, 'know' the Son of God, and 'believe' the Revelation of God.

Receive God's Words

'I have given unto them the words which thou gavest me; and they have received them.' Saved people receive God's words. It was the sure and certain promise of God in the covenant that his people would receive his words from the mouth of his Son, their Surety, by the power of his Spirit (Isaiah 55:11; 59:21). The words of God are found in the mouth of our covenant Surety. The words of God go forth from the mouth of our all-glorious Saviour. And the words of God are received, not by an act of the sinner, but by the mighty operations of God the Holy Spirit.

The words of God are received into the renewed heart like seed sown upon good ground, ground prepared by grace. The words of God are received like the hard, dry, parched earth receives the dew of heaven.

There is no place in God's order of things for the priestly functions of deluded men, sacramental efficacy, or creature contrivances. Salvation is not the result of something you do or of preparations you make. Salvation is altogether in the hand of God. 'Salvation is of the Lord'! It is by his will, by his word, and by his work!

Lost religionists quibble over the words of God. Believers receive his words, as John Gill put it, 'willingly and gladly, with reverence and meekness, with love and thankfulness; so as to understand them and believe them, and so as to be affectionately and closely attached to them.' Believers receive his word, the whole Revelation of God; and his words, all the parts and doctrines of it.

Know Christ

Then the Master says, concerning those who have received his words, 'and (they) have known that I came out from thee'. It is impossible to know the words of God until you are made to receive them by grace. But all who are graciously enabled to receive his words 'know' Christ as he is revealed in the word of God. He is the incarnate God, the Sent One of God, the divinely appointed Substitute and Saviour, and the accepted Sacrifice for sinners.

Believe God's Revelation

'For I have given unto them the words which thou gavest me; and they have received them, and have known surely that I came out from thee, and they have believed that thou didst send me.' It is written, 'A man can receive nothing, except it be given him from heaven' (John 3:27). And when the good and perfect gift of God's salvation is given and received, those to whom it is given and by whom it is received know full well that it was the Lord Jesus Christ the Son of God, whom the Father sent into the world to save his people from their sins, who bought it with his blood, brought it by his grace, and wrought it by his Spirit.

Those who receive the words of God know the Son of God and believe the truth of God; and we gladly give all praise to God, saying, 'Not unto us, O LORD, not unto us, but unto thy name give glory, for thy mercy, and for thy truth's sake' (Psalms 115:1). He chose us. He redeemed us. He called us. He keeps us. He is bringing us home, where we shall forever sing, 'Salvation to our God which sitteth upon the throne, and unto the Lamb' (Revelation 7:10).

Chapter 46

'Sanctify them'

'Sanctify them through thy truth: thy word is truth' (John 17:17).

In this portion of his prayer our Saviour is specifically making intercession for his disciples, those who were present with him on the earth at that time. Then, in verse 20, he tells us that the blessing he sought for them he requested for us as well. So that which our Lord Jesus sought for those disciples, he sought for all who would in time be given faith in him by the Spirit of God. In other words, this is our Saviour's prayer for us, God's elect, for every redeemed sinner, for all who are called of God and born again by his omnipotent grace. This is what he asks of God for every sinner chosen in eternal love and redeemed by his sin-atoning blood upon the cursed tree. 'Sanctify them through thy truth: thy word is truth.' Sinners are sanctified by God through his truth; and his word is his truth. Let us look at our Lord's petition line by line.

'Sanctify them'

Here are three great privileges all of God's elect enjoy by his grace. These three things are true of every saved sinner. By nature, we are all unrighteous and, therefore, unfit to inherit and inhabit the kingdom of God. 'Ye are washed, but ye are sanctified, but ye are justified in the name of the Lord Jesus, and by the Spirit of our God' (1 Corinthians 6:11). These three things are essential elements of God's saving grace. Without them no one is or can be saved.

We must be 'washed', redeemed by the blood of Christ. This redemption, the atonement for our sins, was accomplished for all God's elect when Christ died at Calvary. 'Christ hath redeemed us from the curse of the law, being made a curse for us: for it is written, Cursed is every one that hangeth on a tree' (Galatians 3:13).

We must be 'sanctified' by God the Holy Spirit. There is no salvation apart from sanctification. We must be made holy, or we cannot see God (Hebrews 12:14). This sanctification is accomplished for us and in us experimentally in regeneration, the new birth, when we are made new creatures in Christ, and made to be partakers of the divine nature. 'According as his divine power hath given unto us all things that pertain unto life and godliness, through the knowledge of him that hath called us to glory and virtue: Whereby are given unto us exceeding great and precious promises: that by these ye might be partakers of the divine nature, having escaped the corruption that is in the world through lust' (2 Peter 1:3, 4).

We must be 'justified' before God by his grace. Our justification was accomplished by the Lord God freely and graciously. He has imputed the righteousness of Christ to us, declaring us to be righteous before him. As our sins were imputed to Christ, though he could never sin, so his righteousness has been imputed to every believer, though we could never do righteousness. We are 'justified freely by his grace through the redemption that is in Christ Jesus' (Romans 3:24). 'For he hath made him sin for us, who knew no sin; that we might be made the righteousness of God in him' (2 Corinthians 5:21).

All three of these great privileges are works of grace. We do not wash ourselves, sanctify ourselves, or justify ourselves. God Almighty, by distinct acts of grace, has washed us, sanctified us, and justified us.

All three of these works of grace belong to all believers, without exception. The person who lacks any of these works of God's saving grace has not yet entered into the kingdom of God. He is lost, undone, and perishing in his sins. If you or I die without being washed, sanctified, and justified by the grace of God, we will not be numbered with God's saints in the last day. It is not possible for a person to be saved by the grace of God who is not washed, justified, and sanctified.

We have very little difficulty discussing the matter of being washed by the blood of Christ and justified by his righteousness. Particular, effectual redemption and free justification are matters in which we all rejoice. But when it comes to sanctification, our thinking may not be as clear. Many, I fear, are still confused and a little uncomfortable. Because we are so much influenced by false religion, many of God's saints still imagine that sanctification is something beyond their reach. I want you to understand the doctrine of holy scripture. If you are God's, if you trust Christ, the Lord Jesus Christ, your Saviour, your Advocate, your great High Priest, asks the Father to sanctify you. That means sanctification is yours. You are sanctified. If you trust Christ, God the Holy Ghost declares in 1 Corinthians 6:11 'Ye are sanctified'! That means you are sanctified. Christ is made of God unto you Sanctification. Christ is your Sanctification. But what does that mean? What does it mean to be sanctified? What was our Saviour asking for us when he prayed, 'Sanctify them'?

What do you think of when you hear or read those words? The words 'saints', 'sanctify', 'sanctified', and 'sanctification' are used repeatedly throughout the scriptures. But very few people know what they mean, as they are used by the inspired writers.

Three Errors

We are fairly comfortable in discussing redemption and justification, but not sanctification. With regard to this subject, there is a great deal of confusion; and it needs to be cleared up. Errors regarding the doctrine of sanctification generally fall into one of three categories.

Pentecostalism teaches that sanctification is a second work of grace, whereby the believer is made totally free from sin and the old nature of sin is eradicated from his being. We know that such teaching is wrong for two reasons: first, it is directly contrary to the word of God. 'If we say that we have no sin, we deceive ourselves, and the truth is not in us' (1 John 1:8). Second, it is contrary to every believer's experience. As honest men and women we must confess our sinfulness. Though we are no longer under the dominion of sin, we have a continual struggle with sin. Sin is in us. It is mixed with everything we do. It mars everything we do. If a person says he is without sin, he is a liar. The truth is not in him.

The self-righteous legalist makes sanctification nothing more than an outward, legal morality. To him sanctification is accomplished by his separation from the world, his obedience to religious customs and traditions, and his abstinence from the use of things he considers evil. 'Touch not, taste not, handle not' is his creed.

Most of those who are regarded as orthodox, evangelical Christians teach that sanctification is the progressive increase of the believer in 'personal holiness'. We are told that the child of God attains higher degrees of holiness by his own works in sanctification, until at last he is ripe for heaven, and that sanctification ultimately buds forth into glorification. Among these are both fundamentalists and some who regard themselves as reformed in doctrine.

One writer defined sanctification in these words 'Sanctification is progressive righteousness, which, of course, means that it is incomplete righteousness.' Another wrote, 'Sanctification is the personal holiness of the believer.' Usually this progressive, increasing righteousness is made to be the basis of the believer's assurance here and his heavenly reward hereafter. The words 'progressive righteousness' imply the possibility of perfect righteousness. To suggest that we 'progress in righteousness until we are ripe for heaven' is to suggest the possibility of sinless perfection!

Let us see what God says about sanctification in the book he has written. I am sure you will see that sanctification as it is taught in the Bible is considerably different from the way it is commonly taught in theology books, and from most pulpits. Let us appreciate the writings of men who have been used of God, from whom we may learn much. But when they vary from the word of God, we must vary from them. I have no creed to defend, no confession to uphold, no denomination to answer to, and no catechism to teach, but this: 'Thus saith the Lord'.

I want to show you one thing in this study and clearly demonstrate it from the word of God. Being an essential element of salvation, sanctification is and must be, in its entirety, the work of God's free and sovereign grace in Christ. If salvation is by grace (and it is!), then all that is essential to salvation is by grace alone. Whatever sanctification is, it is the work of God alone. It is this fact, the fact that he is the One who sanctifies us that the Lord uses to encourage obedience in his people (Exodus 31:13).

The Word's Meaning

What is the meaning of the word 'sanctify' as our Lord uses it in John 17:17? When the Saviour prayed, 'Sanctify them', what did he mean? 'Sanctify' is a Bible term. So let's turn to the Bible to find out what it means. The word 'sanctify' is used in three distinct ways in the scriptures.

The first meaning of the word 'sanctify' is 'to set apart', particularly, 'to set apart for God, or for divine service'. Sanctification is taking something that is common and ordinary and setting it apart, separating it unto God's service alone. This is the first and primary meaning of the word as it is used in the Bible.

The seventh day was set apart for God (Genesis 2:3). This is the first time the word 'sanctify' is used in the Bible. 'And God blessed the seventh day, and sanctified it: because that in it he had rested from all his work which God created and made'. The day was not altered at all. It was simply set apart, separated from the other days of the week for God's service alone.

The firstborn of all the families of Israel were set apart for God. 'Sanctify unto me all the firstborn, whatsoever openeth the womb among the children of Israel, both of men and of beast: it is mine' (Exodus 13:2).

The Tabernacle, the altar, and the priesthood were sanctified unto the Lord, set apart for his use alone. 'And I will sanctify the tabernacle of the congregation, and the altar: I will sanctify also both Aaron and his sons, to minister to me in the priest's office' (Exodus 29:44).

It is in this sense that our Lord Jesus Christ says he was sanctified by the Father and sanctified himself (John 10:36; 17:19). He was set apart from all other men to do the will of God by God the Father. And in this sense our Saviour sanctified himself to do the work he was sent to do, to accomplish his Father's will in the redemption and salvation of his people.

Secondly, as the word 'sanctify' is used in the word of God, it means 'to regard as holy', 'to treat as holy', and 'to declare that a person or thing is holy'. For example, God himself is frequently said to be sanctified by his people. We do not make God more holy. And we do not separate God unto himself. But we do regard him as holy, treat him as one who is holy, and declare that he is holy. That is what it is to sanctify the Lord God in your heart. The Lord God commands us to regard him as holy. 'Sanctify the LORD of hosts himself; and let him be your fear, and let him be your dread' (Isaiah 8:13).

Nadab and Abihu were consumed by the Lord when they offered strange fire, because they did not reverence God's holiness (Leviticus 10:3). Moses' sin in smiting the rock the second time, for which he was not allowed to enter the land of promise, was just this. 'Ye believed me not, to sanctify me in the eyes of the children of Israel' (Numbers 20:12). We have an even more familiar illustration of this in what is called 'The Lord's Prayer'. Our Saviour taught us to pray, 'Our Father, which art in heaven, Hallowed be thy name' (Matthew 6:9). The word 'hallowed' is simply another word for 'sanctified'. The meaning is let thy name be reverenced and adored through the whole earth. Let men regard thy name as a holy and sacred thing.

The first meaning of the word 'sanctify' is to set apart for God. The second meaning is to regard, treat, and declare a person or thing as being holy. When a person is sanctified by God, he is regarded by God as one who is holy, declared by God to be holy, and treated by God as one who is holy. All who are sanctified are under God's special care and protection. They are the apple of his eye. They are his anointed. And God says to all creation, 'Touch not mine anointed'!

The third meaning of the word 'sanctify' is 'to actually purify something and make it holy'. This is more than a declaration. This is an actual change in the nature of things. The thing sanctified is not only set apart for God and declared to be holy, it is actually made holy.

When the Lord God was about to come down and give the law at Mount Sinai, the children of Israel were required to make themselves ceremonially holy (Exodus 19:10, 11) in a ceremonial picture of sanctification. And when Israel was about to cross the Jordan River God required them to first be ceremonially purified (Joshua 3:5).

Do you see the basic meanings of the word 'sanctify' as it is used in the scriptures? It is to set apart or separate for God; to regard, treat, and declare something or someone as holy; to purify and make holy.

How Are People Sanctified?

How are the people of God sanctified? As I have already stated, our sanctification, like our redemption and justification, is the work of God Almighty in the trinity of his sacred Persons. We are sanctified by God the Father in election, by God the Son in redemption, and by God the Holy Spirit in regeneration. Sanctification is not something we do for ourselves. It is something God does for us and in us. The words 'sanctify', 'sanctified', 'sanctifieth', and 'sanctification' are used more than thirty times in the New Testament. We are said to be sanctified by the purpose of God, by the blood of Christ, by the Spirit of God, by faith in Christ, and by the word of God. But never, not even once, are we said to sanctify ourselves. Sanctification is the work of God alone!

All believers were sanctified by God the Father in eternal election, being set apart for himself by God's decree, and separated unto him (Jude 1). This is the character of God's distinguishing grace. It sets some people apart from others and sanctifies them unto the Lord. We were secretly set apart for God in his secret, eternal decree of election before the world began. We were legally set apart from Adam's fallen race by the purchase of Christ at Calvary, when he ransomed us from the curse of the law. And we were manifestly set apart and separated unto God by the effectual call of God the Holy Spirit in regeneration.

The doctrine should be clear to all. Every believer has been, in this sense, eternally sanctified, completely set apart by God for God. The practical importance of this glorious doctrine is this. That which has been set apart for God ought never to be used for common purposes again. 'Ye are not your own. For ye are bought with a price: therefore glorify God in your body, and in your spirit, which are God's' (1 Corinthians 6:19, 20). My brother, my sister, we belong to the Lord our God. Let us therefore consecrate ourselves to him and serve him in all things (Romans 12:1, 2). We belong to God. Be assured of this, God Almighty will protect all who belong to him in all their appointed ways, even as he protected the ark of the covenant in the Old Testament (Psalms 91:3-13).

All of God's elect were perfectly sanctified by the blood of Christ when he died as our Substitute (Hebrews 10:10-14). Christ is our Sanctification (1 Corinthians 1:30). We have been and are forever 'sanctified in Christ Jesus' (1 Corinthians 1:2). Believers are addressed throughout the Epistles as 'saints', that is as 'sanctified ones' in Christ. In the Lord Jesus Christ we who believe are regarded by God as perfectly holy, treated as if we were perfectly holy, and declared to be perfectly holy, because in Christ we are perfectly holy!

> With His spotless garments on
> I am as holy as God's Son!

And all believers are actually made holy by God the Holy Ghost in regeneration. Through the instrumentally of gospel preaching, the Spirit of God effectually applies the blood of Christ to the hearts of God's elect, purifying our hearts and implanting a new, holy nature within us. This is regeneration, the new birth. This is our sanctification by the Spirit (2 Thessalonians 2:13, 14; 2 Peter 1:4; 1 John 3:9; 1 John 5:18).

We are a people with two natures, one that is holy and seeks after righteousness, and one that is corrupt and seeks after sin. These two natures are not equal in power. The divine nature rules and reigns, but the evil nature will not bow or serve. While we live in this world we must continue to live with this old, sinful nature. But we do have a new nature created in us in the image of Christ, a nature that cannot sin. It is the old man that sins, not the new. It is written, 'If I do that I would not, it is no more I that do it, but sin that dwelleth in me' (Romans 7:20).

In glorification the old man shall be totally eradicated from us, but not until then. That eradication of the old man is not a gradual, progressive thing. It is the radical, climactic change experienced by God's saints in death, and ultimately in resurrection glory.

Progressive Sanctification

The word of God does not teach the doctrine of progressive sanctification as it is commonly taught and understood by men. Be sure you understand what I mean by that statement. The Bible does not teach that in sanctification our old nature becomes less sinful and more holy. Flesh is flesh it cannot be sanctified. The old man is not sent to the hospital for a cure. He is sent to the cross to be crucified. The Bible does not teach that by sanctification we who believe attain progressively increasing degrees of personal holiness, and thereby improve our acceptance with God. Yet, the scriptures do clearly represent the work of sanctification in the believer as a present, continual work of grace (1 Thessalonians. 1:3-7; 5:23, 24). The child Christ Jesus was perfectly holy. Yet, he grew in that state of holiness. Even so, we are perfectly holy in Christ. We have a perfectly holy nature implanted in us. Yet, the believer grows in grace. Our holiness does not improve. But we grow in that state of holiness (Luke 2:52; 2 Peter 3:18).

Sanctification cannot be properly spoken of as a progressive work. A person is either holy or he is unholy. There is nothing in between. You cannot be more or less holy. But sanctification is a present, continual, on-going work of grace. Being sanctified by God, born again by the Holy Spirit, every believer grows in the grace and knowledge of our Lord Jesus Christ. Every living thing grows. We see more, feel more, do more, know more, repent more, believe more, and love more, as we grow in grace. In sanctification there is an ever-increasing faith, hope, and love in the hearts of God's elect.

Of this I am certain, wherever sanctification is found consecration of the heart increases, conformity to Christ in heart and life increases, commitment to Christ and his cause increases; love, devotion, confidence in, and submission to Christ increases, and confidence in Christ increases.

This growth in grace is the continual operation of God the Holy Spirit in sanctification. 'For it is God which worketh in you both to will and to do of his good pleasure' (Philippians 2:13). To be sanctified is to be separated to God, treated as holy, and made holy.

'through thy truth'

The Lord Jesus prays, 'Sanctify them through thy truth'. Christ is the Truth (John 14:6). He is the embodiment of Truth and the revealer of Truth; but he is more. Christ is the Truth. He is the Truth foreshadowed and typified in all the law and the true fulfilment of all the prophecies of the Old Testament scriptures. Our Lord's prayer here is this. Father sanctify my people, these you have given me through their union with me, through the merit of my blood and righteousness, through the grace they receive from me, and through their faith in me.

'thy word is truth'

'Sanctify them through thy truth: thy word is truth'. Christ is the Truth and Christ is the Word. He is the Word revealed by the word. Our Saviour is saying, Father sanctify my people by your Word. This sanctification is a work of grace accomplished by the Spirit of God through the instrumentality of God's word (2 Thessalonians 2:13, 14; Psalms 119:9-16).

Consecrate

But there's got to be something more in our text. Remember, our Lord is here praying specifically for people who are already born of God, already believers, already his disciples. He is asking God the Father to sanctify people who are already sanctified. 'Sanctify them through thy truth: thy word is truth'. When we read verse 19, we learn exactly what he is asking. 'And for their sakes I sanctify myself, that they also might be sanctified through the truth'.

How did the Lord Jesus sanctify himself? Our blessed Saviour relentlessly dedicated himself, he relentlessly consecrated himself to the will of God and the glory of God, to the redemption and salvation of the people of God, utterly sacrificing himself to God, utterly consecrating himself to God, that we might be utterly consecrated to God, as 'a royal priesthood', serving God day and night. This is beautifully portrayed in Leviticus 8 and 14, where God's priests were ceremonially sanctified by the blood of the sacrifice and the holy anointing oil put upon the tip of their right ears, the thumbs of their right hands, and the great toes of their right feet.

Let us be utterly separated unto God, utterly separated to Christ, utterly separated to the gospel, but never separated from one another. The object of our Saviour's prayer is found in verse 21.

'Sanctify them through thy truth: thy word is truth. As thou hast sent me into the world, even so have I also sent them into the world. And for their sakes I sanctify myself, that they also might be sanctified through the truth. Neither pray I for these alone, but for them also which shall believe on me through their word; That they all may be one; as thou, Father, art in me, and I in thee, that they also may be one in us: that the world may believe that thou hast sent me' (John 17:17-21).

There is never an excuse for believers separating themselves from other believers. The Corinthians had terrible problems; but God never instructed one saint to separate himself from those other saints. The Galatians had horrid evils; but never once were they taught to separate saint from saint. Rather, we are to help the weak, lift the fallen, and forgive the offender (Galatians 6:1, 2).

O Spirit of God, give me this grace. Sanctify me, for Christ's sake. Cause me to be utterly consecrated to my Redeemer!

'Brethren, I count not myself to have apprehended: but this one thing I do, forgetting those things which are behind, and reaching forth unto those things which are before, I press toward the mark for the prize of the high calling of God in Christ Jesus' (Philippians 3:13, 14).

What I ask God to do for me I ask him to do for you. 'And the very God of peace sanctify you wholly; and I pray God your whole spirit and soul and body be preserved blameless unto the coming of our Lord Jesus Christ. Faithful is he that calleth you, who also will do it' (1 Thessalonians 5:23, 24).

'I beseech you therefore, brethren, by the mercies of God, that ye present your bodies a living sacrifice, holy, acceptable unto God, which is your reasonable service. And be not conformed to this world: but be ye transformed by the renewing of your mind, that ye may prove what is that good, and acceptable, and perfect, will of God' (Romans 12:1, 2).

Chapter 47

'thou ... hast loved them as thou hast loved me'

'I in them, and thou in me, that they may be made perfect in one; and that the world may know that thou hast sent me, and hast loved them, as thou hast loved me' (John 17:23).

John 17 contains our Lord's prayer for us as our great High Priest. It not only records his desires for his people, which cannot and will not be denied. What Christ desires, Christ shall have! But this great, intercessory prayer is a very instructive portion of holy scripture, filled with gospel truth. And the text that heads this page teaches us something wonderful, mysterious, and delightful about God's love for his elect, something that is simply astounding. This short, simple statement by our dear Redeemer is full of mysteries I will never be able to comprehend, much less explain. It is itself a profound volume of theology.

Christ In Us

'I in them' The Lord Jesus Christ is in us in a distinctive, unique, saving way. Obviously, as the omnipresent God, Christ is in all the world. As the Creator of all men, he is in all men, giving all the light of conscience by which all are found guilty and condemned from within themselves. As the incarnate God, as a man, our Lord Jesus was once here, dwelling among men. 'The Word was made flesh and dwelt among us'! These things John tells us in chapter one (John 1:5, 9-11, 14).

But when our Lord says, 'I in them', he is telling us that he is in every believing sinner in a special, gracious manner. In regeneration, the new birth, he is revealed in us and to us. Christ is formed in us when we are born of God.

He enters into the chosen, redeemed soul, taking possession of his ransomed one by almighty grace, establishes his throne in the heart, communicates his grace, and grants fellowship with himself, and dwells in the heart. He is to every heaven-born soul, 'Christ in you, the hope of glory'! He is in us by his Spirit, yes. But our text says more. He is personally in us! He is in us as the King in his kingdom, the Head in his members, and the Master in his house.

What wondrous, condescending grace! Christ is in us! Therefore, because he who is holiness dwells in us, we have holiness within, that holy thing which is born of God and cannot sin. Because he who is Light dwells within, we have light and shall never walk in darkness. Because he who is Life dwells within, we have life, eternal life, within and shall never perish. Because Christ dwells within us now in grace, he shall dwell in us forever in glory!

God In Christ

'I in them and thou in me' God the Father is in Christ, not only as one with him in the holy trinity, but also as our God-man Mediator. The Father is in the Son communicating all grace to us through him. The Father, the Son, and the Holy Spirit are in Christ the Mediator in all the fulness of the eternal Godhead. 'In him dwelleth all the fulness of the godhead bodily'! The Father is in the Son graciously now and will show himself in and through him and him alone forever. And the Father will show himself glorious in the Son throughout the endless ages of eternity.

Made Perfect

'I in them and thou in me that they may be made perfect in one'. All this fulness of God in Christ and of Christ in his people is designed for this purpose and shall accomplish it. Because God was in Christ, all his people were made perfect in justification when that man who is God died as our Substitute at Calvary. Because this Christ, in whom all the fulness of God dwells, dwells in us, we are made perfect in sanctification. He has made us holy and righteous, 'meet to be partakers of the inheritance of the saints in light'. Because Christ is both in the Father and in us, because he is in glory, because he is within the veil, because his blood speaks there for us, we shall soon drop this robe of flesh and be made perfect in glory. Then we shall be perfect in knowledge, in holiness, and in peace, joy, and love. Because this great, glorious, gracious, omnipotent Christ is in us and all God's elect are in him, the number of the saved in glory shall be perfect, complete. Not one shall be missing. And we shall be perfectly one. 'I in them and thou in me that they may be made perfect in one and that the world may know that thou hast sent me.' Soon, when he has done all that he purposed must be done, and time is no more, all the world will know who he is!

Loved As

'I in them, and thou in me, that they may be made perfect in one; and that the world may know that thou hast sent me, and hast loved them, as thou hast loved me'. 'Thou hast loved them as thou hast loved me'. Imagine that! What an astounding word this is from our God and Saviour! 'Thou hast loved them as thou hast loved me'. God the Father loved Christ as his own Son, and loved him as our Mediator from everlasting. He loved him when he assumed our humanity. The Father loved him while he walked on this earth as his obedient Son, fulfilling all righteousness for us. Oh, how the Father loved the Son, even when he was made sin for us, especially when he was made sin for us, though justice demanded that he both slaughter him and abandon him, pouring out all the horror of his holy wrath and fury upon him!

The instances and demonstrations of the Father's love to the Son are marvellous to behold. Because the Father loves the Son as our Mediator, he has put all things into his hands, trusting him with all his glory and all the people of his love (Ephesians 1:12). He has made him Head over all things, put all things under his feet, and determined that in all things he shall have the preeminence.

The Father's love for the Son is an eternal, immutable, indestructible love of complacency and delight. It will last forever. That I have no difficulty understanding. But what our Lord tells us here is infinitely gracious and glorious beyond my highest imagination. Our Lord Jesus here declares that God the Father loves us, his people, in exactly the same way as he loves him!

He loves us not merely as his creatures (like a man loves his dog), not merely as the descendants of Adam (as a man loves a man), and certainly not as considered in ourselves (as a man despises and hates his most implacable, obnoxious enemy). But God loves us in his Son, for the sake of his Son, as he loves his Son!

Do you ask, 'How does God display such love for us?' Behold how he loved us! 'Behold, what manner of love the Father hath bestowed upon us'! Does he indeed love us as he loves his own darling Son? Indeed, he does! Did he choose Christ as our Mediator (Isaiah 42:1-4)? So he chose us (Ephesians 1:3-6). Did the Father make a covenant with the Son before the world began (Psalms 89:28)? So he made a covenant with us (Jeremiah 31:31-34; 32:38-40). Did the Father raise the Son from the dead, making him free from sin (1 Peter 4:1, 2)? So he has raised us up from the dead, making us free from sin (Romans 8:1-4). Did the Father supply the Son with all things in daily providence while he walked on earth? So he supplies us! Did the Father send his Spirit and his angels to minister to his Son when he was tempted? So he delivers us out of all our temptations. Does the Father perform all things for the Son? So our God performs all things for us! Does the Father love the Son from everlasting? So he loves us! Does the Father accept the Son? So he accepts us! Does the Father love the Son with utmost pleasure, satisfaction, and delight? So he loves me! 'Thou hast loved them as thou hast loved me'!

> Near, so very near to God, nearer I cannot be.
> For in the person of His Son, I am as near as He!
> Dear, so very dear to God, dearer I cannot be,
> For in the person of His Son, I am as dear as He!
>
> Horatius Bonar

Let my heart be forever humbled, ravished, inspired, and filled with praise to my God for his great love to me. Let my soul be forever exultant, joyful, and at peace! Let my life be forever and alone his!

What a great, glorious gospel truth we have here. It is something that could never be known except by divine revelation. How honouring to our God! It is just like him. How comforting to our souls! To the extent that we are able to believe God's Revelation, our souls shall be comforted.

Our great all-glorious Saviour says, 'Thou hast loved them, as thou hast loved me'. Thus, he tells us that God our Father loves his elect in Christ as he loves Christ himself! That is such an amazing, stupendous thing that were it not written in holy scripture, I would not dare to think it, much less declare it. But there it stands. And, oh, how my soul rejoices in it. It is our Saviour's desire and purpose that the whole world shall know that God loves us as he loves him; and so it shall be! A. W. Pink wrote:

> When God's elect have all been gathered together in one (John 11:52), when the glory which Christ received from the Father has been imparted to them, when they shall have been made perfect in one, then shall the world have such a clear demonstration of God's power, grace, and love toward his people, that they shall know that the One who died to make this glorious union possible was the sent One of the Father, and that they had been loved by the Father as had the Son, for 'When Christ, who is our life shall appear, then shall ye also appear with him in glory' (Colossians 3:4); then 'he shall come to be glorified in his saints and admired in all them that believe ... in that day' (2 Thessalonians 1:10).

That little word 'as' means 'just as', 'even as', 'in proportion as', 'to the same degree as'. When our Lord says, 'Thou hast loved them, as thou hast loved me', this great, little word, 'as', implies at least these three things.

Same Reason

First, there is a similarity of cause between God's love for Christ and his love for us. 'Thou hast loved them, as thou hast loved me'. The Lord God loves us for the same reason he loves his dear Son.

God loves us in Christ. God's love is not a universal sentiment for all men. God's love is in Christ. Apart from Christ, God is a consuming fire. This needs to be understood. These days, men everywhere are taught and universally presume that God loves them. Nothing could be further from the truth. Until you are united to Christ by faith, you have no reason to imagine that God loves you. Our faith in Christ does not cause God to love us. Our faith is the fruit and result of God's eternal love for us. But, until a sinner trusts Christ, only the wrath of God is revealed and known to him; and the wrath of God is upon him. Do you understand that? Until you take refuge in Christ, God's wrath is upon you (John 3:36; Ephesians 2:3).

God loves us for Christ's sake. Thomas Manton rightly observed that 'The elect are made lovely, and fit to be accepted by God, only by Jesus Christ ... The ground of all that love God beareth to us is in Christ.'

We are 'accepted in the beloved'. God accepts our faith, our worship, our works, and our persons only because of Christ, because we are in Christ, and because of what Christ has done for us.

And God the Father loves us for the same reason that he loves his dear Son as our Mediator. Be sure you get this. It will help you. God the Father does not love us for the same reason that he loves his Son as his Son. He loves his Son as his Son necessarily because his Son is one with him in being, perfection, and praise. He cannot but love Christ as God. Else he would cease to love himself. But God's love for Christ as our Mediator is based upon his perfect obedience unto God as our Mediator.

'I am the good shepherd, and know my sheep, and am known of mine. As the Father knoweth me, even so know I the Father: and I lay down my life for the sheep. And other sheep I have, which are not of this fold: them also I must bring, and they shall hear my voice; and there shall be one fold, and one shepherd. Therefore doth my Father love me, because I lay down my life, that I might take it again' (John 10:14-17).

Do you understand what our Lord teaches us here? God's love for us is free and, at the same time, fully deserved. He said, 'I will love them freely' (Hosea 14:4). Yet, his love, mercy, grace, and salvation flow to us upon the grounds of Christ's obedience as our Substitute. He is merciful and gracious to us, forgiving us of all sin, and loves us 'for Christ's sake' (Ephesians 4:32-5:2). God the Father looked upon his Son from eternity as our perfect, obedient Mediator, and, for the sake of his Son, loved us with an everlasting love. Again, Thomas Manton wrote,

> God could not love us with honour to himself, if his wisdom had not found out this way of loving us in Christ ... God was resolved to manifest an infinite love to man, but he would still manifest an infinite hatred against sin; which could not be more fully manifested than by making Christ the ground of our reconciliation ... How could the holy God, the just God ... love such vile and unworthy creatures as we are? The question is answered he loveth us in Christ, and for Christ's sake.

Same Way

Second, this word 'as' suggests a similarity of love. The Lord God loves his people in the same way as he loves his Son. Again, I stress the fact that our Saviour is here comparing the Father's love for him as our Mediator to his love for his elect. Christ, as our Mediator, is the first object of God's love. He loved Christ as the head of his mystical Body, the Church, and us as members. He loved Christ for his own sake. He loves us for Christ's sake.

God the Father loved Christ the God-man as 'the express image of his person' (Hebrews 1:3). So he loves his people who in Christ have been (and those who yet must be) renewed 'after the image of him' (Colossians 3:10; 2 Peter 1:4). He loves Christ as his only begotten Son; and he loves us in Christ as his adopted sons (1 John 3:1). Because the Saviour says, 'Thou hast loved them, as thou hast loved me', we are assured that God loves his elect freely. As we have already seen, the Lord Jesus Christ earned his Father's love as a man by his mediatorial obedience. Yet, when our Saviour came into the world, the Lord God loved the Child freely, delighting in him even before he had fulfilled his will (Isaiah 42:1). He is that One of whom the Father says, 'In whom my soul delighteth'! Even so, he loves us freely (Deuteronomy 7:7, 8; Hosea 14:4).

God loves us tenderly and affectionately. As the Father's love for his Son is a tender, indescribably affectionate love, so is his love for us (Isaiah 62:5; Zechariah 2:8).

God's love for his elect is immutable. As there is no possibility of change in our God (Malachi 3:6, James 1:17), God's love does not change. It cannot be taken from us; and it cannot be destroyed, neither by us nor by hell itself (Romans 8:35-39).

The famous Arminian preacher, founder of the Christian Missionary Alliance denomination, A.W. Tozer, made these statements about the love of God. They are shocking, but they accurately express what the whole religious word believes.

'God must love and will love man until hell has erased the last trace of the remaining image (of God in him). Men are lost now. But they are still loved of God ... I believe that God now loves all lost men ... (But) the day will come when lost man will no longer be loved by God Almighty ... I believe the time will come when God will no longer love lost human beings.'[5]

Such fickle, useless love may be worthy of fickle, useless man, but not of our great and glorious Lord God. Our God does not love today and hate tomorrow. His love is unchangeable.

Same Results

Thirdly, our Lord intends for us to understand that there is a similarity of results, that the effects and fruits, the consequences of God's love to him and his elect are the same. Love that has no effect and bears no fruit is just lip-love; and lip-love is useless love. Love that is never known by the one loved is a frustrated passion that destroys one's own peace and happiness. Love that never sees benefit and blessing upon its object, but only misery and woe, is a tormenting love. But that does not describe the love of God. Oh, no, a thousand times no! God's love toward us, like his love toward his Son as our Mediator, is an effectual, fruitful, beneficial love. Here are five things mutually enjoyed by Christ and his people as the fruit and effect of God's love.

The Revelation Of Secrets

All things are open, common knowledge between people who love one another. As all things are manifest and made known by the Father to the Son as our Mediator (John 1:18; 5:20), so all things are manifest and made known to God's elect by the Son (John 14:21; 15:15).

The Bestowment Of Spiritual Gifts

God's love is a bounteous love. He has given all things to the Son (John 3:34, 35; 17:2; Ephesians 4:8); and he has given all his people all spiritual, heavenly gifts in his Son (Ephesians 1:3).

Strength And Protection In Life

As the Lord Jesus was upheld, strengthened, and protected throughout the days of his obedience to do his Father's will (Isaiah 42:1), so the Lord God upholds,

---

[5] *The Tozer Pulpit*, Volume 8, pp 23-25

strengthens, and protects us, the objects of his love, throughout our days of obedience in this world (2 Corinthians 12:9).

Acceptance Of All We Do For Him

Everything that Christ did for God was accepted and well-pleasing to him because he loved him (Ephesians 5:2). And everything we do for God is accepted and well-pleasing to God through the merits of Christ because he loves us as he loved him (1 Peter 2:5). God our Father accepts our paltry efforts at serving and pleasing him for two reasons: (1) he accepts our poor, sin-stained obedience upon the merit of Christ's perfect obedience. And (2) he accepts our efforts at pleasing him because of his fatherly love for us in Christ.

Honour And Exaltation

The Lord Jesus was honoured and highly exalted by God the Father as the object of his love. He was given preeminence in, possession of, and power over all things (Psalms 2:7, 8; Hebrews 1:8). The Lord God, our heavenly Father, will do the same for us (John 12:26; Revelation 3:21).

Hear the Son of God and rejoice! 'Thou hast loved them, as thou hast loved me'! What a pillow upon which to rest our heads! What a comfort for our poor, aching hearts! What a glorious theme for daily meditation! What a cause for adoration, praise, and worship! We may be despised, misunderstood, abused, and hated of men, but we are loved of God! God our Father loves us even as he loves his darling Son; and he has so loved us from eternity!

'I beseech you therefore, brethren, by the mercies of God, that ye present your bodies a living sacrifice, holy, acceptable unto God, which is your reasonable service. And be not conformed to this world: but be ye transformed by the renewing of your mind, that ye may prove what is that good, and acceptable, and perfect, will of God' (Romans 12:1, 2).

Chapter 48

God's Everlasting Love For His Elect

'Father, I will that they also, whom thou hast given me, be with me where I am; that they may behold my glory, which thou hast given me: for thou lovedst me before the foundation of the world' (John 17:24).

God's everlasting love for his elect is the fountain of all grace and salvation, and the reason for all that he does. In verse 23 our Saviour declares 'I in them, and thou in me, that they may be made perfect in one; and that the world may know that thou hast sent me, and hast loved them, as thou hast loved me.' 'Thou hast loved them, as thou hast loved me'! What a pillow upon which to rest our heads! What a comfort for our poor, aching hearts! What a glorious theme for daily meditation! What a cause for adoration, praise, and worship! We may be despised, misunderstood, abused, and hated of men, but we are loved of God! God our Father loves us even as he loves his darling Son.

In verse 24 the Son of God declares that God the Father has loved us as he loves his Son from eternity! 'Father, I will that they also, whom thou hast given me, be with me where I am; that they may behold my glory, which thou hast given me; for thou lovest me before the foundation of the world.' With those words, our dear Saviour declares that God's love for his elect is an everlasting love. And, as John Gill observed, 'God's everlasting, unchangeable, and invariable love to his elect, through every state and condition into which they come, is written as with a sun-beam in the sacred writings.'

When we dive into the ocean of God's everlasting love for his elect, there is no possibility of us sounding its depths. So when I have said all that I know about it, there will be plenty of room for meditation and further study. I can do nothing more than bring up a few nuggets of gold from this deep mine of infinity. Let me show you five things about God's everlasting love for us in Christ.

The Eternality Of It

God's love for us did not begin yesterday. It is not something born in time. His love for us does not begin with our love for him. 'We love him because he first loved us' (1 John 4:19). God's love for us springs up from eternity, and is the ground of divine predestination, of our election and redemption by Christ, and our calling by God the Holy Spirit (Jeremiah 31:3; Ephesians 1:4-6; Ezekiel 16:8).

The Father loved us 'ere we fell,
And will forever love;
Nor shall the powers of earth or hell
His love from Zion move.

'Twas love that moved Him to ordain
A Surety just and good;
And on His heart inscribe the names
Of all for whom He stood.

Nor is the Surety short of love;
He loves beyond degree;
No less than love Divine could move
The Lord to die for me!

And O what love the Spirit shows!
When Jesus He reveals
To men oppressed with sin and woes,
And all their sorrows heals.

The Three-in-One, the One-in-Three,
In love forever rest;
The chosen shall in glory be
In His love ever blessed.

William Gadsby

All God's acts and works of grace performed for us before the world began arise from and are demonstrations of his everlasting love for us. Election was an act of God's eternal love (Ephesians 1:4). The covenant of grace was established by the triune God in eternity because of his great, everlasting love for us (2 Samuel 23:5; Romans 8:28, 29; 2 Timothy 1:9; Hebrews 13:20). And trusting our souls into the hands of Christ as our Surety was a work of God's eternal love (John 6:39; Ephesians 1:12).

The Immutability Of It

There is no possibility of change in our God (Malachi 3:6; James 1:17). God's love does not change. It cannot be taken from us; and it cannot be destroyed, neither by us nor by hell itself (Romans 8:35-39).

Nothing could be more dishonouring to God than failure (Numbers 14:11-16); but 'He shall not fail'! God's love, like all his gifts bestowed upon men, is without repentance. He will never cease his own to cherish. Those who are loved of God have been loved of God from everlasting, and shall be loved of God to everlasting. His love is eternal both ways. He will not depart from the objects of his love nor cease to do them good, for he cannot change (Jeremiah 32:40; Malachi 3:6; James 1:17).

The salvation of God's elect does not stand upon a precarious foundation of time, but upon the immutable foundation of God's everlasting love. We change often; but there are no changes in his love. Our love is sometimes hot and sometimes cold; but his love is invariably the same. God graciously and wisely changes the dispensations of his providence toward his people, hiding his face and chastening us because of our sin; but his love never changes (Isaiah 54:10; Hebrews 12:5-11). Chastisement is evidence of his love. Even when we sin against him, as we do, God's love does not change. Understand this, and rejoice. God's love toward his elect is from everlasting, and never changes to any degree or for any reason (Psalms 89:19-37; John 13:1).

The Gifts Of It

Love gives. The gifts of God's free and everlasting love are too many for us to calculate. Let me just show you three things that are clearly revealed as the gifts of God's everlasting love to his elect. In comparison with these three, all others, great as they are, must be considered to be far, far less.

The Lord God has given us himself because of his great love for us (Ezekiel 37:27). He says, 'I will be their God, and they shall be my people'. The gift of his Son, the Lord Jesus Christ, to suffer and die as our Substitute was and is the great commendation of his love to us (John 3:16; Romans 5:6-10; 1 John 3:16; 4:10). 'Thanks be unto God for his unspeakable gift'! (2 Corinthians 9:15). The gift of his Spirit to regenerate, call, and seal us in his grace in 'the time of love' is the gift of God's everlasting love to us (Ezekiel 16:8; Titus 3:3-6). John Gill said, 'Indeed, all that God does in time, or will do to all eternity, is only telling his people how much he loved them from everlasting.'

The Distinctiveness Of It

God's love is distinct and distinguishing love. It is utter nonsense to talk about God loving all men. I sometimes hear preachers try to soft peddle God's sovereignty by assuring people that there is a sense in which God loves all men with a love of benevolence though not with a love of complacency and delight. They say God loves all men as his creatures, just as he loves trees and toads. If you can get any comfort from the idea that God loves you like he loves a frog, I guess I should not take that away from you, but it simply is not the teaching of scripture.

God loves his elect distinctively. God does not love all men. I would not emphasize that fact, were it not for the fact that those who teach that God's love is universal are guilty of three horrible crimes. They make the love of God changeable. They make the love of God meaningless. They destroy the greatest motive there is for godliness and devotion. Try telling you wife that you love all women alike. See if that inspires her devotion to you!

The word of God tells us in the plainest terms possible that God's love for his elect is a special, sovereign, distinctive, and distinguishing love (Isaiah 43:1-5; Romans 8:29; Romans 9:11-24). God loves his people delightfully. I mean by that that God delights, takes pleasure in, and is complacent with his elect because of his love for them. God so loves us that he smiles on us perpetually, even when he appears to be frowning upon us!

It is high time that all attempts to divide the love of God into categories, stages, and degrees be laid aside. They do nothing to help men and only obscure the glory and grandeur of our God. If God loves me, he delights in me. If he does not delight in me, he does not love me. Again I say, try telling your wife, 'Honey, I really do love you. I wish you well. I want nothing but the very best for you, and am willing to do anything I can for you. But you do not please me. You are offensive to me. I do not enjoy your company. In fact, I really do not want to look at you.' If you still have a wife tomorrow, let me know.

Our God loves us as he loves his darling Son. That means he is well-pleased with us (Matthew 17:5). The Father and the Son are one; and the Son of God tells us that his 'delights' were with us from eternity (Proverbs 8:31). He could not have used a stronger word than this to express his love for us. The word 'delights' expresses the most intimate, sweet, ravishing pleasure. Can you get hold of this? Our God so delights in us that he says, 'Thou hast ravished my heart, my sister, my spouse: thou hast ravished my heart with one of thine eyes' (Song of Solomon 4:9).

The Efficacy Of It

God's love is more than a wish or desire in his heart to save sinners. God's love for us is an effectual love. That means that those who are the objects of God's love shall be saved, precisely because they are the objects of his love. Otherwise, the love of God is an utterly useless thing. God's love is sovereign (Romans 9:16-18). God's love is sacrificial (1 John 3:16). God's love is saving (Ezekiel 37:27). And God's love is steadfast (John 13:1). Let us rejoice in it!

'I in them, and thou in me, that they may be made perfect in one; and that the world may know that thou hast sent me, and hast loved them, as thou hast loved me. Father, I will that they also, whom thou hast given me, be with me where I am; that they may behold my glory, which thou hast given me: for thou lovedst me before the foundation of the world.'

What an amazing, stupendous revelation of God's love for us! Men tell me that such teaching as this promotes licentiousness and antinomianism, that it discourages godliness and good works; but that is absurd.

When I think of the things we have been meditating upon in this message, that God loved me when I hated him, that he loved me before the world began, that he loves me as he loves my Saviour, that his love for me will never cease, never change, and never vary, these thoughts compel me to love him, and lay me under the greatest obligation possible to reverence him, worship him, devote myself to his glory and his will, and serve his interests while I live in this world (1 John 4:19; 2 Corinthians 5:14; Titus 3:5-8). Does it not do the same for you?

Chapter 49

God's Love In Us

'And I have declared unto them thy name, and will declare it: that the love wherewith thou hast loved me may be in them, and I in them' (John 17:26).

'God is love'. That is who God is and what God is. 'God is love'! God commends his love toward us in the sacrifice of his dear Son, the Lord Jesus Christ (Romans 5:8). The triune God acts in love for us in all his works of grace and providence. The nuptial chariot in which our blessed Saviour carries his Bride through the ages of time is 'paved with love for the daughters of Jerusalem' (Song of Solomon 3:10). 'In love' he 'predestinated us' unto life everlasting! God sheds abroad his love in us in the gift of his Spirit (Romans 5:5). And God's love is made perfect in us when by faith in Christ we are made to know and assured of his love for us (1 John 4:9-19).

The Lord's Prayer

In John 17 the Lord Jesus is about to leave this world. He is going back to the Father. He has told his disciples that they must abide on the earth for a while, that they must endure unceasing trials, heavy troubles, and great tribulation. He has promised to send his Holy Spirit to comfort them. He has promised to help them. He urged them to simply trust him. But he knew their hearts were heavy, anxious, troubled, and fearful. He knew that they were full of doubts and questions. So, just before he goes out from them, just before he goes to die in their room and stead, the Son of God tenderly takes them by the hand, as it were, and says, 'Let us go to God and pray.'

It is this great, high priestly prayer that is before us in John 17. In these 26 verses our Master prays for the complete and perfect salvation of our souls (the salvation of all God's elect). He prays for our preservation (v. 11, 15), our joy (v. 13), our sanctification (v. 17), our union with one another in him (vv. 21-23), our heavenly glory (v. 24), and our complete gratification (v. 24), 'being perfect and entire, wanting nothing'. In this 26th verse, the Lord Jesus makes this wondrous declaration 'I have declared unto them thy name, and will declare it: that the love wherewith thou hast loved me may be in them, and I in them'. With those words our blessed Saviour tells us the meaning of his life, death, and resurrection as our Substitute.

Great Subject

I cannot imagine a subject of greater beauty, a mystery more wondrous, or a motive more inspiring than the love of God. The love of God is an ocean of profound depth, a mine with glorious treasures, and a mystery of inspiring wonders. It is infinitely vast, infinitely full, infinitely rich, and infinitely marvellous!

The love of God is a subject beyond the reach of comprehension in our present state. He who knows the most about it knows very little. Here is a subject into which we may dig and dig as deep as heart and mind will allow, and still never discover all the golden nuggets which lie within it.

Yet, it a subject that is always indescribably delightful, comforting, and instructive for our souls. How many have been converted by the commendation of God's love to sinners in the sacrifice of his darling Son! What has more effectually corrected us from the error of our ways than a fresh reminder of God's love for us? Nothing so effectually reproves our sin, unbelief, and worldliness as the love of God for us. Nothing moves our hearts Godward like the revelation of God's love for us.

May God the Holy Spirit show us something of the wondrous mystery here revealed. 'I have declared unto them thy name, and will declare it: that the love wherewith thou hast loved me may be in them, and I in them.' Here our Saviour speaks about what he had done, what he would do, and why. In a word, he here declares in the hearing of his disciples the entire purpose of his existence in human flesh, summarizes the whole of his work, and asserts that the purpose of it all is this, 'that the love wherewith thou has loved me may be in them, and I in them'!

In Us

The very last word of our Lord's prayer is concerning the love of God for us; but here the love of God for us is made manifest by the love of God in us. This is the last petition which he offers, 'that the love wherewith thou hast loved me may be in them, and I in them.' He means for us to know and enjoy the love of God for us! But there is more here than that. He prays that the love wherewith the Father loved him may itself be in us! He could ask nothing greater than this. He asks that we might be filled with all the fulness of the love of God. In that great request, our dear Saviour asks that we might be filled with all the fulness of God himself, for God is love. God is love, and he in whom loves dwells, dwells in God and God in him.

This is the very beginning of the experience of grace. When God comes to sinners in saving power and grace, he puts his love in them (Romans 5:1-5). Well might we sing with Charles Wesley,

Only love to us be given,
Lord, we ask no other heaven!

Indeed, there is no other heaven here below or yonder above than to enjoy the fulness of his perfect love. This is where the prayer of our great High Priest ends. 'That the love wherewith thou hast loved me may be in them.'

'For this cause I bow my knees unto the Father of our Lord Jesus Christ, Of whom the whole family in heaven and earth is named, That he would grant you, according to the riches of his glory, to be strengthened with might by his Spirit in the inner man; That Christ may dwell in your hearts by faith; that ye, being rooted and grounded in love, May be able to comprehend with all saints what is the breadth, and length, and depth, and height; And to know the love of Christ, which passeth knowledge, that ye might be filled with all the fulness of God' (Ephesians 3:14-19).

God Revealed In Christ

First, the Lord Jesus looks backward and summarizes his entire life and ministry. 'I have declared unto them thy name'. There is no salvation without knowing God. And there is no knowing God apart from the Lord Jesus Christ. Knowledge is not salvation; but there is no salvation without knowledge.

The Son of God came down here in human flesh and dwelt among us, so that we who are weak flesh might know the eternal, infinite, incomprehensible God. He says, 'I have declared unto them thy name'. What a tremendous statement of fact! Here is a man appealing to the righteous judgment of God himself, asserting with absolute, unqualified confidence that he had fully, constantly, and perfectly made known to men all that God is!

The strange thing is that you and I are not astonished by this fact. Some who read these lines have heard it from their infancy, and have heard it so constantly that it no longer seems astonishing. Be astonished, my soul! Here is a man who never learned anything about God, a man who has fully revealed God, a man who is God! This is our Saviour's own account of his whole life and ministry. The meaning of all that he is and all that he did on this earth is just this: he stood here in human flesh and said, 'Look at me. This is God. I AM!'

'If ye had known me, ye should have known my Father also: and from henceforth ye know him, and have seen him. Philip saith unto him, Lord, show us the Father, and it sufficeth us. Jesus saith unto him, have I been so long time with you, and yet hast thou not known me, Philip? He that hath seen me hath seen the Father; and how sayest thou then, Show us the Father? Believest thou not that I am in the Father, and the Father in me? The words that I speak unto you I speak not of myself: but the Father that dwelleth in me, he doeth the works' (John 14:7-10).

As the Father was and is revealed only in Christ, so it is only by Christ that he is revealed to us and in us. The only way men and women can and will know God is by special, divine revelation (Matthew 11:25-27). The knowledge here spoken of is a knowledge Christ gives. 'I have known thee, and these have known that thou hast sent me. And I have declared unto them thy name, and will declare it'. It is not knowledge we pick up as a matter of book learning, but knowledge given us by Christ. It is not knowledge communicated by a preacher, but knowledge granted by God the Holy Spirit.

'At that time Jesus answered and said, I thank thee, O Father, Lord of heaven and earth, because thou hast hid these things from the wise and prudent, and hast revealed them unto babes. Even so, Father: for so it seemed good in thy sight. All things are delivered unto me of my Father: and no man knoweth the Son, but the Father; neither knoweth any man the Father, save the Son, and he to whomsoever the Son will reveal him' (Matthew 11:25-27).

This knowledge distinguishes God's elect from the world. It is the mark by which the elect are made manifest. In the sixth verse of this chapter our Lord says: 'I have manifested thy name unto the men which thou gavest me out of the world: thine they were, and thou gavest them me; and they have kept thy word'. The world does not know the Father, and cannot know him, for it abides in the darkness and death of sin. Judge yourselves therefore by this sure test, and let the love which grows out of gracious knowledge be a token for good unto you.

God's Name Declared

Second, our Saviour looks forward to that which he would yet do. Look at the text again. 'I have declared unto them thy name, and will declare it'. Throughout his life he had declared the Father's name, his character. But he had not yet finished the revelation.

Had the revelation ended here, no son of Adam could ever have known God. He says, 'I have declared unto them thy name, and will declare it'. Go with him to Gethsemane, and hear him declare the name of God. But do not stop in Gethsemane. Go on to Calvary. Pause, my soul, adore and wonder! Here, as I behold the Christ of God suffering all the horrid wrath of God as my Substitute, I see the Lord God himself revealed. Now my soul cries with the prophet, 'Lo, this is our God! We have waited for him! He will save us'!

Only now, through Christ crucified, is it possible for God to be both the righteous God and my righteous Father. Only now, through his precious blood, can the Judge of all the earth, who must do right, embrace us poor, derelict prodigals as the sons of his love!

Lo! In the grace that rescued man
God's brightest form of glory shines!
Here, on the cross, 'tis fairest drawn
In precious blood and crimson lines.

Here I behold His inmost heart,
Where grace and vengeance strangely join,
Piercing His Son with sharpest smart,
To make the purchased treasure mine.

Oh, the sweet wonders of that cross,
Where God the Saviour loved and died!
Her noblest life my spirit draws
From His dear wounds and bleeding side.

Isaac Watts

When God the Holy Spirit comes to sinners in saving mercy, he is sent by the enthroned Christ, who continually declares the Father unto men by the gospel in the saving operations of his grace. When God saves a sinner, not only has the sinner learned who God is, the Father's name has been so declared and manifested in the Son and by the Son in the sinner's heart that the sinner is made to love the God he once despised!

But do not ever imagine that there will be an end to this glorious work. The knowledge of the infinite God comes to us gradually. How slow we are in learning! And when we have learned all that can be learned here, we will have learned but little. Throughout the glory of eternity, the Lord Jesus Christ will be declaring the Father to us.

The Reason

Third, our Saviour tells us the reason for this revelation of God. He says, 'I have declared unto them thy name, and will declare it: that the love wherewith thou hast loved me may be in them, and I in them.' Our Lord's prayer is not that the Father's love may be set upon us, or moved toward us. God does not love us because we know him. He loved us long before we knew him. Paul speaks of 'his great love wherewith he loved us, even when we were dead in trespasses and sins'. Christ did not come to set his Father's love upon the chosen. Oh, no! He did not die to get the Father to love us. He came here and died because God loved us.

'I have declared unto them thy name, and will declare it: that the love wherewith thou hast loved me may be in them, and I in them.' I cannot begin to tell you all that is included in this statement. (A man cannot tell what he does not know, and should not try!) But it is certain that our Lord would have us understand at least these four things.

1. Our Lord Jesus here prays that the love of God for us would be shed abroad in our hearts, assuring us of the Father's love for us (Romans 5:5). Our blessed Saviour would have us enjoy a deep, continuous, undisturbed assurance of the love of God for us. It is this revelation of the love of God that is both the cause and the fruit of faith in Christ.

2. Our great Saviour would have us constantly realise that the love the Father has for us is that same love which he enjoys! 'That the love wherewith thou hast loved me may be in them.'

3. Oh, wonder of wonders! The love wherewith the Father loved his Son is his love to poor sinners in his Son! You are, my brother, my sister, the object of God's delight, even as Christ is, because you are in Christ! I cannot state this more clearly or more wondrously than Spurgeon did, when preaching on this same subject. Here is what C. H. Spurgeon said to his congregation in London, England, many years ago,

> Do not tell me that God the Father does not love you as well as he does Christ: the point can be settled by the grandest matter of fact that ever was. When there was a choice between Christ and his people which should die of the two, the Father freely delivered up his own Son that we might live through him. Oh, what a meeting there must have been of the seas of love that day, when God's great love to us came rolling in like a glorious springtide, and his love to his Son came rolling in at the same time. If they had met and come into collision, we cannot imagine the result; but when they both took to rolling together in one mighty torrent, what a stream of love was there! The Lord Jesus sank

> that we might swim, he sank that we might rise and now we are borne onward forever by the mighty sweep of infinite love into an everlasting blessedness which tongues and lips can never fully set forth. Oh, be ravished with this. Be carried away with it; be in ecstasy at love so amazing, so divine: the Father loves you even as he loves his Son; after the same manner and sort he loveth all his redeemed.

Our love for Christ is a reflection of the Father's love. What a poor word I have chosen to express what I want to say 'reflection'! But how else can I say it? That love which we have for our Saviour is the Father's love for him. It is the love of God in us, created in us, born in us for his Son. The love is mine. I love him. Yet, it is his. He gave me the heart to love him, and put the love in it. Therefore, I can truthfully sing,

> My Jesus, I love thee, I know thou art mine;
> For thee all the follies of sin I resign.

The love of the Father for the Son that dwells in us is that love that beams forth and radiates from God's saints to others (1 John 4:8-14).

Christ In Us

Fourth, observe this in the very last line of this great, great prayer. Yes, our Saviour came here to make God known to men; that the love of God might dwell in us. But there is more. He came here to make God known to us, that the love of God might dwell in us, and that he might dwell in us! 'I have declared unto them thy name, and will declare it: that the love wherewith thou hast loved me may be in them, and I in them.'

The Lord Jesus Christ dwells in his people by faith, assuring us of God's perfect love for us. What can this possibly mean? Obviously, we cannot now comprehend it fully; but soon we shall (John 14:20). For now, it is enough to know that Christ dwelling in us is the assurance of God's love for us and of our hope of glory yet to come (Colossians 1:27; Ephesians 3:14-21). Christ in you is the hope of glory, because Christ in you is the assurance of God's perfect love which 'casteth out all fear' (1 John 4:9-19).

Would you be assured of God's love for you? Would you have God's perfect love in you, that perfect love that 'casteth out all fear' and will give you boldness in the day of judgment? Come, trust my Saviour. 'Believe on the Lord Jesus Christ, and thou shalt be saved'! 'He that believeth on the Son of God hath everlasting life'!

In evil long I took delight,
Unawed by shame or fear;
Till a new object struck my sight,
And stopped my wild career.

I saw One hanging on a tree,
In agonies and blood;
Who fixed His languid eyes on me,
As near His cross I stood.

Sure never to my latest breath,
Can I forget that look
It seemed to charge me with His death,
Though not a word He spoke.

My conscience felt and owned by guilt,
And plunged me in despair;
I saw my sins, His blood had spilt,
And helped to nail Him there.

Alas! I knew not what I did,
But now my tears are vain;
Where shall my trembling soul be hid?
For I the Lord have slain.

A second look He gave, which said,
'I freely all forgive,
This blood is for thy ransom paid,
I died that thou mayst live'.

Thus while His death my sin displays
In all its blackest hue;
Such is the mystery of grace,
It seals my pardon too.

With pleasing grief and mournful joy,
My spirit now is filled;
That I should such a life destroy
Yet live by His I killed!

John Newton

Chapter 50

Gethsemane's Sovereign

'When Jesus had spoken these words, he went forth with his disciples over the brook Cedron, where was a garden, into the which he entered, and his disciples. And Judas also, which betrayed him, knew the place: for Jesus ofttimes resorted thither with his disciples. Judas then, having received a band of men and officers from the chief priests and Pharisees, cometh thither with lanterns and torches and weapons. Jesus therefore, knowing all things that should come upon him, went forth, and said unto them, Whom seek ye? They answered him, Jesus of Nazareth. Jesus saith unto them, I am he. And Judas also, which betrayed him, stood with them. As soon then as he had said unto them, I am he, they went backward, and fell to the ground. Then asked he them again, Whom seek ye? And they said, Jesus of Nazareth. Jesus answered, I have told you that I am he: if therefore ye seek me, let these go their way: That the saying might be fulfilled, which he spake, Of them which thou gavest me have I lost none. Then Simon Peter having a sword drew it, and smote the high priest's servant, and cut off his right ear. The servant's name was Malchus. Then said Jesus unto Peter, Put up thy sword into the sheath: the cup which my Father hath given me, shall I not drink it?' (John 18:1-11).

When our dear Saviour finished his great intercessory prayer as our great High Priest before his Father and our Father in John 17, he arose and walked across the brook Cedron and entered into the Garden of Gethsemane. It was in the Garden of Eden that the first Adam fell, plunged our race into sin, and death, and utter ruin, and lost everything. And our Lord Jesus Christ (the last Adam) came into a garden to restore that which he took not away. It was in a garden where our Saviour sweat great drops of blood falling to the ground, as he anticipated being made sin for us. It was in a garden where he was nailed to the cursed tree, when he suffered and died as our Substitute. It was in a garden where he was buried. And it was in a garden where he came forth in resurrection power, triumphant over death, hell, and the grave! Augustine said, 'It is fitting that the blood of the Physician should there be poured out, where the disease of the sick man first commenced'.

But did you ever notice that of the four inspired Gospel narratives John alone makes no mention of our Saviour's agony in the Garden of Gethsemane? Matthew, Mark, and Luke were all inspired to write about our Saviour's great heaviness and sorrow of heart in Gethsemane with considerable detail. John was inspired to omit that altogether. Why?

I can only guess what the answer to that question may be; but I think, at least in part, the answer is obvious. John's distinct objective throughout his Gospel narrative is to show us the greatness of our Saviour as the Almighty God. So, when he described Gethsemane, he mentioned nothing of weakness and sorrow. He only spoke of majesty, sovereign control, and the assured salvation of God's elect by Christ, our sovereign Saviour.

Symbolic Brook

First, learn that our Saviour's crossing over the brook Cedron was highly symbolic (v. 1).This brook Cedron is the same as the brook Kidron mentioned so often in the Old Testament. You will remember that King David, who was an eminent type of our Saviour, passed over the brook Kidron when he was fleeing from Absalom (2 Samuel 15:23). It was there, at the brook Kidron that King Asa burned his mother's idol and scattered its ashes (2 Chronicles 15:16). Here it was that the good King Josiah caused the polluted vessels of the temple to be burned (2 Kings 23:4). And all the uncleanness found in the house of the Lord in Hezekiah's reign was disposed of in the brook Kidron (2 Chronicles 29:16).

Every year, on the Day of Atonement, the scapegoat was led by a fit man across the brook Kidron and into the wilderness. The word 'Kidron' (Cedron) means 'turbid' or 'blackness'. You can imagine the filth, foulness, and blackness of it. All the blood of all the temple sacrifices ran down into the brook Kidron! There, beside the brook Kidron, all the waste of the sacrifices was burned. What a loathsome, repulsive stream it must have been!

With all that in mind, read Psalms 110:1-7, and see the significance of John's declaration that our Lord Jesus Christ went 'over the brook Cedron' into the Garden of Gethsemane.

'The LORD said unto my Lord, Sit thou at my right hand, until I make thine enemies thy footstool. The LORD shall send the rod of thy strength out of Zion: rule thou in the midst of thine enemies. Thy people shall be willing in the day of thy power, in the beauties of holiness from the womb of the morning: thou hast the dew of thy youth. The LORD hath sworn, and will not repent, Thou art a priest for ever after the order of Melchizedek. The Lord at thy right hand shall strike through kings in the day of his wrath. He shall judge among the heathen, he shall fill the places with the dead bodies; he shall wound the heads over many countries. He shall drink of the brook in the way: therefore shall he lift up the head.'

Obviously, our Saviour did not physically drink the waters of that foul brook Kidron; but, passing over it, he drank of the brook in his way in a spiritual sense. He drank that which is far more foul than that metaphorical brook. Our blessed Saviour took the cup of our iniquities, transgressions, and sins. He drank all the filth and blackness of our sins when he was made sin for us. He drank the cup of trembling, as our divine Surety. Yes, he drank the very dregs of that cup that we might drink the cup of salvation and call upon the name of the Lord; and he did it voluntarily (John 18:11; Isaiah 51:22; Galatians 3:13, 14; Psalms 116:13).

Christless Religion

Second, let us learn that nothing has such a hardening effect upon the heart of man as religion without Christ (vv. 2, 3). Judas was one of the twelve Apostles. Yet, Judas guided the soldiers to the Saviour. John tells us specifically that Judas used his knowledge of the fact that the Lord Jesus often came to Gethsemane for prayer to lead the soldiers to him. There he had often knelt with the Son of God; and there he betrayed him. How shocking! When the band of men and officers approached the Saviour, Judas 'stood with them'.

Yet, this was a man who had been for three years the constant companion of the incarnate God. He had seen the Lord's miracles. He had heard his sermons. Judas had enjoyed the benefit of the Saviour's private instruction. He had professed himself a believer. He had even worked and preached in Christ's name! J. C. Ryle observed: 'From the highest degree of privilege down to the lowest depth of sin, there is but a succession of steps. Privileges misused seem to paralyze the conscience. The same fire that melts wax, will harden clay.'

Beware of resting your hopes of salvation on religious knowledge, however great; or religious advantages, however many. Many there are, I fear, who know all doctrinal truth and are teachers of others, preaching true doctrine zealously, who yet prove reprobate and go down to the pit with Judas! You may bask in the full sunshine of spiritual privileges and have great knowledge, you may be known as a tireless worker for the cause of God, and yet not know God. 'Let him that thinketh he standeth, take heed lest he fall' (1 Corinthians 10:12). Nothing so hardens the heart of man as religion without Christ!

Known Sufferings

Third, we are here taught that our blessed Saviour, the Lord Jesus Christ, knew from the beginning all that must come upon him as our Redeemer. 'Jesus therefore, knowing all things that should come upon him, went forth, and said unto them, Whom seek ye?' (v. 4).

One of the things that must have made our Saviour's sufferings so terrible is the fact that he had perfect knowledge of all the torments he must endure as our Substitute from the beginning. He knew full well all the bitter dregs of the cup before he took it into his holy hands of grace. He knew the scourging, the thorns, the cross, the sin, the curse, the agonizing death that awaited him. No doubt, every time he saw a lamb in the meadow, every time he saw a sacrifice in the temple, he was reminded that he must soon be offered upon the altar of divine justice as the Lamb of God.

Voluntary Substitute

Fourth, the Holy Ghost here teaches us again that our Lord Jesus Christ was our voluntary Substitute. He suffered all that he suffered for us, and died in our place under the wrath of God, by the hands of wicked men, because he desired to do so (vv. 4-11).

'Jesus therefore, knowing all things that should come upon him, went forth, and said unto them, Whom seek ye? They answered him, Jesus of Nazareth. Jesus saith unto them, I am he. And Judas also, which betrayed him, stood with them. As soon then as he had said unto them, I am he, they went backward, and fell to the ground. Then asked he them again, Whom seek ye? And they said, Jesus of Nazareth. Jesus answered, I have told you that I am he: if therefore ye seek me, let these go their way: That the saying might be fulfilled, which he spake, Of them which thou gavest me have I lost none. Then Simon Peter having a sword drew it, and smote the high priest's servant, and cut off his right ear. The servant's name was Malchus. Then said Jesus unto Peter, Put up thy sword into the sheath: the cup which my Father hath given me, shall I not drink it?'

Our Lord Jesus, was the Sovereign even in Gethsemane. Notice, it was he who took the initiative, not the soldiers, the Pharisees, or Judas. He said to those who came to arrest him, 'Whom seek ye?' Thus, he demonstrated with divine force that he was in total control of the situation. When our Lord said, 'I AM', 'they went away backward and fell to the ground'! This is, perhaps, the greatest miracle recorded upon the pages of Inspiration. It was accomplished by the Saviour's mere declaration of his Being. Here is an army of soldiers, with weapons of war, falling backward to the earth, prostrated before the Lord Jesus by the simple words of the incarnate God, 'I Am'! Who but God could have wrought such a miracle?

This, too, was the complete fulfilment of divine prophecy. 'When the wicked, even mine enemies and my foes, came upon me to eat up my flesh, they stumbled and fell' (Psalms 27:2). Isaiah spoke of the same thing (Isaiah 11:1-4).

'And there shall come forth a rod out of the stem of Jesse, and a Branch shall grow out of his roots: And the spirit of the LORD shall rest upon him, the spirit of wisdom and understanding, the spirit of counsel and might, the spirit of knowledge and of the fear of the LORD; And shall make him of quick understanding in the fear of the LORD: and he shall not judge after the sight of his eyes, neither reprove after the hearing of his ears: But with righteousness shall he judge the poor, and reprove with equity for the meek of the earth: and he shall smite the earth with the rod of his mouth, and with the breath of his lips shall he slay the wicked.'

How easily that same breath and those same words might have cast those men down into hell. Do not overlook this. Those very words and that very breath, by which the Lord Jesus gives life, and comfort, and strength to his people, bring death, and judgment, and destruction upon his enemies (Isaiah 51:12; 58:9; 2 Corinthians 2:14-16).

Our dear blessed Saviour took the cup of God's wrath willingly. He was not forced to take it, but was determined to take it (v. 11). Yes, he prayed three times, 'O my Father, if it be possible, let this cup pass from me.' How he trembled at the prospect of being made sin for us and dying under the just curse of God's holy law as our Substitute. Behold, the bloody sweat! Yet, he bowed to his Father's will, saying, 'Not my will, thy will be done'! Then, he rose up from prayer and went out to meet Judas, the Pharisees, the Priests, and the soldiers, healed the wounded soldier, told Peter to put up his sword, and said, 'The cup which my Father hath given me, shall I not drink it?'

The Son of God died as a willing Sacrifice! He is our willing Saviour. He did not die because he could not help it. He did not suffer because he could not escape. All the soldiers of Pilate's army could not have taken him, had he not been willing to be taken. They could not have hurt a hair of his head, had he not given them permission. The Lamb of God, our Saviour, was a willing sufferer, a willing substitute, a willing sacrifice.

He set his heart upon accomplishing our redemption from everlasting. He loved us and gave himself for us, cheerfully, willingly, gladly, in order to make atonement for our sins and save us. This was 'the joy set before him' for which he 'endured the cross and despising the shame'. The Lord Jesus Christ, the Son of God, our great Saviour, is far more willing to save than we are to be saved.

He died as a willing, voluntary Substitute. The Good Shepherd laid down his life for his sheep.

What an example he set before us to follow. In his obedience to his Father, suffering death by his Father's will, he is not only our Redeemer, but our Example, too. The only way we can live in this world in peace is by continually bowing to our Father's will. He is the truly wise man who has learned to say at every stage of his pilgrimage, 'Father, give me what you will, place me where you will, do with me as you will; not my will, but your will be done.' That is the man who has the mind of the Lord Jesus Christ. May God make it mine!

Justice's Demands

Fifth, the death of Christ in the place of his people demands the salvation of all for whom he died (v. 8). Our Saviour here declared to these soldiers, the representatives of law and executioners of justice, 'If you take me, you must let these go their way. You cannot have the Shepherd and the sheep. You cannot punish both the Substitute and those for whom the Substitute is punished. 'Let these go their way'! That was not a request, but a command, a command to which justice must and will acquiesce! Augustus Toplady put it thus:

From whence this fear and unbelief?
Hath not the Father, put to grief
His spotless Son for me?
And will the righteous Judge of men
Condemn me for that debt of sin
Which, Lord, was charged on Thee?

Complete atonement Thou hast made
And to the utmost farthing paid
Whate'er thy people owed;
God's wrath on me cannot take place
If sheltered in Thy righteousness,
And sprinkled with Thy blood?

If Thou hast my discharge procured,
And freely in my room endured
The whole of wrath divine,
Payment God cannot twice demand,
First at my bleeding Surety's hand,
And then again at mine.

Turn, then, my soul, unto thy rest;
The merits of thy great High Priest
Speak peace and liberty;
Trust in His efficacious blood,
Nor fear thy banishment from God,
Since Jesus died for thee.

Tender Watchfulness

Look at verse 8 again, and see this sixth lesson. Our dear Saviour always watches over his people with a keen eye, a tender heart, and omnipotent grace. 'Jesus answered, I have told you that I am he: if therefore ye seek me, let these go their way'.

Here is an instructive picture of all our Saviour's dealings with our souls. He will not allow you who trust him 'to be tempted above that which you are able to bear'. He holds the winds and storms in his hands. He will not allow his own, however sifted and buffeted, to be utterly destroyed. He watches over each of his redeemed tenderly. Like a wise physician, he measures out and mixes our cup with infinite skill, infinite care, and infinite love. Let us lean our souls on this precious truth. In the darkest hour the eye of the Lord Jesus is upon us, and our safety is sure.

Sure Salvation

Seventh, God the Holy Ghost reminds us again that the salvation of God's elect is a matter of absolute certainty. 'That the saying might be fulfilled, which he spake, Of them which thou gavest me have I lost none' (v. 9). God's elect shall never perish! The decree of God demands it. The blood of Christ demands it. The seal of the Spirit demands it.

Would you have this salvation? Would you have this great Saviour? Come to him, and this salvation is yours. Come to him, and he is yours!

Come humble sinner, in whose breast
A thousand thoughts revolve;
Come with your guilt and fear oppressed,
And make this last resolve.

'I'll go to Jesus, though my sins
Like mountains round me close;
I know His courts, I'll enter in,
Whatever may oppose.

'Prostrate I'll lie before His throne,
And there my guilt confess;
I'll tell Him I'm a wretch undone
Without His sovereign grace.'

I'll to the gracious King approach,
Whose sceptre pardon gives;
Perhaps He may command my touch,
And then the suppliant lives!

Perhaps He will admit my plea,
Perhaps will hear my prayer;
But if I perish, I will pray,
And perish only there.

I can but perish if I go,
I am resolved to try;
For if I stay away, I know,
I must forever die.

But if I die with mercy sought,
When I the King have tried,
This were to die (Delightful thought!)
As sinner never died!

Edmund Jones

Chapter 51

Jesus Taken, And Bound, And Led Away

'Then the band and the captain and officers of the Jews took Jesus, and bound him, And led him away to Annas first; for he was father in law to Caiaphas, which was the high priest that same year. Now Caiaphas was he, which gave counsel to the Jews, that it was expedient that one man should die for the people. And Simon Peter followed Jesus, and so did another disciple: that disciple was known unto the high priest, and went in with Jesus into the palace of the high priest. But Peter stood at the door without. Then went out that other disciple, which was known unto the high priest, and spake unto her that kept the door, and brought in Peter. Then saith the damsel that kept the door unto Peter, Art not thou also one of this man's disciples? He saith, I am not. And the servants and officers stood there, who had made a fire of coals; for it was cold: and they warmed themselves: and Peter stood with them, and warmed himself. The high priest then asked Jesus of his disciples, and of his doctrine. Jesus answered him, I spake openly to the world; I ever taught in the synagogue, and in the temple, whither the Jews always resort; and in secret have I said nothing. Why askest thou me? ask them which heard me, what I have said unto them: behold, they know what I said. And when he had thus spoken, one of the officers which stood by struck Jesus with the palm of his hand, saying, Answerest thou the high priest so? Jesus answered him, If I have spoken evil, bear witness of the evil: but if well, why smitest thou me? Now Annas had sent him bound unto Caiaphas the high priest. And Simon Peter stood and warmed himself. They said therefore unto him, Art not thou also one of his disciples? He denied it, and said, I am not. One of the servants of the high priest, being his kinsman whose ear Peter cut off, saith, Did not I see thee in the garden with him? Peter then denied again: and immediately the cock crew' (John 18:12-27).

Here, within the crowded palace of the high priest, they had made a fire to warm themselves, because it was cold. What a striking revelation that is. Just a very few hours earlier, our Lord Jesus knelt in prayer in the open air of Gethsemane. There, as he prayed, he broke out into a bloody sweat. What agony he endured, what a load pressed him down, as he anticipated being made sin for us! There are five things in this part of John's Gospel that stand out as matters of great importance and spiritual instruction. As we follow our Saviour into the palace of Caiaphas the high priest, may God the Holy Spirit, whose word we have before us, be our Teacher.

Adorable Providence

The first thing that strikes me in this portion of holy scripture is the display of God's adorable providence. Our great God rules and overrules all things, abounding toward us in all wisdom and prudence, making known to us the mystery of his will. According to his own good pleasure, he always works 'all things after the counsel of his own will' (Ephesians 1:8-11). Nothing is more wonderful to contemplate or more comforting to remember than that. Never miss, never overlook, never lightly esteem these displays of God's wise and good, adorable providence.

1. John reminds us that this high priest, 'Caiaphas was he, which gave counsel to the Jews, that it was expedient that one man should die for the people' (v. 14). Though Caiaphas did not know God and did not know our Saviour, though he was nothing but a self-serving religious leader, God used him to proclaim as clearly as any man ever did the message of the gospel he despised, substitutionary redemption by the sacrifice of Christ (John 11:50-52).

2. It seems to me that the Holy Spirit inspired John to describe Peter's denial of the Lord Jesus in such a way that we could not miss seeing that the Lord himself placed Peter in the place of temptation. No man is tempted of God; but no temptation comes without God's decree. Our Lord Jesus told Peter how he would deny him three times that very night. Yet, Peter could not have gotten into the high priest's palace had God not placed that disciple there who was known to the high priest (vv. 15, 16). That disciple went in first, got permission for Peter to come in, and then went back to the door and told the door-keeper that Peter had permission to come into the palace.

There Peter would deny the Lord Jesus, displaying that there is no evil that is not in us, no evil we will not perform when left to ourselves, and no strength in us to resist temptation, to resist the devil, or to resist the vile passions of our depraved hearts. There the Lord Jesus would look upon his fallen disciple with the tender eyes of unfailing mercy, love, and grace. There, the Lord Jesus used the maid, the soldier, and the devil to prepare the way for him to make himself more intimately known to Peter, the object of his love (John 21:15-17). There the Lord Jesus would have Peter sifted in the sieve as wheat, that he might make him a more useful preacher and servant of God than he could otherwise be.

3. We again see the display of our great God's adorable providence in using the Jews to accomplish the fulfilment of the sacrificial type. According to the Levitical law (Leviticus 17:1-9), the sacrifice offered to God had to be examined by the high priest before it was offered to God. So Christ our Sacrifice was brought to the high priest before he was sacrificed. Though Caiaphas said nothing about his innocence as the spotless Lamb of God, when Caiaphas sent him to Pilate, Pilate declared him to be without fault (1 Peter 1:17-20). The first thing then that stands out in our text is God's adorable providence.

When carnal reason would demand
Why this or that my God ordained,
My heart in faith, Lord, humbly bend
Before Thy throne, my God and King.

When doubts disturb me and distress,
When darkness seems to block my way,
Oh, give me grace on this to rest,
That thus it seemeth good to Thee!

Be this my joy: My Christ is Lord
And by all things performs His will.
Your providence I would adore,
And calmly, sweetly trust Thee still.

Astonishing Hardness

Second, the Spirit of God here gives us a display of the astonishing hardness of depraved hearts. We see this in the conduct of the men by whom our Lord Jesus was arrested. Some of them were Roman soldiers. Some were servants of the priests and Pharisees. Among them were Judas and the Pharisees. But in one thing they were all alike. They all saw our Saviour's divine power exhibited when they 'went backward and fell to the ground'. All saw the miracle our Lord performed when he touched Malchus' ear and healed him. Yet, all remained unmoved, cold, indifferent, insensible, and hard.

Do you not find that astonishing? They all acted as if they had seen nothing out of the ordinary. 'They made their hearts as an adamant stone' (Zechariah 7:12). They saw these things and hardened their hearts, like Pharaoh, and went on coolly with their callous business. 'They took Jesus, bound him, and led him away'! Oh, how hard the heart of man is! Nothing can break it! Nothing can penetrate it! Nothing but omnipotent grace! Bless God, there is hope for such hard hearts!

John Trapp, quoting one of the ancient writers, said, 'The adamant stone is a legendary stone thought to be the hardest of all stones, harder than flint (Ezekiel 3:9), harder than the nether millstone (Job 41:24). Fire could not burn it, or even cause it to be heated throughout. It could not be broken by a hammer. Yet, this hardest of all stones, when soaked in a goat's blood, is melted, dissolved, and broken. So the hardest heart of the most obstinate sinner is melted, dissolved, and broken when sprinkled with the precious blood of Christ, the sinner's Scapegoat.'

That is our hope and prayer to God for sinners. If God the Holy Spirit sprinkles their hearts with the blood of Christ, if he will apply the blood to them, they will look upon him whom we have pierced and mourn. Miracles will never penetrate fallen man's hard heart. Acts of divine judgment will never break the heart of stone. Affliction will never break it. The law can never break it. Hell itself cannot break the rebel heart of man. But the blood of Christ can!

Amazing Condescension

Third, we have before us a marvellous display of the amazing condescension of our Lord Jesus Christ. Here is the Son of God, our Creator, the Sovereign of the universe, taken prisoner and led away, bound like a common malefactor. He is arraigned before wicked and unjust judges. He is insulted and treated with contempt. He had only to will his deliverance, and he would at once have been free. He had only to command the confusion of his enemies, and they would at once have been confounded.

This Man, Christ Jesus, is the Judge before whose bar Annas and Caiaphas, and all their companions must soon stand, from whom they shall receive a sentence of everlasting damnation. Yet, he condescended to be treated as a malefactor without resisting. 'They took Jesus, and bound him, and led him away' (vv. 12, 13). Imagine that! When he was led away to slaughter, and bound with the sins of his people, our blessed Saviour was led without the camp, to suffer without the gate (Hebrews 13:12). Isaiah tells us that he was 'taken from prison and from judgment' when the Lord God 'laid on him the iniquity of us all' (Isaiah 53:6-8). Deity was arrested that guilty sinners might never be arrested by God's law! Like the sacrifices of old, Christ our Sacrifice was bound to the altar with cords, pinioned and manacled by cords of divine justice as a common malefactor, that common malefactors might never be! The Lord Jesus was bound for our transgressions, bruised for our iniquities, that we by his bondage from chains of darkness might be set free!

Truly the love of Christ to poor sinners is 'a love that passeth knowledge'! To suffer for those we love, those who are in some sense worthy of our affection, is suffering that we can understand. To submit to ill-treatment quietly, when we have no power to resist, is submission that is both graceful and wise. But to suffer voluntarily, when you have the power to prevent it, and to suffer for a people who crave your blood, unasked, unwanted, and unthanked, that is 'love that passeth knowledge'!

Our Lord Jesus was led away captive and dragged before the high priest's bar, not because he could not help himself, but because he had set his whole heart upon us from eternity. By bearing our sins in his own body on the tree, by being made sin for us, and by being punished in our stead, the Son of God was determined to ransom our souls.

He was a willing prisoner, that we might be set free. He was willingly arraigned and condemned, that we might be absolved and declared innocent. 'He suffered for sins, the Just for the unjust, that he might bring us unto God'. 'Though he was rich, yet for our sakes he became poor, that we through his poverty might be rich.' 'He was made sin for us who knew no sin, that we might be made the righteousness of God in him'!

Substitution is the very heart of the gospel. Our dear Saviour suffered and died willingly and unresistingly, because he had come into this world as our Substitute and Surety, determined by substitutionary atonement to purchase our eternal salvation. In all things, our Lord Jesus humbled himself to be both our Substitute and our Example (1 Peter 2:21-25; Philippians 2:5-8).

Our dear Saviour, the Lord Jesus Christ, was our Example in his life and in his death. He said he was our Example in washing the disciples' feet. Our Saviour, by his meekness in suffering for us, made himself an Example for us to follow in suffering. And our Lord Jesus was the Example, the Standard, for all preachers to follow. Look at what he said to Caiaphas about his preaching (vv. 19-21).

'The high priest then asked Jesus of his disciples, and of his doctrine. Jesus answered him, I spake openly to the world; I ever taught in the synagogue, and in the temple, whither the Jews always resort; and in secret have I said nothing. Why askest thou me? ask them which heard me, what I have said unto them: behold, they know what I said.'

Faithful preachers conceal nothing. They preach the gospel with great plainness of speech, determined to be understood. If you want to know what a faithful preacher believes, all you have to do is ask those who hear them.

Abiding Sinfulness

Fourth, God the Spirit here sets before us an undeniable display of the abiding sinfulness that is to be found in all true believers, the corruption that yet remains in every true Christian, and will remain in us as long as we are in this world, in this body of flesh. We see this fact strikingly exemplified in the conduct of the Apostle Peter. There is Peter, that strong, faithful, believing man, forsaking his Master, and acting like a reprobate wretch! There he is running away when he ought to have stood by his Master's side. Do you see him, ashamed to own his Lord when he ought to have confessed him? Hear him three times denying that he knew his Saviour. And all this took place immediately after receiving the Lord's' Supper, after hearing the Saviour's last discourse, after hearing the plainest possible warnings, after hearing his Saviour pray that great prayer as his High Priest that is recorded in the previous chapter, having nothing to gain by his denial!

'Let him that thinketh he standeth take heed lest he fall'! Peter's fall is recorded in the book of God repeatedly, because it is intended to be a lesson to us all. Saved sinners are sinners still. Our only righteousness is the righteousness of Christ. Our only hope before God is Christ. His obedience! His blood! His intercession! Salvation, from start to finish, is by grace alone!

Abounding Grace

The fifth thing set before us in this event is the unfailing, immutable, abounding grace of God our Saviour. 'Where sin abounded grace did much more abound; That as sin hath reigned unto death, even so might grace reign through righteousness unto eternal life by Jesus Christ our Lord' (Romans 5:20, 21). Peter truly loved the Lord Jesus, though he often acted otherwise. So it is with you and me! Peter denied Christ three times; but the Lord Jesus has not denied Peter. So it is with you and me! The Lord Jesus restored Peter by an act of his own free grace; otherwise Peter would never have returned to him. So it is with you and me! Peter did not reap what he sowed. He was not forsaken of God. Christ, his Substitute, reaped what Peter sowed. He was forsaken of God for Peter's sake. So it is with you and me! We are great sinners; and our Lord Jesus Christ is a great Saviour! In him the grace of God superabounds!

Chapter 52

'To this end was I born'

'Then led they Jesus from Caiaphas unto the hall of judgment: and it was early; and they themselves went not into the judgment hall, lest they should be defiled; but that they might eat the passover. Pilate then went out unto them, and said, What accusation bring ye against this man? They answered and said unto him, If he were not a malefactor, we would not have delivered him up unto thee. Then said Pilate unto them, Take ye him, and judge him according to your law. The Jews therefore said unto him, It is not lawful for us to put any man to death: That the saying of Jesus might be fulfilled, which he spake, signifying what death he should die. Then Pilate entered into the judgment hall again, and called Jesus, and said unto him, Art thou the King of the Jews? Jesus answered him, Sayest thou this thing of thyself, or did others tell it thee of me? Pilate answered, Am I a Jew? Thine own nation and the chief priests have delivered thee unto me: what hast thou done? Jesus answered, My kingdom is not of this world: if my kingdom were of this world, then would my servants fight, that I should not be delivered to the Jews: but now is my kingdom not from hence. Pilate therefore said unto him, Art thou a king then? Jesus answered, Thou sayest that I am a king. To this end was I born, and for this cause came I into the world, that I should bear witness unto the truth. Every one that is of the truth heareth my voice. Pilate saith unto him, What is truth? And when he had said this, he went out again unto the Jews, and saith unto them, I find in him no fault at all. But ye have a custom, that I should release unto you one at the passover: will ye therefore that I release unto you the King of the Jews? Then cried they all again, saying, Not this man, but Barabbas. Now Barabbas was a robber' (John 18:28-40).

We have seen our Lord Jesus arrested in the Garden of Gethsemane, dragged as a thief along the dark streets to Annas and then to the palace of Caiaphas the high priest, where he was mocked, slapped, and falsely accused by his foes, and denied by one of his beloved disciples. Then, he is led from Caiaphas' palace to the hall of judgment to be judged by Pilate, the Roman administrator placed over Jerusalem.

You will search the pages of history in vain to find another instance of a person charged with a capital offence arraigned before two different tribunals in a matter of hours. This aspect of our Lord's trial is made even more extraordinary by the fact that he was arraigned before the courts of two nationalities: the one was Jewish and the other Roman. And the courts were of different orders: one was ecclesiastical and the other civil. He was arraigned first before the Jewish Sanhedrin, over which Caiaphas presided, he being 'the high priest the same year' (John 11:49), and then before the Roman court. And so it must have been in order that the scriptures might be fulfilled which foretold the manner of his death.

The closing events of our Lord's life were clearly foretold by the prophets. Thus in the second Psalm we read, 'The kings of the earth set themselves, and the rulers take counsel together, against the LORD, and against his Christ, saying, Let us break their bands asunder, and cast away their cords from us.' There is no uncertainty as to the fulfilment of this prophecy; for the disciples, after reciting these verses of the Psalm, said, 'For a truth, against thy holy child Jesus, whom thou has anointed, both Herod and Pontius Pilate, with the Gentiles and the people of Israel were gathered together for to do whatsoever thy hand and thy counsel determined before to be done' (Acts 4: 24-28).

Thus the great confederacy of Jews and Gentiles, kings of the earth and rulers, having set themselves in defiance against Jehovah and against his Christ, succeeded only in accomplishing what the triune Jehovah had in his eternal counsels decreed before to be done. From the very beginning of time, by all the types and shadows of the law, through all the writings of the Old Testament prophets, throughout the earthly life and ministry of our Lord Jesus Christ, and through all the preaching and writings of the Apostles, in all the book of God, the Lord God revealed to fallen, sinful, hell-bent, hell-deserving sinners the only possible way of salvation for fallen man is the way of the cross, the way of Christ's death and resurrection as the sinners' Substitute.

I must needs go home by the way of the cross,
There's no other way but this;
I shall ne'er get sight of the gates of light,
If the way of the cross I miss.

I must walk by faith in the strait, narrow way,
Faith in His atoning blood!
I can never stand in God's Promised Land,
But by the merit of His blood!

Jessie B. Pounds

The Christ of God must needs have suffered all those things he suffered, in every detail, before he could enter into his promised glory and be the Saviour of his people (Luke 24:25-27).

The blood-thirsty Sanhedrim stayed up all night so that they could plot their course and get the Lord Jesus over to Pilate's judgment hall as early as possible. How they thirsted for his blood! But his thirst was greater than theirs. He thirsted to drink the cup of the Father's wrath for us. He thirsted to drink of that cup for us to very dregs of utmost bitterness, that he might, in love, drink damnation dry!

Stunning Hypocrisy

First, in verses 28-31 we see a stunning display of hypocrisy. Here is a band of religious zealots, the religious leaders of Israel, the Pharisees, the religious leaders of the Pharisees, the Sanhedrim and the high priest of Israel, all plotting together to murder the Lord of Glory, a man whom they knew to be completely innocent of any offence. Yet, they were fearful of being ceremonially defiled by going into the judgment hall!

'Then led they Jesus from Caiaphas unto the hall of judgment: and it was early; and they themselves went not into the judgment hall, lest they should be defiled; but that they might eat the passover. Pilate then went out unto them, and said, What accusation bring ye against this man? They answered and said unto him, If he were not a malefactor, we would not have delivered him up unto thee' (John 18:28-30).

These hardened men were engaged in doing the most abominably wicked thing mortal man ever did. They were in the process of murdering the Messiah. Yet, they talked of being 'defiled', and were very fastidious about the rules for keeping the passover! Our Lord Jesus rightly identified them as hypocrites and vipers.

The conscience of man is as fallen, depraved, and wicked as the rest of our nature. Sometimes it is hardened, seared, dead, and feels nothing. At other times, it is morbidly scrupulous about the matters of religious ceremony and tradition. It is not at all uncommon to find people excessively meticulous about trifling forms and outward ceremonies, while they are detestably immoral. Robbers and murderers are sometimes extremely strict about confessions, and absolutions, and prayers to saints. Fastings and self-imposed austerities in Lent are often followed by vile ungodliness when Lent is over. There is but a step from Lent to Carnival. People who know they are wrong in one direction, often struggle to make things appear right by excess of zeal in another direction. That very zeal is the show of their hypocrisy and their condemnation.

Any form of religion that causes people to focus on outward forms, rites, sacraments, and ceremonies is, to say the least, very suspicious. It may be accompanied by immense zeal and a show of earnestness, but it is not sound. The Pharisees paid tithe of mint, anise, and cummin, and compassed sea and land to make proselytes, while they neglected 'judgment, mercy, and faith' (Matthew 23:23).

Hypocrisy is always mean-spirited and dishonest, though it always seeks to make a show of gentleness, meekness, and brotherly love. These Jews knew that the Lord Jesus had done nothing amiss, that he was completely innocent of all their trumped up and falsified charges. Yet, they said to Pilate, 'If he were not a malefactor, we would not have delivered him up unto thee' (v. 30).

Envy and covetousness, and jealousy and greed are always the motives by which hypocrites are moved to action. The Jews who thirsted for Christ's blood feared the defilement of a Roman judgment hall, and made much ado about keeping the passover! They were moved by envy, covetousness, jealousy and greed. Let their conduct be a beacon to Christians as long as the world stands. That religion is worth nothing which does not make us say with David, 'I esteem all thy precepts concerning all things to be right, and I hate every false way' (Psalms 119:128). That Christianity is worthless which supplants heart worship, heart faith, and heart devotion with an outward show.

God's saints are not hypocrites, but men and women who worship and serve God and one another in sincerity and truth (Philippians 3:3). True faith is 'faith which worketh by love'. 'Man looketh on the outward appearance.' 'The Lord looketh on the heart'!

Prophecy Fulfilled

Second, God's overruling providence compelled the Jews, as they were scheming to crucify the Lord of glory, to bear witness to him whom they crucified (vv. 31, 32).

'Then said Pilate unto them, Take ye him, and judge him according to your law. The Jews therefore said unto him, It is not lawful for us to put any man to death: That the saying of Jesus might be fulfilled, which he spake, signifying what death he should die' (John 18:31, 32).

In verse 31, by acknowledging that they were not allowed by Roman law to execute a criminal, the Jewish Sanhedrim acknowledged that the sceptre of civil government had departed from Judah, and that the time of the Redeemer's revelation had come (Genesis 49:10).

'The sceptre shall not depart from Judah, nor a lawgiver from between his feet, until Shiloh come; and unto him shall the gathering of the people be.'

'Shiloh' is one of the names by which the Messiah was called in the Old Testament. It means 'quiet', 'peaceable', and 'prosperous'. What a great name for our Saviour, who came to make peace between God and men by the blood of his cross! He and he alone gives peace to men. He obtained peace for us. He gives peace to us. He is our Peace!

In verse 32 we are told that the Jews did everything they did with regard to our Saviour's crucifixion, 'That the saying of Jesus might be fulfilled, signifying what death he should die.' Our Lord Jesus repeatedly told his disciples that he must be delivered by the Jews into the hands of the Gentiles, that he might be lifted up from the earth, as the serpent upon the pole (Matthew 20:19; John 12:32, 33, 3:14-16). The Lord God brought it to pass. Both the Jews and the Romans did exactly what the Lord decreed and said they would do, no more and no less.

Spiritual Kingdom

Third, in verses 33-36 our Lord Jesus shows us clearly that his kingdom is altogether spiritual.

'Then Pilate entered into the judgment hall again, and called Jesus, and said unto him, Art thou the King of the Jews? Jesus answered him, Sayest thou this thing of thyself, or did others tell it thee of me? Pilate answered, Am I a Jew? Thine own nation and the chief priests have delivered thee unto me: what hast thou done? Jesus answered, My kingdom is not of this world: if my kingdom were of this world, then would my servants fight, that I should not be delivered to the Jews: but now is my kingdom not from hence' (John 18:33-36).

That is what the Son of God himself has to say about the kingdom of God. His kingdom is not of this world. It is not a carnal, political, civil kingdom. It is not established by worldly power or worldly means. It is not like any earthly kingdom. The kingdom of God is altogether spiritual.

Almost everything we hear preachers say or read from the writings of men about the kingdom of God is totally false. All the popular books about the coming of the kingdom of God and the end of the world promote nothing but carnal notions about future things. Almost everything to be found in the notes of reference Bibles and study Bibles about prophetic things is false. Obviously, I have not read them all; but I have read a few, and I have not yet read even one that sets forth the teaching of holy scripture about the kingdom of God. I urge you to ignore such religious tomfoolery.

And if what I have to say here is not verified by the word of God, count what I say as nothing more than religious tomfoolery. I will go further than that. If what I have to say to you in these chapters is not exactly what God says in his word about his kingdom, ignore me and count what I say as nothing more than religious nonsense.

In Luke our Lord Jesus was accosted by the Pharisees questioning him about his kingdom; and he answered them plainly.

'And when he was demanded of the Pharisees, when the kingdom of God should come, he answered them and said, The kingdom of God cometh not with observation: Neither shall they say, Lo here! or, lo there! for, behold, the kingdom of God is within you. And he said unto the disciples, The days will come, when ye shall desire to see one of the days of the Son of man, and ye shall not see it. And they shall say to you, See here; or, see there: go not after them, nor follow them. For as the lightning, that lighteneth out of the one part under heaven, shineth unto the other part under heaven; so shall also the Son of man be in his day. But first must he suffer many things, and be rejected of this generation' (Luke 17:20-25).

Everything the Pharisees asked our Lord was asked with an evil motive. They never asked anything that they might learn, but only that they might accuse the Lord Jesus of some evil by twisting his words, or deride our Saviour's doctrine. But here, they went even further; they 'demanded' him! What arrogance! What presumption! What hellishness of heart is exposed when sinful men dare to demand anything from the God of glory! Yet, those who made this demand pretended to be the only true worshippers of God!

The word translated 'demanded' means 'accosted' or 'interrogated'. All the Jews, including the Pharisees, were looking for the coming of the kingdom of God. They were looking for the promised Messiah to come and establish his kingdom on earth, making them the rulers over all the world. But this demand has the tone of derision in it. It is as if they said, 'You tell us you are the Messiah, the Son of God, the King. If that is true, where is the kingdom? Do you really expect anyone to believe that such a poor, common man, a man known to keep company with sinners is the Christ of God? How long do you expect us to wait for this kingdom of yours to appear?'

Our Lord Jesus seized the occasion given him by their derision to teach his own disciples and all future disciples some blessed gospel truths. First, he says, 'The kingdom of God cometh not with observation' (v. 20). I can almost picture the puzzled look of utter ignorance upon the faces of those ignorant Pharisees. Our Lord answered these fools according to their folly, only to make them more ignorant, only to give them greater confusion.

Yet, he was at the same time teaching his own disciples who were in the crowd that day, and teaching his disciples of all future days. How Peter, James, and John must have perked up their ears. Mary Magdalene, I am sure, came to a dead silence. 'The kingdom of God cometh not with observation'.

What does that mean? It means that the kingdom of God is not at all like any earthly kingdom. The coming of the kingdom of God cannot be observed by the eye, by watching for signs, marking dates, measuring time, or checking off fulfilled prophecy. Its presence cannot be observed by carnal means, because it is not carnal, but spiritual. Those who expect to observe anything of this kind are sure to be disappointed. They wait and watch in vain for a carnal, material kingdom that will never come, just as the Pharisees did. The Lord Jesus says, 'The kingdom of God cometh not with observation'. These three things, at least, are meant by our Redeemer's words.

The kingdom of God does not come with pomp and pageantry. It does not come with an outward show of any kind. In fact, the translation given in the margin of your Bible is, 'The kingdom of God cometh not with outward show'. The kingdom of God does not come in such a way that men can observe it. God's kingdom is a kingdom no one can see, except he be born again. It is a kingdom none can enter, but by the new birth (John 3:3, 5). No one can discern anything at all about this kingdom, except those who are taught of God and have the mind of Christ (John 3:1-8; 1 Corinthians 2:12-16).

Our Lord's words in Luke 17:20 also mean, perhaps primarily mean, that the Kingdom of God does not come by the observation of religious laws, ceremonies, traditions, and ordinances. The kingdom of God does not come by observing holy days and doing holy things. You do not get into the kingdom of God by receiving imaginary sacraments and doing imaginary good works. The kingdom of God is not a matter of religious dos and taboos (Romans 14:17; Colossians 2:20-23). The fact is, if you and I see something that so impresses our eyes, our natural senses and feelings that we are inclined to think, 'Surely, the kingdom of God is here', we are wrong, dead wrong.

Christ's Mission

Fourth, in verse 37 of John 18, our Saviour declares his mission. 'Pilate therefore said unto him, Art thou a king then? Jesus answered, Thou sayest that I am a king. To this end was I born, and for this cause came I into the world, that I should bear witness unto the truth. Every one that is of the truth heareth my voice'. He was born at Bethlehem to die in the place of his people upon Mount Calvary. He came into the world to bear witness of the truth: the whole gospel, the word of truth. He came to show us the glory of God, to show us God himself. He came to show us how God can be just and justify the ungodly. He came here to glorify the triune God in the salvation of his people (Matthew

1:21). The Son of God came 'to save sinners, of whom I am chief'. Everyone who is of the truth, of God, born of God and taught of God, hears his voice.

Pilate's Declaration

Fifth, Pilate asserts publicly that our blessed Redeemer is without fault. 'Pilate saith unto him, What is truth? And when he had said this, he went out again unto the Jews, and saith unto them, I find in him no fault at all' (v. 38).

First, Pilate asked a sneering, scoffing question. 'What is truth?' he seems to say, as almost all men do today, 'There is no such thing as truth. Truth is one thing to you and another thing to me. No man can tell another man that which is truth'! But that is not the case. 'All the paths of the Lord are mercy and truth' (Psalms 25:10). The scriptures speak repeatedly of 'thy truth', as if to tell us that all truth is wrapped up in one thing. 'For thy mercy is great unto the heavens, and thy truth unto the clouds' (Psalms 57:10). Christ is the Way, the Truth, and the Life. He is the Truth that sprang out of the earth in his incarnation, in his resurrection, and in his ascension (Psalms 85:10, 11). Christ is the Truth by whom and in whom, by whom and with whom God is known.

Then, though he was but a scoffing pagan, Pilate was compelled by God to confess our Saviour's perfect innocence before the law. 'I find in him no fault at all'! He who is our Passover Sacrifice was and must be altogether without fault before the law. Only he who was holy, harmless, undefiled, and separate from sinners could be made sin for us and make us the righteousness of God by the sacrifice of himself.

Substitution Portrayed

Sixth, this chapter closes with a clear, instructive picture of substitution (vv. 39, 40). Here is a picture of the Truth.

'But ye have a custom, that I should release unto you one at the passover: will ye therefore that I release unto you the King of the Jews? Then cried they all again, saying, Not this man, but Barabbas. Now Barabbas was a robber' (John 18:39, 40).

Barabbas was a robber. So are we! You and I have robbed God of his glory and our souls of life and happiness. The Son of God died in Barabbas' place, crucified by wicked hands and slain. Blessed be his name forever, the Son of God died in the place of sinners! Barabbas was released at the passover, when the Lord Jesus died in his place. So were we.

What is truth? This is Truth: God saves sinners by the sacrifice of his own darling Son. He does so justly and righteously, in strict accordance with truth (Galatians 3:13; 1 Peter 2:24; 3:18; 2 Corinthians 5:21). And grace reigns 'through righteousness unto eternal life by Jesus Christ our Lord' (Romans 5:20, 21).

Chapter 53

'Pilate sought to release him'

'Then Pilate therefore took Jesus, and scourged him. And the soldiers platted a crown of thorns, and put it on his head, and they put on him a purple robe, And said, Hail, King of the Jews! and they smote him with their hands. Pilate therefore went forth again, and saith unto them, Behold, I bring him forth to you, that ye may know that I find no fault in him. Then came Jesus forth, wearing the crown of thorns, and the purple robe. And Pilate saith unto them, Behold the man! When the chief priests therefore and officers saw him, they cried out, saying, Crucify him, crucify him. Pilate saith unto them, Take ye him, and crucify him: for I find no fault in him. The Jews answered him, We have a law, and by our law he ought to die, because he made himself the Son of God. When Pilate therefore heard that saying, he was the more afraid; And went again into the judgment hall, and saith unto Jesus, Whence art thou? But Jesus gave him no answer. Then saith Pilate unto him, Speakest thou not unto me? knowest thou not that I have power to crucify thee, and have power to release thee? Jesus answered, Thou couldest have no power at all against me, except it were given thee from above: therefore he that delivered me unto thee hath the greater sin. And from thenceforth Pilate sought to release him: but the Jews cried out, saying, If thou let this man go, thou art not Caesar's friend: whosoever maketh himself a king speaketh against Caesar' (John 19:1-12).

In John 19:12 God the Holy Spirit tells us that 'Pilate sought to release' the Lord Jesus. Pilate was the man who signed the order of execution; but the Spirit of God tells us that 'Pilate sought to release him'. Pilate had no regard for God or for the things of God; but 'Pilate sought to release him'. Without Pilate's order the Lord Jesus would not have been crucified; but Pilate gave the order. Still, 'Pilate sought to release him'. When I read those words, I have to ask, 'Why, then, did Pilate issue the order of execution? Why did Pilate have the Lord of glory crucified?' Only one answer can be given. God ordained it before the world began and brought it to pass in providence.

Let all who read these lines understand that throughout this scene, indeed, throughout every scene of history, it is always the will of God that rules, never the will and devices of men.

God's Sovereignty

There are countless illustrations of God's absolute sovereignty in the holy scriptures. Everywhere the book of God shouts, 'The heavens do rule'! But nothing so marvellously and wondrously sets forth God's absolute sovereignty as his sacrifice of his darling Son in the place of sinners at Calvary.

The triune God purposed to save his people by the slaughter of our Lord Jesus Christ upon the cursed tree before the worlds were made. The Lord God sovereignly ordered all the affairs of providence to bring it to pass, exactly according to his eternal purpose, by Pilate's hand (Acts 4:27, 28). When our Lord's hour had come, when the due time had arrived when God would commend his love toward us in the sacrifice of his darling Son, Pilate gave the order and the hellish deed was performed. The Son of God was murdered by the hands of wicked men! Thus, by the sacrifice of himself, the Lamb of God obtained eternal redemption for sinners.

If you would have that salvation that Christ obtained by the shedding of his own precious blood, trust him. Believe on the Son of God and that salvation is yours. Faith is the evidence of redemption and of redemption applied.

I repeat, nothing displays God's glorious sovereignty like the wondrous accomplishment of redemption by Christ. And, perhaps, the one aspect of our Lord's crucifixion that shows God's sovereign character as God is the fact that Pilate, the Roman governor of Judea, gave the order of crucifixion. Let us look at the record given in this passage of Inspiration.

Here we see our Lord Jesus Christ in Pilate's judgment hall. This passage presents us with a very strange event. Here the Judge of all the earth stands to be judged of wicked men! He that shall soon judge the world in righteousness is judged most unrighteously! He that shall one day sit upon the throne of judgment with ten thousands of his saints and angels, stands as a prisoner before the bar of men!

Justice Perverted

Never in the pages of history was justice so violently and deliberately abused. The Son of God was denied the rights of justice given to a common thief or murderer. Before one witness was produced to testify against him, before any evidence was weighed, the Lord of glory was beaten, mocked, stripped, and abused by the vile hatred of men.

Who can comprehend the depths of humiliation endured by the God-man? That One 'Who, being in the form of God thought it not robbery to be equal with God', now 'made himself of no reputation, and took upon him the form of a servant, and was made in the likeness of men: And being found in fashion as a man, he humbled himself, and became obedient unto death, even the death of the cross'!

Judas made good on his bargain to betray our Lord. No sooner did he kiss the Saviour than the chief priests and Pharisees had Christ's hands bound and led him away. These wolves of the night thirsted for the blood of the Lamb of God. Their malice would not allow any delay. They could not sleep until they had his precious, innocent blood. Therefore, they resolved to kill him as soon as possible. But, so that it would not look like downright murder, they formalized it with a trial. You are familiar with the story.

Sequence Of Events

Let me remind you of the events of that night. Our Redeemer was arrested in the Garden of Gethsemane and hurried along the road which crosses the brook Kidron. Like David, who passed over that brook weeping as he went, our great David passed over the brook weeping as he went. The brook Kidron was that into which all the filth of the Temple sacrifices was thrown. And our dear Saviour walked through that black stream as though he were some foul and filthy thing. He was led into Jerusalem by the sheep-gate, the gate through which the lambs of the Passover were always led. Little did those men understand that they were fulfilling to the very letter those types which God had ordained by the Law of Moses. These wicked men led the Lamb of God to slaughter.

May the Lord himself sanctify our hearts as we follow our Redeemer through his trial and cruel mockery. First, they led Immanuel to the house of Annas, the ex-high priest. There they made a brief call to gratify the blood thirsty wretch with the sight of his victim. Then they hurriedly brought the Son of God to the house of Caiaphas. There the members of the Sanhedrim were assembled, to take counsel against the Lord and against his Anointed. Third, they dragged the Lamb of God through the streets to Pilate's judgment hall. There they sought a legal sentence of execution to be pronounced upon the Lord of glory. Fourth, Pilate sent the crowd to Herod, the governor of Galilee. Finally, the Lord of glory is returned to Pilate's judgment hall. Here he was tried, beaten, mocked, and sentenced to die. This is where we find him in John 19:1-12.

Pilate Overruled

You will not find a more striking and vivid demonstration of God's absolute sovereignty than in Pilate's treatment of the Lord Jesus. First, Pilate was assured of his innocence, acknowledging no less than seven times, 'I find no fault in him'. Second, Pilate desired to release him (Luke 23:20, 22; John 19:12; Acts 3:13). 'Third, Pilate's wife urged him not to sentence the Lord Jesus, but to let him go (Matthew 27:19). Fourth, Pilate tried to bring about his acquittal, telling the Jews to judge him themselves (John 18:31). He sent him to Herod, only for Christ to be returned (Luke 23:7). He tried to get the Jews to have him execute Barabbas (John 18:39, 40). Yet, in the end, Pilate sentenced the Lord of glory to be crucified! Why? Because thus it was ordained from eternity!

Man's will is nothing, when it runs contrary to of God's will! Here was Pilate, the Roman governor of Judea, determined to release the Saviour. Yet, he was prevented from doing so. From all eternity God had decreed that Pilate would sentence his Son to death; and all earth and hell combined could not thwart the purpose of the Almighty. He would not be all-mighty if they could! The Lord Jesus Christ, our Saviour, was 'delivered by the determinate counsel and foreknowledge of God' (Acts 2:23).

As God's servant, Peter fearlessly announced, 'Both Herod and Pontius Pilate, with the Gentiles, and the people of Israel, were gathered together for to do whatsoever thy hand and thy counsel determined before to be done' (Acts 4:27, 28). This is not simply 'Calvinism', it is the explicit declaration of holy scripture; and woe be unto the one who dares to deny it. As Arthur Pink put it: 'Christ had to be sentenced by Pilate because the eternal counsels of Deity had foreordained it'. The Lord Jesus died for sinners both of the Jews and of the Gentiles. Therefore divine wisdom determined that both Jews and Gentiles have a direct hand in his death.

Many object to this. We are told, 'Such doctrine reduces Pilate to a mere robot'! Were that the case, so be it. It is far, far better to reduce a man to a robot than to deny the word of the living God and reduce the Almighty to something less than man. Whether we understand the teaching of scripture or not, it is not ours to argue with or alter the word of God, but to bow in absolute submission to the teaching of the holy scriptures.

Pilate's Responsibility

Yes, God is sovereign, always, everywhere, and in all things. Yet, every man is totally responsible for his own sin. The Gospel records present Pilate to us as a man responsible for his crimes against God. The Lord Jesus addressed himself to Pilate's conscience. 'Everyone that is of the truth heareth my voice'

(John 18:37). God faithfully warned him that the Saviour was a just Man and to do nothing against him (Matthew 27:19). Finally, the Saviour himself told Pilate that he was sinning in holding him (John 19:11).

See that you understand the teaching of holy scripture in this regard. God is absolutely sovereign; and man is fully responsible. Let me show you four things in this passage of holy scripture.

Christ Mocked

First, in verses 1-3, the Spirit of God reminds us of our Saviour's scourging and mockery as our Substitute.

'Then Pilate therefore took Jesus, and scourged him. And the soldiers platted a crown of thorns, and put it on his head, and they put on him a purple robe, And said, Hail, King of the Jews! And they smote him with their hands'.

Having failed in his attempt to release the Lord Jesus by forcing the Jews to choose between him and Barabbas, Pilate ordered the Lord to be scourged; stripped naked, tied to a post, and severely whipped. It appears from verse 12 that Pilate thought that the Jews might be satisfied with that torturous procedure. 'And from thenceforth Pilate sought to release him: but the Jews cried out, saying, If thou let this man go, thou art not Caesar's friend: whosoever maketh himself a king speaketh against Caesar'. Let us never forget that even here, in Pilate's judgment hall, our dear Saviour endured all that he endured as our Substitute, in our room and place (Psalms 89:30-34; Isaiah 53:5).

This scourging was followed by a mock coronation in the soldiers' hall (Matthew 27:26-31). The soldiers wanted to torture him and to mock him, particularly mocking the fact that he was said to be 'the King of the Jews'. The cruel, thorny crown served both purposes. No doubt, that crown of thorns reaches back to Genesis 3:18 in connection with the thorns and thistles promised Adam's sons as a result of the fall. Our blessed Lord 'bore our sins in his own body on the tree'. And, when he was made sin for us, the curse of our sins was made his. He became a curse for us! 'Christ hath redeemed us from the curse of the law, being made a curse for us: for it is written, Cursed is every one that hangeth on a tree' (Galatians 3:13).

Then the soldiers threw a purple robe over his shoulders, put a reed in his hand to represent a king's sceptre (Genesis 49:10), and mockingly marched around him, beating him with their fists, spitting upon him, and saying, 'Hail, King of the Jews'!

Our Saviour was delivered to Pilate charged with making himself King. He was mocked by the soldiers as a king, and he was crucified with this charge written over his head, 'The King of the Jews'. He is indeed the King of kings and Lord of lords. He is owned, received, and acknowledged as such by all who are saved by his grace (Romans 10:9, 10). And one day every creature in heaven, earth, and hell will bow before him and acknowledge him as King of kings and Lord of lords (Philippians 2:9-11).

Innocence Proclaimed

Second, our Saviour's perfect innocence is publicly proclaimed. 'Pilate therefore went forth again, and saith unto them, Behold, I bring him forth to you, that ye may know that I find no fault in him' (v. 4). Pilate was a troubled, confused man. He was afraid of this man, Jesus Christ (Matthew 27:19). He did not want to get the Jews stirred up against him. He was worried that word of this tumult might reach Caesar's ears and endanger his position. When he found no fault in the Lord Jesus, knowing the Jews had an evil motive in the whole affair (Matthew 27:18), he tried one more scheme. Pilate went out before the people and said, 'Behold, I bring him forth to you, that ye may know that I find no fault in him'. I remind you that Pilate publicly proclaimed our Saviour's innocence no less than seven times (John 18:38; 19:4; 19:6 cf. Exodus 12:5; Deuteronomy 17:1; 1 Peter 1:18-20).

Pilate's Fear

Third, we see the judge and executioner trembling before the One he condemned (vv. 6-9).

'When the chief priests therefore and officers saw him, they cried out, saying, Crucify him, crucify him. Pilate saith unto them, Take ye him, and crucify him: for I find no fault in him. The Jews answered him, We have a law, and by our law he ought to die, because he made himself the Son of God. When Pilate therefore heard that saying, he was the more afraid; And went again into the judgment hall, and saith unto Jesus, Whence art thou? But Jesus gave him no answer.'

It was not the people, but the chief priests and officers of the temple who cried, 'Crucify him! Crucify him'! These were men who made great pretensions to piety and religion. They were the religious leaders of the nation. How wicked is the unregenerate heart, especially when it is clothed in religious garb!

Pilate said, 'You crucify him, for I find no fault in him.' Again, Pilate declared our Lord's innocence. By means of this wretched, worthless, wishy-washy politician, our God declared the innocence and holiness of our Lord Jesus Christ (1 Peter 2:21, 22; Isaiah 53:9, 10). Our Savour is the perfect man, bone of our bone and flesh of our flesh, tempted in all points as we are, yet without sin. As such he is our Representative and our Righteousness before God (Romans 5:19; 1 Peter 3:18). In his holy life he honoured the law of God for us; and in his death he satisfied divine justice (Romans 4:25).

The Jews knew exactly what our Lord Jesus claimed about his eternal deity. Liberals, Mormons, Russellites, and others may not be able to discern the meaning of his words, but the Jews did. They understood perfectly what the Lord Jesus had said to them (John 10:30-33). He declared himself to be God; and according to the law, if he were not God, as he claimed, he was to be put to death.

On top of all his other doubts and fears, this new revelation caused Pilate to be terrified. He must have thought, 'Is it possible that this Man is related to deity?' He remembered his wife's dream and her warning. He knew that the Lord Jesus was innocent. He had heard of his life and miracles. He had to have been impressed with the Lord's conduct throughout this whole affair. So Pilate took the Saviour back into the judgment hall and asked, 'Where are you from?' But Christ gave him no answer. He deserved no answer! He had totally ignored every word our Lord spoke, compromised justice by scourging an innocent man, and had no other motive through it all except his own welfare.

Our Saviour gave Pilate no answer, because he did not wish to escape the cross. He was willing to die for us, as our sin-atoning Substitute (Isaiah 53:7).

Sovereignty Asserted

Fourth, our Lord Jesus, even as he stood before Pilate as a common malefactor, wrongfully accused and unjustly condemned, asserted God's sovereignty over his judge and executioner (vv. 10-12).

'Then saith Pilate unto him, Speakest thou not unto me? Knowest thou not that I have power to crucify thee, and have power to release thee? Jesus answered, Thou couldest have no power at all against me, except it were given thee from above: therefore he that delivered me unto thee hath the greater sin. And from thenceforth Pilate sought to release him: but the Jews cried out, saying, If thou let this man go, thou art not Caesar's friend: whosoever maketh himself a king speaketh against Caesar.'

Pilate's reply is natural. He is fearful and afraid. His conscience is troubling him. His whole domain is up in arms over this one Man; and being totally confused at the serenity and calmness of this Jesus, who refuses to defend himself while facing death on a cruel cross, he cried, 'Do you stand in silence and refuse to answer me when you know that I have the power to crucify you or release you? How dare you! Do you know who I am and what power I have?' Our Lord replied, 'You could have no power or authority over me at all, except the power my Father gives to you' (John 3:27; Acts 4:26-28).

Our Lord was saying that Pilate, as Pharaoh, was an instrument used by God to accomplish his purpose and glory, nothing more (Romans 9:17). Robert Hawker rightly observed, 'Jesus looked over the heads of all his foes, to eye the hand of Jehovah in this appointment. And it would be always well for you and for me, and for all the Lord's people to do the same, in all the lesser considerations we meet with in life.'

Pilate's sin was great; but the greater sin belonged to these religious leaders who so grossly sinned against the scriptures they claimed to believe and the light God had given as they heard the Lord Jesus Christ speak (Luke 12:47, 48). Israel knew the scriptures concerning Messiah; Pilate did not; and the 'greater sin' was committed by men who, with the scriptures in their hands, had greater light.

Be warned! Do not heap upon yourself the greater condemnation by trampling underfoot the blood of the Son of God, by crucifying the Lord Jesus afresh by your wilful unbelief!

Pilate's power was God-given power. Pilate's power was 'from above'. He was the governor of Judea because God made him governor. There is no power that is not of God. 'The powers that be are ordained of God'. The source of all earthly power is heavenly. It is not in man or from man, but from the King of kings, the Prince of the kings of the earth. The God of glory put Pilate in his place when the fulness of time was come, so that his darling Son would be crucified by Roman law, as the scriptures of the Old Testament and our Lord Jesus himself had declared he must be (Acts 2:23; 4:27, 28; 13:26-30, 38-41).

'Pilate sought to release him', but he could not because the Lord, our Saviour, was Jehovah's Righteous Servant, Jehovah's voluntary Bond-slave, who sought no release from service because of his love for his Master, his love for his wife, and his love for his children!

Chapter 54

'Behold the man'!

'Then came Jesus forth, wearing the crown of thorns, and the purple robe. And Pilate saith unto them, Behold the man'! (John 19:5).

Pilate, the cowardly, self-serving governor of Judea, has had the Lord Jesus scourged with a whip and severely beaten by his soldiers. Those soldiers stripped him naked, platted a crown of thorns and shoved it into his holy head, put a purple rag on his immaculate shoulders, and stuck a reed for a mock sceptre in his harmless hands. They mocked him, beat him with their fists, and spit all over him. Then, Pilate brought the Lord Jesus out before the Jews, the chief priests, and the Pharisees. When he did, Pilate said, 'Behold, I bring him forth to you, that ye may know that I find no fault in him' (v. 4). 'Then came Jesus forth, wearing the crown of thorns, and the purple robe. And Pilate saith unto them, Behold the man'!

I call your attention to the fact that the name of Pilate was added by our translators, as indicated by the fact that they put his name in italicized letters. So read the text without the name of Pilate added, and you will get another sense of the text altogether. 'Then came Jesus forth, wearing the crown of thorns, and the purple robe and saith unto them, Behold the man'!

The One speaking here is not Pilate, but the Lord Jesus himself. Pilate spoke in verse 4. 'Pilate therefore went forth again, and saith unto them, Behold, I bring him forth to you, that ye may know that I find no fault in him'. But then, it is our blessed Saviour who speaks. He who stood before Pilate in silence, he who spoke not a word to defend himself before the Jews, the chief priests, the Pharisees, the Roman soldiers, or Pilate, when he stepped forth before that crowd of guilty sinners whose hands dripped with his own precious blood, 'wearing the crown of thorns and the purple robe', said 'Behold the Man'! Here, standing before you is the Man you said you have been looking for, the Man of God's appointing, the Man of whom all the scriptures speak. 'Behold the Man'!

Standing before this God-hating, satanically inspired mob of blood-thirsty religious men, men who were about to execute the most violent, lawless deed of history, is the Man for whom the world was made. The Man stood before them, who for three years had healed the sick and done deeds of mercy and kindness, who had revealed his supernatural power as God in countless displays of mercy. These men cried 'Give us the murderer Barabbas! Crucify the Man, crucify him'! And here he stands. His bleeding shoulders covered by the purple robe. His head crowned with thorns. His visage marred and smitten beyond recognition. 'Behold the Man'! That is the message of this book; and that is my message. It is the message God has sent his servants to proclaim to a lost world. 'Behold the Man'!

The Lord Jesus Christ is the Man of whom all the scriptures speak, the Man by whom the triune God saves fallen men.

Bible's Message

'Behold the Man'! It is the great message of the Bible. God's revelation to man is all about one Man, the mediator Man, the God-man, the Man Christ Jesus. From Genesis to Revelation, God says, 'Behold the Man'! Throughout the book of God, our Saviour calls upon his chosen to behold him, to look to him in faith, to trust him, saying again and again, 'Behold the Man' (Judges 13:10, 11; Ezekiel 9:11; Zechariah 6:12, 13).

Throughout the Old Testament, as in the New, the triune Jehovah calls for us to behold this Man, who is God our Saviour. God the Father says, 'Behold the Man' (Isaiah 42:1-4; Matthew 12:18). God the Son says, 'Behold the Man' (Isaiah 65:1; 45:20-22) And God the Holy Ghost says, 'Behold the Man' (John 1:29, 36).

When the Lord Jesus came forth before the high priests and rulers of Israel, having given his back to the scourging and his cheeks to them that plucked off the hair, as the Prophet said he would, the Man Christ Jesus calls upon the multitude standing before him to 'Behold the Man'! Yet, as the Prophet Isaiah also prophesied, he was 'despised and rejected of men' (Isaiah 53:3).

May the Lord God pour upon you and upon me the Spirit of grace and supplication, that we may 'Behold the Man' for sinners slain and live forever in the sweet awareness of his mercy, love, and grace (Zechariah 12:10; 13:1). 'Behold the Man'!

The Covenant Man

Behold our Lord Jesus Christ, the Covenant Man. He stood forth from everlasting as our covenant Surety, in whose image the first man Adam was made. Yes, I know that our Lord's human nature was created in time. His human body and soul were not from everlasting. Yet, he stood forth as our Covenant Head and Surety before the world began. We were from everlasting accepted and blessed of God in him (Ephesians 1:3-7).

The Promised Man

Behold the Lord Jesus, our Divine Saviour, as he is set before us as the promised Man of the Old Testament scriptures. Read the Book of Genesis, and 'Behold the Man'! In the first chapter of Genesis, the earth was brought out of the deep waters of darkness, chaos, death, and judgment (Genesis 1:1-3). Then, at God's command, the earth brought forth vegetation and animal creation. All was garnished with beauty and glory. Finally, on the sixth day of creation, the Lord God created man in the person of our father Adam, and placed him in the Garden of Eden. The Lord God brought forth, out of the dust of the earth and by the breath of his Spirit, by direct creation, a creature which is his offspring. He said, 'Let us make man in our image, and after our own likeness;' and he did it.

All three persons in the eternal Godhead were involved in this creative act. And one of the three, God the Son, knew that at an appointed day, 'in due time', 'when the fulness of time was come', he would take upon himself the nature of that man he created. He is the image of God in whose image Adam was created.

Adam was not a cave-man. He was not a ferocious half-ape, half-man. Adam was not an unintelligent brute. Adam was created in the image of God, filled with wisdom and knowledge. He possessed far greater knowledge than we have ever imagined. He had names for every beast of the field and of the forest. Without a moment's hesitation he named them. Tell me what thousand men together could do so today!

Not only was he brilliant and physically perfect, Adam lived every day in sweet fellowship with the triune God. He enjoyed God's presence all the time, and reigned as king over all the earth.

But soon the scene changed. Adam sinned. He abandoned God in an act of angry rebellion. And fallen man was cursed, cast out of the Garden, and sentenced to death. Doomed to live, generation after generation, under the curse of the fall, in sin, in the sweat of his brow, upon an earth cursed with briars, and thorns, and rocks, and pain, and sickness, and death! There is man: fallen, stripped, lost, ever running and hiding from God! Deeper and deeper he sinks. Sin drags him lower and lower. Darker becomes the night.

But will the Lord God leave him there? Just before he drove Adam and Eve out of the Garden, he promised a Man, a Man to be born of a virgin, the woman's Seed, by whom he would redeem and save his people. 'And I will put enmity between thee and the woman, and between thy seed and her seed; it shall bruise thy head, and thou shalt bruise his heel' (Genesis 3:15). Then the Lord God showed the fallen pair how he would save them by that Man, Christ Jesus, whom he would send into the world. 'Unto Adam also and to his wife did the LORD God make coats of skins, and clothed them' (Genesis 3:21).

From that day on, chosen men, called by grace, lived by faith in that Man who was to come, in and by whom redemption must be accomplished. Throughout the ages of Old Testament history and throughout the writings of Israel's prophets, the Lord God, that is, the Lord Jesus Christ, stood forth, as he did at last in Pilate's judgment hall, and said, 'Behold the Man'! In prophetic promises and redemption prophecies, the Lord God pointed fallen man to the last Man, the Seed of the woman, and for four thousand years cried out to fallen, guilty sinners, 'Behold the Man'! 'Behold My Servant'! 'Behold the Branch'! 'Behold the King'! 'Behold Immanuel'!

'Behold the Man'! God comes down to man as a man, to suffer, to die, to take sin upon himself, to be the Sin Bearer and Sin Offering for his people! 'Behold he cometh', the Lamb of God, to take away sin and sorrow, the curse and the crying, the guilt and the shame, the ruin and the death that plagues fallen man! He comes, that Man, to undo all that the first man Adam did, to restore that which he took not away! 'Behold the Man'! That is the message of the book of God. The Man comes, the One from above, the deathless One, the One who was, and is, and is to come, 'Behold the Man' comes to suffer death and to conquer death, hell, and the grave by the sacrifice of himself, to put away sin by being made sin, to remove the curse by being made a curse! 'Behold the Man'!

The God-Man

Read the first chapter of John's Gospel, and behold the Man again. Here we behold him as the God-man.

'In the beginning was the Word, and the Word was with God, and the Word was God. The same was in the beginning with God. All things were made by him; and without him was not any thing made that was made' (John 1:1-3).

'And the Word was made flesh, and dwelt among us, (and we beheld his glory, the glory as of the only begotten of the Father,) full of grace and truth' (John 1:14).

If there is any verse in the Bible marked with the special emphasis by God the Holy Spirit, surely it is John 1:14. Every word is of immense importance. Here is the glorious person so highly spoken of in the preceding 13 verses of this chapter. The Word who is God is declared to be 'made flesh'. God the Son was 'made flesh'.

The word translated 'flesh' is very strong. The same word is used in Romans 3:20, where we are told no flesh can be justified by the deeds of the law. In Romans 8:3 Christ is said to have been made 'in the likeness of sinful flesh'. The word here translated 'flesh' has the same significance as the Hebrew words used in Genesis 6:12 to speak of 'corrupt' flesh. John could not have used a stronger, more emphatic word to speak of our Saviour's great condescension and humiliation in assuming our nature. Had John merely said, 'The Word was made man', the meaning would not have been so emphatic a declaration of degradation. (Philippians 2:5-8).

'The Word was made flesh'! The Son of God was made what we are, made to be our full nature, body and soul, a complete man. He who is God became man. He did not cease to be God; but he took our human nature into union with his divine nature, so that the Lord Jesus Christ is God and Man, the God-man, our Mediator. 'The Word was made flesh', as Augustine put it in the fourth century, 'Not by changing what he was, but by taking what he was not.' This union of God and Man in one person is indissoluble and forever. Jesus Christ our Saviour, our God-man Mediator is 'the same yesterday, and today, and forever' (Hebrews 13:8).

I have no idea what the length, breadth, height or depth of what I am about to say is; but I cannot help linking these words to those of the Apostle Paul in Ephesians 5:30. 'The Word was made flesh;' and 'we are members of his body, of his flesh, and of his bones'! So is it now, so it has been in all ages of the Church, and so it shall be forever! 'For ye know the grace of our Lord Jesus Christ, that, though he was rich, yet for your sakes he became poor, that ye through his poverty might be rich' (2 Corinthians 8:9).

The Representative Man

As we open the word of God and behold the man Christ Jesus, we have understood nothing until we have been made to see and trust that he is the Representative Man. Oh, may God the Holy Spirit teach you this. 'Behold the Man', the Representative Man, our Saviour!

'Behold the Man'! Thus speaks the Holy Spirit of God in the Gospels. Behold him in his submission to the will of God. Behold him in the display of his power. Listen to his words of eternal life. Behold him in his sinlessness, his perfection, and his loveliness.

But he came for something greater than to live on earth as the perfect man and make the invisible One visible in his person. John the Baptist in his God-given witness states the great truth. 'Behold the Lamb of God which taketh away the sin of the world.' 'Behold the Man' in his life of obedience as our

Representative, bringing in everlasting righteousness. And 'Behold the Man' in his agony, sufferings, and death, as he was made sin for us that we might be made the righteousness of God in him. 'Behold the Man' our Substitute and Surety (Romans 5:12, 18, 19; 5:20, 21; 1 Corinthians 15:21, 22).

'Behold the Man' in Gethsemane. The first man was in a garden of delight, the last Man must also go into a garden, a garden of grief. It is Gethsemane, the garden of sorrow and bloody sweat. We hear the weeping and the wailing, the strong cries and the tears (Hebrews 5). 'Behold the Man' in agony, sweating blood! Now he is what he said in Psalms 22, 'I am a worm, and no man'! The Man of life and glory becomes the willing captive of cruel men.

'Behold the Man' at Gabbatha. After all the dishonour done to him, the cruel scourging, they look upon him with hearts filled with satanic hatred. Here in John 19, we see the Lord Jesus suffering horrid reproach still. Here, at Gabbatha, the Son of God was assaulted by men, by sinners, by the will and the hands of foul, wicked men. Here, at Gabbatha, at Pilate's judgment hall, the Lord Jesus, who was betrayed by his own familiar friend in Gethsemane, was scourged (Matthew 27:26). 'The plowers plowed upon my back: they made long their furrows' (Psalms 129:3). He was mocked by the soldiers and crowned with thorns (Matthew 27:26-29). His beard was plucked from his face (Isaiah 50:6). And here he was condemned to die (John 19:13-16). But our Lord's reproach, our reproach, the reproach of our guilt and sin, the reproach which broke his heart was not over yet.

'Behold the Man' on Golgotha. The Man is nailed to the cursed tree. Where was it done? Scripture says, 'Now in the place where he was crucified there was a garden', 'nigh to the city', 'without the gate' (John 19:21, 41; Hebrews 13:12). The crown of thorns is still upon his blessed head, the head which rested in all eternity upon the Father's bosom. He bears the curse. He bears the shame, bearing our sin in his own body. He makes atonement and satisfies God's infinite justice. 'He who knew no sin was made sin for us'. He bows his thorn-crowned head, and his lips give the great shout of victory, 'It is finished'! 'Behold the Man', our sovereign, successful, satisfied Substitute!

'Behold the Man'! 'Behold the Lamb of God'! He has finished his work. Peace has been made by the blood of the cross! 'Behold the Man'! He is the One, the only One who saves. He has made the new and living way into God's glorious presence. 'Behold the Man'! May God give you grace to behold him, to trust him!

The Risen Man

'Behold the Man', the Risen Man, the Lord Jesus Christ, our Saviour. 'And he made his grave with the wicked, and with the rich in his death; because he had done no violence, neither was any deceit in his mouth. Yet it pleased the LORD to bruise him; he hath put him to grief: when thou shalt make his soul an offering for sin, he shall see his seed, he shall prolong his days, and the pleasure of the LORD shall prosper in his hand. He shall see of the travail of his soul, and shall be satisfied: by his knowledge shall my righteous servant justify many; for he shall bear their iniquities. Therefore will I divide him a portion with the great, and he shall divide the spoil with the strong; because he hath poured out his soul unto death: and he was numbered with the transgressors; and he bare the sin of many, and made intercession for the transgressors' (Isaiah 53:9-12).

'Who was delivered for our offences, and was raised again for our justification. Therefore being justified by faith, we have peace with God through our Lord Jesus Christ: By whom also we have access by faith into this grace wherein we stand, and rejoice in hope of the glory of God. And not only so, but we glory in tribulations also: knowing that tribulation worketh patience; And patience, experience; and experience, hope: And hope maketh not ashamed; because the love of God is shed abroad in our hearts by the Holy Ghost which is given unto us. For when we were yet without strength, in due time Christ died for the ungodly. For scarcely for a righteous man will one die: yet peradventure for a good man some would even dare to die. But God commendeth his love toward us, in that, while we were yet sinners, Christ died for us. Much more then, being now justified by his blood, we shall be saved from wrath through him. For if, when we were enemies, we were reconciled to God by the death of his Son, much more, being reconciled, we shall be saved by his life. And not only so, but we also joy in God through our Lord Jesus Christ, by whom we have now received the atonement' (Romans 4:25-5:11).

'Behold the Man'! The grave is empty. There he stands, that Man who had died, Victor over death, hell, and the grave. He has conquered them forever. He is not a spirit, nor a phantom. 'Behold the Man', the Head of the new creation, the Firstborn among many brethren!

The Ascended Man

'Behold the Man', the Ascended Man, our Lord Jesus Christ. We look up. He has ascended upon high. He passed through the heavens. The power of God lifted up the Man and carried him into the third heaven, into the highest height of all the heavens. We look up and see 'Jesus, who was made a little lower than the angels for the suffering of death, crowned with glory and with honour'. He sits there at the right hand of God. Far above all principalities and powers, and every name that is named. Yonder he sits, the Man, the Man who lived, who died, who was buried, and who rose again. O glorious vision! Oh, for faith to see him in that highest glory, having divine assurance that we, redeemed by him, one with him, shall possess with him the glories above. 'Behold the Man'!

Your great High Priest, your loving Advocate with the Father. 'Behold the Man'! The head of the body, the coming Bridegroom. 'Behold the Man' with all power to give eternal life to chosen, redeemed, helpless sinners! 'Behold the Man'! 'He must reign'! 'Behold the Man' interceding as your Advocate on High!

The Coming Man

'Behold the Man', the Coming Man. 'Behold, he cometh with clouds; and every eye shall see him, and they also which pierced him: and all kindreds of the earth shall wail because of him. Even so, Amen' (Revelation 1:7; 2 Thessalonians 1:7-10; 1 Corinthians 15:49-58).

Soon everything is going to be far different. I see the Man, my Redeemer. I see him leaving the Father's side. He arises from his glorious place. He leaves the mediatorial place. He descends once more. He comes to the air, and gives the commanding shout, the shout which opens the graves of his own, the shout which will gather all his saints together to meet him face to face, to receive the travail of his soul. 'Behold the Man'! We shall 'see him as he is, and shall be like him.' Imagine that! What vision it will be! We shall not see him as the mob saw him, at Gabbatha and Golgotha, but we shall see him in all the fulness of all his glory!

With the enthroned Christ, we shall reign as kings forever! The crown rights over the earth are his. The last Man will restore a ruined creation. There will be a great regeneration. His mighty power will banish the curse. His heel has crushed the serpent's head; and he shall bruise Satan under our feet shortly! 'Behold the Man'! He is upon the throne to rule and reign in righteousness. 'Behold the Man'! The covenant Man, the promised Man, the God-Man, the representative Man, the risen Man, the ascended Man, the coming Man!

'Behold the Man' and live forever! 'Behold the Man'! I see the Lord Jesus standing there in the judgment hall, stretching forth his slashed, bruised, bleeding arms, and hear him saying, 'Behold the Man'! Those words are spoken as a call to faith, a call to utter devotion, and a call to holy communion.

Chapter 55

The Crucifixion Of Our Lord

'When Pilate therefore heard that saying, he brought Jesus forth, and sat down in the judgment seat in a place that is called the Pavement, but in the Hebrew, Gabbatha. And it was the preparation of the passover, and about the sixth hour: and he saith unto the Jews, Behold your King! But they cried out, Away with him, away with him, crucify him. Pilate saith unto them, Shall I crucify your King? The chief priests answered, We have no king but Caesar. Then delivered he him therefore unto them to be crucified. And they took Jesus, and led him away. And he bearing his cross went forth into a place called the place of a skull, which is called in the Hebrew Golgotha: Where they crucified him, and two other with him, on either side one, and Jesus in the midst. And Pilate wrote a title, and put it on the cross. And the writing was, JESUS OF NAZARETH THE KING OF THE JEWS. This title then read many of the Jews: for the place where Jesus was crucified was nigh to the city: and it was written in Hebrew, and Greek, and Latin. Then said the chief priests of the Jews to Pilate, Write not, The King of the Jews; but that he said, I am King of the Jews. Pilate answered, What I have written I have written. Then the soldiers, when they had crucified Jesus, took his garments, and made four parts, to every soldier a part; and also his coat: now the coat was without seam, woven from the top throughout. They said therefore among themselves, Let us not rend it, but cast lots for it, whose it shall be: that the scripture might be fulfilled, which saith, They parted my raiment among them, and for my vesture they did cast lots. These things therefore the soldiers did. Now there stood by the cross of Jesus his mother, and his mother's sister, Mary the wife of Cleophas, and Mary Magdalene. When Jesus therefore saw his mother, and the disciple standing by, whom he loved, he saith unto his mother, Woman, behold thy son! Then saith he to the disciple, Behold thy mother! And from that hour that disciple took her unto his own home. After this, Jesus knowing that all things were now accomplished, that the scripture might be fulfilled, saith, I thirst. Now there was set a vessel full of vinegar: and they filled a spunge with vinegar, and put it upon hyssop, and put it to his mouth. When Jesus therefore had received the vinegar, he said, It is finished: and he bowed his head, and gave up the ghost. The Jews therefore, because it was the preparation, that the bodies should not remain upon the cross on the sabbath day, (for that sabbath day was an high day,) besought Pilate that their legs might be broken, and that they might be taken away. Then came the soldiers, and brake the legs of the first, and of the other which was crucified with him. But when they came to Jesus, and saw that he was dead already, they brake not his legs: But one of the soldiers with a spear pierced his side, and forthwith came there out blood and water. And he that saw it bare record, and his record is true: and he knoweth that he saith true, that ye might believe. For these things were done, that the scripture should be fulfilled, A bone of him shall not be broken. And again another scripture saith, They shall look on him whom they pierced' (John 19:13-37).

How great the love of Christ must be! He voluntarily endured all the agonies of Calvary, all the agonies of death as the cursed one of God upon the cursed tree, for the salvation of poor sinners like you and me!

What a horrid, evil thing sin must be! It could not be atoned for, it could not be forgiven, it could not be removed and washed away, not even by God himself, without the sufferings and death of our Lord Jesus Christ as our Substitute.

This part of John's Gospel gives us information about our Saviour's crucifixion and death at Calvary that is not revealed by Matthew, Mark, and Luke. We are not told why one of the other Gospel writers was inspired to include certain things others were inspired to omit; and we do not need to know why. We are content to know that, both in what they recorded and in what they omitted, all four of the Gospel writers (Matthew, Mark, Luke, and John) wrote by inspiration of God.

These verses describe the sufferings of our Lord Jesus Christ when he was made sin for us and hanged upon the cursed tree. John's brief record of our Lord's crucifixion is not to be read casually, but with great thoughtfulness and adoration. This is an inspired record of the most amazing thing in history. It is amazing and marvellous in our eyes when we remember who suffered these things. It was the Lord Jesus Christ, the Son of God, the Lamb of God, the only truly holy and good man ever to live in this world, the incarnate God, our Saviour! It is amazing and marvellous in our eyes when we remember, too, for whom he suffered (Romans 5:6-8), and why. The cause of his great sorrow and agony of body, soul, and spirit was the fact that the Son of God suffered for sin as the sin-bearer. 'Christ died for our sins'!

Gethsemane

We have seen our Saviour's sorrow in Gethsemane, when he prayed three times, 'O my Father, if it be possible, let this cup pass from me: nevertheless not as I will, but as thou wilt'. Such was the shock of his holy soul at the thought and prospect of being made sin that our Redeemer broke out into a sweat of blood. Luke describes it in these words: 'Being in an agony he prayed more earnestly: and his sweat was as it were great drops of blood falling down to the ground' (Luke 22:44).

Gabbatha

We have seen the scourging of Gabbatha, too. Our Lord was condemned in a mockery of justice at Pilate's judgment hall, called Gabbatha. There he was delivered into the hands of cruel, barbaric Roman soldiers to be scourged. They took him into the common judgment hall where they gathered an entire band of soldiers, between five and twelve hundred of them, to scourge our Saviour. They stripped him. They mercilessly whipped him with a Roman scourge. They mocked him, shoving a crown of thorns into his brow, throwing a purple rag over his shoulders, and putting a reed in his hand, they spit all over him and beat him with their fists!

Golgotha

'Then they led him away to crucify him'! After our Lord was paraded through the streets of Jerusalem as a common criminal, we behold the slaughter at Golgotha. 'And he bearing his cross went forth into a place called the place of a skull, which is called in the Hebrew Golgotha' (v. 17). Hanging upon the cursed tree on Golgotha's hill, the Lord of glory suffered and died in the place of poor, ruined sinners, that sinners like you and me might live forever with God.

'Golgotha' means 'place of a skull'. This was just another name for Calvary. It was called Golgotha because in this place of slaughter people who were stoned to death or crucified were simply covered over with a little dirt. Consequently, in a matter of time skulls and bones were everywhere. But the place of execution is insignificant. The only matters of importance are who is this sufferer? Why was he made to suffer this horrid, cursed death? For whom did he suffer and die? What did he accomplish by his death?

If you could find the actual spot where Christ died and the actual cross on which he was crucified, it would be of no benefit to your soul. You will never find redemption, salvation, and the forgiveness of sin in 'holy places' and religious relics (2 Kings 18:1-4).

Bearing His Cross

The first thing to which I would call your attention is the fact that our blessed Saviour went forth from the judgment hall to Golgotha bearing his cross (vv. 16, 17).

'Then delivered he him therefore unto them to be crucified. And they took Jesus, and led him away. And he bearing his cross went forth into a place called the place of a skull, which is called in the Hebrew Golgotha'.

One portion of the punishment imposed on the vilest criminals was that they were required to carry their own cross when they went to execution. Thus, our Lord Jesus went forth from the judgment hall 'bearing his cross', because he was, in the fullest sense, made sin for us, numbered with the transgressors, reckoned a sinner, and counted a curse for our sakes!

For another thing, this was a fulfilment of the great type of the sin-offering of the Mosaic law. It is written, 'The bullock for the sin offering, and the goat for the sin offering, whose blood was brought in to make atonement in the holy place, shall one carry forth without the camp; and they shall burn in the fire their skins, and their flesh, and their dung' (Leviticus 16:27).

Little did the blinded Jews imagine, when they madly hounded on the Romans to crucify the Lord Jesus outside the gates, that they were unconsciously perfecting the mightiest sin-offering that was ever seen. It is written, 'Wherefore Jesus also, that he might sanctify the people with his own blood, suffered without the gate' (Hebrews 13:12).

Like our Master, let us be content to go forth 'outside the camp', bearing his reproach. Multitudes wear crosses around their necks, as lapel pins, tie tacks, or earrings. Multitudes put crosses on graves, erect crosses on hillsides, and put crosses on stickers. Churches everywhere have crosses on their buildings, and in them. All that is easy and cheap and meaningless! Believers bear the cross. Like our Master, we must be willing to take up our cross daily and follow him. If we are persecuted for our doctrine, so be it. If we are derided for our simplicity of worship, so be it. If we are mocked for our Lord's ordinances, so be it. If we are counted the filth and off-scouring of the earth for our dogmatism and separation from the world, so be it (2 Corinthians 6:14-7:1).

Crucified King

Second, the Holy Spirit tells us that our Lord Jesus Christ was crucified as a King, as 'the King of the Jews' (vv. 13, 14, 19-22). He who hung on the central cross of the three on Golgotha's hill had a royal title over his head: 'JESUS

OF NAZARETH THE KING OF THE JEWS'. Because God ordered it, Pilate wrote out the inscription and stood by it. The inscription was written in Hebrew, Greek, and Latin that it might be read by all Jews, Greeks, and Romans, because our Lord Jesus Christ is indeed the Saviour of men of every nation and the King of all (Philippians 2:9-11).

Even before our Saviour was born, the angel Gabriel declared to his mother, 'He shall be great, and shall be called the Son of the Highest: and the Lord God shall give unto him the throne of his father David: And he shall reign over the house of Jacob forever; and of his kingdom there shall be no end' (Luke 1:32, 33). Almost as soon as he was born, wise men came from the East, saying, 'Where is he that is born King of the Jews?' (Matthew 2:2). The very week before his crucifixion, the multitude who accompanied our Lord at his triumphal entry into Jerusalem 'took branches of palm trees, and went forth to meet him, and cried, Hosanna: Blessed is the King of Israel that cometh in the name of the Lord' (John 12:13). He was born the King. He lived as the King. He died as the King. He arose as the King. He reigns as the King. And he is coming again as the King. Our Lord Jesus Christ is the King of kings and the Lord of lords. He is not your Saviour if he does not reign in your heart as your Lord and King (Luke 14:26-33).

Divine Sovereignty

Third, in the crucifixion of our Lord we see numerous displays of God's absolute sovereignty. Every description of our Saviour's death upon the cursed tree given in holy scripture is replete with these displays of God's total, absolute sovereignty in the whole affair. The four Gospel narratives are filled with them. In this scene of slaughter at Golgotha the Holy Spirit shows us a tremendous display of God's glorious sovereignty in three things.

The two thieves who were crucified with our Lord give us a display of God's sovereign, distinguishing grace in salvation. 'Where they crucified him, and two other with him, on either side one, and Jesus in the midst' (v. 18).

You do not need me to remind you that one of these thieves was plucked as a brand from the burning, from the very jaws of hell, by God's sovereign grace, while the other was left to suffer the just consequences of his sin. Let it never be forgotten by us that if we are saved, we are saved because God did it. The only distinction between you and me and the damned in hell is the distinction that grace has made (1 Corinthians 4:7; 15:10; Romans 9:16).

The fulfilment of scripture by men who had no regard for the scriptures is another great display of God's sovereignty (vv. 23, 24).

'Then the soldiers, when they had crucified Jesus, took his garments, and made four parts, to every soldier a part; and also his coat: now the coat was without seam, woven from the top throughout. They said therefore among themselves, Let us not rend it, but cast lots for it, whose it shall be: that the scripture might be fulfilled, which saith, They parted my raiment among them, and for my vesture they did cast lots. These things therefore the soldiers did.'

These soldiers had no more regard for the scriptures than hogs have for diamonds. Yet they did exactly what God ordained they would do and said they would do (Acts 4:27, 28; 13:27-29). Thus the Lord God makes even his Son's murderers to be his witnesses!

'After this, Jesus knowing that all things were now accomplished, that the scripture might be fulfilled, saith, I thirst. Now there was set a vessel full of vinegar: and they filled a spunge with vinegar, and put it upon hyssop, and put it to his mouth. When Jesus therefore had received the vinegar, he said, It is finished: and he bowed his head, and gave up the ghost' (vv. 28-30).

This mixture of vinegar, flat wine that had gone sour and bitter, mixed with gall was thought to be a mixture that would prolong one's life. It was given by the soldiers because they must, according to God's decree, fulfil the prophecy of Psalms 69:21. 'They gave me also gall for my meat; and in my thirst they gave me vinegar to drink'.

John Gill tells us 'This potion of vinegar with gall, was an aggravating circumstance in our Lord's sufferings, being given to him when he had a violent thirst upon Him; and was an emblem of the bitter cup of God's wrath, he had already tasted of in the garden and was about to drink up.'

Matthew tells us that 'when he had tasted thereof, he would not drink'. Our Lord refused to drink of this mixture because he was determined to suffer the wrath of God for us without any distraction or intoxication of mind. And he refused to drink of it because he would make all to know that he would do nothing to prolong his life, but was willing to die now that his hour, the fulness of time, had come.

Again, we are reminded that the Lord God Almighty was in total control of the affairs on this day of infamy by the fact that these barbaric soldiers did nothing except what God had long before said they would do. The parting of our Lord's garments was a fulfilment of Psalms 22:18. 'They part my garments among them, and cast lots upon my vesture'.

There is another great display of God's sovereignty in the fact that he caused unbelieving, reprobate men to declare his truth, to declare the very essence of the gospel, though they never knew it themselves.

We cannot know for certain, but it may be that it was the testimony of spineless Pilate, the testimony of the wicked, taunting, jeering Jews, and the testimony of the mocking chief priests, scribes, and elders that became the instruments by which God taught that elect thief the gospel and brought him to faith in Christ. Have you ever thought about the testimony that he heard that day? Pilate declared, 'THIS IS JESUS THE KING OF THE JEWS'. The priests, scribes, elders, and people, danced in a drunken, hellish party around Immanuel's cross, and in their blasphemy spoke the truth of God as distinctly as inspired prophets and apostles.

'Thou that destroyest the temple and buildest it in three days'. Though they knew it not, those religious ritualists proclaimed the fact of our Lord's death and resurrection. He destroyed the temple of his body in death; and he raised it up again in three days.

'He saved others; himself he cannot save'. That is the very essence of the gospel! The Son of God died as our Substitute. Because he saved us, he had to sacrifice himself!

'He trusted in God'. Our Lord Jesus Christ, as a man, lived by faith, in all things trusting God his Father. Thus he taught us how to honour, obey, and live for God in this world by faith.

'He said, I am the Son of God'. Our modern infidels choose to ignore it, but those people heard his doctrine plainly. Jesus Christ of Nazareth openly, publicly declared himself to be the Son of God. And that is who he is! He is God and man in one glorious Person. God-Man: the God-Man in Mary's womb, the God-Man in obedience for us, the God-Man dying upon the tree, the God-Man exalted to save!

Real

Fourth, I remind you again that the sufferings and death of the Lord Jesus Christ upon Golgotha's brow were real. Our Lord Jesus endured all the hell of God's wrath for us when he bore our sins in his own body on the cross. He suffered all the wrath of God that we deserved in his body, in his soul, and in his spirit. The listing of his agonies is torturous to read. What must it have been to experience them! The most savage barbarians in history have not been able to equal the tortures heaped upon the Son of God by the Jews and the Romans who crucified him.

J. C. Ryle rightly observed, 'Never let it be forgotten that he had a real human body, a body exactly like our own, just as sensitive, just as vulnerable, just as capable of feeling intense pain.'

Crucifixion was the most indescribably horrid form of execution ever forced upon a human being. The person crucified was stretched out on his back on a piece of timber. His hands were stretched out on the cross piece, and nailed through the wrists to the wood with huge spikes. His feet were crossed one on top of the other and nailed together with a huge mallet driving the spike through them both and fastening them to the wood. Then the Lord Jesus was picked up on the cross and it was dropped into a socket three or four feet deep, with his body attached to it! There he hung, not dying suddenly for no vital organ was touched, in excruciating pain for six long hours. There he hung, naked, shamed, covered from head to foot with the excrement of others men's foul throats and his own holy blood. His head, his hands, his feet oozing with blood, throbbing in pain, the Lord of glory hung there for six indescribable hours of hell.

Yet, his agony of soul was infinitely more excruciating to him than that of his body. The holy Lamb of God was made sin for us! The Son of God was forsaken by his Father. The Lord of glory was slain by the sword of his own holy justice.

Redemption Finished

Fifth, Our dear Saviour, by his sin-atoning sacrifice and death at Calvary, finished the work of redemption. 'When Jesus therefore had received the vinegar, he said, It is finished: and he bowed his head, and gave up the ghost' (v. 30). All the Old Testament types and prophecies were fulfilled. Justice was satisfied. Righteousness was brought in. Sin was put away. The way to God was opened for sinners. Salvation was obtained! 'With his own blood he entered in once into the holy place, having obtained eternal redemption for us'. Behold, the Fountain opened for sin and uncleanness our crucified Lord. 'There is therefore now no condemnation to them which are in Christ Jesus'.

Chapter 56

Seven Words From The Cross

'Now there stood by the cross of Jesus his mother, and his mother's sister, Mary the wife of Cleophas, and Mary Magdalene. When Jesus therefore saw his mother, and the disciple standing by, whom he loved, he saith unto his mother, Woman, behold thy son! Then saith he to the disciple, Behold thy mother! And from that hour that disciple took her unto his own home. After this, Jesus knowing that all things were now accomplished, that the scripture might be fulfilled, saith, I thirst. Now there was set a vessel full of vinegar: and they filled a spunge with vinegar, and put it upon hyssop, and put it to his mouth. When Jesus therefore had received the vinegar, he said, It is finished: and he bowed his head, and gave up the ghost' (John 19:25-30).

How I pray that the Lord God will be pleased to grant me grace that I may live with the cross of our Lord Jesus Christ ever before my mind, with the scenes of my Saviour's redemptive work and glory constantly upon my heart, and the redemption he accomplished for me by his substitutionary death ever flooding my ransomed soul. Let us go again to Mount Calvary, asking God the Holy Spirit to inscribe the things we see and hear upon our hearts, for the glory of his own great name, for Christ's sake. What a scene of infamy we have before us! What a scene of grace! What a scene of the revelation of the glory of God!

Our Lord's Humiliation

The Lord Jesus was hurriedly brought before Pilate, where the Jews slanderously accused him. But Pilate saw their accusations for what they were, nothing but the rantings of envious religionists. Once he found out the Lord

Jesus was a Galilean, he tried to rid himself of the matter and sent him to Herod.

When Herod could not persuade the Son of God to dance before him, he mocked him shamefully and sent him back to Pilate. And that day, those two political jackals became friends. And Pilate, willing to please the Jews, 'delivered Jesus to their will' to be crucified. Pilate, Herod, the high priest, the Jewish mob, and the soldiers were but contemptible little imps, unworthy of further mention. There is but one thing worthy of notice in all that is recorded in the book of God about our Saviour's arrest, mock trial, and crucifixion, one thing they were written down by inspiration of God to reveal, and that is the greatness of our Lord's humiliation for us.

What base contempt and mockery our God and Saviour endured in the house of the high priest, and at the palaces of Pilate and Herod! Truly, 'He humbled himself'! He emptied himself of all the dignity and honour that rightly belongs to him, that he might redeem and save sinners who deserve to be mocked in the fires of hell and held by him in contempt forever. 'For ye know the grace of our Lord Jesus Christ, that, though he was rich, yet for your sakes he became poor, that ye through his poverty might be rich' (2 Corinthians 8:9).

Depravity And Substitution

God the Holy Ghost has given us a terrible, graphic display of the utter depravity of our race and the vile hatred of the human heart for the God of glory! What base, self-serving weaklings men in powerful positions often are! Pilate cared for nothing but himself. Though a man of almost absolute power in his realm, he cowered before the people he ruled, just to gain a moment of approval from them. The whole crowd, religious and reprobate, Jewish and pagan, craved to murder the incarnate God. And Pilate 'delivered Jesus to their will'. What an indictment this is against the will of man!

Yet, there is something glorious here. By the arrangement of divine providence, there was a custom and a man in the scene before us who gave opportunity for our Lord to display everything he had come to accomplish. When Barabbas was released and the Lord Jesus died in his place, it is as though the Saviour had said, 'See this! This is why I came to this hour, to die the Just for the unjust in the place of guilty sinners as their Substitute that they might go free'!

Three Malefactors

It is not by accident that John tells us that they crucified our Lord, 'and two other with him, on either side one, and Jesus in the midst' (v. 18). The obvious indication is that our blessed Redeemer 'was numbered with the transgressors; and he bare the sin of many' (Isaiah 53:12). 'And the scripture was fulfilled, which saith, And he was numbered with the transgressors' (Mark 15:28). Being our Surety and Representative, he stood before the offended law and justice of God as the greatest of all sinners!

'Therefore if any man be in Christ, he is a new creature: old things are passed away; behold, all things are become new. And all things are of God, who hath reconciled us to himself by Jesus Christ, and hath given to us the ministry of reconciliation; To wit, that God was in Christ, reconciling the world unto himself, not imputing their trespasses unto them; and hath committed unto us the word of reconciliation. Now then we are ambassadors for Christ, as though God did beseech you by us: we pray you in Christ's stead, be ye reconciled to God. For he hath made him to be sin for us, who knew no sin; that we might be made the righteousness of God in him' (2 Corinthians 5:17-21).

Seven Statements

Let us look at the seven things our Lord Jesus Christ spoke from the cross, as he hung upon the cursed tree, bearing our sin, suffering all the horror of the wrath of God for us, when he was made sin, that we might be made the righteousness of God in him. I am certain that our Redeemer said many things that are not recorded in the four gospels (Psalms 22, 40, 69). But the Holy Spirit inspired Matthew, Mark, Luke, and John to record seven specific statements spoken by the Lamb of God, as he hung upon the cursed tree as our sin-atoning Sacrifice, bearing all the fury of divine justice and wrath as our Substitute.

These last seven words that fell from the lips of the Lord Jesus Christ are recorded in the book of God by divine purpose and inspiration for our learning, edification, comfort, and hope. This is what God himself declares in Romans 15:4. 'Whatsoever things were written aforetime were written for our learning, that we through patience and comfort of the scriptures might have hope.'

In this Volume of Inspiration God the Holy Ghost has taken very special care to record these seven things spoken by our Lord Jesus Christ, as he was laying down his life for us, to put away our sins by the sacrifice of himself. As he hung upon the cursed tree, bearing our sin, suffering all the horrible fury of the wrath of God for us, when he was made sin for us, that we might be made the righteousness of God in him, the Lord Jesus made seven distinct statements which should ever be held in fond memory in our hearts.

There have been mountains of words and thousands of sermons preached from these seven sayings of Christ from the cross. I cannot add anything to what has already been spoken and written by faithful men. But I do hope that God the Holy Spirit will enable me to give you a glimpse of what I see in them. These are the very words spoken in his humiliation by our great God and

Saviour, spoken as he engaged the forces of hell and endured the indescribable wrath of God in the place of sinners. In these seven words from the cross I see the glorious Person, work, and offices of our Lord Jesus Christ beautifully demonstrated.

A Word Of Forgiveness

The first of those seven statements is found in Luke 23:34. 'Then said Jesus, Father, forgive them; for they know not what they do. And they parted his raiment, and cast lots'. Here I see Christ our Mediator, our High Priest and Advocate pleading for the forgiveness of guilty sinners. Here is the Son of God suffering by the hands of wicked men, suffering with wicked men, suffering as a wicked man, and yet praying for the men who made him suffer. 'There is one God, and one Mediator between God and men', and that Mediator is 'the man Christ Jesus' (1 Timothy 2:5).

We must have a Mediator (Hebrews 5:1). The Mediator must be a man of God's choosing (Hebrews 5:4, 5). The Mediator must pray and be heard (Hebrews 5:7). He must have a sacrifice. Christ's sacrifice was himself, his own life, his blood, his body and his soul! The sacrifice must be offered upon the altar of God. The Altar upon which our Saviour sacrificed himself was the Altar of his own divinity. And the Mediator must have a blessing to bestow. That blessing is God's salvation (Numbers 6:24-26). None but the Lord Jesus Christ meets the qualifications of a mediator between God and men (John 14:6; Romans 8:34; Hebrews 7:25; 1 John 2:1, 2).

A Word Of Assurance

The second word is found in Luke 23:43. The dying thief cried, 'Lord, remember me when thou comest into thy kingdom'! 'And Jesus said unto him, Verily I say unto thee, Today shalt thou be with me in paradise'. Here is a word of salvation and assurance spoken to a believing sinner by Christ our Saviour and King.

Even as he hung upon the cross, suffering untold agony under the wrath of God, Jesus Christ reigned as Lord and King over everything. Do not ever imagine that our Lord Jesus was in anyway the helpless victim of circumstances when he died at Calvary. Even in his death, he was the God of all circumstances and all events. Here is the sovereign King, the Ruler of the kingdom of God, saving whom he will (Romans 9:15). Here is the King of grace opening the door which no mere man can ever open. Here is the Prince of peace giving peace that no man can give. Here is the King of glory promising mercy and eternal life that no man can merit. 'Salvation is of the LORD'! Grace comes from the throne of grace; and the King who sits upon that throne is the Lord Jesus Christ (1 Peter 3:22; John 5:20, 21; 17:2).

A Word Of Tender Care

The third word spoken by our Lord as he hung upon the cross is found in John 19:26, 27. In it I hear Christ, our Representative and Example, speaking a word of tender care.

'When Jesus therefore saw his mother, and the disciple standing by, whom he loved, he saith unto his mother, Woman, behold thy son! Then saith he to the disciple, Behold thy mother! And from that hour that disciple took her unto his own home'.

Even in the agonies of death, under the penalty of sin, enduring the wrath of God, fulfilling the everlasting covenant, accomplishing eternal redemption for us, and satisfying the divine justice, our Lord Jesus Christ did not neglect the responsibilities of manhood. Our Saviour, as our Representative and Example, deliberately gave attention to his responsibilities as a man, even in the time of his dying agony.

Our blessed Saviour fulfilled all righteousness for us, both as our Representative and as our Example. He did everything that it is right for a man to do. He was circumcised. He was subject unto his parents. He was baptised. He attended the synagogue. Our Lord Jesus was 'made of a woman, made under the law, to redeem them that were under the law'. In this, his dying hour, our Redeemer tenderly cared for his mother.

He fulfilled all righteousness as our legal Representative (Romans 5:19); and he fulfilled all righteousness as our Example of righteousness (John 13:13-15; 1 Peter 2:21-24). If we would learn how to live in this world for the glory of God, if we would learn how to serve our generation, if we would learn how to worship God, we must go to Calvary. There we behold the Lamb of God and learn how to live in this world amongst men. There we learn what submission to the will of God involves. At Calvary, we see patience in suffering, learn how to love our brothers and sisters, how to love our husbands and wives (Ephesians 5:25-27), and how to give (2 Corinthians 8:9).

Yet, there is more here than our Lord's care for his mother. When our Saviour said to Mary, 'Woman, behold thy Son', I cannot help thinking that he was saying, 'Behold me now, and remember what I told you when I was just a boy, 'I must be about my Father's business'. Behold me now, and remember the song you sang when I was still in your womb' (Luke 1:46-55).

A Word Of Agony

The fourth word is found in Matthew 27:46. 'And about the ninth hour, (that is at 3:00 in the afternoon, and after three hours of great darkness) Jesus cried with a loud voice, saying, Eli, Eli, lama sabachthani? that is to say, My God, My God, why hast thou forsaken me?'

Here I see Christ our Substitute crying out in agony of soul. This is the only time recorded in scripture that the Lord Jesus Christ spoke to the Father and addressed him as God. Here he takes the lowest place of humanity and cries out to his Father, and our Father, as a creature to be pitied by his Creator. In his great agony, this mighty Man who is God reverts to his childhood, speaking in his native Syrian tongue, not in the Hebrew of his fathers or in the Greek he acquired as he matured.

At the height of his obedience to the Father, the Lord of glory was forsaken by his Father, because we deserved to be forever forsaken of that God whom we have spent our lives forsaking. He was forsaken of God, because he was made sin for us. Reproach now broke his heart.

'My God! My God! Why hast thou forsaken me?' This is a cry arising from depths of infinite anguish no human being can know. It is a cry no mortal mind can comprehend. A mystery no creature can fathom. Martin Luther, after studying and meditating upon this text for hours, closed his Bible, slammed his fists down on his desk and cried, 'God forsaken of God! My God, no man can understand that'!

I will not attempt to explain what no man can understand. But, with a happy broken heart, I rejoice in the fact of this our Substitute's greatest sorrow. He was forsaken of God. That means those sinners for whom he died shall never be forsaken of God (Isaiah 53:9-11; John 3:14-16; Romans 5:6-8; 8:1-4; 2 Corinthians 5:20, 21; 1 Peter 2:24, 25; 1 Peter 3:18; 1 John 4:9, 10).

What an infinitely, horribly evil thing sin is! How holy, just, righteous, and good our God is! O my soul, how great, how infinitely great is the love of God for his people! How anxious, willing, and ready the holy Lord God is to save poor sinners! 'He delighteth in mercy'!

A Word Of Great Need

Our Lord's fifth word from the cross is found in John 19:28. 'After this, Jesus knowing that all things were now accomplished, that the scripture might be fulfilled, saith, I thirst.' Here is Christ the Man expressing his great need and desire. Here we see our Saviour's real humanity. This is the shortest of the seven statements he made on the cross; but it is every bit as instructive as the other six. I am sure it is meant to show us at least these three things about our Saviour.

1. His physical thirst. being in anguish of body, burning with fever, his tongue swollen and cleaving to his jaws, Christ thirsted for water, just like the rich man in hell, as he endured the fire of God's hot, holy wrath for us.

2. His soul's thirst: being forsaken of God, he thirsted in his soul. 'As the hart panteth after the water brooks', so panted his soul for God (Psalms 22:1-21; 40:11-13; 69:1-20).

3. His heart's thirst: the Lord of glory was made sin, made to endure all the horror of God's holy, unmitigated wrath, because he thirsted for the souls of men. He thirsted for his people. He thirsted to be thirsted after. When I hear the Master cry, 'I thirst', I can almost hear his heart crying, 'I will that they also whom thou hast given me be with me where I am, that they may behold my glory'.

A Word Of Accomplishment

'After this, Jesus knowing that all things were now accomplished, that the scripture might be fulfilled, saith, I thirst. Now there was set a vessel full of vinegar: and they filled a spunge with vinegar, and put it upon hyssop, and put it to his mouth. When Jesus therefore had received the vinegar, he said, It is finished: and he bowed his head, and gave up the ghost' (John 19:28-30).

'It is finished'! What a blessed, triumphant word! Our blessed Saviour was not crying a sigh of relief. He was not saying, 'At last, it is over.' Most men leave this world with things unfinished. So many plans unfinished! So many hopes unfulfilled! So many desires unsatisfied! So many works incomplete! So many things they wanted to do, or see, or experience, unfinished! Not so with the Lord Jesus Christ, our great Surety! He accomplished everything he came here to do.

What did he come here to do? Did he come here to do the Father's will (Hebrews 10)? 'It is finished'! Did he come here to save his people (Matthew 1:21)? 'It is finished'! Did he come here to fulfil all the types, promises, and prophecies of the scriptures? 'It is finished'! Did he come here to make an end of sin? Did he come here to put away sin by the sacrifice of himself? 'It is finished'! Did he come here to bring in everlasting righteousness? 'It is finished'! Did he come here to obtain eternal redemption (Hebrews 9:12)? 'It is finished'! Did he come here to redeem us from the curse of the law? 'It is finished'! Did he come here to fulfil and make an end of the law? Did he come here to magnify the law and make it honourable? 'It is finished'!

This is the Surety's cry of accomplished suretyship to the Father. 'It is finished'! 'I have finished the work which thou gavest me to do'! Here our covenant Surety says to his Father, I have finished all the work entrusted into my hands. I have redeemed all the souls entrusted to me. I have ransomed all the sheep. I have found all the lost ones I came to find. All the work is done; fully done, well done, perfectly done!

This is the cry of our great Surety to poor, needy sinners! 'It is finished'! Wrath is finished! Judgment is finished! Sin is finished! Righteousness is finished! Redemption is finished! Justification is finished! Sanctification is finished! Salvation is finished!

'It is finished'! Sinners, hear it:
Hear the dying Saviour's cry;
'It is finished'! Angels sing it,
Sing the praise of Christ on high.
'It is finished'! 'It is finished'!
Tell it through the earth and sky!

Justice now demands salvation
For those souls whose wrath Christ bore;
And it smiles with approbation
On the ransomed evermore!
Grace and mercy, grace and mercy
Freely flow from boundless stores.

Hear the Son of God declare it,
All is done He came to do!
Needy sinners, Hear, believe it. –
Is not this good news to you?
'It is finished'! 'It is finished'!
All is done! Oh, yes, it's true!

'It is finished'! All is over.
Jesus drank damnation dry!
Never can a ransomed sinner
God's salvation be denied!
'It is finished'! 'It is finished'!
Cries our Sur'ty now on High!

Who is he that shall condemn us?
Who shall charge us now with sin?
It is God who justified us,
Christ who died, cries in our name,
'It is finished'! 'It is finished'!
Praised forever be His name!

Thomas Kelly

A Word Of Rest

The Saviour's last word from the cross is found in Luke 23:46 'And when Jesus had cried with a loud voice, he said, Father, into thy hands I commend my spirit: and having said thus, he gave up the ghost.' Our Saviour died with the word of God in his heart and on his lips (Psalms 31:1-5). Here I see Christ our Sabbath entering into rest. Once our great Redeemer had finished his work, he 'cried with a loud voice, and said, Father, into thy hands I commend my spirit: and having said thus, he gave up the ghost.' Thus he entered into his rest and obtained eternal rest for us (Hebrews 4:9-11).

Notice here, our Saviour who had cried, 'My God, My God, Why hast thou forsaken me?' now calls his Father by that endearing name, 'Father'. The storm of God's holy wrath beat fiercely upon his holy soul; but now the storm is nearly over. Only one thing is to be done. He must yet die; but here he seems to say to poor, needy sinners, 'Look here. Look unto me. Behold, now reconciliation is made. Anger is turned away. Judgment is gone'! (Read Isaiah 12:1-6).

Our blessed Saviour committed his spirit into his Father's hands, not Satan's. Some vainly imagine that the Lord Jesus was now taken to hell to be tormented of the devil for three days. That is not so (Hebrews 9:12). He owed Satan nothing. Here he conquered the fiend of hell forever. He committed his spirit into his Father's hands, leaving us an example that we should follow in his steps (1 Peter 2:22-24).

At last, in sovereign majesty, 'He gave up the ghost'. He dismissed his spirit. This Man who is God our Saviour did what none but God could do, who gives life and takes life at his will. 'He gave up the ghost.' That is to say, he dismissed his spirit that we might come now to him and enter into his rest (Matthew 11:28-30).

Chapter 57

Christ Crucified And The Scriptures Fulfilled

'After this, Jesus knowing that all things were now accomplished, that the scripture might be fulfilled, saith, I thirst. Now there was set a vessel full of vinegar: and they filled a spunge with vinegar, and put it upon hyssop, and put it to his mouth. When Jesus therefore had received the vinegar, he said, It is finished: and he bowed his head, and gave up the ghost.'

'The Jews therefore, because it was the preparation, that the bodies should not remain upon the cross on the sabbath day, (for that sabbath day was an high day,) besought Pilate that their legs might be broken, and that they might be taken away. Then came the soldiers, and brake the legs of the first, and of the other which was crucified with him. But when they came to Jesus, and saw that he was dead already, they brake not his legs: But one of the soldiers with a spear pierced his side, and forthwith came there out blood and water. And he that saw it bare record, and his record is true: and he knoweth that he saith true, that ye might believe. For these things were done, that the scripture should be fulfilled, A bone of him shall not be broken. And again another scripture saith, They shall look on him whom they pierced.'

'And after this Joseph of Arimathaea, being a disciple of Jesus, but secretly for fear of the Jews, besought Pilate that he might take away the body of Jesus: and Pilate gave him leave. He came therefore, and took the body of Jesus. And there came also Nicodemus, which at the first came to Jesus by night, and brought a mixture of myrrh and aloes, about an hundred pound weight. Then took they the body of Jesus, and wound it in linen clothes with the spices, as the manner of the Jews is to bury. Now in the place where he was crucified there was a garden; and in the garden a new sepulchre, wherein was never man yet laid. There laid they Jesus therefore because of the Jews' preparation day; for the sepulchre was nigh at hand' (John 19:28-42).

This portion of John's Gospel contains points of deep interest which are silently passed over by Matthew, Mark, and Luke. We are not told why Matthew, Mark, and Luke omit the things John was inspired to record in this portion of holy scripture; and we should not curiously seek to know the reason. It is enough for us to remember that, both in what they recorded and in what they did not record, all four Evangelists wrote by inspiration of God the Holy Ghost.

Our Lord Jesus Christ lived, and died, and was buried in the sure hope and blessed prospect of his resurrection glory, so that sinners trusting him might live, and die, and go to their graves in the sure hope and blessed prospect of his resurrection glory. In this passage of holy scripture God the Holy Ghost sets before us seven facts regarding our dear Saviour's final hours on this earth. May he be pleased to inscribe them upon our hearts.

Scripture Fulfilled

First, 'Christ died for our sins according to the scriptures'. Throughout the biblical accounts of our Lord's crucifixion we read that the things done to him by the hands of wicked men were done 'that the scripture might be fulfilled'. In this nineteenth chapter of John alone we see this fact set before us by divine inspiration three times (John 19:24; Psalms 22:18; John 19:28; Psalms 69:21; John 19:36; Exodus 12:46; Numbers 9:12; Psalms 34:20; Zechariah 12:10).

John here refers to clear and specific prophecies given in Exodus, Numbers, the Psalms, and Zechariah, which received their accomplishment at the cross. I could easily point you to many others. All of these fulfilled prophecies combine to tell us one thing. They tell us that the death of our Lord Jesus Christ at Golgotha was a thing planned, predestined, and prophesied by God. Hundreds of years before it came to pass every part of the solemn transaction was arranged in the divine counsels; and the most minute particulars were revealed to the prophets. From first to last, it was a thing accomplished according to the purpose of God; and every portion of it was in fulfilment of precise divine prophecy. In the highest, fullest sense, when Christ died, he 'died for our sins according to the scriptures' (1 Corinthians 15:3).

I stress this point because I want you to be fully confident that the Bible is indeed the inspired, inerrant book of God, the very word of God. The prophets did not merely foretell Christ's death. They specifically foretold the particulars of his death in detail.

It is impossible to explain so many accomplishments of specific details by any means, except one, 'holy men of God spake as they were moved by the Holy Ghost', and two, 'all scripture is given by inspiration of God'. To say these things are matters of luck, chance, or coincidence is as preposterous and absurd as it is blasphemous.

The only rational account of these prophecies and their fulfilment is the divine inspiration of the Bible. The prophets, who told God's elect the details of the crucifixion of their Redeemer and ours, hundreds of years before it was accomplished, were inspired by the only Lord God who declares the end from the beginning and always performs all his will.

The book of God must never be read as a human composition. It is the word of the living God. The infidel who denies this runs in the face of all reason and credibility. Those who regard the repeated fulfilments of minute prophecies about Christ's death, such as the prophecies about his dress, his thirst, his pierced side, and his bones being unbroken, as the result of chance and not of design, do so in blind rebellion; rebellion that renders them incapable of rational thought regarding the things of God.

Finished Work

Second, we must rest our souls upon the finished work of Christ (vv. 28-30).

'After this, Jesus knowing that all things were now accomplished, that the scripture might be fulfilled, saith, I thirst. Now there was set a vessel full of vinegar: and they filled a spunge with vinegar, and put it upon hyssop, and put it to his mouth. When Jesus therefore had received the vinegar, he said, It is finished: and he bowed his head, and gave up the ghost' (John 19:28-30).

Our Lord's work was accomplished. He had honoured the law in his life of perfect obedience and holiness as our Representative. Now, by his suffering and death under the wrath of God for the sin of his people, he had fully satisfied divine justice as our Substitute (Isaiah 53:4-6). That the scripture might be fulfilled (Psalms 22:15; Psalms 69:21), he cried, 'I thirst'. He suffered the burning thirst of hell (Luke 16:24) that we might drink the water of life and never thirst (John 4:14). Then, once the Lord Jesus had received the vinegar, he cried, 'It is finished', bowed his head, and died. What was finished? The whole will of God in regard to redemption (Hebrews 10:7); the whole work his Father had given him to do (1 Timothy 1:15); the whole Law of God and all the types and ceremonies it contained (Hebrews 10:9-14); the righteousness of God performed, perfected, and imputed to believers (Romans 3:19-24; 10:4; 2 Corinthians 5:21).

The proof that our blessed Surety accomplished all he came to accomplish was his resurrection from the dead (Acts 17:31; Romans 4:25). Salvation and eternal life is the gift of God, not of works on our part, but through the Person and work of our Substitute, the Lord Jesus Christ (Ephesians 2:8, 9; 2 Corinthians 5:18-21). Philip Doddridge says it well,

> 'Tis done, the great transaction's done;
> I am my Lord's and He is mine.

Nothing can be added to his finished work. We rest our souls on a finished work, if we rest them on the work of our Lord Jesus Christ. We need not fear that either sin, or Satan, or law shall condemn us at the last day. We have a Saviour who has done all, paid all, accomplished all, and performed all that is required for our everlasting salvation. We may take up the challenge of the Apostle, 'Who is he that condemneth? It is Christ that died, yea rather, that is risen again, who is even at the right hand of God, who also maketh intercession for us' (Romans 8:34). Trusting Christ, we lack nothing (Colossians 2:9, 10; 1 Corinthians 1:30, 31).

Real Death

Third, our Lord Jesus Christ really did die under the wrath of God as our Substitute. It was late in the afternoon, and the Jews' sabbath day began immediately after sunset. So they urged Pilate to break the legs of the crucified, and hasten their death that their bodies might be taken down and buried before their sabbath began. Dead bodies hanging on crosses would defile their sabbath and their religious ceremonies (Deuteronomy 21:22, 23). What hypocrisy! These self-righteous Pharisees were not concerned about crucifying the Son of God; but they were very conscientious about not defiling their holy day!

So the soldiers broke the legs of the two thieves. But when they came to the Lord Jesus and saw that he was already dead, they broke not his legs. This was not out of compassion for him (as we see in the next verses), but that which restrained them was God's sovereign providence and purpose.

'But one of the soldiers with a spear pierced his side, and forthwith came there out blood and water. And he that saw it bare record, and his record is true: and he knoweth that he saith true, that ye might believe. For these things were done, that the scripture should be fulfilled, A bone of him shall not be broken. And again another scripture saith, They shall look on him whom they pierced' (John 19:34-37).

Our dear Saviour really did die in our place, as our penal Substitute, under the wrath of God. The heart of our blessed Redeemer was pierced. This was not a death stroke. Our Redeemer had already dismissed his spirit. But the piercing of his heart was done to both fulfil the scriptures (Exodus 12:46; Psalms 34:20; Zechariah 12:10; Revelation 1:7) and to demonstrate that his life was gone. Our Lord did not merely faint, or swoon away, or become insensible, as some have dared to insinuate. His heart actually ceased to beat; and he actually died.

This is a matter of great importance. Without a real death, there could be no real sacrifice. Without a real death, there could be no real resurrection. Without a real death and a real resurrection, there is no hope, and we are yet in our sins. The whole gospel of Christ, the whole of true Christianity stands or falls with the reality of our Lord's death and resurrection (1 Corinthians 15:14-17). Though that reckless, hardened Roman soldier never dreamed it, he was the unwitting servant of our God and a mighty helper to our holy faith, when he thrust his spear into our Saviour's side.

Fountain Opened

Fourth, the crucified Lamb of God is a Fountain opened for sin and uncleanness. When the soldier pierced his side and there came out blood and water, John tells us that he saw this and his record is true (1 John 5:6-8). Christ is the Fountain opened for sin and uncleanness, 'In that day there shall be a fountain opened to the house of David and to the inhabitants of Jerusalem for sin and for uncleanness' (Zechariah 13:1).

'This is he that came by water and blood, even Jesus Christ; not by water only, but by water and blood. And it is the Spirit that beareth witness, because the Spirit is truth. For there are three that bear record in heaven, the Father, the Word, and the Holy Ghost: and these three are one. And there are three that bear witness in earth, the Spirit, and the water, and the blood: and these three agree in one' (1 John 5:6-8).

The blood and water from the Lord's side signify both our complete justification and perfect sanctification in him, by him, and with him (1 Corinthians 1:30; Hebrews 10:10-14). Says Toplady,

> Let the water and the blood,
> From Thy riven side which flowed,
> Be of sin the double cure,
> Cleanse me from its guilt and power

Truly God

Fifth, the man Jesus Christ is himself God. If you will compare John's statement in verse 37 with the prophecy from which it is taken in Zechariah 12:10, you cannot fail to see that God the Holy Spirit is here again giving us one of those subtle, but sweet, declarations of our Saviour's divinity.

'And again another scripture saith, They shall look on him whom they pierced' (John 19:37).

'And I will pour upon the house of David, and upon the inhabitants of Jerusalem, the spirit of grace and of supplications: and they shall look upon me whom they have pierced, and they shall mourn for him, as one mourneth for his only son, and shall be in bitterness for him, as one that is in bitterness for his firstborn' (Zechariah 12:10).

The Lord God, speaking by Zechariah, said 'They shall look upon me whom they have pierced'. He who predicted and promised these things was and is the eternal God, the Lord Jehovah. John, writing as an inspired historian, points to Christ and tells us (quoting Zechariah), 'They shall look on him whom they have pierced'. Jesus is Jehovah. The man Christ Jesus is himself God.

Unknown Disciples

Sixth, our Saviour has many disciples unknown to you and me. Many boldly and confidently assert that they know who the Lord's disciples are. They are not hesitant to denounce those who do not agree with them on all matters as reprobate unbelievers. They do not hesitate to denounce as Pharisees and hypocrites all who do not meet their measure. They tell us that a true believer will not be found here, that a child of God would never do that, that anyone who knows God will not follow that path.

I have had people ask me (and they were serious in asking), 'Do you think Solomon was saved?' And I have known many who denounce Joseph of Arimathaea and Nicodemus as hypocrites and unbelievers because they were among the Pharisees and feared the Jews. But God the Holy Spirit tells us plainly that these two men were 'disciples', followers of Christ. Though they were secret disciples, they were still true disciples; and they proved it. When Peter denied him and all forsook him, Joseph and Nicodemus identified themselves with the crucified Son of God.

All are Christ's who trust Christ; but none of us know who the Lord's disciples are, or where they are. Let us therefore be guarded and gracious in our judgment concerning others. Aaron led Israel in the worship of golden calves. Solomon worshipped idols with his wives. Peter sided with the Judaisers at Antioch. Paul took a legal oath at Jerusalem. John fell down to worship an angel. And Joseph of Arimathaea and Nicodemus remained among the Pharisees for a long time, though they were all true followers of Christ.

Burial Not Cremation

Seventh, we bury our dead in hope of the resurrection. Our Saviour's body was buried in the tomb of a rich man, Joseph of Arimathaea, in the anticipation of his resurrection (Psalms 16:9-11). It was necessary that Christ die as our Substitute to do away with sin and death by the sacrifice of himself. It was as necessary that he be 'buried', that his humiliation be complete. A thousand years earlier, our Lord spoke by the Spirit of prophecy and said, 'Thou hast brought me into the dust of death' (Psalms 22:15). And it was necessary, that though he died as one under the sentence of justice, he should have an honourable funeral.

Therefore, in order to fulfil the seemingly contradictory prophecies, in which it was said, 'he is taken from prison and from judgment, and cut off out of the land of the living', yet, contrary to all human probabilities, he must 'make his grave with the wicked, and with the rich in his death' (Isaiah 53:8, 9), these godly men, Joseph of Arimathaea and Nicodemus were raised up by God at the time needed to perform the task of burying our Saviour's holy body.

Our dear Saviour conquered death by his own death. He went into the grave to subdue the power of the grave. And he arose from the dead, in proof that he has triumphed over both death and the grave. In doing so, our Saviour showed the way we shall at last conquer death and the grave by virtue of our union with him.

As our Lord was buried in prospect of the resurrection, we bury our dead, the bodies of our believing brothers and sisters in Christ, in the sure and certain hope of resurrection glory (1 Thessalonians 4:13-18). I am often asked, 'Should I be cremated or buried?' While the scriptures do not give any commandment, they do, in my opinion, clearly indicate that the burial of our bodies is most consistent with the faith of the gospel. Our Lord was buried in the earth; and we confess our Saviour and our faith in him by a burial in believer's baptism. Clearly, there is a connection between burial in hope of the resurrection and our faith in Christ.

Let us often meditate upon the things revealed in this book about our dear Saviour's sufferings and death as our sin-atoning Substitute. Follow him from Gethsemane to Gabbatha and from Gabbatha to Golgotha. Hear his voice, as he cries, 'Behold and see if there be any sorrow like unto my sorrow, which is done unto me, wherewith the Lord hath afflicted me in the day of his fierce anger'!

Read the inscription on the cross. 'He was wounded for our transgressions, he was bruised for our iniquities, the chastisement of our peace was upon him, and with his stripes we are healed'! Matchless love! The Son of God became a man that sinful men might become the sons of God! The Lord Jesus, the holy, harmless, undefiled Lamb of God, who knew no sin, was made sin, that his people might be made the righteousness of God in him.

Neglect not to follow the Saviour to the tomb, in frequent and blessed meditation. 'Come, see the place where the Lord lay.' Glorious triumph is this.

The tomb is empty! Our crucified, risen, ascended Lord holds the keys of death, hell, and the grave. Oh, for grace frequently to visit the garden and the tomb where the body of my Saviour was buried. Here, I would meditate on death with sweet, happy prospect, hope, and anticipation, until he who has the key of David opens my little spot in the earth to receive my body. Even now I hear the voice of comfort and consolation. 'Blessed are the dead which die in the Lord'!

Make sure, that you are 'washed and made white in the blood of the Lamb' (Revelation 7:14). Faith in Christ is the one thing needful. 'He that hath the Son has life, and he that hath not the Son of God hath not life' (1 John 5:12). 'Dost thou believe on the Son of God?' God help you now to believe, for Christ's sake.

Chapter 58

'It is finished'

'When Jesus therefore had received the vinegar, he said, It is finished: and he bowed his head, and gave up the ghost' (John 19:30).

The Son of God has taken upon himself human flesh. He has taken our humanity into union with his divinity. He has lived a life of perfect righteousness as the Representative of his covenant people. He has been all his life long despised and rejected of men, a man of sorrows and acquainted with grief. His enemies have been many. His friends have been few, and those few faithless. At last he is delivered over into the hands of them that hate him. He is crudely arrested in the garden, and arraigned before the courts of law. They robe him in mockery, strip him in shame, and hold him up as a spectacle of ridicule and scorn. He is declared to be perfectly innocent. Yet, the cowardly judge delivers him into the hands of his persecutors. It is written, 'Pilate delivered Jesus to their will'! He is dragged through the streets of Jerusalem. Those who had killed the prophets would now bring upon themselves the blood of the prophets' Master.

The God-man is brought to the hill called Calvary and brutally nailed to the cross. The sun burns upon him. His wounds infect his body with scorching fever. God, his Father, whose will he came to perform, whose purpose he now fulfils, whose people he came to redeem, whose glory he came to uphold, his God and Father forsakes him! Suffering all the concentrated anguish of hell, he cries out, 'My God, my God, why hast thou forsaken me?'

While he hangs there upon the tree, in mortal conflict with sin and Satan, his heart is broken, his limbs are dislocated, and his Father forsakes him. The heavens forsake him. The earth forsakes him. His disciples all forsake him and flee from him. He looks everywhere, but there is none to help. His eye looks all around, but there are none to share his toil. He treads the wine press of the fierceness of the wrath of God alone; and of the people there are none with him.

Yet, on and on he goes; steadily determined to drink the last bitter dregs of that cup which could not pass from his lips if his Father's will is to be done. He says:

'The Lord GOD hath opened mine ear, and I was not rebellious, neither turned away back. I gave my back to the smiters, and my cheeks to them that plucked off the hair: I hid not my face from shame and spitting. For the Lord GOD will help me; therefore shall I not be confounded: therefore have I set my face like a flint, and I know that I shall not be ashamed' (Isaiah 50:5-7).

For the glory of God, for the honour of his holy law, for the redemption of his people, and in order to complete the work for which he came into the world, the Lord Jesus Christ perseveres in his agony, until at last he cries, 'It is finished'! Then he gives up the ghost.

Do you hear this mighty shout of triumph? It is the word of the conquering King. It rings out today with all the freshness and force with which it rang out from Calvary more than two thousand years ago! 'It is finished'! Hear it from the sacred word. Hear it from the Saviour's lips. May God the Holy Ghost give you grace to hear these three words of the sinner's Saviour ringing in your very soul. 'It is finished'! Oh, may all who read these lines enter into the experience of this blessed conquest.

'When Jesus therefore had received the vinegar, he said, It is finished: and he bowed his head, and gave up the ghost.'

I can almost see our Saviour as he looks up to God his Father, as he looks around to the wondering angels of light, as he looks down upon Satan and the demons of hell, and as he looks out over the perishing multitudes of men. When he declares, 'It is finished', he is testifying to heaven and earth and hell that redemption's work is done! I want to show you four things about the finished work of Christ in this study.

The Fact Of It

In the first place, as you hear these words fall from the Saviour's lips, 'It is finished'! I want you to realise the fact of it. When the Lord Jesus Christ died upon the cursed tree, the work of redemption was then and there complete. Nothing was left undone. Nothing more needed to be done. Nothing more could be done. Christ had come into the world to redeem a people unto himself; and those people are redeemed.

'Seventy weeks are determined upon thy people and upon thy holy city, to finish the transgression, and to make an end of sins, and to make reconciliation for iniquity, and to bring in everlasting righteousness, and to seal up the vision and prophecy, and to anoint the most Holy' (Daniel 9:24).

That which Daniel prophesied, the Son of God declares finished by his sacrificial death as our Substitute at Calvary. What did our Saviour mean when he said, 'It is finished?'

He meant that all the types, promises, and prophecies of the Old Testament scriptures were fulfilled and finished forever. The Old Testament scriptures tailor a garment that will fit only one Person, and that Person is the Lord Jesus Christ (Genesis 3:15; 49:10; Psalms 40:6-8; Isaiah 52:13-53:12; Micah 5:2; Malachi 4:2). There is not a single promise, or type, or prophecy of the Old Testament that does not find its perfect and complete fulfilment in Christ. Not only does the garment fit him perfectly, it fits him alone. Only the Lord Jesus Christ fits the character of that One who was promised in the Old Testament. He is a Prophet like Moses and a Deliverer like Joshua. He is a Priest like Aaron and like Melchisedec. He is a King like David and like Solomon. He is the Lamb that was slain and the Scapegoat that was not slain. He is the Turtledove that was dipped in blood and the Priest who killed the bird. He is the Altar and the Tabernacle. He is the Mercy-Seat and the Shewbread. He is the Sacrifice and the Sacrificer. Everything in the Old Testament points to Christ.

When our Lord said, 'It is finished', he meant that all the typical sacrifices of the ceremonial law were completely fulfilled and, therefore, forever abolished (Hebrews 10:1-14). Judaism today is just as idolatrous as Romanism. God has put aside forever the carnal ordinances of the Old Testament. 'God is Spirit: and they that worship him must worship him in spirit and in truth' (John 4:24).

When the Lord Jesus cried, 'It is finished', he meant that all the duties and commandments of the moral law of God were now perfectly fulfilled and that the rule of the law was, therefore, ended and abolished forever. 'For Christ is the end of the law for righteousness to every one that believeth' (Romans 10:4). The age of sonship has come; and the sons of God are no longer subject to the tutelage and discipline of the law. All who are taught of God are made willing servants in the day of his power. Those who give from a willing heart generously do not need a law to compel them to pay a legal tax. Those who rest in Christ do not need to be ordered to keep a sabbath day. Our lives are a perpetual Sabbath. Those who love Christ do not need the ball and chain of the law to make them do what is right for the glory of Christ.

When he cried, 'It is finished', our blessed Lord proclaimed that the way of access has been opened up to God. The veil of the temple was torn in two, from top to bottom, telling us that a way was opened for sinful man to approach the holy God (Hebrews 10:19-22).

When the Lord Jesus Christ cried, 'It is finished', he declared that he had perfectly accomplished the redemption of his people (Galatians 3:13; Hebrews 9:12). The work his Father gave him to do was done. All that he had agreed upon in the covenant of grace as our Surety, he had now fulfilled (John 17:4). He had brought in an everlasting righteousness. He had satisfied divine justice. The debt was paid. The debtors discharged. By his one offering for sin upon the cursed tree, the atonement was accomplished, propitiation was made, reconciliation between God and his covenant people was complete; and he perfected forever them that are sanctified. The cup of wrath was drained. The whip of justice was worn out on his back. The curse of the law fell on him and the thunder of Sinai was silenced. He swallowed up the sword of God's infinite wrath and justice in his holy soul. He had annihilated the sins of his people. He had conquered Satan. He had defeated death.

'It is finished'! Oh, child of God, I want you to recognise this blessed fact. In the substitutionary death of Christ at Calvary, the Old Testament scriptures are fulfilled, the typical sacrifices of the ceremonial law are forever abolished, the commandments of the moral law are all perfectly and representatively performed for us and fulfilled for us the way of access to God is open and the redemption of our souls is accomplished.

The Result Of It

In the second place, as you hear these words, sounded out by our mighty Saviour, 'It is finished', I want you to rejoice in the result of it. Did you hear the Son of God say, 'It is finished?' Believe it, my friend. It is true. The Lord Jesus Christ, by his representative life and vicarious atonement in our place, has finished the work of redemption for us. And having finished the work which the Father gave him to do, there are certain inevitable consequences which must follow. The death of Christ was an effectual atonement for sin. Let me briefly show you what some of the results of our Lord's sacrifice are.

Because of our Saviour's finished work, the covenant of God's grace has been ratified and put into force (Hebrews 9:15-17). The covenant was signed and sealed before all worlds. It was ordered in all things and sure by God's eternal decree. But when Christ said, 'It is finished', that covenant was put into force by blood. Not one stipulation of the covenant could ever be broken, not one promise could ever fail. All the blessings of the covenant were made sure to all of God's elect by the blood of Christ. Though he died to put his will in force, our crucified Redeemer lives in heaven to see to it that his will is executed (Isaiah 53:10-12).

Because of the finished work of our Lord Jesus Christ, God Almighty, in his perfect holiness, is both just and the Justifier of guilty sinners (Romans 3:24-26). Since the God-man died, there is hope for sinners! Through the propitiatory atonement of Christ, God can be just and still justify the ungodly. Indeed, the justice of God demands that all for whom Christ died must go free.

Because of the finished work of Christ, the Holy Spirit has come down from heaven to gather out God's elect (Galatians 3:13, 14; John 16:7-14). Since the Holy Spirit has been poured out upon all flesh, the gospel is sent into all the world. The gospel of God's free, sovereign, saving grace in Christ is a worldwide message (Joel 2:32). 'Whosoever shall call upon the name of the Lord shall be saved.'

Because of the finished work of Christ, the salvation of God's elect is sure and secure (John 6:39). He who entered into heaven with his own blood, having obtained eternal redemption for his people, will see to it that his people all have the eternal redemption he obtained for them.

Every sinner bought by blood
Shall at last be brought to God.
Truth and justice make it plain
Jesus did not die in vain!

None for whom the Saviour bled
Can be severed from their Head.
Called by grace! Kept forever!
Jesus is a mighty Saviour!

Not one soul for whom Christ shed his blood at Calvary shall ever perish. All of his elect shall be saved. All of his redeemed ones are secure. Justice demands it! 'He shall see of the travail of his soul and shall be satisfied'. Our sins are gone. The law has no claim upon us. Christ cannot fail (Isaiah 45:23-25). That means every blood-bought soul shall be with Christ in glory!

Because of the finished work of our Lord Jesus Christ, the glory of God is revealed in the gospel (2 Corinthians 4:6; 2 Timothy 1:9, 10). In the cross of Christ we see all the marvellous attributes of the eternal Godhead brilliantly displayed. His holiness and his goodness, his justice and his mercy, his truth and his grace, his immutability and his wisdom, his greatness and his love.

Because of his finished work as our Redeemer, the Lord Jesus Christ is exalted to the throne of universal monarchy to rule over all flesh (Philippians 2:9-11; Psalms 2:8).

The Experience Of It

The work of redemption which secured the salvation of all God's elect was completed at Calvary by Christ alone. Its results were immediately effected. When he died in my place, and I died in him, my soul was as safe and secure under his blood as it is today. But I did not know it until he came by the power of his Spirit and brought me into the experience of it.

So, in the third place, when you hear the Saviour say, 'It is finished', I want you to know the experience of it. In preaching the gospel, we proclaim to men the good news of full redemption, the glad tidings of full atonement, and the comforting message of full pardon. We know nothing of a possible redemption, a partial redemption, or a potential redemption. We proclaim an accomplished redemption. We declare to sinners everywhere that for all who look to Christ, 'the warfare is over' (Isaiah 40:1, 2).

How can a poor, lost, spiritually dead sinner enter into the experience of Christ's finished work? I can tell you this: if ever you come to experience the finished work of Christ in everlasting salvation, it will be the result of his work and his work alone. The Lord must send his word to heal your soul, or you will never be saved (Psalms 107:20; Ephesians 1:13). The Lord must send his Spirit into your heart, or you cannot live. Christ himself must be revealed to you and in you, or you cannot believe (Galatians 1:15, 16; Philippians 3:3). When God reveals Christ in your heart, he gives you faith to trust him, he proclaims peace in your soul, he breaks the iron chains of your sin, and he causes your troubled soul to find rest in him (Psalms 107:1-31). Only he can do it!

The Cause Of It

In the fourth place, as you hear the Lord Jesus Christ cry, 'It is finished', I want you to see and appreciate the cause of it. Why should the Lord Jesus Christ endure the painful, shameful, ignominious death of the cross for me? What caused the Son of God to stand as my Surety and agree to finish the work of my soul's redemption? What motivated our Lord in this blessed work? The book of God tells us. It was his Father's will (Psalms 40:7, 8). There was no other possible means of saving us (Galatians 2:21). He loved us, and he was determined to have us (Malachi 3:17). And the Lord our God was determined to glorify himself by saving us (Psalms 106:8; Ephesians 2:7).

'It is finished'! God will never accept the works of your hands; but he has accepted the work of his Son's hand. Will you rest your soul upon the finished work of Christ alone?

‘It is finished’

Nothing, either great or small;
Nothing, sinner, no;
Jesus did it, did it all,
Long, long ago!

When He, from His lofty throne,
Stooped to do and die,
Everything was fully done;
Hearken to His cry

‘It is finished’! Yes indeed,
Finished every jot.
Sinner, this is all you need.
Tell me, Is it not?

Weary, working, plodding one,
Why toil you so?
Cease your doing, all was done,
Long, long ago!

Till to Jesus’ work you cling
By a simple faith,
Doing is a deadly thing.
Doing ends in death!

Cast your deadly ‘doing’ down,
Down at Jesus’ feet.
Stand in Him, in Him alone,
Gloriously complete!

James Procter

‘Not unto us, O LORD, not unto us, but unto thy name give glory, for thy mercy, and for thy truth’s sake’ (Psalms 115:1).

Chapter 59

Lessons From The Resurrection

'The first day of the week cometh Mary Magdalene early, when it was yet dark, unto the sepulchre, and seeth the stone taken away from the sepulchre. Then she runneth, and cometh to Simon Peter, and to the other disciple, whom Jesus loved, and saith unto them, They have taken away the Lord out of the sepulchre, and we know not where they have laid him. Peter therefore went forth, and that other disciple, and came to the sepulchre. So they ran both together: and the other disciple did outrun Peter, and came first to the sepulchre. And he stooping down, and looking in, saw the linen clothes lying; yet went he not in. Then cometh Simon Peter following him, and went into the sepulchre, and seeth the linen clothes lie, And the napkin, that was about his head, not lying with the linen clothes, but wrapped together in a place by itself. Then went in also that other disciple, which came first to the sepulchre, and he saw, and believed. For as yet they knew not the scripture, that he must rise again from the dead. Then the disciples went away again unto their own home. But Mary stood without at the sepulchre weeping: and as she wept, she stooped down, and looked into the sepulchre, And seeth two angels in white sitting, the one at the head, and the other at the feet, where the body of Jesus had lain. And they say unto her, Woman, why weepest thou? She saith unto them, Because they have taken away my Lord, and I know not where they have laid him. And when she had thus said, she turned herself back, and saw Jesus standing, and knew not that it was Jesus. Jesus saith unto her, Woman, why weepest thou? whom seekest thou? She, supposing him to be the gardener, saith unto him, Sir, if thou have borne him hence, tell me where thou hast laid him, and I will take him away. Jesus saith unto her, Mary. She turned herself, and saith unto him, Rabboni; which is to say, Master. Jesus saith unto her, Touch me not; for I am not yet ascended to my Father: but go to my brethren, and say unto them, I ascend unto my Father, and your Father; and to my God, and your God. Mary Magdalene came and told the disciples that she had seen the Lord, and that he had spoken these things unto her' (John 20:1-18).

I once read about an old woman, a believer, whose age began to take its toll on her, especially on her memory. At one time, she knew much of the Bible by heart. Eventually only one precious, little portion stayed with her: 'I know whom I have believed, and am persuaded that he is able to keep that which I have committed unto him against that day'. Soon, part of that slipped from her mind, as well. She would be found often quietly repeating what she could of the text. Family and friends would hear her going over it again and again. – 'That which I have committed unto him'. Just before she slipped out of this world into glory, her children noticed her lips moving, and they bent over to hear what she was saying. She was repeating just one word, 'him ... him ... him'. She had lost her memory of the whole Bible and of everything else, but one word. Yet, she had the whole Bible and had everything in that one word 'him'. This blessed book is all about 'him'. I want you to know, trust, love, and worship 'him'. May God the Holy Spirit now set our hearts on 'him'.

John 20 takes us from Christ's death upon the cursed tree as our sin-atoning Substitute to his resurrection. He who was delivered up to the painful, shameful, ignominious death of the cross because of our sins which were made his own, arose from the dead because of our justification accomplished by his death, by his satisfaction of divine justice with his own blood. But I am not interested in merely convincing people that the doctrine of the resurrection is true. I want to know, and I want you to know him who is himself 'the resurrection and the life'. May God give us grace to know him and the power of his resurrection.

Like Matthew, Mark, and Luke, John dwells on these two great events with peculiar fulness and specificity. We need not wonder why. The whole gospel of the grace of God, the whole of our saving faith, the whole salvation of our souls hangs on these facts: 'That Christ died for our sins according to the scriptures; and that he was buried, and that he rose again the third day according to the scriptures' (1 Corinthians 15:3, 4). What are the lessons God the Holy Ghost intends for us to learn from this portion of holy scripture?

Forgiveness And Love

First, we are reminded that those who are forgiven most love most (Luke 7:36-50). The first one John names among those who came to the Saviour's tomb is Mary Magdalene. The history of this faithful woman is not given in any detail in the word of God. We only know that she was one out of whom the Lord had cast 'seven devils' (Mark 16:9; Luke 8:2). Mary had been possessed of the devil and wasted her life serving him, until the Lord Jesus saved her by his grace. From that day on, Mary was always by his side, following him, hanging on his every word, and observing his wondrous works.

It was this woman, if I am not mistaken, who anointed the Lord Jesus in the house of Simon the leper. The Master was referring to her when he asked Simon, 'Who will love most?' He was referring to her when he said, 'Her sins, which are many, are forgiven; for she loved much: but to whom little is forgiven, the same loveth little' (Luke 7:47).

Mary's gratitude to our Lord for his deliverance of her soul from the clutches of hell and for his forgiveness of her sins was a gratitude that knew no bounds. Mary Magdalene had been forgiven much; and she loved much. She felt that she owed so much to the Saviour. She felt strongly that there was nothing too great to do for Christ, and nothing too much to sacrifice for him. Mary was the last at the cross. Mary was the first at the sepulchre. Mary arose early and came to the tomb while it was still dark. Having been forgiven much, Mary loved much. Having received much, she loved much; and loving much, she did much, constrained only by a heart of love for and gratitude to her Saviour.

The fact is, the more fully and more deeply we are aware of our depravity and sin, the more we will cherish our Saviour and the forgiveness of our sins by his blood. To whom much is forgiven, the same love much. Where sin is not deeply and painfully felt, little is done for Christ. The man who is deeply conscious of his own guilt and corruption, and deeply convinced that without the blood, the death, the grace, and intercession of Christ he would sink forever into the lowest hell, that is the man who will spend and be spent for the Saviour. That is the man who thinks, 'I can never do enough for my Redeemer'. Spirit of God, make me such a man! Give me Mary's sense of indebtedness, gratitude, and love for 'the Son of God who loved me and gave himself for me'! Show me more of myself! Show me more of Christ! Show me more of God's amazing grace to me in him!

When we begin to realise the greatness of our sin and the greatness of Christ's forgiveness, then, only then, can we begin to understand what the Apostle Paul meant when he said, 'The love of Christ constraineth us; because we thus judge, that if one died for all, then were all dead: and that he died for all, that they which live should not henceforth live unto themselves, but unto him which died for them, and rose again' (2 Corinthians 5:14, 15).

Take my life and let it be
Consecrated, Lord, to Thee!

Different Personalities

Second, God the Holy Ghost here reminds us again that God's saints are not all alike in personality and temperament. When Mary Magdalene told Peter and John, 'They have taken away the Lord out of the sepulchre, and we know not where they have laid him' (v. 3), as they ran to the sepulchre and arrived at the place, all three acted differently.

They all ran to the sepulchre; but John, the disciple whom Jesus loved, outran Peter and reached the empty grave first. John stooped down and looked in, but went no further. Peter, a bit more zealous and impulsive, ran right into the sepulchre that he might see with his own eyes. Mary, apparently, came somewhat more slowly back to the tomb and quietly waited to see what Peter and John would do and say. They all loved the Lord Jesus and trusted him. The hearts of these three believers were, no doubt, full of hopes, and fears, and anxieties, and expectations, all tangled together. Yet each behaved in their own characteristic fashion. Without question, these things were intentionally written by the Spirit of God for our learning.

We should always remember that there are great differences of personality and temperament among God's saints. All are redeemed, justified, and sanctified. All are washed in the blood of Christ. All live and walk in the Spirit. All seek the glory of God. But God's saints are not all alike. We do not do things exactly the same way. We do not all react to things the same way.

If we will remember this simple fact, it will save us much trouble in the journey of life and prevent many unkind and uncharitable thoughts and words. We should never judge one another harshly, or think ill of others, because they do not see or feel things exactly as we do, or because things do not affect them in the same way they affect us. The flowers in the Lord's garden are not all of one colour and of one scent, though they are all planted by one Spirit and are all in his garden. The subjects of his kingdom do not all look alike or always act alike, though they all love the same Saviour and all have their names written in the same Book of Life. The Church of Christ has some in its ranks who are like Peter, and some who are like John, and some who are like Mary. Some are fathers, some are elders, some are young men, some are mothers, some are children; but all are God's. Let us always treat them as such. All who trust the Lord Jesus are loved and chosen of God the Father. All who trust him are loved and redeemed by God the Son. All who are born again are loved and called by God the Spirit.

'If there be therefore any consolation in Christ, if any comfort of love, if any fellowship of the Spirit, if any bowels and mercies, fulfil ye my joy, that ye be likeminded, having the same love, being of one accord, of one mind. Let nothing be done through strife or vainglory; but in lowliness of mind let each esteem other better than themselves. Look not every man on his own things, but every man also on the things of others. Let this mind be in you, which was also in Christ Jesus' (Philippians 2:1-5).

Much Ignorance

Third, we must never forget that there is much ignorance in true believers. 'For as yet they knew not the scripture, that he must rise again from the dead' (v. 9). That fact seems utterly incredible. For three years the Lord's disciples had heard him declare repeatedly that his resurrection from the dead would be the proof of his messiahship and the means by which he would take his seat upon the throne of heaven as the Son of David. Yet, it appears that none of them, except Mary, had paid any attention to his words in that regard. These were true believers; but they were very ignorant of some very important gospel truths.

If the Lord's disciples remained so ignorant of this simple, vital fact, after sitting under his ministry for three years, no faithful gospel preacher should be surprised to find that those who hear him are ignorant of a few things. The one thing needful is not a head full of knowledge, but a heart full of Christ! 'Christ in you, the Hope of glory'!

Some things we must know if we would be saved. We must know our sinfulness and guilt before God. We must know Christ and his accomplishments as our Saviour and Redeemer. We must know that salvation is by the grace of God, through faith in Christ.

The extent to which one man may have true grace with much ignorance and another may have much knowledge and no grace is one of the greatest mysteries in world. It is a mystery that only the day of judgment will unravel. Let us then seek knowledge, and be ashamed of ignorance. But above all, let us make sure that Christ is ours. Let us make our calling and election sure, trusting the Son of God as our only Lord and Saviour!

Baseless Fears

Fourth, let us learn from this portion of holy scripture that our countless fears and sorrows are, for the most part, to be attributed to our own ignorance and unbelief. We are told that Mary stood at the sepulchre weeping, and wept as if nothing could comfort her.

Only John was inspired of God to record the conversation that took place between Mary Magdalene and the Lord Jesus in verses 11-18. Yet, this is, in my opinion, the most heart touching account of our Lord's many appearances after his resurrection.

When Peter and John went to their homes, Mary stayed at the sepulchre. Love to her Lord would not let her leave the place where he had been laid.

Where he was now, she did not know. What had become of him, she could not tell. But she could not drag herself away from the empty tomb, where Joseph and Nicodemus had laid her Lord. And her loving attachment to the Lord Jesus was richly honoured. Mary Magdalene saw the angels whom Peter and John never observed. Mary Magdalene heard those angels speak words of comfort to her heart. Mary Magdalene was the first to see our Lord Jesus after he rose from the dead, the first to hear his voice, the first to hold conversation with him.

Blessed are those who wait to find the Saviour! Mary stood there at the place where the Lord Jesus was last seen, waiting for him. There she stands in silence, weeping with great sorrow, looking in, not knowing how to leave the sacred spot. Let us wait like Mary in the house of God to worship him, before the preaching of the gospel to hear his word, at the Lord's Table to remember him. Like the spouse of old, let us send out the anxious inquiry, 'Saw ye him whom my soul loveth?' (Song of Solomon 3:3). 'I charge you, O daughters of Jerusalem, if ye find my Beloved, that ye tell him, that I am sick of love' (Song of Solomon 5:8).

Yet, we are told that Mary stood there 'weeping' (v. 11). She wept in great sorrow and fear, as if nothing could comfort her. She wept when the angels spoke to her. She wept when the Lord Jesus himself spoke to her. But her sorrows and fears were completely baseless. Had she only known what had happened, was happening, and would soon happen, she would have been dancing and rejoicing.

O my brother, my sister, how readily we must identify ourselves with Mary in this! We often weep when we should really rejoice. We cry too much, like Jacob, 'All these things are against me', when in reality, our God is working all things together for our good! If we could see as God sees, if we knew what he knows, in every circumstance, in every event, we would give thanks and praise to him. I can hear you say, 'But, pastor, we can't see as God sees or know what he knows'. I understand that; but we ought to be able to trust him. 'Rejoice evermore. Pray without ceasing. In everything give thanks: for this is the will of God in Christ Jesus concerning you' (1 Thessalonians 5:16-18).

Christ Near

Fifth, the Spirit of God reminds us here that the Lord Jesus is very near, even when, perhaps especially when, we are altogether unaware of his presence. Mary complained, 'They have taken away my Lord, and I know not where they have laid him' (v. 13). Yet, all the while her risen Lord was right beside her, with body, and flesh, and bones. Her tears were needless. Her anxiety was unnecessary. Like Hagar in the wilderness, she had a well of water by her side; but she had no eyes to see it. Child of God, when your heart is empty, he is near to fill it. When your heart is cold, he is near to warm it. When your soul is languishing, he is near to revive it. When you are weak, he is near to strengthen you. When you are fallen, he is near to lift you up.

'Rejoice in the Lord alway: and again I say, Rejoice. Let your moderation be known unto all men. The Lord is at hand. Be careful for nothing; but in everything by prayer and supplication with thanksgiving let your requests be made known unto God. And the peace of God, which passeth all understanding, shall keep your hearts and minds through Christ Jesus' (Philippians 4:4-7).

Discoveries Of Christ

Sixth, every discovery we have of Christ is the result of him discovering himself to us. Though the Lord Jesus was standing in front of her, and talking with her, Mary did not and could not know him until he made himself known to her (vv. 15, 16). So it is with us. We cannot know the Lord Jesus either before we are converted or after we are converted, except he make himself know to us (Isaiah 65:24; 2 Corinthians 4:6; 1 John 4:19, 20).

Union With Christ

Seventh, let us learn and rejoice to know that all that is Christ's is ours in him. 'Jesus saith unto her, Touch me not; for I am not yet ascended to my Father: but go to my brethren, and say unto them, I ascend unto my Father, and your Father; and to my God, and your God' (v. 17). There was nothing wrong with Mary touching him. He later commanded Thomas to do so. But the Lord was saying to Mary, 'There is no need for you to be clinging to my body. I have something for you to do. Go tell my disciples that I have risen from the dead' 'Mary Magdalene came and told the disciples that she had seen the Lord, and that he had spoken these things unto her' (v. 18). It is not the physical presence of Christ that we need, but his grace and spiritual presence. The Lord Jesus has left us here to tell others that he has accomplished redemption by the sacrifice of himself, risen from the dead, and sits on the throne of grace to give repentance and remission of sins to needy sinners.

'Go to my brethren, and say unto them, I ascend unto my Father, and your Father; and to my God, and your God'. Be sure you get this. Roll it over in sweet meditation and joy, with praise and thanksgiving. Carry it with you through the day and through the night, as you make your pilgrimage through this world. Child of God, all that is Christ's is yours and mine in him! His Father is our Father. His God is our God. His obedience is our obedience. His death is our death. His reward is our reward. His inheritance is our inheritance. His glory is our glory. His safety is our safety. We are one with him as he is one with the Father!

Chapter 60

The Tomb Was Not Empty

‘The first day of the week cometh Mary Magdalene early, when it was yet dark, unto the sepulchre, and seeth the stone taken away from the sepulchre. Then she runneth, and cometh to Simon Peter, and to the other disciple, whom Jesus loved, and saith unto them, They have taken away the Lord out of the sepulchre, and we know not where they have laid him. Peter therefore went forth, and that other disciple, and came to the sepulchre. So they ran both together: and the other disciple did outrun Peter, and came first to the sepulchre. And he stooping down, and looking in, saw the linen clothes lying; yet went he not in. Then cometh Simon Peter following him, and went into the sepulchre, and seeth the linen clothes lie, And the napkin, that was about his head, not lying with the linen clothes, but wrapped together in a place by itself. Then went in also that other disciple, which came first to the sepulchre, and he saw, and believed. For as yet they knew not the scripture, that he must rise again from the dead. Then the disciples went away again unto their own home. But Mary stood without at the sepulchre weeping: and as she wept, she stooped down, and looked into the sepulchre, And seeth two angels in white sitting, the one at the head, and the other at the feet, where the body of Jesus had lain. And they say unto her, Woman, why weepest thou? She saith unto them, Because they have taken away my Lord, and I know not where they have laid him. And when she had thus said, she turned herself back, and saw Jesus standing, and knew not that it was Jesus. Jesus saith unto her, Woman, why weepest thou? whom seekest thou? She, supposing him to be the gardener, saith unto him, Sir, if thou have borne him hence, tell me where thou hast laid him, and I will take him away. Jesus saith unto her, Mary. She turned herself, and saith unto him, Rabboni; which is to say, Master. Jesus saith unto her, Touch me not; for I am not yet ascended to my Father: but go to my brethren, and say unto them, I ascend unto my Father, and your Father; and to my God, and your God. Mary Magdalene came and told the disciples that she had seen the Lord, and that he had spoken these things unto her' (John 20:1-18).

We who believe in the risen Christ have entered into his rest, because he is resting at the right hand of the Father. We rest in Christ, the risen Redeemer, because his work is finished. His resurrection is the pledge that he has perfected forever them that are sanctified. He has finished all the salvation of his people; and we are complete in him. It is my hope that God the Holy Spirit will enable me to set before you some restful thoughts, as we make a pilgrimage to the new tomb of Joseph of Arimathea, and see the place where the Lord lay.

Once Died

The very first thing that must be remembered is this: Christ Jesus once died. 'For in that he died, he died unto sin once: but in that he liveth, he liveth unto God' (Romans 6:10). So, as we gather around the place where the Lord Jesus slept 'with the rich in his death', seeing the stone rolled from the mouth of the tomb, we know he is not there. Yet, he assuredly was once there. 'He was crucified, dead, and buried.' He was as dead as the dead whose bodies are buried in the cemetery down the road. Though he could see no corruption, though he could not be held by the bands of death beyond the predestined time, yet he was once dead. There was a time when there was no light in his eye, no sound in his ear, no thought in his mind, and no word in his mouth, because there was no pulse of life in his heart. Christ died for our sins. He did not merely appear to be dead. He died unto sin once, because he was made sin for us. He was, therefore, buried in the sepulchre. A dead man is a fit occupant of the silent tomb. But, blessed be his name, he is not there now! He is risen from the dead. We look to the risen Christ as our only Saviour and our only salvation (Romans 4:25-5:11). As we take another look at this portion of holy scripture, I want to call your attention to some memorials of the fact that our blessed Saviour was once in the tomb, memorials that he has left for us in the tomb.

'Moreover, brethren, I declare unto you the gospel which I preached unto you, which also ye have received, and wherein ye stand; by which also ye are saved, if ye keep in memory what I preached unto you, unless ye have believed in vain. For I delivered unto you first of all that which I also received, how that Christ died for our sins according to the scriptures; and that he was buried, and that he rose again the third day according to the scriptures' (1 Corinthians 15:1-4).

Sweet Spices

What memorials of this fact can be found in the tomb? How are they to be used by us? First, the Lord Jesus left sweet spices in the tomb. When he arose, he did not take those costly spices in which his body was wrapped with him. He left them behind. Joseph had brought about one hundred pounds of myrrh and aloes, and the sweet aroma of those spices remained in the tomb. That tomb must have smelled like a perfume store when Peter and John stepped into it.

What a blessed thought that is, when taken in a spiritual sense! Our Lord Jesus has filled the grave with sweet fragrances. It no longer smells of corruption and foul decay, but we can sing:

Why should we tremble to convey
The Christian to the tomb?
There the dear flesh of Jesus lay,
And left a long perfume.

The graves of all the saints He blessed,
And softened every bed;
Where should the dying members rest,
But with their dying Head?

Thence He arose, ascending high,
And showed our feet the way;
Up to the Lord we, too, shall fly,
At that great rising-day.

Then let the last loud trumpet sound,
And bid our kindred rise:
Awake, ye nations under ground;
Ye saints, ascend the skies.

Isaac Watts

That bed awaiting our bodies beneath the earth is now perfumed with costly spices and decked with sweet flowers. There, the truest Friend we have, once laid his holy head. The angel's first word to the women who came to the tomb was, 'Fear not ye' (Matthew 28:5). We should never draw back with fear from the grave. Our Lord was once there; and where he goes no terror can remain.

'Yea, though I walk through the valley of the shadow of death, I will fear no evil: for thou art with me; thy rod and thy staff they comfort me' (Psalms 23:4).

Grave Clothes

Next, we see here that our Saviour left his grave clothes behind him in the tomb. When John stooped down and looked into the sepulchre, he saw the grave clothes carefully folded by themselves, lying to one side. Our Lord Jesus did not leave behind him a mouldy shroud, but, as John tells us in verse 5, 'linen clothes'.

He left those grave clothes for us to look upon as tokens of his fellowship with us in our low estate, as reminders that as he has cast aside the garments of death, so shall we. When he arose from his chamber, he left his bedclothes behind. And when we drop these bodies in death, as we ascend up to heaven, we will leave these garments of death behind (Psalms 17:5; 27:13; Isaiah 57:1, 2; 2 Corinthians 4:16-5:9).

Look at it another way. We have seen old tattered flags hung up in places as the memorials of victory, memorials of defeated enemies and battles won. So in the tomb where the Saviour vanquished death, his grave clothes are hung up as the trophies of his victory over death and assurances to us that we have been made more than conquerors through him that loved us. 'O death, where is thy sting? O grave, where is thy victory?'

Take one more look at those linen grave clothes in the fragrant tomb. Do they not lay before your eye of faith as emblems of his righteousness, that righteousness by which he merits heavenly glory as our Surety, that righteousness he has made ours, by which we are made 'meet to be partakers of the inheritance of the saints in light'? Nothing makes the grave more comfortable than the blessed assurance that we are the very righteousness of God in Christ Jesus. The garments of salvation we wear before our God are the blessed linen garments of perfect righteousness (Psalms 132:7-9; Revelation 14:4, 5; 19:6-9)

The Napkin

Then, John tells us that Peter saw 'the napkin that was about his head' carefully folded up and laid by itself. 'Then cometh Simon Peter following him, and went into the sepulchre, and seeth the linen clothes lie, and the napkin, that was about his head, not lying with the linen clothes, but wrapped together in a place by itself.'

I see that napkin in my Saviour's tomb still. It is the handkerchief with which the Lord God wipes every tear from my eyes. The widow and the orphan, the widower and the broken-hearted father, mourning brothers, and sisters, and friends, take this handkerchief and wipe their tears away forever.

'Thus saith the LORD; Refrain thy voice from weeping, and thine eyes from tears: for thy work shall be rewarded, saith the LORD; and they shall come again from the land of the enemy' (Jeremiah 31:16). 'Thy dead men shall live, together with my dead body shall they arise. Awake and sing, ye that dwell in dust: for thy dew is as the dew of herbs, and the earth shall cast out the dead' (Isaiah 26:19).

And with this same handkerchief, he wipes away all other tears from our eyes. Tears of repentance, tears of trouble, tears of fear, and tears of bereavement, all our tears our heavenly Father sweetly dries with this handkerchief of grace (Revelation 7:17; 21:4).

Angels

Our Lord Jesus left something else in his tomb. He left angels behind him and made the grave,

> A cell which angels use
> To come and go with heavenly news.

Angels were not in the tomb before, but, at his resurrection, they descended. One rolled away the stone; and others sat where the Saviour's body once laid. I have never read that our Master has recalled the angels from the sepulchres of his saints. And we are assured that when his Lazaruses die, the angels of God carry their souls into the bosom of their Lord; and their bodies, too, shall be watched by guardian spirits, as surely as Michael kept the body of Moses until the resurrection.

A Way Out

Another thing was left behind in the tomb by our blessed Redeemer: a way out. He left an open passage from the tomb. The stone was rolled away. Why? Does he not by this remind us that death is, for God's elect, a prison without bars or doors? The open tomb tells me there is a Door open in heaven. The risen Christ is the Way out of death for us. Blessed be his name, he is the Way, the Way of Life, the Way out of spiritual death!

> From darkest night to brilliant light,
> O praise His name, He lifted me!

And he who is the Way of Life, the Way out of spiritual death, is also for his ransomed ones, the Way out of physical death and the Way out of the second death (Revelation 20:1-6). Our mighty Samson has pulled up the posts and carried away the gates of the grave with all their bars. The key is taken from the girdle of death and is held in the hand of the Prince of Life. As Peter, when he was visited by the angel, found that his chains fell off, while iron gates opened to him of their own accord, so shall the saints find ready escape at the resurrection morning. Yes, we shall sleep awhile, each one in his resting-place; but we shall rise again in the morning, for the stone is rolled away. A mighty Angel rolled away the stone, for it was very great, and when he had done the deed, he sat down upon the stone. His garment was white as snow, and his face like lightning, and as he sat on the stone, he seemed to say to death and hell, 'Roll it back again if you can.' That mighty Angel who rolled away the stone from the tomb for us is Christ himself!

Light

Our risen Saviour left one more thing behind in his tomb. Tombs are places of darkness. But our Lord Jesus left in his tomb the light of life. God 'hath saved us, and called us with an holy calling, not according to our works, but according to his own purpose and grace, which was given us in Christ Jesus before the world began, but is now made manifest by the appearing of our Saviour Jesus Christ, who hath abolished death, and hath brought life and immortality to light through the gospel: whereunto I am appointed a preacher, and an apostle, and a teacher of the Gentiles' (2 Timothy 1:9-11).

Our Lord has gone into the tomb and illuminated it with his presence, 'the lamp of his love is our guide through the gloom'. He has brought life and immortality to light by the gospel; and now in every cemetery there is a light which shall burn through the watches of earth's night till the day break and the shadows flee away, and the resurrection morn shall dawn.

When I have breathed my final breath
And dropped this robe of flesh in death,
When my appointed work is done
And my allotted time is gone,
Don't stand around my grave and cry.
I'll not be there. I did not die.

My Saviour came to call me home,
And I with Him to heav'n have gone!
Now I am free from sin and pain;
And with the glorified I reign!
Don't stand around my grave and cry.
I'm glorified! I did not die!

Seated with Jesus on His throne,
Glorified by what He has done,
I am a trophy of His grace.
Rejoicing, I behold His face:
Don't stand around my grave and cry.
I am with Christ! I did not die!

My body lies beneath the clay
Until the resurrection day.
In that day when Christ comes again,
Body and soul unite again!
Don't stand around my grave and cry.
Rejoice with me! I did not die!

Chapter 61

'Then were the disciples glad'

'Mary Magdalene came and told the disciples that she had seen the Lord, and that he had spoken these things unto her. Then the same day at evening, being the first day of the week, when the doors were shut where the disciples were assembled for fear of the Jews, came Jesus and stood in the midst, and saith unto them, Peace be unto you. And when he had so said, he shewed unto them his hands and his side. Then were the disciples glad, when they saw the Lord. Then said Jesus to them again, Peace be unto you: as my Father hath sent me, even so send I you. And when he had said this, he breathed on them, and saith unto them, Receive ye the Holy Ghost: Whose soever sins ye remit, they are remitted unto them; and whose soever sins ye retain, they are retained. But Thomas, one of the twelve, called Didymus, was not with them when Jesus came. The other disciples therefore said unto him, We have seen the Lord. But he said unto them, Except I shall see in his hands the print of the nails, and put my finger into the print of the nails, and thrust my hand into his side, I will not believe. And after eight days again his disciples were within, and Thomas with them: then came Jesus, the doors being shut, and stood in the midst, and said, Peace be unto you. Then saith he to Thomas, Reach hither thy finger, and behold my hands; and reach hither thy hand, and thrust it into my side: and be not faithless, but believing. And Thomas answered and said unto him, My Lord and my God. Jesus saith unto him, Thomas, because thou hast seen me, thou hast believed: blessed are they that have not seen, and yet have believed. And many other signs truly did Jesus in the presence of his disciples, which are not written in this book: But these are written, that ye might believe that Jesus is the Christ, the Son of God; and that believing ye might have life through his name' (John 20:18-31).

'Mary Magdalene came and told the disciples that she had seen the Lord, and that he had spoken these things unto her.' This was our Lord's first appearance after his resurrection from the dead (Mark 16:9). Matthew tells of another appearance to the women as they went to tell his disciples (Matthew 28:9, 10). Luke and Mark tell us that he appeared to two disciples as they were going to Emmaus (Luke 24:13-34; Mark 16:12, 13). These appearances were all on the same day on which he arose. They all took place on Sunday, the first day of the week. The Apostle Paul reports other appearances of the Lord Jesus during the time between his resurrection and his ascension (1 Corinthians 15:3-7).

After our Lord's resurrection from the dead, the disciples gathered for worship and breaking of bread on Sunday, the first day of the week, the day of Christ's resurrection. On this day the Lord arose and first appeared to his disciples. Never again did the disciples observe a legal sabbath. The gospel sabbath of faith in Christ began with the resurrection on Sunday morning.

Sunday is not, as many call it, 'the Christian Sabbath'. Christ is our Sabbath. We rest in him. Perhaps John is speaking of Sunday when he writes of 'the Lord's Day' (Revelation 1:10); but it is not a sabbath day. After the resurrection of our Lord, the disciples met on Sunday, the first day of the week, for worship, preaching, fellowship, breaking bread, and praise. We do not read anywhere in the New Testament of any congregation of Christians meeting on the Jewish Sabbath or observing any kind of sabbath day. The Apostles preached to the Jews assembled on Saturday; but no record is found of them meeting on Saturday for worship. There is no record of them again observing a legal sabbath day of any kind, to any degree. Our Sabbath is Christ (Hebrews 4:3-10). We observe the sabbath spiritually by faith, resting in the Saviour. Christ is our Rest, not a day but the Saviour himself! All legal sabbath day observance is strictly forbidden in the New Testament (Colossians 2:16-23).

'Then the same day at evening, being the first day of the week, when the doors were shut where the disciples were assembled for fear of the Jews, came Jesus and stood in the midst, and saith unto them, Peace be unto you. And when he had so said, he shewed unto them his hands and his side. Then were the disciples glad, when they saw the Lord.' Nothing gladdens the hearts of God's elect like the manifest presence of our Lord Jesus Christ, bestowing his grace and speaking peace to our hearts. Child of God, as you think about your risen Saviour, here are seven things which ought to make your heart glad.

The Peace He Gives

First, we are reminded that the peace Christ gives gladdens the hearts of his people. Twice the Lord Jesus addressed these disciples with the sweet, gentle, gracious words, 'Peace be unto you'. He who 'spake as never man spake' said nothing without meaning. He spoke to these disciples with special emphasis because of their present state of mind, with special reference to the events of the last few days, and with special reference to their future days. 'Peace' and not blame, 'peace' and not fault-finding, 'peace' and not rebuke, was the first word this little band of believers heard from their Master's lips after he arose from the tomb.

The Lord Jesus sent Mary to these disciples to prepare them for this most gracious visit; and what a refreshing and soul-satisfying visit it must have been! We hear no upbraiding for their recent desertions, nothing of reproach for their unbelief, no scolding for their failures, all was mercy, love, and grace!

'Peace on earth' was the song of the heavenly host, when Christ was born. Peace and rest of soul was the general subject he continually preached for three years. Peace, and not riches, was the great legacy he left with the eleven the night before his crucifixion. It was in full keeping with the tenor of all our Lord's dealings, that, when he came to his disciples after his resurrection, his first word should be 'Peace'. It was a word to soothe and calm their minds.

Peace is the key-note of the gospel we preach, the gospel he has sent us to preach: peace with God, peace by the blood of his cross, peace from God, the peace of God, peace between God and man by the precious blood of atonement, and peace between man and man by the gift of his grace. Christ has sent us to preach peace, spread peace, and practise peace.

Any religion, like that of Mahomet, which makes converts with the sword, is not from above, but from beneath. Any religion, like that of Rome, that burns men at the stake to promote its own success, carries with it the stamp of hell and of antichrist. That religion which is the religion of the Prince of Peace is that which preaches, spreads, practises, and promotes peace; real, true peace.

Assuring Revelations

Second, how greatly our hearts are gladdened by those blessed, sweet revelations of our Lord Jesus which assure us of his accomplishments as our Mediator. Can you imagine what that first meeting of the Church after the Lord's death must have been like? The disciples had heard the reports of the Lord's resurrection; but they did not believe them (Mark 16:12, 13; Luke 24:11). They must have been terribly confused, very fearful, shamefully unbelieving, yet a little hopeful.

Then the Lord Jesus appeared in their midst and showed them his wounds! Our Lord Jesus very gently and graciously gave his beloved disciples this remarkable, assuring evidence of his resurrection and of their redemption. He showed them 'his hands and his side'.

Without question, the Saviour was, in this action, both identifying himself to them and assuring them that he had really risen from the dead in a real body.

He bade them see with their own eyes, that he had a real material body, and that he was not a spirit or a ghost. 'Handle me and see', were his words. 'A spirit hath not flesh and bone, as ye see me have', he said (Luke 24:39). Great indeed was the condescension of our blessed Master in thus coming down to the feeble faith of his disciples!

Yet, there is more here than a mere proof of our Lord's bodily resurrection. Showing them his hands and side and feet, our Lord Jesus showed them assuring tokens of redemption with which he entered into heaven as our Representative, tokens of redemption that would everlastingly plead for them in glory.

The Lord had said in his commission to Mary that she should say to his brethren, 'I ascend unto my Father, and your Father, to my God, and your God'. By showing them his wounds he said, 'In my ascension, these wounds will appear for you. And all the petitions you send to heaven by me, I will put into these pierced hands and present you and your prayers to our Father and our God'.

The primary reason for showing the disciples his wounds was to convince them that he had indeed risen and that the reports given by the women and the two disciples (which they did not believe – Mark 16:12, 13; Luke 24:11) were true. But the wounds and scars of our Lord Jesus were and forever shall be proof of his great love for those whom he redeemed, and evidence of our full salvation in and by him (Isaiah 53:4-6).

The disciples rejoiced and were glad when it finally dawned upon them that it was their Lord standing in their midst, that he was alive again and that he had accomplished redemption by the sacrifice of himself. As these disciples were then made glad when they saw the Lord, so we are made glad with every spiritual manifestation of our crucified, risen, ascended, exalted Saviour today as we seek to worship him in private and in our public assemblies of worship with his saints.

Our Commission

Third, I want us to see that we are sent by our Saviour into this world, just as he was sent by his Father, for the salvation of his elect (vv. 21-23).

'Then said Jesus to them again, Peace be unto you: as my Father hath sent me, even so send I you. And when he had said this, he breathed on them, and saith unto them, Receive ye the Holy Ghost: Whose soever sins ye remit, they are remitted unto them; and whose soever sins ye retain, they are retained.'

The Lord Jesus has left us here as his witnesses, that we might preach his gospel to all men, for the salvation of his elect. This is our commission (Matthew 28:18-20; John 17:18-20; 2 Timothy 2:1, 2; 1 Timothy 4:13-16). By the preaching of the gospel, the sins of eternity-bound men and women are either remitted or retained (2 Corinthians 2:14-16). How honoured and how glad we ought to be to have this trust given to us!

Neglected Worship

Fourth, if you will look at verses 24 and 25, you will see that when we absent ourselves from the house of God, when we neglect the assembly of God's saints for worship, we deprive ourselves of great blessings.

'But Thomas, one of the twelve, called Didymus, was not with them when Jesus came. The other disciples therefore said unto him, We have seen the Lord. But he said unto them, Except I shall see in his hands the print of the nails, and put my finger into the print of the nails, and thrust my hand into his side, I will not believe.'

Our Lord had appeared to his disciples and convinced them that he had indeed risen from the dead. He had given them the Holy Spirit to empower them for their ministry to the world. But Thomas was not present with them when the Lord appeared.

We do not know where he was or why he was not there, but there is a lesson to be learned from his absence. He missed the joy of seeing the risen Lord. He missed hearing our Lord's words of peace. And he missed the peace and assurance itself as evidenced by his words in the next verse, 'I will not believe'.

The Spirit of God tells us plainly that we must not forsake the assembling of ourselves together (Hebrews 10:25). Such neglect leads to spiritual leanness, snares, and temptations, and to missed blessings. The house of God, the gathered Church of God assembled for worship, is the place were God our Saviour meets with his people and makes himself known (Matthew 18:20). This is the place from which he sends out his word. Public worship is the most important aspect of every believer's life (Hebrews 10:23-29).

Restoring Grace

Fifth, in verses 26-29 we see how gracious and merciful our Saviour is to his poor, weak, sinful people in the exercise of his indescribable restoring grace.

'And after eight days again his disciples were within, and Thomas with them: then came Jesus, the doors being shut, and stood in the midst, and said, Peace be unto you. Then saith he to Thomas, Reach hither thy finger, and behold my hands; and reach hither thy hand, and thrust it into my side: and be not faithless, but believing. And Thomas answered and said unto him, My Lord and my God. Jesus saith unto him, Thomas, because thou hast seen me, thou hast believed: blessed are they that have not seen, and yet have believed.'

The disciples found Thomas and with great joy and assurance of faith told him that they had 'seen the Lord'. They not only had the testimony of the women and the angels, but they saw him with their own eyes. Still, Thomas said, 'Except I shall see in his hands the print of the nails, and put my finger into the print of the nails, and thrust my hand into his side, I will not believe'.

Thomas was present at the raising of Lazarus, and had heard Christ himself say that he would rise from the dead. He now had the testimony of his friends that the Lord was risen. Still he did not believe. How great and inexcusable our unbelief is! How stubborn these vile hearts are! Yes, there is in us all 'an evil heart of unbelief' that soon would depart from our God (Hebrews 3:12).

> Prone to wander, Lord, I feel it!
> Prone to leave the God I love!
> Here's my heart, oh take and seal it,
> Seal it for Thy courts above!

Thank God, he overrules our unbelief and is faithful to us when we are unfaithful to him (2 Timothy 2:13). Where sin abounds, his grace much more abounds!

Christ's Divinity

Sixth, our hearts are made glad by every reminder that he who is our Saviour is himself our God, as Thomas confessed him to be. What a glorious confession Thomas gave once the Lord Jesus, in his boundless mercy, had granted him restoring grace. 'My Lord and my God'! Blessed be his name, Jesus Christ is God! None but God could redeem us, justify us, make us holy, and bring us to heaven.

Wonders Performed

Seventh, our hearts ought to be made glad every time we are reminded that all the wonders performed by our Lord Jesus Christ in this world are designed for us, that we might believe (vv. 30, 31).

'And many other signs truly did Jesus in the presence of his disciples, which are not written in this book: But these are written, that ye might believe that Jesus is the Christ, the Son of God; and that believing ye might have life through his name'.

Everything our great God and Saviour does is a wonder. 'Thou art the God that doest wonders' (Psalms 77:14). And he does his wonders for us, for the everlasting salvation of chosen sinners (Romans 8:28). By believing on Christ, and through his blessed name, we have eternal life, access to the throne, and acceptance before God (Acts 2:36; 4:11, 12; Romans 3:19-24; 4:22-25; 1 John 5:10-13). Wondrous grace!

Chapter 62

'on this wise showed he himself'

'After these things Jesus shewed himself again to the disciples at the sea of Tiberias; and on this wise shewed he himself. There were together Simon Peter, and Thomas called Didymus, and Nathanael of Cana in Galilee, and the sons of Zebedee, and two other of his disciples. Simon Peter saith unto them, I go a fishing. They say unto him, We also go with thee. They went forth, and entered into a ship immediately; and that night they caught nothing. But when the morning was now come, Jesus stood on the shore: but the disciples knew not that it was Jesus. Then Jesus saith unto them, Children, have ye any meat? They answered him, No. And he said unto them, Cast the net on the right side of the ship, and ye shall find. They cast therefore, and now they were not able to draw it for the multitude of fishes. Therefore that disciple whom Jesus loved saith unto Peter, It is the Lord. Now when Simon Peter heard that it was the Lord, he girt his fisher's coat unto him, (for he was naked,) and did cast himself into the sea. And the other disciples came in a little ship; (for they were not far from land, but as it were two hundred cubits,) dragging the net with fishes. As soon then as they were come to land, they saw a fire of coals there, and fish laid thereon, and bread. Jesus saith unto them, Bring of the fish which ye have now caught. Simon Peter went up, and drew the net to land full of great fishes, an hundred and fifty and three: and for all there were so many, yet was not the net broken. Jesus saith unto them, Come and dine. And none of the disciples durst ask him, Who art thou? knowing that it was the Lord. Jesus then cometh, and taketh bread, and giveth them, and fish likewise. This is now the third time that Jesus shewed himself to his disciples, after that he was risen from the dead' (John 21:1-14).

How does the Lord Jesus show himself? How does our blessed Saviour make himself known to his people? When does he come to his own? When does he make himself known? We should always come to the house of God and to the word of God desiring to see our blessed Saviour and hear his voice. 'He standeth behind our wall, he looketh forth at the windows, showing himself through the lattice' (Song of Solomon 2:9). We come to his word, and come to his house in public worship with his saints, hoping that our Lord Jesus will be pleased to look forth at the window of his word and show himself through the lattice of his ordinances, as we gather in his name for prayer, praise, and the preaching of the gospel.

Did he not promise, 'Where two or three are gathered together in my name, there am I in the midst of them' (Matthew 18:20)? Did he not tell us, 'He that hath my commandments, and keepeth them, he it is that loveth me: and he that loveth me shall be loved of my Father, and I will love him, and will manifest myself to him' (John 14:21)? Yet, how often we are compelled to ask, 'Lord, how is it that thou wilt manifest thyself unto us, and not unto the world?' (John 14:22).

How does the Lord Jesus show himself? We might find some answers to that question in this closing chapter of John's Gospel. 'On this wise showed he himself'. After our Lord arose from the dead, he appeared to Mary and twice to his disciples, and showed himself to seven of the disciples who had gone to Galilee according to his instructions (Matthew 28:10, 16). These appearances were more than just physical appearances in order that they could see him and know that he lives. They were more than mere proofs of his resurrection. In these post-resurrection appearances our blessed Saviour manifested himself in his divine majesty, his resurrected glory, his love and compassion for his people, and his finished redemptive work, showing forth his glory as our risen, triumphant Saviour.

Recorded Appearances

As we have previously noted (p. 542), there are twelve recorded appearances of our Lord Jesus Christ after his resurrection in the New Testament. Of course, there may have been others; we do not know (Acts 1:3). These twelve are recorded for us in the book of God, let me list them again. Our Saviour appeared,

To Mary Magdalene (John 20:11-18).
To the women (Matthew 28:9, 10).
To Cleopas and his companion (Luke 24:13-35).
To Simon (Luke 24:34; 1 Corinthians 15:5).

To the Disciples, Thomas being absent (John 20:19-23).
To the Disciples, Thomas being present (John 20:24-29).
To the Seven at the Sea of Galilee (John 21:1-14).
To the Disciples on the mountain in Galilee (Matthew 28:16-20).
To the Five Hundred (1 Corinthians 15:6).
To James, the Lord's brother (1 Corinthians 15:7).
To the Disciples on Olivet, near Jerusalem (Acts 1:4-11; Luke 24:50, 51).
To Paul on the road to Damascus (Acts 9:3-7).

Special Revelation

But after his resurrection, our Lord Jesus never showed himself to anyone except his disciples. And they saw him only as he made himself known to them. Though he stood before them and spoke to them, though they saw him physically, none could see him and know who he was except by special revelation, except Christ reveal himself to them. So it is now.

This fact is important. By it we see that the resurrection was never intended to be a proof of anything to unbelievers. This fact also teaches us that any profitable sight of our Lord Jesus Christ, any sight of him that is beneficial to our souls, any saving sight and knowledge of the Lord Jesus Christ is spiritual. Not carnal, not academic, not visionary, but spiritual! We cannot see the Lord Jesus, at any time, or know his presence, or hear his voice, except as he is pleased to make himself known to us. All who are yet without Christ, without life, without faith, without God, and without hope, must forever remain as they are unless the Lord Jesus makes himself known to them by the mighty operations of his grace (2 Corinthians 4:6; Genesis 1:1-3).

The same thing is true of us who are the Lord's. Though we are born again, though we live by faith in Christ, though we live in the Spirit, walk in the Spirit, and are filled with the Holy Ghost, as all heaven-born souls are, we cannot, at any time, in any circumstances, or under any conditions, see and know our blessed Saviour, except he make himself known to us by the wonderful, mighty operations of his grace on our behalf. Though the Lord Jesus stood before Mary and talked to her, she did not see him and did not know him until he made himself known to her. Though the risen Saviour walked with and taught those disciples on the road to Emmaus, they did not see him and did not know him until he made himself known to them. Though the Saviour miraculously stepped into their midst on that first day, that first Sunday evening after he was risen, they did not see him and did not know him until he made himself known to them. The same is true of us today! O blessed Saviour, graciously make yourself known to our souls day by day, and hour by hour, that we may walk joyfully with you!

The only way we can see the Lord Jesus Christ, the only way we can behold the glory of God in the Person and work of his dear Son is by faith in Christ; and that faith by which we behold him is his own gift of grace. 'On this wise showed he himself.' This appearance of our Lord Jesus to his disciples at the sea of Tiberias indicates that there are specific times when the Saviour comes to his own; and that he always comes to us for a specific reason, to give us grace to help in our time of need. Here are seven specific seasons when we may expect our dear Saviour to show himself to us as he does not to the world.

Undeserving

First, the Lord Jesus shows himself to his chosen when we are most undeserving. He came to these poor disciples after a night of great fault and of sad failure (vv. 2, 3).

'There were together Simon Peter, and Thomas called Didymus, and Nathanael of Cana in Galilee, and the sons of Zebedee, and two other of his disciples. Simon Peter saith unto them, I go a fishing. They say unto him, We also go with thee. They went forth, and entered into a ship immediately; and that night they caught nothing.'

Seven of the disciples were assembled together in a certain place not far from the Sea of Galilee or Tiberias. Peter said, 'Boys, I'm going back to my fishing business.' Fishing was his business and occupation before he met the Master. Peter, having denied the Saviour, unsure of his Master's purpose for him, and being a man of action more than contemplation and waiting, decided to go back to the boats and nets. It seems clear to me that Peter turned his back on preaching the gospel, and made up his mind to return to his former occupation, fishing.

The other disciples were ready to follow where Peter led, and they said, 'Wait up, we'll go with you.' Obviously, they still owned their boats and nets. Why they kept them, we are not told; but they did; and those boats and nets became a snare to their souls. Let every preacher be warned. Sell all and follow Christ. Make it your business to disentangle yourself from the cares of this world. Make it your relentless determination to be continually 'separated unto the gospel of God' (Romans 1:1).

Those poor, fallen preachers all of whom had forsaken the Saviour, Peter who had denied him, went back to their fishing business, entered one of their ships, as they had done all their lives, and fished all night. But on this night something very unusual happened. They caught nothing!

Our Lord Jesus is sovereign over the fish of the sea; and he graciously kept his fallen disciples from having any success that night. 'They had been called', Pastor Henry Mahan wrote, 'to be fishers of men, not fishermen of this sort.' Failure and disappointment are often instruments our God uses to prepare us for some blessed, sweet experience of his grace. If the Lord permits his own to fall, it is that he might lift us up and, in the lift, reveal himself the more gracious and glorious.

Daybreak

Second, our dear Saviour shows himself to his chosen at daybreak. 'But when the morning was now come, Jesus stood on the shore: but the disciples knew not that it was Jesus' (v. 4). In the Revised Version those words are translated, 'When the day was now breaking, Jesus stood on the shore.' Whenever the Lord Jesus comes to us and shows himself to us, it is the breaking of a fresh, new day to our souls (Isaiah 12:1-6; 25:9).

When Christ first appears to his elect in conversion, the daybreak of grace is begun in the heaven-born soul! When the Day Star (2 Peter 1:19) arises in our hearts, when the Sun of Righteousness (Malachi 4:2) arises in our souls, with healing in his wings, a new day begins! And when the blessed Saviour shows himself after a season of darkness, it is the breaking of day to our souls. Sorrow may endure for the night; but joy comes in the morning when he appears!

Confession

Third, the Son of God shows himself to his chosen, sweetly forcing us to make confession of our need of him (vv. 4, 5). Morning dawned and the Lord Jesus stood on the shore. The disciples were only about one hundred yards offshore. They could both see him and hear him; but they did not know that it was the Lord. He asked if they had caught any fish; and they said, 'No'.

He did not ask this question for information, or because he did not know the answer. He asked, 'Children, have ye taken any meat?' to draw their attention to the fact that their return to their old occupation was a total failure, to sweetly and graciously force them to confess their complete failure and inability, to make them attentive to the miracle he was about to perform, and to prepare them for the great revelation of his goodness. Robert Hawker calls our attention to the fact that,

> The want of success in those fishers, and the Lord Jesus early in the morning standing on the shore, formed a blessed occasion for the manifestation of his person and grace, which were to follow. When the Lord is about to reveal himself to his people, how graciously he sometimes prepares the way for the greater display of his love.

Have we not proved, again and again, that our dear Saviour can and does supply all the needs of his redeemed (Philippians 4:19)?

His Greatness

Fourth, our Lord Jesus Christ shows himself to his chosen to display his greatness as God our Saviour. 'And he said unto them, Cast the net on the right side of the ship, and ye shall find' (v. 6).

I have no idea how to adequately explain this. Experienced fishermen are not likely to obey the instructions of a stranger standing on the shore. Yet, at the command of the Lord Jesus to 'cast the net on the right side of the ship', they obeyed without hesitation. They had toiled all night to no purpose, and now that the day was breaking, they had given up all hope. But the authoritative voice of that stranger on the shore, so full of promise, was heard and immediately obeyed.

This is an obvious display of our Lord's absolute sovereignty. He never commands anything that is not done! The disciples had no idea who it was that spoke to them; but they obeyed his voice as readily and quickly as the angels of heaven obey the voice of the Almighty.

Our Lord will sometimes leave us to ourselves, not only to show us how utterly impotent we are, but also to make us know more fully his divine greatness as God our Saviour, and to teach us to look to him, not to ourselves, for everything.

Success

Fifth, our gracious Master shows himself to his chosen to give us success. Look at verse 6 again. 'They cast therefore, and now they were not able to draw it for the multitude of fishes'! By this great display of his power, the Lord Jesus made himself known to these disciples he so dearly loved (vv. 7, 8).

'Therefore that disciple whom Jesus loved saith unto Peter, It is the Lord. Now when Simon Peter heard that it was the Lord, he girt his fisher's coat unto him, (for he was naked,) and did cast himself into the sea. And the other disciples came in a little ship; (for they were not far from land, but as it were two hundred cubits,) dragging the net with fishes.'

No doubt they remembered another incident similar to this (Luke 5:4-11). No doubt they also remembered the parable by which the Lord Jesus had taught them (Matthew 13:47-51). Gospel preaching is compared to fishing, but with a net, never with a hook and line. If you fish with a hook, you have to cover the hook and deceive the fish. If you fish with a hook and bait, the catch depends in some measure on the skill of the fisherman. But, if you fish with a net, everything depends on God. You have to wait for God to put the fish in the net!

Both the disciples and the fish obeyed the Lord Jesus. At his command, the disciples cast the net on the right side of the ship; and 153 fish swam into the net on the right side of the ship!

As I read this story I cannot help thinking, how near and dear to his heart the Lord's people must be! He says now as much as he did then, 'Children, have ye any meat? Cast on the right side, and ye shall find.' If we fail to seek our spiritual sustenance from him, he will be found of them that seek him not. Oh, how often the Lord Jesus makes himself known by his gracious acts as well as by his word! He makes himself known by his providence and by his grace in countless instances where we least expected him.

Surely, these gospel preachers were taught by this experience, and we should be, that the success of our labour in the gospel is the Lord's doing alone. Nothing depends on us. Everything depends on him!

Provision

Sixth, our ever gracious Saviour, Jehovah-Jesus, Jehovah-jireh, shows himself to his chosen to provide our needs (vv. 9-11).

'As soon then as they were come to land, they saw a fire of coals there, and fish laid thereon, and bread. Jesus saith unto them, Bring of the fish which ye have now caught. Simon Peter went up, and drew the net to land full of great fishes, an hundred and fifty and three: and for all there were so many, yet was not the net broken.'

Even in his resurrection body, the Lord Jesus was not unmindful of the bodies of his cold and hungry disciples. This is another manifestation of his love and care for his own. The meal provided was not a sumptuous feast; but it was according to his manner as the Shepherd of his flock and according to their need. And it was miraculously provided.

The Son of God always goes before us in his providential arrangements for our souls. How we ought to rejoice in every token of his eternal purpose, his sovereign providence, and his special prevenient grace, all exercised on our behalf!

Communion

Seventh, the Lord Jesus shows himself to his chosen to give us the joy of sweet communion with himself (vv. 12-14).

'Jesus saith unto them, Come and dine. And none of the disciples durst ask him, Who art thou? knowing that it was the Lord. Jesus then cometh, and taketh bread, and giveth them, and fish likewise. This is now the third time that Jesus showed himself to his disciples, after that he was risen from the dead.'

Our dear Saviour, the Lord Jesus Christ, has a way of giving, whereby he makes himself known. 'And it came to pass, as he sat at meat with them, he took bread, and blessed it, and brake, and gave to them. And their eyes were opened, and they knew him; and he vanished out of their sight' (Luke 24:30, 31). Here are these poor, sinful, fallen disciples sitting with the risen Lord of glory. As they sat down to breakfast with the Master, they must have recalled how he had once fed the multitudes with the same fare as he now fed them, a few fish and a loaf of bread (John 6:1-14). They were awestruck in his presence. How utterly unworthy they must have felt, yet how welcome!

We usually have the most conscious, humbling sense of ourselves when the Lord Jesus makes himself known to us in his most bounteous and free acts of mercy, love, and grace. When the all gracious Christ of God and the poor, needy sinner meet, the sweetest fellowship known to man on this earth commences! None of the disciples asked any questions, for they knew that it was the Lord. Their doubts, unbelief, and questions about his resurrection were all resolved by his presence!

The disciples came from their defeat, frustration, and failure at sea to find a fire kindled and a meal of bread and fish prepared for them by the Son of God. What a lesson there is in this for those who preach the gospel! We are unable to provide anything in our own strength, but by his grace, he will fully meet all our needs. His grace is sufficient! The Saviour's provisions are so complete that nothing of ours need be added. The command, when he provides, is simply, 'Come and dine, for all things are ready'.

So it is in redemption. 'Christ is all and in all'. All we bring to him is our emptiness, our need, and our sin. We stand before him for his spiritual blessings as these weary, hungry disciples stood before that meal. It was all provided by their loving Lord. The law demands; but Christ gives (1 Corinthians 1:30, 31; Colossians 2:9, 10; Ephesians 1:3-6). The hymn writer C. B. Widmeyer wrote,

1 Jesus has a table spread
Where the saints of God are fed,
He invites His chosen people, "Come and dine";
With His manna He doth feed
And supplies our every need:
Oh, 'tis sweet to sup with Jesus all the time!

Refrain:
"Come and dine," the Master calleth, "Come and dine";
You may feast at Jesus' table all the time;
He Who fed the multitude, turned the water into wine,
To the hungry calleth now,

2 “Come and dine.” The disciples came to land,
Thus obeying Christ’s command,
For the Master called unto them, “Come and dine”;
There they found their heart’s desire,
Bread and fish upon the fire;
Thus He satisfies the hungry every time. [Refrain]

3 Soon the Lamb will take His bride
To be ever at His side,
All the host of heaven will assembled be;
Oh, ’twill be a glorious sight,
All the saints in spotless white;
And with Jesus they will feast eternally. [Refrain]

Eat, friends. Come and dine. ‘Behold, all things are now ready’!

Chapter 63

‘lovest thou me?’

‘So when they had dined, Jesus saith to Simon Peter, Simon, son of Jonas, lovest thou me more than these? He saith unto him, Yea, Lord; thou knowest that I love thee. He saith unto him, Feed my lambs. He saith to him again the second time, Simon, son of Jonas, lovest thou me? He saith unto him, Yea, Lord; thou knowest that I love thee. He saith unto him, Feed my sheep. He saith unto him the third time, Simon, son of Jonas, lovest thou me? Peter was grieved because he said unto him the third time, Lovest thou me? And he said unto him, Lord, thou knowest all things; thou knowest that I love thee. Jesus saith unto him, Feed my sheep’ (John 21:15-17).

This is the third, perhaps even the fourth time that the Lord has shown himself to Peter after his resurrection. Until now not a word had passed between them. Peter had not spoken to the Saviour; and the Lord Jesus had not spoken directly to Peter. The matter of Peter’s denial of the Lord Jesus has not been mentioned, neither by the Lord Jesus, nor by Peter. How Peter must have longed to speak to his Lord privately, to confess his shame and beg forgiveness; but the Lord Jesus had not allowed it. Now Christ is alone with Peter, at some distance from the other disciples. And it is the Lord Jesus who opens the conversation. What will he say? How will he reprove this fallen one? How will he deal with Peter’s sin?

‘Lovest thou me?’ A more important question could not be considered. More than two thousand years have passed since our Lord Jesus first asked Peter this question. But it is just as searching and useful today as it was then. Love is something everyone understands. It is a feeling, an emotion, a passion that God has implanted in the human nature. Everybody loves somebody. No one is incapable of love. May God the Holy Ghost make a place in our hearts for the Lord Jesus Christ, who alone is worthy of all the love of our hearts. Oh, for grace to love him who loved us and gave himself for us!

This is not a matter of fanaticism, enthusiasm, or emotionalism. It is a subject that deserves the reasonable consideration of everyone who professes faith in Christ and claims to be a Christian. The Son of God asks, 'Lovest thou me?' This is a simple fact: All true Christians love Christ (1 John 4:19), and any who do not love Christ are not Christians, are not believers, and are not saved.

Christ's Purpose

First, I want to show you that our Lord's purpose in squeezing this confession of love from Peter was altogether gracious. The test our Saviour put to Peter, by which he would prove his sincerity to him, was love. The Lord Jesus did not ask, 'Have you honoured me, or obeyed me, or what proofs can you give of performing your duties toward me, or do you live for me? He asked just one thing: 'Lovest thou me?'

Many have imagined that our Saviour asked Peter this question three times to remind him of the fact that he had denied him three times; but there is no indication that that was the case. In fact, I am confident it was not our Lord's intention here to aggravate Peter's sense of guilt and shame, but to prove to his dear disciple his grace toward him and his interest in that grace.

The well-known and long proved love and grace of Christ Jesus to his elect inclines me to think that the Saviour asked Peter this question ('Lovest thou me?') three times that he might give his fallen child the opportunity to openly repeat his own assurance of his love for Christ three times. Having declared, with assurance, 'Lord, I truly do love you', was the Lord's way of making Peter understand that his threefold denial was no indication of his true character as a child of God. That was not really Peter, but sin dwelling in him (Romans 7:15-20).

Instead of being a display of our Lord's displeasure, his appearance and conversation with Peter appears to me to have been one of those countless instances we have on record of the tenderness of our dear Saviour to his people, by which he repeatedly shows us where sin abounds grace much more abounds! When his chosen display great weakness, he manifests great grace. When we fall, he lifts us up, and in the sweet exercise of his grace to us enables us to show greater love to him. Our Lord's gracious intention in squeezing this open confession of love from Peter is manifest when we realise that the very thing that terrifies the hypocrite comforts the true believer; and that is our Lord's omniscience. 'Thou knowest all things'! He knows what I am by nature, what I have done, what he has done for me, what he has made me by his grace, and what I am in him. It is written, 'By his knowledge shall my righteous servant justify many'! And here Peter confesses, 'Thou knowest all things; thou knowest that I love thee.'

How very gracious our Saviour is! He came to Peter in his despair, when in a state of great shame, and squeezed from him this firm confession of love for his Saviour at a time when no one else could have done so. Not only that, the Lord Jesus further assured Peter that he had committed to him the care of his lambs and his sheep. It is as if the Saviour had said, 'Yes, Peter, I am fully aware of your great love for me, so much so that I trust to your care the people of my love'!

Pastor's Work

Second, it is the work of every under-shepherd, the work of every gospel preacher, the work of every pastor to feed the Lord's sheep. Christ is the great Shepherd of the sheep. He is the great Pastor of his flock. It is Christ himself who feeds his sheep. He is both the life and sustenance of all his fold. He is the Bread of Life and the Water of Life. His flesh is meat indeed; and his blood is drink indeed.

Yet, our dear Saviour condescends to give his flock under-shepherds, under-pastors, according to his own heart, to feed his people with knowledge and understanding (1 Peter 5:1-4). The Lord's faithful under-shepherds feed his lambs, his young ones, gently. These pastors feed the sheep of the fold and lead them. The first and primary qualification of a pastor is love for Christ. A man's abilities as a speaker and a leader, even if he possesses the greatest possible knowledge, are nothing without this love of the heart for Christ.

Believer's Love

Third, I want you to see that every true believer loves the Lord Jesus Christ. Many are utterly confused about what a Christian is. Many foolishly imagine that anyone raised in a 'Christian country', or in a 'Christian home', or in a country under the influence of Christianity is a Christian. Many think that all who profess faith in Christ, all who have been baptised in the name of Christ, all who attend the worship of Christ are Christians. But it is not so. A Christian is a person who has been redeemed by the precious blood of Christ. A Christian is one who has been born again by the Spirit of Christ. A Christian is one who lives by faith in Christ. A Christian is a person who seeks in all things to follow, obey, and honour Christ. But there is more. A Christian is a person who loves the Lord Jesus Christ. If a person truly loves Christ, all is well, if not, all is wrong (John 8:42; 1 Corinthians 16:22).

Love for Christ is the inseparable companion of saving faith (1 Corinthians 13:13; Galatians 5:6). Love cannot usurp nor take the place of faith. It is not love that unites the soul with Christ, but faith. It is not love that draws the waters of grace from the wells of salvation, but faith. It is not love that brings peace to the conscience, but faith. But wherever faith lives, love lives.

Love is the motive and mainspring of all work for Christ (2 Corinthians 8:7). Very little, if anything, is done for Christ from a sense of duty, or merely from a knowledge of right and wrong. The heart must be interested before the hands will be engaged. Those who have done great things in the name of Christ were not men who merely held to a creed. They were people who loved a Person! Duty tithes. Love gives. Duty goes to church. Love comes to worship. Duty reads the word. Love seeks to understand it. Duty will do some things for Christ. Loves lives for Christ!

Love for Christ is the common point of unity for all believers. We may have many differences with our brethren in other churches and denominations. But here we are one. All true Christians love Christ. Love for Christ gives us a common meeting point. Love for Christ gives us unity. Love for Christ dissolves cultural, racial, and social differences (Colossians 3:11).

Love for Christ will be the distinguishing mark of all the redeemed in heaven. That multitude which no man can number will be of one mind. Old differences will be forgotten. Old carnal debates will be dropped. In heaven around the throne of grace, all will be of one mind and one heart. All will love Christ (Revelation 1:5, 6).

The Cause

Would you know the secret of this love? What is it that causes saved sinners to love the Son of God? Read 1 John 4:19, and learn the secret. 'We love him because he first loved us'. No son or daughter of Adam ever loved Christ by nature. 'The carnal mind is enmity against God'. But all who are born of God love Christ 'because he first loved us'.

His love for us precedes our love for him by eternity (Jeremiah 31:3). His love for us exceeds our love for him by infinity (Romans 5:8; 1 John 3:16; 4:9, 10). And Christ's love for us is the cause of our love for him, 'We love him because he first loved us'!

'We love him' because of who he is, and because of what he has done for us. He chose us in everlasting love and redeemed us with his own precious blood, kept us for himself throughout the days of our rebellion and unbelief unto the appointed time of our calling. He called us by omnipotent mercy, effectually creating life and faith in us by his grace. He has forgiven us, justified us, sanctified us, and made us 'meet to be partakers of the inheritance of the saints in light'! And it is our dear Saviour who keeps us in the midst of our countless trials, temptations and falls, and will not let us go! Therefore, we love him.

'We love him because' of all he is doing for us in providence, working all things together for our good (Romans 8:28), all his unfailing intercession on our behalf in heaven, and because of his daily, all-sufficient grace and unfailing mercies. Should any believer be asked, 'Why do you love the Lord?' he has his own 'because' to give.

'I love the LORD, because he hath heard my voice and my supplications. Because he hath inclined his ear unto me, therefore will I call upon him as long as I live. The sorrows of death compassed me, and the pains of hell gat hold upon me: I found trouble and sorrow. Then called I upon the name of the LORD; O LORD, I beseech thee, deliver my soul. Gracious is the LORD, and righteous; yea, our God is merciful. The LORD preserveth the simple: I was brought low, and he helped me. Return unto thy rest, O my soul; for the LORD hath dealt bountifully with thee. For thou hast delivered my soul from death, mine eyes from tears, and my feet from falling. I will walk before the LORD in the land of the living. I believed, therefore have I spoken: I was greatly afflicted: I said in my haste, All men are liars. What shall I render unto the LORD for all his benefits toward me? I will take the cup of salvation, and call upon the name of the LORD' (Psalms 116:1-13).

Love Can Be Known

Yet, there are some who would have us to believe that this matter of love for Christ is something that cannot be known in this world. So I want you to see in the last place that love for Christ, or the lack of it, is something that can and should be known. Love is not ambiguous. It is not something we have to guess about. And love for Christ is something that a person may and should know.

J. C. Ryle wrote, 'How do we know whether we love any person here upon earth? In what manner does love show itself between people in this world? Between husband and wife? Between parent and child? Between brother and sister? Between friend and friend? Let these questions be answered by common sense and observation … and the knot before us is untied.' Then he gave eight simple marks by which love is known. By these eight things, if we will be honest with ourselves, every person reading these lines can answer the Lord's question 'Lovest thou me?' If I love a person …

I like to think about him. He dwells in my heart (Ephesians 3:17).
I like to hear about him.
I like to read about him.
I like to please him.
I like his friends.

I am jealous to promote and protect his name and honour.
I like to talk to him.
I like to be with him.

Consider this question seriously. Examine it carefully. And answer it honestly 'Lovest thou me?' 'Yea, Lord, thou knowest all things, thou knowest that I love thee'. I do not love him as I should. I do not love him as I would. And I do not love him as I hope I soon shall. But I do love him.

Do not I love Thee, O my Lord?
Behold my heart and see;
And turn each odious idol out
That dares to rival Thee.

Thou knowest I love Thee, dearest Lord;
But, oh, I long to soar
Far from the sphere of mortal joys,
And learn to love Thee more!

Philip Doddridge

If you do not love Christ, it is because you do not know Christ. Your soul is in great danger! You are lost, a child of wrath, and the wrath of God is upon you. The only remedy for your lack of love is a revelation of Christ in you. Make it your business to attend the ministry of the word. Hear the gospel, for 'faith cometh by hearing, and hearing by the word of God.' Pray for the grace of God the Holy Spirit. Believe on the name of the Lord Jesus Christ.

If you love Christ, don't ever be ashamed for others to see it and know it. Witness for him. Live for him. Work for him. Devote yourself to him (Romans 12:1, 2). We cannot love Christ too fully, live for him too thoroughly, confess him too boldly, or devote ourselves to him too heartily. 'To whom much is forgiven, the same loveth much'!

Chapter 64

'what is that to thee?'

'Verily, verily, I say unto thee, When thou wast young, thou girdedst thyself, and walkedst whither thou wouldest: but when thou shalt be old, thou shalt stretch forth thy hands, and another shall gird thee, and carry thee whither thou wouldest not. This spake he, signifying by what death he should glorify God. And when he had spoken this, he saith unto him, Follow me. Then Peter, turning about, seeth the disciple whom Jesus loved following; which also leaned on his breast at supper, and said, Lord, which is he that betrayeth thee? Peter seeing him saith to Jesus, Lord, and what shall this man do? Jesus saith unto him, If I will that he tarry till I come, what is that to thee? follow thou me. Then went this saying abroad among the brethren, that that disciple should not die: yet Jesus said not unto him, he shall not die; but, If I will that he tarry till I come, what is that to thee? This is the disciple which testifieth of these things, and wrote these things: and we know that his testimony is true. And there are also many other things which Jesus did, the which, if they should be written every one, I suppose that even the world itself could not contain the books that should be written. Amen' (John 21:18-25).

In the New Testament, every time anyone came to our Lord and complained to him about what someone else was doing, or was not doing, what someone else might do or might not do, he rebuked them sharply (Luke 9:49, 50; 10:38-50; John 21:18-25).

Background
The Lord Jesus gave his last message to his disciples. You can read the Saviour's final instructions to his Church in chapters 13-16. In chapter 17, he

offered his great high priestly prayer to God the Father as our Mediator. Then, in chapter 18, we see him in the garden, praying with Peter, James, and John, anticipating all that he must suffer as our Substitute, when a band of soldiers, led by Judas, came to arrest him.

When these soldiers came to arrest him, Peter arose immediately to defend his Master, without regard for his own life (v. 10). Our Saviour voluntarily gave himself up to be crucified by wicked men, but only upon the condition that his own elect would be spared (vv. 8-12). The Saviour was led away to the judgment hall, where Peter denied him three times (18:27).

Then, our blessed Substitute accomplished our redemption by the sacrifice of himself upon the cursed tree (19:28-30). On the third day,[6] early in the morning, the Lord Jesus Christ arose from the grave, triumphing over it for us (20:1-17). He appeared to Mary Magdalene and the other Mary. He appeared to the disciples, Thomas being absent. Then he appeared to them one week later when Thomas was present. Now, in chapter 21, he appears a third time to his disciples, specifically to restore Peter, to confirm his love to Peter, and to confirm (in Peter's own mind) Peter's love to him.

We have seen how the conversation unfolded. When Peter had publicly confessed, 'Lord, thou knowest all things, thou knowest that I love thee', the Lord gave him this charge 'Feed my sheep'. Peter had denied his Master three times. Here he confesses his heartfelt love for Christ three times, and is commissioned by the Lord three times to feed his people. Now, read verse 22. 'Jesus saith unto him, If I will that he tarry till I come, what is that to thee? follow thou me.'

The Question

'What is that to thee?' That is the question I want to address. John concludes his gospel narrative, and our Lord Jesus here concludes his time on earth by teaching Peter and us a lesson that is very hard for us to learn. We must leave God's servants and God's people to God's care. 'Who art thou that judgest another man's servant? to his own master he standeth or falleth. Yea, he shall be holden up: for God is able to make him stand' (Romans 14:4).

God's people are God's people. They are not yours; and they are not mine. They are his. God's servants are God's servants. They are not yours; and they are not mine. They are his. I sure wish we could learn that! They are not to be

[6] There seems to be a difficulty here. It is obvious that our Lord, being crucified on Friday afternoon and resurrected on Sunday morning was in the grave (to our way of thinking) only one full day (Saturday), the Friday evening preceding it and Sunday morning following it. But that is no problem at all. The Jews calculated any part of a night or day as a whole. Calculating as they did, our Lord was in the tomb the day and night of Friday, the day and night of Saturday, and the night (the time preceding dawn) and day of Sunday.

judged by us. They are not to be controlled by us. Their lives are not to be run by us. Religion binds people. Christ sets them free.

It is absolutely none of your business or mine how someone else serves Christ. It is none of your business or mine what someone else does for his Master, or does not do. It is none of your business or mine what someone else gives, or does not give. The Lord God Almighty is perfectly capable of taking care of his own. Besides, most of us have a full time job, with plenty of overtime, taking care of ourselves! So let us 'study to be quiet, and to do our own business, and to work with our own hands', as we have been commanded (1 Thessalonians 4:11). It is absolutely none of your business or mine how someone else serves Christ. 'To his own Master he stands or falls'.

Grace Assured

The Lord Jesus told Peter how that he would be required to suffer and die for the glory of God. Impetuous and sometimes fickle in his youth, Peter was assured that, in the end, he would be faithful unto death. And he was. He was crucified because of his faithfulness to Christ. When the Lord Jesus gave Peter this word of assurance, he said to him, 'Follow me' (vv. 18, 19).

'Verily, verily, I say unto thee, When thou wast young, thou girdedst thyself, and walkedst whither thou wouldest: but when thou shalt be old, thou shalt stretch forth thy hands, and another shall gird thee, and carry thee whither thou wouldest not. This spake he, signifying by what death he should glorify God. And when he had spoken this, he saith unto him, Follow me.'

An Evil Question

Then, as they walked along the beach, Peter saw John following. That is what a disciple is supposed to do. But when Peter saw John, he said, 'Lord, you have told me what I must do, but what about John, what is he to do?' (vv. 20, 21).

'Then Peter, turning about, seeth the disciple whom Jesus loved following; which also leaned on his breast at supper, and said, Lord, which is he that betrayeth thee? Peter seeing him saith to Jesus, Lord, and what shall this man do?'

That may appear to be a perfectly innocent question; but it was horribly evil. It was a question that arose from Peter's proud heart. It ought never to have been asked. It was a question that would, if entertained, be sure to cause a division among the Lord's disciples and lead to other evils. At that point, the Lord must have stopped, turned to Peter, and looking squarely into his eyes, he gave this stern admonition and reproof 'If I will that he tarry till I come, what is that to thee? Follow thou me' (v. 22).

Here is a message directly from the lips of the Lord Jesus Christ to you and me. He says, 'What is that to thee? Follow thou me'! It is our responsibility in all things ever to follow Christ; but it is never our responsibility to determine what another disciple is doing, or even concern ourselves about what another is doing or not doing. If we could learn this one thing, it would put an end to every problem there is in the church and kingdom of God. All the strife and division that exists among true believers can be traced to this one, proud evil. We all concern ourselves with what others are doing and not doing, when we ought to concern ourselves only with what the Lord would have us do.

Our Primary Responsibility

Our primary responsibility in life is to follow Christ. I know the consequences, ramifications, and implications of what I am saying. I know what it will cost us if we dare to do what the Lord commands. But, oh how I pray that God will give us grace to hear and obey his word.

The main business of your life and mine, the primary, all-consuming business of your life and mine is to follow Christ. We live in vain if we do not live for God! Indeed, it were better for you and me had we never been born, than that we should live and die without Christ. The Lord Jesus says to you and me, 'Follow me … Follow thou me'!

This is the command of the gospel. Many today try to separate salvation from discipleship. They suggest that there may be faith in Christ without the following of Christ. But that is not so. In Bible terms, to believe on Christ is to follow Christ (Matthew 4:18-22; 16:24-26; 19:20-22).

If you are yet without Christ, you would be wise to make the salvation of your immortal soul the primary concern of your life. Make your soul your first care, if necessary, to the neglect of all other things. What shall it profit you, if you should gain the whole world and lose your own soul? If you are without Christ, you are under the wrath of God, cursed and condemned because of your sin. If you die without Christ, you shall forever suffer the wrath of God in hell. Will you follow Christ and be forever saved; or will you follow your own devices and be forever damned? (Deuteronomy 30:15, 19).

To follow Christ is to seek him. To follow Christ is to trust him. To follow Christ is to submit to his dominion as your Lord. To follow Christ is to be saved by him. 'Believe on the Lord Jesus Christ, and thou shalt be saved.' This is the Lord's commandment to you: 'Follow thou me'!

This is also the character of faith. Faith follows Christ. My brothers and sisters in the grace of God, having been saved by Christ, having been washed in his precious blood, robed in his perfect righteousness, and born again by his Holy Spirit, our Master's word to us is 'Follow thou me'!

The main, primary, all-encompassing business of our lives is to follow Christ. When sin is pardoned and salvation is secure, the one thing we must do is follow Christ. Peter was a believer, a preacher, and an Apostle. And this was our Lord's command to him: 'Follow me … follow thou me'! C. H. Spurgeon said, 'The one thing we are to aim at is, to tread in Christ's footsteps, to do what he did; and, as far as he is imitable by us, to do it as he did it, and to be as he was in the midst of the sons and daughters of men.' It is our business in this world to imitate the Son of God in all things. That is what the grace of God teaches all who are taught of God (Titus 2:11-14).

A disciple is one who learns to live the life his teacher lives. Discipleship is more than getting to know what the teacher teaches. It is getting to be what the teacher is. And Christianity is more than believing the doctrine of Christ. Christianity is following Christ. It is seeking to mould my life after Christ. If I am a child of God, I am not a follower of Calvin, Gill, or Spurgeon, or any other mere man. I am a follower of Christ. I seek to mould my doctrine, my thoughts, my words, my character, and my deeds after the example of Christ. Christ himself is the rule and pattern of my life (John 13:15; 1 Peter 2:21).

We are trees of God's planting, set in his vineyard to bring forth fruit for God's praise. If we would do what we were created to do, we must follow Christ. This is the life, the character, and the business of faith (Philippians 3:7-21).

God has given every believer a place, position, and gifts in which to serve him, which no one else can occupy. This is the vocation to which we are called. No matter what your earthly occupation is, if you are in Christ, you are first and foremost his servant. That is your occupation. God has put you where you are, with the gifts, talents, abilities, and opportunities you have to influence and minister to other people, people no one else can reach, for the glory of his name. All saved sinners are missionaries. All saved sinners are his witnesses. That is what a missionary is, his witness! All saved sinners are martyrs, men and women who voluntarily lay down their lives for him, in his cause.

I do not believe that any child of God was created just to run a business, keep records, build houses, connect water pipes, sell insurance, or teach school There is something greater for you and me to do. We were created to serve the cause of God our Saviour in the place of our calling, for the glory of his name (1 Corinthians 7:20-24). God has put you and me where we are, with the gifts, talents, and means we have to seek the salvation of those people who are under our influence for the glory of his name (John 20:21; Hebrews 12:1, 2). This is your life's business, occupation, and calling: 'Follow thou me'!

Voluntary Subjugation

If we would follow Christ, we must subject everything to his sovereign will. When Peter learned what he must suffer and endure for Christ, he looked at John and said, 'And what shall this man do?' And the Lord's answer to him was, 'What is that to thee? Follow thou Me'!

If we would follow Christ, we must not concern ourselves with the responsibilities of others. It is true that we are all members of the body of Christ. And we work and labour together for one cause the glory of God. All God's people together preach his word, feed his sheep, and promote his glory. But each individual believer is the Lord's servant. And we must recognise that every man stands or falls before his own Master. We must each be occupied with our own responsibilities, our own ministries, our own calling, and our own faithfulness. We must not concern ourselves with how, when, or where God is pleased to use others. We gladly help others as they serve Christ (missionaries, churches, pastors, etc.). But we must not seek to govern others in their service for Christ. We leave them in the hands of God. And we must not allow ourselves to be turned aside by others from our own responsibilities.

I am not responsible for what God has called you to do. But I am responsible for what he has called me to do. What God does with you is his business. What you do for God is your business and his, not mine. What I do for God is my business and his, not yours (Romans 14:4). God give us grace to cease being busybodies about other people's business (1 Thessalonians 4:11; 1 Peter 4:14-16).

If we would follow Christ, we must not concern ourselves with foolish and unlearned questions (2 Timothy 2:22-24). If we would follow Christ, we must not concern ourselves with our own personal interests, needs, or relations. We must lose our life if we would save it. I must follow Christ whether my family follows him or not. I must follow Christ regardless of personal preference. I must follow Christ regardless of personal cost and do so willingly (2 Timothy 2:8-10.

Most Reasonable

It is most reasonable that we should confine ourselves to this one life-long occupation. 'Follow thou me'! I know that I am calling for costly commitment, commitment that requires of us many things contrary to the flesh, things that are often misunderstood and misrepresented by people around us. I am calling for you and me to give ourselves in unreserved, voluntary, whole-hearted commitment to the Lord Jesus Christ and the gospel of his grace. Our Master says to you and me, 'Follow thou me'. His command is most reasonable. He bought us (1 Corinthians 6:19, 20). Shall we take what belongs to Christ and waste it upon vanity?

Our powers are so limited. I know some of my own limitations. I would like to use what little ability God has given me and the brief time available in the work of following Christ, preaching the gospel, and seeking to bring others to know, trust, worship, and follow him.

Our time is so limited! 'The time is short' (1 Corinthians 7:29). Let us therefore redeem the time we have (Ephesians 5:16) and use it wisely, following Christ!

My brother, my sister, do not allow anyone to divert you from the straight path of obedience to Christ. To that, above everything else, we have been called. How I pray that we might, each of us, live to glorify God, that we might each be like an arrow shot from Christ's bow, by his own pierced hand, to the target of God's glory. Let nothing turn us aside from the path of obedience.

I wonder what God would have us to do, individually and collectively, as members of the church and kingdom of God in this day. I wonder what God might do with us, if we will but obey his command and follow Christ. What does he yet have for us to do for Christ? What will he yet do with us in the service of his kingdom?

If you are God's, you are all free men and women, free born children of God, I shall not prescribe for you what to do. I simply call upon you to obey the direction of God the Holy Ghost and follow Christ. Perhaps, as you read these lines, you are thinking, 'What can I do?' You are Christ's witness; so tell sinners about him. Use your time and money and ability to further the gospel. Tell perishing sinners around you what wondrous things God has done for you and in you by his grace. Make it your business to minister to, to serve, God's children in this world.

Do everything you can to help one another along the way; but do not sit in judgment over, or try to manipulate one another. What another does or does not do is absolutely none of your business or mine. Regarding all such matters, the Lord Jesus says to us, 'What is that to thee? Follow thou me'! Follow Christ. This is the command of the gospel. Follow Christ. This is the life of faith. If we do follow Christ now by faith, soon we will follow him home to heaven (John 13:36).

Chapter 65

'other things'

'And there are also many other things which Jesus did, the which, if they should be written every one, I suppose that even the world itself could not contain the books that should be written. Amen' (John 21:25).

This is John's inspired concluding statement to his Gospel narrative. This is the very last thing God the Holy Ghost inspired his servant to pen about the earthly history of our Lord Jesus Christ. What are these 'other things' our Lord Jesus did while he walked on this earth, of which we are told nothing in the book of God? Why are we not told about them? Why are we told about so many things, but not about these 'other things?'

Certainly these 'other things' do not refer to our Saviour's doctrine, which is fully revealed in holy scriptures, which are able to make chosen, redeemed sinners wise unto salvation. But there were many things done by our Saviour which are not written in the book of God. Much about his childhood, his family, and his manhood are simply and wisely unrevealed. And there were certainly many 'other things' done by our Lord which God the Holy Ghost chose not to have the inspired writers record, things Matthew, Mark, Luke, and John omitted from the Four Gospels; sermons and prayers, conversations he had with his disciples and others on different occasions, and other signs and wonders, and miraculous operations which were done by him.

World Cannot Receive

Had all that our Saviour done been written out on paper, with all the details relating to them explained, John says, 'I suppose that even the world itself could not contain the books that should be written.' That is quite a statement. 'I suppose that even the world itself could not contain the books that should be written.'

Perhaps John is referring to the fact that the world cannot receive the things of God. God has wisely given us the record of our Redeemer's incarnation, life, ministry, and doctrine in his word, which may be read with ease and delight. Here we are given everything relevant to the whole of Christianity and all that is needful to be known for the salvation of our souls.

Christ's eternal deity
Christ's incarnation
His miracles
His doctrine
His righteous obedience
His vicarious sufferings
His substitutionary death
His triumphant resurrection
His ascension into heaven
His glorious exaltation
His sovereign reign
His heavenly intercession
His glorious second advent

These things cannot and will not be understood by the world. The natural man cannot receive them, and will not bear them. Rather, the world rejects and despises them. The gospel of God is foolishness to the world.

John's words in this passage are not hyperbole. In addition to these wonders of mercy, love, and grace accomplished by God our Saviour, John began his Gospel by telling us that 'All things were made by him'. If one were to attempt to even summarise all God's works of creation and providence, the world itself could not contain the resulting volumes!

Other Things

But what about those 'other things?' Let us go back to John 20:30, 31 and see what God the Holy Ghost would have us learn by the omission of so many, many 'other things' from the book of God. Why did he leave so many things out of this book that might easily have been included in it? Why are so many, many 'other things' omitted and only very specific, wondrous things revealed? John 20:30, 31 tells us. 'And many other signs truly did Jesus in the presence of his disciples, which are not written in this book: But these are written, that ye might believe that Jesus is the Christ, the Son of God; and that believing ye might have life through his name.'

The word of God was written that we might believe that 'Jesus is the Christ, the Son of God', and that 'believing we might have life through his name.'

The Design Of Holy Scripture

First, John tells us plainly that the purpose, the design, the intention of holy scripture is that we might believe that Jesus is the Christ, the Son of God. Holy scripture is not the mother of doubt, but of faith. The book of God was written to give us confidence toward God by revealing a sure, indisputable line of fact and truth regarding the person and work of our Lord Jesus Christ. 'Many other signs truly did Jesus in the presence of his disciples, which are not written in this book: But these are written, that ye might believe that Jesus is the Christ'. Obviously, John is referring specifically to the person and work of our Saviour as recorded by himself and the other Gospel writers. But that which John tells us here is equally true of the entire volume of holy scripture.

Luke 24

Read Luke 24:13-35. That which is here revealed is so precious, so sweet, so heavenly that it hardly needs explanation. Indeed, it cannot be explained to any who have not experienced it for themselves. As they walked together, our Lord Jesus opened the scriptures to his two disciples. 'Beginning at Moses and all the prophets, he expounded unto them in all the scriptures the things concerning himself.' Robert Hawker, commenting on those words, wrote, 'Hence we are taught, as plain as words can make it, that the whole body of scripture is concerning the Lord Jesus Christ.'

Our Lord Jesus Christ is the Pearl of great price in this field of his divine revelation. As he drew near these two disciples in the way, may he draw near to us every time we open the book of God. As he opened to them the scriptures, may he open the scriptures to us by his Spirit. As his presence and his doctrine caused their hearts to burn within them, may he cause our hearts to burn within us when we read and study the sacred volume.

The fact is we have read the Bible with no profit to our souls and no understanding of its message until we realise that the message of holy scripture is the person and work of our Lord Jesus Christ. The purpose of the Bible is the revelation of Christ.

I fully agree with Martin Luther, who wrote, 'There is not a word in the Bible which can be understood without reference to the cross ... As we go to the cradle only in order to find the baby, so we go to the scriptures only to find Christ.'

Robert Murray M'Cheyne, who lived long before anyone dreamed of electric lights, said to his congregation at Christ's Church in Dundee, Scotland, 'When you are reading a book in a dark room, and find it difficult, you take it to a window to get more light. So take your Bible to Christ.'

Christ is the scope of scripture, the sum and substance of divine revelation. Take Christ out of this book and all that is left is processed wood, with gilded edges, wrapped in leather covers.

One Message

The Bible is a book about the Lord Jesus Christ. How I wish I could get every man who claims to be a preacher to see this! With regard to the book of God, Christ is 'the key of knowledge'. Without the key, men can never unlock the chest and discover its riches. They just fumble. The Bible is not a book about science, but the book about Christ. This is not a book about morality, but the book about Christ. This is not a book about history, politics, philosophy, or law. It is not even a book about prophecy, church dogma, or theology. This is a HIM-BOOK. It is all about HIM, the Lord Jesus Christ. It is not enough just to preach the book, we are sent of God to preach the message of the book, and the message of this book is Jesus Christ and him crucified. There is not a page in this book that does not speak of Christ, not a page!

The Son of God tells us plainly that he is the message and theme of holy scripture, that he is the living Word of whom the written word speaks. He said, 'Search the scriptures; for in them ye think ye have eternal life: and they are they which testify of me' (John 5:39). 'And beginning at Moses and all the prophets, he expounded unto them in all the scriptures the things concerning himself … And he said unto them, These are the words which I spake unto you, while I was yet with you, that all things must be fulfilled, which were written in the law of Moses, and in the prophets, and in the psalms, concerning me. Then opened he their understanding, that they might understand the scriptures, And said unto them, Thus it is written, and thus it behoved Christ to suffer, and to rise from the dead the third day: And that repentance and remission of sins should be preached in his name among all nations, beginning at Jerusalem' (Luke 24:27, 44-47).

The Apostle Paul shows us that the preaching of Christ is synonymous with preaching all the counsel of God, for Christ is all the counsel of God. In Acts 20:26, 27 he said, to the Ephesian elders, 'Wherefore I take you to record this day, that I am pure from the blood of all men. For I have not shunned to declare unto you all the counsel of God'. In 1 Corinthians 2:2 he wrote, to the Church at Corinth, 'I determined not to know any thing among you, save Jesus Christ, and him crucified'. In both places, he is telling us the same thing. Christ and him crucified is all the counsel of God, for all that God Almighty has purposed, decreed, revealed, and given to the sons of Adam is in Jesus Christ and him crucified. The Bible, the word of God, is a book with one message; and that one message is redemption, righteousness, and eternal life in Christ.

The word of God is preached only when the gospel of Christ is preached (1 Peter 1:23-25). All the Old Testament scriptures speak of Christ, point us to Christ, and call us to faith in Christ (Genesis 3:15; 22:13, 14; 49:10; Deuteronomy 18:15-18; Job 19; Psalms 2:7, 8; 24; 45:6, 7; 110:3; Proverbs 8:22, 23; Song of Solomon; Isaiah 53; Micah 5:2; Zechariah 12:10; Malachi 3:1). In addition to the direct prophecies about the coming of Christ, God gave numerous types and pictures to foreshadow his coming, there are typical people, typical events, typical things, typical places, typical laws and ceremonies, and sabbath days (Colossians 2:16, 17). The doctrine and message of the entire New Testament is the Lord Jesus Christ. The ordinances of worship prescribed in the New Testament are designed to focus our hearts upon Christ. It is the preacher's business to preach Christ. The American Puritan, Cotton Mather instructed his students with these wise and needful words of counsel,

> Among all the subjects with which you feed the people of God, I beseech you, let not the true Bread of Life be forgotten; but exhibit as much as you can of the glorious Christ unto them; yea, let the motto upon your whole ministry be, "Christ is all!"

What a blessing it would be if every man who claims to speak for God, who claims to be a gospel preacher, would heed those words! How blessed the church of God would be if those who fill her pulpits were determined to preach and teach nothing but Jesus Christ and him crucified!

That was Paul's determination (1 Corinthians 2:2). It ought to be every preacher's. Any man who is sent of God to preach is sent of God to preach Christ crucified, always, in all places, in all his fulness (1 Corinthians 1:17-25). Christ crucified is 'all the counsel of God' (Acts 20:27).

He is the singular subject of holy scripture. He is the sum and essence of all true doctrine. He is the life of gospel ordinances. He is the secret ingredient of all true worship. He is the mercy-seat in whom God meets with men. He is the motive of all godliness, obedience, service, and devotion. He is the reward of heavenly glory. Jesus Christ is our God! Jesus Christ is our Saviour. And Jesus Christ is salvation. He is the Way to heaven; and he is Heaven. He is the Revealer of truth; and he is Truth. He is the Giver of life; and he is Life.

The word of God might be compared to that alabaster box that was brought into Simon's house in Bethany (Mark 14:1-9) containing 'ointment of spikenard very precious'. When the box was broken and the ointment poured out, the sweet fragrance filled the room. Gospel preachers are like the woman who brought the box and broke it open. They come to the house of God with the word of God, break it open, and as they expound the scriptures, the sweet fragrance of Christ crucified fills the house. In the book of God 'Christ is all'!

When we talk about divine sovereignty, we are declaring that Jesus Christ is Lord. When we proclaim God's glorious work of predestination, we are showing how that sinners have been predestinated to be conformed to the image of Christ. God's election is his choice of some to everlasting salvation in Christ and for Christ's sake. Total depravity, a thoroughly biblical doctrine, is God's revelation of our need of Christ. Limited atonement is the biblical assurance of effectual redemption and grace by Christ, the declaration that all for whom Christ died shall be saved. Irresistible grace, or effectual calling, is the almighty, irresistible revelation of Christ in the soul by God the Holy Spirit, which causes the chosen to come to him. Regeneration is the implanting of Christ in us. Justification is the imputation of Christ's righteousness to all his redeemed. Faith is trusting Christ. Sanctification is Christ being formed in us, begun in regeneration and consummated in glorification. Perseverance is Christ holding our hearts by grace and keeping us in life and faith. Baptism is the believer's public confession of faith in Christ. Being symbolically buried in the watery grave and raised with him, we confess our faith in his finished work of redemption as our Substitute. The Lord's Supper is our blessed remembrance of Christ. Eternal life is knowing Christ. Heaven is being with Christ and like Christ, perfectly and forever. Preaching is telling people about Christ. Anything else is not preaching. Call it what you may; but it is not preaching!

Let Christ be preached, exalted in all his saving grace and glory, in the power of God the Holy Spirit, and God's elect will leave the house of God saying, as the two disciples in Luke 24, 'Did not our heart burn within us, while he talked with us by the way, and while he opened to us the scriptures?'

Beginning at Genesis and going right through the Book of Revelation, God the Holy Ghost tells us, 'These are written that ye might believe that Jesus is the Christ, the Son of God.' The Bible is a wonderful library of sixty-six books. Yet, there is such a unity about it that it is one book, with one message. And this one book has but one design. The whole book of God, and every portion of it, was 'written that ye might believe that Jesus is the Christ, the Son of God.'

What a lesson this is for all who write or speak for God! Let us labour for this one thing, that we may lead immortal souls to believe that Jesus is the Christ, the Son of God. God give me grace to preach and write to bring you to Christ, not to promote a creed, not to build a denomination, not to maintain a history, not to promote myself, but 'that ye might believe that Jesus is the Christ, the Son of God.' The book of God was not written that we might know all about Christ, but that we might know Christ, that we might 'believe that Jesus is the Christ, the Son of God'!

The Object Of Saving Faith

I have deliberately used the bulk of this final study in John's Gospel showing you that the purpose, the design, the intention of holy scripture is that we might believe that Jesus is the Christ, the Son of God. Now, in the second place, let me briefly show you the singular object of saving faith. Faith is believing Christ. The singular object of saving faith is Christ. What does that mean? Sadly, I fear that very few know the answer. But John gives us the answer. To believe Christ is to believe that 'Jesus is the Christ, the Son of God' (1 John 2:22; 5:1). Faith in Christ involves believing 'that Jesus is the Christ', to believe that the man, Jesus of Nazareth, actually, effectually accomplished all that the prophets of the Old Testament said Christ would accomplish (Isaiah 53; Daniel 9:24).

C. H. Spurgeon once passed by a known church building where the gospel of Christ was denied and mocked, but never preached. This sign outside announced the title of the message for that week 'Crucifiction'.

Though 'crucifixion' and 'crucifiction' sound the same when pronounced, there is a vast difference between the two. The religious world of our day has not shifted much in its opinion about what really happened at Calvary. While some deny the fact that Jesus of Nazareth was crucified at Calvary, nearly all in our day deny what he accomplished. The majority of the preaching that goes on today denies the effectual redemption and salvation accomplished by Christ's blood sacrifice and righteousness obedience (Philippians 2:7-9; Hebrews 2:17; 9:12). When you preach that his blood was shed for all humanity without exception, but it never really secured and accomplished salvation for anyone, you are preaching 'crucifiction'.

Thank God the scriptures do not teach 'crucifiction'. The scriptures plainly teach us the glorious and successful work our Lord Jesus Christ accomplished for his people on the cross (Matthew 1:21; Hebrews 9:12). His crucifixion means sin is atoned (1 John 4:10), justice is satisfied (Galatians 3:13), the law of God is honoured (Isaiah 42:21), everlasting righteousness is established and brought in (Romans 5:19-21; Philippians 3:9), salvation is accomplished (John 17:4; 19:30), and God's elect are ransomed (Acts 20:28). That is why the apostle Paul was determined to know, rejoice in, and preach nothing except Jesus Christ and him crucified (1 Corinthians 2:2). This is also why he refused to glory except in the cross of the Lord Jesus Christ (Galatians 6:14).

Do you believe in 'crucifixion' or 'crucifiction?' The difference is eternal life in Christ Jesus, or the just condemnation in Adam (Romans 5:19). If Christ did not effectually put away sin (Hebrews 9:26) and accomplish salvation

(John 17:4; 19:30), your hope of redemption is mere fiction and utterly false, not reality and truth (Galatians 2:20, 21; 1 John 5:21).

The Connection Of Life With Faith

Third, John shows us the connection of life with faith.

'But these are written, that ye might believe that Jesus is the Christ, the Son of God; and that believing ye might have life through his name' (John 20:31).

May God the Holy Spirit be pleased to seal the message of this book to your heart, causing you to 'believe that Jesus is the Christ; and that believing, ye might have life through his name'. Faith in Christ does not give you eternal life. The gift of life eternal brings with it all the fulness of grace by God the Holy Spirit, who works faith in us, causing us to believe. You will never have eternal life, if you do not trust Christ. But, if you trust the Lord Jesus Christ, eternal life is yours. You have eternal life. 'He that believeth on the Son hath everlasting life; and he that believeth not the Son shall not see life, but the wrath of God abideth on him' (John 3:36).

Amen

Index Of Bible Verses

Genesis
1:1-3 419, 483
1:2 311
1:26, 27 165, 247
1:26-28 165
2:3 358
2:7 247
2:18-24 245
2:18-25 249
3 247
3:15 105, 420, 453, 509
3:18 413
3:21 420
4:1-4 105
4:1-8 53
4:3-8 35
5:1, 2 247
6:5 326
6:12 421
7:23 99
17:1 325
22:8 99
22:8-14 105
22:13, 14 99, 337, 509
28:16 194
43:8, 9 109
49:10 405, 413, 453, 509
49:22 216

Exodus
3:5 341
3:6 57
5:21-23 198
8:32-9:3 172
12:5 414
12:13 105
12:46 444, 446
13:2 358
14:13 59
15:26 337
17:8-15 337
19:10, 11 359
21:1-6 276
29:44 358
31:13 337, 358
33:18-23 100
33:19 100
34:5-7 100

Leviticus
4 320
5 320
8 363
10:3 359
14 363
16:27 428
17:1-9 397
19:1, 2 324
20:7 324
21 106
21:16-21 106
22 106
22:17-24 106
22:21 106, 325

Numbers
6:24-26 436
9:12 444
12:13 43
14:11-16 375
20:12 359

Deuteronomy
7 272
7:7, 8 370
17:1 414
18:15-18 509
18:18, 19 352
21:22, 23 446
30:15, 19 500

Joshua
3:5 359

Judges
6:24 337
11 136
13:10, 11 418
16:20 194

Ruth
1:16, 17 136
4:14, 15 99

1 Samuel
2:1 99
2:30 120, 137
5:1-7:17 195
16:7 325
17:45-51 99

2 Samuel
6:21 282
15:23 388
23:5 109, 280, 375

1 Kings
17:14-16 99
19:9-14 49

2 Kings
18:1-4 428
23:4 388

2 Chronicles
15:16 388
29:16 388

Job
1:20-23 99
2:9, 10 99
5:8 119
11:12 131
19 509
19:25, 26 101
19:25-27 72
39:5 131
41:24 398
42:6 58
42:10 99

Psalms
2:7,8 372, 509
2:8 123, 456
4:8 68
11:4-7 317
14:2, 3 326
15:4 79
16:9, 10 145
16:9-11 449
17:5 470
19:1 94
22 105, 422, 435
22:1-21 439
22:15 445, 449
22:18 430, 444
23:1 337
23:4 470
24 509
24:3, 4 326
25:10 408
25:14 349
27:2 391
27:13 470
29:3-11 49
31:1-5 441
31:2 119
31:21-23 300
34:20 444, 446
35:1 119
35:19 35, 293
36:6 198
40 435
40:6-8 453
40:7, 8 456
40:11-13 439
40:12 110
41:9 216
45:2 233
45:6, 7 509
51:1-5 325
51:3-5 315
51:4, 5 314
51:5 247, 326
51:7 213
51:11 311
57:2 212
57:10 408
58:3 247
65:4 280, 281
68:18 311
68:18-20 160
69 435
69:1-7 298
69:1-20 439
69:3-6 110
69:4 293, 295
69:9 110
69:15 83
69:19, 20 110
69:21 430, 444, 445
73 198
73:22, 23 300
76:10 95, 195
77:13, 19 198
77:14 480
80:8-19 255
80:15, 17 261
80:17 164
81:10 302
82:6 36
85:9-13 150, 159
85:10 100
85:10, 11 408
87:7 262
89:19 165
89:19-37 375
89:28 367
89:28-34 300
89:30-34 413
89:30-36 28
91:3-13 360
93:3 83
106:8 159, 456
106:43-45 300
107:1-31 456
107:20 456
109:3, 4 216
109:6-8 350
110:1-7 388
110:3 138, 509
111:2 198
115:1 289, 354, 457
116:1-13 495
116:13 389
119:9-16 362
119:49 118
119:71 262
119:81 118
119.114 118
119:128 404
119:154 119
121:1-8 230
125:3 222
127:2 68
129:3 422
130:5 118
132:7-9 470
139:15, 16 163
149:2 128

Proverbs
1:22-33 292
1:23-33 23, 171
1:33 295
3:5, 6 160
8 241
8:22, 23 509
8:31 376
14:12 344
16:4 59, 95, 159, 195
16:6 150
17:15 173
28:5 177
28:26 118
29:1 23, 171, 292

Ecclesiastes
3:11 23
3:14 28, 263
5:12 68
7:2, 4 42
9:7-10 267
12:6, 7 60

Song Of Solomon
1:7, 13 115
1:12 120
1:14 255
2:8 129
2:9 482
2:17 63
3:3 464
3:6 129
3:10 379
4:9 376
5:2 49, 115
5:8 464
7:11, 12 255
8:5-7 82
8:6 185
8:11-13 255

Isaiah
1:16-20 326
1:18 295
5:7 261
6 173
6:1-7 325
6:1-13 172
6:5 58
6:9, 10 23
8:13 359
8:20 170
9:6 165
11:1-4 391
12:1-6 441, 485
14:24 285
14:26, 27 285
25:9 485
26:3 230
26:19 471
28:14-20 266
30:18 81
32:12 165
38:14 119
40:1, 2 150, 236, 456
40:3 90
40:4 46
42:1 272, 370, 371
42:1-4 367, 418
42:4 149
42:21 327, 511
43:1-5 376
43:21 59
43:26 101
45:12 344
45:20-22 150, 418
45:21 312
45:23-25 455
46:9-11 285
46:13 285
50:5-7 158, 277, 452
50:6 422
51:12 391
51:22 389
52:7 16
52:7, 8 205
52:13-53:12 453
53 89, 105, 509, 511
53:1 172
53:1-12 165
53:3 418
53:4-6 445, 478
53:4-8 110
53:5 16, 413
53:5, 6 346
53:6-8 399
53:7 415
53:8 23, 110
53:8, 9 449
53:9 165
53:9, 10 414
53:9-11 438
53:9-12 423
53:10 30
53:10, 11 29, 149
53:10-12 108, 136, 145, 455
53:12 434
54:10 28, 375
55:1 296
55:3 296
55:6, 7 296
55:8 344
55:8, 9 141
55:11 353
56:10, 11 14
57:1, 2 470
57:14 46, 90
58:9 391
59:16 78
59:21 353
60:14 222
62:5 370
62:11 125
63:14 95
64:6 326
65:1 89, 418
65:24 465
66:8 101

Jeremiah
2:24 131
3:15 12, 17, 91
6:13 14
17:9 118, 326
23:6 109, 248, 295, 323, 324, 327, 336, 337, 346
29:11-13 321
29:12, 13 90
31:3 23, 28, 195, 273, 374, 494

31:12 128
31:16 471
31:31-34 23, 367
32:38-40 367
32:38-41 226, 257, 263
32:40 375
32:41 235
33:12-16 17
33:16 109, 248, 323, 327
50:20 111, 329, 331

Lamentations
1:12, 14 158
3:24 118
3:25 89

Ezekiel
3:9 398
9:11 418
16 273
16:1-14 273
16:6-8 307, 321
16:8 346, 374, 376
16:63 197
18:20 173, 325
20:37 188, 321
33:7-9 92
33:11 180
33:14-16 182
33:19 182
34:2 14
34:29 261
36:27 307
36:33-38 101
37:1-14 321
37:14 307
37:27 375, 377
48:35 337

Daniel
4 124
7:13, 14 164
9:24 105, 135, 327, 453, 511

9:25 128
9:26 122
12:2 69
12:10 105

Hosea
1-3 81
14:4 295, 369, 370
14:7 261
14:8 255, 262

Joel
2:32 311, 455

Micah
5:2 453, 509
7:18 180

Habakkuk
3:4 124

Zechariah
2:8 370
3:1-9 206
6:12, 13 418
7:12 398
9:9 125, 127
11:17 15
12:10 307, 321, 418, 444, 446-448, 509
13:1 196, 197, 263, 321, 418, 447
13:7 165

Malachi
3:1 514
3:6 370, 375
3:17 456
3:18 218
4:1, 2 105
4:2 453, 485

Matthew
1:21 23, 286, 312, 334, 407, 439, 511
2:2 429
3 159
3:15 327
4:18-22 500
5:17 327
5:19 326
5:20 324
5:48 324
6:9 345, 359
6:9-16 267
7:7 89
7:7-11 267
8:17 40
10:22 26
10:25 22
11:25, 26 280
11:25-27 382
11:25-30 294
11:27 343
11:28-30 129, 296, 441
12:18 418
13:47-51 486
13:58 97
16:13-17 164
16:24-26 500
17 159
17:5 329, 376
18:20 89, 479, 482
19:20-22 500
19:26 67
20:2 116
20:16 283
20:19 405
21:4, 5 125
21:42 127
21:45 127
22:14 283
23:23 404
24:44 166
25:13 166
25:31 163
25:34-40 119
26:10 153
26:12 117
26:14-16 217
26:63-67 164
27:19 412-414

27:26 422
27:26-29 422
27:18 414
27:26-31 413
27:46 437
27:54 149
28:5 469
28:9, 10 74, 476, 482
28:10, 16 482
28:16-20 74, 483
28:18 336, 343
28:18-20 478

Mark
2:1-5 91
2:28 163
4:40 229
6:3 161
6:5, 6 97
7:20-23 294
7:37 179
9:23, 24 101
9:24 229
13:47-51 486
14:1-9 509
14:6 153
14:6-9 117
14:21 218
15:28 435
16:7 226
16:9 461, 476
16:12, 13 476-478
16:15, 16 49
16:16 180

Luke
1:32, 33 429
1:46-55 437
2:25 105, 306
2:52 361
4:25-32 294
4:30 124
5:4-11 486
5:17-26 163
7 324
7:35 116
7:36-50 460
7:38 197
7:47 116, 461
8:2 461
8:11-15 266
9:31 202
9:49, 50 497
9:51 149
10 115
10:7 14
10:21 348
10:38-50 497
11:26 218
12:37 213
12:40 166
12:47, 48 416
14:25-33 52
14:26-33 429
15:2 195
15:7, 10 69
16:15 261, 294, 326
16:24 445
16:29-31 119
17:20 407
17:20-25 406
18:8 166
19:5 49
19:10 137, 166
20:37, 38 57
22:15 114
22:31, 32 253
22:44 427
23:7 412
23:20, 22 412
23:34 436
23:43 436
23:46 441
24 510
24:11 477, 478
24:13-34 476
24:13-35 74, 482, 507
24:21 135
24:25-27 403
24:27 508
24:30, 31 488
24:34 74, 482
24:39 478
24:44-47 105, 508
24:50, 51 74, 483

John
1:1 106
1:1-3 420
1:1, 18 334
1:4, 5 143
1:5 365
1:8 357
1:9-11 365
1:10, 11 143
1:11 292
1:11-13 343
1:14 59, 250, 365, 420
1:18 96, 150, 371
1:29 105, 107
1:29, 36 418
2:4 135
2:19 127
2:23-25 119
3:1-8 407
3:3, 5 407
3:3-8 321, 343
3:5, 6 248
3:8 346
3:13 163
3:14-16 405, 438
3:16 145, 149, 342, 375
3:17, 18 181
3:19, 20 181
3:21 181
3:27 354, 415
3:34 371
3:35 260, 272, 336
3:36 343, 346, 369, 512
4:2 206
4:10 306
4:14 445
4:24 453
5:19-27 163
5:20 272, 371, 336
5:20, 21 436
5:20-24 159
5:22 331
5:23 292
5:25 51, 52, 56,
74, 134
5:25-29 101
5:28, 29 69, 75
5:29 76
5:39 508
5:40 50
5:43 344

6:1-14	488
6:26	98
6:28, 29	182
6:37	91, 195
6:37-39	336
6:37-40	29, 50, 74, 294, 343
6:39	109, 375, 455
6:44	50
6:44, 45	294
6:45	176
6:47-51	294
6:53	294
6:61-65	294
6:62	163
6:63	88, 266, 343, 352
6:70	219
7:30	135
7:39	127, 311
7:53-8:1	137
8:12	177
8:19	343
8:26-28	352
8:31	26
8:40	294
8:42	493
8:42-45	21
8:44	209
8:59	55, 124
9:11	92
10:6-21	11
10:10	343
10:11	110
10:11, 15	23
10:14-17	369
10:16-18	158, 182, 272, 277
10:17, 18	149
10:19-30	19
10:24-28	343
10:25-33	294
10:26	20
10:27, 28	350
10:27-30	25, 263
10:29, 30	30
10:30	292
10:30-33	415
10:31-42	33
10:33	164
10:36	165, 359
10:1-57	39
11:1-12:11	49
11:11	65
11:11-46	55
11:14	51
11:16	65
11:21	66
11:25, 26	71, 74
11:32	66
11:33	66
11:36	77
11:37	66
11:39	87
11:40	93, 95, 99
11:43	49, 51
11:43-46	98
11:44	49
11:47-57	103
11:49	402
11:50-52	396
11:52	368
11:57	124
12:1-7	153
12:1-11	113
12:9	134
12:9-11	53
12:12-19	121
12:13	429
12:14, 15	125
12:20-26	154
12:20-33	133
12:24	127
12:26	372
12:27, 28	96
12:27-30	153, 154
12:28	350
12:29-33	138, 160
12:31-33	141
12:31-34	161, 164
12:32, 33	147, 405
12:34	162
12:35-43	167
12:44-50	175
12:47-50	353
13:1	180, 181, 209, 375, 377
13:1-20	194, 202
13:4, 5	205
13:7	194
13:10	195, 262
13:12-15	211
13:13-15	437
13:15	211, 501
13:17	214
13:18-31	215
13:31	221
13:31, 32	159
13:31-14:1	221
13:34, 35	214
13:35	214
13:36	503
13:36-38	226
14:1	177, 226, 227
14:1-3	227, 346
14:1-20	240, 241, 246, 248
14:1-31	233
14:6	318, 362, 436
14:6-9	336
14:6-10	177
14:7-10	382
14:13	302
14:15-20	250
14:16	302, 305, 320
14:16, 17	306
14:17	307
14:20	385
14:21	371, 482
14:22	482
15:1-6	244
15:1-8	259, 260
15:1-27	253
15:9	269, 270, 281
15:13	273, 275
15:15	272, 371
15:16	279, 280, 302
15:18	36
15:22-25	291
15:25	35, 292
15:26	305, 308
16:1	298
16:1-33	297
16:7	305, 310
16:7-11	308, 319, 320, 321, 323
16:7-14	309, 455
16:7-16	305

16:8 313
16:8-11 314, 317
16:10 316, 323
16:12, 13 308
16:12-14 318
16:13 321
16:14-16 308
16:16 127
16:20 338
16:23 302
16:28 334
16:33 53, 221
17:1, 4 96
17:1-5 135, 163
17:1-26 333
17:2 108, 123, 145, 436
17:3 126, 341
17:4 454, 511, 512
17:4, 5 272
17:5 331
17:8 347-349
17:9 23
17:9-11 30
17:15 30
17:17 355, 358
17:17-21 363
17:18-20 478
17:19 359
17:20 23, 30, 331
17:22 73
17:23 250, 365
17:24 62, 74, 231, 373
17:26 379
18:1-11 387
18:2-9 218
18:6 124
18:11 389
18:12-27 396
18:28-30 403
18:28-40 401
18:31 412
18:31, 32 404
18:33-36 405
18:37 413
18:38 414
18:39, 40 408, 412
19:1-12 409, 411
19:4 414
19:5 417
19:6 414
19:11 413
19:12 409, 412
19:13-16 422
19:13-37 426
19:21, 41 422
19:24 444
19:25-30 433
19:26, 27 437
19:28 438, 444
19:28-30 439, 445
19:28-42 444
19:30 150, 336, 451, 511, 512
19:34-37 446
19:36 444
19:37 448
20:1-18 460, 468
20:11-18 74, 482
20:18-31 475
20:19-23 74, 483
20:20 301
20:21 92, 501
20:22 257
20:24-29 74, 483
20:30, 31 506
20:31 512
21:1-14 74, 481, 483
21:15-17 226, 397, 491
21:18-25 497
21:25 505

Acts
1:3 73, 482
1:4-11 74, 483
1:6 135
2:23 143, 150, 412, 416
2:23, 36 295
2:32-36 126
2:33 311
2:36 480
3:13 412
3:21 178
3:25, 26 292
4:11 480
4:24-28 402
4:26-28 415
4:27, 28 295, 410, 412, 416, 430
7:54-59 164
7:55-58 61
7:56 162
8:26-39 89
9:3-7 74, 483
10:38 35
10:43 105, 150
13:26-30 416
13:27-29 430
13:38, 39 107
13:38-41 416
13:48 23, 343
14:22 228, 303
15:9 263
16:31 50
17:22, 23 344
17:30, 31 337
17:31 317, 331, 445
18:24-28 126
20:26, 27 508
20:27 509
20:28 136, 511
20:29 16
20:31 16
26:26 122

Romans
1:1 484
1:9 16
1:15, 16 145
1:16 182
1:18-20 170
1:25 344
1:28 171
3:3, 4 172, 173
3:12 325
3:19-24 295, 445, 480
3:20 421
3:20-26 328
3:22 109
3:24 356
3:24-26 100, 107, 135, 150, 206, 312, 317, 334, 336, 455

3:28-31 109
3:31 182
4:8 30, 331
4:20-22 99
4:22-25 480
4:25 328, 414, 445
4:25-5:11 423, 468
5:1-5 381
5:5 119, 379, 384
5:5-11 322
5:6-8 84, 149, 223, 276, 427, 438
5:6-10 375
5:8 145, 311, 379, 494
5:9-11 330
5:10 29
5:10, 11 61
5:12 51, 73, 247, 326, 328, 422
5:12-19 165
5:17-21 328
5:18, 19 327, 422
5:18-21 73, 327
5:19 109, 316, 334, 414, 437, 511
5:19-21 511
5:20, 21 400, 408, 422
6:4 242
6:6, 7 73
6:8 242
6:9-11 73
6:10 468
6:11 330
6:14, 15 210
6:15 144
6:23 23, 169, 342
7:1-4 210
7:4 73, 144
7:11-24 247, 330
7:17-20 492
7:18 58, 330
7:20 361
7:24 68
7:24, 25 342
8:1 331
8:1-4 181, 316, 323, 367, 438
8:1-17 307
8:3 421
8:3, 4 109
8:7 21, 34
8:7, 8 294
8:11 58
8:15 345
8:17 331
8:17, 18 272
8:23 267
8:26 267
8:28 100, 212, 337, 480, 495
8:28, 29 375
8:28-30 73, 283, 286, 328
8:29 376
8:29, 30 23, 109, 273
8:30 28
8:31-34 29
8:32 295, 329
8:32-34 331, 346
8:32-39 144
8:34 316, 323, 333, 436, 446
8:34, 35 118
8:35 195
8:35-37 303
8:35-39 370, 375
9:4-23 216
9:5 36
9:6 195
9:10-24 23
9:11 285
9:11-18 283
9:11-24 171, 173, 376
9:13 23
9:15 436
9:16 27, 87, 170, 265, 429
9:16-18 377
9:17 95, 415
9:21-24 95
9:31-10:4 324
10:1-4 210
10:4 144, 445, 453
10:9, 10 414
10:13-17 90, 349
10:17 145
10:21 171
11:5-7 283
11:7-10 292
11:29 28
11:33-36 199
11:33-12:2 31
11:36 59, 95, 100, 159
12:1, 2 360, 363, 372, 496
12:12 119
14:4 498, 502
14:5 211
14:8 57
14:9 123
14:11-17 211
14:17 407
15:4 118, 217, 435
16:20 144, 179

1 Corinthians

1:2 339, 360
1:17-25 509
1:17-2:2 145
1:18 182
1:21 90
1:26-29 116
1:26-31 224
1:30 260, 360, 447, 488
1:30, 31 255, 318, 324, 327, 446
2:2 508, 509, 511
2:9, 10 301
2:9-12 57
2:12-16 177, 301, 407
2:14 21
3:21-23 267
3:22 57, 68
4:7 24, 206, 218, 429
4:15 16

5:7, 8	114
6:9-11	197, 263, 331
6:11	273, 355, 356
6:19, 20	360, 502
7:20-24	501
7:29	503
9:7-14	14
9:16	90, 92
10:12	120, 389
10:13	224
10:31	120, 160
12:12, 27	74
13:1-13	214
13:13	494
15:1	26
15:1-4	468
15:1-8	73
15:3	444
15:3, 4	460
15:3-7	476
15:5	74, 482
15:6	74, 483
15:7	74, 483
15:10	263, 429
15:14, 17	346
15:14-17	447
15:17	73
15:19	71
15:20	74
15:20, 51	67
15:21, 22	422
15:21, 23	74
15:24-28	166, 336
15:35-44	75
15:40-49	70
15:42-58	44
15:45	247
15:45, 47	165
15:47-49	74
15:49-58	424
15:51-58	232, 234
15:51-59	75
15:56, 57	67
16:22	493

2 Corinthians

2:4	16
2:14	303
2:14-16	114, 352, 391, 479
2:15, 16	160
2:17	16, 353
3:5	260, 352
4:1-7	16
4:3, 4	23
4:3-7	24
4:6	94, 177, 308, 455, 465, 483
4:16-5:9	470
4:17-5:9	230
5:1-9	60
5:4	58
5:10	331
5:10, 11	76, 167, 296
5:14	377
5:14, 15	225, 461
5:14-16	211
5:17	52, 247, 263, 321, 329
5:17-19	296
5:17-21	118, 151, 329, 435
5:18-21	446
5:20, 21	296, 438
5:21	80, 110, 205, 310, 324, 327, 356, 408, 445
6:1, 2	50, 296
6:14-7:1	52, 428
7:1	52
8:7	494
8:9	80, 129, 205, 421, 434, 437
9:15	375
12:9	265, 372
12:10	256, 265
13:5	196
13:14	307

Galatians

1:4, 5	29
1:6-8	125
1:15, 16	456
2:19, 20	144
2:20	173, 181, 242
2:20, 21	512
2:21	456
3:10	325, 326
3:13	87, 107, 156, 310, 316, 334, 356, 408, 413, 454, 511
3:13, 14	80, 110, 300, 307, 309, 311, 389, 455
3:24	325
3:24-26	210
3:28	134
4:3-9	144
4:4, 5	261
4:4-6	300, 334
4:19	16
5:1-4	210
5:2-4	125
5:6	494
5:14	214
5:16, 17	246
5:16-22	247
5:17	58
5:22, 23	211, 261, 262, 267
5:23, 24	330
6:1, 2	363
6:6	14
6:14	143, 145, 151, 224, 511
6:15	134

Ephesians

1:1-14	285
1:3	332, 371
1:3, 4	279
1:3-6	73, 135, 204, 244, 255, 272, 328, 367, 488
1:3-7	109, 419
1:3-14	79, 109, 306, 321
1:4	375
1:4-6	285, 286, 374
1:5-7	59

1:6 96, 107, 109, 204, 338
1:8-11 396
1:11 331
1:11, 12 261, 285
1:12 96, 338, 367, 375
1:12-14 300
1:13 109, 456
1:13, 14 30, 307, 308, 321, 352
1:14 58, 96, 338
1:19 101
1:19, 20 51, 173
1:21, 22 123
1:22 79
1:22, 23 74, 244
1:23 249, 255
2:1-4 28
2:1-5 134
2:1-7 55
2:1-10 51, 74
2:3 369
2:4-6 72
2:5, 6 44, 72
2:6 242
2:7 96, 272, 286, 329, 338, 456
2:7-9 168
2:8 50, 101, 173
2:8, 9 446
2:8-10 168
3:14-19 83, 270, 381
3:14-21 385
3:17 495
4:4-6 338
4:8 371
4:11-16 318
4:18 66
4:22-24 246, 247
4:24 248
4:30 58
4:32-5:2 370
5:2 165, 372
5:14 90
5:16 503
5:20 178
5:23-32 272
5:25-27 29, 191, 207, 437
5:25-32 240
5:27 111
5:30 249, 421

Philippians
1:3 16
1:6 30
1:21-24 224
1:22 61
1:29 173
2:1-5 115, 463
2:1-8 214
2:1-11 205
2:5-7 334
2:5-8 205, 399, 421
2:5-11 272
2:7-9 511
2:8-11 145, 160
2:9-11 123, 166, 308, 414, 429, 456
2:13 362
2:14-18 115
2:15 209
2:16 266
2:21 14
3:3 404, 456
3:7-15 144
3:7-21 501
3:9 511
3:13, 14 363
3:21 60, 70, 74, 75
4:1 16
4:4-7 465
4:4-8 128
4:19 267, 486

Colossians
1:12 249, 273, 329, 331
1:15 165
1:19-22 107
1:20-22 312
1:23 26
1:25-29 16
1:27 73, 240, 247, 249, 328, 330, 385
2:1 16
2:6 229
2:9 260
2:9, 10 176, 249, 446, 488
2:9-15 74
2:10-12 101
2:11 242
2:12 51, 242
2:13-15 74
2:14 144, 173
2:14-16 210
2:16, 17 114, 509
2:16-23 476
2:20-23 407
3:4 368
3:9, 10 247
3:10 370
3:11 134, 498

1 Thessalonians
1:3 118
1:4, 5 52, 343
1:5 352
2:19 16
3:9 16
4:11 499, 502
4:13-18 44, 63, 69, 75, 232, 234, 449
4:14 58, 67
5:9 218, 219
5:10 67
5:12, 13 205
5:16-18 464
5:18 178
5:23, 24 363

2 Thessalonians
1:7-10 59, 75, 232, 234, 424
1:10 368
2:10-12 23
2:11, 12 307
2:11-14 24
2:13 273, 339
2:13, 14 286, 287, 361, 362
2:13-17 219

1 Timothy
1:1 118
1:2 16
1:15 107, 445
2:2 210
2:5 135, 436
3:16 106, 240
4:1-5 211
4:13-16 478
5:17, 18 14
6:3 210
6:6-8 68
6:14-16 106

2 Timothy
1:9 23, 109, 204, 287, 375
1:9, 10 245, 288, 328, 455
1:9-11 73, 286, 472
1:12 118, 136
2:1, 2 478
2:8-10 502
2:13 480
2:19 29
2:22-24 502
3:12 303
3:16, 17 37, 125

Titus
2:11-14 501
2:12 209
2:14 29
3:3-6 376
3:4-7 206, 263
3:5 197
3:5-8 377

Philemon
10 16

Hebrews
1:1-3 108, 164, 335
1:3 165, 197, 370
1:6-9 164
1:8 372
2:1-3 180
2:6-9 164
2:13 29, 111, 336
2:14, 15 74
2:15 318
2:17 511
2:17, 18 166
3:6, 14 26
3:12 480
4:3 106, 109, 204
4:3-10 476
4:9-11 441
4:12 266
4:14, 15 107
4:14-16 344
4:15 166
4:16 107, 235
5:1 436
5:2 166
5:4, 5 436
5:7 156, 436
6:16-20 257
6:20 111, 331
7:22 23, 108
7:25 166, 333, 346, 436
7:26 107
8:1 107
8:10-12 150
9:12 107, 110, 150, 439, 441, 454, 511
9:14-17 150, 197
9:15-17 454
9:22 206, 311, 312
9:26 110, 346, 511
9:27 331
10:1-14 108, 453
10:5 261
10:5-10 135, 158, 312, 334
10:7 444
10:9-14 445
10:10 339
10:10-14 107, 360, 447
10:11-14 334
10:12 111
10:19 312
10:19-22 107, 454
10:23-29 479
10:25 479
11:1 20, 257
11:4 35
12:1, 2 69, 338, 501
12:2 155
12:5-11 375
12:14 248, 324, 325, 356
13:7, 17 16
13:8 421
13:12 398, 422, 428
13:14 230
13:20 375

James
1:2-4 262
1:17 370, 375
1:18 267, 352

1 Peter
1:2 279, 286, 287, 339
1:3-5 263
1:7 262
1:15 325
1:15, 16 324
1:16 325
1:17-20 397
1:18-20 107, 346, 414
1:18-21 196
1:18-25 150
1:23-25 145, 182, 266, 352, 509
2:5 329, 372
2:6-8 23
2:7, 8 171, 173
2:9 279
2:21 211, 501
2:21, 22 414
2:21-24 437
2:21-25 399
2:22-24 441
2:24 110, 408
2:24, 25 438

3:18 343, 408, 414, 438
3:22 436
5:1-3 91
5:1-4 493
5:6, 7 230

2 Peter
1:3, 4 356
1:4 247, 248, 328, 330, 361, 370
1:10 196
1:16-21 37
1:19 485
1:20, 21 125
3:18 361

1 John
1:1 352
1:3, 4 338
1:7, 9 206
1:7-9 196, 197
1:7-10 321
1:7-2:2 329
1:8 357
1:9 197
2:1, 2 30, 110, 197, 254, 302, 312, 436
2:15-17 143
2:20 178, 318
2:20, 27 27
2:20-27 301
2:22 511
2:22, 23 176
2:23, 24 125
3:1 272, 370
3:1, 2 62
3:1-9 308
3:5 111
3:5-9 330
3:5-12 209
3:9 247, 248, 328, 330, 361
3:10, 13 35
3:16 17, 145, 149, 223, 311, 375, 377, 494
3:16, 17 198, 214
3:19 29
3:23 211, 251
3:23, 24 182, 225
4:2 125, 176
4:4 303
4:8 214
4:8-14 385
4:9 145
4:9, 10 149, 223, 311, 322, 438, 494
4:9-11 84, 214
4:9-19 379, 385
4:10 511
4:15 176
4:15-19 274
4:16-19 322
4:17 308
4:19 295, 374, 377, 492, 494
4:19, 20 465
5:1-3 118
5:1-13 308
5:6-8 447
5:7 36, 250, 306, 344
5:7-12 118
5:10 295, 316
5:10-13 480
5:11 342
5:12 450
5:18 361
5:20 336
5:21 512

3 John
5-8 92

Jude
1 328, 338, 360
4 23, 171, 173, 210
4-11 219
19 307
21 191, 231, 274
24 207
24, 25 107, 111, 136, 191

Revelation
1:5, 6 107, 494
1:7 424, 446
1:10 476
1:13 162
2:17 206
3:20 115
3:22 372
4:11 59, 95, 159
5:9, 10 107
5:9-13 338
5:11-14 230
7:1-17 230
7:9-17 145
7:10 354
7:14 303, 450
7:17 471
8:1 213
12:7-10 144
13:8 105, 109, 204
14:1-4 230
14:4 267
14:4, 5 470
14:13 69
14:14 162
19:1-9 230, 303
19:6-9 470
20:1-6 472
20:6 44, 51, 55, 74
20:11-15 329
20:12, 13 331
21:1-5 332
21:2-5 329
21:3-7 339
21:4 471
21:5 143
21:7 179
21:27 248, 324
22:1-6 329
22:3 69
22:3-6 332
22:11 331

Index Of Bible Verses

www.ingramcontent.com/pod-product-compliance
Lightning Source LLC
Chambersburg PA
CBHW020457100426
42812CB00024B/2683

9781908475084